I0868606

Fundamentals of Institutional Asset Management

Fundamentals of Institutional Asset Management

Frank J. Fabozzi
EDHEC Business School, France

Francesco A. Fabozzi
Stevens Institute of Technology, USA

World Scientific

NEW JERSEY • LONDON • SINGAPORE • BEIJING • SHANGHAI • HONG KONG • TAIPEI • CHENNAI • TOKYO

Published by

World Scientific Publishing Co. Pte. Ltd.

5 Toh Tuck Link, Singapore 596224

USA office: 27 Warren Street, Suite 401-402, Hackensack, NJ 07601

UK office: 57 Shelton Street, Covent Garden, London WC2H 9HE

Library of Congress Cataloging-in-Publication Data
Names: Fabozzi, Frank J., author. | Fabozzi, Francesco A., author.
Title: Fundamentals of institutional asset management / Frank J. Fabozzi,
EDHEC Business School, France, Francesco A. Fabozzi, Stevens Institute of Technology, USA.
Description: USA : World Scientific, 2020. | Includes bibliographical references and index.
Identifiers: LCCN 2020032969| ISBN 9789811220029 (hardcover) |
ISBN 9789811220036 (paperback) | ISBN 9789811221590 (ebook) |
ISBN 9789811221606 (ebook other)
Subjects: LCSH: Institutional investments--Management. | Asset allocation. | Portfolio management.
Classification: LCC HG4521 .F258 2020 | DDC 332.67/253--dc23
LC record available at https://lccn.loc.gov/2020032969

British Library Cataloguing-in-Publication Data
A catalogue record for this book is available from the British Library.

Copyright © 2021 by World Scientific Publishing Co. Pte. Ltd.

All rights reserved. This book, or parts thereof, may not be reproduced in any form or by any means, electronic or mechanical, including photocopying, recording or any information storage and retrieval system now known or to be invented, without written permission from the publisher.

For photocopying of material in this volume, please pay a copying fee through the Copyright Clearance Center, Inc., 222 Rosewood Drive, Danvers, MA 01923, USA. In this case permission to photocopy is not required from the publisher.

For any available supplementary material, please visit
https://www.worldscientific.com/worldscibooks/10.1142/11819#t=suppl

Desk Editors: Ramya Gangadharan/Lum Pui Yee

Typeset by Stallion Press
Email: enquiries@stallionpress.com

Frank J. Fabozzi
To my wife Donna, my children Karly, Patricia, and Francesco

Francesco A. Fabozzi
To my mother and to the memory of my Aunt Lucy

Preface

This book provides the fundamentals of asset management. The 19 chapters are grouped into six parts. Each chapter begins with learning objectives. At the end of each chapter, there is a comprehensive list of the key points covered in the chapter.

Part One provides an explanation of the key activities involved in asset management (Chapter 1) and the various forms of risk (Chapter 2). The four chapters in Part Two describe the investment vehicles and asset classes: equities (Chapter 3), debt instruments (Chapter 4), collective investment vehicles and alternative assets (Chapter 5), and financial derivatives (Chapter 6).

Part Three covers theories about portfolio selection and asset pricing. The fundamentals about measuring return and risk are the subject of Chapter 7. Chapter 8 covers what is popularly known as *modern portfolio theory*, despite being introduced almost 70 years ago by Professor Harry Markowitz, the 1990 co-recipient of the Nobel Memorial Prize in Economic Sciences. This theory, also referred to as mean-variance analysis, provides a framework for the construction of efficient portfolios — portfolios that offer the maximum expected return for a given level of risk. The implementation of mean-variance analysis is not straightforward. There are issues associated with the estimation of the inputs required in the optimization model that must be employed to obtain efficient portfolios. These implementation issues are also explained in Chapter 8. In Chapter 9, the fundamentals of asset pricing models — models that describe the relationship between some measure of risk and expected return — are explained. The two most well-known asset pricing models — the capital asset pricing model and the arbitrage pricing theory model — are both covered in the chapter, as well as a brief introduction to factor models commonly used in practice.

The five chapters in Part Four cover common stock analysis and portfolio management. Stock analysts rely on financial analysis in evaluating a company's operating performance and financial condition. The tools of financial analysis are covered in Chapter 10. Methods for valuing a company's stock based on discounted cash flow models and relative valuation models are explained in Chapter 11. The wide range of common stock strategies are covered in Chapters 12 and 13. In Chapter 12, we discuss the concept of market efficiency and its implications for investment strategies. The remainder of that chapter covers investment strategies when investors believe that the market is price-efficient. These strategies are referred to as beta strategies. Active equity strategies, also referred to as alpha strategies, are the subject of Chapter 13. In that chapter, we also describe the reasons how an asset manager generates the realized return (return attribution analysis), the capacity issue associated with investment strategies, and the fundamentals of backtesting an investment strategy. How equity derivatives are used to control the risk of a common stock portfolio is the subject of Chapter 14.

Four chapters are the subject of Part Five, which is devoted to bond analytics and portfolio management. Chapter 15 explains how bonds are priced and the various yield measures used by practitioners. The measures for quantifying interest rate risk are the subject of Chapter 16. In addition, in that chapter we discuss various credit risk measures. Bond portfolio strategies, indexing and active, are explained in Chapter 17. Unlike indexing in the equity market, indexing a bond portfolio is quite challenging. To control a bond portfolio's interest rate risk and credit risk, derivatives are used. The instruments and how they are used to control risk are explained and illustrated in Chapter 18.

There has been considerable growth in multi-asset funds — funds where the asset manager invests in not only equities and bonds, but also alternative assets. The strategies used in managing multi-asset portfolios are the subject of Chapter 19, the one chapter comprising Part Six.

The Companion Book

This book covers the fundamentals of institutional asset management. There is a companion book, *Asset Management: Tools and Issues*, coauthored by Frank J. Fabozzi, Francesco A. Fabozzi, Marcos López de Prado and Stoyan V. Stoyanov, that provides a description of the analytical tools used in asset management as well as more in-depth explanations of specialized topics covered in *Fundamentals of Institutional Asset*

Management. Here we provide a brief description of each chapter in the current book and the reason based on our experience in the industry and in teaching undergraduate and graduate students why we decided to cover these topics in the companion book.

The first chapter describes asset management companies. The characteristics of asset management companies are described, how they differ from wealth management companies, and how traditional asset management companies differ from hedge funds. The governing document between a client and an asset management company is the investment management agreement. The basic terms of this agreement are described in the chapter and the appendix to the chapter is a sample investment management agreement. What clients are looking for from their asset manager, how the industry is changing, and what is needed to build the asset management company of the future are also described in this chapter.

Understanding the fundamentals of accounting is needed by those seeking to be security analysts. To analyze a company, an equity analyst uses traditional financial statement analysis coupled with an investigation of a company's management and an economic analysis of a company's position in an industry. But an understanding of financial statements is also necessary for those who are quantitative analysts. This is because a company's fundamental factors are constructed from its financial statements. Yet, blindly accepting numbers from a company's financial statement without realizing that alternative accounting treatments may be possible, and the discretion given to management in making financial performance more attractive, could distort the recommendation of an equity analyst or the use of incorrectly computed factor measures incorporated into a quantitative model. In Chapter 2, the key financial statements are reviewed, and the assumptions made in preparing financial statements are explained. There is no explanation of the mechanics of preparing financial statements (i.e., no debit and credit mechanics). This chapter provides a good review for those who have not had a course in financial accounting.

The largest non-government sector of the investment-grade bond market is the residential mortgage-backed securities sector. So, any bond portfolio manager should be familiar with the products in this sector: mortgage pass-through securities, collateralized mortgage-backed securities, and stripped mortgage-backed securities. In Chapter 3, we describe these securitized products and explain how and why they are created. The mechanics for creating these products, referred to as structuring a pool of assets or loans, is also used in creating asset-backed securities.

Statistical and operations research tools commonly used in quantitative asset management are covered in Chapters 3 through 7. Chapter 4 covers financial econometrics: regression analysis, principal component analysis, and time-series models for volatility (ARCH and GARCH).

In asset management, the performance of a portfolio or investment strategy will often depend on the outcome of many random variables, with changes in every variable impacting performance proceeding along a substantial number of possible paths. Because these eventualities make it impractical to evaluate all possible combinations of outcomes in order to assess the risks, Monte Carlo simulation is employed. The basics of Monte Carlo simulation are covered in Chapter 5, as well as several asset management applications.

An optimization model prescribes the best course of action to be pursued in order to achieve an objective. The optimization models used in most asset management applications such as asset allocation, portfolio construction, and portfolio rebalancing are mathematical programming models. The various types of mathematical programming models used for optimization in asset management and several applications are described in Chapter 6.

Asset managers have relied on financial econometric tools described to identify the relations among financial and economic variables. These tools are also used to identify patterns in data, but the application in this area is limited. However, machine learning promises to change that by allowing researchers to use modern nonlinear and highly dimensional techniques. After explaining how machine learning differs from financial econometrics, Chapter 7 describes machine learning, provides a brief overview of machine learning tools, and explains the various applications to asset management. The chapter also explains how to develop machine learning strategies. Formulating such strategies is non-trivial, and their misuse can lead to disappointing results.

In the classical asset allocation problem (more popularly referred to as modern portfolio theory as formulated by Harry Markowitz), variance is used as a proxy for risk. However, the variance penalizes symmetrically both positive and negative returns. In Chapter 8, extensions of mean-variance analysis capturing asymmetry of risk by means of a risk measure or an asymmetric measure of dispersion focusing on the features which are most relevant for asset allocation decision-making are described. These features include the capacity to capture the skewness and kurtosis present in observed asset returns, the tail-dependence which is most relevant for extreme losses, and, most importantly, consistency with the principle of diversification. Because it is common to use alternative risk measures in conjunction with a distributional assumption for asset returns, in Chapter 8 the most popular distributional hypotheses focusing on what makes the extended frameworks different from mean-variance analysis are reviewed. Every extension of mean-variance analysis is consistent with a risk-reward ratio which can be used as a measure of risk-adjusted performance.

In describing various theories in finance and describing various strategies, short selling and/or leveraging are key. The ability to borrow securities in the market when short selling, financing a position to create leverage, and using a portfolio of holdings as collateral to generate incremental returns falls into the area of securities finance and collateral management. Chapter 9 discusses securities lending and other vehicles used in securities finance and collateral management. The focus in this chapter is on equities. Repurchase agreements, commonly used to fund positions in the bond market, are the subject of Chapter 10.

Chapters 11 through 14 delve into quantitative equity strategies. The issues in implementing quantitative research are discussed in Chapter 11. In that chapter, we describe the process of performing quantitative research, how to convert research into implementable trading strategies, the issues associated with the quantitative approach to asset management, the common objective of a quantitative research process, and issues in selecting a sample and methodology for estimating a model.

The wide range of quantitative equity strategies is then discussed in Chapter 12. The chapter begins by describing the differences between the fundamental and quantitative approaches to asset management. Then we set forth a taxonomy of quantitative equity strategies and describe multifactor strategies, asset allocation strategies, factors strategies, event-based strategies, statistical arbitrage strategies, textual strategies, alternative data strategies, and thematic/macro strategies. After describing these strategies, the process for developing quantitative strategies is explained, along with a description of the five properties of a good quantitative investment model and strategy.

The challenges in implementing equity factor investing are the subject of Chapter 13 where a description of the current state of factor research is surveyed. Equity transaction and trading costs are described in Chapter 14. Although we briefly described these costs in Chapter 13 of this book, the discussion in the companion book is much more comprehensive.

As explained in Chapter 13 of this book, there are two types of factor models: return forecast factor models and risk forecast factor models. Chapters 15 and 16 of the companion book demonstrate how risk forecast factor models are used for equity and bond portfolio management, respectively.

In the last two chapters of the book, the issues and methodologies for backtesting investment strategies are covered. Chapter 17 describes the biases associated with backtesting and provides an overview of the three commonly used methodologies and the advantages and disadvantages of each. The focus is on the walk-forward method. Also described in Chapter 17 is the information that should be disclosed to clients regarding the results from backtesting a proposed investment strategy. In Chapter 18, the focus is on the use of the Monte Carlo simulation method for backtesting and its advantages over other methods for backtesting an investment strategy.

About the Authors

Frank J. Fabozzi is editor of *The Journal of Portfolio Management* and co-editor/co-founder of *The Journal of Financial Data Science.* He is Professor of Finance at EDHEC Business School. Over the past 35 years, he has held professorial positions at MIT, Yale, Princeton, and New York University. He is a trustee of the BlackRock closed-end fund complex. He has authored more than 120 books and more than 200 articles in peer-reviewed journals. He is the CFA Institute's 2007 recipient of the C. Stewart Sheppard Award and the CFA Institute's 2015 recipient of the James R. Vertin Award. He was inducted into the Fixed Income Analysts Society Hall of Fame in November 2002. He earned the designations of Chartered Financial Analyst (CFA) and Certified Public Accountant (CPA). He received his BA and MA in economics in 1970 from The City College of New York where he was elected to Phi Beta Kappa, and received a PhD in economics in 1972 from the City University of New York. In 1994 he was awarded an Honorary Doctorate of Humane Letters from Nova Southwestern University.

Francesco A. Fabozzi is a doctoral student in data science at the Stevens Institute of Technology. He is the managing editor of *The Journal of Financial Data Science*. He has worked as a research associate at NYU's Courant Institute in the Department of Mathematical Finance. He is on the Curriculum Board of the Financial Data Professionals Institute (FDP Institute). He interned at AQR in the firm's machine learning group. Francesco assisted in the authoring of *Global Financial Markets*. He earned a BA in economics in 2018 from Princeton University and an MS in financial analytics in 2019 from the Stevens Institute of Technology.

Acknowledgments

We would like to acknowledge the assistance of the following organizations and individuals:

- The data and the optimization model for the asset allocation illustration using mean-variance analysis in Chapter 8 were from *Portfolio Visualizer* developed by Tuomo Lampinen of Silicon Cloud Technologies (https://www.portfoliovisualizer.com/)
- Parts of Chapter 10 draw from Frank Fabozzi's writings with Pamela Peterson Drake of James Madison University.
- Parts of Chapter 11 on equity valuation models draw from Frank Fabozzi's writings with Pamela Peterson Drake of James Madison University and Glen Larsen, Jr. of Indiana University.
- The equity style investing section in Chapter 13 draws from Frank Fabozzi's writings with Eric H. Sorensen of Panagora Asset Management.
- Feedback and discussions on parts of Chapter 13 were provided by Jennifer Bender of State Street Global Advisors, Ananth Madhavan and Ron Kahn of BlackRock Financial Management, Eric Sorensen of Panagora Asset Management, and Joseph Cerniglia.
- Parts of Chapter 14 draw from Frank Fabozzi's writings with Bruce Collins.

Contents

PART I

Asset Management and Risk

Chapter 1

Overview of Asset Management

Learning Objectives

After reading this chapter, you will understand:

- what asset management is;
- the difference between institutional and individual investors;
- the major activities of the asset management process: setting investment objectives; establishing an investment policy; selecting an investment strategy; constructing and monitoring the portfolio; and measuring and evaluating investment performance;
- what is meant by non-liability driven investment objectives and liability driven investment objectives;
- what is meant by a liability;
- the difference between defined benefit and defined contribution pension plans;
- what a benchmark is and how it is used;
- what is the asset allocation decision and the different asset allocation strategies;
- what is meant by an asset class, traditional asset classes, and alternative assets;
- the characteristics of developed market countries, emerging market countries, and frontier market countries;
- what is meant by a client's investment beliefs and why these beliefs are important;
- the types of investment constraints faced by an asset manager;
- the different types of investment strategies;
- why the broadest categorization of investment strategies are active and passive strategies;
- why the assumed market price efficiency impacts whether an active or passive strategy is selected;
- what tasks are involved in the construction and monitoring of a portfolio;

- what is meant by rebalancing a portfolio; and
- the issues involved in measuring and evaluating performance.

Asset management is the process of managing the funds of clients. Other terms commonly used to describe this process are *investment management*, *portfolio management*, and *money management*. Accordingly, the individual who manages a portfolio of investments is referred to as an asset manager, investment manager, portfolio manager, or money manager. We will use these terms interchangeably throughout this book. In industry jargon, an asset manager "runs money". The 10 largest asset management firms in the world based on assets under management (AUM) in U.S. dollars as of the first quarter of 2019 are (1) BlackRock ($6.84 trillion AUM), (2) The Vanguard Group ($5.6 trillion AUM), (3) Charles Schwab ($3.7 trillion), (4) JPMorgan Chase ($1.9 trillion AUM), (5) State Street Global Advisors ($3.12 trillion AUM), (6) Fidelity ($3.0 trillion AUM), (7) Allianz Global Investors ($2.5 trillion AUM), (8) PIMCO ($1.9 trillion AUM), (9) BNY Mellon ($1.9 trillion AUM), and (10) Amundi ($1.71 trillion AUM) Lemke [2019]. The largest 20 asset management firms in the world have a combined AUM of $44.9 trillion. Of the top 20, 12 are headquartered in the United States, three in France, two in Switzerland, and two in Germany (Fischer [2019]).

The asset management process requires an understanding of the various investment vehicles, the way these investment vehicles are valued and traded in the financial market, and the various strategies that can be used to select the investment vehicles that should be included in a portfolio in order to accomplish a client's investment objectives.

Investors can be classified as either individual investors or institutional investors. Individual investors are referred to as *retail investors*. They are the *asset owners* and can either invest directly or use the services of an institutional investor. *Institutional investors* include pension funds (private and public), insurance companies (property & casualty, life, and health), endowments and foundations, registered investment companies (mutual funds/open-end and closed-end funds), depository institutions (commercial banks, savings & loan associations, and credit unions), and hedge funds. A *financial advisor* is someone who advises individual investors about investment matters. Financial advisors whose clients are high-net worth individuals are referred to as *wealth managers*. Every year *The Wall Street Journal* publishes the list of the top wealth management firms. In 2019, the top five in terms of U.S. dollars were (1) Bank of America Global Wealth & Investment Management ($1.35 trillion AUM: 20,000 wealth managers in over 750 branches), (2) Morgan Stanley Wealth Management ($1.26 trillion AUM; 15,600+ wealth managers in 600 branches), (3) J.P. Morgan Private Bank ($774 billion AUM; 1,300 wealth managers in 48 branches), (4) Wells Fargo ($604 billion AUM; 15,000 wealth managers in 1,468 branches), and (5) UBS Wealth Management ($601 billion; 7,100 wealth managers in 208 branches).

The purpose of this book is to describe the process of asset management, focusing on the strategies for institutional investors. However, the basic principles are applicable to individual investors.

In this chapter, we provide an overview of the asset management process and, by means of this overview, layout the sections of the book and chapters to follow.

In practice, the management of portfolios for institutional investors is typically done by a portfolio management team. The asset management process in which members of the team are involved includes the following five major activities:

1. Setting investment objectives.
2. Establishing an investment policy.
3. Selecting an investment strategy.
4. Constructing and monitoring the portfolio.
5. Measuring and evaluating investment performance.

This is a cyclical process where performance evaluation may result in changes to the objectives, policies, strategies, and composition of a portfolio.

Setting Investment Objectives

Setting investment objectives starts with a thorough analysis of the investment objectives of the client whose funds are being managed. Although we might think of institutional investors hiring a third party to manage its funds, that is typically not the case. Large institutional investors will first decide whether to manage part of the funds themselves (internal management) or whether to use third-party managers (external management) or a combination of the two.

Classification of Investment Objectives

In general, we can classify the investment objectives of institutional investors into two broad categories: non-liability-driven objectives and

Vanguard Strategic Equity Fund

Investment Objective: The Fund seeks to provide long-term capital appreciation.

Principal Investment Strategies: The Fund invests in small- and mid-capitalization domestic equity securities based on the advisor's assessment of the relative return potential of the securities. The advisor selects securities that it believes offer an appropriate balance between strong growth prospects and reasonable valuations relative to their industry peers. The advisor does this by using a quantitative process to evaluate all of the securities in the Fund's benchmark, the MSCI US Small + Mid Cap 2200 Index, while seeking to maintain a risk profile similar to that of the Index. Under normal circumstances, at least 80% of the Fund's assets will be invested in equity securities.

Vanguard 500 Index Fund

Investment Objective: The Fund seeks to track the performance of a benchmark index that measures the investment return of large-capitalization stocks.

Principal Investment Strategies: The Fund employs an indexing investment approach designed to track the performance of the Standard & Poor's 500 Index, a widely recognized benchmark of US stock market performance that is dominated by the stocks of large US companies. The Fund attempts to replicate the target index by investing all, or substantially all, of its assets in the stocks that make up the Index, holding each stock in approximately the same proportion as its weighting in the Index.

Vanguard Emerging Markets Stock Index Fund

Investment Objective: The Fund seeks to track the performance of a benchmark index that measures the investment return of stocks issued by companies located in emerging market countries.

Principal Investment Strategies: The Fund employs an indexing investment approach designed to track the performance of the FTSE Emerging Markets All Cap China A Inclusion Index, a market-capitalization-weighted index that is made up of approximately 4,027 common stocks of large-, mid-, and small-cap companies located in emerging markets around the world. The Fund invests by sampling the Index, meaning that it holds a broadly diversified collection of securities that, in the aggregate, approximates the Index in terms of key characteristics. These key characteristics include industry weightings and market capitalization, as well as certain financial measures, such as price/earnings ratio and dividend yield.

Vanguard FTSE Social Index Fund

Investment Objective: The Fund seeks to track the performance of a benchmark index that measures the investment return of large- and mid-capitalization stocks.

Principal Investment Strategies: The Fund employs an indexing investment approach designed to track the performance of the FTSE4Good US Select Index. The Index is composed of the stocks of companies that have been screened for certain social and environmental criteria by the Index sponsor, which is independent of Vanguard. The Index is market-capitalization weighted and includes primarily large- and mid-cap US stocks that have been screened for certain criteria related to the environment, human rights, health and safety, labor standards, and diversity. The Index excludes companies involved with weapons, tobacco, gambling, alcohol, adult entertainment, and nuclear power. The Fund attempts to replicate the Index by investing all, or substantially all, of its assets in the stocks that make up the Index.

FIGURE 1: From Summary Prospectus of Mutual Funds

liability-driven objectives. As the name indicates, those institutional investors that fall into the first category can manage their assets without regard to satisfying any liabilities. An example of an institutional investor that is not driven by liabilities is a regulated investment company which includes open-end regulated funds (called mutual funds) and closed-end regulated funds. Figure 1 shows the investment objectives of mutual funds managed by The Vanguard Group as set forth in the summary prospectus.[1]

[1]When a security is being sold to the public, it must file a legal document with a regulatory agency. In the United States, that regulatory agency is the Securities and Exchange Commission (SEC). One type of security is a share in an investment company, which we will describe in more detail in Chapter 5.

The second category includes institutional investors that must meet contractually specified liabilities. A *liability* is a cash outlay that must be made at a specific future date in order to satisfy the contractual terms of an obligation. An institutional investor is concerned with both the *amount* and *timing* of liabilities, because its portfolio of assets must produce the cash flow to meet any payments it has promised to make in a timely manner. Here are two examples of institutional investors that face liabilities:

1. Life insurance companies have a wide range of investment-oriented products. One such product is a *guaranteed investment contract* (GIC). For this product, a life insurance company guarantees an interest rate on the funds given to it by a customer. With respect to the GIC account, the investment objective of the asset manager is to earn a return greater than the rate guaranteed.
2. There are two types of pension plans offered by the sponsor of a plan. The sponsor can be a corporation, a state government, or a local government. The two types of pension plans that can be sponsored are a defined contribution or a defined benefit plan. For a *defined contribution plan*, the sponsor need only provide a specified amount for an employee to invest and the employee is then responsible for investing those funds. The plan sponsor has no further obligation. However, in the case of a *defined benefit plan*, the plan sponsor has agreed to make specified payments to the employee after retirement. Thus, the plan sponsor has created a liability against itself, and in managing the assets of a defined benefit pension plan, the asset manager must earn a return adequate to meet those future pension liabilities.

Some institutional investors may have accounts that have both non-liability-driven objectives and liability-driven objectives. For example, a life insurance company may have a GIC account (which as explained above is a liability-driven objective product) and a variable annuity account. With a variable annuity account, an investor makes either a single payment or a series of payments to the life insurance company and in turn the life insurance company (1) invests the payments received and (2) makes payments to the investor at some future date. The payments that the life insurance company makes will depend on the investment performance of the insurance company's asset manager. While the life insurance company does have a liability, it does not guarantee any specific dollar payment.

Benchmark

Regardless of the type of investment objective, to evaluate the performance of an asset manager, a *benchmark* will be established. The determination of a benchmark is in some cases simple. In the case of a liability-driven objective, the benchmark is typically a return target. For example, the California Public Employee's Retirement System (CalPERS) has a liability-driven objective and has established as its benchmark a 7% return.[2] The benchmark is accompanied by the imposition of the permitted volatility for the portfolio return. As we explain in later chapters, the volatility of a portfolio's return is measured by the standard deviation of returns. This is a statistical measure of volatility. CalPERS target benchmark is 7% with a volatility of no more than 13%.

In the case of a non-liability-driven objective, the benchmark is typically the asset class in which the assets are invested. For example, later in this chapter we describe the major asset classes. One such asset class is large capitalization stocks. There are several benchmarks for that asset class and the client and asset manager will jointly determine which one to use.

It is not always simple to determine the benchmark. Today, regulated investment companies have created funds that invest in multiple asset classes. Such funds, referred to as *multi-asset funds*, the subject of Chapter 19, will often have a return objective that is based on some absolute return.

Typically, asset management firms or external consultants work with the client to determine the benchmark.

Establishing an Investment Policy

The second major activity in the asset management process is establishing policy guidelines to satisfy the investment objectives. Setting policy begins with the *asset allocation decision*. That is, a decision must be made as to how the funds to be invested should be distributed among the major asset classes that we describe below.

---

[2]See Saret, Zhan, and Mitra [2017]. A study of public pension funds by the Center for Retirement Research at Boston College reported that as of 2015, the average public pension plan had a long-term target return of 7.6% down from a target return of 8% in 2001 (see Munnell and Aubry [2016]).

To appreciate how important the asset allocation decision is, we briefly review two major studies that have looked at historical performance and the asset class mix. Brinson, Hood, and Beebower [1986] investigated the performance of US pension plans over the period 1974–1983. They found that about 94% of the average return variation can be explained by the asset mix. A study by Ibbotson and Kaplan [2000] found that about 90% of returns can be explained by the asset mix, confirming the findings of the study done 14 years earlier. Subsequent studies further confirm the critical importance of the asset allocation decision.

In this section, we first describe the asset classes and then explain asset allocation strategies.

Asset Classes

Asset allocation strategies involve the allocation of the portfolio funds among the asset classes. But what is an asset class? In practice, an asset class is determined in terms of the investment attributes that the members of an asset class share. These investment characteristics include (1) the principal factors that impact the value of the asset class; (2) a similar risk and return characteristic; and (3) a common legal or regulatory structure. Based on this way of defining an asset class, we can look at asset classes in terms of the correlation of their expected rate of return. The correlation of the expected rate of return of those assets within an asset class will be very high. In contrast, the correlation between the expected rate of return between two asset classes is low.

Asset classes are also classified based on the type of capital market where they are traded. The capital markets throughout the world are classified as developed, emerging (developing), and frontier (pre-emerging) capital markets. Two attributes differentiate these three capital markets.[3] They are the development of a country's economy and the development of its capital markets. A country's economic development refers primarily to its per capita income and its potential growth rate. *Developed market countries* are characterized by higher levels of per capita income but lower potential growth. The development of their capital markets refers to the size of

[3] "What is the Difference between a Developed, Emerging, and Frontier Market?" May 11, 2012. http://www.nasdaq.com/article/what-is-the-difference-between-a-developed-emerging-and-frontier-market-cm140649.

their market capitalization, the level of liquidity, and the development of their supporting regulatory and legal bodies. These characteristics affect the growth potential, risk, and liquidity of investments in their markets. Developed market countries are found mostly in North America, Western Europe, and Australasia.

Emerging market countries, also called *developing market countries*, share some of the characteristics of a developed country but not all of them. Loucks, Penicook, and Schillhorn [2008, p. 340] describe what is meant by an emerging market as follows:

> Emerging market issuers rely on international investors for capital. Emerging markets cannot finance their fiscal deficits domestically because domestic capital markets are poorly developed and local investors are unable or unwilling to lend to the government. Although emerging market issuers differ greatly in terms of credit risk, dependence on foreign capital is the most basic characteristic of the asset class.

Developing market countries include Brazil, Russia, India, and China (as a group, popularly referred to as BRIC); Portugal, Ireland, Italy, Greece, Spain (PIIGS); and other countries. China and India are the two largest developing market countries.

A *frontier market country* or *pre-emerging market country* characterizes a country whose economy is slower than developing market countries. One characteristic of frontier markets is that there is a lack of transparency and information. As a result, there is considerable difference in whether securities are properly priced in the market. There are 29 countries that are included in market indexes comprising frontier countries.[4]

Along with the designation of asset classes comes a barometer to be able to quantify the performance of the asset class — the risk, return, and the correlation of the returns with different asset classes. The barometer is called a "benchmark index", "market index", or simply "index". An example would be the Standard & Poor's 500. We describe many more indexes in later chapters. The indexes are also used by investors to evaluate

[4]They include Argentina, Bahrain, Bangladesh, Burkina Faso, Benin, Croatia, Estonia, Guinea-Bissau, Ivory Coast, Jordan, Kenya, Kuwait, Lebanon, Lithuania, Kazakhstan, Mauritius, Mali, Morocco, Niger, Nigeria, Oman, Romania, Serbia, Senegal, Slovenia, Sri Lanka, Togo, Tunisia, and Vietnam.

the performance of professional managers that they hire to manage their assets.

The different asset classes

In developed market countries, the major asset classes are (1) cash equivalents, (2) equities (common stocks), (3) bonds, and (4) real assets. The convention is to refer to cash equivalents, equities, and fixed income as *traditional asset classes.* Those asset classes that are not one of the traditional asset classes include real assets such as real estate and commodities, as well as hedge funds. The non-traditional asset classes are referred to as *alternative assets.*

From the perspective of a US investor, the three traditional major asset classes can be extended to create other asset classes as follows:

(1) Cash Equivalents: This asset class includes securities that are characterized as having a low-risk, low return profile. The securities that fall into this asset class are US Treasury bills, commercial paper, certificates of deposit, and bankers' acceptance.

(2) Stock Asset Classes: The broad asset class of equities or common stock is typically classified based on the following:

- the size of the company;
- whether the stock exhibits the characteristics of a growth stock or a value stock;
- whether the stock is issued by a domestic or foreign corporation;
- whether the stock is that of a public or private company.

The size of a company is measured in terms of its *market capitalization* (or simply *market cap*) which is computed by multiplying the market value of each share of the corporation's common stock by the number of shares of common stock outstanding. For example, in January 2020, IRobot Corporation (IRobot) had approximately 28.27 million common shares of common stock outstanding and the price at that time was about $54.78 per share.[5] Multiplying 28.27 million by $54.78 gives a market cap for IRobot of approximately $1.55 billion.

[5]Information about the number of shares outstanding for a company can be found at Yahoo!Finance (https://finance.yahoo.com/) under the tab "Statistics". Also, in this tab the market cap is shown.

Based on market cap, the following stock asset classes are used, although not every financial advisor or asset manager agrees with these cut-off values for market cap:

- mega-cap stocks (greater than \$200 billion);
- large-cap stocks (\$10 billion to \$200 billion);
- mid-cap stocks (\$2 billion to \$10 billion);
- small-cap stocks (\$300 million to \$2 billion);
- micro-cap stocks (\$50 million to \$300 million);
- nanocap stocks (less than \$50 million).

Based on the above market cap classifications, IRobot is a micro-cap stock.

In practice, stocks with a market cap greater than or equal to \$10 billion are referred to as large-cap stocks and therefore incorporate mega-cap stocks. Also, in practice, stocks with a market cap that is less than \$2 billion are classified as small cap stocks and therefore include micro-cap and nanocap stocks. So, IRobot would be classified as a small cap stock.

Equities are also classified based on attributes referred to as "growth" and "value". Although the market cap of a company is easy to determine given the market price per share and the number of shares outstanding, how does one define "value" and "growth" stocks? We'll describe how this is done in Chapter 13.

(3) Bond Asset Classes: For US bonds, also referred to as fixed-income securities, the following are classified as asset classes: (1) US government bonds, (2) corporate bonds, (3) US municipal bonds (i.e., state and local bonds), (4) residential mortgage-backed securities, (5) commercial mortgage-backed securities, and (6) asset-backed securities. In turn, several of these asset classes are further segmented by the credit rating of the issuer (we discuss credit ratings in Chapter 2). For example, for corporate bonds, investment-grade (i.e., high credit quality) corporate bonds and non-investment grade corporate bonds (i.e., speculative quality) are treated as two separate asset classes.

Asset Allocation Strategies

Asset allocation strategies fall into the following two categories: (1) strategic asset allocation and (2) dynamic asset allocation.

Strategic asset allocation strategy

A *strategic asset allocation strategy* can loosely be characterized as a long-term asset allocation decision, in which the investor seeks to assess an appropriate long-term "normal" asset mix that offers the greatest prospects for strong long-term rewards to accomplish the investment objectives. The key in a strategic asset allocation strategy is the establishment of a fixed allocation to each asset class in which the asset manager is permitted to invest. In assessing the strategic asset allocation strategy, the investor will take into consideration risk tolerance, the potential returns from each asset class, the various risks associated with each asset class, the correlations between the returns of each pair of asset classes, and capital market conditions. The tools for performing this analysis are described in Chapter 18.

In practice, a strategic asset allocation strategy will allow for a narrow range for the deviation from the specified allocation for each asset class. For example, suppose that the strategic asset allocation strategy specifies that 55% be invested in equities. Each day as prices change, the portfolio's allocation to equities may deviate from 55%. The strategic asset allocation may permit a deviation of 2% so that the portfolio allocation to equities is permitted to range from 53% to 57%. Once the actual portfolio is outside of that range, the asset manager must act to bring the portfolio's allocation to equities into compliance by either buying (if the portfolio's allocation to equities is below the range) or selling equities (if the portfolio's allocation to equities is above the range).

For example, as mentioned earlier, CalPERS established a target return of 7% with a volatility of no more than 13%. For 2018, CalPERS' board of trustees selected the following strategic asset allocation that it felt, based on capital market conditions and the relevant risks, would realize its investment objective: 50% in global equity, 28% fixed income, 13% real assets, 8% private equity, and 1% liquidity. In the news release on this asset allocation, CalPERS stated: "In making its decision, the Board reviewed recommendations from CalPERS team members, external pension and investment consultants, and input from employer and employee stakeholder groups."[6]

An investor pursuing a strategic asset allocation strategy may not permit the asset manager to deviate from the fixed asset mix specified

[6] "CalPERS Selects Asset Allocation for Investment Portfolio," December 18, 2017. https://www.calpers.ca.gov/page/newsroom/calpers-news/2017/asset-allocation-selected-for-investment-portfolio.

(or violate the boundaries for a specific asset class). Consequently, since once the allocations are made to each asset class, no changes are permitted, a strategic asset allocation strategy is a passive asset allocation strategy. However, investors may allow an asset manager to deviate from the fixed allocation to an asset class in order to enhance the expected return through short-term gains to a given asset class. This asset allocation strategy is referred to as *tactical asset allocation.* Perceived short-term gains can be realized based on a variety of strategies that we describe throughout this book. Tactical asset allocation is not a single, clearly defined strategy. There are many variations and nuances that are involved in building a tactical allocation strategy. Given that the strategy is to seek short-term return enhancement opportunities, it is referred to as an active asset allocation strategy. The risk in this asset allocation strategy is that there could be considerable short-term losses that result in the strategic asset allocation strategy failing to meet the investment objectives.

Dynamic asset allocation strategy

A criticism of the strategic asset allocation strategy is that it considers only capital market conditions at the outset of the investment period and thereby fails to adapt to changes in capital market conditions. In contrast to a strategic asset allocation strategy, in a *dynamic asset allocation strategy* the asset mix (i.e., the allocation among the asset classes) is mechanistically shifted in response to changing capital market conditions. Also, unlike a strategic asset allocation strategy, no fixed allocation is established for each asset class. The asset manager is free to alter the asset mix based on expectations about each asset classes' performance. The asset manager shifts funds out of the asset classes that are expected to perform poorly and into those expected to perform the best. The performance of the portfolio is, of course, determined by the asset manager's skill in assessing the future performance of each asset class. Moreover, transaction costs are higher than for a strategic asset allocation strategy because of the rebalancing of the portfolio to capitalize on the expected performance of asset classes.

Like the tactical asset allocation strategy, the dynamic asset allocation strategy is an active asset allocation strategy. The difference between these two active asset allocation strategies is that the tactical asset allocation strategy requires that the asset manager return to the fixed allocation as specified by the strategic asset allocation strategy; the asset manager for the dynamic asset allocation does not have a fixed allocation to an asset class that must be adhered to.

Client's Investment Beliefs

A client's *investment beliefs* — their values and priorities — provide the foundations for the management of the investment portfolio, providing the guidelines in decision-making. Investment beliefs also guide clients in selecting asset managers who best share their beliefs. In a survey based on published investment beliefs, Slager and Koedijk [2007] find that there are three essential elements for investment beliefs: "(1) a clear view of the capital markets (the inefficiencies to exploit, the risk/return relation, the relation between asset pricing and investment horizon); (2) a competent organization (cost-effectiveness, organization-specific values); and (3) a view on societal issues that affect investments (sustainable investments, corporate governance)."[7]

The CalPERS Board of Administration, for example, adopted 10 investment beliefs in September 2013. These investment beliefs are shown in Figure 2. While not shown in Figure 2, for each investment belief there are several actionable statements (identified as sub-beliefs) that offer implementation insights. For example, consider Investment Belief 7 ("CalPERS

Investment Belief 1: Liabilities must influence the asset structure

Investment Belief 2: A long time investment horizon is a responsibility and an advantage

Investment Belief 3: CalPERS investment decisions may reflect wider stakeholder views, provided they are consistent with its fiduciary duty to members and beneficiaries

Investment Belief 4: Long-term value creation requires effective management of three forms of capital: financial, physical and human

Investment Belief 5: CalPERS must articulate its investment goals and performance measures and ensure clear accountability for their execution

Investment Belief 6: Strategic asset allocation is the dominant determinant of portfolio risk and return

Investment Belief 7: CalPERS will take risk only where we have a strong belief we will be rewarded for it

Investment Belief 8: Costs matter and need to be effectively managed

Investment Belief 9: Risk to CalPERS is multi-faceted and not fully captured through measures such as volatility or tracking error

Investment Belief 10: Strong processes and teamwork and deep resources are needed to achieve CalPERS goals and objectives

FIGURE 2: Ten Investment Beliefs Adopted by CALPERS Board of Administration
Source: CalPERS Beliefs. Our Views Guiding us into the Future. https://www.calpers.ca.gov/docs/board-agendas/201702/pension/item7-01.pdf.

[7]More about investment beliefs can be found in the book by Koedijk and Slager [2011].

will take risk only where we have a strong belief we will be rewarded for it"). The four sub-beliefs are as follows:

- "An expectation of a return premium is required to take risk; CalPERS aims to maximize return for the risk taken.
- Markets are not perfectly efficient, but inefficiencies are difficult to exploit after costs.
- CalPERS will use index tracking strategies where we lack conviction or demonstrable evidence that we can add value through active management.
- CalPERS should measure its investment performance relative to a reference portfolio of public, passively managed assets to ensure that active risk is being compensated at the Total Fund level over the long-term."

Figure 3 shows the four investment beliefs of another public pension retirement system, the Missouri State Employees' Retirement System (MOSERS).

Investment Constraints

In the development of an investment policy, the following factors must be considered:

- Client-imposed constraints.
- Regulatory constraints.
- Tax considerations.

Client-imposed constraints

Examples of client-imposed constraints would be restrictions that specify the types of securities in which a manager may invest and concentration limits on how much or little may be invested in a particular asset class or in a particular issuer. Today, one of the most popular client-imposed constraints on allocations to particular companies and industries is *responsible investing*. Based on minimum environmental factors (E), social responsibility factors (S), and corporate governance factors (G), a list of firms that fail in one or more of these criteria are removed as investment candidates for non-financial reasons. Responsible investing, also referred to as environmental, social, and governance (ESG) investing is described in Chapter 13.

Where the objective is to meet the performance of a particular market or customized benchmark, there may be a restriction as to the degree to which

- **Portfolio construction should focus first on the allocation and balancing of risk; it is the allocation of risk that drives portfolio returns.** While investment returns receive a lot of public attention, understanding and balancing risks across asset classes improves the consistency of returns for a given level of risk and thus provides more stability in the contribution rate for the employer. Returns are the end product, where risks are the ingredients.
- **Diversification is critical because the future is unknown.** Reliable diversification requires a fundamental understanding of the economic drivers of risk and return. MOSERS' policy portfolio has been built upon the premise that very little is known about what the future holds. Therefore it is rational to construct a portfolio that is believed to combat various economic conditions.
- **Every investment should be examined in the context of its potential return from beta (market return) and alpha (value added return); while separation is not always possible, every effort should be made to distinguish the two distinct return components.** Beta is the return which is expected to be earned by investing passively within a specific asset class or compensated risk premium. Exposures to beta can be purchased cheaply, and over long periods of time, the beta return should be positive and coincide with the risk associated with a given asset class. In contrast, alpha is the return generated through a manager's ability to select particular investments that perform better than the asset class as a whole. Alpha is a zero-sum game.

  Regardless of the source of the return, it is important to construct the portfolio based on a conscious decision to include a certain amount of beta exposure in the portfolio and a certain amount of alpha exposure. By consciously selecting this balance within the portfolio, staff is better able to manage the risks of the portfolio while ensuring the RRO is achieved.

- **Flexibility to opportunistically alter the portfolio away from risk-balanced when markets are driven to extremes as result of short-term economic cycles is an important portfolio management tool.** As a result of the cyclical nature of the economy, asset classes or investment strategies may be more or less attractive relative to others in given time frames, thus marginal flexibility in the allocation policy provides the system with the opportunity to capitalize on this cyclicality within prudent risk constraints. Under circumstances where the valuations of a particular asset class are compelling, it may make sense to modify the portfolio's allocation at the margins in order to capitalize on attractively valued opportunities without exposing the fund to additional risk.

FIGURE 3: Investment Beliefs of Missouri State Employees' Retirement System (MOSERS)
Source: https://www.mosers.org/Investments/Investment-Policy/Investment-Beliefs.aspx.

the manager may deviate from some key characteristics of the benchmark. For example, throughout this book we will discuss certain portfolio risk measures that are used to quantify different types of risks. The three major examples are tracking error risk for any type of asset class and market risk which is measured by beta for common stock portfolios and duration for bond portfolios. These portfolio risk measures provide an estimate of the portfolio's exposure to changes in key factors that affect a portfolio's performance — the market overall in the case of a portfolio's beta and the general level of interest rates in the case of a portfolio's duration.

Typically, a client will not set a specific value for the level of risk exposure. Instead, the client restriction may be in the form of a maximum on the level of the risk exposure or a permissible range for the risk measure relative to the benchmark's risk. For example, a client may restrict the portfolio's duration to be +0.5 or −0.5 of the client-specified benchmark. Thus, if the duration of the client-imposed benchmark is 4, the manager has the discretion of constructing a portfolio with a duration between 3.5 and 4.5.

Regulatory constraints

There are many types of regulatory constraints. These involve constraints on the asset classes that are permissible as well as concentration limits on investments. A *concentration limit* is a constraint on the maximum exposure to what may be included in a portfolio. It could be a maximum exposure to an asset class, a sector of the market, a company, or a country. Moreover, in making the asset allocation decision, consideration must be given to any risk-based capital requirements that may be imposed on a client by its regulators. For depository institutions and insurance companies, the amount of statutory capital required is related to the quality of the assets in which the institution has invested. For example, for regulated investment management companies (e.g., mutual funds), there are restrictions on the amount of leverage (i.e., amount of borrowed funds relative to equity) that can be used.

Tax considerations

Tax considerations are important for several reasons. First, certain institutional investors such as pension funds, endowments, and foundations are exempt from federal income taxation. Consequently, the asset classes in which they invest will not be those that are tax-advantaged investments. Second, there are tax factors that must be incorporated into the investment policy. For example, while a pension fund might be tax-exempt, there may be certain assets or the use of some investment vehicles in which it invests whose earnings may be taxed.

Selecting an Investment Strategy

Selecting an investment strategy that is consistent with the investment objectives and investment policy guidelines of the client or institution is another major activity in the asset management process. The broadest categorization of investment strategies is active and passive strategies.

An *active strategy* uses available information and forecasting techniques to seek a better performance than a portfolio that is simply diversified broadly. Essential to all active strategies are expectations about the factors that have been found to influence the performance of an asset class. For example, with active common stock strategies this may include forecasts of future earnings, dividends, or price/earnings ratios. With bond portfolios that are actively managed, expectations may involve forecasts of future interest rates and sector spreads. Active portfolio strategies involving foreign securities may require forecasts of local interest rates and exchange rates.

A *passive strategy* involves minimal expectational input, and instead relies on diversification to match the performance of some market index. In effect, a passive strategy assumes that the marketplace will efficiently reflect all available information in the price paid for securities. Between these extremes of active and passive strategies, several strategies have sprung up that have elements of both. For example, the core of a portfolio may be passively managed with the balance being actively managed.

A useful way of thinking about active versus passive strategies is in terms of the following three activities performed by the manager: (1) portfolio construction (deciding on the securities to buy and sell), (2) trading of securities, and (3) portfolio monitoring. Generally, active managers devote most of their time to portfolio construction. In contrast, with passive strategies managers devote less time to this activity.

In the bond area, there are several strategies classified as *structured portfolio strategies*. A structured portfolio strategy is one in which a portfolio is designed to achieve the performance of some predetermined liabilities that must be paid out. These strategies are frequently used when trying to match the funds received from an investment portfolio to the future liabilities that must be paid and are therefore referred to as *liability-driven strategies*.

Given the choice among active and passive management, which should be selected? The answer depends on the client's (1) view of how "price efficient" the market is, (2) investment beliefs, (3) risk tolerance, and (4) liabilities structure (if any).

By marketplace *price efficiency*, we mean how difficult it would be to earn a greater return than a passive strategy after adjusting for the risk associated with a strategy and the transaction costs associated with implementing that strategy. We will discuss the different forms of market efficiency and the implications for a client's selection of an investment strategy in Chapter 11.

Formulating an Active Strategy

Asset managers formulate active strategies that they propose to clients or prospective clients. The various categories of active strategies are described throughout this book. In formulating portfolio strategies an asset manager will be guided by investment beliefs.

Before proposing these strategies to clients or potential clients, and even to the senior management of the asset management firm, the asset management team must test the strategy using historical return data. The testing of a potential strategy is referred to as *backtesting*. There are various methodologies and statistical pitfalls in backtesting; these are briefly described in Chapter 13 and in more detail in Chapters 17 and 18 in the companion volume of this book.

Constructing and Monitoring the Portfolio

Once a portfolio strategy is selected, the asset manager must select the assets to be included in the portfolio. The following are involved in this major activity of the asset management process:

- Producing realistic and reasonable return expectations and forecasts.
- Constructing an efficient portfolio.
- Monitoring, controlling, and managing risk exposure.
- Managing trading and transaction costs.

In seeking to produce realistic and reasonable return expectations, the asset manager has several tools available that we describe in this book. An active asset manager will seek to identify mispriced securities or market sectors. This information is then used as input to construct an *efficient portfolio*. An efficient portfolio is defined as a portfolio that offers the greatest expected return for a given level of risk or, equivalently, the lowest risk for a given expected return. The specific meaning of return and risk cannot be provided at this time. As we develop our understanding of asset management throughout this book, we will be able to quantify what we mean by these terms.

Once a portfolio is constructed, the asset manager must monitor the portfolio to determine how the portfolio's risk exposure may have changed given prevailing market conditions and information about the assets in the portfolio. The current portfolio may no longer be efficient and, as a result, the asset manager is likely to rebalance the portfolio in order to produce an efficient portfolio.

Transaction costs critically impact investment performance. The costs associated with managing a portfolio go beyond brokerage costs for transacting in securities. We briefly describe these costs in Chapter 13 and in more detail in Chapter 14 in the companion volume. Transactions costs must be considered not only in the initial construction of the portfolio but also when the portfolio must be rebalanced. *Rebalancing of a portfolio* means the asset manager alters the holdings of the portfolio.

Measuring and Evaluating Performance

The measurement and evaluation of investment performance involves two activities. The first activity is performance measurement, which involves properly calculating the return realized by an asset manager over some time interval referred to as the *evaluation period.* It may seem that this would be a straightforward calculation, but, as we will see in Chapter 7, there are several important issues that must be addressed in developing a methodology for calculating a portfolio's return. Different methodologies can lead to quite disparate results, making it difficult to compare the relative performance of different asset managers.

The second activity is performance evaluation, which is concerned with two issues: (1) determining whether the asset manager added value by outperforming the established benchmark and (2) determining how the asset manager achieved the calculated return. For example, in Part Three of this book we describe several strategies that the manager of a stock portfolio can employ. Did the asset manager achieve the return by market timing, by buying undervalued stocks, by buying low-capitalization stocks, by overweighting specific industries, and so on? The decomposition of the performance results to explain the reasons why those results were achieved is called *performance attribution analysis.* Moreover, performance evaluation requires the determination of whether the asset manager achieved superior performance (i.e., added value) by skill or by luck.

Key Points of the Chapter

- Asset management is the process of managing money.
- Investors can be classified as either individual investors (retail investors) or institutional investors.
- Institutional investors include pension funds, insurance companies, endowments and foundations, registered investment companies, depository institutions, and hedge funds.
- The five major activities of the asset management process include: setting investment objectives; establishing an investment policy; selecting an investment strategy; constructing and monitoring the portfolio; and measuring and evaluating investment performance.
- Setting investment objectives starts with a thorough analysis of the investment objectives of the client whose funds are being managed.
- The investment objectives of institutional investors are classified as either non-liability-driven objectives or liability-driven objectives.
- To evaluate the performance of an asset manager, a benchmark will be established.
- In the case of a liability-driven objective, the benchmark is typically a return target; in the case of a non-liability-driven objective, the benchmark is typically the asset class in which the assets are invested.
- Setting policy to satisfy investment objectives begins with the asset allocation decision (i.e., how the funds to be invested should be distributed among the major asset classes).
- Empirical studies consistently confirm the critical importance of the asset allocation decision on investment performance.
- An asset class is based on the investment attributes that the members of an asset class share: (1) the principal factors that impact the value of the asset class; (2) similar risk and return characteristic; and (3) common legal or regulatory structure.
- Based on investment attributes for defining an asset class, one can look at asset classes in terms of the correlation of their expected rate of return; the correlation of the expected rate of return for assets within the same asset class will be very high, while the correlation between the expected rate of return between two different asset classes is low.
- Asset classes are also classified based on the type of capital market where they are traded: developed, emerging (developing), and frontier (pre-emerging) capital markets.

- The two attributes that differentiate capital markets are the development of a country's economy and the development of its capital markets.
- In developed market countries, the major asset classes are (1) cash equivalents, (2) equities (common stocks), (3) fixed-income (bonds and loans), and (4) real assets.
- The convention is to refer to cash equivalents, equities, and fixed income as traditional asset classes; those asset classes that are not one of the traditional asset classes include real assets such as real estate and commodities, as well as hedge funds.
- The non-traditional asset classes are referred to as alternative assets.
- The broad asset class of equities or common stock is typically classified based on the size of the company, whether the stock exhibits the characteristics of a growth stock or a value stock, whether the stock is issued by a domestic or foreign corporation, and whether the stock is that of a public or private company.
- The size of a company is measured in terms of its market capitalization which is computed by multiplying the market value of each share of the corporation's common stock by the number of shares of common stock outstanding
- For US bonds, also referred to as fixed income securities, the following are classified as asset classes: (1) US government bonds, (2) corporate bonds, (3) US municipal bonds (i.e., state and local bonds), (4) residential mortgage-backed securities, (5) commercial mortgage-backed securities, and (6) asset-backed securities.
- The two types of asset allocation strategies are strategic asset allocation and dynamic asset allocation.
- Generally speaking, a strategic asset allocation strategy is a long-term asset allocation decision, in which the investor seeks to assess an appropriate long-term "normal" asset mix that offers the greatest prospects for strong long-term rewards to accomplish the investment objectives.
- The key in a strategic asset allocation strategy is the establishment of a fixed allocation to each asset class in which the asset manager is permitted to invest.
- In practice, a strategic asset allocation strategy will allow for a narrow range for the deviation from the specified allocation for each asset class.
- In a tactical asset allocation strategy, an investor allows an asset manager to deviate from the fixed allocation to an asset class in order to enhance the expected return to the asset class through short-term gains.

- In contrast to a strategic asset allocation strategy, in a dynamic asset allocation strategy the allocation among the asset classes is mechanistically shifted in response to changing capital market conditions; unlike a strategic asset allocation strategy, no fixed allocation is established for each asset class.
- When using a dynamic asset allocation strategy, the asset manager is free to alter the asset mix based on expectations about each asset classes' performance, shifting funds out of the asset classes that are expected to perform poorly and into those expected to perform the best.
- A client's investment beliefs provide the foundations for the management of the investment portfolio, the client's values and priorities provide guidelines in decision-making.
- Investment beliefs guide clients in selecting asset managers who best share their beliefs.
- In the development of an investment policy, client-imposed constraints, regulatory constraints, and tax considerations must be considered.
- The broadest categorization of investment strategies is active and passive strategies.
- An active strategy uses available information and forecasting techniques to seek a better performance than a portfolio that is simply diversified broadly.
- Essential to all active strategies are expectations about the factors that have been found to influence the performance of an asset class.
- A passive strategy involves minimal expectational input, and in contrast to active strategies relies on diversification to match the performance of some market index.
- A passive strategy assumes that the marketplace will efficiently reflect all available information in the price paid for securities.
- Between the extremes of active and passive strategies, several strategies have sprung up that have elements of both.
- A structured portfolio strategy is one in which a portfolio is designed to achieve the performance of some predetermined liabilities that must be paid out.
- A structured portfolio strategy is used when trying to match the funds received from an investment portfolio to the future liabilities that must be paid and are therefore referred to as liability-driven strategies.
- A client's considerations in deciding between an active and passive management strategy include (1) view of how "price efficient" the market

is, (2) investment beliefs, (3) risk tolerance, and (4) liabilities structure (if any).

- Marketplace price efficiency means that it is difficult to earn a greater return than a passive strategy after adjusting for the risk associated with a strategy and the transaction costs associated with implementing that strategy.
- Before proposing any strategy to clients or potential clients, the asset manager must test the strategy using historical return data.
- Backtesting is the procedure for testing a potential strategy.
- Once a portfolio strategy is selected, portfolio construction involves the asset manager's selection of the specific assets to be included in the portfolio.
- To construct a portfolio, the asset manager needs to produce realistic and reasonable return expectations and forecasts.
- An active asset manager will seek to identify mispriced securities or market sectors and use this information as input to construct an efficient portfolio.
- An efficient portfolio is defined as a portfolio that offers the greatest expected return for a given level of risk or, equivalently, the lowest risk for a given expected return.
- Once a portfolio is constructed, the asset manager must monitor the portfolio to determine how the portfolio's risk exposure may have changed given prevailing market conditions and information about the assets in the portfolio.
- Transaction costs critically impact investment performance.
- Transaction costs associated with managing a portfolio are more than brokerage costs for transacting in securities and these costs must be considered not only in the initial construction of the portfolio but also when the portfolio must be rebalanced.
- The measurement and evaluation of investment performance involves measuring performance using the proper calculation of return and evaluating the reason for the performance.
- There are several important issues that must be addressed in developing a methodology for calculating a portfolio's return since different methodologies can lead to quite disparate results, making it difficult to compare the relative performance of different asset managers.
- Performance evaluation involves two issues: (1) determining whether the asset manager added value by outperforming the established benchmark

and (2) determining how the asset manager achieved the calculated return.
- Performance attribution analysis involves the decomposition of the performance results to explain the reasons for those results.

References

Brinson, G. P., R. Hood, and G. L. Beebower, 1986. "Determinants of portfolio performance," *Financial Analysts Journal*, July/August: 133–136.

Fischer, M. S., 2019. "World's top 20 biggest asset managers: 2019," *ThinkAdvisor*. Available at https://www.thinkadvisor.com/2019/08/07/worlds-top-20-biggest-asset-managers-2019/?slreturn=20200115114729.

Ibbotson, R. G. and P. D. Kaplan, 2000. "Does asset allocation policy explain 40%, 90%, or 100% of performance?" *Financial Analysts Journal*, January/February: 26–33.

Koedijk, K. and A. Slager, 2011. *Investment Beliefs: A Positive Approach to Institutional Investing*. London: Palgrave MacMillan.

Lemke, T. 2019. "The 10 largest investment management companies worldwide," *The Balance*. Available at https://www.thebalance.com/which-firms-have-the-most-assets-under-management-4173923.

Loucks, M., J. A. Penicook, and U. Schillhorn, 2008. "Emerging markets debt," in *The Handbook of Finance*, Vol. 1, F. J. Fabozzi (ed.). Hoboken, NJ: John Wiley & Sons, pp. 339–346.

Munnell, A. H. and J-P. Auby, 2016. "The funding of state and local pensions: 2015–2020," Center for Retirement Research at Boston College, *State and Local Pension Plans, No. 50*, June: 1–14.

Saret, J. N., B. Zhan, and S. Mitra, 2017. "Investment return assumptions of public pension funds," *Pension & Investments*, March 23. Available at https://www.pionline.com/article/20170323/ONLINE/170319953/investment-return-assumptions-of-public-pension-funds.

Slager, A. and K. Koedijk, 2007. "Investment eliefbs," *Journal of Portfolio Management*, 33(3): 77–84.

Chapter 2

The Different Types of Risks in Investing

Learning Objectives

After reading this chapter, you will understand:

- the general meaning of risk;
- the distinction between risk and uncertainty;
- the difference between systematic risk and unsystematic risk;
- the relationship between systematic risk and non-diversifiable risk, and between unsystematic risk and idiosyncratic risk/diversifiable risk;
- what is meant by investment risk and the different types of investment risks: price risk, credit risk, inflation risk, liquidity risk, and foreign-exchange rate risk;
- what is meant by a risk factor;
- what market beta is and how it is related to price risk;
- what the duration of a bond measures and how it is related to a bond's price risk; and
- the different forms of credit risk/counterparty risk.

Throughout this book, we will use the word "risk". An Internet search on the word "risk" shows results in excess of 42 million. With respect to investments, clients typically view risk as the potential that there will be a negative outcome relative to what was expected. As we will see, that is too general a definition of risk. Here, we will explain the various types of investment risk which will be discussed further in later chapters.

Risk vs. Uncertainty

Let's begin by distinguishing between what is meant by "risk" and what is meant by "uncertainty". Although these terms are commonly used interchangeably, there is a difference between the two. As we will see when we discuss how asset managers construct portfolios, they rely on their beliefs about the factors that are expected to impact the performance of the assets that are candidates for inclusion in their portfolio. In formulating those beliefs about the possible outcomes, asset managers can draw on the field of probability theory to quantify the risk associated with potential outcomes. That is, asset managers are assumed to be able to express their beliefs in the form of probabilities. Economists make a distinction between risk and uncertainty based on how probabilities are derived.

Frank Knight [1921] argued that "risk" applies to decision-making in which the outcome of the decision is unknown, but the decision-maker can fairly accurately quantify the probability associated with each outcome that may arise from that decision. Knight called this "measurable risk" or "risk proper". Knight viewed "uncertainty" as situations in which the decision-maker cannot know all the information needed in order to obtain all the probabilities associated with the potential outcomes and referred to this as "unmeasurable uncertainty" or "true uncertainty". Today we refer to it as "Knightian uncertainty".[1]

An example given by Knight should help us understand Knight's distinction between risk and uncertainty. Consider an urn that includes red and black balls. Two individuals are asked to draw a ball from the urn. Because the first individual has no information about the number of red and number of black balls in the urn, she might assume that there is an equal probability of drawing a ball of either color. Unlike the first individual, the second individual has information that the urn contains three red balls for each black ball. Because of this information, the second individual knows that for every four balls in the urn, three are red and, therefore, the probability of drawing a red ball is 75% and the probability of drawing a black ball is 25%. According to Knight, the second individual faces risk while the first individual faces uncertainty.

We can cast this illustration in terms of an investment decision. Consider an analyst evaluating two companies for possible inclusion in a portfolio. The first is a publicly traded company started in 1950 and which has filed

[1] A similar distinction between risk and uncertainty was made by John Maynard Keynes [1921]. He argued that there is risk that can be calculated and another sort of risk that he labeled "irreducible uncertainty". Keynes recognized that there are decisions where risks cannot be computed because attempting to do so would require relying on assumptions about the future that have no basis in probability theory.

information with the SEC and has trading information available since its inception. The second company is a start-up that has not generated significant revenue. In evaluating the prospects of the two companies in terms of future price performance, the analyst might view the decision for the publicly traded company in terms of risk and the private company in terms of uncertainty.

There is a long-running debate among economists about the relevance of the distinction between risk and uncertainty in decision-making. Some economists argue that the two concepts are the same while others argue that the distinction is crucial. For asset managers, there is strong evidence that the distinction is important in decision-making. This evidence comes from the global financial crisis of 2008–2009. There are several causes of this crisis which led to the Great Recession. However, one of the major factors that market observers believe contributed to the financial crisis was the failure of the statistical models used to manage the risk of financial institutions to provide a warning about the financial difficulties that lay ahead. It appears that the management of financial institutions believed that they had adequate statistical models for measuring risk so as to prevent a major collapse in the financial system. That is, management of financial institutions failed to recognize that they were dealing with situations that involved Knightian uncertainty.

Black Swans and Uncertainty

Recently, there have been other forms of uncertainty that have been popularized. These forms of uncertainty are events that are not even contemplated as potential outcomes prior to their occurrence. The first of these is the distinction between "known unknowns" and "unknown unknowns". The second is the notion of black swan-type events.

The notion of "known unknowns" and "unknown unknowns" was popularized by then US Secretary of Defense Donald Rumsfeld in response to a question at a February 12, 2002 news briefing regarding the lack of evidence that linked the government of Iraq with the supply of weapons of mass destruction to terrorist groups.[2] His response was as follows:

> Reports that say that something hasn't happened are always interesting to me, because as we know, there are known knowns;

[2]While Rumsfeld popularized the terms, the terms "known, known–unknown, and unknown–unknown" risks are familiar to those in the field of project management. See Wideman [1992].

> there are things we know we know. We also know there are known unknowns; that is to say we know there are some things we do not know. But there are also unknown unknowns – the ones we don't know we don't know.

Taleb [2005, 2010] has popularized the term "black swan event" to characterize a high-impact, hard-to-predict, and rare event that is beyond the realm of normal expectations that would be formed based on historical events that have occurred in financial markets, technology, and the sciences. In the context of asset management, a "high-impact event" means that the event has a large monetary impact on an investment, a trading position, or a portfolio. A black swan event is a surprise to an asset manager, and even after the event has occurred, the asset manager makes up an excuse for its occurrence by providing an explanation. Linking this to Knightian uncertainty, black swan events are presumed not to exist.

Total Risk, Systematic Risks, and Unsystematic Risks

To be able to estimate an asset's fair value and how that asset's value will change over time, the factors that drive (i.e., affect) asset valuation must be determined. Because the factors affect asset valuation, they are referred to as *risk factors*. However, for simplicity in our discussion here we will refer to them as simply "factors".

In general, risks can be divided into two categories: systematic risks and unsystematic risks. *Systematic risks* are the risks that affect the valuation of *all* assets within an asset class. These risks are also referred to as *common risk factors*. Some of these factors are expected to affect all asset classes. For example, in the Spring of 2019, there was concern about the impact of a potential trade war with China on the earnings of US companies. This concern drove down the price of the stock of most companies, despite the US economy showing strong economic growth and companies reporting earnings that were better than expected by stock analysts. In later chapters, we discuss systematic factors for common stocks and bonds.

In addition to systematic risks, there are factors that may be unique to the issuer of a particular asset. This risk is referred to as *unsystematic risk*. Other names given to systematic risk are *idiosyncratic risk*, *company-specific risk*, and *unique risk*. Examples of idiosyncratic risk for a company would be a strike by its employees, an uninsured natural disaster that destroys a principal manufacturing plant, the expropriation of major overseas manufacturing facilities by the government of the country in which the facilities are located, or a litigation against a company for patent infringement.

Diversification, Total Risks, Systematic Risks, and Unsystematic Risks

Theories about the pricing of assets are the subject of Chapter 9. These theories assert that in financial markets that operate efficiently in pricing assets, investors should only be compensated for accepting systematic risks. That is, the price of an asset in such a market embodies compensation for only systematic risks. The explanation for this is that the other component of risk, unsystematic risks, can be eliminated by constructing a diversified portfolio. Unlike unsystematic risks, investors cannot eliminate systematic risks by creating a diversified portfolio. Because of this characteristic of systematic risks, they are also labeled *non-diversifiable risks* and unsystematic risk is also labeled *diversifiable risk*. That is, we have the following relationships:

$$\text{Total risk} = \text{Systematic risk} + \text{Unsystematic risk}$$

$$\text{Systematic risk} = \text{Common risk} = \text{Non-diversifiable risk}$$

$$\text{Unsystematic risk} = \text{Idiosyncratic risk} = \text{Unique risk} = \text{Diversifiable risk}$$

There is ample empirical evidence gathered over the past 50 years that supports the relationship between total risks, systematic risks, and unsystematic risks, and their effect on diversification.[3] In portfolio theory, which we describe in Part Two of this book, we will see that the total risk of a stock is measured by the standard deviation of the stock's return. (We'll show how this is calculated in Chapter 7.) Similarly, the total risk of a portfolio is measured by the standard deviation of the portfolio returns.

Empirical studies have calculated for randomly selected common stock, the total risks of portfolios of common stock with a varying number of company stocks. What was calculated from randomly constructed portfolios is the average standard deviation of the portfolio return. These studies show that total risk declines as the number of holdings increases. Adding more stocks gradually tends to eliminate the unsystematic risk, leaving only systematic risk.

[3]The first such study was by Wagner and Lau [1971].

The major findings of these studies on the impact of diversification on the risk of a portfolio of common stock are as follows:

- The average return is unrelated to the number of issues in the portfolio, yet the standard deviation of return declines as the number of holdings increases.
- At a portfolio size of about 20 randomly selected common stocks, the level of total portfolio risk is reduced such that what is left is only systematic risk.
- For individual stocks, the average ratio of systematic risk to total risk is about 30%.
- On the average, approximately 40% of the single-security risk is eliminated by forming randomly selected portfolios of 20 stocks. Additional diversification yields rapidly diminishing reduction in risk. The improvement is slight when the number of securities held is increased beyond, say, 10.
- The return on a diversified portfolio follows the market closely with the ratio of systematic risk to total risk exceeding 90%.

Major Investment Risks

Now let's focus on the major investment risks that investors face that can result in performance that is less than what was expected. These risks include (1) price risk, (2) credit risk, (3) inflation risk, (4) liquidity risk, and (5) foreign-exchange rate risk. Here we give a brief description of each risk and discuss them further in later chapters. Also, by understanding these risks, one can understand why financial instruments, known as financial derivatives, can be used to control each of these risks.

Price Risk

Asset prices change over time. *Price risk* is the risk that an asset's price will change adversely. Whether there is a price increase or decrease, the price risk that an investor is exposed to depends on the investor's position. An investor can have either a long position or a short position in the asset. A *long position* means that an investor owns the asset or is considering purchasing the asset. An investor in a long position benefits from an increase in the asset's price, but realizes a loss if the asset's price declines.

In a *short position*, an investor has sold or plans to sell an asset that it does not own. An investor who has a short position in an asset will benefit if the price decreases. Although selling an asset that is not owned, referred to as *short selling*, may sound like an illegal act, it is not in financial markets. In fact, the ability to sell short is a critical aspect of financial markets because it allows asset prices to reflect their true value. More will be said in later chapters about the role of short selling in financial markets, as well as the mechanism available to investors who want to short sell. What is important here is that for a short position, price risk is the risk that the price will increase.

Let's look at the price movement of Apple Inc. (ticker symbol APPL) on the following three selected dates over the period April 23, 2019 to May 3, 2019:

$$\text{April 23, 2019 \$207.48,}$$

$$\text{April 30, 2019 \$200.67,}$$

$$\text{May 3, 2019 \$211.75.}$$

Suppose the investor purchased the stock of Apple on April 23, 2019 for $207.48 per share. The price risk that this investor faces is that the price per share would decline below $207.48. On April 30, 2019, Apple's price traded at $200.67, which would have resulted in a loss of $6.81 per share if the stock had been sold on that day.

Suppose that the investor sold Apple short on April 3, 2019 for $200.67 per share anticipating a decline in the stock's price. A few days later, the investor observes that the price has continued to increase and now expects that the price will increase further. Because of this belief, the investor decides to close out the position on May 3, 2019 by buying Apple at $211.75 per share and use that purchase to cover the short position in Apple. Since the investor sold Apple short for $200.67 per share and purchased it for $211.75 per share, the investor will realize a loss of $11.08 per share.

From the example we can clearly see that price risk is the risk of an adverse price movement for an asset, which could result from either an increase or a decrease in an asset's price, depending on the investor's position. A long position's price risk is that the price will decline; a short position's price risk is that the price will increase. While in our illustration we used common stock as an example, price risk applies to any asset.

To understand what causes price risk, we must understand what factors cause an asset's price to change. So, to determine price risk, we must at least understand qualitatively what factors influence an asset's price. In practice, to implement a portfolio strategy or construct a portfolio, an asset manager must be able to quantify the influence that each factor has on performance. Given that the factors that an asset manager identifies drive an asset's price, the asset manager must develop a model that links an asset's price sensitivity to the factors. Such models are referred to as *asset pricing models.* Given an asset pricing model, an asset manager can measure an asset's price risk exposure to each factor. That is, there may not be one measure of price risk for an asset, but one for each factor that the asset manager considers influences the asset's price. The exposure of an asset to a factor is referred to as its *factor beta.* The factor beta is estimated using various statistical models incorporating historical returns for the asset. These factor betas are measures of systematic factors and are discussed in Chapter 13.

One common factor beta is *market beta.* It measures how sensitive a stock's price is to a movement in the "general market". For common stock, the general market means the common stock market. We will discuss various stock market indices in Chapter 3. Typically, the Standard & Poor's 500 (S&P 500) is used as a proxy for the stock market. Information about the market beta of a stock is available on *Yahoo!Finance.* For example, here is the market beta for the common stock of three companies as of May 3, 2019:

Walmart	0.66,
3M Company	1.09,
Facebook	1.30.

The market beta is interpreted as follows: It is the sensitivity of the price of a stock to a change in the stock market. Consider Walmart's market beta of 0.66, where the general market is proxied by the S&P 500. A market beta of 0.66 means that if the S&P 500's value changes by 1%, then the approximate price change for Walmart's stock will be 0.66%. So, if the S&P 500 changed by 5%, the Walmart's stock will change by approximately 3.3% (5% × 0.66). In contrast, a 5% change in the S&P 500 will have a much greater impact on the price change of the stock of Facebook. That stock's price will change by 6.5% (5% × 1.30).

Only a few companies have a market beta that is negative. A market beta of 1 means that the stock tends to move in lockstep with the general market. It is sometimes said the stock is neutral to the general market. A company that has a stock that has a beta greater than 1 is said to be an aggressive stock; a company that has a stock that is positive but less than 1 is said to be a defensive stock.[4]

Once we know the market beta of the individual stocks in a portfolio, a portfolio's beta can be calculated as a weighted average of the beta of the stock holdings.

Price risk for bonds

Bonds are also exposed to price risk. There are several factors that impact a bond's price that we discuss in detail in Chapter 15, but here we will look at how changes in the level of interest rates are relevant to the pricing of a particular issuer's bonds. In general, if interest rates change, the price of a bond will change in the opposite direction. The quantitative measure of a bond's price sensitivity to changing interest rates is called its *duration*, a measure that we will show how to calculate in Chapter 16. This measure is interpreted as follows: It is the approximate percentage change in the price of a bond for a 100 basis point change in interest rates.[5] A bond with a duration of 5 means that if interest rates change by 100 basis points, then the bond's price will change by approximately 5%. For a 200-basis-point change in interest rates, the bond's price will change by approximately 10%. As with a common stock portfolio's market beta, a bond portfolio's duration is a weighted average of the duration of the bonds in the portfolio.

To aid asset managers to control price risk for a portfolio or an individual asset, there are financial instruments that can be used. These financial instruments are called *derivative instruments* and we describe those that have been used to control price risk in later chapters.

Credit Risk

Credit risk refers to situations where one or both parties to a transaction will be adversely affected by the other party not fulfilling its contractual obligation.

Counterparty risk is the risk that the other party to a transaction (called the counterparty) fails to fulfill the obligations set forth in the contractual agreement. There are many transactions involving asset managers

[4]The terms "aggressive stock" and "defensive stock" are also used in describing other attributes of a company's stock.

[5]A basis point is equal to 0.01%. So, 100 basis points is equal to 1%. A 50-basis-point change is equal to 0.5% and a 150-basis-point change is equal to 1.5%.

that expose them to counterparty risk. Let's use two examples to illustrate counterparty risk. The first example is from a transaction called securities lending and the second is from a derivatives transaction.

Securities lending is part of a more general area called *securities finance*. To illustrate securities lending, suppose that asset manager A has sold short 10,000 shares of Apple stock at $200.67 per share on April 30, 2019. This means that at some future time, asset manager A must deliver 10,000 shares of Apple to its broker to settle the short contract. Asset manager A can borrow the 10,000 shares and we'll assume here that the shares are borrowed from asset manager B (from a different asset management firm) who owns the shares and is willing to lend them. To make the transaction simple, let's assume that the securities lending agreement calls for asset manager A giving to asset manager B the value of the 10,000 Apple shares at the time, $2,006,700, as collateral for lending the 10,000 shares to asset manager A. Assume also that the agreement allows asset manager B to require asset manager A to return the shares upon requesting to do so. A few days later on May 3, 2019, the price of Apple's stock increased to $211.75 and, as a result, suppose that asset manager B believes this would be a good time to sell the 10,000 shares. Asset manager B would contact asset manager A to return the stock. What happens if asset manager A cannot return the stock for some reason? Although asset manager B has $2,006,700 that it received from asset manager A, it does not have possession of the stock. The 10,000 shares of Apple stock now have a market value of $2,117,500. By asset manager A failing to perform by not returning the 10,000 shares of Apple, asset manager B realizes a loss of $110,000 (= $2,117,500 – $2,006,700).

For our second example of counterparty risk, suppose that on April 23, 2019 asset manager C enters into a transaction with asset manager D in which the two parties agree to the following. For a sum of $10,000 paid by asset manager C to asset manager D at the time the agreement is entered into, asset manager D agrees to allow asset manager C to purchase from it 10,000 shares of Apple stock for $209 per share on May 3, 2019. As will be explained in Chapter 14, this transaction is a special type of derivative instrument called an option. (At the time of the transaction, the price of a share of Apple was $207.48.) Hence, this agreement allows asset manager C to benefit from a rise in the price of Apple stock above $209 per share. No matter what happens to Apple's stock price on May 3, 2019, asset manager C foregoes the $10,000 payment to enter the agreement. On May 3, 2019, Apple's stock price was $211.75 per share. This transaction would generate a profit for asset manager C as follows. Asset manager C would purchase

10,000 shares of Apple's stock from asset manager D at the agreed upon price of $209 per share. This would require the payment of $2,090,000. Asset manager C's total cost of acquiring the 10,000 Apple shares would be $2,100,000 which is the $2,090,000 needed to purchase the shares plus the $10,000 paid to asset manager D to enter the agreement on April 30, 2019. The value of the 10,000 Apple shares on May 3, 2019 would be $2,117,500, resulting in a profit of $17,500. However, suppose that when asset manager C requests that asset manager D perform on its part of the agreement, this counterparty does not have the financial ability to do so. Asset manager C will have lost a profit of $17,500. This is counterparty risk. Notice that in this example, it is only asset manager C that faces counterparty risk. This is because once asset manager D makes the payment of $10,000 at the outset of the agreement, it does not worry about asset manager C performing.

The simplified type of derivative transaction just described is one that is commonly used by asset managers. What we will see is that derivatives fall into two categories: exchange-traded derivatives and over-the-counter (OTC) derivatives. With exchange-traded derivatives, the counterparty is an organized exchange where the derivative is traded. Thus, in a derivative transaction entered into by an asset manager, once the trade is completed, the exchange becomes the counterparty. Historically, there has never been a failure of an exchange to perform on its obligations. Consequently, for exchange-traded derivatives, counterparty risk is viewed as minimal. In our second illustration above, asset manager C would more than likely have used an exchange-traded derivative rather than use asset manager D as a counterparty, which thereby exposed itself to the counterparty risk of asset manager D.

In contrast to an exchange-traded derivative, an OTC derivative can expose one or both parties to considerable counterparty risk as can be seen from the second illustration above. An example of counterparty risk that underscores the critical importance of counterparty risk was the bankruptcy of a major financial institution, Lehman Brothers Holding Inc., in September 2008. The firm was a major investment banking firm that was the counterparty in many private transactions involving derivative instruments. Its bankruptcy resulted in the failure to satisfy its obligations in derivative transactions.

Another type of counterparty risk is default risk. This occurs when a borrower of funds fails to satisfy its contractual obligation to make timely payment of interest and repayment of the amount borrowed. The lender of the funds, referred to as the *creditor*, is exposed to counterparty risk because the borrower, referred to as the *debtor*, may fail to satisfy its obligation. Lending agreements include loans, notes, and bonds. For example, when an individual borrows money from a bank to purchase a home, the lending arrangement exposes the lending bank to default risk — the risk that the borrower will fail to repay the loan. When Apple in April 2013 issued $17 billion of bonds, the purchasers of those bonds (the creditors) were exposed to default risk — the risk that Apple will not be able to make the interest payments and repay the principal when it comes due.

To quantify default risk financial analysis of the ability of the issuer or counterparty to meet its obligations can be performed by a member of the portfolio team or can be obtained from an independent third party. This type of analysis is known as *credit analysis*. The portfolio team of most large institutional investors has a dedicated group that performs credit analysis of debt obligations in which the portfolio manager is considering investing in or already has a position in. The same group will evaluate the creditworthiness of current and potential future counterparties. Asset managers who do not have access to their own credit analysis use (to different degrees) opinions about default risk as provided by the *credit rating agencies* who perform credit analysis and cast their opinion in the form of a *credit rating*.

The three major rating agencies are Standard & Poor's Corporation, Moody's Investors Service, Inc., and Fitch Ratings. In all rating systems, the term *high grade* means low credit risk, or conversely, a high probability of future payments. The highest-grade bonds are denoted by Moody's by the symbol Aaa, and by S&P and Fitch by the symbol AAA. The next highest grade is denoted by the symbol Aa (Moody's) or AA (S&P and Fitch). For the third grade all rating systems use A. The next three grades are Baa or BBB, Ba or BB, and B, respectively. There are also C grades. Moody's uses 1, 2, or 3 to provide a narrower credit quality breakdown within each class, and S&P and Fitch use plus and minus signs for the same purpose. Bonds rated triple A (AAA or Aaa) are said to be *prime*, double A (AA or Aa) are of *high quality*, single-A issues are called *upper medium grade*, and triple-B issues are *medium grade*. Lower-rated bonds are said to have speculative elements or to be distinctly speculative. Bond issues assigned a rating in the top four categories are referred to as *investment-grade bonds*. Issues that carry a rating below the top four categories are referred to as *non-investment-grade bonds*, *high-yield bonds* or *junk bonds*. Thus, the bond market can be divided into two sectors, the investment-grade and non-investment-grade markets.

Liquidity Risk

An important attribute of an asset is its liquidity. However, there is no uniformly accepted definition of what it is. Several studies have defined liquidity in terms of the ability of an investor to trade an asset at short notice at a low cost and without having a significant adverse impact on the asset's price. *Liquidity risk* for an asset can then be defined as the risk that when an asset manager executes a trade for that asset, market conditions at the time of the trade will be such that the cost will be higher and there will be a significant adverse impact on the price at which the trade is executed.

The liquidity of an asset is important because it allows an asset manager the flexibility to rebalance a portfolio in order to implement an investment strategy. One way of viewing liquidity of an asset is in terms of the potential loss that may be incurred by a portfolio where that asset is held should the asset manager want to sell that asset immediately rather than engaging in a costly and time-consuming search to identify a buyer who is willing to pay a higher price. An asset's degree of liquidity can vary depending on how much an asset manager seeks to sell or buy. Although an asset manager may find that liquidity is good when transacting in a small quantity of an asset, that may not be the case when a large quantity is involved. That is, an asset may be liquid for a small quantity traded but illiquid if a large quantity is involved in the transaction.

Inflation Risk

Clients are interested in realizing returns that adjust for the rate of inflation. For example, suppose that an asset manager generates a one-year return of 7% ignoring the impact of inflation. The return generated is referred to as the *nominal return*. The nominal return, however, does not indicate how much the client's purchasing power has increased. A better indication of the increased purchasing power is the *real return*, which is calculated as the difference between the nominal return and the actual rate of inflation as measured by some inflation index. In the United States, the Consumer Price Index is typically used. The risk that the real return will be negative, or equivalently, that the nominal return earned is less than the inflation rate, is referred to as *inflation risk*.

Asset classes expose clients to different degrees of inflation risk. Historically, stocks and real estate have been found to expose investors to less inflation risk than bonds. Given that each asset class has a different exposure to inflation risk, a portfolio comprising different asset classes will have different exposure to inflation risk, depending on how much is allocated to each asset class.

Foreign Exchange Rate Risk

The cash flow of a financial instrument can be denominated in any currency (e.g., US dollars, euros, Japanese yen, British pound sterling). The currency may not be in the home currency of the investor. For example, a US investor can invest in a bond issued by the French government whose interest payments and principal are paid in euros. When the denomination of the cash flow is not the same as the investor's domestic currency, then that investor is basically taking two risks. The first risk is that the investor is exposed to the asset's price risk. The second risk that the investor is exposed to is that the value of the currency in which the cash flows are denominated will depreciate relative to the investor's domestic currency. If the investor has a long position, there is the risk that the exchange rate will change at the time of receipt of the cash flow such that fewer units of the domestic currency are realized. This risk is referred to as *foreign exchange rate risk* or *currency risk.*

Most currencies are *convertible currencies.* This means that the currency can be freely exchanged into another currency. However, there is the risk that the foreign government may prevent its currency from being fully converted into convertible currency. The risk is known as *convertibility risk* and is therefore a risk associated with investing in an asset whose cash flow is not denominated in the investor's domestic currency.

Key Points

- The word "risk" can mean many different things in asset management.
- The risks that affect the value of an asset can be classified as systematic risks and unsystematic risks.
- Systematic risks or common risk factors are those risks that affect the valuation of all assets within an asset class.
- Systematic risks are also referred to as non-diversifiable risks because they cannot be diversified away.
- Unsystematic risk is a risk that is unique to an issuer and for that reason is also referred to as unique risk.

- Because unsystematic risk can be diversified away in a portfolio, it is referred to as diversifiable risk.
- Broadly speaking, investment risk refers to the probability that the outcome realized by an investment or an investment strategy will be below what the investor expected.
- Investment risk includes price risk, credit risk, inflation risk, liquidity risk, and foreign exchange rate risk.
- Price risk is the risk of an adverse movement in an asset's price that could result from an increase or decrease in an asset's price, depending on the investor's position: a long position's price risk is that the price will decline and a short position's price risk is that the price will increase.
- Credit risk encompasses default risk and counterparty risk.
- Credit rating agencies assess the credit risk of an issuer of a debt obligation and cast their opinion in the form of a credit rating.
- Risk factors, or simply factors, are the variables that affect an asset's price.
- An asset pricing model is a model that shows how factors affect an asset's price.
- Given an asset pricing model, one can measure an asset's price risk exposure to each factor, which is referred to as an asset's factor beta.
- Market beta is a measure of price risk associated with how a stock or a portfolio responds to the movement of the stock market.
- The duration of a bond indicates its price sensitivity to changes in interest rates.
- Inflation risk, also referred to as purchasing power risk, is the risk that the real return earned will be less than the inflation rate; that is, inflation risk is the risk of earning a negative real return.
- An asset's liquidity risk is the risk that when an investor executes a trade for that asset, prevailing market conditions will be such that the cost will be higher and there will be a significant adverse impact on the price at which the trade is executed.
- Foreign exchange rate risk, also referred to as currency risk, is the risk that the currency in which a cash flow is paid (i.e., the foreign currency) will depreciate relative to the investor's domestic currency.

References

Keynes, J. M., 1921. *Treatise on Probability.* New York: MacMillan.

Knight, F., 1921. *Uncertainty, Risk, and Profit.* New York: Houghton Mifflin.

Taleb, N. N., 2005. *Foolishness by Randomness: The Hidden Role of Chance in Life and in the Markets.* New York: Random House.

Taleb, N. N., 2010. *The Black Swan: The Impact of the Highly Improbable*, 2nd edition. New York: Random House.

Wagner, W. H. and S. Lau, 1971. "The effect of diversification on risk," *Financial Analysts Journal*, November–December: 2–7.

Wideman, R. M., 1992. *Project and Program Risk Management: A Guide to Managing Project Risks and Opportunities.* Newtown Square, PA: Project Management Institute.

PART II
The Investment Vehicles

Chapter 3

Fundamentals of Equities

Learning Objectives

After reading this chapter, you will understand:

- what equity ownership means;
- sub-asset equity classes based on market capitalization and growth vs. value;
- the venues where stocks are traded;
- the different types of alternative trading systems;
- what is pre-trade and post-trade transparency;
- why investors use alternative trading systems;
- trading mechanisms such as the types of orders, short selling, and margin transactions;
- trading arrangements to accommodate institutional traders, such as block trades and
- program trades;
- the federal regulations dealing with market volatility (trading limits and circuit breakers), short selling, and insider trading;
- the role played by stock market indexes and how they are constructed;
- the various types of stock market indexes: country, regional, and global;
- the three methods for constructing a stock market index;
- the use of stock market indexes in asset management.

To raise funds for operating a business, a corporation issues various financial instruments. They can be either an equity security or a debt instrument. An equity security represents an ownership interest in a corporation. In contrast to an equity security, a debt instrument is a debt obligation of the issuing corporation and is the subject of the next chapter. Equity securities entitle the holder of the security to the earnings of the corporation when those earnings are distributed in the form of dividends. Should a corporation be liquidated, an investor is entitled to a pro rata share of the corporation's remaining equity.

Equity securities fall into two categories: common stock and preferred stock. The difference between these two forms of equity securities lies in the degree to which they may participate in any distribution of earnings and the priority given to each in the distribution of assets in the case of a liquidation of the company. Typically, preferred stockholders are entitled to a fixed dividend, which they receive before common stockholders may receive dividends. We discuss preferred stock later in this chapter. While technically preferred stock is a form of equity, it is referred to as senior corporate security and treated as part of the fixed-income securities market.

In this chapter, we describe the different equity sub-asset classes, the venues where equity trading takes place in the United States, trading mechanics and trading arrangements used by individual and institutional investors, and stock market indexes.

Equity Asset Classes

In Chapter 1, we explained that equity, or common stock, is one of the three traditional asset classes. Common stock can be further divided into sub-classes based on some fundamental characteristic of the company. The two fundamental characteristics used to create sub-asset classes in the equity market are the size of the company and what is referred to as value/growth companies.

The size classification is based on a company's *market capitalization* or market cap. This measure is calculated by multiplying the stock's market price by the number of shares outstanding. As explained in Chapter 1, in the United States, sub-asset classes are used based on market cap, the three major ones being large-cap stocks, mid-cap stocks, and small-cap stocks.

The second classification method is based on whether a company's stock is characterized as a value stock or a growth stock. At this point, what constitutes value and growth is difficult to explain — it is nowhere as simple as classification by market cap. This classification arises due to what is referred to as investment style, a topic we discuss in Chapter 13. There are two styles that have come to be accepted by market participants: value investing and growth investing. Value investing is an investment approach that involves identifying and then taking a position in stocks that are undervalued. The companies whose stock fall into this category, value stocks, are classified based on fundamental financial information about the company which we describe in Chapter 13. Growth investing involves investing in companies whose stock price is estimated to grow at a rate that is greater than the average growth rate of the market in general. Companies whose stock is believed to have this characteristic are referred to as growth stocks.

The Stock Market

Over the past 60 years, there have been significant changes to the market where stocks are traded. In addition to changes mandated by market regulators, there are two reasons for this. The first reason is due to market trading being dominated by large institutional investors rather than retail (individual) or small investors. This is referred to as the "institutionalization" of the stock market and this has important implications for the design of equity trading systems because the demands made by institutional investors are different from those made by individual investors.

The second reason for the significant change in the way stocks are traded is due to innovations largely attributable to advances in computer technology. It is for this reason that the nature of equity trading is dominated by the use of computers to generate orders. As a result, the former chairwomen of the Securities and Exchange Commission (SEC), Mary Jo White, referred to stock trading as "algorithmic trading" and the equity market has been referred to as an "algorithmic marketplace". This is in contrast to how equity markets previously operated, which has been referred to as a "manual market".

Prior to 2001, stock prices were transacted in eighths or thirty-seconds of a dollar. In 2000, the SEC permitted stocks to be traded in pennies. Allowing price increments to be a penny is referred to as "decimalization".

US Venues for Trading Stocks

The different venues where stocks are traded can be viewed in terms of their listing on an exchange. According to federal securities law, there are two categories of traded stocks. The first is *exchange-traded stocks*, also referred to as "listed" stocks. The second category of traded stocks is what is called *over-the-counter stocks* (OTC stocks). These stocks are also referred to as *non-exchange-traded stocks* or *unlisted stocks*.

Each trading venue provides information in terms of pre-trade transparency and post-trade transparency. *Pre-trade transparency* is provided in the venue's order book. The *order book* is a list of the orders that are received by the trading venue for a particular stock. Although this information is helpful to market participants because it provides an indication of the liquidity and depth of the market for that stock (i.e., it provides market transparency), there are institutional traders that prefer not to have that information disclosed. We'll discuss the reasons why later. *Post-trade transparency* is the disclosure of trades that have been executed on the trading venue.

Exchange market for listed stocks

Exchange markets are physical locations that comprise members who utilize the exchange facilities and systems to trade listed stocks. For a stock to be listed on an exchange, it must comply with the requirements established by the exchange. Even after being listed, exchanges may delist a company's stock if it fails to satisfy the exchange requirements.

There are regional stock exchanges and national stock exchanges. The New York Stock Exchange (NYSE) is the major national stock exchange in the United States that trades listed stocks and we will discuss it shortly.

The four regional exchanges are the Boston, Chicago, Pacific, and Philadelphia stock exchange and these exchanges are smaller than the national stock exchanges. On regional stock exchanges, companies that are listed are primarily those that (1) could not meet the listing requirements of a national stock exchange or (2) could satisfy the requirements for listing on a national stock exchange but prefer not to be listed. Although rare these day, there are companies that are listed on a national stock exchange as well as on the regional exchange, referred to as "dually listed stocks".

New York Stock Exchange

The NYSE is the major national exchange that trades listed stocks. Trading takes place by NYSE members in what is called a centralized continuous auction market at a designated location on the trading floor which is called a *post*. The post is populated by brokers who represent their customers who seek to transact (buy or sell) the stocks traded at the post. There may be more than one company's stock traded at the post. At the post, there is one individual, called the *specialist*, who is the market maker for each stock. The auction process conducted by a specialist in a stock must be done in a manner that maintains an orderly market and public orders must be given over trading for the specialist's own account.

Exchange market for unlisted stocks

The OTC market is the market for unlisted stocks and comprises two markets. The first is the Nasdaq Stock Market, a national securities exchange registered with the SEC that trades unlisted stocks. Despite being referred to as a market for unlisted stocks, certain "listing requirements" must be fulfilled for a company's stock to be traded on the Nasdaq Stock Market. Nevertheless, exchange-traded stocks are referred to as "listed", and stocks traded in the Nasdaq Stock Market are said to be "unlisted". The second part of the OTC market is for truly unlisted stocks (i.e., stocks not traded on the Nasdaq Stock Market). This market is called the *third market.*

The Nasdaq Stock Market has three tiers. They are the Nasdaq Global Select Market, the Nasdaq Global Market, and the Nasdaq Capital Market. While the corporate governance requirements for all tiers are the same, the financial and liquidity requirements for listing on each tier differs. The Nasdaq Global Select Market has the most stringent financial and liquidity requirements than the other two tiers. In terms of market capitalization, The Nasdaq Global Select Market includes large market capitalization stocks, the Nasdaq Global Market includes mid capitalization stocks, and the Nasdaq Capital Market includes small capitalization stocks.

Basically, the Nasdaq is a telecommunications network linking geographically dispersed market-making participants. Price quotations are provided by the Nasdaq electronic quotation system. Unlike the NYSE, there is no central trading floor. Consequently, the Nasdaq functions can be fairly described as an electronic "virtual trading floor". The stock of more than 4,100 companies is traded in the Nasdaq system. There are more than 500 dealers that provide competing bids to buy and offers to sell Nasdaq stocks. The dealers, referred to as market makers, are obligated to continuously post firm two-sided quotes good for most stocks, promptly report trades, and stand ready to execute against their quotes.

Alternative trading systems

An alternative trading system (ATS) is a trading venue regulated by the SEC that serves as an alternative to trading on exchanges and for after-hours trading. Electronic communication networks (ECNs) and crossing networks are the two types of ATSs.

Electronic communications networks

ECNs display quotes that reflect actual orders and provide ECN members with an anonymous means for entering orders. Transparency, anonymity, automated service, and reduced transaction costs are provided by an ECN. ECNs provide pre-trade transparency about orders and post-trade transparency about executed trades. For this reason, ECNs are said to be light pool markets (or LIT markets). This is in contrast to equity trading venues that do not provide pre-trade transparency. Such venues are referred to as dark pools, which we will discuss shortly. However, recently some ECNs are going dark while some dark pools are now providing pre-trade transparency (i.e., they are being LIT).

Institutional and retail investors, market makers, and broker–dealers are subscribers to ECNs. The different types of orders described in the next section can be used. ECN and the orders will then be posted by the ECN for other subscribers to view. The orders will then be matched by the ECN to complete the execution. Typically, the parties to the trade remain anonymous to each other. For the publicly disclosed trade execution report, the ECN is identified as the counterparty to the trade.

The ECN charges a fee for its service. The fee involves a rebate to the party in the trade depending on whether that party adds liquidity to or removes liquidity from the ECN's order book, while a fee is charged to the counterparty. Adding or removing liquidity depends on the type of order placed by a party. We describe the different types of orders in the next section. An example of an order that adds liquidity is a limit order that is not immediately executable while a market order that is immediately executable removes liquidity from the ECN's order book. Incentives in the form of higher rebates or lower fees may be offered to subscribers based on the volume of trades.

Crossing networks

Institutional investors who want to "cross" trades using a computer matching of buyers and sellers directly can use a crossing network. In a crossing network, this type of ATS batch processes aggregate orders for execution at specified times. Pre-trade transparency varies with the particular crossing network. Those crossing networks that do not provide pre-trade transparency (i.e., no public displaying of orders) are dark pools. However, there are some dark pools that are either moving in the direction of pre-trade transparency or have done so already. The next section discusses the types of orders that can be placed when trading in a dark pool.

Although post-trade transparency is required for dark pools because federal regulations specify that executed transactions are treated as OTC trades and therefore less information is required than for a trade on the NYSE, the lack of pre-trade transparency means that dark pools provide institutional investors with several benefits. The first benefit is that there is less leakage of information contained in an order. The reason why information leakage is critical for an institutional investor is that the executed trade could be part of a proprietary trading strategy. An institutional investor would be concerned about the potential for a displayed order providing information to its competitors about its strategy. The second benefit is that it eliminates the risk of broker–dealers and other traders executing trades ahead of large orders in order to take advantage of the potential price movement resulting from the trade. This is referred to as *front running* a trade and would result in trading costs higher than in the absence of a public display of an order. The third benefit is it will reduce market impact costs, a cost that we discuss later in this chapter. Finally, by avoiding the use of a broker–dealer as an intermediary for the trade, commissions are avoided that might be more than in a direct exchange between counterparties offered by means of a dark pool.

Based on the minimum size of transactions that can be traded for each order, dark pools are classified as a *block-oriented dark pool* and *streaming liquidity pool*. The former sets a minimum size for each order, such as 5,000 shares, while the latter has no minimum size for any order. There are other characteristics of dark pools in addition to trade size such as ownership of the dark pool, who is allowed to trade in a dark pool, price and order discovery, liquidity levels and types, accessibility, and the existence of liquidity partners.

Order Execution

The result of the large number of alternative venues for trading stocks has resulted in a stock market that can best be described as a fragmented marketplace. This makes the processing of orders complicated. Consequently, understanding the process by which an order is executed once it is placed with a broker is critical because how the broker ultimately executes the order affects the price at which the trade is executed. This then impacts a trade's overall effective cost.

After receiving an order, a broker must decide how to execute the order. That is, the broker must decide which of the trading venues to use to execute the order. In selecting a trading venue, it is the obligation of the broker to find the one that will provide the "best execution" that is reasonably available for customer orders. That is, the broker will evaluate which trading venue will provide the customer with the most favorable terms.

There are three key factors that a broker will evaluate when selecting the trading venue to obtain the best execution for customer orders. The first factor is whether the broker can obtain a better price than quoted in the market when the order is placed. This is referred to as "price improvement". The second factor is the probability that the order can in fact be executed on a given trading venue. The speed of execution is the third factor considered by the broker. This is important when using a market order (explained later) to place an order because in a fast-moving market, any delays in the execution of an order can result in an inferior price than the market price at the time the order was received.

A customer has the option to take the selection decision away from the broker and instead instruct the broker to use a particular venue to execute an order. The broker may impose a fee for the trade in such cases. In the absence of a customer specifying a venue, the broker's decision as to which venue to direct the order to is as follows. For a stock that is listed on an exchange, the broker has three choices: (1) direct the order to the exchange where the stock is listed, (2) direct the order to a regional exchange, or (3) direct the order to a firm that stands ready to execute the order at publicly quoted prices (such firms are referred to as third market makers). If the order involves an unlisted stock traded on the Nasdaq, the broker may send the order to a market maker on the Nasdaq.

Regional stock exchanges, third-party market makers, and many Nasdaq market makers attempt to induce brokers to route an order to their venue. They do so by paying brokers a fee referred to as *payment for order flow* and the payment amount is based on the number of shares directed. This is permitted with the approval and knowledge of the customer. This authorization is obtained by the broker when the account is opened. The brokerage firm must notify the customer annually as to whether they receive payment for order flow as well as on each confirmation.

There are two other alternatives that a broker has in routing an order. The first is using an ECN. The second is "internalizing" an order. This involves the broker routing the order to a division of the broker's firm that can execute the order and is referred to as the *internalization of an order*, also popularly referred to as the *upstairs market*. Orders that are routed internally are fulfilled from the firm's own inventory.

Trading Mechanics

In this section, we describe the key features involved in trading stocks. In the next section, we discuss trading arrangements that were developed specifically for coping with the trading needs of institutional investors.

Types of Orders and Trading Priority Rules

When an investor wants to buy or sell a share of common stock, the price and conditions under which the order is to be executed must be communicated to a broker. The simplest type of order is the *market order*, an order to be executed at the best price available in the market. If the stock is listed and traded on an organized exchange, the best price is assured by the exchange rule that when more than one order on the same side of the buy/sell transaction reaches the market at the same time, the order with the best price is given priority. Thus, buyers offering a higher price are given priority over those offering a lower price; sellers asking a lower price are given priority over those asking a higher price.

Another priority rule of exchange trading is needed to handle the receipt of more than one order at the same price. Most often, the priority in executing such orders is based on the time of arrival of the order — the first orders in are the first orders executed — although there may be a rule that gives higher priority to certain types of market participants over other types of market participants who are seeking to transact at the same price. For example, on exchanges, orders can be classified as either *public orders* or orders of those member firms dealing for their own account (both nonspecialists and specialists). Exchange rules require that public orders be given priority over orders of member firms dealing for their own account.

The danger of a market order is that an adverse move may take place between the time the investor places the order and the time the order is executed. To avoid this danger, the investor can place a *limit order* that designates a price threshold for the execution of the trade. A *buy limit order* indicates that the stock may be purchased only at the designated price or lower. A sell limit order indicates that the stock may be sold at the designated price or higher. The key disadvantage of a limit order is that there is no guarantee that it will be executed at all; the designated price may simply not be obtainable. A limit order that is not executable at the time it reaches the market is recorded as an unexecuted limit order that is maintained by the security specialist who works at the stock exchange.

The *limit order book* is where these unexecuted limit orders for a specific stock are maintained.

A limit order is a *conditional order* that is executed only if the limit price or a better price can be obtained. Another type of conditional order is the *stop order*, which specifies that the order is not to be executed until the market moves to a designated price, at which time it becomes a market order. A *buy stop order* specifies that the order is not to be executed until the market rises to a designated price, that is, until it trades at or above, or is bid at or above, the designated price. A *sell stop order* specifies that the order is not to be executed until the market price falls below a designated price — that is, until it trades at or below, or is offered at or below, the designated price. A stop order is useful when an investor cannot watch the market constantly. Profits can be preserved or losses minimized on a stock position by allowing market movements to trigger a trade. In a sell (buy) stop order, the designated price is lower (higher) than the current market price of the stock. In a sell (buy) limit order, the designated price is higher (lower) than the current market price of the stock.

There are two dangers associated with stop orders. Stock prices sometimes exhibit abrupt price changes, so the direction of a change in a stock price may be quite temporary, resulting in the premature trading of a stock. Also, once the designated price is reached, the stop order becomes a market order and is subject to the uncertainty of the execution price noted earlier for market orders.

A *stop-limit order*, a hybrid of a stop order and a limit order, is a stop order that designates a price limit. In contrast to the stop order, which becomes a market order if the stop is reached, the stop-limit order becomes a limit order if the stop is reached. The stop-limit order can be used to cushion the market impact of a stop order. The investor may limit the possible execution price after the activation of the stop. As with a limit order, the limit price may never be reached after the order is activated, which therefore defeats one purpose of the stop order — to protect a profit or limit a loss.

An investor may also enter a *market-if-touched order*. This order becomes a market order if a designated price is reached. A market-if-touched order to buy becomes a market order if the market falls to a given price, while a stop order to buy becomes a market order if the market rises to a given price. Similarly, a market if touched order to sell becomes a market order if the market rises to a specified price, while the stop order to sell becomes a market order if the market falls to a given price. We can think of the stop order as an order designed to get out of an existing position at an acceptable price (without specifying the exact price), and the market if touched order as an order designed to get into a position at an acceptable price (also without specifying the exact price).

Orders may be placed to buy or sell at the open or the close of trading for the day. An opening order indicates a trade to be executed only in the opening range for the day, and a closing order indicates a trade is to be executed only within the closing range for the day.

An investor may enter orders that contain order cancellation provisions. A *fill-or-kill order* must be executed as soon as it reaches the trading floor or it is immediately canceled. Orders may designate the time period for which the order is effective — a day, week, or month, or perhaps by a given time within the day. An *open order*, or *good-till-canceled order*, is good until the investor specifically terminates the order.

Orders are also classified by their size. A *round lot* is typically 100 shares of a stock. An *odd lot* is defined as less than a round lot.

Margin Transactions

Investors can borrow cash to buy securities and use the securities themselves as collateral. A transaction in which an investor borrows to buy shares using the shares themselves as collateral is referred to as *buying on margin*. By borrowing funds, an investor creates leverage. The funds borrowed to buy the additional stock will be provided by the broker, and the broker gets the money from a bank. The interest rate that banks charge brokers for these funds is the *call money rate* (also referred to as the *broker loan rate*). The broker charges the borrowing investor the call money rate plus a service charge.

The brokerage firm is not free to lend as much as it wishes to the investor to buy securities. Federal securities law prohibits brokers from lending more than a specified percentage of the market value of the securities. The *initial margin requirement* is the proportion of the total market value of the securities that the investor must pay as an equity share, and the remainder is borrowed from the broker. The Board of Governors of the Federal Reserve (the Fed) has the responsibility to set initial margin requirements and changes it as an instrument of economic policy. Initial margin requirements vary for stocks and bonds.

The Fed also establishes a *maintenance margin requirement*. This is the minimum proportion of (1) the equity in the investor's margin account to

(2) the total market value. If the investor's margin account falls below the minimum maintenance margin (which would happen if the share price fell), the investor is required to put up additional cash. The investor receives a margin call from the broker specifying the additional cash to be put into the investor's margin account. If the investor fails to put up the additional cash, the broker has the authority to sell the securities in the investor's account.

To illustrate the maintenance requirement, assume that an investor buys 100 shares of a stock at \$120 per share for a total cost of \$12,000. Assume that the initial margin is 50% and the maintenance margin is 25%. The initial margin requires that the investor put up \$6,000 (50% of \$12,000) in cash or some other form of acceptable equity. The balance of the \$12,000 purchase (\$6,000), must be borrowed. The stock price can decline to \$80 before falling below the maintenance margin. To understand why, the value of the 100 shares purchased on margin then would have a value of \$8,000 (\$80 × 100 shares). With a loan of \$6,000, the equity in the account is \$2,000 (\$8,000 – \$6,000), or 25% of the account value (\$2,000/\$8,000 = 25%). If the price of the stock decreases below \$80, the investor must deposit more equity to bring the equity level up to the 25% level.

Trading Arrangements for Institutional Investors

With the increase in trading by institutional investors, trading arrangements were developed in order to better suit institutional investors' needs. Institutional investor needs include trading in large size and trading groups of stocks, both at a low commission and with low market impact. This has resulted in the evolution of special arrangements for the execution of certain types of orders commonly sought by institutional investors: (1) orders requiring the execution of a trade of a large number of shares of a given stock and (2) orders requiring the execution of trades in a large number of different stocks at or near the same time as possible. The former types of trades are called *block trades*; the latter are called *program trades*. An example of a block trade would be a mutual fund seeking to buy 15,000 shares of the stock of Procter & Gamble. An example of a program trade would be a pension fund wanting to buy shares of 100 names (companies) at the end of a trading day ("at the close").

The institutional arrangement that has evolved to accommodate these two types of institutional trades is a network of trading desks of the major securities firms and other institutional investors that communicate with each other by means of electronic display systems and telephones. This network is the upstairs market. Participants in the upstairs market play a key role by providing liquidity to the market so that such institutional trades can be executed, and by arbitrage activities that help to integrate the fragmented stock market.

Block trades

On the NYSE, block trades are defined as trades of at least 10,000 shares of a given stock. Since the execution of large numbers of block orders places strain on the specialist system in the NYSE, special procedures have been developed to handle them. Typically, an institutional customer contacts its salesperson at a brokerage firm, indicating that it wishes to place a block order. The salesperson then gives the order to the block execution department of the brokerage firm. Note that the salesperson does not submit the order to be executed to the exchange where the stock might be traded or, in the case of an unlisted stock, try to execute the order on the Nasdaq system. The sales traders in the block execution department contact other institutions to attempt to find one or more institutions that would be willing to take the other side of the order. That is, they use the upstairs market in their search to fill the block trade order. If this can be accomplished, the execution of the order is completed.

If the sales traders cannot find enough institutions to take the entire block, then the balance of the block trade order is given to the firm's market maker. The market maker must then make a decision as to how to handle the balance of the block trade order. There are two choices. First, the brokerage firm may take a position in the stock and buy the shares for its own account. Second, the unfilled order may be executed by using the services of competing market makers. In the former case, the brokerage firm is committing its own capital.

Program trades

Program trades involve the buying and selling of a large number of names simultaneously. Such trades are also called basket trades because effectively a "basket" of stocks is being traded. The NYSE defines a program trade as any trade involving the purchase or sale of a basket of at least 15 stocks with a total value of $1 million or more. Some examples of why an institutional investor may want to use a program trade are (1) deployment of new cash into the stock market, (2) implementation of a decision to move funds invested in the bond market to the stock market (or vice versa), and (3) rebalancing the composition of a stock portfolio because of a change in investment strategy. A mutual fund portfolio manager can, for example, move funds quickly into or out of the stock market for an entire portfolio of stocks through a single program trade. All these strategies are related to asset allocation. Another reason why an institutional investor may have a need to execute a program trade is in implementing an indexing strategy that we describe in Chapter 12.

There are several commission arrangements available to an institutional investor for a program trade and each arrangement has numerous variants. Considerations in selecting one (in addition to commission costs) are the risk of failing to realize the best execution price; and the risk that the brokerage firms to be solicited about executing the program trade will use their knowledge of the program trade to benefit from the anticipated price movement that might result — in other words, that they will front-run the transaction. From a dealer's perspective, program trades can be conducted in two ways, namely on an agency basis and on a principal basis. An intermediate type of program trade, the agency incentive arrangement, is an additional alternative. A program trade executed on an *agency basis* involves the selection by the investor of a brokerage firm solely on the basis of commission bids (cents per share) submitted by various brokerage firms.

The brokerage firm selected uses its best efforts as an agent of the institutional investor to obtain the best price. Such trades have low explicit commissions. To the investor, the disadvantage of the agency program trade is that, while commissions may be the lowest, the execution price may not be the best because of impact costs and the potential front-running by the brokerage firms solicited to submit a commission bid. The investor knows in advance the commission paid, but does not know the price at which the trades will be executed.

Related to the agency basis is an *agency incentive arrangement*, in which a benchmark portfolio value is established for the group of stocks in the program trade. The price for each "name" (i.e., specific stock) in the program trade is determined as either the price at the end of the previous day or the average price of the previous day. If the brokerage firm can execute the trade on the next trading day such that a better-than benchmark portfolio value results — a higher value in the case of a program trade involving selling, or a lower value in the case of a program trade involving buying — then the brokerage firm receives the specified commission plus some predetermined additional compensation. In this case, the investor does not know in advance the commission or the execution price precisely, but has a reasonable expectation that the price will be better than a threshold level.

If the brokerage firm does not achieve the benchmark portfolio value, the program variants come into play. One arrangement may call for the brokerage firm to receive only the previously agreed-upon commission. Other arrangements may involve sharing the risk of not realizing the benchmark portfolio value with the brokerage firm. That is, if the brokerage firm falls short of the benchmark portfolio value, it must absorb a portion of the shortfall. In these risk-sharing arrangements, the brokerage firm is risking its own capital. The greater the risk sharing the brokerage firm must accept, the higher the commission it will charge.

The brokerage firm can also choose to execute the trade on a principal basis. In this case, the dealer would commit its own capital to buy or sell the portfolio and complete the investor's transaction immediately. Since the dealer incurs market risk, it would also charge higher commissions. The key factors in pricing principal trades are liquidity characteristics, absolute dollar value, nature of the trade, customer profile, and market volatility. In this case, the investor knows the trade execution price in advance, but pays a higher commission.

To minimize front-running, institutional investors often use other types of program trade arrangements. They call for brokerage firms to receive, not specific names and quantities of stocks, but only aggregate statistical information about key portfolio parameters. Several brokerage firms then bid on a cents per share basis on the entire portfolio (also called blind baskets), guaranteeing execution at either the closing price (termed market-at-close) or a particular intraday price to the customer. Note that this is a principal trade.

Algorithmic trading

Traditionally, orders for stock executions have been conducted by traders who execute the trades on a trading desk for a portfolio manager or whomever determines what trades should be executed. Traders are judged to have "market information and savvy" which permits them to conduct the trades at a lower cost and with less market impact than the portfolio manager conducting the trades on a less formal basis themselves.

The effectiveness of these traders is often measured by execution evaluation services, and traders are often compensated partially on the basis of their effectiveness. But some observers believe that the traders, in the interest of maximizing their compensation, may have different incentives than the portfolio managers and do not optimize the portfolio manager's objectives — this is referred to as an agency effect. In addition, some think that trades could be conducted more efficiently by electronic systems as opposed to human traders.

Due to improved technology and quantitative techniques, as well as regulatory changes, electronic trading systems have been developed to supplement or replace human traders and their trading desks. Such trading is called algorithmic trading or algo trading.

Algorithmic trading is a relatively recent type of trading technique whereby an overall trade (either buy or sell) is conducted electronically in a series of small transactions instead of one large transaction. Such trades are conducted via computers, which make the decision to trade or not trade depending on whether recent price movements indicate whether the market will be receptive to the intended trade at the moment or, instead, will cause the price to move significantly against the intended price. Algorithmic trading also permits the traders to hide their intentions.

The advent and wide use of algos is due primarily to both technology and regulation. The technology element is based on faster and cheaper technological systems to execute via improved quantitative methods. A subset of algorithmic trading is high-frequency trading. High-frequency trading is used by traders to capitalize on infinitesimal price discrepancies that periodically exist in the market.

Soft Dollars Arrangements

Investors often choose their broker–dealer based on who will give them the best execution at the lowest transaction cost on a specific transaction, and also based on who will provide complementary services (such as research) over a period of time. As explained earlier, order flow can also be "purchased" by a broker–dealer from an investor with "soft dollars". In this case, the broker–dealer provides the investor, without explicit charge, services such as research or electronic services, typically from a third party for which the investor would otherwise have had to pay "hard dollars" to the third party, in exchange for the investor's order flow. Of course, the investor pays the broker–dealer for the execution service.

According to such a relationship, the investor preferentially routes their order to the broker–dealer specified in the soft dollar relationship and does not have to pay "hard dollars", or real money, for the research or other services. This practice is called paying "soft dollars" (i.e., directing their order flow) for the ancillary research. For example, client A preferentially directs his order flow to broker–dealer B (often a specified amount of order flow over a specified period, such as a month or year) and pays the broker–dealer for these execution services. In turn, broker–dealer B pays for some research services provided to client A. Very often, the research provider is a separate firm, say, firm C. Thus, soft dollars refer to money paid by an investor to a broker–dealer or a third party through commission revenue rather than by direct payments.

The disadvantage to the broker–dealer is that they have to pay hard dollars (to the research provider) for the client's order flow. The disadvantage to the client is that they are not free to "shop around" for the best bid or best offer, net of commissions, for all their transactions, but have to trade an agreed amount of transaction volume with the specific broker–dealer. In addition, the research provider may give a preferential price to the broker–dealer. Thus, each of these participants in the soft dollar relationship experiences some advantages, but also a disadvantage.

The SEC provides a three-step test for analyzing the suitability of a soft dollar arrangement. First, the particular product or service under the arrangement qualifies as an eligible research or brokerage service. Second, whether the product or service of the arrangement truly provides lawful and appropriate assistance in an adviser's investment decision-making responsibilities. Finally, whether client commissions paid are reasonable given the value of the products or services provided by the broker–dealer.

Trading Regulations Imposed by Federal Securities Law

There are regulations imposed by federal securities law that impact trading. The regulations involve market volatility, short selling, and insider trading.

Market volatility rules

Market volatility rules involve trading limit rules and circuit breakers.

Trading limit rules

Trading limits (or *price limits*) establish a minimum price limit below which a market price index level may not decline. If this occurs, there is a mandated termination of trading, at least at prices below the specified price (the price limit) for a specified period of time. The reason for the pause in trading is to "give the market a breather" to at least calm emotions. There are two different types of price limits for circuit breakers and trading collars.

A circuit breaker is a temporary halting of trading during a severe market decline. Two types of circuit breakers have been adopted to deal with significant market volatility, market-wide circuit breakers and single-stock circuit breakers. *Market-wide circuit-breaker* rules are implemented depending on the level of market volatility. The trading could halt temporarily or, in the case of extreme market volatility, the market could close before the normal close of the trading session. *Single-stock circuit-breaker* rules involve what are referred to as the "limit up-limit down" rules. The intention of the limit up-limit down rule is to prevent trades in individual stocks from being executed outside a specified price band. The price band is established as a percentage level above and below the stock's average price, where the average price is computed over the immediately preceding 5-minute trading period. Failure of the price of a stock trading outside the price band to return to a price within the band within 15 seconds results in a 5-minute trading halt.

Short selling rules

A *short sale* is the sale of a security not owned by an investor and is referred to as *short selling*. The expectation of an investor who shorts a security is that the price will decline, so that the investor can purchase the security at a future date at a price less than the price at which the security was sold. Short selling is illegal only if it is done by an investor with an intent to manipulate the market. An example of such a manipulate practice would be an investor entering into a series of transactions with the intent of depressing a stock's price so as to induce the purchase or sale of that stock by others.

There are SEC rules dealing with short sales. These rules include the alternative uptick rule and rules applied to what is called "naked" short selling. Recognizing that short selling can be beneficial for the efficiency of the stock market but could potentially have a harmful impact on the stock market, the SEC adopted the alternative uptick rule. To prevent the further driving down of a stock's price that has declined more than 10% in one day, this rule specifies that once the 10% trigger has occurred, those who own the stock can sell their shares before short sellers are allowed to do so.

Although the mechanism for selling short involves borrowing the shorted stock to cover the sale, there are short sales where no borrowing occurs or no arrangement is made for borrowing in time for the settlement of the shorted security to the buyer. This is referred to as naked short selling and is not necessarily a violation of SEC rules. However, there is the potential in a naked short sale that the short seller may not be able to deliver the shorted stock. When the short seller does not deliver the stock at the required settlement date, a "fail" occurs. For this reason, the SEC imposes certain requirements on the broker–dealer to deal with the problems associated with failed trades. The key requirement, referred to as the "locate requirement", calls for the broker–dealer to have a reasonable basis for believing that the short seller can borrow the stock so as to deliver it on the settlement date prior to executing the trade. The broker–dealer is required to document this before the short sale is executed.

Insider Trading Rules

The SEC describes illegal insider trading activity as the trading in a security that is "in breach of a fiduciary duty or other relationship of trust and confidence, while in possession of material, non-public information about the security".[1] The laws dealing with insider trading are shaped by judicial opinions. Therefore, there is no legal definition of what insider trading activity is and must be determined on a case-by-case basis under the antifraud provisions of the federal securities laws (principally Section 10(b) of the Securities Exchange Act of 1934).

Examples of insiders and illegal insider trading are corporate officers, directors, and employees who trade their corporation's stock following the acquisition of information that is a significant, confidential corporate development. Insider trading violations extend to others who may have received a tip ("tippees") from a person (the "tipper") who had access to material, non-public information.[2]

Stock Market Indexes

Stock market indexes provide a benchmark for evaluating the performance of asset managers. In general, stock market indexes rise and fall in fairly similar patterns. The indexes do not move in exactly the same ways at all

[1] See the SEC web site: http://www.sec.gov/answers/insider.htm.

[2] Not all trading by insiders is illegal. Corporate insiders can legally buy or sell the stock of their corporation as long as the trading activity is not based on material, nonpublic information.

times. The differences in movement reflect the different ways in which the indexes are constructed. The three factors that enter into that construction are as follows: (1) the universe of stocks represented by the sample underlying the index, (2) the relative weights assigned to the stocks included in the index, and (3) the method of averaging across all the stocks in the index.

US Stock Market Indexes

The stocks included in a stock market index must be combined in certain proportions, and each stock must be given a weight. The three main approaches to weighting are (1) weighting by the market capitalization of the stock's company, which is the value of the number of shares times the price per share; (2) weighting by the price of the stock; and (3) equal weighting for each stock, regardless of its price or the firm's market value. With the exception of the Dow Jones Industrial Average (DJIA), the index cited most often by the popular press, all the most widely used indexes by professional investors are market value-weighted. The DJIA is a price-weighted average.

Stock market indicators can be classified into three groups: (1) those produced by stock exchanges based on all stocks traded on the respective exchange, (2) those produced by organizations that subjectively select the stocks to be included in an index, and (3) those in which stock selection is based on an objective measure, such as the market capitalization of the company.

The first group includes the New York Stock Exchange Composite Index, which reflects the market value of all stocks traded on the exchange. Although it is not an exchange, the Nasdaq Composite Index falls into this category because the index represents all stocks tracked by the Nasdaq system.

The two most popular stock market indicators in the second group are the DJIA and Standard & Poor's 500 stock index (S&P 500). The DJIA is constructed from 30 of the largest and most widely held US industrial companies. The companies included in the average are those selected by Dow Jones & Company, the publisher of *The Wall Street Journal*. The S&P 500 index represents stocks chosen from the two major national stock exchanges and the OTC market. The stocks in the index at any given time are determined by a committee of the Standard & Poor's Corporation, which may occasionally add or delete individual stocks or the stocks of entire industry groups. The aim of the committee is to capture present overall stock market conditions as reflected in a broad range of economic indicators.

Some indexes represent a broad segment of the stock market while others represent a particular sector, such as technology, energy (primarily oil and gas), or financials. In addition, because the notion of an equity investment style is widely accepted in the investment community, early acceptance of equity style investing has led to the creation and proliferation of published style indexes. By style it is meant that there is a focus on growth versus value or on small versus mid- versus large-market capitalization. Earlier in this chapter, we listed the different classifications of market capitalization. As for growth versus value, growth is the term applied to the stock of companies with high earnings growth expectations. For growth investors, the current price of the shares is less important than future company fundamentals. That is, the stock is expected to appreciate as the company continues to generate improvements in its future earnings and cash flow. In contrast, a value strategy involves investing in stocks that the market has somehow undervalued.

In a third group are the Wilshire indexes and Russell indexes. The Wilshire indexes are produced by Wilshire Associates and published jointly with the Dow Jones & Company. The Russell indexes are produced by the Frank Russell Company. The criterion for inclusion in each of these indexes is solely a firm's market capitalization. The most comprehensive index is the Wilshire 5,000, which now includes more than 6,700 stocks, up from 5,000 at its inception. The Wilshire 4,500 includes all stocks in the Wilshire 5000 except those in the S&P 500. Thus, the shares in the Wilshire 4,500 have a smaller capitalization than those in the Wilshire 5,000. The Russell 3,000 encompasses the 3,000 largest companies in terms of their market capitalization. The Russell 1,000 is limited to the largest 1,000 of those, and the Russell 2,000 has the remaining smaller firms.

Country, Regional, and Global Stock Indexes

There are stock market indexes for individual countries, regional stock market indexes, and global stock market indexes. As for the United States, news organizations and financial advisory services create indexes. Here we present only an overview of the major ones.

Country stock market indexes

The stock indexes just described are for stocks traded in the United States. Here we briefly describe some of the major non-US national stock market indexes of developed countries.

United Kingdom

The major trading venue in the United Kingdom is the London Stock Exchange (LSE). There are several market value indexes that have been created for selected stocks trading on the LSE, all created by the *Financial Times*. These indexes are referred to as "FTSE" indexes, which stand for Financial Times Stock Exchange and nicknamed "Footsie". The FTSE 100 Index is the most popular index. This includes the shares of the largest 100 UK firms and the aggregate market value of these 100 companies makes up most of the market value of all UK equities.

The other indexes are the FTSE 350 Index (which combines the 350 largest UK firms), the FTSE SmallCap Index, and the FTSE All-Share Index (which is the aggregation of the largest UK stocks plus the stocks in the FTSE SmallCap Index).

Germany

In Germany, the major German stock market index is the Deutscher Aktienindex, abbreviated DAX, created by the Frankfurter Wertpapierbörse (FWB). The FWB is more commonly referred to as the Frankfurt Stock Exchange. The DAX 30 comprises the 30 most actively traded shares listed on the FWB. The German newspaper *Frankfurter Allgemeine Zeitung* (FAZ) also produces a popular German stock market index comprising the 100 largest companies listed on the FWB.

France

In France, the major trading of stocks takes place on the Euronext Paris, formerly known as the Paris Bourse. The electronic trading system on the Euronext is the *Cotation Assistée en Continu*, abbreviated CAC, and translated as "continuous assisted trading". The exchange produces the most popular stock market index called the CAC 40 Index and includes the 40 largest French companies (in terms of market capitalization) traded on the exchange.

Japan

The major stock exchange in Japan is the Tokyo Stock Exchange (TSE). The companies traded on the exchange are divided into three sections depending on market capitalization. The first section includes the largest companies and the second section includes the mid-size companies. The

Mothers Section is the TSE's third section and includes start-up companies. The name "Mothers" Section is an acronym for "market of the high-growth and emerging stocks". The most popular stock market index is the Nikkei 225 Stock Average, which includes the TSE's largest 225 companies in the first section. This index, calculated in the same way as the DJIA, is created by the publisher of Japan's top financial publication, *Nihon Keizai Shimbun.*

China

There are three major exchanges in the Chinese stock market: the Hong Kong Stock Exchange (SEHK), the Shanghai Stock Exchange (SSE), and the Shenzhen Stock Exchange (SZE). The SSE and SZE are the two mainland exchanges. Most of the large-cap stocks in China are large state-owned enterprises (SOEs). There are listed and unlisted stocks. The Chinese stock market indexes are based entirely on listed stocks, that is, stocks listed on one of the exchanges. The listed stocks consist of about 50% SOEs and 50% private stocks.

There are three different types of shares listed and traded on the three Chinese stock exchanges, A, B, and H shares. Two classes of stocks are traded for every listed company on the SSE and SZSE: A-shares and B-shares. A-shares are traded mainly among domestic Chinese investors and are quoted in yuan. B-shares are traded mainly among international investors and are quoted in US dollars and Hong Kong dollars, depending on the exchange.

The major stock indexes in China are the Hang Seng Index (HIS), the Shanghai Composite Index, the Shenzhen Component Index, and the CSI 300 Index. The HSI is a market capitalization-weighted stock market index traded on the SEHK that includes 50 companies representing about 58% of the capitalization of companies on that exchange. The Shanghai Stock Exchange Composite Index (SH Comp.) is a capitalization-weighted index which tracks the price performance of all the A-shares and B-shares listed on the SSE. The Shenzhen Composite Index (SZSE Component Index), the major index of the Shenzhen Stock Exchange (SZSE), is an index of 500 stocks traded on this exchange. The CSI 300, produced by China Securities Index Company, is a market capitalization-weighted index of 300 A-share stocks which are listed on the two mainland stock exchanges. The S&P China 500 (CNY) includes 500 of the largest, most liquid Chinese companies.

Regional stock market indexes

There are stock market indexes that measure the performance of regions of the world: Europe, Asia, and Latin America.

Europe

For Europe, an index provider STOXX Ltd. created two popular regional stock market indexes: the EURO STOXX 50 and the STOXX Europe 600. The EURO STOXX 50 comprises the 50 blue chip companies that are supersector leaders (i.e., largest and most liquid stocks) in the eurozone. The STOXX Europe 600 includes companies from 17 European countries (not just those in the Eurozone). The 600 companies in this index are large and small capitalization companies. S&P produces the S&P 350 which has 350 European stocks. FTSE has a series of regional stock market indexes for Europe.

Asia

S&P and Dow Jones have produced indexes for the Asian region. The S&P Asia 50 index includes companies traded on the Hong Kong, Singapore, South Korean, and Taiwan stock exchanges. The Dow Jones Asian Titans 50 Index includes 25 blue chip Japanese companies and 25 non-Japanese companies in Asia. Dow Jones also produces a small cap index, the Dow Jones Asia/Pacific Small-Cap Total Stock Market Index. FTSE created two indexes for Southeast Asia: FTSE/ASEAN and FTSE/ASEAN 40.

Latin America

The S&P Latin American 40 Index includes 40 blue chip companies in five Latin American countries: Brazil, Chile, Columbia, Mexico, and Peru. The 40 companies included in the index represent approximately 70% of the market capitalization of Latin American countries.

Global stock market indexes

The two major providers of global stock market indexes are Morgan Stanley Capital Index (MSCI) and the *Financial Times.*

MSCI global stock market indexes

The MSCI database of publicly traded stocks throughout the world is used to create more than 28,000 indexes. MSCI has created a series of stock market indexes that are used to represent the aggregate (global) markets of the world and multiple regions. MSCI also creates indexes based on companies in developed and emerging markets.

The MSCI ACWI Index includes developed and emerging market countries. Removing the emerging market countries from that index gives the MSCI World Index, which consists of 23 developed countries. For developed countries excluding the United States and Canada, there is the MSCI Europe, Australasia, and the Far East (MSCI EAFE) Index. This index includes 21 developed countries. There are five MSCI EAFE indexes: MSCI EAFE Large Cap Index (the largest 70% of the companies), the MSCI EAFE Standard (the largest 85% of the companies), the MSCI Investable Market Index (largest 99% of the companies), the MSCI EAFE Mid-Cap Index (comprising those companies in the 71st% and 85th%), and MSCI EAFE Small Cap Index (comprising those companies in the 85th% and 99th%).

The MSCI Emerging Markets Index includes large- and mid-cap stocks of emerging market countries. This index has roughly 830 companies, representing about 85% of the market cap of the 24 emerging market countries. For frontier countries, there is the MSCI Frontier Markets Index, which covers about 99% of these countries.

Financial Times global stock market indexes

Like MSCI, the *Financial Times* has produced a series of global stock market indexes called the FTSE Global Equity Index Series. The series includes about 7,400 different companies throughout the world. The series includes the FTSE All-World Index, FTSE All-World ex-US Index, FTSE Developed Markets Index, FTSE Emerging Markets Index, FTSE Global All Cap Index, FTSE Global Small Cap Index, and FTSE Global Small Cap Index Series. The FTSE All-World BRIC Index includes the largest and most liquid companies in Brazil, Russia, India, and China.

Issues with Stock Market Indexes

There are two issues with stock market indexes. The first is how the index is constructed. The second issue is the use of indexes in asset management.

Methodologies for Constructing a Stock Market Index

There are three methodologies for constructing a stock market index. By a methodology we mean the rule for determining the weight assigned to each stock comprising the index. The three methods that have been used are market capitalization weighting, equal weighting, and price weighting.

The *market capitalization weighting* (or market cap weighting) simply weights each stock as a percentage of its market capitalization relative to the market capitalization of all the stocks comprising the index. Consider, for example, the S&P 500 which is a market cap index. As of January 2019, the market capitalization was approximately $23 trillion. At the same time, the market capitalization of Apple was about $711.9 billion. Apple's weight in the S&P 500 index at that time was then about 3.1% ($711.9 billion/$23 trillion). The top 10 market cap stocks in the S&P 500 index comprise about 20% of the entire index. Most stock market indexes use the market cap weighting methodology.

In an *equal weighted methodology* for constructing an index, each stock is weighted based on the number of stocks in the index. So, for an index that has W stocks, each stock has a weight of $1/W$. Some index providers will create an equal weighted index even if they have a market cap weighted index. For example, there is an equal weighted version of the S&P 500 Index, the S&P 500 Equal Weight Index. That index has 500 stocks,[3] and each stock has a weight of 1/500 or 0.2%. As a result, despite Apple's size, it will have the same weight in the index as Tiffany & Co., which would have a weight of about 0.05% in the S&P 500 market cap weighted index.

Finally, the price weighted methodology weights by the price of each stock. The price of each stock in the index is first summed. Suppose that the sum of the stock prices is $\$X$ and that the price of an individual stock is $\$x$. Then the weight assigned to that stock is $\$x/\$X$. This methodology makes no economic sense. The reason that it is mentioned here is that it is used in the construction of the Dow Jones Industrial Average. Historically, that is the way that the index has been constructed since it was published in May 1986.

The Use of Stock Market Indexes in Asset Management

Stock market indexes are used as a benchmark for the evaluation of the performance of asset managers. Typically, a client will select a benchmark

---

[3] Because there are several companies that have two share classes, there are actually 505 stock symbols. Alphabet, for example, is the parent company of Google which has two shares in the S&P 500 index, GOOGL which is its Class A stock and COOG which is its Class C stock.

that an asset manager agrees to measure performance against. When a manager is retained to match an index, the strategy is referred to as *indexing* or a *beta strategy*. We discuss these strategies in Chapter 12. The stock market indexes that represent sectors or sub-sectors are used as a benchmark for mutual fund managers and the managers of exchange-traded funds (collective investments described in Chapter 5) to provide asset owners with an investment vehicle that gives exposure to different sectors or sub-sectors of the stock market. When a manager is retained to outperform the index after management fees, the strategies employed are called *active strategies* or *alpha strategies* and they are the subject of Chapter 13.

A major criticism of the market cap weighted indexes is that they are dominated by large cap companies. This large cap bias reduces exposure to relatively new companies that may have significant growth potential and price appreciation. As a result, alternative stock market indexes have been developed. We will discuss this further in Chapter 12 where we discuss a strategy called smart beta.

Key Points

- Equity securities represent an ownership interest in a corporation.
- Holders of an equity security have the right to receive the earnings of the corporation when those earnings are distributed in the form of dividends.
- Equity securities include common stock and preferred stock.
- Since preferred stock has priority over the common stock in the distribution of dividends and in the liquidation of a corporation, this form of equity is referred to as a senior corporate security.
- The two fundamental characteristics used to create sub-asset classes in the equity market are the size of the company and what is referred to as value/growth companies.
- Factors that have contributed to the major change in the structure of the equity market include (1) the institutionalization of the stock market as a result of a shift away from retail (individual) investors to large institutional investors, (2) changes in government regulation of the market, and (3) innovation owing largely to advances in computer technology.
- The shifting of the stock market from one that had been dominated by retail investors to one that is now dominated by institutional investors has resulted in the redesigning of equity trading systems to accommodate the types of trading required by institutional investors.

- Equity trading in the United States typically occurs either on a national securities exchange or on an alternative trading system.
- The different types of venues where stock trading occurs can be classified in terms of their listing on an exchange are exchange-traded stocks (also called "listed" stocks) and OTC (unlisted) stocks.
- Disclosure of a stock's supply and demand by a trading venue is referred to as pre-trade transparency and is measured by the bid-ask prices for a stock.
- The major exchange on which listed stocks are traded is the NYSE where trading is done in a centralized continuous auction market at a designated location by a single specialist who is the market maker for each stock.
- Specialists are required to conduct the auction process and maintain an orderly market in one or more designated stocks.
- The OTC market is the market for unlisted stocks and comprises two markets: (1) the Nasdaq Stock Market (a national securities exchange registered with the SEC) which trades unlisted stocks and (2) the OTC market for truly unlisted stocks (i.e., stocks not traded on the Nasdaq Stock Market), which is referred to as the third market.
- An alternative trading system (ATS) is a trading venue that serves as an alternative to trading on exchanges and for after-hours trading.
- Electronic communication networks (ECNs) and crossing networks are the two types of ATS.
- ECNs display quotations that reflect actual orders and provide subscribers with an anonymous way to enter orders.
- ECNs provide both pre-trade transparency about orders and post-trade transparency about executed trades and are referred to as light pool markets.
- Crossing networks are an ATS where orders are aggregated for execution at specified times, with pre-trade transparency varying by the crossing networks.
- Dark pools are crossing networks that do not provide pre-trade transparency.
- The absence of public orders (i.e., no pre-trade transparency) in crossing networks provides institutional investors several benefits: they reduce information leakage contained in an order, avoid front-running of large orders, and lower market-impact costs.

- In deciding where to execute a customer's order, a broker has an obligation to find the "best execution" that is reasonably available for customer orders.
- When a broker is evaluating which of the alternative trading venues would obtain the best execution, the following are considered (1) a better price than quoted in the market when the order is placed, (2) the likelihood that the order will be executed, and (3) the speed of execution.
- The internalization of an order occurs when a broker routes an order to a division of his or her firm for execution.
- The US equity market is referred to as a fragmented market because some orders for a given stock are handled differently from other orders.
- Different types of orders may be submitted to transact in the stock market.
- The most common type of order is a market order — an order that must be filled immediately at the best price.
- Other types of orders (e.g., stop and limit orders) are filled only if the market price reaches a price specified in the order.
- Because institutional investors tend to place orders of larger sizes and with a large number of names (specified stocks), there are special trading arrangements that have evolved to accommodate these investors.
- Block trades are trades of 10,000 shares or more of a given stock or trades with a market value of $200,000 or more.
- Program trades (basket trades) involve the simultaneous transactions in a large number of names.
- Buying on margin is a transaction in which an investor borrows part of the funds needed to buy shares using the shares themselves as collateral for the loan.
- In a margin transaction, the funds borrowed to buy the additional stock are provided by the broker and the investor is charged the call money rate or broker loan rate to borrow the funds.
- Institutional investors have developed computer-automated programs to enter trading orders to minimize the costs associated with trading — the use of computer programs for this purpose is known as algorithmic trading.
- High-frequency trading is a subset of algorithmic trading used by traders to capitalize on infinitesimal price discrepancies that periodically exist in the market.

- Order flow can be "purchased" by a broker–dealer from an investor with "soft dollars".
- When order flow is purchased, the broker–dealer provides the investor, without charge, services such as research or electronic services, typically from a third party.
- Trading or price limits specify a minimum price limit, below which the market price index level may not decline as a result of an institutionally mandated termination of trading, at least at prices below the specified price (the price limit), for a specified period of time.
- There are two types of circuit breakers — conditions precipitating a temporary halting of trading during a severe market decline: market-wide circuit breakers and single-stock circuit breakers.
- The two rules that the SEC has adopted to deal with short sales are the alternative uptick rule and naked short selling rule.
- The reason for the alternative uptick rule is to restrict short sellers from further driving down the price of a stock that has fallen more than 10% in a single trading day from the closing price on the previous trading day.
- With naked short selling — a short sale where no borrowing of the stock occurs or no arrangement is made for borrowing in time for the settlement of the shorted stock with the buyer — the risk is that the short seller is not able to deliver the stock shorted.
- The SEC describes illegal insider trading activity as trading in a security that is "in breach of a fiduciary duty or other relationship of trust and confidence, while in possession of material, non-public information about the security".
- What constitutes insider trading has been developed on a case-by-case basis under the antifraud provisions of the federal securities laws.
- The stocks included in a stock market index must be combined in certain proportions, and each stock must be given a weight.
- Stock market indexes can be classified into three groups: (1) those produced by stock exchanges and include all or a subset of stocks traded on the exchange, (2) those for which a committee subjectively selects the stocks to be included in the index (e.g., the S&P 500 index), and (3) those for which the stocks selected are based solely on the stocks' market capitalizations.
- There are stock market indexes for individual countries, regional stock market indexes, and global stock market indexes.
- There are various methodologies for constructing a stock market index.

- The market capitalization weighting (or market cap weighting) weights each stock as a percentage of its market capitalization relative to the market capitalization of all the stocks comprising the index.
- In an equal weighted methodology for constructing an index, each stock is weighted based on the number of stocks in the index.
- The price weighted methodology involves first summing the price of all stocks in the index and then assigning a weight to each stock based on the ratio of the stock's price relative to the sum of the price of all stocks in the index.
- Stock market indexes are used as benchmarks for evaluating the performance of an asset manager pursuing an indexing or an active stock strategy.

Chapter 4

Fundamentals of Debt Instruments

Learning Objectives

After reading this chapter, you will understand:

- the key features of debt instruments: maturity value, par value, coupon rate, provisions for paying off the debt obligation, options granted to debtholders, currency denomination, and covenants;
- where debt instruments are traded;
- what are investment-grade and non-investment grade debt obligations;
- what interest rate risk is and how it is measured;
- what call and prepayment risk are;
- the major sectors of the debt market (1) Treasury securities market, (2) federal agency securities market, (3) corporate debt market, (4) municipal bonds market, (5) asset-backed securities market, and (6) non-US bond market;
- the types of securities issued by the US Department of the Treasury;
- the two types of federal agencies that issue securities;
- what are corporate bonds and bank loans;
- tax-exempt and taxable municipal bonds;
- the different types of municipal bonds issued;
- what is meant by securitization;
- the different types of securitized products;
- the different types of agency residential mortgage-backed securities: pass-through securities, collateralized mortgage obligations, and stripped mortgage-backed securities;
- non-US bonds: sovereign bonds, supranational bonds, and global bonds;
- the Eurobond market;
- the different types of bond indexes.

In its simplest form, a *debt instrument* is the financial obligation of an entity that promises to pay a specified sum of money at specified future dates. The payments are made up of two components: (1) the repayment of the amount of money borrowed and (2) interest. The entity that promises to make the payment is called the issuer of the security or the borrower. Debt instruments include bonds and bank loans.

Features of Debt Instruments

The key features of debt instruments are maturity, par value, coupon rate, provisions for paying off the debt obligation, options granted to debtholders, currency denomination, and covenants. In a bond agreement, the legal contract that sets forth all of these important bond terms is the *indenture*.

Maturity

Unlike common stock, which has a perpetual life, debt obligations have a date on which they mature. The number of years over which the issuer has promised to meet the conditions of the obligation is referred to as the *term to maturity*. The maturity of a bond refers to the date that the debt will cease to exist, at which time the issuer will redeem the bond by paying the amount borrowed. The maturity date of a bond is always identified when describing a bond. For example, a description of a bond might state "due 12/15/2030".

The practice in the bond market is to refer to the "term to maturity" of a bond as simply its "maturity" or "term". Despite sounding like a fixed date in which the bond matures, there are provisions that may be included in the indenture that grants either the issuer or the bondholder the right to alter a bond's term to maturity. These provisions, which will be described later in this chapter, include call provisions, put provisions, conversion provisions, and accelerated sinking fund provisions.

The debt market is categorized based on the debt instrument's term to maturity: short-term, intermediate-term, and long-term. The classification is somewhat arbitrary and varies among market participants. A common classification is that short-term bonds have a maturity ranging from 1 to 5 years, intermediate-term bonds have a maturity from 5 to 12 years, and long-term bonds have a maturity that exceeds 12 years. Typically, the maturity of a bond does not exceed 30 years. There are, of course, exceptions. For example, Walt Disney Company issued 100-year bonds in July 1993 and the Tennessee Valley Authority issued 50-year bonds in December 1993.

The term to maturity of a debt instrument is important for two reasons in addition to indicating the time period over which the debtholder can expect to receive interest payments and the number of years before the amount borrowed will be repaid in full. The first reason is that the yield offered on a debt instrument depends on the time to maturity. At any given point in time, the relationship between the debt instrument's yield and maturity (called the term structure of interest rates) indicates how debtholders are compensated for investing in debt instruments with different maturities. The second reason is that a debt instrument's price will fluctuate over its life as market interest rates change. The degree of price volatility of a debt instrument is dependent on its maturity. More specifically, all other factors being constant, the longer the maturity of a debt instrument, the greater the price volatility resulting from a given change in interest rates. This will be discussed in more detail in Chapter 16, where we discuss the fundamental analysis of debt instruments.

Par Value

The *par value* of a debt instrument is the amount that the issuer agrees to repay the debtholder by the maturity date. This amount is also referred to as the *principal, face value, redemption value*, or *maturity value.*

Because debt instruments have a different par value, the practice is to quote the price of a debt instrument as a percentage of its par value. A value of 100 means 100% of par value. So, for example, if a debt instrument has a par value of $1,000 and is selling for $850, this debt instrument would be said to be selling at 85. If a debt instrument with a par value of $100,000 is selling for $106,000, the debt instrument is said to be selling for 106.

Coupon Rate

The annual interest rate that the issuer agrees to pay each year is called the *coupon rate.* The annual amount of the interest payment made to debtholders during the term of the debt instrument is called the *coupon* and is determined by multiplying the coupon rate by the debt instrument's par value. For example, a debt instrument with a 6% coupon rate and a par value of $1,000 will pay annual interest of $60.

When describing a debt instrument, the coupon rate is indicated along with the maturity date. For example, the expression "5.5s of 2/15/2034" means a debt instrument with a 5.5% coupon rate maturing on 2/15/2034.

For bonds issued in the United States, the usual practice is for the issuer to pay the coupon in two semiannual installments. Mortgage-backed securities and asset-backed securities, two debt instruments that we describe later, typically pay interest on a monthly basis. For debt instruments issued in some markets outside the United States, coupon payments are made only once per year.

In addition to indicating the coupon payments that the debtholder should expect to receive over its term, the coupon rate also affects the debt instrument's price sensitivity to changes in market interest rates. All other factors being constant, the higher the coupon rate, the less the price will change in response to a change in market interest rates. This will be demonstrated in Chapter 16.

There are securities that have a coupon rate that increases over time according to a specified schedule. These securities are called *step-up notes* because the coupon rate "steps up" over time. For example, a 5-year step-up note might have a coupon rate that is 5% for the first 2 years and 6% for the last 3 years. Or, the step-up note could call for a 5% coupon rate for the first 2 years, 5.5% for the third and fourth years, and 6% for the fifth year. When there is only one change (or step up), as in our first example, the issue is referred to as a single step-up note. When there is more than one increase, as in our second example, the issue is referred to as a *multiple step-up note.*

Not all debt instruments make periodic coupon payments. *Zero-coupon debt instruments*, as the name indicates, do not make periodic coupon payments. Instead, the holder of a zero-coupon debt instrument realizes interest at the maturity date. The aggregate interest earned is the difference between the maturity value and the purchase price. For example, if an investor purchases a zero-coupon debt instrument for 63, the aggregate interest at the maturity date is 37, the difference between the par value (100) and the price paid (63). The reason why certain investors like zero-coupon debt instruments is that they eliminate one of the risks that we will discuss later, reinvestment risk. The disadvantage of a zero-coupon debt instrument is that the accrued interest earned each year is taxed despite the fact that no actual cash payment is made.

There are debt instruments whose coupon payment is deferred for a specified number of years. That is, there is no coupon payment for the deferred period and then at some specified date coupon payments are made until maturity. These debt instruments are referred to as *deferred interest securities.*

A coupon-bearing security need not have a fixed interest rate over the term of the debt instrument. There are debt instruments that have an interest rate that is variable. These debt instruments are referred to as *floating-rate securities.* In fact, another way to classify debt markets is the fixed-rate market and the floating-rate market. Floating-rate securities appeal to institutional investors such as depository institutions (commercial banks, savings and loan associations, and credit unions) because they provide a better match against their funding costs which are typically floating-rate debt.

The interest rate is adjusted on specific dates, referred to as the *coupon reset date.* There is a formula for the new coupon rate, referred to as the *coupon reset formula* that has the following generic formula:

$$\text{Coupon reset formula} = \text{Reference rate} + \text{Quoted margin}$$

The quoted margin is the additional amount that the issuer agrees to pay above the reference rate. The quoted margin need not be a positive value. It could be subtracted from the reference rate.

A floating-rate security may have a restriction on the maximum coupon rate that will be paid at a reset date. The maximum coupon rate is called a *cap.* Because a cap restricts the coupon rate from increasing, a cap is an unattractive feature for the debtholder. A floating-rate security may have a minimum coupon rate, which is called a *floor.* This feature is attractive to the debtholder.

While the reference rate for most floating-rate securities is an interest rate or an interest rate index, there are some issues where this is not the case. Instead, the reference rate can be some financial index such as the return on the Standard & Poor's 500 index or a non-financial index such as the price of a commodity or the consumer price index.

Typically, the coupon reset formula on floating-rate securities is such that the coupon rate increases when the reference rate increases and decreases when the reference rate decreases. There are issues whose coupon rate changes in the opposite direction of the change in the reference rate. Such issues are called *inverse floaters* or *reverse floaters.*

Accrued interest

The coupon interest payment is made to the debtholder of record. Thus, if an investor sells a debt instrument between coupon payments and the buyer holds it until the next coupon payment, then the entire coupon interest earned for the period will be paid to the buyer of the debt instrument since the buyer will be the holder of record. The seller of the debt instrument gives up the interest from the time of the last coupon payment to the time until the debt instrument is sold. The amount of interest over this period that will be received by the buyer even though it was earned by the seller is called *accrued interest.* In the United States and many other countries, the buyer must compensate the seller for the accrued interest. The amount that the buyer pays the seller is the agreed-upon price for the debt instrument plus accrued interest. This amount is called the *full price.* The agreed-upon bond price without accrued interest is called the *clean price.*

A debt instrument in which the buyer must pay the seller accrued interest is said to be trading *cum-coupon.* If the buyer forgoes the next coupon payment, the debt instrument is said to be trading *ex-coupon.* In the United States, debt instruments are always traded cum-coupon. There are debt markets outside the United States where bonds are traded ex-coupon for a certain period before the coupon payment date.

There are exceptions to the rule that the buyer must pay the seller accrued interest. The most important exception is when the issuer has not fulfilled its promise to make the periodic payments. In this case, the issuer is said to be in default. In such instances, the debt instrument's price is sold without accrued interest and is said to be traded *flat.*

Provisions for Paying Off Debt Instruments

The issuer of a debt instrument agrees to repay the principal by the stated maturity date. The issuer can agree to repay the entire amount borrowed in one lump sum payment at the maturity date. That is, the issuer is not required to make any principal repayments prior to the maturity date. Such debt instruments are said to have a *bullet maturity.*

Debt instruments backed by pools of loans (mortgage-backed securities and asset-backed securities) often have a schedule of principal repayments. Such debt obligations are said to be *amortizing securities.* For many loans, the payments are structured so that when the last loan payment is made, the entire amount owed is fully paid off. Another example of an amortizing feature is a debt instrument that has a sinking fund provision. This provision for repayment of a bond may be designed to liquidate all of an issue by the maturity date, or it may be arranged to repay only a part of the total by the maturity date.

A debt instrument may have a call provision granting the issuer an option to retire all or part of the issue prior to the stated maturity date.

Some issues specify that the issuer must retire a predetermined amount of the issue periodically. These provisions are discussed next.

Call and refunding provisions

An issuer generally wants the right to retire a debt instrument prior to the stated maturity date because it recognizes that at some time in the future the general level of interest rates may fall sufficiently below the issue's coupon rate so that redeeming the issue and replacing it with another issue with a lower coupon rate would be economically beneficial. This right is a disadvantage to the bondholder since proceeds received must be reinvested at a lower interest rate. As a result, an issuer who wants to include this right as part of a bond offering must compensate the bondholder when the issue is sold by offering a higher coupon rate, or equivalently, accepting a lower price than if the right is not included.

The right of the issuer to retire the issue prior to the stated maturity date is referred to as a *call provision* and is more popularly referred to as a *call option*. A debt instrument with this provision is referred to as a *callable bond*. If an issuer exercises this right, the issuer is said to "call the bond". The price which the issuer must pay to retire the issue is referred to as the *call price*. There may not be a single call price, but a call schedule, which sets forth a call price based on when the issuer may exercise the option to call the debt instrument.

When a debt instrument is issued, the issuer may be restricted from calling it for a number of years. In such situations, the debt instrument is said to have a *deferred call*. The date at which the debt instrument may first be called is referred to as the *first call date*. However, not all issues have a deferred call. If a bond issue does not have any protection against early call, then it is said to be a *currently callable issue*. But most new debt instruments, even if currently callable, usually have some restrictions against certain types of early redemption. The most common restriction is prohibiting the refunding of the debt instrument for a certain number of years. Refunding a debt instrument means redeeming it with funds obtained through the sale of a new bond issue.

Call protection is much more absolute than refunding protection. While there may be certain exceptions to absolute or complete call protection in some cases, it still provides greater assurance against premature and unwanted redemption than does refunding protection. Refunding prohibition merely prevents redemption only from certain sources of funds, namely the proceeds of other debt issues sold at a lower cost. The debtholder is only protected if interest rates decline, and the borrower can obtain lower-cost money to pay off the debt.

Debt instruments can be called in whole (the entire issue) or in part (only a portion). When less than the entire issue is called, the specific debt instruments to be called are selected randomly or on a pro rata basis. Generally, the call schedule is such that the call price at the first call date is a premium over the par value and scaled down to the par value over time. The date at which the issue is first callable at par value is referred to as the *first par call date*. The call prices in a call schedule are referred to as the *regular* or *general redemption* prices.

Prepayment provision

Amortizing securities backed by loans have a schedule of principal repayments. However, individual borrowers typically have the option to pay off all or part of their loan prior to the scheduled principal repayment date. Any principal repayment prior to the scheduled date is called a *prepayment*. The right of borrowers to prepay is called the prepayment option.

Basically, the prepayment option is the same as a call option. However, unlike a call option, there is no call price that depends on when the borrower pays off the issue. Typically, the price at which a loan is prepaid is at par value.

Sinking fund provision

A *sinking fund provision* included in a bond indenture requires the issuer to retire a specified portion of an issue each year. Usually, the periodic payments required for sinking fund purposes will be the same for each period. A few debt instruments might permit variable periodic payments, where payments change according to certain prescribed conditions set forth in the indenture. The alleged purpose of the sinking fund provision is to reduce credit risk. This kind of provision for repayment of debt may be designed to liquidate all of a debt instrument by the maturity date, or it may be arranged to pay only a part of the total by the end of the term. If only a part is paid, the remainder is referred to as a *balloon maturity*. Many indentures include a provision that grants the issuer the option to retire more than the amount stipulated for the scheduled sinking fund retirement. This is referred to as an accelerated sinking fund provision.

Options Granted to Debtholders

A debt instrument could grant the debtholder and the issuer an option to take some action against the other party. The most common type of option embedded in a debt instrument is a call option discussed already. This option is granted to the issuer. There are two options that can be granted to the debtholder: the right to "put" the issue and the right to convert the issue to the issuer's common stock.

A debt instrument with a put provision grants the debtholder the right to sell the debt instrument (that is, force the issuer to redeem the debt instrument) at a specified price on designated dates. A debt instrument with this provision is referred to as a *putable debt instrument.* The specified price is called the *put price.* Typically, a debt instrument is putable at par value if it is issued at or close to par value. For a zero-coupon debt instrument, the put price is below par. The advantage of the put provision to the debtholder is that if after the issue date market rates rise above the issue's coupon rate, the debtholder can force the issuer to redeem the debt instrument at the put price and then reinvest the proceeds at the prevailing higher rate.

A *convertible debt instrument* is an issue giving the debtholder the right to exchange the debt instrument for a specified number of shares of the issuer's common stock. Such a feature allows the debtholder to take advantage of favorable movements in the price of the issuer's common stock. An *exchangeable debt instrument* allows the debtholder to exchange the issue for a specified number of shares of common stock of a corporation different from the issuer of the bond.

Currency Denomination

The payments that the issuer makes to the debtholder can be in any currency. For debt instruments issued in the United States, the issuer typically makes both coupon payments and principal repayments in US dollars. However, there is nothing that forces the issuer to make payments in US dollars. When the debt instrument is issued, the issuer may make payments in some other specified currency. For example, payments may be made in euros or yen.

An issue in which payments to bondholders are in US dollars is called a *dollar-denominated issue. A non-dollar-denominated issue* is one in which payments are not denominated in US dollars. There are some issues whose coupon payments are in one currency and their principal payment is in another currency. An issue with this characteristic is called a *dual-currency issue.*

Some issues allow either the issuer or the bondholder the right to select the currency in which a payment will be paid. This option effectively gives the party with the right to choose the currency the opportunity to benefit from a favorable exchange rate movement.

Covenants

Covenants establish rules for several important areas of operations for borrowers. These provisions are safeguards for the debtholder because they attempt to limit some issuer behavior that could increase the credit risk faced by the debtholder.

Trading Venues

Unlike common stock that can trade on an exchange or in the over-the-counter (OTC) market, the principal secondary market for debt instruments is the OTC market. A concern of investors is the degree of market transparency. In the United States, the reporting system of the Financial Industry Regulatory Authority (FINRA), the *Trade Reporting and Compliance Engine* (TRACE), requires that all broker–dealers who are members of FINRA must, under a set of rules approved by the SEC, report transactions in certain bonds to TRACE. At the end of each trading day, market aggregate statistics are published on market activity for certain types of bonds. The end-of-day recap information provided includes (1) the number of securities and total par amount traded, (2) advances, declines, and 52-week highs and lows, and (3) the 10 most active investment-grade, high-yield, and convertible bonds for the day.

In the case of corporate bond trading, traditionally the OTC market was conducted by telephone and based on broker–dealer trading desks that took principal positions in corporate bonds in order to fulfill the buy and sell orders of their customers. There has been a transition away from this traditional form of bond trading and toward electronic trading. Electronic bond trading makes up more than a third of corporate bond trading. The major advantages of electronic trading over traditional corporate bond trading in the OTC market are (1) the ability to provide liquidity to the markets,

(2) enhanced price discovery (particularly for less liquid markets), (3) the use of new technologies, and (4) trading and portfolio management efficiencies. As an example of the advantages, a portfolio manager can load buy and sell orders in a website, trade from these orders, and then clear these orders. There are five types of electronic bond trading systems: auction systems, cross-matching systems, interdealer systems, client-to-dealer systems, and single-dealer systems.

Risks Associated with Investing in Debt Instruments

Debt instruments may expose an investor to one or more of the following risks: (1) interest rate risk, (2) call and prepayment risk, (3) credit risk, (4) liquidity risk, (5) exchange rate or currency risk, or (6) inflation or purchasing power risk. In Chapter 2, we reviewed the last four risks. So here we describe just the first two risks.

Interest Rate Risk

The price of a typical debt instrument changes in the opposite direction of the change in interest rates. That is, when interest rates rise, a debt instrument's price will fall; when interest rates fall, a debt instrument's price will rise.

The reason for this inverse relationship between price and changes in interest rates or changes in market yields is as follows. Suppose investor X purchases a hypothetical 6% coupon 20-year bond at par value ($100). The yield for this bond is 6%.[1] Suppose that immediately after the purchase of this debt instrument two things happen. First, market interest rates rise to 6.50% so that if an investor wants to buy a similar 20-year debt instrument, a 6.50% coupon rate would have to be paid by the issuer in order to offer the debt instrument at par value. Second, suppose investor X wants to sell the debt instrument. In attempting to sell it, investor X would not find an investor who would be willing to pay par value for a debt instrument with a coupon rate of 6%. The reason is that any investor who wanted to purchase this debt instrument could obtain a similar 20-year debt instrument with a coupon rate that is 50 basis points higher, 6.5%. What can the investor

[1]In Chapter 15, we explain how to compute the yield of a debt instrument given its coupon rate and maturity.

do? The investor cannot force the issuer to change the coupon rate to 6.5%. Nor can the investor force the issuer to shorten the maturity of the debt instrument to a point where a new investor would be willing to accept a 6% coupon rate. The only thing that the investor can do is adjust the debt instrument's price so that at the new price the buyer would realize a yield of 6.5%. This means that the price would have to be adjusted down to a price below par value. The new price must be $94.4469. While we assumed in our illustration an initial price of par value, the principle holds for any purchase price. Regardless of the price that an investor pays for a debt instrument, an increase in market interest rates will result in a decline in a debt instrument's price.

Suppose instead of a rise in market interest rates to 6.5%, they decline to 5.5%. Investors would be more than happy to purchase the 6% coupon, 20-year issue for par value. However, investor X realizes that the market is only offering investors the opportunity to buy a similar debt instrument at par value with a coupon rate of 5.5%. Consequently, investor X will increase the price until it offers a yield of 5.5%. That price is $106.0195.

Since the price of a debt instrument fluctuates with market interest rates, the risk that an investor faces is that the price of a debt instrument held in a portfolio will decline if market interest rates rise. This risk is referred to as *interest rate risk* and is a major risk faced by investors in the debt market.

Features of a debt instrument that affect interest rate risk

The interest rate risk of a debt instrument's price depends on its maturity and coupon rate, as well as any embedded options (call and put provisions). We summarize the properties of a debt instrument with respect to maturity, coupon rate, and level of interest rates as follows:

> **Property 1:** For a given maturity and initial yield, the lower the coupon rate, the greater the debt instrument's price sensitivity to changes in market interest rates.
> **Property 2:** For a given coupon rate and initial yield, the longer the maturity of a debt instrument, the greater its price sensitivity to changes in market interest rates.
> **Property 3:** For a given coupon rate and maturity, the lower the level of interest rates, the greater the debt instrument's price sensitivity to changes in market interest rates.

When we describe the analytics of debt instruments in Chapter 16, we demonstrate these properties. In addition to the two features of a debt instrument (maturity and coupon rate), a debt instrument's price also depends on any embedded option such as a call provision. We discuss this later when we cover call risk.

Measuring interest rate risk

Investors are interested in estimating the price sensitivity of a debt instrument to changes in market interest rates. The measure commonly used to approximate the percentage price change is duration. *Duration* gives the approximate percentage price change for a 100-basis-point (one percentage point) change in interest rates. For example, suppose that the duration of a debt instrument is 4. This means that the debt instrument will change by approximately 4% if interest rates change by 100 basis points. For a 50-basis-point change, this debt instrument's price will change by approximately 2% (4% divided by 2).

Chapter 16 explains the concept of duration further and its measurement.

Call and prepayment risk

As explained earlier, a debt instrument may include a provision that allows the issuer to retire or call all or part of the issue before the maturity date. From the debtholder's perspective, the following are the disadvantages of call provisions:

- The debt instrument's cash flow pattern is not known with certainty.
- Because the issuer will call the debt instrument when interest rates have dropped, the debtholder is exposed to reinvestment risk. This is the risk that the debtholder will have to reinvest the proceeds when the bond is called at a lower interest rate.
- The capital appreciation potential of a debt instrument will be reduced because the price of a callable debt instrument may not rise much above the price at which the issuer is entitled to call the issue.

Because of these disadvantages faced by the investor, a callable debt instrument is said to expose the investor to *call risk*.The same disadvantages apply to debt instruments that can prepay. In this case, the risk is referred to as *prepayment risk*.

Sectors of the Debt Market

The US bond market is the largest debt market in the world. The major sectors of the debt market are the (1) Treasury securities market, (2) federal agency securities market, (3) corporate debt market, (4) municipal bond market, (5) asset-backed securities market, and (6) non-US bond market.

US Treasury Securities

The securities issued by the US Department of the Treasury (US Treasury hereafter) are called *Treasury securities* or just *Treasuries.* Because they are backed by the full faith and credit of the US government, market participants throughout the world view them as having virtually no credit risk. Hence, the interest rates on Treasury securities are treated as the benchmark, default-free interest rates. There are two types of marketable Treasury securities issued: fixed principal securities and inflation-indexed securities. The securities are issued via a regularly scheduled auction process.

The US Treasury issues two types of *fixed principal securities*: discount securities and coupon securities. Discount securities are called *Treasury bills*; coupon securities are called *Treasury notes* and *Treasury bonds.*

Types of securities issued by the Treasury

Treasury bills are issued at a discount to par value, have no coupon rate, and mature at face value. Generally, Treasury bills can be issued with a maturity of up to 2 years. The US Treasury typically issues only certain maturities. The practice of the US Treasury is to issue Treasury bills with maturities of 4 weeks, 13 weeks, 26 weeks, and 52 weeks.

The US Treasury issues securities with initial maturities of 2 years or more as coupon securities. Coupon securities are issued at approximately par and, in the case of fixed principal securities, mature at par value. They are not callable. *Treasury notes* are coupon securities issued with original maturities of more than 2 years but no more than 10 years. The US Treasury issues a 2-year note, a 5-year note, and a 10-year note. Treasuries with original maturities greater than 10 years are called Treasury bonds. The US Treasury issues a 30-year bond.

The US Treasury issues coupon securities that provide inflation protection and are popularly referred to as *Treasury inflation-protected securities* (TIPS). They do so by having the principal increase or decrease based on the rate of inflation such that when the security matures, the investor receives the greater of the principal adjusted for inflation or the original principal. The US Treasury issues a 5-year TIPS, a 10-year TIPS, and a 20-year TIPS. TIPS work as follows. The coupon rate on an issue is set at a fixed rate, the rate being determined via the auction process, just like fixed principal Treasury securities. The coupon rate is referred to as the *real rate* because it is the rate that the investor ultimately earns above the inflation rate. The inflation index used for measuring the inflation rate is the non-seasonally-adjusted US City Average All Items Consumer Price Index for All Urban Consumers (CPI-U).

Treasury securities are issued via an auction process. The most recently auctioned Treasury coupon securities for each maturity are referred to as *on-the-run issues* or *current coupon issues*. Treasury coupon securities auctioned prior to the current coupon issues are referred to as *off-the-run issues* and are not as liquid as on-the-run issues and therefore offer a higher yield than the corresponding on-the-run Treasury issues.

Stripped Treasury securities

The US Treasury does not issue zero-coupon notes or bonds. However, because of the demand for zero-coupon instruments with virtually no credit risk, the private sector has created such securities using a process called *coupon stripping*.

To illustrate the process, suppose that $2 billion of a 10-year fixed principal Treasury note with a coupon rate of 5% is purchased by a dealer firm to create zero-coupon Treasury securities. The cash flow from this Treasury note is 20 semiannual payments of $50 million each ($2 billion times 0.05 divided by 2) and the repayment of principal of $2 billion 10 years from now. As there are 21 different payments to be made by the US Treasury for this note, a security representing a single payment claim on each payment is issued, which is effectively a zero-coupon Treasury security. The amount of the maturity value or a security backed by a particular payment, whether coupon payment or principal repayment, depends on the amount of the payment to be made by the US Treasury on the underlying Treasury security. In our example, 20 zero-coupon Treasury securities each have a maturity value of $50 million, and one zero-coupon Treasury security, backed by the principal, has a maturity value of $2 billion. The maturity dates for the zero-coupon Treasury securities coincide with the corresponding payment dates by the US Treasury.

Zero-coupon Treasury securities are created as part of the US Treasury's Separate Trading of Registered Interest and Principal of Securities (STRIPS) program to facilitate the stripping of designated Treasury securities.

Federal Agency Securities

Federal agency securities can be classified by the type of issuer — federally related institutions and government-sponsored enterprises. Federal agencies that provide credit for certain sectors of the credit market issue two types of securities: debentures and mortgage-backed securities. We review the former type here and the latter in the next section of this chapter.

Federally related institutions are arms of the federal government and generally do not issue securities directly into the marketplace. Federally related institutions include the Export– Import Bank of the United States, the Tennessee Valley Authority, the Commodity Credit Corporation, the Farmers Housing Administration, the General Services Administration, the Government National Mortgage Association, the Maritime Administration, the Private Export Funding Corporation, the Rural Electrification Administration, the Rural Telephone Bank, the Small Business Administration, and the Washington Metropolitan Area Transit Authority.

With the exception of securities of the Tennessee Valley Authority (TVA) and the Private Export Funding Corporation, the securities are backed by the full faith and credit of the US government. The federally related institution that has issued securities in recent years is the TVA.

Government-sponsored enterprises (GSEs) are privately owned, publicly chartered entities. They were created by Congress to reduce the cost of capital for certain borrowing sectors of the economy deemed to be important enough to warrant assistance. GSEs issue securities directly in the marketplace. There are five GSEs that currently issue debentures: Freddie Mac, Fannie Mae, Federal Home Loan Bank System, Federal Farm Credit System, and the Federal Agricultural Mortgage Corporation. Fannie Mae, Freddie Mac, and Federal Home Loan Bank are responsible for providing credit to the housing sectors. The Federal Agricultural Mortgage Corporation provides the same function for agricultural mortgage loans. The Federal Farm Credit Bank System is responsible for the credit market in the agricultural sector of the economy.

With the exception of the securities issued by the Farm Credit Financial Assistance Corporation, GSE securities are not backed by the full faith and credit of the US government, as is the case with Treasury securities. Consequently, investors purchasing GSEs are exposed to credit risk. However, a bailout program for Fannie Mae and Freddie Mac has resulted in some of their debt instruments being backed by the US Treasury.

Corporate Debt

Corporate debt instruments can be classified as bonds and bank loans. They are also classified by the industry of the issuer: utilities, transportations, industrials, banks, and finance (non-banks). Within these five general categories finer breakdowns are often made to create more homogeneous groupings. For example, utilities are sub-divided into electric power companies, gas distribution companies, water companies, and communication companies. Transportations are divided further into airlines, railroads, and trucking companies. Industrials are the catchall class and the most heterogeneous of the groupings with respect to investment characteristics because this category includes all kinds of manufacturing, merchandising, and service companies.

Corporate bonds

The corporate bond market can be classified into the investment-grade sector and the speculative-grade sector. The latter sector — referred to as the *non-investment grade bond sector*, *high-yield bond sector*, and *junk bond sector* — includes bond issues rated below investment grade by the rating agencies (that is, BBB — and lower by Standard & Poor's and Fitch Ratings and Baa3 and lower by Moody's). They may also be unrated, but not all unrated debt is speculative.

Several types of issuers fall into the non-investment grade bond sector. These include (1) original issuers, (2) fallen angels, and (3) restructuring and leveraged buyouts. *Original issuers* may be young, growing corporations lacking the stronger balance sheet and income statement profile of many established corporations, but often with lots of promise. Also called venture capital situations or growth or emerging market companies, the bond is often sold with a story projecting future financial strength. There are also the established operating firms with financials neither measuring up to the strengths of investment-grade corporations nor possessing the weaknesses of companies on the verge of bankruptcy.

Fallen angels are companies with a previously investment-grade-rated debt that have come upon hard times with deteriorating balance sheet and income statement measures. They may be in default or near bankruptcy. In these cases, investors are interested in the workout value of the debt in a reorganization or liquidation, whether within or without the bankruptcy courts. Some refer to these issues as "special situations". Over the years they have fallen on hard times; some have recovered, and others have not. General Motors Corporation and Ford Motor Company are examples of fallen angels. From 1954 to 1981, General Motors Corp. was rated AAA by S&P; Ford Motor Co. was rated AA by S&P from 1971 to 1980. In August 2005, Moody's lowered the rating on both automakers to junk bond status.

Restructurings and *leveraged buyouts* are companies that have deliberately increased their debt burden with a view toward maximizing shareholder value. The shareholders may be the existing public group to which the company pays a special extraordinary dividend, with the funds coming from borrowings and the sale of assets. Cash is paid out, net worth decreased and leverage increased, causing the credit ratings to be downgraded on existing debt. Newly issued debt gets junk bond status because of the company's weakened financial condition. In a leveraged buyout (LBO), a new and private shareholder group owns and manages the company. The bond issue's purpose may be to retire other debt from banks and institutional investors incurred to finance the LBO.

Security for corporate bonds

A corporate bond can be secured or unsecured. In the case of a secured bond, either real property (e.g., real estate) or personal property (e.g., equipment) may be pledged to offer security beyond that of the general credit standing of the issuer. With a *mortgage bond*, the issuer has granted the bondholders a lien against the pledged assets. A *lien* is a legal right to sell mortgaged property to satisfy unpaid obligations to bondholders.

Some companies do not own fixed assets or other real property, and so have nothing on which they can give a mortgage lien to secure bondholders. Instead, they own securities of other companies; these are holding companies and the other companies are subsidiaries. To satisfy the bondholders' desire for security, the issuer grants investors a lien on stocks, notes, bonds, or whatever other kind of financial assets it owns. These assets are termed collateral (or personal property), and bonds secured by such assets are called *collateral trust bonds*.

Debenture bonds are not secured by a specific pledge of property, but that does not mean that bondholders have no claim on the property of issuers. Debenture bondholders have the claim of general creditors on all assets of the issuer not pledged specifically to secure other debt. And they even have a claim on pledged assets to the extent that those assets have value greater than necessary to satisfy secured creditors. *Subordinated debenture bonds* are issues that rank after secured debt, after debenture bonds, and often after some general creditors in the claim on assets and earnings in the case of the bankruptcy of the company.

Convertible bonds

A *convertible bond* grants the bondholder the right to convert the bond into a predetermined number of shares of common stock of the issuer. The number of shares of common stock that the bondholder will receive from exercising the option of a convertible bond is called the *conversion ratio.* The conversion privilege may extend for all or only some portion of the convertible bond's life, and the stated conversion ratio may change over time. It is always adjusted proportionately for stock splits and stock dividends. At the time of issuance of a convertible bond, the issuer effectively grants the bondholder the right to purchase the common stock at a price equal to: par value of convertible bond/conversion ratio.

This price is referred to in the prospectus as the *stated conversion price.* Almost all convertible bonds are callable by the issuer. Typically, there is a non-call period (i.e., a time period from the time of issuance that the convertible bond may not be called). There are some issues that have a provisional call feature that allows the issuer to call the issue during the non-call period if the price of the stock reaches a certain price. The call price schedule of a convertible bond is specified at the time of issuance. The call price typically declines over time.

A put option grants the bondholder the right to require the issuer to redeem the issue at designated dates for a predetermined price. Some convertible bonds are putable. Put options can be classified as "hard" puts and "soft" puts. A hard put is one in which the convertible bond must be redeemed by the issuer only for cash. In the case of a soft put, the issuer has the option to redeem the convertible bond for cash, common stock, subordinated notes, or a combination of the three.

Bank loans

As an alternative to the issuance of securities, a corporation can raise funds by borrowing from a bank. Bank loans to corporate borrowers have a floating interest rate. There are two types of bank loans: investment-grade loans and leveraged loans. As the name suggests, an *investment-grade loan* is a bank loan made to corporate borrowers that have a credit rating that is investment-grade. These loans are held in the loan portfolio by the originating bank and therefore institutional investors typically do not have the opportunity to participate in these types of loans. The second type of bank loan to a corporation is a *leveraged loan*. These loans are made to corporations with a credit rating that is below-investment-grade. These loans can be sold to institutional investors.

Syndicated bank loans

A *syndicated bank loan* is one in which a group (or syndicate) of banks provides funds to the borrower. The reason why a group of banks is needed is because the amount sought by a corporate borrower might be too large for any one bank to be exposed to the credit risk of that borrower. Therefore, the syndicated bank loan is used by corporate borrowers who seek to raise a large amount of funds in the loan market rather than through the issuance of securities. The syndication may include using the securitization process described later in this chapter to create *collateralized loan obligations* (CLOs) and is therefore an important part of the corporate bank loan market.

Syndicated bank loans are called *senior bank loans* because of their priority position over subordinated lenders (bondholders) with respect to repayment of interest and principal. A syndicated loan is typically structured so that it is amortized according to a predetermined schedule, and repayment of principal begins after a specified number of years.

Syndicated bank loans can be traded in the secondary market or securitized to create CLOs. The trade association that has been the main advocate of commercial loans as an asset class is the Loan Syndications and Trading Association (LSTA).

Municipal Bonds

Issuers of *municipal bonds* include municipalities, counties, towns and townships, school districts, and special service system districts. Included in the category of municipalities are cities, villages, boroughs, and incorporated towns that have received a special state charter. A special purpose service system district, or simply special district, is a political subdivision created to foster economic development or related services to a geographical area. Special districts provide public utility services (water, sewers, and drainage) and fire protection services. Public agencies or instrumentalities include authorities and commissions.

There are both tax-exempt and taxable municipal securities. "Tax-exempt" means that interest on a municipal security is exempt from federal income taxation. The tax exemption of municipal securities applies to interest income, not capital gains. The exemption may or may not extend to taxation at the state and local levels. The state tax treatment depends on (1) whether the issue from which the interest income is received is an "in-state issue" or an "out-of-state issue"; and (2) whether the investor is an individual or a corporation. The treatment of interest income at the state level varies by state.

Most municipal securities that have been issued are tax exempt. Municipal securities are commonly referred to as tax-exempt securities, although taxable municipal securities have been issued and are traded in the market.

Types of municipal bonds

There are basically two types of municipal security structures: tax-backed debt obligations and revenue bonds.

Tax-backed debt obligations are secured by some form of tax revenue. The broadest type of tax-backed debt obligation is the general obligation debt. General obligation bond pledges include unlimited and limited tax general obligation debt. The stronger form is the unlimited tax general obligation debt because it is secured by the issuer's unlimited taxing power (corporate and individual income taxes, sales taxes, and property taxes) and is said to be secured by the full faith and credit of the issuer. A limited tax general obligation debt is a limited tax pledge because for such debt there is a statutory ceiling on the tax rates that may be levied to service the issuer's debt.

Revenue bonds are the second basic type of security structure found in the municipal bond market. These bonds are issued for enterprise financings that are secured by the revenues generated by the completed projects themselves, or for general public-purpose financings in which the issuers pledge to the bondholders the tax and revenue resources that were previously part of the general fund. Revenue bonds can be classified by the type of financing. These include utility revenue bonds, transportation revenue bonds, housing revenue bonds, higher education revenue bonds, health care revenue bonds, seaport revenue bonds, sports complex and convention center revenue bonds, and industrial development revenue bonds.

Some municipal securities have special security structures. These include prefunded bonds and insured bonds. An issuer may find it attractive to refund a bond issue. Often, a refunding takes place when the original bond issue is escrowed or collateralized by direct obligations guaranteed by the US government. Such bonds are known as *pre-refunded bonds*. Such bonds, if escrowed with securities guaranteed by the US government, have little, if any, credit risk and are therefore the safest municipal bonds available. *Insured bonds* are credit enhanced by an unconditional guarantee of a commercial insurance company. The insurers of municipal bonds are typically monoline insurance companies that are primarily in the business of providing guarantees. While almost half of municipal bonds were insured prior to 2007, beginning in 2008 there has been very little issuance of insured bonds.

Asset-Backed Securities

An *asset-backed security* (ABS) is a debt instrument backed by a pool of loans or receivables. ABSs are also referred to as *securitized products*. The process for the creation of asset-backed securities is referred to as *securitization*. Here we only briefly describe the general principles of securitization and then briefly describe the wide range of securitized products. In Chapter 3 in the companion volume, we illustrate the securitization process and provide more details on the products and how they are valued.

The securitization process

We will use an illustration to show how a securitized product is created. Suppose that Superior Medical Equipment Inc. manufactures high-quality medical equipment. Although the company has cash sales, the bulk of its sales come from installment sales contracts. (An installment sale contract is a loan to the buyer of the medical equipment wherein the buyer agrees to repay Superior Medical Equipment Inc. over a specified period of time for the amount borrowed plus interest.) The medical equipment purchased is the collateral for the loan. We will assume that the loans are all for 5 years.

We will assume that Superior Medical Equipment has more than $200 million of installment sales contracts. We will further assume that the company wants to raise $200 million. Rather than issuing corporate bonds for $200 million, the treasurer of the company decides to raise the funds through a securitization. To do so, Superior Medical Equipment will set up a legal entity referred to as a *special-purpose vehicle* (SPV).

In our illustration, the SPV that is set up is called SME Asset Trust (SMEAT). Superior Medical Equipment will then sell to SMEAT $200 million of the loans. Superior Medical Equipment Inc. will receive from SMEAT $200 million in cash, the amount of funds it wanted to raise. SMEAT obtains the $200 million by selling securities that are backed by the $200 million of loans. The securities are the ABSs we referred to earlier. In the prospectus for a securitization, these securities are usually referred to as "certificates".

In a securitization, there is a transaction structure. This refers to the securities created, the rules that set forth the way in which the losses are to be distributed among the securities in the structure, the rules for the distribution of interest each month among the securities in the structure, and the rules for the distribution of principal repayment among the securities in the structure. The rules are referred to as the structure's "waterfall".

Let's look at some different types of structures. In the simplest structure, suppose the SMEAT issues three bond classes, A, B, and C. These bond classes are commonly referred to as *tranches*. Recall that the total amount of the receivables is $200 million and that the par amount of the bond classes sold is the same amount. Assume that the par value of bond class A is $160 million, bond class B is $30 million, and bond class C is $10 million, and that the rules for the distribution of the losses from the pool of receivables backing this securitization are as follows:

- Losses on the pool of receivables are first allocated to bond class C up to $10 million (the par amount of that bond class).
- Subsequent losses on the pool of receivables are then allocated to bond class B up to $30 million (the par amount of that bond class) above the $10 million loss absorbed by bond class C.
- Finally, should losses on the pool of receivables exceed $40 million, losses are then absorbed by bond class A.

For the distribution of principal when it is paid by the borrowers, the rules are as follows:

- Pay bond class A with all principal received up to the amount of its par value ($160 million).

- Once bond class A is fully repaid its par amount of $160 million, the principal received is distributed to bond class B up to its par value of $30 million.
- Finally, after bond class B is paid off, any additional principal is paid to bond class C.

Note that in this structure, bond class C is providing credit support against losses from the pool of receivables for bond class A and bond class B up to $10 million. Moreover, bond class B is providing credit support against losses from the pool of receivables for bond class A up to an additional $30 million above that provided by bond class C. For this reason, we say that bond class B and bond class C are *subordinated bond classes*. Because bond class C is the first to absorb the losses, it is referred to as the *first-loss piece*. We also say that since bond class A is not providing credit support for the other two bond classes, it is referred to as the *senior bond class*. The structure itself is referred to as a *senior-subordinated structure*.

Each of the bond classes will receive a credit rating. The senior bond class will receive the highest credit rating and the two subordinated bond classes will receive a lower credit rating. More specifically, bond class B will receive a lower credit rating than bond class A, but a higher credit rating than bond class C because bond class B is being provided credit support by bond class C.

Types of securitized products

Many types of assets have been securitized. Securitized products are backed by two types of assets: non-real estate receivables/loans and real estate mortgage loans. Non-real estate receivables/loans cover a wide range of securitized products, the largest sectors being credit card receivables ABS, auto loan receivables ABS, student loan ABS, and CLOs. Securitization of real estate assets (i.e., real estate loans) is by far the largest sector.

The two types of real estate property mortgages that have been securitized are residential mortgage loans and commercial mortgage loans. The securities created from the former are called *residential mortgage-backed securities* (RMBS) and by the latter are called *commercial mortgage-backed securities* (CMBS). In turn, the RMBS can be further classified as agency RMBS and private-label (or non-agency) RMBS.

Agency RMBS are those issued by three government-related entities and form by far the largest sector in the investment-grade bond market.

Private-label RMBS are issued by any other entity. Because of the credit risk associated with private-label RMBS, they require credit enhancement to provide some form of credit protection against default on the pool of assets backing a transaction. Credit enhancement mechanisms are typical in ABS transactions. In the case of agency RMBS, the credit enhancement is either a government guarantee or the guarantee of a government-sponsored enterprise.

In what follows, we provide a brief description of agency RMBS because of its size. They comprise not only the largest sector in the securitized product market, but also consistently comprise at least one-third of the entire investment-grade debt market. Fundamentally, a bond portfolio manager who is not familiar with this market will be at a disadvantage. The RMBS sector is where there are opportunities for bond portfolio managers to enhance returns because of the complexity of these securities, particularly the private-label RMBS sector.

Agency RMBS

A residential mortgage is a loan secured by the collateral of some specified real estate property that obliges the borrower to make a predetermined series of payments. The interest rate on the mortgage loan is called the *note rate*. The fundamental unit in an agency RMBS is the pool. At its lowest common denominator, the pool is a collection of a large number of residential mortgage loans with similar (but not identical) characteristics — loans with a commonality of attributes such as note rate, term to maturity, credit quality, loan balance, and type of residential mortgage design.

The transformation of groups of residential mortgage loans with common attributes into RMBS occurs using one of two mechanisms. Loans that meet the underwriting guidelines of three entities — Ginnie Mae, Fannie Mae, and Freddie Mac — are securitized as an agency pool. Although Ginnie Mae (Government National Mortgage Association) is an agency of the US government, carrying the full faith and credit of US government, Fannie Mae and Freddie Mac are government-sponsored enterprises. Despite this distinction, the RMBS issued by these three entities are referred to as agency RMBS and we review the different types of agency RMBS here. There are three types of agency RMBS: pass-through securities, collateralized mortgage obligations, and stripped RMBS.

The second mechanism is the securitization of residential mortgage loans that do not qualify for agency pools and these are the non-agency or "private-label" RMBS. These types of securities do not have an agency guarantee, but are credit enhanced by one of several mechanisms.[2]

Before we describe the three types of agency RMBS, let's describe the cash flow characteristics of residential mortgage loans because that is what investors in any RMBS will receive. Although a mortgagor may select from many types of mortgage loans, we will use the most common mortgage design: the level payment, fixed-rate mortgage because our purpose here is to understand the basic cash flow characteristics of a mortgage loan. The basic idea behind the design of the level-payment, fixed-rate mortgage, or simply level-payment mortgage, is that the borrower pays for an agreed-upon period of time, called the maturity or term of the mortgage. Thus, at the end of the term, the loan has been fully amortized.

For a level-payment mortgage, each monthly mortgage payment consists of two components: (1) interest of 1/12 of the fixed annual note rate times the amount of the outstanding mortgage balance at the beginning of the previous month and (2) a repayment of a portion of the outstanding mortgage balance (principal).

The difference between the monthly mortgage payment and the portion of the payment that represents interest equals the amount that is applied to reduce the outstanding mortgage balance. The monthly mortgage payment is designed so that after the last scheduled monthly mortgage payment of the loan is made, the amount of the outstanding mortgage balance is zero (i.e., the mortgage is fully repaid). Thus, the portion of the monthly mortgage payment applied to interest declines each month, and the portion applied to reducing the mortgage balance increases. The reason for this is that because the mortgage balance is reduced with each monthly mortgage payment, the interest on the mortgage balance declines. Since the monthly mortgage payment is fixed, an increasingly larger portion of the monthly payment is applied to reduce the principal in each subsequent month.

For the mortgagee, the cash flow from the mortgage loan is not the same as what the mortgagor pays. This is because of a servicing fee and guarantee fee that must be paid. Every mortgage loan must be serviced. The monthly cash flow from a mortgage loan, regardless of the mortgage

[2]One type of non-agency RMS is a subprime RMBS and it is the problems in this securitized product that led to the subprime mortgage crisis that began in the summer of 2007.

design, can, therefore, be divided into three parts: (1) the servicing and guarantee fees, (2) the interest payment net of the two fees, and (3) the scheduled principal repayment (referred to as amortization).

One cannot assume that the mortgagor would not pay off any portion of the mortgage balance prior to the scheduled due date. Payments made in excess of the scheduled principal repayment are called *prepayments*. Prepayments occur for several reasons. First, borrowers prepay the entire mortgage balance when they sell their home. Second, borrowers may be economically motivated to pay off the loan as market rates fall below the loan's note rate. This reason for prepaying a mortgage loan is referred to as refinancing. Third, in the case of borrowers who cannot meet their mortgage obligations, the property is repossessed and sold. The proceeds from the sale are used to pay off the mortgage loan. Finally, if the property is destroyed by a fire or if another insured catastrophe occurs, the insurance proceeds are used to pay off the mortgage loan.

The effect of prepayments is that the cash flow from a mortgage is not known with certainty — by this, we mean that the amount and the timing of the cash flow is uncertain. Consequently, ignoring defaults, the mortgagor knows that as long as the loan is outstanding, interest will be received, and the principal will be repaid at the scheduled date each month. On the maturity date of the mortgage loan, the investor would recover the amount lent. What the mortgagee does not know — the uncertainty — is for how long the mortgage loan will be outstanding and, therefore, the timing of the principal payments.

We now describe the three types of agency RMBS: agency pass-through securities, agency collateralized mortgage obligations, and agency stripped RMBS.

Agency mortgage pass-through securities

In an *agency mortgage pass-through security*, or simply an agency pass-through, the monthly cash flow from the pool of mortgage loans is distributed on a pro rata basis to the investors. The monthly cash flow that may be distributed to the investors consists of three components: (1) interest net of the servicing and guarantor fees, (2) regularly scheduled principal payments (amortization), and (3) prepayments.

As just noted, the difficulty for investors in estimating the cash flow is due to prepayments. This risk, as explained earlier in this chapter, is called prepayment risk. The estimation or prediction of prepayments is critical in valuing and assessing the interest rate risk of not just an agency pass-through but any residential RMBS. Dealer firms and large asset management firms have developed models for doing so, referred to as prepayment models. These models are beyond the scope of our discussion.

The key here is that because of prepayment risk, the cash flow is uncertain. Typically the way that investors gauge the uncertainty is by computing the average life of an RMBS based on different prepayment assumptions. For example, assume the following for an agency pass-through that an investor is considering purchasing:

Prepayment Speed Assumed	Average Life
Very fast prepayments	2 years
Fast prepayments	4 years
Moderate prepayments	11 years
Slow prepayments	18 years
Very slow prepayments	22 years
No prepayments	26 years

Looking at the above, the investor sees a wide range in the average life based on the prepayment speeds. Would an investor in this agency pass-through own a short-term investment (say 2 years) or a very long-term investment (say 22 years)? The investor does not know. Thus, an investor must be aware of the impact of prepayment risk. Although there is no credit risk with an agency RMBS, there is considerable prepayment risk. Recognizing this, dealers have developed the next agency RMBS product, the agency collateralized mortgage obligation, that redistributes prepayment risk among different bond classes in a structure.

Agency collateralized mortgage obligations

A collateralized mortgage obligation (CMO) is a security backed by a pool of agency pass-through securities. Agency CMOs are structured so that there are several classes of bondholders with varying average lives so that institutional investors can select the average life range that best suits their needs and the degree to which they want to be exposed to prepayment risk.

In a CMO, the principal payments from the underlying pool of pass-through securities are used to retire the bond classes on a priority basis as specified in the prospectus.

Although we will not explain the wide range of bond classes or tranches created in a CMO structure, we will provide a few for the purposes of showing how they are created (structured) and how they alter the investment characteristics relative to agency pass-through securities from which they were created: sequential-pay bonds, planned amortization class bonds, and support bonds.[3]

The simplest type of CMO structure is the *sequential-pay structure*. In structuring an agency deal, there are only rules specified for the distribution of principal and interest. (There are no rules for deals with defaults and delinquencies because payments are guaranteed by either Ginnie Mae, Fannie Mae, and Freddie Mac.) Suppose that the CMO contains four bond classes, A, B, C, and D and the following are the rules for the distribution of interest from the collateral and the principal:

- **Rule for distribution of interest:** The monthly interest is distributed to each bond class on the basis of the amount of principal outstanding at the beginning of the month.
- **Rule for the distribution of principal:** All monthly principal (i.e., regularly scheduled principal and prepayments) is distributed first to bond class A until it is completely paid off. After bond class A is completely paid off its par amount, all monthly principal payments are made to bond class B until it is completely paid off. After bond class B is completely paid off its par amount, all monthly principal payments are made to bond class C until it is completely paid off its par amount. Finally, after bond C is completely paid off, all monthly principal payments are made to bond class D.

These are simple but powerful rules, in that they redistribute the prepayment risk among the four bond classes. Remember that prepayment risk cannot be eliminated. It can only be redistributed among the bond classes. For example, the average life over a wide range of assumed prepayment speeds for bond class A might be from 6 months to 4 years. Although there is still variability in the average life, it is far less than that of an

[3]For a more detailed description of the different types of CMO bond classes, see Fabozzi, Bhattacharya, and Berliner [2011].

agency pass-through security. So an investor considering buying a short-term RMBS would be concerned with buying the pass-through whose average life varies from 2 years to 26 years. In contrast, bond class A would be more appealing. Let's look at an investor interested in a long-term RMBS, say at least 15 years. Suppose that the average life of bond class D is from 14 years to 22 years. Although there is a wide variation in the average life for this bond class, it is a better investment than the pass-through security that can have an average life as short as 2 years if the prepayment speed is very fast.

A *planned amortization class* (PAC) can reduce the variance of the average life of some bond classes (the PAC bond classes) but at the same time increase the variance of the average life of the non-PAC bond classes (called the support bond classes). Let's suppose that there are three PAC bond classes and one support bond class in the structure. The rules for the payment of interest are the same as in the sequential-pay CMO. However, the rule for the payment of principal is different. The reason is that the schedule of principal payments is generated at two prepayment speeds. The rule for the distribution of the principal would be as follows:

- **Rule for the distribution of principal:** Principal is distributed first to bond class A each month according to the schedule. Any principal from the collateral that exceeds the scheduled amount for that month is paid to bond class D. After bond class A is completely paid off its par amount, principal payment is made to bond class B each month based on the scheduled payment. Any principal from the collateral that exceeds the monthly scheduled amount is paid to bond class D. After bond class B is completely paid off its par amount, principal is paid to bond class C each month based on the scheduled payment. Any principal from the collateral that exceeds the monthly scheduled amount is paid to bond class D. After bond class C is fully paid off, principal payments each month are made to bond class D.

What this rule for the distribution of monthly principal does is that if actual prepayments are roughly in the range of the two prepayment speeds used to create the PAC principal schedule for bond classes A, B, and C, then the investor will know what the average life will be. That is, there is less prepayment risk than in a sequential-pay CMO and certainly much less than in a pass-through security. Since the prepayment risk cannot be eliminated but can be redistributed, how are the PAC bond classes (A, B, and C) getting the benefit of lower prepayment risk? That must come from the support bond (D) in this structure. Basically, support bonds have substantial prepayment risk. It could, for example, have an average life from 1 year to 28 years!

Agency stripped mortgage-backed securities

A pass-through security distributes the cash flow from the underlying pool of mortgage loans on a pro rata basis to the investors: An *RMBS stripped mortgage-backed security* (stripped MBS) is created by altering that distribution of principal and interest from a pro rata distribution to an unequal distribution. In the most common type of stripped RMBS, all of the interest is allocated to one class — the *interest only class* — and all of the principal to the other class — the *principal-only class.* The rationale for investing in these securities is either to use them as hedging vehicles in the managing of a mortgage portfolio or using them for speculative purposes because of their substantial interest rate risk.

Non-US Bonds

Non-US bonds are issued by the national government and their subdivisions, supranational entities, and corporations (non-financial and financial corporations).

Sovereign bonds

Sovereign bonds are those issued by the central government of a country. The largest government bond market outside of the United States is the Japanese government bond market, followed by the markets in Italy, Germany, and France.

As explained earlier, in the US government bond market the interest payments and principal payment can be separated and sold as separate securities. Many Euro government bonds are stripped to create zero-coupon securities. Sovereign governments also issue inflation-linked bonds. The largest non-US government issuer of inflation-linked bonds is the United Kingdom, followed by France. These bonds, popularly referred to as *linkers* in Europe, are typically linked to some consumer price index of the country.

Sovereign bonds are rated by credit rating agencies and their ratings are referred to as "sovereign ratings". The two general categories used by rating agencies in deriving their ratings are economic risk and political risk. The former category is an assessment of the ability of a government to satisfy its obligations. Both quantitative and qualitative analyses are used in assessing economic risk. Political risk is an assessment of the willingness of a government to satisfy its obligations. A government may have the ability to pay, but may be unwilling to do so. Political risk is assessed based on qualitative analysis of the economic and political factors that influence a government's economic policies.

There are two ratings assigned to each national government. The first is a local currency debt rating and the second is a foreign currency debt rating. The reason for distinguishing between the two types of debts is that, historically, the default frequency differs by the currency denomination of the bond. Specifically, defaults have been greater on foreign currency-denominated debt. The reason for the difference in default rates for local currency debt and foreign currency debt is that if a government is willing to raise taxes and control its domestic financial system, it can generate sufficient local currency to meet its local currency debt obligation. This is not the case with foreign currency-denominated debt. A national government must purchase foreign currency to meet a debt obligation in that foreign currency and therefore has less control with respect to its exchange rate. Thus, a significant depreciation of the local currency relative to a foreign currency in which a debt obligation is denominated will impair a national government's ability to satisfy such obligations.

Supranational bonds

A supranational is an entity that is formed by two or more central governments through international treaties. The purpose for creating a supranational is to promote economic development for the member countries. Two examples of supranational institutions are the International Bank for Reconstruction and Development, popularly referred to as the World Bank, and the Inter-American Development Bank.

Global bond markets

From the perspective of a given country, the global bond market can be classified into an internal bond market and an external bond market.

Internal bond market

The *internal bond market* can be decomposed into two markets, the *domestic bond market* and the *foreign bond market*. The domestic bond market is where issuers domiciled within the country issue bonds and where those bonds are subsequently traded.

The foreign bond market of a country is where bonds of issuers not domiciled in the country are issued and traded. For example, in the United States, the foreign bond market is the market where bonds are issued by non-US entities and then subsequently traded. Bonds traded in the US foreign bond market are nicknamed "Yankee bonds". In Japan, a yen-denominated bond issued by a non-Japanese entity and subsequently traded in Japan's bond market is part of the Japanese foreign bond market. Yen-denominated bonds issued by non-Japanese entities are nicknamed "samurai bonds". Foreign bonds in the United Kingdom are referred to as "bulldog bonds", those in the Netherlands are referred to as "Rembrandt bonds", and those in Spain are referred to as "matador bonds".

External bond market

The external bond market, commonly referred to as the offshore bond market or, more popularly, the *Eurobond market*, includes bonds with the following three distinguishing features: (1) are underwritten by an international syndicate, (2) at issuance are offered simultaneously to investors in a number of countries, and (3) are issued outside the jurisdiction of any single country.

The Eurobond market is divided into sectors depending on the currency in which the issue is denominated. For example, when a Eurobond is denominated in US dollars, it is referred to as a *Eurodollar bond.* A Eurobond denominated in Japanese yen is referred to as a *Euroyen bond.* Issuers of Eurobonds include national governments and their subdivisions, corporations (financial and non-financial), and supranationals.

There are five types of Eurobond structures: straight bonds, subordinated notes, floating-rate notes, convertibles, and asset-backed securities. A *Euro straight bond* is the traditional fixed-rate coupon bond. They are issued on an unsecured basis and are usually issued by high-quality entities. With subordinated notes, the rights of the bondholder are subordinate to the rights of other creditors. There are floating-rate Eurobonds with the various types of coupon reset formulas described earlier in this chapter.

Bond Indexes

There are numerous US bond market indexes. Bond indexes are classified based on one or more of the following characteristics with respect to the bonds that are included in the index: (1) bond sectors included in the index, (2) industries, (3) maturity of the bonds in the index, and (4) credit rating of the bonds in the index. The commonly used bond indexes are all market-capitalization weighted.[4]

There are several index providers that have created broad-based market indexes. The broad-based US bond market index most commonly used was originally developed by the now defunct Lehman Brothers. In November 2008, Lehman Brothers sold its bond indexes to Barclays which now has bond indexes called the Bloomberg Barclays indexes. The most popular broad-based market index, which includes more than 6,000 issues, is the Bloomberg Barclays US Aggregate Bond Index. This index includes only investment-grade bond issues.

Generally, broad-based bond index providers create sector indexes. For example, Bloomberg Barclays produces the following sector indexes: Barclays US Treasury Bond Index, Barclays US Government-Related Bond Index, Barclays US Agencies Bond Index, Barclays US Corporate Bond Index, Barclays US Securitized Bond Index, Barclays US MBS Index, Barclays US ABS Index, and Barclays US CMBS (ERISA Only) Index. All of these indexes include only investment-grade issues.

Industry bond indexes available from Bloomberg Barclays are the Bloomberg Barclays US Industrial Bond Index, Bloomberg Barclays US Utility Bond Index, and Bloomberg Barclays US Financial Institutions Bond Index. With respect to maturity, Bloomberg Barclays creates an index based on the maturity of Treasury securities. This includes Bloomberg Barclays US 1–3 Year Treasury Bond Index, Bloomberg Barclays US 3–7 Year Treasury Bond Index, Bloomberg Barclays US 7–10 Year Treasury Bond Index, Bloomberg Barclays US 10–20 Year Treasury Bond Index, and Bloomberg Barclays US 20+ Year Treasury Bond Index.

The bond indexes of Bloomberg Barclays described above include only investment-grade issues. Corporate bond indexes that include non-investment-grade (i.e., high-yield) corporate bonds have been created by several providers. The Bloomberg Barclays US High Yield Bond Index is an example of such an index.

While the bond indexes created by Bloomberg Barclays are used by institutional investors and by exchange-traded funds, there are other index

[4]As with market capitalization-weighted indexes, there have been criticisms regarding the appropriateness of using market-capitalization bond indexes and, as a result, alternative schemes have been proposed. See Goltz and Campani [2011] and Siegel [2003].

providers such as the BoA Merrill Lynch Fixed Income Indices (ICE BoAML Bond Indices).

Key Points

- The debt market is categorized based on the debt instrument's term to maturity: short-term (1–5 years), intermediate-term (5–12 years), and long-term (longer than 12 years).
- In addition to indicating the final date that the debt will be repaid, the maturity date is also important because (1) yield offered on a debt instrument depends on it and (2) the degree of price volatility of a debt instrument is dependent on it.
- The par value of a debt instrument is the amount that the issuer agrees to repay the debtholder by the maturity date.
- Because debt instruments have a different par value, the practice is to quote the price of a debt instrument as a percentage of its par value.
- The coupon rate is the annual interest rate that the issuer agrees to pay each year.
- A debt instrument may have a fixed rate or a floating rate.
- For a floating-rate debt instrument, the interest rate is adjusted on specific dates (coupon reset date) as specified by the coupon reset formula.
- There are debt instruments that have a zero-coupon rate; they do not make periodic coupon payments and the holder of a zero-coupon debt instrument realizes interest at the maturity date.
- Provisions that permit the issuer to pay off a debt instrument prior to the maturity date are call and refunding provisions, prepayment provision, and sinking fund provision.
- Options that may be granted to the debtholder are a put provision and a conversion provision (i.e., converting the bond for common stock).
- The payments that the issuer makes to the debtholder can be in any currency.
- Unlike common stock that can trade on an exchange or in the OTC market, the principal secondary market for debt instruments is the OTC market.
- Debt instruments may expose an investor to one or more of the following risks: (1) interest rate risk, (2) call and prepayment risk, (3) credit risk, (4) liquidity risk, (5) exchange rate or currency risk, (6) inflation or purchasing power risk.

- The price of a typical debt instrument changes in the opposite direction from the change in interest rates. That is, when interest rates rise, a debt instrument's price will fall; when interest rates fall, a debt instrument's price will rise.
- Interest rate risk for an investor who owns a debt instrument is that its price will decline if interest rates rise and is the major risk faced by investors.
- There are three properties of interest rate risk: (1) for a given maturity and initial yield, the lower the coupon rate, the greater the debt instrument's price sensitivity to changes in market interest rates, (2) for a given coupon rate and initial yield, the longer the maturity of a debt instrument, the greater its price sensitivity to changes in market interest rates, and (3) for a given coupon rate and maturity, the lower the level of interest rates, the greater the debt instrument's price sensitivity to changes in market interest rates.
- Duration is a measure of the price sensitivity of a debt instrument to changes in market interest rates; the measure gives the approximate percentage price change for a 100-basis-point change in interest rates.
- For a debtholder, there are three disadvantages of a debt instrument that has a provision allowing the issuer to retire or call all or part of the issue before the maturity date: (1) the cash flow pattern is not known with certainty, (2) there is reinvestment risk, and (3) when interest rates decline, the capital appreciation potential will be reduced.
- The major sectors of the debt market are the (1) Treasury securities market, (2) federal agency securities market, (3) corporate debt market, (4) municipal bond market, (5) asset-backed securities market, and (6) non-US bond market.
- The US Treasury issues two types of fixed principal securities: discount securities and coupon securities. Discount securities are called Treasury bills; coupon securities are called Treasury notes and Treasury bonds.
- TIPS, issued by the US Treasury, are coupon securities that provide inflation protection.
- Dealers have created zero-coupon Treasury securities through the process of coupon stripping; the resulting securities are referred to Treasury STRIPS.
- Federal agency securities include federally related institutions and government-sponsored enterprises.
- Corporate debt instruments can be classified as bonds and bank loans.

- The corporate bond market can be classified into the investment-grade sector and the non-investment grade bond sector.
- The non-investment-grade sector includes bond issues rated below investment grade by the rating agencies (that is, BBB− and lower by Standard & Poor's and Fitch Ratings and Baa3 and lower by Moody's).
- A corporate bond can be secured or unsecured. In the case of a secured bond, either real property (e.g., real estate) or personal property (e.g., equipment) may be pledged to offer security beyond that of the general credit standing of the issuer.
- With a mortgage bond, the issuer has granted the bondholders a lien against the pledged assets.
- Debenture bonds are not secured by a specific pledge of property, but that does not mean that bondholders have no claim on the property of issuers; the bondholders have the claim of general creditors on all assets of the issuer not pledged specifically to secure other debt.
- A convertible bond grants the bondholder the right to convert the bond into a predetermined number of shares of common stock of the issuer.
- There are two types of bank loans made to corporations: (1) investment-grade loans which are loans made to corporations that have a credit rating that is investment-grade and (2) leverage loans made to corporations that have a credit rating that is below investment grade.
- Municipal bonds are issued by municipalities, counties, towns and townships, school districts, and special service system districts.
- Although there are both tax-exempt and taxable municipal securities, most municipal bonds are tax-exempt.
- Tax-exempt means that interest is exempt from federal income taxation; the tax exemption of municipal securities applies to interest income, not capital gains.
- There are basically two types of municipal security structures: tax-backed debt obligations and revenue bonds.
- Tax-backed debt obligations are secured by some form of tax revenue; the broadest type of tax-backed debt obligations are general obligation debts.
- Revenue bonds are issued for enterprise financings that are secured by the revenues generated by the completed projects themselves, or for general public-purpose financings in which the issuers pledge to the bondholders the tax and revenue resources that were previously part of the general fund.

- An ABS is a debt instrument backed by a pool of loans or receivables and is often referred to as a securitized product.
- An ABS is created via the securitization process.
- Securitized products are backed by two types of assets: non-real estate receivables/loans and real estate mortgage loans.
- Non-real estate receivables/loans cover a wide range of securitized products, the largest sectors being credit card receivables ABS, auto loan receivables ABS, student loan ABS, and CLOs.
- Securitization of real estate assets (i.e., real estate loans) is by far the largest sector.
- The two types of real estate property mortgages that have been securitized are residential mortgage loans and commercial mortgage loans.
- The securities created from real estate mortgage loans are RMBS and CMBS.
- RMBS can be further classified as agency RMBS and private-label (or non-agency). The former sector of the securitized product market is not only the largest sector but a large sector in the investment-grade bond market as well.
- Agency RMBS are created from loans that meet certain underwriting standards established by the three issuers of these securities: Ginnie Mae, Fannie Mae, and Freddie Mac.
- Ginnie Mae (Government National Mortgage Association) is an agency of the US government, carrying the full faith and credit of the US government, while Fannie Mae and Freddie Mac are government-sponsored enterprises.
- The three types of agency RMBS are agency pass-through securities, agency collateralized mortgage obligations, and agency stripped RMBS.
- A major risk of investing in an agency RMBS is the uncertainty about the cash flow due to the prepayments.
- In an agency pass-through, the monthly cash flow from the pool of mortgage loans is distributed on a pro rata basis to the investors, and this exposes investors to significant prepayment risk as gauged by the considerable range of the average life under different prepayment speeds.
- A CMO is a security backed by a pool of pass-through securities. Agency CMOs are structured so that there are several classes of bondholders with varying average lives so that institutional investors can select the average life range that best suits their needs and the degree to which they want to be exposed to prepayment risk.

- Although prepayment risk cannot be eliminated, it can be redistributed among bond classes in a CMO based on the rules for the distribution of interest and principal.
- A sequential-pay CMO structure is the simplest type of CMO where there are bond classes that are paid off sequentially, resulting in average life variability that is more acceptable to institutional investors.
- A planned amortization class CMO is another type of CMO structure that can reduce the variance of the average life of some bond classes (the PAC bond classes), but at the same time increase the variance of the average life of the non-PAC bond classes (called the support bond classes).
- In contrast to a pass-through security which distributes the cash flow from the underlying pool of mortgage loans on a pro rata basis to the investors, an agency stripped mortgage-backed security is created by altering that distribution of principal and interest from a pro rata distribution to an unequal distribution.
- For the most common type of stripped MBS, all of the interest is allocated to one class — the interest only class — and all of the principal to the other class — the principal-only class.
- Interest-only and principal-only securities have substantial interest rate risk.
- Non-US bonds are issued by the national government and their subdivisions, supranational entities, and corporations (non-financial and financial corporations).
- From the perspective of a given country, the global bond market can be classified into an internal bond market and an external bond market.
- The internal bond market can be decomposed into two markets, the domestic bond market and the foreign bond market.
- The domestic bond market is where issuers domiciled within the country issue and trade bonds; the foreign bond market of a country is where bonds of issuers not domiciled in the country are issued and traded.
- The external bond market is commonly referred to as the offshore bond market, or, more popularly, the Eurobond market.
- Bond indexes are classified based on one or more of the following characteristics with respect to the bonds that are included in the index: (1) bond sectors included in the index, (2) industries, (3) maturity of the bonds in the index, and (4) credit rating of the bonds in the index.
- The commonly used bond indexes used are all market-capitalization weighted.

References

Fabozzi, F. J., A. K. Battacharya, and W. S. Berliner, 2011. *Mortage-Backed Securities: Products, Structuring, and Analytical Techniques: Second Edition.* Hoboken, NJ: John Wiley & Son.

Goltz, F. and C. Campani, 2011. *Review of Corporate Bond Indices: Construction Principles, Return Heterogeneity, and Fluctuations in Risk Exposures.* EDHEC-Risk Institute Publication.

Siegel, L. B., 2003. *Benchmarks and Investment Management.* Charlottesville, Virginia: The Research Foundation of the Association for Investment Management and Research.

Chapter 5

Collective Investment Vehicles and Alternative Assets

Learning Objectives

After reading this chapter, you will understand:

- collective investment vehicles and the reason for investing in them;
- what an investment company is and the different types of investment companies: open-end funds (mutual funds) and closed-end funds;
- how net asset value (NAV) is calculated;
- what exchange-traded funds (ETFs) are;
- the similarities and differences between ETFs and closed-end funds;
- the use of ETF shares by investors;
- what a hedge fund is, and the different types of hedge funds;
- the general characteristics of a hedge fund;
- the different types of commodity investments and the different reasons for investing in them (indirect investment in stocks of natural resource companies, commodity mutual funds, and commodity futures);
- what is meant by private equity and how an investor can gain exposure to this alternative asset class via a venture capital fund;
- the structure of a venture capital fund and the capital commitment made by investors;
- what is commercial property and the different types of commercial property;
- the four sectors of the commercial real estate market: private commercial real estate equity market, public commercial real estate equity market, private commercial real estate debt market, and public commercial real estate debt market;
- the reasons for investing in commercial real estate;
- the various vehicles for investing in private commercial real estate equity;
- the different types of real estate investment trusts;

- what a commercial loan is;
- the ways of investing in private commercial real estate debt and public commercial real estate debt; and
- what a commercial mortgage-backed security is.

In Chapters 3 and 4, we discussed equities and debt instruments. In this chapter, we cover collective investment vehicles and alternative assets. *Collective investment vehicles* involve the pooling of funds by investors and then the investment of those funds in certain assets and asset classes. Three major advantages of the indirect ownership of securities by investing in collective investment vehicles are the risk reduction through diversification, professional management of assets, and possible favorable tax treatment.

Collective investment vehicles include investment companies, exchange traded funds, hedge funds, venture capital funds, and real estate investment trusts. As investment vehicles, asset managers may find them appealing because they allow them to obtain exposure to some asset or asset class. In this chapter, we describe the various collective investment vehicles.

In addition to collective investment vehicles, we describe alternative asset classes. Traditional asset classes include equities (the subject of Chapter 3) and debt (the subject of the previous chapter). Alternative asset classes include commodities, private equity, and commercial real estate.

We begin with a description of investment companies, ETFs, and hedge funds. These collective investment vehicles allow investors to obtain exposure to the alternative asset classes. Specialized ETFs and hedge funds allow exposure to commodities and commercial real estate. Real estate investment trusts are another collective investment vehicle for investing in commercial real estate. To invest in private equity, a venture capital fund is the collective investment vehicle that is used by investors.

Investment Companies

Investment companies include open-end funds, closed-end funds, and unit trusts. Shares in investment companies are sold to the public and the proceeds are invested in a diversified portfolio of securities. The value of a share of an investment company is called its *net asset value* (NAV). The two types of costs borne by investors in open-end funds are the shareholder sales charge or load and the annual fund operating expense. There is a wide range of investment companies that invest in different asset classes and with different investment objectives.

Types of Investment Companies

There are three types of investment companies: open-end funds, closed-end funds, and unit trusts.

Open-end funds (mutual funds)

Open-end funds, commonly referred to as *mutual funds*, are portfolios of securities, mainly stocks, bonds, and money market instruments. There are several important aspects of mutual funds.

- First, investors in mutual funds own a pro rata share of the overall portfolio.
- Second, the asset manager of the mutual fund manages the portfolio, that is, buys some securities and sells others (this characteristic is unlike unit investment trusts, discussed later).
- Third, the value or price of each share of the portfolio, called the NAV, equals the market value of the portfolio minus the liabilities of the mutual fund divided by the number of shares owned by the mutual fund investors. That is,

$$\text{NAV} = \frac{\text{Market value of portfolio} - \text{Liabilities}}{\text{Number of shares outstanding}}.$$

  For example, suppose that a mutual fund with 20 million shares outstanding has a portfolio with a market value of \$315 million and liabilities of \$15 million. The NAV is

$$\text{NAV} = \frac{\$315{,}000{,}000 - \$15{,}000{,}000}{20{,}000{,}000} = \$15.00.$$

- Fourth, the NAV or price of the fund is determined only once each day, at the close of the day. For example, the NAV for a stock mutual fund is determined from the closing stock prices for the day.
- Fifth, and very importantly, all new investments into the fund or withdrawals from the fund during a day are priced at the closing NAV (investments after the end of the day or on a non-business day are priced at the next day's closing NAV).

The total number of shares in the fund increases if there are more investments than withdrawals during the day, and vice versa. This is the reason such a fund is called an "open-end" fund. For example, assume that at the beginning of the day a mutual fund portfolio has a value of $1 million, there are no liabilities, and there are 10,000 shares outstanding. Thus, the NAV of the fund is $100. Assume that during the day $5,000 is deposited into the fund, $1,000 is withdrawn, and the prices of all the securities in the portfolio remain constant. This means that 50 shares were issued for the $5,000 deposited (since each share is $100) and 10 shares redeemed for $1,000 (again, since each share is $100). The net number of new shares issued is then 40. Therefore, at the end of the day there will be 10,040 shares and the total value of the fund will be $1,004,000. The NAV will remain at $100.

If, instead, the prices of the securities in the portfolio change, both the total size of the portfolio and, therefore, the NAV will change. In the previous example, assume that during the day the value of the portfolio doubles to $2 million. Since deposits and withdrawals are priced at the end-of-day NAV, which is now $200 after the doubling of the portfolio's value, the $5,000 deposit will be credited with 25 shares ($5,000/$200) and the $1,000 withdrawn will reduce the number of shares by 5 shares ($1,000/$200). Thus, at the end of the day there will be 10,020 shares in the fund with a NAV of $200, and the value of the fund will be $2,004,000. (Note that 10,020 shares × $200 NAV equals $2,004,000, the portfolio value).

Overall, the NAV of a mutual fund will increase or decrease due to an increase or decrease in the price of the securities in the portfolio, respectively. The number of shares in the fund will increase or decrease due to the net deposits into or withdrawals from the fund, respectively. And the total value of the fund will increase or decrease for both reasons.

Closed-end funds

The shares of a closed-end fund are very similar to the shares of common stock of a corporation. The new shares of a closed-end fund are initially issued by an underwriter for the fund. And after the new issue, the number of shares remains constant. This is the reason such a fund is called a "closed-end" fund. After the initial issue, there are no sales or purchases of fund shares by the fund company as there are for open-end funds. The shares are traded on a secondary market, either on an exchange or in the over-the-counter market.

Investors can buy shares either at the time of the initial issue (as discussed below), or thereafter in the secondary market. Shares are sold only on the secondary market. The price of the shares of a closed-end fund is determined by the supply and demand in the market in which these funds are traded. Thus, investors who transact closed-end fund shares must pay a brokerage commission at the time of purchase and at the time of sale.

The NAV of closed-end funds is calculated in the same way as for open-end funds. However, the price of a share in a closed-end fund is determined by supply and demand, so the price can fall below or rise above the NAV per share. Shares selling below NAV are said to be "trading at a discount", while shares trading above NAV are "trading at a premium".

Consequently, there are two important differences between open-end funds and closed-end funds. First, the number of shares of an open-end fund varies because the fund sponsor will sell new shares to investors and buy existing shares from shareholders. Second, by doing so, the share price is always the NAV of the fund. In contrast, closed-end funds have a constant number of shares outstanding because the fund sponsor does not redeem shares and sell new shares to investors (except at the time of a new underwriting). Thus, the price of the fund shares will be determined by supply and demand in the market and may be above or below NAV, as discussed above. Although the divergence of the price from NAV is often puzzling, in some cases the reasons for the premium or discount are easily understood. For example, a share's price may be below the NAV because the fund has a large built-in tax liability and investors are discounting the share's price for that future tax liability. (We'll discuss this tax liability issue later in this chapter.) A fund's leverage and resulting risk may be another reason for the share's price trading below NAV. A fund's shares may trade at a premium to the NAV because the fund offers relatively cheap access to, and professional management of, stocks in another country about which information is not readily available or transactions are difficult or expensive for small investors.

Under the Investment Company Act of 1940, closed-end funds are capitalized only once. They make an initial public offering (IPO) and then their shares are traded on the secondary market, just like any corporate stock, as discussed earlier. The number of shares is fixed at the IPO; closed-end funds cannot issue more shares. In fact, many closed-end funds become leveraged to raise more funds without issuing more shares.

An important feature of closed-end funds is that the initial investors bear the substantial cost of underwriting the issuance of the funds' shares.

The proceeds that the managers of the fund must invest is equal to the total paid by the initial buyers of the shares minus all costs of issuance. These costs normally include selling fees or commissions paid to the retail brokerage firms that distribute the shares to the public. The commissions are strong incentives for retail brokers to recommend these shares to their retail customers, and for investors to avoid buying these shares on their initial offering.

As explained later in this chapter, ETFs pose a threat to both mutual funds and closed-end funds. ETFs are essentially hybrid closed-end vehicles, which trade on exchanges and typically trade very close to NAV.

Since closed-end funds are traded like stocks, the cost to any investor of buying or selling a closed-end fund is the same as that of a stock. The obvious charge is the stockbroker's commission. The bid-offer spread of the market on which the stock is traded is also a cost.

Unit trusts

A *unit trust* is similar to a closed-end fund, in that the number of unit certificates is fixed. Unit trusts typically invest in bonds. They differ in several ways from both mutual funds and closed-end funds that specialize in bonds. First, there is no active trading of the bonds in the portfolio of the unit trust. Once the unit trust is assembled by the sponsor (usually a brokerage firm or bond underwriter) and turned over to a trustee, the trustee holds all the bonds until they are redeemed by the issuer. Typically, the only time the trustee can sell an issue in the portfolio is if there is a dramatic decline in the issuer's credit quality. As a result, the cost of operating the trust will be considerably less than costs incurred by either a mutual fund or a closed-end fund.

Second, unit trusts have a fixed termination date, while mutual funds and closed-end funds do not. Third, unlike the mutual fund and closed-end fund investor, the unit trust investor knows that the portfolio consists of a specific portfolio of bonds and has no concern that the trustee will alter the portfolio. While unit trusts are common in Europe, they are not common in the United States.

All unit trusts charge a sales commission. The initial sales charge for a unit trust ranges from 3.5% to 5.5%. In addition to these costs, there is the cost incurred by the sponsor to purchase the bonds for the trust that an investor indirectly pays. That is, when the brokerage firm or bond underwriting firm assembles the unit trust, the price of each bond to the trust also includes the dealer's spread. There is also often a commission if the units are sold.

Fund Sales Charges and Annual Operating Expenses

There are two types of costs borne by investors in mutual funds. The first is the shareholder fee, usually called the sales charge or load. For securities transactions, this charge is called a *commission*. This cost is a "one time" charge debited to the investor for a specific transaction, such as a purchase, redemption, or exchange. The type of charge is related to the way the fund is sold or distributed.

The second cost is the annual fund operating expense, usually called the *expense ratio*, which covers the funds' expenses, the largest of which is for investment management. This charge is imposed annually. The *management fee*, also called the *investment advisory fee*, is the fee charged by the investment advisor for managing a fund's portfolio.

Other expenses include primarily the costs of (1) custody (holding the cash and securities of the fund); (2) the transfer agent (transferring cash and securities among buyers and sellers of securities and the fund distributions, etc.); (3) independent public accountant fees; and (4) directors' fees.

Types of Funds by Investment Objective

Mutual funds have been created to satisfy the various investment objectives of investors. In general, there are stock funds, bond funds, money market funds, and alternative investment funds. Within each of these categories, there are several subcategories of funds. There are also US-only funds, international funds (no US securities), and global funds (both US and international securities).

There are also passive and active funds. Passive (or indexed) funds are designed to replicate one of the market indexes discussed in Chapter 12. Active funds, on the other hand, attempt to outperform a market index by actively trading the fund portfolio. There are also many other categories of funds, as discussed below. Each fund's objective is stated in its prospectus, as required by the SEC and the "1940 Act", as discussed in what follows.

Stock funds differ by:

- The average market capitalization ("market cap") (large, mid, and small) of the stocks in the portfolio.

- Style (growth, value, and blend).
- Sector — "sector funds" specialize in one particular sector or industry, such as technology, healthcare, or utilities.

Bond funds differ by the creditworthiness of the issuers of the bonds in the portfolio (for example, US government, and investment-grade and high-yield corporates) and by the maturity (or duration) of the bonds (long, intermediate, and short.) There is also a category of bond funds called municipal bond funds whose interest income is exempt from federal income taxes.

Exchange-Traded Funds

There are two criticisms that have been leveled against mutual funds. First, because mutual fund (open-end fund) shares are priced only at the closing (i.e., end of trading day), an investor who wants to transact in mutual funds can only do so at the close of the day at the closing price. That is, because there are no intraday prices, transactions (i.e., purchases and sales) prior to the close of the day are not allowed. Second, from an investor's perspective, mutual funds are an inefficient tax structure: redemptions by current shareholders of the fund can trigger taxable capital gains (or losses) for shareholders who remain in the fund.

Unlike mutual funds, because closed-end funds are listed on an exchange, they trade throughout the trading day. That does not mean that the first criticism of mutual funds does not apply to closed-end funds. This is because there is typically a difference, in some cases a large difference, between the NAV of the closed-end's underlying portfolio and the closed-end fund's market price. When the NAV exceeds the fund's market price, it is said to be *trading at a discount*; when the NAV is less than the fund's market price, it is said to be *trading at a premium*.

Consequently, mutual funds and closed-end funds have a NAV, but the latter are exchange traded and therefore a market value is available throughout the trading day. This permits investors to use trading strategies such as shorting and levering with closed-end funds. In contrast, mutual fund shares are always exchanged at a price equal to NAV because at the end of each trading day the sponsor will always issue new fund shares or redeem outstanding fund shares at the NAV.

It would be ideal to have an investment vehicle that embodied a combination of the desirable aspects of mutual funds (open-end funds) and closed-end funds. That is, it would be ideal to have an investment vehicle that can be transacted throughout the trading day like a stock (as is a closed-end fund) at a price equal to the continuously known NAV (that is, the price is not at a premium or at a discount to its NAV). An investment vehicle with these two attributes exists: an ETF. Like mutual funds, ETFs require a sponsor. In addition to providing seed money to initiate the ETF and advertising and marketing the ETF, a sponsor (or provider) must do the following:

- Develop or select the index that the ETF's portfolio will seek to match the performance.
- Retain a key player, authorized participants (whose function is explained next).
- Manage the portfolio.

Another characteristic of open-end funds is that they trade throughout the day at a price that is very close to their NAV. What mechanism will force an ETF's market price to trade very close to the portfolio's NAV? This is accomplished as follows. An agent is commissioned to arbitrage between the ETF's stock price and the NAV to keep their values equal. The agent, referred to as an *authorized participant*, would do this by buying the cheap ETF and selling the expensive underlying portfolio (at NAV) when the ETF's price is below the NAV, and vice versa. This arbitrage performed by the authorized participant would tend to maintain the ETF's price very close (or equal) to that of the NAV. In practice, there is more than one authorized participant. Authorized participants are mainly large institutional traders who have contractual agreements with ETF providers.

For the arbitrage mechanism to work, the composition and the NAV of the ETF's portfolio must be known and continuously traded throughout the trading day. When the portfolio is a known index (such as the S&P 500 Index), this requirement is met. For example, for the S&P 500, the 500 stocks in the index are very liquid and their prices and the value of the index are quoted continuously throughout the trading day. The arbitrage process is not feasible for the typical actively managed mutual fund because the composition of the fund's portfolio is not known throughout the trading day. The reason is that mutual funds are only required to make the fund's holdings public four times a year, and then only 45 days after the date of the portfolio report.

Consequently, ETFs are feasible for indexes, but not on typical actively managed mutual funds. The original ETFs were based on well-known stock and bond indexes, both US and international. This was followed by ETFs based on narrower sector indexes covering financial, health care, industrial, natural resources, precious metals, technology, utilities, real estate, and others. These were, in turn, followed by ETFs based on new and often narrow indexes, specifically designed for ETFs. There is now an effort to develop ETFs on actively managed funds.

Uses of ETFs

ETFs provide a cost-effective means for both institutional and individual investors to gain exposure to asset classes and sectors through either passively or actively managed ETFs. ETFs can be used to alter exposure to asset classes of the US market as well as by using ETFs that have a non-US benchmark index, avoiding the custodian and transaction costs associated with creating an exposure to non-US markets.

An active portfolio manager who wants to alter exposure to a sector of the market can do so by using an ETF that is passively managed. For example, let's consider an active equity portfolio manager who is seeking to outperform the S&P 500 index and wants to do so by increasing exposure to a sector of the equity market that the portfolio manager believes will outperform the other sectors. That is, the portfolio manager wants to overweight exposure to that sector. This can be done by using an appropriate ETF. To make the example more concrete, suppose that the portfolio manager wants to overweight the health care sector of the S&P 500 index. This can be done by purchasing shares of, say one of the following sector ETFs: Vanguard Healthcare ETF, iShares US Healthcare ETF, or Health Care Select Sector SPDR Fund.

Because ETFs are traded on an exchange, ETF shares can be purchased on margin and can be sold short. This means that they can be used by portfolio managers to create leverage and be used to reduce exposure to the index. Moreover, a portfolio can use the types of orders that are available for taking a position in stocks (such as stop orders and limit orders), which were discussed in Chapter 3.

Hedge Funds

In this section, we describe hedge funds. There is no universally accepted definition of a hedge fund. For our purposes, we can characterize hedge funds as follows. The managers of hedge funds employ a wide range of trading strategies and techniques in an attempt to earn superior returns. The strategies used by a hedge fund can include one or more of the following, which are discussed in more detail in later chapters: (1) leverage, or the use of borrowed funds, (2) short selling, (3) arbitrage, or the simultaneous buying and selling of related financial instruments to realize a profit from the temporary misalignment of their prices; and (4) risk control, using of derivatives to reduce the risk of loss. What is clear is that hedge funds do not hedge, which means they do not seek to eliminate risk. In fact, they are willing to take on considerable risks, but constantly monitor those risks and control those using derivatives.

The management fee structure for hedge funds is a combination of a fixed fee based on the market value of assets managed plus a share of the positive return. The latter is a performance-based compensation referred to as an *incentive fee.*

In evaluating hedge funds, investors are interested in the absolute return generated by the asset manager, not the relative return. *Absolute return* for a portfolio is simply the return realized. The relative return is the difference between the actual return and the return on some benchmark or index. The use of absolute return rather than relative return for evaluating an asset manager's performance in managing a hedge fund is quite different from the criteria used to evaluate the performance of an asset manager in managing the other types of portfolios discussed in this chapter.

Types of Hedge Funds

There are various ways to categorize the different types of hedge funds. Anson [2006] proposes the following four broad categories: market directional, corporate restructuring, convergence trading, and opportunistic.

- **Market directional hedge fund:** The fund manager retains some exposure to "systematic risk". Within the category of market directional hedge funds, there are hedge funds that pursue the following strategies: equity long/short strategies, equity market timing, and short selling.

- **Corporate restructuring hedge fund:** The hedge fund manager positions the portfolio to capitalize on the anticipated impact of a significant corporate event. These events include a merger, an acquisition, or bankruptcy.
- **Convergence trading hedge funds:** The hedge fund manager seeks to identify potential misalignments of prices and/or yields that are expected to move back to or "converge" to an assumed relationship. The hedge fund manager positions the portfolio to benefit from the convergence.
- **Opportunistic hedge funds:** In this type of fund, the hedge fund manager has the broadest mandate compared to the other hedge fund categories. The hedge fund manager can make specific bets on stocks or currencies or they could have well-diversified portfolios. One type of hedge fund that falls into this group is a global macro hedge fund. The hedge fund manager for this type of fund invests opportunistically, based on macroeconomic considerations in any market in the world. They take large positions depending upon the hedge fund manager's forecast of changes in interest rates, currency movements, monetary policies, and macroeconomic indicators. Hedge funds will also invest in other hedge funds as a part of their holdings. That is, the portfolio of a fund of hedge funds consists of interests in other hedge funds. The hedge fund manager tactically reallocates capital across hedge fund strategies when it is believed that certain hedge fund strategies will do better than others.

Commodities

Commodities represent an alternative asset class that is characterized by its heterogeneity. The quality of commodities is not standardized; every commodity has its own specific properties. A common way to classify them is to distinguish between soft and hard commodities. *Hard commodities* include energy, precious metals, and industrial metals sectors. *Soft commodities* are usually weather-dependent, perishable commodities from the agricultural sector serving consumption purposes, such as grains, soybeans, or livestock.

Investing in commodities differs greatly from traditional asset classes. Commodities are real assets — primarily consumption goods as opposed to investment goods. They have an intrinsic value and provide utility by use in industrial manufacturing or in consumption.

Furthermore, supply is limited because in any given period, commodities have only a limited availability. For example, although renewable commodities such as grains can be produced virtually without limitation, their yearly harvest is strictly limited. Moreover, there is a strong seasonal component in the supply of certain commodities. Although metals can be mined almost all year, agricultural commodities such as soybeans depend on the harvesting cycle.

Proponents of investing in commodity markets argue that commodities are considered an effective means for investors to diversify traditional portfolios. The diversification benefits of commodities are twofold. First, returns from investing in commodities tend to exhibit a low (and sometimes even negative) correlation with equity and bond returns. Second, commodity returns exhibit a high positive correlation with the rate of inflation. Therefore, during periods of rising prices, commodities as real assets can function as effective inflation hedges.

Despite the low correlation of commodity returns with stock and bond returns, in general when markets decline, commodities may also decline. However, because commodities can be characterized as a heterogeneous alternative asset class, specific sectors of the commodity market can behave quite differently. In fact, some commodity sectors may have a negative correlation with equity and bond returns.

Investing in the Commodities Market

The most obvious way to invest directly in commodities is by purchasing the physical goods at the cash market (also referred to as the spot market). However, there are several financial instruments that an asset manager can use to participate in the commodity markets:

- indirect investment in stocks of natural resource companies;
- commodity mutual funds;
- commodity futures.

Commodity stocks

An asset manager can take a position (long or short) in commodity stocks. *Commodity stocks* are natural resource companies that generate a majority of their earnings by buying and selling physical commodities. In general, the term "commodity stock" cannot be clearly differentiated. It consists of listed companies that are related to commodities (i.e., those that explore, mine, refine, manufacture, trade, or supply commodities to other companies). Such an indirect investment in commodities (e.g., the purchase of petrochemical stocks) is an insufficient substitute for a direct investment.

Investors do not receive direct exposure to commodities by investing in such stocks, because listed natural resource companies all have their own characteristics and inherent risks. They take action in order to limit exposure to their commodity product by hedging appropriately. One study shows that these sector-specific stocks are only slightly correlated with commodity prices, and hence prices of commodity stocks do not completely reflect the performance of the underlying market (see Georgiev [2005]). The reason for this low correction is that there are other price-relevant factors such as the company's strategic position, management quality, capital structure (the debt/equity ratio), the expectations and credit rating of the company, profit growth, risk sensitivity, as well as information transparency and information credibility.

Stock markets also show quick and more sensible reactions to expected developments that can impact the company's value. Hence, there are other factors affecting commodity stock prices that differ from a pure commodity investment. Moreover, natural resource companies are subject to operational risk caused by human or technical failure, internal regulations, or external events.

Commodity funds

In contrast to an investment in commodity stocks, one can actively invest in a commodity fund. A commodity fund is an example of a collective investment vehicle. It offers the opportunity to obtain diversification benefits with moderate transaction costs. Commodity funds differ in terms of management style, allocation strategy, geographic and temporal investment horizon, the denominated currency, and investment behavior. There are active and passive funds (i.e., index tracking funds).

With an index-oriented investment, an asset manager can obtain exposure to commodities or an individual commodity sector. Such an investment can be done cost-effectively using the following two types of financial products: ETFs on commodity indexes, and commodity index certificates closely tied to commodity indexes. We discussed ETFs earlier in this chapter. *Commodity index certificates* constitute legal obligations that can be quickly and fairly cheaply issued by banks. The term of a certificate is normally restricted to a fixed date. However, there are also open-end certificates. An advantage of commodity ETFs over certificates is the non-existing credit risk of the issuer.

Commodity futures

In Chapter 6, we discuss derivative instruments. They include two fundamental products: futures contracts and options. A futures contract is an instrument that is traded on an organized exchange which allows for the buying and selling of "something" in the future. The "something" that can be bought or sold in the future is referred to as the "underlying". We'll see all the different types of underlying assets in the next chapter. A futures contract where the underlying is a commodity product is called a *commodity future*. Investors in commodity futures can profit from price movements of the underlying commodity without having to fulfill the logistical or storage requirements connected with a direct purchase of the commodity product. The advantages of a position in futures lie in the tremendous flexibility and leveraged nature of the futures position due to the low capital requirements to take a position, referred to as the "initial margin". The initial margin is only a fraction of the value of the underlying commodity, which gives the investor in these instruments leverage. Furthermore, the futures markets are characterized by a high degree of liquidity and low transaction costs. By holding long or short positions, investors can profit from rising and falling markets.

In Chapter 6, where we cover the mechanics of taking a position in any futures contract, we will see that an investor must be prepared to put in capital beyond the initial margin. This additional amount that the investor must put up is referred to as "variation margin". Failure to deliver variation margin when the futures contract moves against the investor will result in the exchange where the futures contract is traded, closing out the position.

Private Equity

Private equity provides the long-term equity base of a company that is not listed on any exchange and therefore cannot raise capital via the public stock market. Private equity provides the working capital that is used to help private companies grow and succeed. It is a long-term investment process that requires patient due diligence and hands on monitoring.

Here, we focus on the best known of the private equity categories: venture capital. *Venture capital* is the supply of equity financing to companies in various stages of their development prior to going public and therefore potential investors are exposed to a high level of risk that the company may fail. Venture capitalists finance these high-risk, illiquid, and unproven ideas by purchasing senior equity stakes while the firms are still privately held. Venture capitalists are willing to underwrite new ventures with untested products and bear the risk of no liquidity only if they can expect a reasonable return for their efforts.

Venture capitalists have two roles within the industry. Raising money from investors is just the first part. The second is to invest that capital with start-up companies. Venture capitalists are not passive investors. Once they invest in a company, they take an active role either in an advisory capacity or as a director on the board of the company. They monitor the progress of the company, implement incentive plans for the entrepreneurs and management, and establish financial goals for the company. Besides providing management insight, venture capitalists usually have the right to hire and fire key managers, including the founders. They also provide access to consultants, accountants, lawyers, investment bankers, and most importantly, other businesses that might purchase the start-up company's product.

Typically, venture capital firms specialize in one or more stages of a startup firm's business and by industry. The stages of a startup company are the early stage, the expansion stage, and the acquisition/buyout stage.

Venture Capital Funds

To obtain the funds to invest in startup companies, venture capital firms raise capital from individual and institutional investors. An investor does not invest in the venture capital firm but in a particular fund managed by the firm and referred to as a *venture capital fund*. Investors can invest in private equity through a venture capital fund. Unlike investors in the other collective investment vehicles discussed in this chapter, an investor in a venture capital fund must commit funds for a long period of time, typically at least 10 years. Venture capital firms earn fees in two ways: management fees and a percentage of the profits earned by the venture fund.

The limited partnership is the typical legal structure used in creating a venture capital fund. There are general partners and limited partners. The venture capital firm is the general partner in a venture capital fund. The general partners are responsible for managing the fund, which means evaluating and selecting the portfolio of companies in which the venture capital fund invests. All of the fund's partners will commit to a specific investment amount at the formation of the limited partnership.

The limited partners sign a *commitment letter* which obligates them to make cash contributions when requested to do so. The venture capital firm receives the cash to invest as investors fulfill the terms of their commitment agreement. No cash contributions are made by the limited partners until they are called on by the general partner to do so. This is referred to as "taking down" the commitment and is done by the general partner making a "capital call". The general partner will make a capital call when startup companies are identified in which the venture capital fund's management team wants to invest. Capital is committed not only by the limited partners but also by the general partner, the venture capital firm. With the venture capital firm committing its own capital, there is an alignment of the interests of the investors and the venture capital firm. The venture capital fund's income and capital gains are not taxed at the partnership level, but instead are passed through to the investors, who are then taxed.

Commercial Real Estate

Real estate is property that includes land, any structures built on it (i.e., buildings), and any natural resources that reside on the property. Real-estate properties are classified as either residential properties or commercial properties. Residential real estate includes one- to four-family properties. Although individuals and some investors might purchase residential real estate property as an investment, this is typically not the reason for the purchase. Commercial real estate includes income-producing properties. The major commercial property types are multifamily housing, apartment buildings, office buildings, industrial properties (including warehouses), shopping centers, hotels, health care facilities (e.g., senior housing care facilities), and timberlands.

In this section, we discuss commercial real estate as an investment outlet.

Reasons for Investing in Commercial Real Estate

There are several reasons put forth to support the inclusion of commercial real estate as part of an investor's portfolio.[1] There have been empirical studies that investigated whether these alleged reasons can be supported.

First, this non-traditional asset class allows an investor to reduce portfolio risk by combining asset classes that respond in different ways to expected and unexpected events. As such, commercial real estate is a portfolio diversifier and risk reducer. Without having covered the notion of the construction of efficient portfolios — the subject of Chapter 8 — this means that from a universe of investment candidates, the inclusion of commercial real estate in a portfolio will give a higher expected return for a given level of risk than a portfolio that does not include commercial real estate. The reason for this, as explained in Chapter 8, is the low return correlation between commercial real estate with other asset classes. Several studies find that the return correlations between real estate and stocks, real estate and bonds, and real estate and cash are such that real estate is a good diversifier.

Second, several empirical studies have reported that commercial real estate has generated attractive returns even after adjusting for the risk of investing in a financial instrument.

Third, commercial real estate is said to provide a hedge against unexpected inflation or deflation. The explanation as for why real estate is an inflation hedge is if the inflation rate exceeds the expected inflation rate, the returns on real estate will compensate for the surprise, helping to offset the negative response to excess inflation of other assets in the portfolio. The question is whether this can be empirically supported for all property types (i.e., offices, warehouses, retail, and apartments). One study concludes that although private equity real estate is a very useful partial inflation hedge, the degree of inflation-hedging ability is not uniform across property types (see Hudson-Wilson, Fabozzi, and Gordon [2003]).

The fourth reason it is argued that investors should include commercial real estate in a balanced portfolio is that this asset class is an important part of the investment universe. Consequently, failure to allocate any amount of a portfolio to commercial real estate cannot be justified on a theoretical basis.

The final reason for investing in commercial real estate is that it generates strong cash flows to the portfolio. The need of investors for regular distributions of cash varies. There are investors whose objective is to generate

[1]These are arguments given in Hudson-Wilson, Fabozzi, and Gordon [2003].

a higher portfolio return relative to a benchmark return who find the need for strong cash flows to be of less importance than investors who need cash to satisfy liabilities. For investors who need cash to meet liabilities, the appeal of an asset class that exhibits strong cash flows is important. One study analyzes the relative income returns on commercial real estate and compares them with those of bonds and stocks. They find that real estate is a far superior producer of steady income for investors. For investors seeking to earn a higher proportion of their total portfolio return in the form of realized income rather than unrealized capital appreciation, real estate has a far greater chance of accomplishing this.

Sectors of the Commercial Real Estate Market

The commercial real estate market is divided into four sectors: (1) private commercial real estate equity sector, (2) public commercial real estate equity sector, (3) private commercial real estate debt sector, and (4) commercial real estate debt sector. We describe each of these sectors and how an investor can obtain exposure to each market as follows.

Private commercial real estate equity

The private commercial real estate equity market is the sector where there is equity exposure to commercial real estate that does not involve the use of a publicly traded investment vehicle. Exposure to the private commercial real estate equity market by an asset manager can be done in two ways: direct purchase of property and a private real estate investment trust.

A real estate investment trust (REIT) is a collective investment vehicle that is classified as either a private REIT or a public REIT. A *private REIT* is not traded on an exchange nor is it registered with the Securities and Exchange Commission (SEC). A *public REIT* is traded on an exchange and therefore must be registered with the SEC. REITs are further classified as equity REITs and debt REITs. An asset manager who wants exposure to the private commercial real estate equity market will do so (if permitted) by investing in a private equity REIT.

Public commercial real estate equity

The public commercial real estate equity market provides exposure to real estate using publicly traded collective investment vehicles. There are three types of collective investment vehicles: *public equity REITs*, *real estate operating companies* (REOCs), and ETFs.

Equity REITs can be classified as diversified REITs, sector REITs, and specialty REITs. As the name suggests, a *diversified REIT* invests in all four of the major commercial property types. The holdings of a *sector REIT* are restricted to specific commercial property types. There are office REITs, industrial REITs, retail REITs, lodging REITs, residential REITs, health care REITs, self-storage REITs, and timberland REITs. A *specialty REIT* invests in a unique mix of property types that are not included within the major REIT property types. Examples are gas stations, golf courses, racetracks, and movie theaters.

There are REIT indexes to evaluate the performance of this sector of the commercial property market. The most popular REIT indices are the MSCI US REIT index and the Dow Jones Equity All REIT index. REOCs invest in real estate and issue shares to the public that are traded on an exchange. However, there are two differences between a REOC and a REIT. First, a REOC is afforded more flexibility than a REIT as to the types of real estate investments in which they may invest. Second, a REOC will reinvest the earnings generated into the company rather than distributing earnings to shareholders as a REIT does.

Private commercial real estate debt

Private commercial real estate debt is held as either directly issued commercial mortgages held in funds and/or commingled vehicles or whole loans (i.e., single commercial mortgage that has not been securitized). Commercial mortgage loans are mortgage loans for income-producing properties.

A commercial mortgage loan exposes the lender to credit risk. For commercial mortgage loans, the lender relies on the ability of the borrower to repay and has no recourse to the borrower if the payment terms are not satisfied. That is, commercial mortgage loans are non-recourse loans. This means that the lender can look only to the income-producing property backing the loan for interest and principal repayment. Because of the credit risk, lenders rely on various measures to assess the credit risk. The two most used measures of potential credit risk are the debt-to-service coverage ratio and the loan-to-value ratio.

For residential mortgage loans, only prepayment penalty mortgages provide some protection for the lender against prepayments. For commercial mortgage loans, call protection can take the following forms: a prepayment lockout, prepayment penalty points, yield maintenance charges, and defeasance. A prepayment lockout is a contractual agreement that prohibits any prepayments during a specified period of time, called the *lockout period.* The lockout period can be from two to 10 years. After the lockout period, call protection usually comes in the form of either prepayment penalty points or yield maintenance charges. Prepayment penalty points are predetermined penalties that must be paid by the borrower if the borrower wishes to refinance. For example, 5 – 4 – 3 – 2 – 1 is a common prepayment penalty point structure. A yield maintenance charge is designed to make the lender indifferent as to the timing of prepayments. The yield maintenance charge, also called the make-whole charge, makes it uneconomical to refinance solely to get a lower mortgage rate. With defeasance, the borrower provides sufficient funds for the servicer to invest in a portfolio of Treasury securities that replicates the cash flows that would exist in the absence of prepayments.

Commercial mortgage loans are typically balloon loans, requiring substantial principal payment at the end of the loan's term. The risk that a borrower will not be able to make the balloon payment because the borrower either cannot arrange for refinancing at the balloon payment date or cannot sell the property to generate sufficient funds to pay off the balloon balance is called *balloon risk.* Because the term of the loan will be extended by the lender during the workout period, balloon risk is also referred to as *extension risk.*

Public commercial real estate debt

Public commercial real estate debt includes REITs that invest in mortgage debt and commercial mortgage-backed securities (CMBS). REITs that invest in mortgage debt represent a small part of the REIT market. A CMBS is a debt instrument created through the securitization process described in Chapter 4. That is, a CMBS is a securitized product which we discuss in what follows.

Many types of commercial loans can be sold by the loan's originator as a commercial whole loan or structured into a CMBS transaction. A CMBS is a security backed by one or more commercial mortgage loans. In a CMBS, loans of virtually any size (from as small as \$1 million to single property transactions as large as \$200 million) can be securitized.

In the United States, CMBS, like residential MBS described in Chapter 4, can be issued by Ginnie Mae, Fannie Mae, Freddie Mac, and private entities. All of the securities issued by Ginnie Mae, Fannie Mae, and Freddie Mac are consistent with their mission of providing funding for residential housing. This includes securities backed by nursing home projects and health care facilities. Securities issued by Ginnie Mae are backed by the Federal Housing Administration — insured multifamily housing loans. These loans are called project loans. From these loans, Ginnie Mae creates project loan pass-through securities. The securities can be backed by a single project loan on a completed project or by one or more project loans. Freddie Mac and Fannie Mae purchase multifamily loans from approved lenders and either retain them in their portfolio or use them as collateral for a security. This is no different from what these two entities do with single-family-housing mortgage loans that they acquire. Although securities backed by Ginnie Mae, Fannie Mac, and Freddie Mac constitute the largest sector of the residential mortgage-backed securities (RMBS) market, it is the securities issued by private entities that constitute by far the largest sector of the CMBS market.

CMBS are backed by either newly originated or seasoned commercial mortgage loans. Most CMBS are backed by newly originated loans. CMBS can be classified by the type of loan pool. The first type of CMBS consists of loans backed by a single borrower. Usually, such CMBS are backed by large properties, such as regional malls or office buildings. The investors in this type of CMBS are insurance companies. The second type of CMBS consists of those backed by loans to multiple borrowers. This is the most common type of CMBS and is backed by a variety of property types. The most prevalent form of a deal backed by commercial mortgage loans to multiple borrowers is a conduit deal. These deals are created by investment banking firms that establish a conduit arrangement with mortgage bankers to originate commercial mortgage loans specifically for the purpose of securitizing them (i.e., of creating CMBS). The mortgage bankers originate and underwrite loans using the capital provided by the investment banking firm. There are multiple-borrower CMBS deals that combine loans that are included in conduit deals with a large or “mega” loan. These CMBS deals are called fusion deals or hybrid deals. Fusion-type deals dominate the US CMBS market and are an important, but not dominant, sector outside the United States.

Key Points

- Collective investment vehicles are products created through the pooling of funds.

- By investing in a collective investment vehicle, an investor obtains an equity interest in the fund's net assets.
- The NAV of a collective investment vehicle is the difference between the market value of the assets and its liabilities divided by the number of shares outstanding.
- The advantages of collective investment vehicles compared to direct investment in assets and asset classes are better portfolio diversification, better liquidity, professional management expertise, and possibly favorable tax treatment.
- Asset managers are both managers of collective investment vehicles and investors in them.
- When an asset management firm manages a collective investment vehicle, the firm receives compensation through a management fee and possibly an incentive fee.
- An investment company is a collective investment vehicle that sells shares to the public and invests the proceeds in a diversified portfolio of securities, with each share representing a proportionate interest in the underlying portfolio of securities.
- Investment companies are further classified as open-end funds (also called mutual funds) and closed-end funds.
- A wide range of funds with many different investment objectives are available.
- Exchange-traded funds (ETFs) are collective investment vehicles that overcome two major drawbacks of open-end mutual funds: the pricing of mutual fund transactions only at the end of the trading day and tax inefficiencies.
- ETFs are like open-end mutual funds, in that they trade based on net asset value (NAV), but unlike open-end funds, they trade like stocks.
- The asset manager of an ETF is responsible for managing the portfolio so as to replicate as closely as possible the return of the benchmark index.
- There is no universally accepted definition of a hedge fund (a collective investment vehicle), but they share common attributes in seeking to generate superior returns: use of leverage, short selling, arbitrage, and risk control.
- Despite the term "hedge" in describing these entities, they do not completely hedge their positions.
- Hedge funds can be categorized as market directional, corporate restructuring, convergence trading, and opportunistic.

- Venture capital firms provide financing for startup companies and specialize by sector and the stage of financing of a startup.
- Venture capital firms create venture capital funds, for which they seek investors. Investors in a venture capital fund commit to a specific investment amount, but only have to provide cash when there is a capital call by the venture capital firm as specified by the commitment letter.
- The legal structure used for a venture capital fund is a limited partnership.
- Capital for a venture capital fund is committed not only by outside investors but also by the venture capital firm itself, thereby aligning the interests of the outside investors and the venture capital firm.
- Commodities represent an alternative asset class that is characterized by its heterogeneity.
- The quality of commodities is not standardized because every commodity has its own specific properties.
- A common way to classify commodities is to distinguish between hard commodities (which include energy, precious metals, and industrial metals sectors) and soft commodities (which include weather-dependent, perishable commodities from the agricultural sector).
- Proponents of investing in commodity markets argue that commodities are considered an effective means for investors to diversify traditional asset class portfolios due to their returns exhibiting a low (and sometimes even negative) return correlation with equity and bond markets and a high positive correlation with the rate of inflation.
- Although one can invest directly in commodities by purchasing the physical goods in the cash (spot) market, there are several financial instruments that an asset manager can use to participate in commodity markets: indirect investment in stocks of natural resource companies, commodity mutual funds, and commodity futures.
- The major commercial property types are multifamily housing, apartment buildings, office buildings, industrial properties (including warehouses), shopping centers, hotels, health care facilities (e.g., senior housing care facilities), and timberlands.
- There are four sectors of the commercial real-estate market: (1) private commercial real estate equity market, (2) public commercial real estate equity market,(3) private commercial real estate debt market, and (4) public commercial real estate debt market.
- The reasons often given for investing in commercial real estate are to (1) reduce portfolio risk in a diversified portfolio, (2) generate absolute returns in excess of the risk-free rate, (3) hedge against unexpected

inflation or deflation, (4) constitute a part of a portfolio that is a reasonable reflection of the overall investment universe, and (5) generate strong cash flows to the portfolio.

- Real estate investment trusts (REITs), a collective investment vehicle, are publicly traded stocks that represent an interest in an underlying pool of real estate properties. Just as with closed-end funds, the market price can differ from the NAV.
- Private commercial real estate equity is held by investors as individual assets or in commingled vehicles such as private REITs.
- Public commercial real estate equity is structured as real estate investment trusts or real estate operating companies, both entities issuing shares to the public that are traded on an exchange.
- There are exchange-traded funds available to obtain exposure to the public commercial real estate equity sector.
- Equity REITs can be classified as diversified REITs, sector REITs, and specialty REITs.
- Commercial mortgage loans are non-recourse mortgage loans for income-producing properties that expose the lender to credit risk.
- Call protection for commercial mortgage loans includes prepayment lockout, defeasance, prepayment penalty points, and yield maintenance charges.
- Public commercial real estate debt is structured as commercial mortgage-backed securities and REITs that invest in mortgage debt.
- CMBS are securitized products backed by commercial mortgage loans with the deal backed by either loans to a single borrower, loans to multiple borrowers (called conduit deals), or a combination of loans that are included in conduit deals with a large or "mega" loan, referred to as fusion or hybrid deals.

References

Anson, M. J. P., 2006. *Handbook of Alternative Assets: Second Edition*, Hoboken, NJ: John Wiley & Sons.

Georgiev, G., 2005. "Benefits of commodity investment: 2005 update," Center for International Securities and Derivatives Markets. Available at http://www.starkresearch.com/resources/documents/commodities/2005%20benefitsofcommodities.pdf.

Hudson-Wilson, S., F. J. Fabozzi, and J. N. Gordon, 2003. "Why real estate?" *Journal of Portfolio Management*, 29(5): 12–25.

Chapter 6

Basics of Financial Derivatives

Learning Objectives

After reading this chapter, you will understand:

- the fundamental features of a futures and forward contract;
- the differences between futures and forward contracts;
- the risk/return relationship of a futures and forward contract position and why it is referred to as a linear payoff derivative;
- how the theoretical price of a futures/forward contract is determined;
- the fundamental features of a swap;
- the relationship between a swap and a forward contract and why swaps are linear payoff derivatives;
- the fundamental features of an option;
- the difference between a put and call option;
- the difference between a futures contract and an option contract;
- the risk/return relationship of an option position and why an option is referred to as a nonlinear payoff derivative;
- the basic components of the price of an option;
- the factors that influence the option price;
- the fundamental features of a cap and a floor;
- why a cap and a floor are economically equivalent to a package of options;
- why a cap and a floor are nonlinear payoff derivatives.

Derivative instruments, or simply derivatives, are contracts that essentially derive their value from the behavior of cash market instruments such as stocks, stock indexes, bonds, currencies, and commodities that underlie the contract. There are three general categories of derivatives: (1) futures and forwards, (2) options, and (3) swaps. Derivatives are either traded on an exchange or in the *over-the-counter* (OTC) market. That is, there are exchange-traded derivatives and OTC derivatives. Exchange-traded derivatives are standardized contracts. An advantage of OTC derivatives over exchange-traded derivatives is that they offer asset managers customized solutions for their investment strategy. In fact, one of the keys to the success of OTC derivatives is the flexibility of the payoff structures that can be created. A key difference between exchange-traded and OTC derivatives is that the former are guaranteed by the exchange, while the latter are the obligation of the non-exchange entity that is the counterparty. Thus, the user of an OTC derivative is subject to credit risk or counterparty risk.

In this chapter, we explain only the fundamental features of the three types of derivatives (futures/forwards, options, and swaps). Derivatives can be used for both controlling risk or in an investment strategy to enhance portfolio returns. While our description of derivatives here is general, there are specific derivatives that fall into the category of equity derivatives, interest rate derivatives, credit derivatives, commodity derivatives, and currency derivatives. When we discuss how derivatives are used in Chapters 14 and 18, we describe the specific contracts that are used.

Futures and Forward Contracts

Futures and forward contracts are derivatives that have a similar structure and risk/return profile. As explained below, futures are exchange-traded products while forward contacts are OTC products.

Futures Contracts

A futures contract is an agreement between a buyer and a seller in which the buyer agrees to take delivery of "something" at a specified price at the end of a designated period of time. The seller agrees to make the delivery of "something" at a specified price at the end of a designated period of time. Of course, no one buys or sells anything when entering into a futures contract. Rather, those who enter into the contract agree to buy or sell a specific amount of a specific item at a specified future date. When we speak of the "buyer" or the "seller" of a contract, we are simply adopting the jargon of the futures market, which refers to parties of the contract in terms of their future obligation.

Let's look closely at the key elements of a futures contract. The price at which the parties agree to transact in the future is called the *futures price*. The designated date at which the parties must transact is called the *settlement date* or *delivery date*. The "something" that the parties agree to exchange is called the *underlying*. Again, a futures contract is a financial instrument that is traded on an exchange.

To illustrate, suppose the underlying for a futures contract is asset XYZ, and the settlement is three months from now. Assume further that Benjamin buys this futures contract, and Shihong sells this futures contract, and the price at which they agree to transact in the future is $100. Then $100 is the futures price. At the settlement date, Shihong will deliver asset XYZ to Benjamin and Benjamin will pay Shihong the futures price of $100.

When an investor takes a position in the market by buying a futures contract, the investor is said to be in a *long position* or to be *long futures*. If, instead, the investor's opening position is the sale of a futures contract, the investor is said to be in a *short position* or *short futures*.

The buyer of a futures contract will realize a profit if the futures price increases; the seller of a futures contract will realize a profit if the futures price decreases. For example, suppose that one month after Benjamin and Shihong take their positions in the futures contract, the futures price of asset XYZ increases to $120. Benjamin, the buyer of the futures contract, could then sell the futures contract and realize a profit of $20. Effectively, at the settlement date, he has agreed to buy asset XYZ for $100 and can then sell asset XYZ in the market for $120. Shihong, the seller of the futures contract, will realize a loss of $20. If the futures price falls to $40 and Shihong buys back the contract at $40, she realizes a profit of $60 because she agreed to sell asset XYZ for $100 and now can buy it for $40. Benjamin would realize a loss of $60. Thus, if the futures price decreases, the buyer of the futures contract realizes a loss while the seller of the futures contract realizes a profit.

Liquidating a position

Most financial futures contracts have settlement dates in the months of March, June, September, or December. This means that at a predetermined time in the contract settlement month, the contract stops trading, and a price is determined by the exchange for settlement of the contract. For example, on January 4 suppose Benjamin buys and Shihong sells a futures contract that settles on the third Friday of March of the same year. Then, on that date, Benjamin and Shihong must perform — Benjamin agreeing to buy asset XYZ at $100, and Shihong agreeing to sell asset XYZ at $100. The exchange will determine a settlement price for the futures contract for that specific date. For example, if the exchange determines a settlement price of \$130, then Benjamin has agreed to buy asset XYZ for \$100 but can settle the position for \$130, thereby realizing a profit of \$30. Shihong would realize a loss of \$30.

Instead of Benjamin or Shihong entering into a futures contract on January 4 that settles in March they could have selected a settlement in June, September, or December. The contract with the closest settlement date is called the *nearby futures contract.* The *next futures contract* is the one that settles just after the nearby contract. The contract farthest away in time from settlement is called the *most distant futures contract.*

A party to a futures contract has two choices regarding the liquidation of the position. First, the position can be liquidated prior to the settlement date. For this purpose, the party must take an offsetting position in the same contract. For the buyer of a futures contract, this means selling the same number of identical futures contracts; for the seller of a futures contract, this means buying the same number of identical futures contracts. An identical contract means the contract for the same underlying and the same settlement date. So, for example, if Benjamin buys one futures contract for asset XYZ with settlement in March on January 4, and wants to liquidate a position on February 14, he can sell one futures contract for asset XYZ with settlement in March. Similarly, if Shihong sells one futures contract for asset XYZ with settlement in March on January 4, and wants to liquidate a position on February 22, she can buy one futures contract for asset XYZ with settlement in March. A futures contract on asset XYZ that settles in June of the same year is not the same contract as a futures contract on asset XYZ that settles in March in the same year.

The alternative is to wait until the settlement date. At that time, the party purchasing a futures contract accepts delivery of the underlying; the party that sells a futures contract settles the position by delivering the underlying at the agreed upon price. For some futures contracts that we shall describe in later chapters, settlement is made in cash only. Such contracts are referred to as *cash settlement contracts.*

A useful statistic for measuring the liquidity of a contract is the number of contracts that have been entered into but not yet liquidated. This figure is called the contract's *open interest.* An open interest figure is reported by an exchange for every futures contract traded on that exchange.

The role of the clearinghouse

Associated with every futures exchange is a clearinghouse which performs several functions. One of these functions is to guarantee that the two parties to the transaction will perform. Because of the clearinghouse, the two parties need not worry about the financial strength and integrity of the other party taking the opposite side of the trade. After initial execution of an order, the relationship between the two parties ends. The clearinghouse interposes itself as the buyer for every sale and as the seller for every purchase. Thus, the two parties are free to liquidate their positions without involving the other party in the original trade, and without worry that the other party may default.

Margin requirements

When a position is first taken in a futures contract, the investor must deposit a minimum dollar amount per contract as specified by the exchange. This amount, called *initial margin*, is required as a deposit for the contract. The initial margin may be in the form of an interest-bearing security such as a US Treasury bill. The initial margin is placed in an account, and the amount in this account is referred to as the *investor's equity*. As the price of the futures contract changes at the end of each trading day, the value of the investor's equity in the position changes.

At the end of each trading day, the exchange determines the "settlement price" for the futures contract. The settlement price is different from the closing price, which is the price of the security for the final trade of the day (whenever that trade occurred during the day). By contrast, the settlement price is that value which the exchange considers to be representative of trading at the end of the trading day. The exchange uses the settlement price to *mark to market* the investor's position (i.e., record the value of the investor's position based on the current market price) so that any gain or loss from the position is quickly reflected in the investor's equity account at the end of the trading day.[1]

Maintenance margin is the minimum level by which an investor's equity position may fall as a result of unfavorable price movements before the investor is required to deposit additional margin. The maintenance margin requirement is a dollar amount that is less than the initial margin

[1]Although there are initial and maintenance margin requirements for buying securities on margin as explained in Chapter 3, the concept of margin differs for securities and futures. When securities are acquired on margin, the difference between the price of the security and the initial margin is borrowed from the broker. The security purchased serves as collateral for the loan, and the investor pays interest. For futures contracts, the initial margin, in effect, serves as "good-faith" money, an indication that the investor will satisfy the obligation of the contract. Normally, no money is borrowed by the investor.

requirement. It sets the floor that the investor's equity account can fall to before the investor is required to furnish additional margin.

The additional margin deposited, called *variation margin*, is an amount necessary to bring the equity in the account back to its initial margin level. Unlike initial margin, variation margin must be in cash, not interest-bearing instruments. Any excess margin in the account may be withdrawn by the investor. If a party to a futures contract who is required to deposit variation margin fails to do so within 24 hours, the futures position is liquidated by the clearinghouse. The variation margin must be cash.

What is critical to understand by an asset manager who elects to use futures contracts is that cash must be available to satisfy any request for variation margin. Many potentially successful investment strategies have been terminated because the asset manager could not meet the call for additional margin.

Leveraging aspect of futures

When taking a position in a futures contract, a party need not put up the entire amount of the investment. Instead, the exchange requires that only the initial margin be invested. To see the implications, suppose Benjamin has \$100 and wants to invest in asset XYZ because he believes its price will appreciate. If asset XYZ is selling for \$100, he can buy one unit of the asset in the cash market (i.e., the market where goods are delivered upon purchase). His payoff will then be based on the price action of one unit of asset XYZ.

Suppose that the exchange where the futures contract for asset XYZ is traded requires an initial margin of only 5%, which in this case would be \$5. Then Benjamin can purchase 20 contracts with his \$100 investment. (This example ignores the fact that Benjamin may need funds for variation margin.) His payoff will then depend on the price action of 20 units of asset XYZ. Thus, he can leverage the use of his funds. The degree of leverage equals 1/margin rate. In this case, the degree of leverage equals 1/0.05, or 20. While the degree of leverage available in the futures market varies from contract to contract, as the initial margin requirement varies, the leverage attainable is considerably greater than in the cash market.

At first, the leverage available in the futures market may suggest that the market benefits only those who want to speculate on price movements.

This is not true. As we shall see, futures markets can be used to reduce price risk. Without the leverage possible in futures transactions, the cost of reducing price risk using futures would be too high for many market participants.

Forward Contracts

A *forward contract*, just like a futures contract, is an agreement for the future delivery of the underlying at a specified price at the end of a designated period of time. Futures contracts are standardized agreements as to the delivery date (or month) and quality of the deliverable, and are traded on organized exchanges. A forward contract differs, in that it is usually non-standardized (that is, the terms of each contract are negotiated individually between buyer and seller), there is no clearinghouse, and secondary markets are often non-existent or extremely thin. Unlike a futures contract, which is an exchange-traded derivative, a forward contract is an OTC derivative.

Because there is no clearinghouse that guarantees the performance of a counterparty in a forward contract, the parties to a forward contract are exposed to *counterparty risk*, the risk that the other party to the transaction will fail to perform. Futures contracts are marked to market at the end of each trading day. Consequently, futures contracts are subject to interim cash flows because additional margin may be required in the case of adverse price movements or because cash may be withdrawn in the case of favorable price movements. A forward contract may or may not be marked to market.

When the counterparties are two high-credit-quality entities, the two parties may agree not to mark positions to market. However, if one or both of the parties are concerned with the counterparty risk of the other, then positions may be marked to market. Thus, when a forward contract is marked to market, there are interim cash flows just as with a futures contract. When a forward contract is not marked to market, then there are no interim cash flows.

Other than these differences, what we said about futures contracts applies to forward contracts, too.

Pricing of Futures and Forward Contracts

When using derivatives, a market participant should understand the basic principles of how they are valued. While there are many models that have been proposed for valuing financial instruments that trade in the cash (spot) market, the valuation of all derivative models are based on arbitrage arguments.

Basically, this involves developing a strategy or a trade wherein a package consists of a position in the underlying (that is, the underlying asset or instrument for the derivative contract) and borrowing or lending so as to generate the same cash flow profile of the derivative. The value of the package is then equal to the theoretical price of the derivative. If the market price of the derivative deviates from the theoretical price, then the actions of arbitrageurs will drive the market price of the derivative toward its theoretical price until the arbitrage opportunity is eliminated.

In developing a strategy to capture any mispricing, certain assumptions are made. When these assumptions are not satisfied in the real world, the theoretical price can only be approximated. Moreover, a close examination of the underlying assumptions necessary to derive the theoretical price indicates how a pricing formula must be modified to value specific contracts.

Here we present the theoretical prices of futures and forward contracts. The pricing of these contracts is similar. If the underlying asset for both contracts is the same, the difference in pricing is due to differences in features of the contract that must be dealt with by the pricing model. So what we present here is the basic model for pricing futures contract. By "basic" we mean that we are extrapolating from the nuisances of the underlying for a specific contract. How the theoretical price for futures and forward contracts is derived and the issues associated with applying the basic pricing model to some of the more popular futures contracts are described in derivatives books.

The theoretical futures price can be demonstrated to be:

$$\text{Theoretical futures price} = \text{Cash market price}$$

$$+ (\text{Cash market price}) \times (\text{Financing cost} - \text{Cash yield}).$$

In this basic pricing formula, "Financing cost" is the interest rate to borrow funds and "Cash yield" is the payment received from investing in the asset as a percentage of the cash price.

For example, suppose that the cash price (also called the spot price) for the underlying is \$100, the financing cost is 3%, and the cash yield is 4%. Then the theoretical futures price is

$$\$100 + [\$100 \times (3\% - 4\%)] = \$99.$$

Note that the futures price can be above or below the cash price depending on the difference between the financing cost and cash yield. The difference between these rates is called the *net financing cost*. A more commonly used term for the net financing cost is the *cost of carry*, or simply, carry. *Positive carry* means that the cash yield exceeds the financing cost. Notice that while the difference between the financing cost and the cash yield is a negative value, carry is said to be positive. *Negative carry* means that the financing cost exceeds the cash yield. The following is a summary of the effect of carry on the difference between the futures price and the cash market price:

Positive carry	Futures price will sell at a discount to cash price.
Negative carry	Futures price will sell at a premium to cash price.
Zero	Futures price will be equal to the cash price.

At the settlement date of the futures contract, the futures price must equal the cash market price. The reason is that a futures contract with no time left until delivery is equivalent to a cash market transaction. Thus, as the delivery date approaches, the futures price will converge to the cash market price. This fact is evident from the formula for the theoretical futures price. The financing cost approaches zero as the delivery date approaches. Similarly, the yield that can be earned by holding the underlying approaches zero. Hence, the cost of carry approaches zero, and the futures price approaches the cash market price.

Swaps

A *swap* is an agreement involving two counterparties, calling for each counterparty to exchange periodic payments. The amount of the payments exchanged is based on some predetermined principal, called the *notional amount* or *notional principal*. The amount each counterparty pays to the other is the agreed-upon periodic rate times the notional amount. The only cash payments exchanged between the parties are the agreed-upon payments, not the notional amount.

To illustrate a swap, consider the following swap agreement in which payments are exchanged once a year for the next 5 years. The counterparties to the swap are an asset manager and a bank. The notional amount of this swap is \$100 million. Every year for the next 5 years, the asset manager agrees to pay the bank 4% per year, while the bank agrees to pay the asset manager the interest rate on some reference rate. Therefore, every year the asset manager will pay \$4 million (4% × \$100 million) to the bank. The amount that the bank pays the asset manager depends on the reference rate when the payment must be made. For example, if the reference rate is 3%, the bank pays the asset manager \$3 million (3% × \$100 million).

It is difficult to appreciate at this stage why an asset manager would want to use a swap. However, certain types of swaps are commonly used by asset managers in controlling portfolio risk, as will be explained in Chapter 18. In the meantime, understanding the economics of a swap explains why it is a popular derivative.

The Economics of a Swap

If we look carefully at a swap, we can see that it is not a new derivative instrument. Rather, it can be decomposed into a package of derivative instruments that we have already discussed. To understand this, consider our illustrative swap between the asset manager and the bank. Every year for the next 5 years the asset manager agrees to pay the bank 4% per year, while the bank agrees to pay the reference rate to the asset manager. Because the notional amount is \$100 million, the asset manager agrees to pay \$4 million. Alternatively, we can rephrase this transaction as follows: Every year for the next 5 years, the bank agrees to deliver to the asset manager "something" (the reference rate) and to accept a payment of \$4 million. The arrangement can be rephrased as follows: The two parties enter into multiple forward contracts. One party agrees to deliver something at some time in the future, and the other party agrees to accept delivery. The reason for saying that there are multiple forward contracts is that the agreement calls for making the exchange each year for the next 5 years.

Even though a swap may be nothing more than a package of forward contracts, it is not a redundant contract for several reasons. First, in many markets with forward and futures contracts, the longest maturity does not extend out as far as that of a typical swap. Second, a swap is a more transactionally efficient instrument, which means that in one transaction an entity can effectively establish a payoff equivalent to a package of forward contracts. The forward contracts would each have to be negotiated separately. Third, the liquidity of certain types of swaps is more liquid than many forward contracts, particularly long-dated (i.e., long-term) forward contracts.

Types of Swaps

Swaps are classified based on the characteristics of the swap payments. The five types of swaps include interest rate swaps, interest rate-equity swaps, equity swaps, and currency swaps. A fifth derivative instrument that has the word "swap" in its name is a "credit default swap", but it is really an option-type instrument, which we describe in Chapter 18.

In an *interest rate swap*, the counterparties swap payments in the same currency based on a specified interest rate benchmark. For example, one of the counterparties can pay a fixed interest rate and the other party can pay a floating interest rate. The floating interest rate is commonly referred to as the reference rate.

In an *interest rate-equity swap*, one party exchanges a payment based on a reference rate and the other party exchanges a payment based on the return of some equity index. The payments are made in the same currency.

In an *equity swap*, both parties exchange payments in the same currency based on some equity index. Finally, in a *currency swap*, the two parties agree to swap payments based on different currencies.

Options

An option is a contract in which the *option seller* grants the *option buyer* the right to enter into a transaction with the seller to either buy or sell the underlying at a specified price on or before a specified date. The specified price is called the *strike price* or *exercise price* and the specified date is called the *expiration date*. The option seller grants this right in exchange for a certain amount of money called the *option premium* or *option price*. The option seller is also known as the *option writer*, while the option buyer is the option holder. The asset that is the subject of the option is the underlying. The underlying can be an individual stock, a stock index, a bond, or even another derivative instrument such as a futures contract. The option writer can grant the option holder one of two rights. If the right is to purchase the underlying, the option is referred to as a *call option*. If the right is to sell the underlying, the option is referred to as a *put option*.

An option can also be categorized according to when it may be exercised by the buyer. This is referred to as the *exercise style*. A *European option* can only be exercised at the option's expiration date. An *American option*, in contrast, can be exercised any time on or before the expiration date. An option that can be exercised before the expiration date but only on specified dates is called a *Bermuda option* or an *Atlantic option*.

The terms of exchange are represented by the contract unit and are standardized for most contracts. The option holder enters into the contract with an opening transaction. Subsequently, the option holder then has the choice to exercise or to sell the option. The sale of an existing option by the holder is a closing sale.

Let's use an illustration to demonstrate the fundamental option contract. Suppose that Diego buys an American call option for $3 (the option price) with the following terms:

- The underlying is one unit of asset ABC.
- The exercise price is $100.
- The expiration date is three months from now.

At any time up to and including the expiration date, Diego can decide to buy from the writer of this option one unit of asset ABC, for which he will pay a price of $100. If it is not beneficial for Diego to exercise the option, he will not — how he decides when it is beneficial is explained shortly. Whether Diego exercises the option or not, the $3 he paid for it will be kept by the option writer. If Diego buys a put option rather than a call option, then he would be able to sell asset ABC to the option writer for a price of $100.

The maximum amount that an option buyer can lose is the option price. The maximum profit that the option writer can realize is the option price. The option buyer has substantial upside return potential, while the option writer has substantial downside risk. We investigate the risk-reward relationship for option positions later in this section.

Differences between Options and Futures Contracts

Note that, unlike in a futures contract, one party to an option contract is not obligated to transact — specifically, the option buyer has the right but not the obligation to transact. The option writer does have the obligation to perform. In the case of a futures contract, both buyer and seller are obligated to perform. Of course, a futures buyer does not pay the seller to accept the obligation, while an option buyer pays the seller the option price. Consequently, the risk-reward characteristics of these derivative contracts are also different. In the case of a futures contract, the buyer of the contract realizes a dollar-for-dollar gain when the price of the futures contract increases and suffers a dollar-for-dollar loss when the price of the futures contract decreases. The opposite occurs for the seller of a futures contract. Because of this relationship, futures and forward contracts are said to have a "linear payoff". Since swaps are nothing more than a package of forward positions, swaps are linear payoff derivatives.

Options do not provide this symmetric risk–reward relationship. The most that the buyer of an option can lose is the option price. While the buyer of an option retains all the potential benefits, the gain is always reduced by the amount of the option price. The maximum profit that the writer may realize is the option price; this is offset against substantial downside risk. Because of this characteristic, options are said to have a nonlinear payoff.

The difference in the type of payoff between futures and options is extremely important because asset managers can use futures to protect against symmetric risk and options to protect against asymmetric risk.

Listed Options vs OTC Options

Options, like other financial instruments, may be traded either on an organized exchange or in the OTC market. An option that is traded on an exchange is referred to as a listed option or an *exchange-traded option*. An option traded in the OTC market is called an *OTC option* or a *dealer option*. The advantages of a listed option are as follows. First, the exercise price and expiration date of the contract are standardized. Second, as in the case of futures contracts, the direct link between buyer and seller is severed after the trade is executed because of the interchangeability of listed options. The clearinghouse associated with the exchange where the option trades performs the same function in the options market that it does in the futures market. Finally, the transactions costs are lower for listed options than for OTC options.

The higher cost of an OTC option reflects the cost of customizing the option for the many situations where an asset manager seeking to use an option to manage risk needs to have a tailor-made option because the standardized listed option does not satisfy its objectives. While an OTC option is less liquid than a listed option, this is typically not of concern to the user of such an option. The explosive growth in OTC options suggests that portfolio managers find that these products serve an important investment purpose.

Risk and Return Characteristics of Options

Now we illustrate the risk and return characteristics of the four basic option positions:

- Buying a call option (long a call option).
- Selling a call option (short a call option).
- Buying a put option (long a put option).
- Selling a put option (short a put option).

We use asset XYZ as the underlying in our illustration. The illustrations assume that each option position is held to the expiration date and is not exercised early. Also, to simplify the illustration, we assume that the underlying for each option is for one unit of asset XYZ and we ignore transaction costs.

Buying call options

Assume that there is a call option on asset XYZ that expires in one month and has a strike price of \$100. The option price is \$3. Suppose that the current or spot price of asset XYZ is \$100. The profit and loss will depend on the price of asset XYZ at the expiration date. In Figure 1, the solid line shows the profit and loss profile at the expiration date for buying a call option. The buyer of a call option benefits if the price rises above the strike price. If the price of asset XYZ is equal to \$103, the buyer of a call option

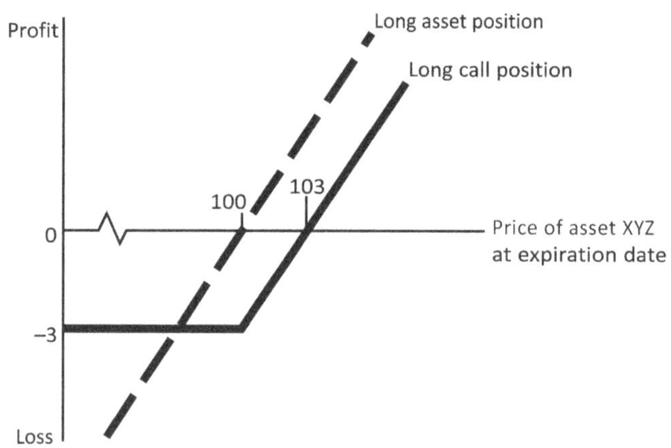

FIGURE 1: Profit/Loss Profile at Expiration of a Long Call Position and a Long Asset Position

breaks even. The maximum loss is the option price, and there is substantial upside potential if the stock price rises above $103.

It is worthwhile to compare the profit and loss profile of the call option buyer with that of an investor taking a long position in one share of asset XYZ. The payoff from the position depends on asset XYZ's price at the expiration date. The broken line in Figure 1 provides this comparison. This comparison clearly demonstrates the way in which an option can alter the risk–return profile for investors. An investor who takes a long position in asset XYZ realizes a profit of $1 for every $1 increase in asset XYZ's price. As asset XYZ's price falls, however, the investor loses dollar for dollar. If the price drops by more than $3, the long position in asset XYZ results in a loss of more than $3. The long call position, in contrast, limits the loss to only the option price of $3 but retains the upside potential, which will be $3 less than for the long position in asset XYZ. Which alternative is better, buying the call option or buying the asset? The answer depends on what the investor is attempting to achieve.

We can also use this hypothetical call option to demonstrate the speculative appeal of options. Suppose an investor has strong expectations that asset XYZ's price will rise in one month. At an option price of $3, the speculator can purchase 33.33 call options for each $100 invested. If asset XYZ's price rises, the investor realizes the price appreciation associated with 33.33 units of asset XYZ. With the same $100, however, the investor can purchase only one unit of asset XYZ selling at $100, thereby realizing the appreciation associated with one unit if asset XYZ's price increases. Now, suppose that in one month the price of asset XYZ rises to $120. The long call position will result in a profit of $566.50 [($20 × 33.33) – $100], or a return of 566.5% on the $100 investment in the call option. The long position in asset XYZ results in a profit of $20, only a 20% return on $100.

This greater leverage attracts investors to options when they wish to speculate on price movements. There are drawbacks to this leverage, however. Suppose that asset XYZ's price is unchanged at $100 at the expiration date. The long call position results in this case in a loss of the entire investment of $100, while the long position in asset XYZ produces neither a gain nor a loss.

Writing call options

To illustrate the option seller's, or writer's, position, we use the same call option we used to illustrate buying a call option. The profit/loss profile

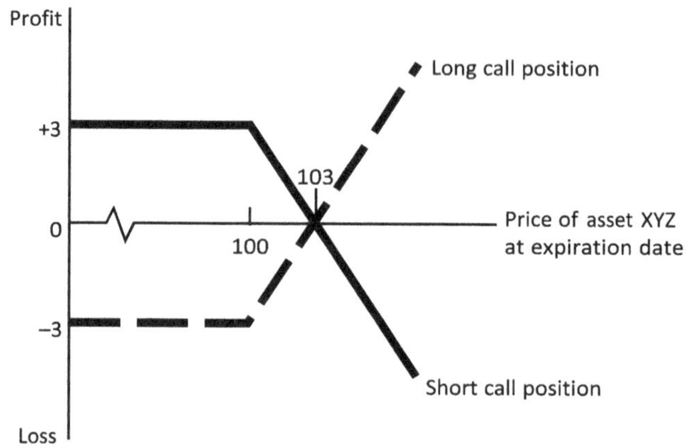

FIGURE 2: Profit/Loss Profile at Expiration for a Short Call Position and a Long Call Position

at expiration of the short call position (that is, the position of the call option writer) is the mirror image of the profit and loss profile of the long call position (the position of the call option buyer). That is, the profit of the short call position for any given price for asset XYZ at the expiration date is the same as the loss of the long call position. Consequently, the maximum profit the short call position can produce is the option price. The maximum loss is not limited because it is the highest price reached by asset XYZ on or before the expiration date, less the option price; this price can be indefinitely high. This can be seen in Figure 2, which shows the profit/loss profile for a short call position, as well as the profit/loss profile at expiration for a long call position.

Buying put options

To illustrate a long put option position, we assume a hypothetical put option on one unit of asset XYZ with one month to expiration and a strike price of \$100. Assume that the put option is selling for \$2 and the price of asset XYZ is \$100. The profit or loss for this position at the expiration date depends on the market price of asset XYZ. The buyer of a put option benefits if the price falls.

The profit/loss profile at expiration of a long put position is shown in Figure 3. As with all long option positions, the loss is limited to the option price. The profit potential, however, is substantial: the theoretical maximum profit is generated if asset XYZ's price falls to zero in the case

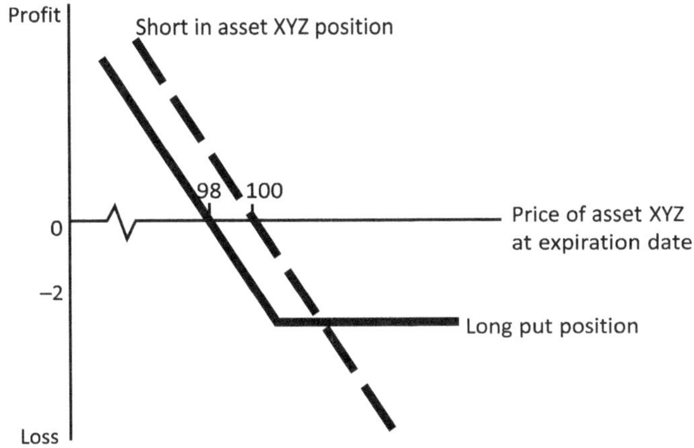

FIGURE 3: Profit/Loss Profile at Expiration for a Long Put Position and a Short Position

of a put option. Contrast this profit potential with that of the buyer of a call option. The theoretical maximum profit for a call buyer cannot be determined beforehand because it depends on the highest price that can be reached by asset XYZ before or at the option expiration date.

To see how an option alters the risk-return profile for an investor, we again compare it with a position in asset XYZ. The long put position is compared with a short position in asset XYZ because such a position would also benefit if the price of the asset falls. A comparison of the two positions is shown in Figure 3. While the investor taking a short asset position faces all the downside risk as well as the upside potential, an investor taking the long put position faces limited downside risk (equal to the option price) while still maintaining upside potential reduced by an amount equal to the option price.

Writing put options

The profit and loss profile for a short put option is the mirror image of the long put option. The maximum profit to be realized from this position is the option price. The theoretical maximum loss can be substantial should the price of the underlying fall; if the price were to fall all the way to zero, the loss would be as large as the strike price less the option price. Figure 4 depicts this profit/loss profile at expiration for both a short put position and a long put position.

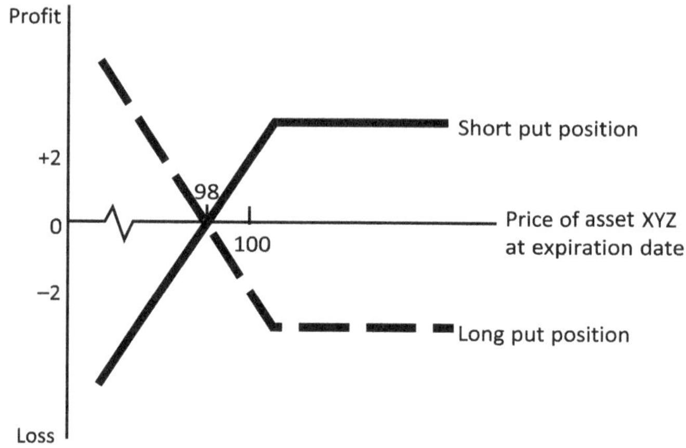

FIGURE 4: Profit/Loss Profile at Expiration for a Short Put Position and a Long Put Position

Summary of profit/loss from option positions

To summarize, buying calls or selling puts allows the investor to gain if the price of the underlying rises. Buying calls gives the investor unlimited upside potential, but limits the loss to the option price. Selling puts limits the profit to the option price, but provides no protection if the price of the underlying falls, with the maximum loss occurring if the price of the underlying falls to zero.

Buying puts and selling calls allows the investor to gain if the price of the underlying falls. Buying puts gives the investor upside potential, with the maximum profit realized if the price of the underlying declines to zero. However, the loss is limited to the option price. Selling calls limits the profit to the option price, but provides no protection if the price of the underlying rises, with the maximum loss being theoretically unlimited.

The Option Price

As with futures and forward contracts, the theoretical price of an option is also derived based on arbitrage arguments. However, the pricing of options is not as simple as the pricing of futures and forward contracts. Here we provide only the basic components and the factors that affect the value of an option. The most popular option pricing model is the one developed in Black and Scholes [1973] and is referred to as the *Black-Scholes option pricing model.*

Basic components of the option price

The theoretical price of an option is made up of two components: the intrinsic value and a premium over the intrinsic value.

Intrinsic value

The *intrinsic value* is the option's economic value if it is exercised immediately. If no positive economic value would result from exercising immediately, the intrinsic value is zero. An option's intrinsic value is easy to compute given the price of the underlying and the strike price. For a call option, the intrinsic value is the difference between the current market price of the underlying and the strike price. If that difference is positive, then the intrinsic value equals that difference; if the difference is zero or negative, then the intrinsic value is equal to zero. For example, if the strike price for a call option is $100 and the current price of the underlying is $109, the intrinsic value is $9. That is, an option buyer exercising the option and simultaneously selling the underlying would realize $109 from the sale of the underlying, which would be covered by acquiring the underlying from the option writer for $100, thereby netting a $9 gain.

An option that has a positive intrinsic value is said to be *in-the-money*. When the strike price of a call option exceeds the underlying's market price, it has no intrinsic value and is said to be *out-of-the-money*. An option for which the strike price is equal to the underlying's market price is said to be *at-the-money*. Both at-the-money and out-of-the-money options have intrinsic values of zero because it is not profitable to exercise them. Our call option with a strike price of $100 would be (1) in-the-money when the market price of the underlying is more than $100; (2) out-of-the-money when the market price of the underlying is less than $100, and (3) at-the-money when the market price of the underlying is equal to $100.

For a put option, the intrinsic value is equal to the amount by which the underlying's market price is below the strike price. For example, if the strike price of a put option is $100 and the market price of the underlying is $95, the intrinsic value is $5. That is, the buyer of the put option who simultaneously buys the underlying and exercises the put option will net $5. The underlying will be sold to the writer for $100 and purchased in the market for $95. With a strike price of $100, the put option would be (1) in-the-money when the underlying's market price is less than $100; (2) out-of-the-money when the underlying's market price exceeds $100; and (3) at-the-money when the underlying's market price is equal to $100.

We summarize the relations in Table 1.

TABLE 1: Intrinsic Value of Options

	Call Option	Put Option
If Asset Price > Strike Price		
Intrinsic value	Asset price — Strike price	Zero
Jargon	In-the-money	Out-of-the-money
If Asset Price < Strike Price		
Intrinsic value	Zero	Strike price — Asset price
Jargon	Out of the money	In the money
If Asset Price = Strike Price		
Intrinsic value	Zero	Zero
Jargon	At the money	At the money

Time premium

The *time premium* of an option, also referred to as the *time value* of the option, is the amount by which the option's market price exceeds its intrinsic value. The time premium consists of a volatility component and a leverage component. The volatility component is expressed as the expectation of the option buyer that at some time prior to the expiration date, changes in the market price of the underlying will increase the value of the rights conveyed by the option. Because of this expectation, the option buyer is willing to pay a premium above the intrinsic value. The leverage component is the carry cost of the underlying, which is positive for calls but negative for puts.

The volatility component is positive for both calls and puts. For example, if the price of a call option with a strike price of \$100 is \$12 when the underlying's market price is \$104, the time premium of this option is \$8 (\$12 minus its intrinsic value of \$4). Had the underlying's market price been \$95 instead of \$104, then the time premium of this option would be the entire \$12 because the option has no intrinsic value. All other things being equal, the option's time premium will increase with the amount of time remaining to expiration.

An option buyer has two ways to realize the value of an option position. The first way is by exercising the option. The second way is to sell the option in the market. In the first example above, selling the call for \$12 is preferred to exercising the call because the exercise will realize only \$4 (the intrinsic value), but the sale will realize \$12. As this example shows, exercise causes the immediate loss of any time premium. It is important to note that there are circumstances under which an option may be exercised prior to the expiration date. These circumstances depend on whether the total proceeds at the expiration date would be greater by holding the option as opposed to exercising and reinvesting any received cash proceeds until the expiration date.

Factors that influence the option price

The six factors that affect the price of an option include as follows:

- Market price of the underlying;
- Strike price of the option;
- Time to expiration of the option;
- Expected volatility of the underlying's return over the life of the option;
- Short-term, risk-free interest rate over the life of the option;
- Anticipated cash payments on the underlying over the life of the option.

The impact of each of these factors may depend on whether (1) the option is a call or a put, and (2) whether the option is an American option or a European option. Table 2 summarizes how each of the six factors listed above affects the price of a put and a call option. Here, we briefly explain why these factors have these particular effects. In the well-known Black-Scholes option pricing model mentioned above, the first five factors are included.

1. **Market price of the underlying asset:** The option price will change as the price of the underlying changes. For a call option, as the underlying's price increases (all other factors being constant), the option price increases. The opposite holds for a put option: As the price of the underlying increases, the price of a put option decreases.

TABLE 2: Summary of Factors that Affect the Price of an Option

	Effect of an Increase of Factor on	
Factor	**Call Price**	**Put Price**
Market price of underlying	Increase	Decrease
Strike price	Decrease	Increase
Time to expiration of option	Increase	Increase
Expected asset return volatility	Increase	Increase
Short-term, risk-free interest rate	Increase	Decrease
Anticipated cash payments	Decrease	Increase

2. **Strike price:** The strike price (or exercise price) is fixed for the life of the option. All other factors being equal, the lower the strike price, the higher the price for a call option. For put options, the higher the strike price, the higher the option price.
3. **Time to expiration of the option:** After the expiration date, an option has no value. All other factors being equal, the longer the time to expiration of the option, the higher the option price. This is because as the time to expiration decreases, less time remains for the underlying's price to rise (for a call buyer) or fall (for a put buyer), and therefore, the probability of a favorable price movement decreases. Consequently, as the time remaining until expiration decreases, the option price approaches its intrinsic value.
4. **Expected volatility of the underlying's return over the life of the option:** All other factors being equal, the greater the expected volatility of the underlying's return (as measured by the standard deviation), the more the option buyer would be willing to pay for the option, and the more an option writer would demand for it. This occurs because the greater the expected volatility, the greater the probability that the movement of the underlying's price will change so as to benefit the option buyer at some time before expiration.
5. **Short-term, risk-free interest rate over the life of the option:** Buying the underlying requires an investment of funds. Buying an option on the same quantity of the underlying makes the difference between the underlying's price and the option price available for investment at an interest rate at least as high as the risk-free rate. Consequently, all other factors being constant, the higher the short-term, risk-free interest rate, the greater the cost of buying the underlying and carrying it to the expiration date of the option. Hence, the higher the short-term, risk-free interest rate, the more attractive the option will be relative to the direct purchase of the underlying. As a result, the higher the short-term, risk-free interest rate, the greater the price of an option.
6. **Anticipated cash payments on the underlying over the life of the option:** Cash payments — dividends in the case of common stock and interest in the case of bonds — on the underlying tend to decrease the price of a call option because the cash payments make it more attractive to hold the underlying than to hold the option. For put options, cash payments on the underlying tend to increase the price.

Caps and Floors

Caps and floors are derivatives in which for a fee (premium), one of the counterparties agrees to compensate the other if a designated reference is different from a predetermined level. The party that receives the payment if the designated reference differs from a predetermined level and pays the fee to enter into the agreement is called the buyer. The party that agrees to make the payment if the designated reference differs from a predetermined level is called the seller.

The agreement is called a *cap* when the seller agrees to pay the buyer if the designated reference exceeds the predetermined level. The agreement is referred to as a *floor* when the seller agrees to pay the buyer if a designated reference falls below a predetermined level.

The designated reference could be a specific interest rate such as LIBOR, the rate of return on some domestic or foreign stock market index such as the S&P 500 or the FTSE 100 (a UK stock market index), or an exchange rate such as the exchange rate between the US dollar and the euro. The predetermined level is called the *strike*. As with a swap, a cap and a floor are based on a notional amount.

In general, the payment made by the seller of the cap to the buyer on a specific date is determined by the relationship between the designated reference and the strike. If the former is greater than the latter, then the seller pays the buyer the following:

$$\text{Notional amount} \times (\text{Actual value of designated reference} - \text{Strike})$$

If the designated reference is less than or equal to the strike, then the seller pays the buyer nothing.

For a floor, the payment made by the seller to the buyer on a specific date is also determined by the relationship between the strike and the designated reference. If the designated reference is less than the strike, then the seller pays the buyer the following:

$$\text{Notional amount} \times (\text{Strike} - \text{Actual value of designated reference}).$$

If the designated reference is greater than or equal to the strike, then the seller does not pay the buyer anything.

Let's illustrate a floor agreement. Suppose that an asset manager enters into a 3-year floor agreement with a bank with a notional amount of

$50 million. The terms of the floor specify that if the return on the S&P 500 is less than 3% on December 31 each year for the next 3 years, the bank (the seller of the floor) will pay the asset manager the difference between 3% (the strike) and the return realized on the S&P 500 index (the designated reference). The fee that the buyer agrees to pay the bank each year is $300,000. The payment made by the bank to the asset manager on December 31 for the next 3 years based on the performance of the S&P 500 index for that year will be as follows. If the actual return on the S&P 500 index is less than 3%, then the bank (the seller of the floor) pays

$$\$50 \text{ million} \times (3\% - \text{Actual return on S\&P 500 index}).$$

If the actual return on the S&P 500 index in the first year of the floor is 1%, the bank pays the asset manager $1 million. If the actual return on the S&P 500 is greater than or equal to 3%, then the bank pays nothing at that time.

The Economics of a Cap and Floor

In a cap or floor, the buyer pays a fee that represents the maximum amount the buyer can lose and the maximum amount the seller of the agreement can gain. The only party required to perform is the seller. The cap buyer benefits if the designated reference rises above the strike because the seller must compensate the buyer. The buyer of a floor benefits if the designated reference falls below the strike because the seller must compensate the buyer.

In essence, the payoff of these contracts is the same as in an option. Buying a cap has a similar payoff to that of buying a call option. A call option buyer pays a fee and benefits if the value of the option's underlying asset (or equivalently, the designated reference) is higher than the strike price at the expiration date. Similarly, buying a floor has a similar payoff to that of buying a put option. A put option buyer pays a fee and benefits if the value of the option's underlying asset (or equivalently, the designated reference) is less than the strike price at the expiration date. An option seller is only entitled to the option price. The seller of a cap or floor is only entitled to the fee.

Thus, a cap and a floor can be viewed as simply a package of options and therefore these derivatives have a nonlinear payoff.

Key Points

- In futures and forward contracts, the buyer (the long) agrees to accept delivery of the underlying at the settlement date and the seller (the short) agrees to make delivery of the underlying at the delivery date with the price of the transaction being the futures price.
- Futures contracts are exchanged traded products and forward contracts are OTC products.
- In a futures contract, both parties are required to put up the initial margin.
- Every trading day, the position of both parties in a futures contract is marked to market, with additional (variation) margin required if the equity in the position falls below the maintenance margin.
- The clearinghouse associated with the futures exchange guarantees that the parties to the futures contract will satisfy their obligations and therefore counterparty risk is minimal.
- A forward contract differs from a futures contract, in that the parties to a forward contract are exposed to the risk of non-performance by the counterparty and unwinding a position in a forward contract may be difficult due to a thin or non-existent secondary market.
- A buyer (seller) of a futures contract realizes a profit if the futures price increases (decreases) while the buyer (seller) of a futures contract realizes a loss if the futures price decreases (increases).
- Futures and forward contracts are linear payoff derivatives.
- Futures and forward contracts provide investors with substantial leverage.
- In a swap, the counterparties agree to exchange periodic payments.
- The dollar amount of the payments exchanged in a swap is based on the notional amount.
- A swap offers the risk/return profile of a package of forward contracts and is therefore a linear payoff derivative.
- An option grants the buyer of the option the right either to buy (in the case of a call option) or to sell (in the case of a put option) the underlying asset to the seller (writer) of the option at a stated price (the strike or exercise price) by a stated date (the expiration date).
- The option price (option premium) is the amount the option buyer pays to the option writer.

- There are different option exercise styles: an American option allows the option buyer to exercise the option at any time up to and including the expiration date, while a European option may be exercised only at the expiration date.
- Option buyers cannot realize a loss that is more than the option price and has all the upside potential; the maximum gain that the option writer (seller) can realize is the option price but is exposed to all the downside risk.
- Because of the payoff profile of an option, it is referred to as a nonlinear payoff derivative.
- Dealer-created or OTC options are customized to satisfy the desires of institutional investors.
- The intrinsic value and the time premium are the two components of the option price.
- The intrinsic value is the economic value of the option if it is exercised immediately (except if no positive economic value results from exercising immediately, in which case the intrinsic value is zero).
- The time premium is the amount by which the option price exceeds the intrinsic value.
- Six factors influence the option price: (1) the current price of the underlying asset, (2) the strike price of the option, (3) the time remaining to the expiration of the option, (4) the expected price volatility of the underlying asset, (5) the short-term risk-free interest rate over the life of the option, and (6) anticipated cash payments on the underlying asset.
- A cap is an agreement whereby the seller agrees to pay the buyer when a designated reference exceeds a predetermined level (the strike).
- A floor is an agreement whereby the seller agrees to pay the buyer when a designated reference is less than a predetermined level (the strike).
- The designated reference could be a specific interest rate, the rate of return on some stock market index, or an exchange rate.
- From an economic perspective, a cap and a floor are equivalent to a package of options and are therefore nonlinear payoff derivatives.

Reference

Black, F. and M. Scholes, 1973. "The pricing of options and corporate liabilities," *Journal of Political Economy*, 81(3): 637–654.

PART III

Modern Portfolio Theory and Asset Pricing

Chapter 7

Measuring Return and Risk

Learning Objectives

After reading this chapter, you will understand:

- the various methodologies for computing return: arithmetic average rate of return, time-weighted rate of return, and dollar-weighted rate of return;
- what the compounded annual growth rate (CAGR) is;
- the assumptions made in computing sub-period returns and the drawbacks of each method;
- how returns are annualized;
- the various risk measures that are used in evaluating performance;
- the normal distribution and the evidence as to whether asset returns follow a normal distribution;
- the limitations of the standard deviation of returns as a measure of risk;
- the desirable properties of investment risk measures;
- well-known dispersion measures and safety-first measures of risk;
- how to measure market risk (beta) for common stock;
- what is meant by a drawdown and measures of drawdown risk;
- how tracking error is used to measure portfolio risk versus a benchmark and the determinants of tracking error;
- the difference between forward-looking and backward tracking error, and;
- the various risk-adjusted return measures (reward-risk ratios): Sharpe ratio, Treynor ratio, the Sortino ratio, and the information ratio.

In evaluating performance of an asset manager, an investment strategy, or an investment vehicle, the first step is to calculate the actual return realized. Several methodologies for computing the actual return are explained in this chapter. Performance evaluation must take into account the risks associated with any investment. Although we described the various types of risks in Chapter 2, in this chapter we will explain and illustrate several measures to quantify risk. A more detailed discussion of how these risk measures are calculated is provided in Chapter 8 of the companion book. Reward-risk ratios combine return (or reward) from an investment relative to its risk. Four reward-risk ratios are described at the end of this chapter.

Measuring Return

Here we will discuss how to evaluate the investment performance of an asset manager. In doing so, we must distinguish between performance measurement and performance evaluation. *Performance measurement* involves the calculation of the return realized by an asset manager over some time interval that we refer to as the *evaluation period.* There are several important issues that must be addressed in developing a methodology for calculating a portfolio's return over the evaluation period.

Performance evaluation is concerned with two issues: (1) determining whether the asset manager added value by outperforming the established benchmark; and (2) determining how the asset manager achieved the calculated return. For example, as explained in Chapter 13, there are several strategies the manager of a stock portfolio can employ. Did the asset manager achieve the return by market timing, buying undervalued stocks, buying low-capitalization stocks, overweighting specific industries, and so on? The decomposition of the asset manager's performance in order to explain the reasons why those results were achieved is called *performance attribution analysis.* Moreover, performance evaluation requires the determination of whether the asset manager achieved superior performance (i.e., added value) by skill or by luck.

The starting point for evaluating the performance of an asset manager is measuring return. This might seem quite simple, but several practical issues make the task complex because one must consider any cash distributions made from a portfolio during the evaluation period.

Alternative Return Measures

The dollar return realized on a portfolio for any evaluation period (i.e., a year, month, or week) is equal to the sum of:

- the difference between the market value of the portfolio at the end of the evaluation period and the market value at the beginning of the evaluation period;
- any distributions made from the portfolio.

It is important that any capital or income distributions from the portfolio to a client or beneficiary of the portfolio be considered.

The *rate of return*, or simply *return*, expresses the dollar return in terms of the amount of the market value at the beginning of the evaluation period. Thus, the return can be viewed as the amount (expressed as a fraction of the initial portfolio value) that can be withdrawn at the end of the evaluation period while maintaining the initial market value of the portfolio intact.

In equation form, the portfolio's return can be expressed as follows:

$$R_p = \frac{MV_1 - MV_0 + D}{MV_0}, \tag{1}$$

where R_P is the return on the portfolio, MV_1 is the portfolio market value at the end of the evaluation period, MV_0 is the portfolio market value at the beginning of the evaluation period, D is the cash distributions from the portfolio to the client during the evaluation period.

To illustrate the calculation of a return, assume the following information for the asset manager of a common stock portfolio: The portfolio's market value at the beginning and end of the evaluation period is \$25 million and \$28 million, respectively, and, during the evaluation period, \$1 million is distributed to the client from investment income. Therefore,

$$MV_1 = \$28{,}000{,}000; \quad MV_0 = \$25{,}000{,}000; \quad D = \$1{,}000{,}000.$$

Then

$$R_p = \frac{\$28{,}000{,}000 - \$25{,}000{,}000 + \$1{,}000{,}000}{\$25{,}000{,}000} = 0.16 = 16\%.$$

There are three assumptions in measuring return as given by Equation (1). The first assumption is that cash inflows into the portfolio from dividends or interest that occur during the evaluation period, but are not distributed to clients, are reinvested in the portfolio. For example, suppose that during the evaluation period, \$2 million is received from dividends. This amount is reflected in the market value of the portfolio at the end of the period.

The second assumption is that if there are distributions from the portfolio, they either occur at the end of the evaluation period or are held in the form of cash until the end of the evaluation period. In our example, \$1 million is distributed to the client. But when did that distribution occur? To understand why the timing of the distribution is important, consider two extreme cases: (1) the distribution is made at the end of the evaluation period, as assumed by Equation (1); and (2) the distribution is made at the beginning of the evaluation period. In the first case, the asset manager had the use of the \$1 million to invest for the entire evaluation period. By contrast, in the second case, the asset manager loses the opportunity to invest the funds until the end of the evaluation period. Consequently, the timing of the distribution will affect the return, but this is not considered in Equation (1).

The third assumption is that there is no cash paid into the portfolio by the client. For example, suppose that sometime during the evaluation period the client gives an additional \$1.5 million to the asset manager to invest. Consequently, the market value of the portfolio at the end of the evaluation period, \$28 million in our example, would reflect the contribution of \$1.5 million. Equation (1) does not reflect that the ending market value of the portfolio is affected by the cash paid in by the client. Moreover, the timing of this cash inflow will affect the calculated return.

Thus, while the return calculation for a portfolio using Equation (1) can be evaluated for any length of time — such as 1 day, 1 month, 5 years — from a practical point of view, the assumptions of this approach limit its application. The longer the evaluation period, the more likely the assumptions will be violated. For example, it is highly likely that there may be more than one distribution to the client and more than one contribution from the client if the evaluation period is 5 years. Therefore, a return calculation made over a long period of time, if longer than a few months, would not be very reliable because of the assumption underlying the calculations that all cash payments and inflows are made and received at the end of the period.

Not only does the violation of the assumptions make it difficult to compare the returns of two asset managers over some evaluation period, but it is also not useful for evaluating performance over different periods. For example, Equation (1) will not give reliable information to compare the performance of a 1-month evaluation period and a 3-year evaluation period. To make such a comparison, the return must be expressed per unit of time, for example, per year.

The way to handle these practical issues is to calculate the return for a short unit of time such as a month or a quarter. We call this return the sub-period return. To get the return for the evaluation period, the sub-period returns are then averaged. So, for example, if the evaluation period is 1 year, and 12 monthly returns are calculated, the monthly returns are the sub-period returns, and they are averaged to get the 1-year return. If a 3-year return is sought, and 12 quarterly returns can be calculated, quarterly returns are the sub-period returns, and they are averaged to get the 3-year return. The 3-year return can then be converted into an annual return by the straightforward procedure described later.

Three methodologies have been used in practice to calculate the average of the sub-period returns:

- the arithmetic average rate of return;
- the time-weighted rate of return (also called the compounded growth rate and geometric rate of return);
- the dollar-weighted return.

Table 1 compares these methods side by side. We explain the interpretation and limitations below.

TABLE 1: Three Methods for Averaging Sub-period Returns

Method	**Interpretation**	**Limitations**
Arithmetic average (mean) rate of return	Average value of the withdrawals (expressed as a fraction of the initial portfolio market value) that can be made at the end of each sub-period while keeping the initial portfolio's market value intact.	Overvalues total return when sub-period returns vary greatly. Assumes the maintenance of initial market value.
Time-weighted (geometric) rate of return (compounded growth rate)	The compounded rate of growth of the initial portfolio's market value during the evaluation period.	Assumes all proceeds are reinvested.
Dollar-weighted rate of return (internal rate of return)	The interest rate that will make the present value of the sum of the sub-period cash flows (plus the terminal market value) equal to the initial market value of the portfolio.	Is affected by client contributions and withdrawals beyond the control of the money manager.

Arithmetic average (mean) rate of return

The *arithmetic average rate of return* or *arithmetic mean rate of return* is an unweighted average of the sub-period returns. The general formula is

$$R_A = \frac{R_{P1} + R_{P2} + \cdots + R_K}{K}, \tag{2}$$

where R_{A} is the arithmetic average rate of return, R_{Pk} is the portfolio return for sub-period k as measured by Equation (1), where $k = 1, \ldots, K$, and K is the number of sub-periods in the evaluation period.

For example, consider the following monthly portfolio values and corresponding monthly portfolio returns for a \$1,000 investment:

Month (k)	Ending Portfolio Value	Monthly Portfolio Return (%)
1	\$1,040.00	4.0
2	\$1,102.40	6.0
3	\$1,124.45	2.0
4	\$1,101.96	−2.0

Therefore, $R_{P1} = 0.04$, $R_{P2} = 0.06$, $R_{P3} = 0.02$, $R_{P4} = -0.02$, and $K = 4$:

$$R_A = \frac{0.04 + 0.6 + 0.02 + (-0.02)}{4} = 0.025 = 2.5\%.$$

There is a major problem with using the arithmetic average rate of return. To see this problem, suppose the initial market value of a portfolio is \$28 million, and the market values at the end of the next 2 months are \$56 million and \$28 million, respectively, and assume that there are no distributions or cash inflows from the client for either month. Then, using Equation (1), we find the sub-period return for the first month (R_{P1}) is 100%, and the sub-period return for the second month (R_{P2}) is −50%. The arithmetic average rate of return using Equation (2) is then 25%. Not a bad return! But think about this number. The portfolio's initial market value was \$28 million. Its market value at the end of 2 months is \$28 million. The return over this 2-month evaluation period is zero. Yet, Equation (2) says it is a whopping 25%.

Thus, it is improper to interpret the arithmetic average rate of return as a measure of the average return over an evaluation period. The proper interpretation is as follows: It is the average value of the withdrawals (expressed as a fraction of the initial portfolio market value) that can be made at the end of each sub-period while keeping the initial portfolio market value intact.

Time-weighted rate of return

The *time-weighted rate of return* measures the compounded rate of growth of the initial portfolio market value during the evaluation period if all cash distributions are reinvested in the portfolio. This rate of return is also commonly referred to as the *compounded growth rate* and the *geometric mean return* because it is computed by compounding the portfolio sub-period returns calculated from Equation (1). The general formula is

$$R_T = [(1 + R_{P1})(1 + R_{P2}) \cdots (1 + R_{PN})]^{1/K} - 1, \tag{3}$$

where R_T is the time-weighted rate of return, and R_{Pk} and K are as defined earlier.

Using the monthly returns in our example ($R_{P1} = 0.04$, $R_{P2} = 0.06$, $R_{P3} = 0.02$, $R_{P4} = -0.02$) in Equation (3), we get

$$R_T = [(1 + 0.04)(1 + 0.06)(1 + 0.02)(1 - 0.02]^{1/4} - 1,$$

$$R_T = [(1.04)(1.06)(1.02)(0.98)]^{1/4} - 1 = 0.0246 = 2.45\%.$$

Consider once again the problem that arises when using the arithmetic average rate of return in the case where the monthly portfolio return is 100% in the first month and −50% in the second month. The return was zero, but the arithmetic average rate of return is 25%. Now let's use the monthly returns to calculate the time-weighted rate of return:

$$R_T = \{(1 + 1.00)[1 + (-0.50)\}^{1/2} - 1 = [(2.00)(0.50)]^{1/2} - 1 = 0\%.$$

As can be seen, the time-weighted average rate of return gives the correct return, zero.

The arithmetic average rate of return and time-weighted rate of return will generally give different values for the portfolio return over some evaluation period. This is because, in computing the arithmetic average rate of return, the amount invested is assumed to be maintained (through additions or withdrawals) at its initial portfolio market value. The time-weighted rate of return, on the other hand, is the return on a portfolio that varies in size because of the assumption that all proceeds are reinvested.

In general, the arithmetic average rate of return will exceed the time-weighted average rate of return. We can see this in our example where the arithmetic average rate of return is 2.5% and the weighted-time rate of return is 2.4%. The exception is in the special situation where all the sub-period returns are the same, in which case the averages are identical. The magnitude of the difference between the two averages is smaller the less the variation in the sub-period returns over the evaluation period.

Note that it is not necessary to know the sub-period returns in order to calculate the time-weighted average rate of return if the beginning and ending portfolio values are known. The formula is then

$$R_T = \left[\frac{\text{Ending portfolio value}}{\text{Beginning portfolio value}}\right]^{1/K} - 1. \tag{4}$$

In our example, \$1,000 is the beginning portfolio value (i.e., the initial investment). The ending portfolio value is \$1,101.96. Therefore,

$$R_T = \left[\frac{\$1{,}101.96}{\$1{,}000{,}00}\right]^{1/4} - 1 = 2.45\%.$$

This agrees with the calculation using Equation (3).

The time-weighted rate of return must be annualized as explained later in this section. Since the time-weighted rate of return is also called the compounded growth rate, when it is annualized it is called the CAGR. The second column in Table 2 shows the CAGR for equity asset classes over the period January 1, 1995 to May 31, 2019 and January 1, 2005 to May 31, 2019.

Dollar-weighted rate of return

The *dollar-weighted rate of return* is computed by finding the interest rate that will make the present value of the cash flows from all the sub-periods in the evaluation period plus the terminal market value of the portfolio equal to the initial market value of the portfolio. The cash flow for each sub-period reflects the difference between the cash inflows due to investment income (i.e., dividends and interest) and to contributions made by the client to the portfolio and the cash outflows reflecting distributions to the client. Notice that it is not necessary to know the market value of the portfolio for each sub-period to determine the dollar-weighted rate of return.

The dollar-weighted rate of return is simply an internal rate of return calculation, and, hence, it is also called the *internal rate of return*.

TABLE 2: CAGR, Standard Deviation of Returns, Maximum Drawdown, and Reward-Risk Ratios for Equity Asset Classes

Asset Class	CAGR (%)	St. Dev. (%)	Max. Drawdown (%)	Sharpe Ratio	Sortino Ratio	US Mkt Correlation
For the period 1/1/1995 to 5/31/2019						
US stock market	9.64	15.01	−50.89	0.54	0.77	1.0
US large cap	9.59	14.64	−50.97	0.54	0.79	1.0
US large cap value	9.23	14.81	−54.85	0.52	0.74	0.9
US large cap growth	10.06	15.79	−53.58	0.54	0.79	1.0
US mid cap	11.22	16.42	−54.14	0.59	0.87	1.0
US mid cap value	11.02	15.88	−56.51	0.60	0.87	0.9
US mid cap growth	10.21	18.73	−54.48	0.49	0.72	0.9
US small cap	9.91	18.87	−53.95	0.48	0.69	0.9
US small cap value	10.77	17.76	−56.13	0.54	0.78	0.9
US small cap growth	9.93	20.08	−53.52	0.46	0.67	0.9
US micro cap	11.46	18.96	−56.61	0.55	0.82	0.8
For the period 1/1/2005 to 5/31/2019						
US stock market	8.15	14.40	−50.89	0.53	0.76	1.00
US large cap	7.96	13.93	−50.97	0.53	0.76	1.00
US large cap value	7.23	14.16	−54.85	0.48	0.67	0.97
US large cap growth	9.06	14.63	−47.19	0.58	0.86	0.97
US mid cap	8.59	16.33	−54.14	0.51	0.73	0.97
US mid cap value	8.12	16.28	−56.51	0.49	0.69	0.97
US mid cap growth	8.57	16.97	−54.48	0.50	0.71	0.95
US small cap	8.30	18.27	−53.95	0.46	0.67	0.96
US small cap value	7.39	18.25	−56.13	0.42	0.60	0.94
US small cap growth	9.10	18.82	−53.52	0.49	0.72	0.94
US micro cap	4.91	19.02	−56.61	0.28	0.40	0.89

The general formula for the dollar-weighted return is

$$V_0 = \frac{C_1}{(1+R_D)} + \frac{C_2}{(1+R_D)^2} + \cdots + \frac{C_N + V_N}{(1+R_D)^N}, \tag{5}$$

where R_D is the dollar-weighted rate of return, V_0 is the initial market value of the portfolio, V_K is the terminal market value of the portfolio, C_k is the cash flow for the portfolio (cash inflows minus cash outflows) for sub-period k, where $k = 1, 2, \ldots, K$.

For example, consider a portfolio with an initial market value of $100,000 and capital withdrawals of $5,000 at the end of each of the next 3 months and no cash inflows from the client in any month, and a market value at the end of the third month of $110,000. Then $V_0 = \$100{,}000$, $K = 3$, $C_1 = C_2 = C_3 = \$5{,}000$, $V_3 = \$110{,}000$, and R_D is the interest rate that satisfies the following equation:

$$V_0 = \frac{\$5{,}000}{(1+R_D)} + \frac{\$5{,}000}{(1+R_D)^2} + \frac{\$5{,}000 + \$110{,}000}{(1+R_D)^3}.$$

It can be verified that the interest rate that satisfies the above expression is 8.1%. This, then, is the dollar-weighted rate of return.

The dollar-weighted rate of return and the time-weighted rate of return will produce the same result if no withdrawals or contributions occur over the evaluation period and if all investment income is reinvested. The problem with the dollar-weighted rate of return is that it is affected by factors that are beyond the control of the asset manager. Specifically, any contributions made by the client or withdrawals that the client requires will affect the calculated return. This may make it difficult to compare the performance of two asset managers. Despite this limitation, the dollar-weighted rate of return does provide useful information. It indicates information about the growth of the fund that a client will find useful. This growth, however, is not attributable to the performance of the asset manager because of contributions and withdrawals.

Annualizing returns

The evaluation period may be less than or greater than 1 year. Typically, return measures are reported as an average annual return. This requires the annualization of the sub-period returns. The sub-period returns are usually calculated for a period of less than 1 year for the reasons described earlier.

The sub-period returns are then annualized using the following formula:

$$\text{Annual return} = (1 + \text{Average period return})^{\text{Number of periods in year}} - 1.$$

So, for example, suppose the evaluation period is 3 years, and a monthly period return is calculated. Suppose further that the average monthly return is 2%. Then the annual return would be

$$\text{Annual return} = (1.02)^{12} - 1 = 26.8\%.$$

Suppose, instead, that the period used to calculate returns is quarterly, and the average quarterly return is 3%. Then the annual return is

$$\text{Annual return} = (1.03)^{4} - 1 = 12.6\%.$$

Measuring Risk

In Chapter 2, we described different risk concepts. Here we will discuss concepts of risk drawn from probability theory as well as addressing the issue of whether there is one measure of risk that can be used. We begin with a brief description of key concepts of probability theory. A more detailed description of risk measures is provided in Chapter 8 in the companion volume.

Basics of Probability Theory

A probability measures the decision-maker's degree of belief in the likelihood of a given outcome. A decision-maker may formulate a probability based on empirical evidence. For example, if an asset manager wants to estimate the probability that the return on the S&P 500 will increase by more than 1% in a given month, the asset manager can look at historical returns on the S&P 500 and base this probability on the percentage of times that a return greater than 1% occurred. In some instances, however, empirical evidence may not be available. The asset manager, then, draws on a variety of information and experience to formulate a probability.

A *random variable* is a variable for which a probability can be assigned to each possible value that can be taken by the variable. A *probability distribution* or *probability function* is a function that describes all the values that the random variable can take on, and the probability associated with each. A *cumulative probability distribution* is a function that shows the probability that the random variable will attain a value less than or equal to each value that the random variable can take.

Describing a probability distribution

In describing a probability distribution function, it is common to summarize it by using various measures. The four most commonly used measures are: (1) location, (2) dispersion, (3) asymmetry, and (4) concentration in tails.

The first way to describe a probability distribution function is by some measure of *central value* or *location*. The various measures that can be used are the mean or average value, the median, or the mode. The relationship among these three measures of location depends on the skewness of a probability distribution function that we will describe later. The most commonly used measure of location is the *mean*.

Another measure that can help us describe a probability distribution function is the dispersion or how spread out the values of the random variable can realize. Various measures of dispersion are the *range*, *variance*, and *mean absolute deviation*. The most commonly used measure is the variance. The variance measures the dispersion of the values that the random variable

TABLE 3: Risk and Reward- Risk Ratios for Equity Asset Classes Based on Monthly Returns: 1/1/1995–5/31/2019 and 1/1/2005–5/31/2019

Asset Class	CAGR (%)	St. Dev. (%)	Max. Drawdown (%)	Sharpe Ratio	Sortino Ratio	US Mkt Correlation
For the period 1/1/1995 to 5/31/2019						
US stock market	9.64	15.01	−50.89	0.54	0.77	1.0
US large cap	9.59	14.64	−50.97	0.54	0.79	1.0
US large cap value	9.23	14.81	−54.85	0.52	0.74	0.9
US large cap growth	10.06	15.79	−53.58	0.54	0.79	1.0
US mid cap	11.22	16.42	−54.14	0.59	0.87	1.0
US mid cap value	11.02	15.88	−56.51	0.60	0.87	0.9
US mid cap growth	10.21	18.73	−54.48	0.49	0.72	0.9
US small cap	9.91	18.87	−53.95	0.48	0.69	0.9
US small cap value	10.77	17.76	−56.13	0.54	0.78	0.9
US small cap growth	9.93	20.08	−53.52	0.46	0.67	0.9
US micro cap	11.46	18.96	−56.61	0.55	0.82	0.8
For the period 1/1/2005 to 5/31/2019						
US stock market	8.15	14.40	−50.89	0.53	0.76	1.00
US large cap	7.96	13.93	−50.97	0.53	0.76	1.00
US large cap value	7.23	14.16	−54.85	0.48	0.67	0.97
US large cap growth	9.06	14.63	−47.19	0.58	0.86	0.97
US mid cap	8.59	16.33	−54.14	0.51	0.73	0.97
US mid cap value	8.12	16.28	−56.51	0.49	0.69	0.97
US mid cap growth	8.57	16.97	−54.48	0.50	0.71	0.95
US small cap	8.30	18.27	−53.95	0.46	0.67	0.96
US small cap value	7.39	18.25	−56.13	0.42	0.60	0.94
US small cap growth	9.10	18.82	−53.52	0.49	0.72	0.94
US micro cap	4.91	19.02	−56.61	0.28	0.40	0.89

Source: Data obtain from and calculations provided by *Portfolio Visualizer*, www.portfoliovisualizer.com.

can realize relative to the mean. It is the average of the squared deviations from the mean. The variance is in squared units. By taking the square root of the variance, one obtains the *standard deviation.* The calculation of the variance can be done on standard calculators and software, so we do not describe its calculation here. The *mean absolute deviation* takes the average of the absolute deviations from the mean.

Table 3 shows the standard deviation for various equity asset classes over two periods based on monthly returns: January 1, 1995 to May 31, 2005 and January 1, 2005 to May 31, 2019.

There are other measures that may be critical for assessing a portfolio's risk depending on the probability distribution of the return of the assets. The use of only the mean and variance assumes that the return distribution of the assets follows a normal distribution, as explained later in this chapter.

A probability distribution may be symmetric or asymmetric around its mean. A popular measure for the asymmetry of a distribution is called

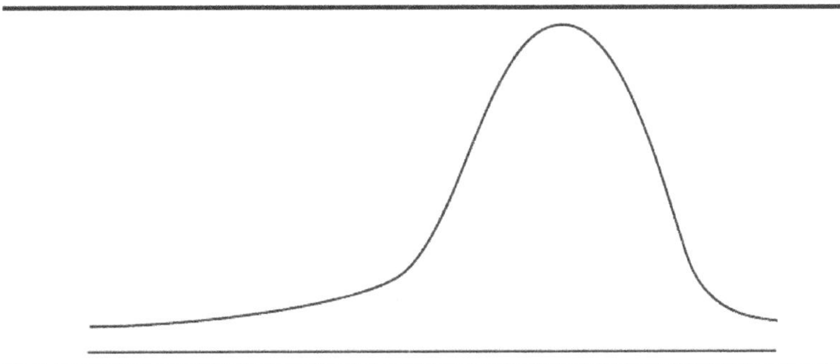

(a)

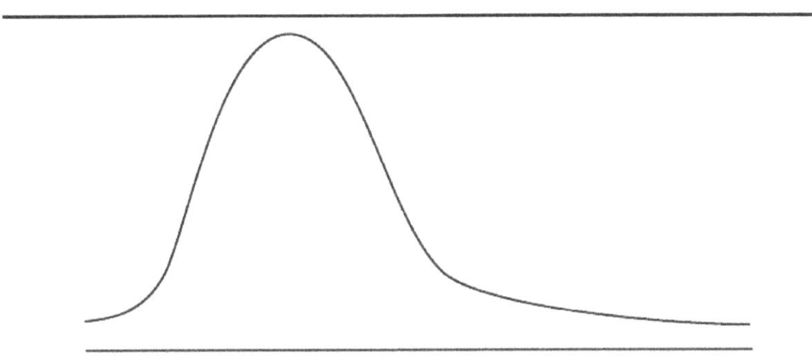

(b)

FIGURE 1: Skewed Distributions. (a) Distribution Skewed to the Left and (b) Distribution Skewed to the Right

its *skewness*. A negative skewness measure indicates that the distribution is skewed to the left; that is, compared to the right tail, the left tail is elongated (see Figure 1(a)). A positive skewness measure indicates that the distribution is skewed to the right; that is, compared to the left tail, the right tail is elongated (see Figure 1(b)).

Additional information about a probability distribution function is provided by measuring the concentration (mass) of potential outcomes in its tails. The tails of a probability distribution function contain the extreme values. In portfolio management and analysis applications, it is the tails that provide information about the potential for very poor returns. The fatness of the tails of the distribution is related to the *peakedness* of the distribution around its mean or center. The joint measure of peakedness and tail fatness is called *kurtosis*.

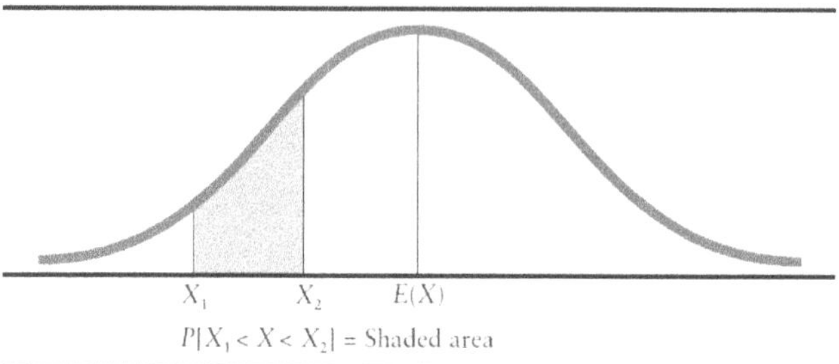

FIGURE 2: Example of a Normal Distribution (or Normal Curve)

In the parlance of the statistician, the four measures described above are called *statistical moments* or simply *moments*. The mean is the *first central moment* and is also referred to as the *expected value*. The variance is the second central moment, skewness is a rescaled third central moment, and kurtosis is a rescaled fourth central moment.[1]

Normal Distribution: A probability distribution that is frequently assumed in portfolio management, despite the absence of supporting empirical evidence, is the *normal distribution* depicted in Figure 2. For this distribution, also referred to as the *Gaussian distribution*, the area under the curve between any two points on the horizontal axis is the probability of obtaining a value between those two values. For example, the probability of realizing a value for the random variable X that is between X_1 and X_2 in Figure 2 is shown by the shaded area.

The entire area under the normal curve is equal to 1. The normal distribution has the following properties:

- The point in the middle of the normal curve is the expected value for the distribution.
- The distribution is symmetric around the expected value. That is, half the distribution is to the left of the expected value, and the other half is to the right. Thus, the probability of obtaining a value less than the expected value is 50%. The probability of obtaining a value greater than the expected value is also 50%.

[1]The definition of skewness and kurtosis is not as unified as for the mean and the variance. The various skewness calculations are the so-called Fishers' skewness and the Pearson's skewness, which equals the square of the Fisher's skewness. The same holds true for kurtosis: there is the Pearson's kurtosis and Fishers' kurtosis (sometimes referred to as excess kurtosis), which can be obtained by subtracting three from Pearson's kurtosis.

- The probability that the actual outcome will be within a range of one standard deviation above the expected value and one standard deviation below the expected value is 68.3%.
- The probability that the actual outcome will be within a range of two standard deviations above the expected value and two standard deviations below the expected value is 95.5%.
- The probability that the actual outcome will be within a range of three standard deviations above the expected value and three standard deviations below the expected value is 99.7%.

If the return distribution is normally distributed, then the variance is a useful measure of risk. The distribution is symmetric, so outcomes (area under the normal distribution curve) above and below the expected value are equally likely. However, there are both empirical studies of real-world financial markets as well as theoretical arguments that would suggest that the normal distribution assumption should be rejected.[2]

Desirable Features of Investment Risk Measures

The failure of asset return distributions to follow a normal distribution leads to the question of how risk should be measured. There is a growing literature in finance that has proposed alternative risk measures. However, the measures proposed are highly technical and we can only provide the very basics here and leave the rest for Chapter 8 in the companion book. We begin with a discussion of the desirable features of investment risk measures.

Although in asset management the variance of a portfolio's return has been the most commonly used measure of investment risk, different investors adopt different investment strategies when seeking to realize their investment objectives. Consequently, it is difficult to believe that investors have come to accept only one definition of risk. Regulators of financial institutions and commentators about risk measures proposed by regulators have offered alternative definitions of risk.

Balzer [2001] argues that a risk measure is investor specific and, therefore, there is "no single universally acceptable risk measure." He suggests the following three features that an investment risk measure should

[2]There is considerable empirical evidence on this. For a discussion of these studies as well as theoretical challenges as to why return distributions would be normally distributed, see Rachev, Menn, and Fabozzi [2005].

capture[3]: relativity of risk, multidimensionality of risk, and asymmetry of risk.

The *relativity of risk* means that risk should be related to performing worse than some alternative investment or benchmark. Balzer [1994, 2001] and Sortino and Satchell [2001], among others, have proposed that investment risk might be measured by the probability of the investment return falling below a specified risk benchmark. The risk benchmark might itself be a random variable, such as a liability benchmark (for example, an insurance product), the inflation rate or possibly inflation plus some safety margin, the risk-free rate of return, the bottom percentile of returns, a sector index return, a budgeted return, or other alternative investments. Each benchmark can be justified in relation to the goal of the asset manager. Should performance fall below the benchmark, there could be major adverse consequences for the asset manager.

In addition, the same investor could have multiple objectives and hence multiple risk benchmarks. Thus, risk is also a multidimensional phenomenon. However, an appropriate choice of the benchmarks is necessary to avoid an incorrect evaluation of opportunities available to investors. For example, historically, too often little recognition is given to liability targets by some institutional investors. This is the major factor contributing to the underfunding of US corporate pension sponsors of defined benefit plans (see Ryan and Fabozzi [2002]).

Intuition suggests that risk is an asymmetric concept related to the downside outcomes, and any realistic risk measure must value and consider upside and downside differently. The standard deviation considers the positive and the negative deviations from the mean as a potential risk. Thus, in this case, over-performance relative to the mean is penalized just as much as underperformance.

Alternative Risk Measures for Portfolio Selection

There is a heated debate on risk measures that should be used by asset managers. Here we will describe the various portfolio risk measures proposed in the literature. However, we do not include the mathematical formulation for each of these measures in this chapter, leaving that to Chapter 8 in the companion book.

[3]There are other features Balzer suggests but they are not discussed here.

According to the literature on portfolio theory, there are two disjointed categories of risk measures: dispersion measures and safety-risk measures. We describe some of the most well-known dispersion measures and safety-first measures next.

Dispersion measures

The variance or standard deviation of returns is a dispersion measure. Several alternative portfolio mean dispersion approaches have been proposed in the last few decades. The most commonly used measure (and easiest to understand) is the mean-absolute deviation. The *mean-absolute deviation* (MAD) dispersion measure is based on the absolute value of the deviations from the mean rather than the squared deviations as in the case of the mean-standard deviation. The MAD is more robust with respect to outliers (i.e., observations in the tail of the return distribution).

Safety-first risk measures

Many researchers have suggested *safety-first risk measures* as a criterion for decision-making under uncertainty. In these models, a benchmark or a disaster level of returns is identified. The objective is the maximization of the probability that the returns are above that level. Thus, most of the safety-first risk measures proposed in the literature are linked to the benchmark-based approach. Some of the most well-known safety-first risk measures proposed in the literature are (1) classical safety-first, (2) value at risk, and (3) conditional value at risk/expected tail loss.

In the classical safety-first portfolio choice problem as formulated by Roy [1952], the risk measure is the probability of loss or, more generally, the probability of portfolio return less than some specified value. In terms of implementation, generally, this approach involves solving a much more complex optimization problem to find the optimal portfolios in comparison to the mean-variance model.[4]

Probably the most well-known downside risk measure is *value at risk* (VaR). This measure is related to the percentiles of loss distributions and measures the predicted maximum loss at a specified probability level (for example, 95%) over a certain time horizon (for example, 10 days). The main characteristic of VaR is that of synthesizing a single value for the possible

[4]More specifically, it involves a complex mixed integer linear programming problem. This optimization is explained in Chapter 6 in the companion book.

losses which could occur with a given probability in a given temporal horizon. This feature, together with the (very intuitive) concept of maximum probable loss, allows investors to figure out how risky a portfolio trading position is. There are various ways to calculate the VaR of a security or a portfolio, but a discussion of these methodologies is beyond the scope of this chapter and are described in Chapter 8 in the companion book.

Despite the advantages cited for VaR as a measure of risk, it does have limitations. The major one is that it ignores returns beyond the VaR (i.e., it does not consider the concentration of returns in the tails beyond VaR). To overcome this limitation, Artzner, Delbaen, Eber, and Heath [1999] propose the *conditional value at risk* (CVaR) as an alternative risk measure. CVaR, also called *expected shortfall* or *expected tail loss*, measures the expected value of portfolio returns given that VaR has been exceeded. CVaR is a coherent risk measure, and portfolio selection using this risk measure can be reduced to a linear optimization problem.

Measuring Market Risk (Beta)

An important measure of risk for common stocks is market risk. As explained in Chapter 12, market risk is a major systematic risk that common stock investors face. It measures the sensitivity of a stock or a stock portfolio to a change in the stock market. The proxy for the stock market is a broad-based stock market index such as the S&P 500.

The following statistical model is used to estimate the sensitivity of a stock or a stock portfolio:

$$R_t = \alpha + \beta R_{M,t} + \varepsilon_t,$$

where R_t is the return on a stock or portfolio in period $t (t = 1, \dots, T)$, $R_{M,t}$ is the return on the stock market index in period $t (t = 1, \dots, T)$, ε_t is the error term $(t = 1, \dots, T)$, and β and α are the parameters to be estimated. β (beta) is the estimated market risk and α (alpha) is the estimate for the intercept term.

The above model is referred to as the *market model* and is simply a regression model.[5] There is no need to go through the calculations necessary to obtain the estimated value of the parameter of interest, β. For example,

[5]The market model was introduced by Sharpe [1963]. Some vendors and academics use the excess returns in calculating beta. The excess return is found by subtracting a suitable risk-free rate from the stock's or portfolio's return and from the market's return. This is referred to as the risk-premium form of the market model.

the following estimated β for five stocks was reported by *Yahoo!Finance* on August 2018:

Procter & Gamble (PG)	0.39
Verizon Communications (VZ)	0.67
International Business Machines (IBM)	1.02
iRobot (IRBT)	1.13
Netflix (NFLX)	1.39

In estimating beta, *Yahoo!Finance* uses monthly price changes for the company's stock and the monthly change of the S&P 500 index. Three years of monthly percentage price changes (36 months) are used (when available). Thus, the company's monthly stock price changes are regressed on the returns of the S&P 500 percentage index changes. The corresponding intercept term is the α and the coefficient on the S&P returns is the stock's β.

Drawdown Risk

Investors are concerned with capital preservation if they invest in a particular investment vehicle or an investment strategy. The concern is that the investment vehicle or investment strategy will incur a significant decline in value. *Drawdown* is the difference in the investment value if an investor purchases an investment vehicle or invests in an investment strategy at its peak value, maintained the position until it declined to the time before it rose in value again, and then sold before it turned up in value. The difference between any peak value that was reached and the low value before the value increased is the drawdown. A drawdown can be computed for a specific time period such as quarterly or annually.

For example, suppose an investor invests \$1.25 million in an investment strategy and it doubles in value to \$2.5 million but then declines to \$1 million and then rises in value. The drawdown in this case is \$1.5 million (\$2.5 million − \$1 million). Drawdown is typically calculated not in dollar terms, but as a percentage of the peak value. In our example, it would be 60% (\$1.5 million/\$2.5 million).

Maximum drawdown is the decline in the investment's value from its maximum value over some time period. The maximum value for this measure is 100%. The larger the maximum drawdown, the greater the risk. To illustrate, consider the same investment as in the previous paragraph. Suppose that after the investment value reaches \$1 million it rises in value to $3 million and then declines to $750,000 before it rises in value again. The maximum value in this example is $3 million. The drawdown from this maximum value is 75% ($3 million − $750,000) and therefore is the maximum drawdown. The maximum drawdown is expressed as a negative value. Thus, in our example, the maximum drawdown would be expressed as −75%. Table 3 shows the maximum drawdown for two different time periods for several equity asset classes.

The *maximum drawdown duration* is the longest amount of time for the maximum drawdown. It is measured as the longest amount of time between peak prices. It can be argued that the maximum drawdown duration is a better measure of drawdown risk than maximum drawdown. For example, consider the two measures for the following two investment vehicles:

Investment Vehicle	Maximum Drawdown (%)	Maximum Drawdown Duration
A	14	3 months
B	8	9 months

Some investors might prefer A to B even though A has a higher maximum drawdown.

Another measure is the *average drawdown* during a period. Suppose that an investor is looking at drawdown over a quarter. The investor could calculate all the realized drawdowns during the quarter and then calculate the average of these drawdowns. This average drawdown is useful in assessing whether the maximum drawdown might have been the result of a rare event.

The *Calmar ratio* is the ratio of the annual growth rate of an investment over a period of time divided by the maximum drawdown during the same time period.[6] This measure is typically used to measure drawdown risk for hedge funds. A large value for the Calmar ratio indicates that a hedge fund's return has historically not been at risk for large drawdowns. A lower Calmar ratio indicates that the drawdown risk is higher.

[6]The Calmar ratio stands for the California Managed Account Reports ratio. It was suggested by Young [1991].

Tracking Error as a Measure of Portfolio Risk

The risk of a portfolio can be measured by the standard deviation of portfolio returns. This statistical measure provides a range around the average return of a portfolio within which the actual return over a period is likely to fall with some specific probability. The mean return and standard deviation (or volatility) of a portfolio can be calculated over a period of time.

The standard deviation or volatility of a portfolio or a market index is an absolute number. An asset manager or client can also ask what the variation of the return of a portfolio is relative to a specified benchmark. Such variation is called the portfolio's *tracking error.*

Specifically, tracking error measures the dispersion of a portfolio's returns relative to the returns of its benchmark. That is, tracking error is the standard deviation of the portfolio's *active return* where active return is defined as follows:

$$\text{Active return} = \text{Portfolio's actual return} - \text{Benchmark's actual return}.$$

The average active return is called the *alpha.*

To find the tracking error of a portfolio, it is first necessary to specify the benchmark. The tracking error of a portfolio, as indicated, is its standard deviation relative to the benchmark, *not* its total standard deviation. Table 4 presents the information used to calculate the tracking error for a hypothetical portfolio and benchmark using 30 monthly observations. The fourth column in the table shows the active return for each month. The monthly average active return is 0.297%. Annualizing this value by multiplying by the square root of 12 (since the returns analyzed are monthly) gives 3.57% and is the alpha. The monthly standard deviation of the monthly active returns is 0.669%. To get the tracking error, this value is then annualized by multiplying by the square root of 12. Therefore, the tracking error is 2.32%.

A portfolio created to match the benchmark index (that is, an index fund) that regularly has zero active returns (i.e., always matches its benchmark's actual return) would have a tracking error of zero. But a portfolio that is actively managed and takes positions substantially different from the benchmark would likely have large active returns, both positive and negative, and thus would have an annual tracking error of, say, 5–10%.

Given the tracking error, a range for the possible portfolio active returns and corresponding range for the portfolio returns can be estimated assuming

TABLE 4: Tracking Error: Data and Calculation

Month	Portfolio (%)	Benchmark (%)	Active (%)	
1	2.90	2.72	0.18	
2	−0.66	−1.09	0.43	
3	−0.97	−0.35	−0.62	
4	0.96	0.34	0.62	
5	−0.22	0.23	−0.45	
6	2.19	2.91	−0.72	
7	−0.39	−0.08	−0.31	
8	−0.31	−1.16	0.85	
9	3.19	2.11	1.08	
10	−0.02	−0.40	0.38	
11	−0.56	−0.42	−0.14	
12	0.92	0.71	0.21	
13	1.10	1.25	−0.15	
14	1.01	−0.37	1.38	
15	2.20	1.98	0.22	
16	−0.12	−1.33	1.21	
17	−0.87	−0.20	−0.67	
18	0.60	0.72	−0.12	
19	2.12	0.95	1.17	
20	0.63	0.89	−0.26	
21	1.52	1.92	−0.40	
22	1.91	1.89	0.02	
23	−0.63	−1.66	1.03	
24	0.84	0.90	−0.06	
25	1.73	−0.25	1.98	
26	1.81	0.98	0.83	
27	1.40	0.96	0.44	
28	1.02	1.03	−0.01	
29	−0.41	−0.95	0.54	
30	1.92	1.66	0.26	
Average monthly active return				0.297
Standard deviation of monthly of active returns =				0.669
Annualizing				
Annual average active return = Monthly average active return × 12 = Alpha				3.568
Annual std dev = monthly std dev × $12^{.5}$ = Tracking error =				2.317

that the active returns are normally distributed. For example, assume the following:

Benchmark = S&P 500,

Expected return on S&P 500 = 20%,

Tracking error relative to S&P 500 = 2%.

Number of Standard Deviations	Range for Portfolio Active Returns	Corresponding Range Probability for Portfolio Returns	
1	±2%	18–22%	67%
2	±4%	16–24%	95%
3	±6%	14–26%	99%

An asset manager can pursue a blend of an active and passive (e.g., indexing) strategy. That is, a manager can construct a portfolio such that a certain percentage of the portfolio is indexed to some benchmark index and actively manage the balance. Assume that the passively managed portion (that is, the indexed portion) has a zero-tracking error relative to the index. For such a strategy, we can show (after some algebraic manipulation) that the tracking error for the overall portfolio would be as follows:

$$\begin{aligned}&\text{Portfolio tracking error relative to index}\\&\quad = (\text{Percent of portfolio actively managed})\\&\qquad \times (\text{Tracking error of the actively managed portion relative to index}).\end{aligned}$$

An *enhanced index fund* differs from an index fund, in that it deviates from thc benchmark index holdings in small amounts and hopes to slightly outperform the benchmark index through those small deviations. In terms of an active/passive strategy, the asset manager allocates a small percentage of the portfolio to be actively managed. The reason is that in case the bets prove detrimental, the underperformance would be small. Thus, realized returns would always deviate from index returns only by small amounts. There are many enhancing strategies.

Suppose that an asset manager whose benchmark is the S&P 500 pursues an enhanced indexing strategy by allocating only 5% of the portfolio to be actively managed and the other 95% indexed. Assume further that the tracking error of the actively managed portion is 15% with respect to the S&P 500. The portfolio would then have a tracking error calculated as follows:

$$\begin{aligned}&\text{Percent of portfolio actively managed relative to S\&P 500} = 5\%,\\&\text{Tracking error relative to S\&P 500} = 15\%,\\&\text{Portfolios tracking error relative to S\&P 500} = 5\% \times 15\% = 0.75\%.\end{aligned}$$

Forward-looking vs. backward-looking tracking error

In Table 4, the tracking error of the hypothetical portfolio is shown based on the active returns reported. However, the performance shown is the result of the asset manager's decisions during those 30 weeks with respect to portfolio positioning issues such as beta, sector allocations, style tilt (that is, value vs. growth), and stock selections. Hence, we can call the tracking error calculated from these trailing active returns a *backward-looking tracking error* or an *ex post tracking error.*

One problem with a backward-looking tracking error is that it does not reflect the effect of current decisions by the asset manager on the future active returns and hence the future tracking error that may be realized. If, for example, the asset manager significantly changes the portfolio beta or sector allocations today, then the backward-looking tracking error that is calculated using data from prior periods would not accurately reflect the current portfolio risks going forward. That is, the backward-looking tracking error will have little predictive value and can be misleading regarding portfolio risks going forward.

The asset manager needs a forward-looking estimate of tracking error to accurately reflect the portfolio risk going forward. This is done in practice by using the services of a commercial vendor that has a model, called a *multifactor risk model*, which has defined the risks associated with a benchmark index. Statistical analysis of the historical return data of the stocks in the index are used to obtain the factors and quantify their risks. (This involves the use of variances and correlations.) Using the asset manager's current portfolio holdings, the portfolio's current exposure to the various factors can be calculated and compared to the benchmark's exposures to the factors. Using the differential factor exposures and the risks of the factors, a *forward-looking tracking error* for the portfolio can be computed. This tracking error is also referred to as the *predicted tracking error* and *ex ante tracking error.*

There is no guarantee that the forward-looking tracking error at the start of, say, a year would exactly match the backward-looking tracking error calculated at the end of the year. There are two reasons for this. The first is that as the year progresses and changes are made to the portfolio, the forward-looking tracking error estimate would change to reflect the new exposures. The second is that the accuracy of the forward-looking tracking error depends on the extent of the stability in the variances and correlations that were used in the analysis. The average of forward-looking tracking error estimates obtained at different times during the year will be reasonably close to the backward-looking tracking error estimate obtained at the end of the year.

Each of these estimates has its uses. The forward-looking tracking error is useful in risk control and portfolio construction. An asset manager can immediately see the likely effect on tracking error of any intended change in potential strategies and eliminate those that would result in a tracking error beyond the client's tolerance for risk. The backward-looking tracking error can be useful for assessing actual performance analysis, such as the information ratio, a return/risk measure described later in this chapter.

Risk-Adjusted Return: Reward-Risk Ratio

Now that we know how to calculate the return or reward that should be used in evaluating portfolio performance and the various risk measures, a *risk-adjusted return* can be calculated. The risk-adjusted return is calculated as a reward-risk ratio. The reward can be measured on an absolute or relative basis. Reward-risk ratios that use *absolute* rewards in the numerator are measured as the difference between the realized return and the risk-free rate, or zero. When the reward is measured on a *relative* basis, it is the difference between the realized return and a benchmark selected by the client.

The four most common risk-adjusted return measures (reward-risk ratios) are the Sharpe ratio, Treynor ratio, the Sortino ratio, and the information ratio.[7]

Sharpe Ratio

The most popular reward-risk ratio that measures the reward on an absolute basis is the *Sharpe ratio*, named in honor of its developer, William Sharpe (1966). He initially referred to the ratio as the "reward-to-variability ratio". The risk-free return is used to reduce the realized return in this reward-risk ratio as follows:

$$\text{Sharpe ratio} = \frac{\text{Realized portfolio return} - \text{Risk-free rate of return}}{\text{Standard deviation of the realized portfolio return}}.$$

[7]These four reward-risk ratios are not the only ones that use different measures of risk. A comprehensive discussion of the wide range of reward-risk ratios is provided by Cheridito and Kromer [2013]. They introduce three families of reward-risk ratios and study their properties.

The numerator in the Sharpe ratio is called the *excess return*. That is,

$$\text{Sharpe ratio} = \frac{\text{Excess return}}{\text{Standard deviation of the realized portfolio return}}.$$

The risk-free rate is the interest rate on a Treasury bill whose maturity is equal to the length of the time horizon over which the portfolio return is calculated.

The Sharpe ratio measures how much excess return the asset manager earned for the extra volatility accepted for investing in risky assets rather than holding the risk-free rate.

The calculation of the Sharpe ratio involves computing the numerator for each time period and then calculating the average excess return. This is illustrated using the data in Table 5 using the portfolio return for 30 months for the same fund shown in Table 4. The realized returns are shown in the second column and the third column shows the monthly risk-free rate. For example, for month 1, the annual risk-free rate is 5.4% and dividing by 12 gives a monthly risk-free rate of 0.45%. The fourth column gives the excess return which is found by subtracting from the realized portfolio return the risk-free rate. The average excess monthly portfolio return is 0.354%. Annualized by multiplying by 12 gives 4.25% and is the numerator of the Sharpe ratio. The standard deviation of the realized monthly returns is 1.17%. Annualizing by multiplying 1.17% by the square root of 12 gives 4.05%, which is the denominator of the Sharpe ratio. Therefore, the Sharpe ratio for the portfolio over the 30 months is

$$\text{Sharpe ratio} = \frac{4.25\%}{4.05\%} = 1.05$$

We annualized the Sharpe ratio when using monthly returns by annualizing the monthly returns by multiplying the average return by 12 and the standard deviation by the square root of 12. In general, annualizing based on returns that are less than annual is done as follows:

$$\text{Annualized Sharpe ratio} = \sqrt{F} \times (\text{Sharpe ratio based on } F),$$

where F is the time period over which the return is calculated. That is, when monthly returns are used, F is 12. When weekly returns are used, F is 52. Daily is a little tricky. $F = 252$ is used because there are 252 trading days in a year. Note that in our illustration above, we multiply

TABLE 5: Sharpe Ratio: Return Data and Calculation

Month	Portfolio (%)	Risk-free (%)	Excess (%)	
1	2.90	0.45	2.45	
2	−0.66	0.42	−1.08	
3	−0.97	0.40	−1.37	
4	0.96	0.42	0.54	
5	−0.22	0.43	−0.65	
6	2.19	0.49	1.70	
7	−0.39	0.50	−0.89	
8	−0.31	0.52	−0.83	
9	3.19	0.53	2.66	
10	−0.02	0.53	−0.55	
11	−0.56	0.56	−1.12	
12	0.92	0.58	0.34	
13	1.10	0.49	0.61	
14	1.01	0.48	0.53	
15	2.20	0.49	1.71	
16	−0.12	0.42	−0.54	
17	−0.87	0.45	−1.32	
18	0.60	0.45	0.15	
19	2.12	0.45	1.67	
20	0.63	0.45	0.18	
21	1.52	0.40	1.12	
22	1.91	0.40	1.51	
23	−0.63	0.45	−1.08	
24	0.84	0.45	0.39	
25	1.73	0.45	1.28	
26	1.81	0.52	1.29	
27	1.40	0.52	0.88	
28	1.02	0.52	0.50	
29	−0.41	0.49	−0.90	
30	1.92	0.49	1.43	
Average monthly excess return				0.354
Standard deviation of monthly realized returns =				1.17
Annualizing				
Annual average excess return = Monthly average excess return × 12				4.25
Annual std dev = Monthly std dev × $12^{.5}$ =				4.06
Sharpe ratio =				1.05

the numerator by 12 and the denominator by the square root of 12, which is equivalent to multiplying the monthly Sharpe ratio by the square root of 12.

The Sharpe ratio has come under attack by researchers and practitioners because it (1) uses the standard deviation (variance) as a measure of risk, which fails to recognize that the return distribution is likely to be skewed as discussed earlier in this chapter and (2) uses the risk-free rate as a benchmark to compare performance.

The Sharpe ratio is not only used for portfolio performance but also for the performance of asset classes and individual assets. Table 3 shows the Sharpe ratio for two periods for several equity asset classes.

Treynor Ratio

Another measure of absolute return is the *Treynor ratio* formulated by Jack Treynor [1965]. The numerator is the same as the Sharpe ratio, but the risk measure is different. Rather than the standard deviation of the return, market risk as measured by the beta of the portfolio is used. That is,

$$\begin{aligned}\text{Treynor ratio} &= \frac{\text{Realized portfolio return-Risk-free rate of return}}{\text{Beta}}\\ &= \frac{\text{Excess return}}{\text{Beta}}.\end{aligned}$$

This measure is typically used for evaluating stocks or common stock portfolios.

The numerator is the same as in the Sharpe ratio. So, using the realized returns shown in the second column of Tables 4 and 5, the numerator is 4.25%. We discussed beta earlier in this chapter. For the realized returns and benchmark returns in Table 3, it can be shown that the beta is 0.82. Therefore,

$$\text{Treynor ratio} = \frac{\text{Excess return}}{\text{Beta}} = \frac{4.25\%}{0.82} = 5.18.$$

Sortino Ratio

A well-known reward-risk ratio that measures reward on a relative return basis is the Sortino ratio, as described in Sortino and van der Meer [1991] and Sortino and Price [1994]. The *Sortino ratio* addresses the criticism of the Sharpe ratio of using the standard deviation of realized returns. The Sortino ratio uses, as the measure of relative performance a client-specified *minimum acceptable return* (MAR). The risk measure is not the standard deviation of the realized returns but the standard deviation of the realized returns that are below the client-specified minimum acceptable return. Effectively, rather than looking at total volatility (i.e., standard deviation), the risk measure only considers bad volatility, which is returns below the minimum acceptable return. That is, the Sortino ratio is

$$\text{Sortino ratio} = \frac{\text{Realized portfolio return} - \text{Minimum acceptable return}}{\text{Standard deviation of the realized returns below the minimum acceptable return}}.$$

We will illustrate the calculation using the portfolio realized returns in Tables 4 and 5. We will use as the minimum acceptable return 0%. Table 6 shows the data for the calculation of the Sortino ratio. From Table 6, it can be seen that the annual realized return is 9.92%. Since in our illustration the numerator of the Sortino ratio, the minimum acceptable return, is assumed to be zero, the numerator is simply the annual realized return. Care must be taken in calculating the denominator. The third column shows the returns below the minimum acceptable return. There are only 11 months where the asset manager failed to earn a positive return. It is those months that are used to calculate the standard deviation. The annual standard deviation of the realized return below the minimum acceptable rate is 1.90. Therefore,

$$\text{Sortino ratio} = \frac{9.92\%}{1.90\%} = 5.21.$$

As with the Sharpe ratio, the Sortino ratio can be used to evaluate the performance of asset classes and individual assets. Table 6 shows for two time periods and several equity asset classes the Sortino ratio assuming that the MAR is zero.

Information Ratio

Because of the importance of comparing the performance of an asset manager to the performance of its competitors, Sharpe [1994] proposed a measure that takes into account tracking error of an actively managed portfolio. The ratio proposed is called the *information ratio*, calculated as follows:

$$\text{Information ratio} = \frac{\text{Alpha}}{\text{Backward-looking tracking error}}.$$

The reward is *alpha*, which is measured by the average of the active returns over a time period. The risk is the backward-looking tracking error

TABLE 6: Sortino Ratio: Data and Calculation

Minimum Acceptable Return (MAR) = 0%				
Month	**Portfolio (%)**	**Port–MAR (%)**	**Squared**	
1	2.90			
2	−0.66	−0.66	0.436	
3	−0.97	−0.97	0.943	
4	0.96			
5	−0.22	−0.22	0.048	
6	2.19			
7	−0.39	−0.39	0.152	
8	−0.31	−0.31	0.096	
9	3.19			
10	−0.02	−0.02	0.000	
11	−0.56	−0.56	0.314	
12	0.92			
13	1.10			
14	1.01			
15	2.20			
16	−0.12	−0.12	0.014	
17	−0.87	−0.87	0.757	
18	0.60			
19	2.12			
20	0.63			
21	1.52			
22	1.91			
23	−0.63	−0.63	0.397	
24	0.84			
25	1.73			
26	1.81			
27	1.40			
28	1.02			
29	−0.41	−0.41	0.168	
30	1.92			
Number negative				11
Average monthly return — MAR				0.83
Standard deviation of monthly MAR =				0.55
Annualizing				
Annual realized return = Monthly realized return × 12				9.92
Annual std dev = Monthly std dev $\times 12^{.5}$ =				1.90
Sortino ratio =				5.21

described earlier and is the standard deviation of a portfolio's active return. The higher the information ratio, the better the asset manager performed relative to the risk assumed.

To illustrate the calculation of the information ratio, consider the active returns for the hypothetical portfolio shown in Table 3. The annual average active return or alpha is 3.57%. Since the backward-looking tracking error is 2.32%, the information ratio is

$$\text{Information ratio} = \frac{3.57\%}{2.32\%} = 1.54.$$

Key Points

- In evaluating performance of an asset manager, an investment strategy, or an investment vehicle, the first step is to calculate the actual return realized.
- Performance measurement involves the calculation of the return realized by an asset manager over an evaluation period.
- There are several important issues that must be addressed in developing a methodology for calculating a portfolio's return over the evaluation period.
- Performance evaluation is concerned with determining whether the asset manager added value by outperforming the established benchmark and determining how the asset manager achieved the calculated return.
- Performance evaluation must take into account the risks associated with any investment.
- The dollar return realized on a portfolio for any evaluation period is equal to (1) the sum of the difference between the portfolio's market value at the end of the evaluation period and the market value at the beginning of the evaluation period, and (2) any distributions made from the portfolio.
- The assumptions in computing a return are that (1) cash inflows into the portfolio occur during the evaluation period but are not distributed or reinvested in the portfolio, (2) if there are distributions, they either occur at the end of the evaluation period or are held in the form of cash until the end of the evaluation period, and (3) there is no cash paid into the portfolio by the client.
- The three methodologies used to calculate the sub-period returns are the arithmetic average rate of return, the time-weighted rate of return, and the dollar-weighted return.
- The arithmetic average rate of return or arithmetic mean rate of return is an unweighted average of the sub-period returns.
- It is improper to interpret the arithmetic average rate of return as a measure of the average return over an evaluation period.

- The time-weighted rate of return (also called the compounded growth rate and geometric mean return) measures the compounded rate of growth of the initial portfolio market value over the evaluation period if all cash distributions are reinvested in the portfolio.
- When the compounded growth rate is annualized, it is called the CAGR.
- The dollar-weighted rate of return is computed by finding the interest rate that will make the present value of the cash flows from all the sub-periods in the evaluation period plus the terminal market value of the portfolio equal to the initial market value of the portfolio.
- The dollar-weighted rate of return and the time-weighted rate of return will produce the same result if no withdrawals or contributions occur over the evaluation period and if all investment income is reinvested.
- The problem with the dollar-weighted rate of return is that it is affected by factors that are beyond the control of the asset manager.
- The normal distribution (or Gaussian distribution) is frequently assumed for asset returns despite the absence of empirical evidence to support this distribution.
- It has been argued that risk is investor specific and therefore there is no universal measure of risk.
- According to the literature on portfolio theory, two disjointed categories of risk measures can be defined: dispersion measures and safety-risk measures.
- The variance (standard deviation) and mean-absolute deviation are dispersion measures.
- With safety-first risk measures, there is a benchmark or a disaster level of returns identified, with the objective being to maximize the probability that the returns are above that level.
- Some of the most well-known safety-first risk measures are (1) classical safety-first, (2) value at risk, and (3) conditional value at risk/expected tail loss.
- An important measure of risk for common stock is market risk as measured by beta.
- Beta is estimated using the market model using regression analysis.
- Investors are concerned with capital preservation if they invest in a particular investment vehicle or an investment strategy and this risk is measured using various drawdown measures.
- Drawdown is the difference in the investment value if an investor purchases an investment vehicle or invests in a strategy at its peak value,

maintains the position until it declines to the time before rising in value again, and then sells before it turns up in value.

- Maximum drawdown is the decline in the investment's value from its maximum value over some time period.
- The maximum drawdown duration is the longest amount of time for the maximum drawdown and is measured by the longest amount of time between peak prices.
- The Calmar ratio is the ratio of the annual growth rate of the investment over a period of time divided by the maximum drawdown during the same time period.
- Tracking error is the standard deviation of the portfolio's active return where active return is the difference between the portfolio's actual return and the benchmark's actual return.
- Backward-looking tracking error or *ex post* tracking error is computed based on the actual (historical) performance of a portfolio.
- Forward-looking tracking error (also called predicted tracking error and *ex ante* tracking error) is the forecasted tracking error based on some multifactor model.
- A risk-adjusted return measure is a reward in a reward-risk ratio that can be measured on an absolute or relative basis.
- Reward-risk ratios that use absolute rewards in the numerator measure it as the difference between the realized return and the risk-free rate, or zero.
- When the reward is measured on a relative basis in calculating a reward-risk ratio, it is the difference between the realized return and a benchmark selected by a client.
- The four most common risk-adjusted return measures (reward-risk ratios) are the Sharpe ratio, Treynor ratio, the Sortino ratio, and the information ratio.
- The Sharpe ratio and the Treynor ratio use absolute rewards, but use different measures of risk (the standard deviation of returns for the Sharpe ratio and beta for the Treynor ratio).
- The Sortino ratio and the information ratio use relative rewards.
- The Sortino ratio calculates the reward relative to a client-selected minimum acceptable return and calculates the standard deviation using only returns below the minimum acceptable return.
- The information ratio uses the alpha (average of the active returns) as the reward and tracking error as the risk measure.

References

Artzner, P., F. Delbaen, J. M. Eber, and D. Heath, 1999. "Coherent measures of risk," *Mathematical Finance*, 9: 203–228.

Balzer, L. A., 1994. "Measuring investment risk: A review." *Journal of Investing* 3(3): 47–58.

Balzer, L. A., 2001. "Investment risk: A unified approach to upside and downside returns," in *Managing Downside Risk in Financial Markets: Theory, Practice and Implementation*, edited by F. A. Sortino and S. E. Satchell (pp. 103–155). Oxford: Butterworth-Heinemann.

Cheridito, P. and E. Kromer, 2013. "Reward-risk ratios," *Journal of Investment Strategies*, 3(1): 1–16.

Rachev, S. T., C. Menn, and F. J. Fabozzi, 2005. *Fat-Tailed and Skewed Asset Return Distributions: Implications For Risk Management, Portfolio Selection, and Option Pricing.* Hoboken, NJ: John Wiley & Sons.

Roy, A. D., 1952. "Safety-first and the holding of assets," *Econometrica*, 20: 431–449.

Ryan, R. and F.J. Fabozzi, 2002. "Rethinking pension liabilities and asset allocation," *Journal of Portfolio Management*, 28(4): 7–15.

Sharpe, W. F., 1963. "A simplified model for portfolio analysis," *Management Science*, 9(2): 277–293.

Sharpe, W. F., 1966. "Mutual fund performance," *Journal of Business*, 39(Suppl.): 119–138.

Sharpe, W. F., 1994. "The Sharpe ratio," *Journal of Portfolio Management*, 21(1): 49–58.

Sortino, F. A. and L. N. Price, 1994. "Performance measurement in a downside risk framework," *Journal of Investing*, 3: 50–58.

Sortino, F. and S. Satchell, 2001. *Managing Downside Risk in Financial Markets.* Oxford: Butterworth-Heinemann.

Sortino, F. and R. van der Meer, 1991. "Downside risk," *Journal of Portfolio Management*, 17(4): 27–31.

Treynor, J., 1965. "How to rate management of investment funds," *Harvard Business Review*, 43: 63–75.

Young, T. W., 1991. "Calmar ratio: A smoother tool," *Futures*, 20(1): 40.

Chapter 8

Portfolio Theory: Mean-Variance Analysis and the Asset Allocation Decision

Learning Objectives

After reading this chapter, you will understand:

- what mean-variance analysis as formulated by Harry Markowitz is and how it is used in the asset allocation decision;
- the concept of portfolio diversification;
- portfolio theory's assumptions about how investors make decisions and about return distributions;
- the importance of the correlation between two assets in measuring a portfolio's risk;
- what is meant by a feasible portfolio and a set of feasible portfolios;
- what is meant by the efficient set or efficient frontier;
- what is meant by an optimal portfolio, and how an optimal portfolio is selected from all the portfolios available on the efficient frontier;
- the criticisms of portfolio theory, and;
- the issues associated with the implementation of portfolio theory in practice.

In this chapter, we will explain a theory about how investors should construct a portfolio. The model for portfolio construction was developed in 1952 by Harry Markowitz and, despite being developed almost 70 years ago, is still referred to as *modern portfolio theory.*[1] Because this theory for portfolio construction uses as inputs the mean and variance of portfolio returns, the theory is commonly referred to *as mean-variance analysis.*

[1] The theory was first presented in an article by Markowitz [1952] and further developed in Markowitz [1959].

This framework for portfolio construction is one of the two principal theories in asset management. Prior to the development of mean-variance analysis, asset managers would often speak of risk and return but failed to quantify these important measures and apply them in portfolio construction. Moreover, asset managers would focus on the risks of individual assets without understanding how combining those into a portfolio could affect a portfolio's risk. In the next chapter, an economic theory called the *capital asset pricing model* is explained and is the second principal theory in asset management. This theory, which provides the relationship between risk and expected return,[2] is used to determine how assets should be priced in the market. It does so by estimating what return market participants should expect for an asset given its risk and how risk should in fact be measured.

The statistical concepts that the reader should be familiar with to understand and appreciate these two theories are the mean, variance (standard deviation), correlation, covariance, and regression analysis. These concepts are covered in any introductory statistics textbook. We described several of these concepts in the previous chapter. For a further discussion of these concepts as well as explaining the distributional properties exhibited by asset returns and alternative return distributions, see Rachev, Menn, and Fabozzi [2005].

Although the two theories are the cornerstone of much of investment theory, they have been under constant attack. This should not be surprising in the intellectual development of any field. As mentioned earlier, portfolio theory was formulated in 1952 by Markowitz and is still referred to as "modern" portfolio theory. Today, there are a good number of extensions of portfolio theory as formulated by Markowitz. These extensions are not a criticism of the intellectual contribution by Markowitz but indicate how to modify the assumptions and how to deal with issues associated with the implementation of the theory.

Applications of Mean-Variance Analysis

Mean-variance analysis is applied in asset management in two ways: asset allocation and portfolio selection. One of the most important investment

[2]As confirmation of the importance of these theories, in October 1990 the Alfred Nobel Memorial Prize in Economic Science was awarded to Harry Markowitz, the developer of portfolio theory, and to William Sharpe, one of the developers of capital market theory.

decisions that an asset manager or a client must make is how to allocate funds among the different asset classes to meet investment objectives. The decision as to how to allocate a portfolio's funds across asset classes is referred to as the asset allocation decision, which we discussed in Chapter 1. In the asset allocation decision, mean-variance analysis does not provide the specific securities or assets that should be included in the portfolio but only how much should be allocated to each asset class. Consequently, the output of mean-variance analysis when used for making the asset allocation decision indicates what percentage of the portfolio should be allocated to cash, large cap stocks, mid-cap stocks, small cap stocks, non-US stocks, US government bonds, investment-grade corporate bonds, non-investment grade bonds, securitized products, and alternative assets. There is no information provided by mean-variance analysis as to which specific securities should be held in the portfolio. That is, the output of mean-variance analysis may indicate the best portfolio to be constructed on behalf of a client. For example, suppose that the output states that the manager should allocate 30% to large cap stocks. So if the portfolio has $100 million, the analysis would indicate $30 million should be allocated to large cap stocks but not which specific large cap stocks should be included.

The second way mean-variance analysis is used is in constructing a portfolio to determine which specific securities within an asset class should be included in the portfolio. This is the portfolio selection decision. For example, an asset manager seeking to construct a portfolio of large cap stocks can use mean-variance analysis to do so. In this application, the output of mean-variance analysis will identify, from the universe of large cap stocks from which the asset manager may select, the specific ones that should be included in the portfolio and the percentage of each stock that should be included. So, for example, if a $30 million portfolio consisting of large cap stocks is to be constructed, mean-variance analysis will indicate the stocks of the specific companies that should be included in the portfolio and what percentage of each stock should be included. For example, the output might indicate that the large cap stocks to be included are 4% of Apple Inc. ($1.2 million), 5% of Amazon.com ($1.5 million), 6% of Johnson & Johnson ($1.8), and so on. The portfolio would then consist of $30 million of large cap stocks.

Our focus in this chapter is on the mean-variance framework applied to the asset allocation decision.

Asset Allocation and Portfolio Diversification

Investors often talk about "diversifying" their portfolio. An investor who diversifies constructs a portfolio in such a way as to reduce portfolio risk without sacrificing returns. This is certainly a goal that investors should seek. However, the question is how to do this in practice.

Some investors would say that including assets across all asset classes could diversify a portfolio. For example, an investor might argue that a portfolio should be diversified by investing in stocks, bonds, and real estate. While that might be reasonable, two questions must be addressed in constructing a diversified portfolio. First, how much should be invested in each asset class? Should 40% of the portfolio be in stocks, 50% in bonds, and 10% in real estate, or is some other allocation more appropriate? Second, once the allocation is determined, which specific stocks, bonds, and real estate should the investor select?

Some investors who focus only on one asset class, such as common stock, argue that these portfolios should also be diversified. By this they mean that an investor should not place all his or her investment funds in the stock of one corporation but should invest in the stocks of many corporations. Here too several questions must be answered to construct a diversified portfolio. First, which corporations should be represented in the portfolio? Second, how much of the portfolio should be allocated to the stock of each corporation?

Prior to the development of portfolio theory as presented in this chapter, although investors often talked about diversification in general terms, they did not have the analytical tools with which to answer the questions posed above. For example, Leavens [1945] wrote:

> An examination of some fifty books and articles on investment that have appeared during the last quarter of a century shows that most of them refer to the desirability of diversification. The majority, however, discuss it in general terms and do not clearly indicate why it is desirable.

Assuming risks are independent, Leavens then shows how an investor can benefit from diversification. What is noteworthy is his final paragraph, in which he cautions investors that the assumption that risks are independent for each security is important but in practice is not likely to hold. He wrote,

> Diversification among companies in one industry cannot protect against unfavorable factors that may affect the whole industry; additional diversification among industries is needed for that purpose. Nor can diversification among industries protect against cyclical factors that may depress all industries at the same time.

Seven years later, Markowitz [1952] independently formulated portfolio theory, which quantified the notion expressed in Leavens' insights by using basic statistical concepts. As we will see, the Markowitz diversification strategy that we explain in this chapter is primarily concerned with the degree of covariance/correlation between asset returns in a portfolio as a measure of portfolio risk, rather than with the risk of each asset in isolation.

Mean-Variance Analysis Applied to the Asset Allocation Decision

The portfolio in the asset allocation decision consists of asset classes, not individual assets. In making the asset allocation decision in portfolio construction, investors seek to maximize the expected return given some level of risk they are willing to accept. (Alternatively stated, investors seek to minimize the risk they are exposed to given some target expected return.) Portfolios that satisfy this requirement are called *efficient portfolios*. Portfolio theory tells us how to achieve efficient portfolios. Because Markowitz is the developer of portfolio theory, efficient portfolios are sometimes referred to as "Markowitz efficient portfolios".

To construct an efficient portfolio of risky assets, it is necessary to make some assumption about how investors behave in making investment decisions. A reasonable assumption is that investors are *risk averse*. A risk-averse investor when faced with two investments with the same expected return but two different levels of risk will prefer the one with the lower risk. Given a choice of efficient portfolios from which an investor can select, an *optimal portfolio* is the one most preferred.

To construct an efficient portfolio, an investor needs to be able to estimate the expected return for each asset class that is a candidate for inclusion in the portfolio, and not only to specify some measure of risk but also measure that risk for each asset class. There are different quantitative measures of risk and these are described in the previous chapter and in more detail in Chapter 8 of the companion volume. The one selected in Markowitz portfolio theory is the variance or the standard deviation.

Expected Portfolio Return

The expected value of a portfolio's return, or simply the expected portfolio return, is the weighted average of the expected value of the return for each asset class over the time period. Mathematically,

$$E(R_p) = w_1 E(R_1) + w_2 E(R_2) + \cdots + w_K E(R_K), \tag{1}$$

where $E(R_p)$ is the expected portfolio return, $E(R_k)$ is the expected return for asset class k ($k = 1, \ldots, K$), w_k is the weight of asset class k in the portfolio (i.e., the market value of asset class k as a proportion of the market value of the total portfolio) at the beginning of the period, K is the number of asset classes that are candidates for inclusion in the portfolio.

The weights used in calculating a portfolio's expected return are the percentage or proportion of the portfolio allocated to that asset class. If an asset class is not selected, its weight is zero. It is the weights that we are seeking to determine.

For example, consider the asset allocation decision for CalPERS, the retirement program for the state government of California. CalPERS' board has decided to use four major asset classes: growth stocks, income (bonds), real estate, and trust level assets.[3] Therefore, in Equation (1), $K = 4$. The asset allocation strategy could be even more detailed in terms of asset classes. For example, CalPERS invests in the following two subclasses for growth stocks: public equity and private equity. For the real assets asset class, CalPERS uses the following subclasses: real estate, forestland, infrastructure, liquidity, and inflation. Combined with income (bonds) and trust level assets, there would be nine asset classes (i.e., $K = 9$). The key to remember here is that no individual securities are being selected.

When implementing the theory, the mean return from historical returns, adjusted where necessary by the analysts of the asset management team, is used in Equation (1). As can be seen from Equation (1), the calculation of the expected portfolio return is simple once the expected return for each asset class is estimated: it is simply a weighted linear combination of the

[3]Trust level assets include absolute return strategies, multi-asset class strategies, and overlay, transition, and plan level strategies.

asset classes that are candidates for inclusion in the portfolio. As we will see, however, measuring the portfolio's risk is not as straightforward.

Measuring Portfolio Risk

The measure of risk used in Markowitz portfolio theory is the variance, and hence the theory is also referred to as mean-variance theory. Here we explain how a portfolio's risk is calculated and the role of the covariance of asset class returns. We assume that the variance of the return for each asset class that is a candidate for inclusion in the asset allocation decision has been calculated from historical returns.

Two-asset class portfolio

To simplify, we will assume that there are only two asset classes. The portfolio variance is calculated as follows:

$$\sigma^2(Rp) = (w_1)^2\sigma^2(R_1) + (w_2)^2\sigma^2(R_2) + 2(w_1)(w_2)\text{cov}(R_1, R_2), \tag{2}$$

where $\sigma^2(Rp)$ is the portfolio variance, $\sigma^2(R_1)$, $\sigma^2(R_2)$ is the variance of asset class 1 and asset class 2, respectively, w_1, w_2 are the portfolio allocation (weight) of asset class 1 and asset class 2, respectively, $\text{cov}(R_1, R_2)$ is the covariance between the returns for the two asset classes.

As can be seen from Equation (2), the covariance between the two asset classes is introduced. The covariance is a measure of the dependence structure or covariability between two random variables. In our application, the two random variables are the returns for asset classes 1 and 2.

An alternative to measuring the covariability of two random variables is to determine the correlation. The correlation between random variables is the covariance of the two random variables divided by the product of their standard deviations. Applying this formula to the returns for asset classes 1 and 2, we have

$$\text{cor}(R_1, R_2) = \text{cov}(R_1, R_2)/[\sigma(R_1)\sigma(R_2)],$$

where $\text{cor}(R_1, R_2)$ is the correlation between the returns of the two asset classes. Solving for the covariance,

$$\text{cov}(R_1, R_2) = \sigma(R_1)\sigma(R_2)\text{cor}(R_1, R_2). \tag{3}$$

Substituting Equation (3) into Equation (2) for the covariance, the portfolio variance can be rewritten as

$$\sigma^2(Rp) = (w_1)^2\sigma^2(R_1) + (w_2)^2\sigma^2(R_2) + 2(w_1)(w_2)\text{cor}(R_1, R_2)/[\sigma(R_1)\sigma(R_2)]. \tag{4}$$

General asset class case

The mathematics for the two-asset case is not complicated. Moving from the two-asset class case to the general case in which there are more than two assets gets a little trickier. For example, the three-asset class case (i.e., asset classes 1, 2, and 3) where the portfolio variance is defined in terms of variances and covariances is as follows:

$$\begin{aligned}\sigma^2(R_p) = {} & (w_1)^2\sigma^2(R_1) + (w_2)^2\sigma^2(R_2) + (w_3)^2\sigma^2(R_3)\\ & + 2(w_1)(w_2)\text{cov}(R_1, R_2) + 2(w_1)(w_3)\text{cov}(R_1, R_3)\\ & + 2(w_2)(w_3)\text{cov}(R_2, R_3).\end{aligned} \tag{5}$$

In general, for a portfolio with K asset classes, the portfolio variance is given by

$$\sigma^2(R_p) = \sum_{k=1}^{K}\sum_{h=1}^{K} w_k w_h \text{cov}(R_k, R_h). \tag{6}$$

In Equation (6), the K variances are the cases in which $k = h$ results, and the covariance between every pair of assets is when $k \neq h$ results.

Role of Correlation in Determining Portfolio Risk and the Diversification Effect

Let's illustrate the expected portfolio return and portfolio risk using a simple two-asset class portfolio. This allows us to assess the role that the correlation plays in determining portfolio risk. Suppose we have the following information for the two asset classes, 1 and 2:

Asset	$E(R_i)$	$\sigma(R_i)$
1	12%	30%
2	18%	40%

Let's assume that the portfolio has equal weights for both assets (i.e., $w_1 = w_2$). Based on this information, the expected portfolio return from Equation (1) is

$$E(R_p) = 0.50(12\%) + 0.50(18\%) = 15\%.$$

From Equation (4), the portfolio variance is

$$\begin{aligned}\sigma^2(Rp) &= (0.5)^2(30\%)^2 + (0.5)^2(40\%)^2 \\ &\quad + 2(0.5)(0.5)(30\%)(40\%)\,\mathrm{cor}(R_1, R_2), \\ &= 625 + 600\,\mathrm{cor}(R_1, R_2).\end{aligned}$$

Taking the square root of the above equation, we obtain the standard deviation:

$$\sigma(Rp) = [625 + 600\,\mathrm{cor}(R_1, R_2)]^{0.5}.$$

We can now see how portfolio risk changes for our two-asset class portfolio with different correlations between the returns of the two asset classes. We know that the correlation ranges from -1 to $+1$. Let's examine the following three cases for $\mathrm{cor}(R_1, R_2)$: -1, 0, and 1. Substituting into the equation above for the correlation for these three cases of $\mathrm{cor}(R_1, R_2)$, we get:

$\mathrm{cor}(R_1, R_2)$	-1	0	$+1$
$\sigma(Rp)$	5%	25%	35%

As can be seen, as the correlation between the expected returns on asset classes 1 and 2 increases from -1.0 to 0.0 to 1.0, the standard deviation of the expected portfolio return increases from 5% to 35%. Note that although the portfolio risk changes with the correlation, the expected portfolio return remains 15% for each case.

This example clearly illustrates the effect of diversification based on the mean-variance framework. The principle of diversification in the mean-variance framework states that as the correlation (covariance) between the returns for asset classes that are combined in a portfolio decreases, so does the variance (hence the standard deviation) of the return for the portfolio. This is the result of the degree of correlation between the asset class returns.

As can be seen, investors can construct a portfolio to maintain expected portfolio return but lower portfolio risk by combining assets with lower (and preferably negative) correlations. However, in practice, very few asset classes have small to negative correlations with other asset classes. The problem, then, becomes one of searching among asset classes in an effort to identify the portfolio (i.e., asset allocation) with the minimum portfolio risk for a given level of expected portfolio return, or, equivalently, the highest expected portfolio return for a given level of portfolio risk.

Constructing Portfolios

Constructing a portfolio that represents the asset allocation as suggested results in portfolios that have the highest expected return for a given level of risk. As explained earlier, portfolios that have this attribute are referred to as efficient portfolios. To construct efficient portfolios, the following assumptions about how investors select assets are made:

- *Mean-Variance Assumption*: Only the expected value and the variance are used by investors in making asset selection decisions.
- *Risk-Aversion Assumption*: Investors are risk averse, which means that when faced with a decision about which of two asset classes to invest in when both have the same expected return but different levels of risk, investors will prefer the asset class with the lower risk.
- *Homogeneous Expectations Assumption*: All investors have the same expectations regarding expected return, variance, and covariance for all risky asset classes.
- *One-Period Horizon Assumption*: All investors have a common one-period investment horizon.
- *Optimization Assumption*: In constructing portfolios, investors seek to achieve the highest expected return for a given level of risk.

The construction of efficient portfolios given the universe of potential asset classes requires several calculations. For a universe of K asset classes, there are $(K^2 - K)/2$ unique covariances to calculate. Hence, for a portfolio with say eight asset classes, there are 28 covariances. That does not seem so onerous, although as explained later, there is the problem of misestimation of these 28 values. However, the problem of computing many estimates and the introduction of estimation risk increases exponentially when mean-variance is applied to the selection of individual assets as opposed to asset classes. For example, suppose that mean-variance is applied to construct a portfolio of small cap stocks and there are 350 candidate stocks for inclusion in the portfolio. Then there are 61,075 covariances that must be estimated!

The solution to the asset allocation problem can be be determined by solving the following optimization problem:

$$\text{Minimize: } \sigma^2(R_p) = \sum_{k=1}^{K}\sum_{h=1}^{K} w_k w_h \operatorname{cov}(R_k, R_h),$$

$$\text{Subject to: } E(R_p) = w_1 E(R_1) + w_2 E(R_2) + \cdots + w_K E(R_K).$$

The above optimization problem determines the minimum portfolio variance subject to a given level of expected portfolio return. For each level of expected return, the portfolio that minimizes portfolio risk can be calculated.

The specific optimization program used to solve the above problem for a given level of risk is quadratic programming. Although the algorithm used to solve a quadratic programming problem is covered in a course in management science (operations research), it is unnecessary to understand the algorithm for appreciating how efficient portfolios are constructed in the application of mean-variance analysis. Instead, we will just provide an illustration to show the results of the optimization process. To do so, we will use our earlier two-asset class portfolio illustration, for asset class 1 and asset class 2. Recall that for two asset classes, $E(R_1) = 12\%$, $\sigma(R_1) = 30\%$, $E(R_2) = 18\%$, and $\sigma(R_2) = 40\%$. In our earlier illustration we did not make any assumption about the correlation between the two assets. Here, however, we will assume that $\operatorname{cor}(R_1, R_2) = -0.5$. The expected portfolio return and the standard deviation for five different portfolios (A, B, C, D, and E) made up of varying proportions of asset classes 1 and 2 are shown in Table 1.

TABLE 1: Portfolio Expected Returns and Standard Deviations for Five Asset Allocations for Asset Classes 1 and 2 Assuming a Correlation of −0.5

Portfolio	w_1	w_2	$E(R_P)$	$\sigma(R_p)$
1	100%	0%	12.0%	30.0%
2	75	25	13.5	19.5
3	50	50	15.0	18.0
4	25	75	16.5	27.0
5	0	100	18.0	40.0

Note: $E(R_1) = 12\%$; $\sigma(R_1) = 30\%$; $E(R_2) = 18\%$; $\sigma(R_2) = 40\%$; $\operatorname{Cor}(R_1, R_2) = -0.5$.

Feasible portfolios

Any portfolio that an investor can construct given the universe of candidate asset classes is referred to as a *feasible portfolio*. The five portfolios (i.e., five asset allocations) shown in Table 1 are all feasible portfolios in which the risk is measured in terms of the portfolio's standard deviation. The collection of all feasible portfolios is called the *set of feasible portfolios*, or simply the *feasible set*.

In our illustration, where only two asset classes are candidates for inclusion in a portfolio, it is easy to graphically show the feasible set. The feasible set, shown in Figure 1, is a curve that represents those combinations of portfolio risk and expected portfolio return that are attainable by constructing portfolios from all possible combinations of asset class 1 and asset class 2. The five portfolios in Table 1 are identified on the curve representing the feasible set. Beginning with portfolio 1 and proceeding to portfolio 5, the allocation to asset class 1 goes from 100% of the portfolio to 0%, while the allocation to asset class 2 goes from 0% to 100% — therefore, all possible combinations of asset class 1 and asset class 2 lie between portfolio 1 and portfolio 5 (i.e., the curve labeled 1–5 in Figure 1). In the case of two asset classes, any other asset allocation to the two asset classes not lying on this curve is not attainable, since there is no mix of asset classes 1 and 2 that can be created. It is for this reason that curve 1–5 is the feasible set.

Figure 1 shows the feasible set for the two-asset class case. The general case, in which there can be more than two asset classes, is shown in

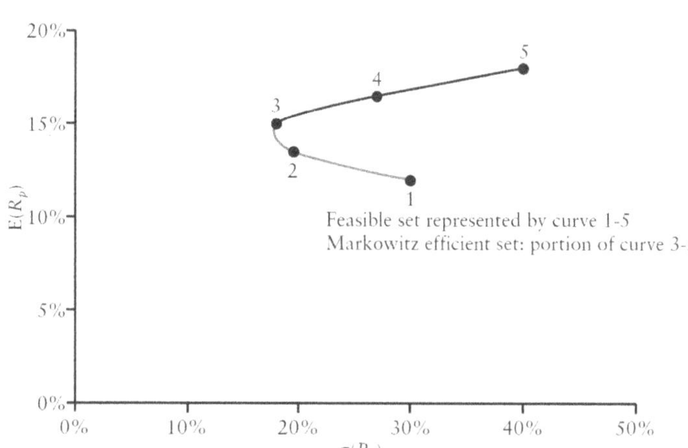

FIGURE 1: Feasible and Efficient Portfolios for Asset Classes 1 and 2

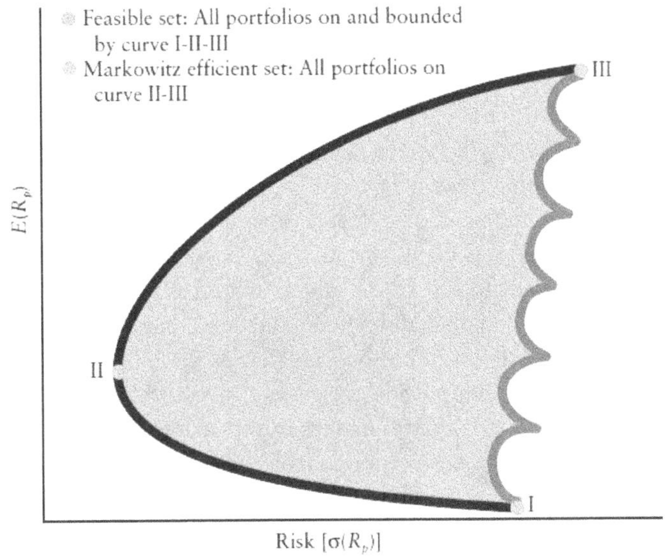

FIGURE 2: Feasible and Efficient Portfolios with More Than Two Asset Classes

Figure 2.[4] For the general asset class case, the feasible set is not a curve as shown in Figure 1 for the two-asset class case but instead is the shaded area in Figure 2 and it borders. The reason is that unlike in the two-asset class case, it is possible to create portfolios that result in combinations for the expected portfolio return and portfolio risk that not only lie on curve I-II-III in Figure 2 but also in the shaded area.

Efficient portfolios

An *efficient portfolio* is one that gives the highest expected return for the feasible set of portfolios with the same risk. It is also referred to as the *Markowitz efficient portfolio* and *mean-variance efficient portfolio.* For each level of portfolio risk there is an efficient portfolio, and the collection of all efficient portfolios is referred to as the set of efficient portfolios, or simply the *efficient set* or *Markowitz efficient set.* On a graph, the efficient set is referred to as the *efficient frontier.*

[4]Note that Figure 2 is for illustrative purposes only. The actual shape of the feasible set will depend on the expected return and standard deviation of returns for the assets chosen and the correlation between all pairs of asset returns.

Figure 1 shows the part of the feasible set for our two-asset class case that represents the efficient set. While the feasible set is shown by the curve 1–5, the efficient set or efficient frontier is the portion of the curve 3–5 that is part of the feasible set. These portfolios offer the highest expected portfolio return for a given level of portfolio risk. Of the five portfolios (i.e., asset allocations) shown in Table 1, only three, portfolios 3, 4, and 5, are part of the efficient set. The reason for excluding the remaining two portfolios of the feasible set from the efficient set — portfolio 1, with $E(R_p) = 12\%$ and $\sigma(R_p) = 20\%$, and portfolio 2, with $E(R_p) = 13.5\%$ and $\sigma(R_p) = 19.5\%$ — is because there is at least one portfolio among the efficient set (e.g., portfolio 3) that has a higher expected portfolio return and a lower portfolio risk than either portfolio 1 or portfolio 2. Also, portfolio 4 has a higher expected portfolio return and a lower portfolio risk than portfolio 1. In fact, the entire portion of the feasible set represented by the curve 1–3 (excluding portfolio 3) is not efficient since for any portfolio representing a combination of expected portfolio return and portfolio risk there is a portfolio among the efficient set that has the same portfolio risk and a higher expected portfolio return, or the same expected portfolio return and a lower portfolio risk, or both. Another way of saying this is that for any portfolio among the portion of the feasible set given by curve 1–3 (excluding portfolio 3), there exists a portfolio that dominates it by having the same expected portfolio return but a lower risk, or the same portfolio risk and a higher expected portfolio return, or a lower portfolio risk as well as a higher expected portfolio return. For example, portfolio 4 dominates portfolio 1, and portfolio 3 dominates both portfolios 1 and 2.

Again, Figure 1 represents the special case of only two asset classes. Figure 2 shows the general asset class case. As can be seen, the efficient set is given by curve II-III because it can be easily observed that all the feasible portfolios represented on that portion of the curve dominate the portfolios in the shaded area. Note that any portfolio above the efficient set cannot be constructed given the expected return and risk for each asset class and their correlations.

Selecting the Optimal Portfolio

It makes economic sense that the portfolio (i.e., asset allocation) that should be selected by an investor is one that is in the efficient set (i.e., lies somewhere on the efficient frontier). The efficient portfolios represent a trade-off between expected portfolio return and portfolio risk. How does the investor select which portfolio in the efficient set is the best one? Intuitively, one key element missing from the framework described thus far is the investor's tolerance for risk. Well, that is precisely what is missing, and for an investor to select the best portfolio given his or her risk tolerance, risk must be introduced. Remember that within the mean-variance framework, risk is the portfolio's variance/standard deviation of returns.

Utility theory and the optimal portfolio

In the economic "theory of choice", the concept used to represent a trade-off is an investor's utility function. This concept, formulated by John von Neumann and Oscar Morgenstern [1994], is applied when a decision-maker is faced with a set of choices. The decision-maker in our case is an investor, and the choices are the efficient portfolios contained in the efficient set. So, before we discuss how an investor can select a portfolio from the efficient set, we will provide a review of the concept of a utility function.

A *utility function* assigns a (numerical) value to all possible choices faced by a decision-maker, and the larger the assigned value of a particular choice, the greater the utility derived from that choice. The objective is to maximize the decision-maker's utility subject to one or more constraints. In introductory microeconomics, utility functions are used in describing the trade-off between different consumer goods with the objective of maximizing utility subject to a budget constraint. In our application to portfolio theory, the trade-off is between a portfolio's expected value and that portfolio's risk. The constraint imposed is that the allocation of the portfolio's funds must be such that the weights (i.e., the w_i's in the above equations) sum to 1.

The efficient portfolios offer different levels of portfolio expected return and portfolio risk, such that the greater the portfolio's expected return, the greater the portfolio risk. Investors are faced with the decision of choosing one of the efficient portfolios where the portfolio's expected return is a desirable commodity that increases the level of utility and risk is an undesirable commodity that decreases the level of utility. Therefore, investors obtain different levels of utility from different combinations of expected portfolio return and portfolio risk. The utility obtained from any possible such combination is expressed by the utility function. Put simply, the utility function expresses the preferences of investors for different combinations of perceived portfolio risk and expected return. Utility functions can be expressed mathematically. However, that is unnecessary for our purpose,

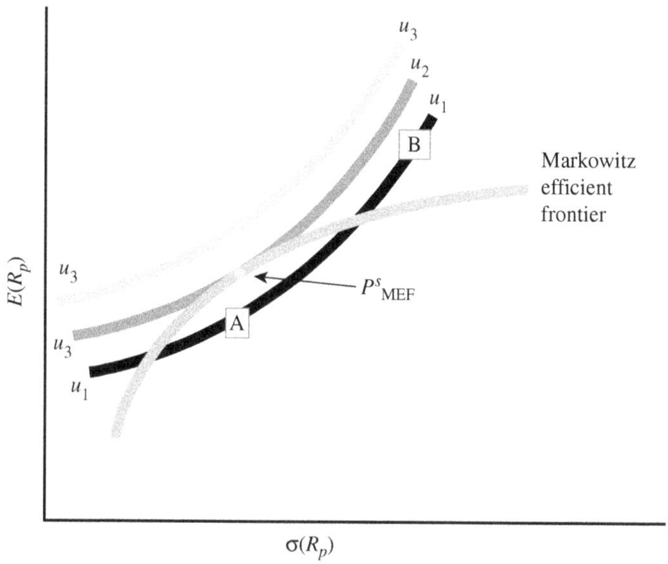

u_1, u_2, u_3 = indifference curves with $u_1 < u_2 < u_3$

P^s_{MEF} = optimal portfolio on Markowitz efficient frontier

FIGURE 3: Selection of Optimal Portfolio with Different Indifference Curves (Utility Function)

which is to understand conceptually the general idea about how the decision is made by an investor. So instead of mathematically expressing a utility function, we will show it graphically. Figure 3 shows three utility curves, labeled u_1, u_2, and u_3. The horizontal axis measures portfolio risk and the vertical axis measures the portfolio expected return. Each curve represents a set of portfolios with different combinations of portfolio risk and expected portfolio return. All the points on the same curve identify combinations of portfolio risk and expected portfolio return that, based on the investor's preferences, offer the same level of utility. Because they offer the same level of utility, each curve is referred to as an *indifference curve*. For example, on the indifference curve u_1 in the figure, two points, A and B are shown. The two points represent two portfolios (i.e., two asset allocations), with the portfolio corresponding to B having a higher portfolio expected return than the portfolio corresponding to A, but also having a higher risk. Because the two portfolios lie on the same indifference curve, the investor has an equal preference for (or is indifferent to) the two portfolios — or, for that matter, any portfolio on the curve.

Note two things about the indifference curves. First, the slope of the indifference curve is positive, and this is so for a rational economic reason: at the same level of utility, the investor requires a higher expected portfolio return in order to accept a higher portfolio risk. Second is the positioning of each indifference curve. The utility the investor receives is greater the farther the indifference curve is from the horizontal axis because that indifference curve represents a higher expected portfolio return at every level of portfolio risk. Thus, for the three indifference curves shown in Figure 3, u_3 has the highest utility and u_1 the lowest.

Given a choice from the set of efficient portfolios, the *optimal portfolio* is the one that is most preferred by the investor, where preference is represented by the investor's utility function. Figure 3 demonstrates graphically how this is done. In the figure, there are three indifference curves representing an investor's utility function. On the same figure is the efficient frontier. From this display, it is possible to determine the optimal portfolio for the investor with the indifference curves shown. Remember that the investor wants to get to the highest indifference curve achievable given the efficient frontier. Considering that requirement, the optimal portfolio is represented by the point where an indifference curve is tangent to the efficient frontier. In Figure 3, that is portfolio P^*_{MEF}. For example, suppose that P^*_{MEF} corresponds to portfolio D in Figure 2. We know from Table 1 that this portfolio is made up of 25% of asset class 1 and 75% of asset class 2, with $E(R_p) = 16.5\%$ and $\sigma(R_p) = 27.0\%$.

Consequently, for the investor with preferences with respect to portfolio expected return and portfolio risk as determined by the shape of the indifference curves represented in Figure 3 and expectations for asset class 1 and asset class 2 inputs (expected returns and variance-covariance) represented in Table 1, portfolio D is the optimal portfolio because it maximizes the investor's utility. If this investor had a different preference for portfolio expected return and portfolio risk, a different optimal portfolio would be selected.

At this point in our discussion, a natural question is how to estimate an investor's utility function so that the indifference curves can be determined. Unfortunately, there is little guidance about how to construct a utility function. In general, economists have not been successful in estimating utility functions. The inability to estimate utility functions does not mean that the theory is flawed. What it does mean is that in practice, once an investor constructs the efficient frontier, the investor has to use some other criteria for the selection of which efficient portfolio is the optimal portfolio. There are several possible criteria, and these are discussed in what follows.

Other criteria for selecting the optimal portfolio

The optimization model for mean-variance analysis computes the minimum variance for a given level of risk. A criterion used in practice for selecting the optimal portfolio is to select from all the efficient portfolios the one that has the smallest variance. This portfolio is called the *global minimum variance portfolio* or GMV portfolio.

In the previous chapter, we described several reward-risk ratios. Each of these ratios can be used to select the optimal portfolio. A common one is the Sharpe ratio. Other reward-risk ratios involve the selection of the benchmark such as the information ratio or a minimum acceptable rate in the case of the Sortino ratio. Other criteria could be the minimization of the drawdown metric.

Finally, in Chapter 8 of the companion book we discuss other risk measures. The minimum of any of these other risk measures can be used to select the optimal portfolio from the efficient frontier.

An Illustration of Asset Allocation Selection Using Mean-Variance Analysis

To illustrate the asset allocation decision using mean-variance analysis, we will use Portfolio Visualizer developed by Tuomo Lampinen of Silicon Cloud Technologies, LLC, which is available online.

For our illustration, we will use the following six US asset classes: (1) large-cap stocks, (2) mid-cap stocks, (3) small-cap stocks, (4) micro-cap stocks, (5) long-term Treasury securities, and (6) long-term corporate bonds. The data used in the model will be monthly returns from 1/1/1995 to 5/31/2019. The data are provided by Portfolio Visualizer. Panel (a) of Table 2 shows the historical average return[5] and standard deviation for all of the asset classes. Also shown are the measures described in the previous chapter (maximum drawdown, Sharpe ratio, and Sortino ratio). Panel (b) of Table 2 shows the correlation between each asset class.

[5]The historical average return is calculated as the compound average growth rate (CAGR) over the time period.

TABLE 2: Data for Illustration

(a) Average return and standard deviation of returns for six asset classes and other measures

Asset Class	Mean Return %	St. Dev. %	Max. Drawdown %	Sharpe Ratio	Sortino Ratio
US large cap	9.49	14.64	−50.97	0.54	0.79
US mid-cap	11.22	16.42	−54.14	0.59	0.87
US small cap	9.91	18.87	−53.95	0.48	0.69
US micro-cap	11.46	18.96	−56.61	0.55	0.82
Long-term treasury	7.39	10.11	−16.68	0.53	0.88
Long-term corporate bonds	7.54	8.51	−16.82	0.63	1.01

(b) Correlations for the asset class returns

Asset class	US Large Cap	US Mid-cap	US Small Cap	US Micro-cap	Long-Term Treasury	Long-Term Corporate Bonds
US large cap	—	0.91	0.83	0.76	−0.22	0.09
US mid-cap	0.91	—	0.93	0.84	−0.23	0.10
US small cap	0.83	0.93	—	0.89	−0.26	0.05
US micro-cap	0.76	0.84	0.89	—	−0.31	−0.00
Long-term treasury	−0.22	−0.23	−0.26	−0.31	−0.82	0.82
Long-term corporate bonds	0.09	0.10	0.05	−0.00	0.82	—

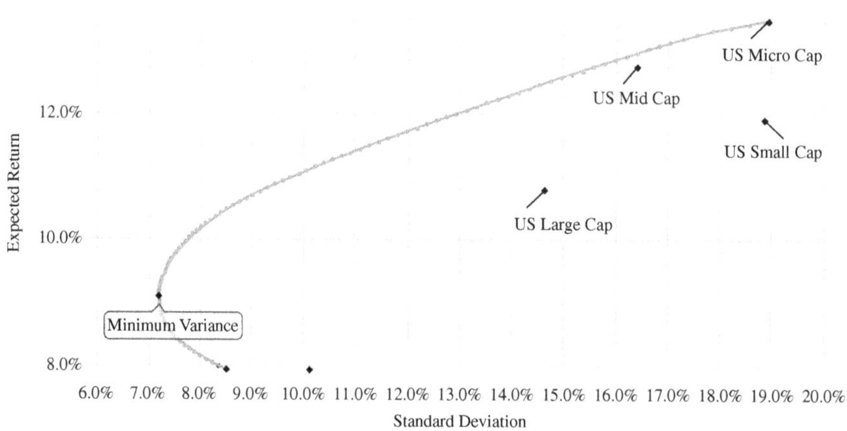

FIGURE 4: Efficient Frontier (Starting at the Minimum Variance): January 1995–May 2019

Figure 4 shows the efficient frontier as well as the location of each asset class on the standard deviation-expected return graph. Table 3 shows 40 efficient portfolios obtained from the optimization. Shown for each portfolio is the allocation to each asset class and the expected portfolio return and portfolio standard deviation.

Which portfolio or asset allocation is the optimal one? The criterion for selecting the optimal portfolio from the efficient set must be determined. As explained earlier in this chapter, in practice a criterion must be selected by the investor. The last column in Table 3 shows the Sharpe ratio for each portfolio. The criterion could be minimization of the portfolio variance or maximization of the Sharpe ratio. The minimum variance portfolio, the GMV portfolio in our illustration, is efficient portfolio 22 and for the Sharpe ratio maximization it is portfolio 36.[6] The optimal portfolio based on each of these criterion along with the portfolio composition are shown in the second and third columns of Table 4. Note the dramatic difference in the asset allocation based on the two optimization objectives.

The efficient frontier and the optimal portfolio for the six asset classes thus far are based on an unconstrained optimization. That is, no restrictions were imposed on the amount that can be allocated to any of the asset classes. Suppose that an investor imposes the restrictions shown in panel (a) in Table 5.

[6]Note that for both optimization objectives there are two efficient portfolios that have the same optimization value. The software identified which was the lowest portfolio variance and maximum Sharpe ratio.

TABLE 3: 40 Efficient Frontiers

Efficient Portfolio	US Large Cap (%)	US Mid-cap (%)	US Small Cap (%)	US Micro-Cap (%)	Long-Term Treasury (%)	Long-Term Corporate Bonds (%)	Expected Return* (%)	Standard Deviation* (%)	Sharpe Ratio*
1	0.00	0.00	0.00	0.00	0.43	99.57	7.93	8.51	0.658
2	1.94	0.00	0.00	0.00	6.85	91.22	7.98	8.36	0.676
3	3.88	0.00	0.00	0.00	9.36	86.76	8.04	8.23	0.694
4	5.82	0.00	0.00	0.00	11.87	82.31	8.09	8.11	0.711
5	7.76	0.00	0.00	0.00	14.38	77.85	8.15	7.99	0.729
6	9.70	0.00	0.00	0.00	16.90	73.40	8.20	7.88	0.746
7	11.65	0.00	0.00	0.00	19.41	68.95	8.26	7.78	0.762
8	13.59	0.00	0.00	0.00	21.92	64.49	8.31	7.69	0.778
9	15.53	0.00	0.00	0.00	24.43	60.04	8.37	7.61	0.794
10	17.47	0.00	0.00	0.00	26.95	55.58	8.42	7.53	0.809
11	19.41	0.00	0.00	0.00	29.46	51.13	8.48	7.47	0.823
12	21.35	0.00	0.00	0.00	31.97	46.67	8.53	7.42	0.836
13	22.02	0.00	0.00	0.66	34.00	43.32	8.59	7.37	0.849
14	21.74	0.00	0.00	1.82	35.66	40.78	8.64	7.34	0.861
15	21.45	0.00	0.00	2.98	37.33	38.25	8.70	7.30	0.872
16	21.16	0.00	0.00	4.14	38.99	35.71	8.75	7.27	0.884
17	20.87	0.00	0.00	5.29	40.65	33.18	8.81	7.25	0.894
18	20.59	0.00	0.00	6.45	42.32	30.64	8.86	7.23	0.904
19	20.30	0.00	0.00	7.61	43.98	28.11	8.92	7.21	0.914
20	20.01	0.00	0.00	8.77	45.64	25.57	8.97	7.20	0.923
21	19.73	0.00	0.00	9.93	47.31	23.04	9.03	7.19	0.932

(Continued)

TABLE 3: (*Continued*)

Efficient Portfolio	US Large Cap (%)	US Mid-cap (%)	US Small Cap (%)	US Micro-Cap (%)	Long-Term Treasury (%)	Long-Term Corporate Bonds (%)	Expected Return* (%)	Standard Deviation* (%)	Sharpe Ratio*
22	19.44	0.00	0.00	11.09	48.97	20.50	9.08	7.19	0.94
23	19.15	0.00	0.00	12.24	50.63	17.97	9.14	7.19	0.947
24	18.87	0.00	0.00	13.40	52.30	15.43	9.19	7.20	0.954
25	18.58	0.00	0.00	14.56	53.96	12.90	9.25	7.21	0.960
26	18.29	0.00	0.00	15.72	55.63	10.36	9.30	7.22	0.966
27	18.00	0.00	0.00	16.88	57.29	7.83	9.36	7.24	0.971
28	17.61	0.16	0.00	17.95	58.92	5.36	9.41	7.27	0.975
29	16.34	1.73	0.00	18.26	60.21	3.47	9.47	7.30	0.979
30	15.06	3.29	0.00	18.57	61.51	1.57	9.53	7.33	0.982
31	13.67	4.93	0.00	18.88	62.52	0.00	9.58	7.36	0.986
32	11.72	6.89	0.00	19.20	62.20	0.00	9.64	7.40	0.988
33	9.77	8.84	0.00	19.51	61.87	0.00	9.69	7.44	0.99
34	7.83	10.80	0.00	19.83	61.54	0.00	9.75	7.49	0.991
35	5.88	12.76	0.00	20.15	61.21	0.00	9.80	7.53	0.992
36	3.93	14.72	0.00	20.47	60.88	0.00	9.86	7.59	0.993
37	1.98	16.68	0.00	20.78	60.55	0.00	9.91	7.64	0.993
38	0.03	18.64	0.00	21.10	60.22	0.00	9.97	7.70	0.992
39	0.00	19.20	0.00	21.65	59.16	0.00	10.03	7.77	0.991
40	0.00	19.72	0.00	22.20	58.08	0.00	10.08	7.84	0.989

Note: **Ex ante* values shown for portfolio return and volatility. *Ex ante* Sharpe ratio calculated using historical 1-month Treasury bill returns as the risk-free rate (2.33% annualized).

TABLE 4: Optimal Portfolio (Asset Allocation) Based on Minimum Variance and Maximum Sharpe Ratio (No Constraints)

	Minimum Variance Portfolio	**Maximum Sharpe Ratio**
Efficient portfolio number	22	36
Portfolio expected return	9.08%	9.86%
Portfolio std. deviation	7.19%	7.59%
Allocation		
US large cap	19.44%	3.93%
US mid-cap	0.00%	14.72%
US small cap	0.00%	0.00%
US micro-cap	11.09%	20.47%
Long-term treasury	48.97%	60.88%
Long-term corporate bonds	20.50%	0.00%

TABLE 5: Optimal Portfolio (asset allocation) Based on Minimum Variance and Maximum Sharpe Ratio (with constraints)

(a) Minimum and maximum allocation constraints

Asset Class	**Minimum Allocation (%)**	**Maximum Allocation (%)**
US large cap	10	25
US mid-cap	10	25
US small cap	10	25
US micro-cap	0	15
Long-term treasury	10	25
Long-term corporate bonds	10	25

(b) Optimal portfolio

	Minimum Variance Portfolio (%)	**Maximum Sharpe Ratio (%)**
Portfolio expected return	9.79	9.65
Portfolio std. deviation	8.50	10.07
Allocation		
US large cap	24.75	13.65
US mid-cap	10.00	11.35
US small cap	10.00	10.00
US micro-cap	4.25	15.00
Long-term treasury	25.00	25.00
Long-term corporate bonds	25.00	25.00

Issues with Mean-Variance Analysis

Portfolio theory as formulated by Markowitz, as described in this chapter, proposes how investors make investment decisions to construct efficient portfolios. This is a normative theory. That is, it is a theory that describes a norm of behavior that investors should pursue in constructing a portfolio and making asset allocation decisions. And if investors do follow that norm of behavior in constructing portfolios, the portfolio selected would be an efficient portfolio. So, the criticisms of portfolio theory focus on the assumptions on which the theory is built. After we discuss these criticisms, we will look at the issues associated with implementing modern portfolio theory.

Attack on the Assumptions

Certain assumptions made in portfolio theory were identified earlier in the chapter: the mean-variance assumption, the risk-aversion assumption, the homogeneous expectations assumption, the one-period horizon assumption, and the optimization assumption. The mean-variance, homogeneous expectations, and one-period horizon assumptions have come under attack. The major attack on these assumptions has been raised by financial economists from the field of behavioral finance.

The mean-variance assumption states that the appropriate measure of risk considered by an investor is the variance of the distribution of portfolio returns. There are limitations on the use of variance as a measure of risk when asset returns are not normally distributed. As explained in the previous chapter, the preponderance of empirical evidence indicates that asset returns are not normally distributed. More specifically, asset returns are skewed and exhibit fat tails. The implication of fat tails is that there is more risk in the tails of the distribution than suggested by assuming normally distributed returns.

The homogeneous expectations assumption holds that every investor has the same expectations about the inputs: means, variances, and correlations of returns. Insofar as investors typically do not have access to the same data, it is unlikely that this assumption holds. About the one-period assumption, the theory does not specify what the length of the period should be.

Implementation Issues

There are practical issues associated with implementing the mean-variance model. Specifically, estimation errors in the forecasts significantly affect the

TABLE 6: Optimal Portfolio Selected Based on GMV with Different Starting Dates to Estimate the Inputs

	January 1, 1995 to May 31, 2019 (%)	**January 1, 2000 to May 31, 2019 (%)**	**January 1, 2005 to May 31, 2019 (%)**	**January 1, 2014 to May 31, 2019 (%)**
Portfolio expected return	9.08	7.61	7.41	7.85
Portfolio std. deviation	7.19	7.19	7.25	6.31
Allocation				
US large cap	19.44	26.98	28.32	22.19
US mid-cap	0.00	0.00	0.00	0.00
US small cap	0.00	0.00	0.00	0.00
US micro-cap	11.09	8.06	9.82	6.45
Long-term treasury	48.97	54.35	56.64	3.70
Long-term corporate bonds	20.50	10.60	5.22	67.66

resulting portfolio weights. Studies have shown that estimation error for the expected returns tend to exert more influence than estimation error for the variances and covariances (for example, see Best and Grauer [1991, 1992] and Chopra and Ziemba [1993]). Furthermore, it turns out that errors in the variances are about twice as important as errors in the covariances (for example, see Best and Grauer [1991, 1992]). For this reason, Michaud [1998] refers to mean-variance optimization techniques as "error maximizers" that can produce extreme or nonintuitive weights for some assets in the portfolio.

Remember that the inputs for the illustration are based on returns from January 1, 1995 to May 31, 2019. Table 6 demonstrates how sensitive the optimal allocation is if a different starting date is used. The optimal portfolios shown in the table are the GMV portfolios. As can be seen, the allocations change dramatically based on the starting date for estimating the inputs.

Extensions and Alternatives to Mean-Variance Analysis

Mean-variance analysis is the most popular theory for asset allocation and portfolio selection. The model has been extended to overcome the criticisms of this approach that we just discussed. To overcome the problem of errors in estimating the inputs, mean-variance analysis has been cast as a robust optimization problem.[7] A very different approach to portfolio construction

[7]See, for example, Kim, and Fabozzi [2016].

that has been successfully used in the asset allocation decision is risk parity. This approach will be discussed in Chapter 19.

Key Points

- Portfolio theory, developed by Harry Markowitz, explains how investors should construct efficient portfolios and select the best or optimal portfolio among all efficient portfolios.
- Markowitz portfolio theory differs from previous approaches to portfolio theory, in that Markowitz demonstrated how the key parameters to the portfolio selection problem should be measured.
- There are only two statistical moments used in constructing a portfolio, expected return and risk as measured by the variance (or standard deviation) of returns, and hence the technique is referred to as mean-variance analysis.
- The goal of diversifying a portfolio is to reduce a portfolio's risk without sacrificing the portfolio's expected return.
- The goal of portfolio selection can be cast in terms of not just the expected return and variance of returns but also the correlation (or covariance) between assets.
- A portfolio's expected return is simply a weighted average of the expected return of each asset in the portfolio, with the weight assigned to each asset being equal to the market value of the asset in the portfolio relative to the total market value of the portfolio.
- The risk of an asset is measured by the variance or standard deviation of its return.
- Unlike the expected return, a portfolio's risk is not a simple weighting of the standard deviation of the individual assets in the portfolio.
- Portfolio risk is affected by the correlation between the return of the assets in the portfolio: the lower the correlation/covariance, the smaller the portfolio risk.
- Mean-variance analysis is used in making the asset allocation decision and in selecting the specific securities to be included in the portfolio.
- Mean-variance analysis assumes that investors are risk-averse, and all have the same expectation about the inputs and have a single period investment horizon.
- In mean-variance analysis, it is assumed that the returns are normally distributed.

- The mean-variance optimization problem is to create an efficient portfolio which is the portfolio that minimizes the portfolio variance for a given expected portfolio return (or equivalently maximizes the expected portfolio return for a given portfolio variance).
- From the efficient set, the optimal portfolio must be selected.
- In portfolio theory, utility theory is used to determine the optimal portfolio.
- In practice, the criterion to select the optimal portfolio does not rely on utility theory.
- A criterion that can be used by an investor to select the optimal portfolio is the smallest variance from among all the efficient portfolios and the resulting optimal portfolio is referred to as the minimum variance portfolio.
- Another criterion that can be used by an investor to select the optimal portfolio is to determine the maximum of some reward-risk ratio such as the Sharpe ratio.
- Other metrics can be used to select the optimal portfolio.
- A criticism of the mean-variance framework is that it ignores moments such as skewness and fat tails that have been observed for asset returns in real-world financial markets.
- Proponents of behavioral finance have attacked mean-variance analysis because, in their view, investors do not make investment decisions in the manner assumed by portfolio theory.
- One of the most serious difficulties in implementing the Markowitz framework (as it would be for any framework requiring estimates) is the impact of forecasts for the individual means, standard deviations, and pairwise correlations in the portfolios generated.
- There are extensions of mean-variance analysis and other approaches for dealing with the asset allocation problem.

References

Best, M. J. and R. T. Grauer, 1991. "On the sensitivity of mean-variance-efficient portfolios to changes in asset means: Some analytical and computational results," *Review of Financial Studies*, 4(2): 315–342.

Best, M. J. and R. T. Grauer, 1992. "Sensitivity analysis for mean-variance portfolio problems," *Review of Financial Studies*, 1(1): 17–37.

Chopra, V. K. and W. T. Ziemba, 1993. "The effect of errors in means, variances, and covariances on optimal portfolio choice," *Journal of Portfolio Management*, 19(2): 6–11.

Kim, W. C., J. H. Kim and F. J. Fabozzi, 2016. *Robust Equity Portfolio Management.* Hoboken, NJ: John Wiley & Sons.

Leavens, D. H., 1945. "Diversification of investments," *Trusts and Estates*, 80: 469–473.

Markowitz, H. M., 1952. "Portfolio selection," *Journal of Finance*, 7(1): 77–91.

Markowitz, H. M., 1959. *Portfolio Selection: Efficient Diversification of Investments*, Cowles Foundation Monograph 16. New York: John Wiley & Sons.

Michaud, R., 1998. *Efficient Asset Allocation: A Practical Guide to Stock Portfolio Optimization and Asset Allocation.* Boston: Harvard Business School Press.

Rachev, S. T., C. Menn, and F. J. Fabozzi, 2005. *Fat-Tailed and Skewed Asset Return Distributions: Implications for Risk Management, Portfolio Selection, and Option Pricing.* Hoboken, NJ: John Wiley & Sons.

Sharpe, W. F., 1964. "Capital asset prices," *Journal of Finance*, 19(3): 425–442.

Chapter 9

Asset Pricing Theories

Learning Objectives

After reading this chapter, you will understand:

- what an asset pricing model is;
- the characteristics of asset pricing models;
- what is meant by the risk premium offered on an asset;
- the difference between systematic risk and unsystematic risk;
- what the capital asset pricing model is and the role of the market portfolio;
- the behavioral and capital market assumptions underlying the capital asset pricing model;
- the risk factor in the capital asset pricing model;
- what the risk premium is in the capital asset pricing model;
- the meaning of the capital market line and the security market line;
- the major findings of empirical tests of the capital asset pricing model and their implications;
- what is meant by the low-volatility anomaly and its implications;
- the several extensions of the capital asset pricing model;
- what the arbitrage pricing theory is and what it says about systematic risk factors;
- the three types of multifactor models used in practice: fundamental factor models, macroeconomic factor models, and statistical factor models, and;
- systematic risk factors included in the Fama–French–Carhart models.

Asset pricing models, the subject of this chapter, describe the relationship between risk and expected return. When we refer to asset pricing models in this chapter, we mean the expected return investors require given the risk associated with an investment. The most well-known equilibrium pricing models are the *capital asset pricing model* (CAPM) developed in the

1960s and its subsequent extensions. We also describe the *arbitrage pricing theory* (APT), an asset pricing model developed in the mid-1970s.

Characteristics of an Asset Pricing Model

In well-functioning capital markets, an investor should be rewarded for accepting the various risks associated with investing in an asset. Risks are also referred to as "risk factors" or "factors." We can express an *asset pricing model* in general terms based on risk factors as follows:

$$E(R_i) = f(F_1, F_2, F_3, \ldots, F_N), \tag{1}$$

where $E(R_i)$ is the expected return for asset i, F_k is the risk factor k, and N is the number of risk factors.

Equation (1) says that the expected return is a function of N risk factors. The trick is to figure out what the risk factors are and to specify the precise relationship between expected return and the risk factors. We can fine-tune the asset pricing model given by Equation (1) by thinking about the minimum expected return we would want from investing in an asset. There are securities issued by the US Department of the Treasury that offer a known return if held over some time period. The expected return offered on such securities is called the *risk-free return* or the *risk-free rate* because they are believed to have minimal default risk. When investing in an asset other than such securities, investors will demand a premium over the risk-free rate. That is, the expected return that an investor will require is

$$E(R_i) = R_f + \text{Risk premium},$$

where R_f is the risk-free rate.

The "risk premium" or additional return expected over the risk-free rate depends on the risk factors associated with investing in the asset. Thus, we can rewrite the general form of the asset pricing model given by Equation (1) as follows:

$$E(R_i) = R_f + f(F_1, F_2, F_3, \ldots, F_N). \tag{2}$$

Risk factors can be divided into two general categories. The first category is risk factors that cannot be diversified away. That is, no matter what the investor does, the investor cannot eliminate these risk factors. These risk factors are referred to as *systematic risk factors* or *non-diversifiable risk factors*. The second category is risk factors that can be eliminated via diversification. These risk factors are unique to the asset and are referred to as *unsystematic risk factors* or *diversifiable risk factors*.

Capital Asset Pricing Model

The first asset pricing model derived from economic theory is the *capital asset pricing model* (CAPM).[1] The CAPM formalizes the relationship that should exist between asset returns and risk if investors behave in a hypothesized manner. More specifically, it builds on a theory of portfolio selection that we describe in the previous chapter, mean-variance analysis. The CAPM is a theory that hypothesizes how investors who select assets based on mean-variance analysis behave. In turn, that behavior determines how assets should be priced and the appropriate measure of risk for which investors should be compensated.

The CAPM has only one systematic risk factor — the risk of the overall movement of the market. This risk factor is referred to as *market risk*. So, in the CAPM, the terms "market risk" and "systematic risk" are used interchangeably. By "market risk" it is meant the risk associated with holding a portfolio consisting of all assets, called the *market portfolio*. As will be explained later, in the market portfolio an asset is held in proportion to its market value to the market value of all assets. So, for example, if the total market value of all assets is $\$X$ and the market value of asset j is $\$Y$, then asset j will comprise $\$Y/\$X$ of the market portfolio.

The CAPM is given by the following formula:

$$E(R_i) = R_f + \beta_i[E(R_M) - R_f], \tag{3}$$

where $E(R_M)$ is the expected return on the "market portfolio", $E(R_i)$ is the expected return on asset i, and β_i is the measure of systematic risk of asset i relative to the "market portfolio".

Although we have provided a description based on asset i, Equation (3) holds for a portfolio.

Let's look at what this asset pricing model says. The expected return for an asset i according to the CAPM is equal to the risk-free rate plus a risk premium. The risk premium is

$$\text{Risk premium in the CAPM} = \beta_i[E(R_M) - R_f].$$

[1]The CAPM was developed by Sharpe (1964), Lintner (1965), Treynor (1961), and Mossin (1966).

First look at *beta* (β_i) in the risk premium component of the CAPM. Beta is a measure of the sensitivity of the return of asset i to the return of the market portfolio. A beta of 1 means that the asset or portfolio has the same quantity of risk as the market portfolio. A beta greater than 1 means that the asset or portfolio has more market risk than the market portfolio, and a beta less than 1 means that the asset or portfolio has less market risk than the market portfolio.

The second component of the risk premium in the CAPM is the difference between the expected return on the market portfolio, $E(R_M)$, and the risk-free rate. It measures the potential reward for taking on market risk that exceeds what can be earned by investing in an asset that offers a risk-free rate.

Taken together, the risk premium is a product of the quantity of market risk (as measured by beta) and the potential compensation of taking on market risk (as measured by $[E(R_M) - R_f]$).

Let's use some values for beta to see if all of this makes sense. Suppose that a portfolio has a beta of zero. That is, the return for this portfolio has no market risk. Substituting zero for β into the CAPM given by Equation (3), we would find that the expected return is just the risk-free rate. This makes sense since a portfolio that has no market risk should have an expected return equal to the risk-free rate.

Consider a portfolio that has a beta of 1. This portfolio has the same market risk as the market portfolio. Substituting 1 for β in the CAPM given by Equation (3) results in an expected return equal to that of the market portfolio. Again, this is what one should expect for the return of this portfolio since it has the same market risk exposure as the market portfolio.

If a portfolio has greater market risk than the market portfolio, beta will be greater than 1 and the expected return will be greater than that of the market portfolio. If a portfolio has less market risk than the market portfolio, beta will be less than 1 and the expected return will be less than that of the market portfolio.

Assumptions of the CAPM

The CAPM is an abstraction of the real-world capital markets and, as such, is based on assumptions. These assumptions simplify matters a great deal, and some of them may even seem unrealistic. However, these assumptions make the CAPM more tractable from a mathematical standpoint. The CAPM assumptions are as follows:

- **Assumption 1:** In constructing a portfolio, investors base their decision as to what to include in a portfolio on the expected return and variance of returns of assets.
- **Assumption 2:** Investors are rational and risk averse.
- **Assumption 3:** Investors all invest for the same period of time.
- **Assumption 4:** Investors have the same expectations about the expected return and variance of all assets.
- **Assumption 5:** There is a risk-free asset and investors can borrow and lend any amount at the risk-free rate.
- **Assumption 6:** Capital markets are completely competitive and frictionless.

The first four assumptions deal with the way investors make decisions. The last two assumptions relate to characteristics of the capital market. These assumptions require further explanation. Many of these assumptions have been challenged, resulting in modifications of the CAPM. There is a branch of financial theory, called behavioral finance, which is highly critical of these assumptions.

Assumption 1 says that when investors decide how to construct a portfolio, the inclusion of assets is based on the expected return and variance of asset returns that are candidates for inclusion in the portfolio. Using the variance of asset returns in the construction of portfolios is the measure of risk that is used by investors. This approach to constructing a portfolio using mean-variance analysis was described in the previous chapter. What was explained in that chapter is that investors use mean-variance analysis to construct efficient portfolios. An efficient portfolio is one that gives the maximum expected return for a given level of risk. Since there is an efficient portfolio for every level of risk, we can talk in terms of the set of efficient portfolios, and on a graph, it is referred to as the efficient frontier. Since the CAPM is built off of mean-variance analysis, some of the criticism of that approach for portfolio construction also applies to the CAPM.

Assumption 2 indicates that to accept greater risk, investors must be compensated by the opportunity of realizing a higher return. We refer to the behavior of such investors as being risk averse.[2] What this means is that if an investor faces a choice between two portfolios with the same expected return, the investor will select the portfolio with the lower risk. Certainly, this is a reasonable assumption.

By Assumption 3, all investors are assumed to make investment decisions over some single-period investment horizon. The theory does not specify how long that period is (i.e., 6 months, 1 year, 2 years, etc.). The investment decision process is more complex than that, with many investors having more than one investment horizon. Nonetheless, the assumption of a one-period investment horizon is necessary to simplify the mathematics of the theory.

To obtain the set of efficient portfolios in developing the CAPM, it is assumed that investors have the same expectations with respect to the inputs that are used to derive the efficient portfolios: asset expected returns and variances, as well as the statistical measures of correlations/covariances of returns explained in the previous chapter that are needed to apply mean-variance analysis. This is Assumption 4 and is referred to as the "homogeneous expectations assumption".

The existence of a risk-free asset and unlimited borrowing and lending at the risk-free rate, Assumption 5, is important in the CAPM. This is because, as explained in the previous chapter, efficient portfolios are created for portfolios consisting of risky assets. No consideration is given to how to create efficient portfolios when a risk-free asset is available. In the CAPM, it is assumed not only that there is a risk-free asset but also that an investor can borrow funds at the same interest rate offered on a risk-free asset. This is a common assumption in many economic models developed in finance despite the fact it is well known that there is a different rate at which investors can borrow and lend funds. The notion that investors can borrow funds to buy securities means that investors can create a leveraged portfolio. This assumption that investors are not averse to borrowing funds to leverage a portfolio is important because in Chapter 19 we present an approach to creating a diversified portfolio called "risk parity". That approach assumes that investors are in fact reluctant to use leverage.

---

[2]This is an oversimplified definition. A more rigorous definition of risk aversion is described by a mathematical specification of an investor's utility function. However, this complexity need not be of concern here.

Finally, Assumption 6 specifies that the capital market is perfectly competitive. In general, this means the number of buyers and sellers is sufficiently large, and all investors are small enough relative to the market so that no individual investor can influence an asset's price. Consequently, all investors are price takers, and the market price is determined where there is an equality of supply and demand. In addition, according to this assumption, there are no transaction costs or impediments that interfere with the supply of and demand for an asset. Economists refer to these various costs and impediments as "market frictions". The costs associated with market frictions generally result in buyers paying more than in the absence of market frictions and sellers receiving less. The existence of market frictions also explains why investors may have an aversion to the use of leverage.

In economic modeling, the model is modified by relaxing one or more of the assumptions. There are extensions and modifications of the CAPM, but they will not be discussed here.[3] No matter the extension or modification, the basic implications are unchanged: Investors are only rewarded for taking on systematic risk, and in the case of the CAPM, the only systematic risk is market risk.

Capital Market Line

Let's now look at the notion of an efficient frontier using Figure 1. In the figure, risk is shown on the horizontal axis and the measure used to represent risk is the standard deviation of the portfolio's return. The standard deviation of portfolio's return is the square root of the variance.

The figure shows the efficient frontier from the theory of portfolio selection in the previous chapter. Every point on the efficient frontier is the maximum expected portfolio return for a given level of risk.

As explained in the previous chapter, the curve indicated by "efficient frontier" is derived assuming that investors construct portfolios using mean-variance analysis. For example, look at point P_A. One can interpret this point as follows. It is an efficient portfolio which gives the maximum expected portfolio return for a given level of risk (i.e., standard deviation of portfolio return). Equivalently, it is the minimum risk that the investor must accept to obtain that expected portfolio return.

---

[3]The best known one is the zero-beta version of the CAPM developed by Black [1972]. The version assumes that there is no risk-free asset. There is considerable debate in financial economics about whether a risk-free asset exists.

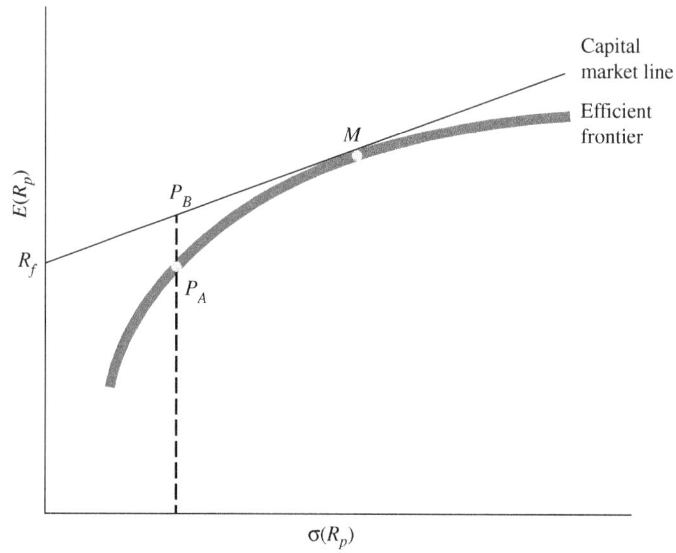

FIGURE 1: The Capital Market Line

In creating an efficient frontier using mean-variance analysis, there is no consideration of a risk-free asset. The efficient frontier changes, however, once a risk-free asset is introduced and assuming that investors can borrow and lend at the risk-free rate (Assumption 6). This is illustrated in Figure 1 by the straight line that is tangent to the efficient frontier at point M. The line from the risk-free rate that is tangent to portfolio M is called the *capital market line* (CML).

Every combination of the risk-free asset and the efficient portfolio denoted by point M is shown on the line drawn from the vertical axis starting at the risk-free rate tangent to the efficient frontier. The point of tangency, M, represents portfolio M. All the portfolios on the line are feasible for the investor to construct. Portfolios to the left of portfolio M represent combinations of risky assets and the risk-free asset. Portfolios to the right of M include purchases of risky assets made with funds borrowed at the risk-free rate. Such a portfolio is called a *leveraged portfolio* because it involves the use of borrowed funds.

Let's compare a portfolio on the CML to a portfolio on the efficient frontier with the same risk. For example, compare portfolio P_A, which is on the efficient frontier, with portfolio P_B, which is on the CML and therefore comprises some combination of the risk-free asset and the efficient portfolio

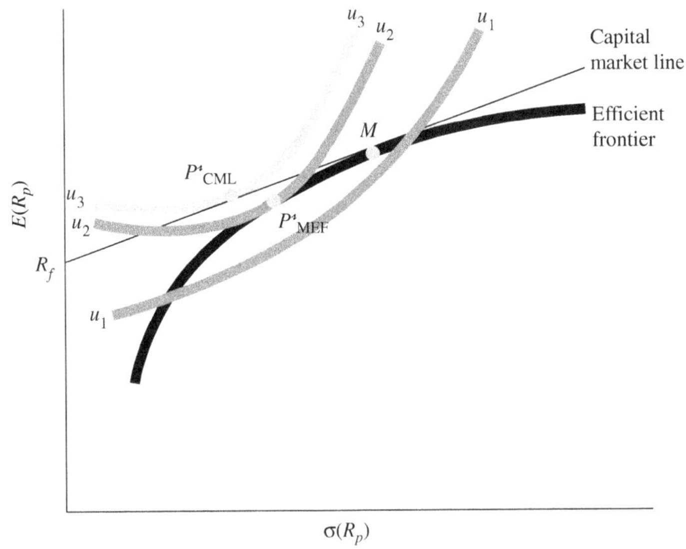

u_1, u_2, u_3 = indifference curves with $u_1 < u_2 < u_3$
M = market portfolio
R_f = risk-free rate
P^*_{CML} = optimal portfolio on capital market line
P^*_{MEF} = optimal portfolio on efficient frontier

FIGURE 2: Optimal Portfolio and the Capital Market Line

M. Notice that for the same risk, the expected return is greater for P_B than for P_A. By Assumption 2, a risk-averse investor will prefer P_B to P_A. That is, P_B will dominate P_A. In fact, this is true for all but one portfolio on the CML: portfolio M, which is on the efficient frontier.

With the introduction of the risk-free asset, we can now say that the portfolio that an investor will select will depend on the investor's risk preference. This can be seen in Figure 2, which is the same as Figure 1 but has the investor's indifference curves included. The investor will select the portfolio on the CML that is tangent to the highest indifference curve, u_3 in the exhibit. Note that without the risk-free asset, an investor could only get to u_2, which is the indifference curve that is tangent to the efficient frontier. Thus, the opportunity to borrow or lend at the risk-free rate results in a capital market where risk-averse investors will prefer to hold portfolios consisting of combinations of the risk-free asset and some portfolio M on the efficient frontier.

The formula for the CML is

$$E(R_p) = R_f + \left[\frac{E(R_M) - R_f}{\sigma(R_M)}\right] \sigma(R_p).$$

Now that we know that portfolio M is pivotal to the CML, we need to know what portfolio M is. That is, how does an investor construct portfolio M? Fama [1970] demonstrated that portfolio M must consist of all assets, and each asset must be held in proportion to its market value relative to the total market value of all assets. That is, portfolio M is the "market portfolio" described earlier. So, rather than referring to the market portfolio, we can simply refer to the "market".

Risk premium in the CML

With homogeneous expectations, $\sigma(R_M)$ and $\sigma(R_p)$ are the market's consensus for the expected return distribution for portfolio M and portfolio p. The risk premium for the CML is

$$\left[\frac{E(R_M) - R_f}{\sigma(R_M)}\right] \sigma(R_p).$$

Let's examine the economic meaning of the risk premium. The numerator of the first term is the expected return from investing in the market beyond the risk-free return. It is a measure of the reward for holding the risky market portfolio rather than the risk-free asset. The denominator is the market risk of the market portfolio. Thus, the first term measures the reward per unit of market risk. Since the CML represents the return offered to compensate for a perceived level of market risk, each point on the CML is a balanced market condition, or equilibrium. The slope of the CML (that is, the first term) determines the additional return needed to compensate for a unit change in market risk. That is why the slope of the CML is also referred to as the *equilibrium market price of risk*.

The CML says that the expected return on a portfolio is equal to the risk-free rate, plus a risk premium equal to the market price of risk (as measured by the reward per unit of market risk), multiplied by the quantity of risk for the portfolio (as measured by the standard deviation of the portfolio). That is,

$$E(R_i) = R_f + (\text{Market price of risk} \times \text{Quantity of risk}),$$

where the market price of risk is the difference between the expected market return and the risk-free rate.

Systematic and non-systematic risk

Now we know that a risk-averse investor who makes decisions based on expected returns and variance (i.e., mean-variance analysis) should construct an efficient portfolio using a combination of the market portfolio and the risk-free rate. The combinations are identified by the CML. Based on this result, an asset pricing model that shows how a risky asset should be priced can be derived. In the process of doing so, we can fine-tune our thinking about the risk associated with an asset. Specifically, we can show that the appropriate risk that investors should be compensated for accepting is not the variance of an asset's return but some other quantity. To do this, let's take a closer look at risk.

We can do this by looking at the variance of the portfolio. It can be demonstrated that the variance of the market portfolio containing N assets is equal to

$$\text{var}(R_p) = w_{1M}\,\text{cov}(R_1, R_M) + w_{2M}\,\text{cov}(R_2, R_M) + \cdots + w_{NM}\,\text{cov}(R_N, R_M)$$

where w_{iM} is equal to the proportion invested in asset i in the market portfolio.

Notice that the portfolio variance does not depend on the variance of the assets comprising the market portfolio, but rather their covariance with the market portfolio. Sharpe [1964] defined the degree to which an asset co-varies with the market portfolio as the asset's *systematic risk*. More specifically, he defined systematic risk as the portion of an asset's variability that can be attributed to a common factor. Systematic risk is the minimum level of risk that can be obtained for a portfolio by means of diversification across a large number of randomly chosen assets. As such, systematic risk is that which results from general market and economic conditions that cannot be diversified away.

Sharpe defined the portion of an asset's variability that can be diversified away as *non-systematic risk*. It is also sometimes called unsystematic risk, idiosyncratic risk, diversifiable risk, unique risk, residual risk, and company-specific risk. This is the risk that is unique to an asset.

Consequently, total risk (as measured by the variance) can be partitioned into systematic risk as measured by the covariance of asset i's return with the market portfolio's return and non-systematic risk. The relevant risk for decision-making purposes is the systematic risk. We will see how to measure systematic risk later.

How diversification reduces non-systematic risk for portfolios is illustrated in Figure 3. The vertical axis shows the standard deviation of the

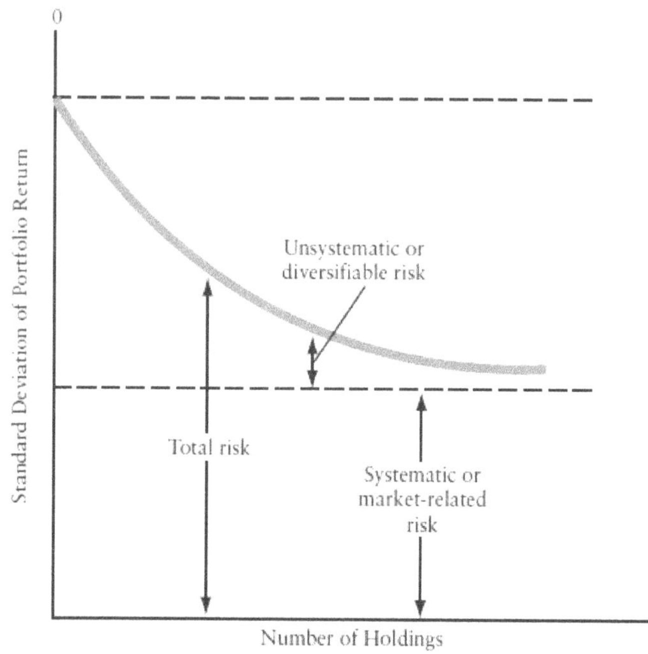

FIGURE 3: Systematic and Unsystematic Portfolio Risk

portfolio return. The standard deviation of the portfolio return represents the total risk for the portfolio (systematic plus non-systematic). The horizontal axis shows the number of holdings of different assets (e.g., the number of common stock held of different issuers). As can be seen, as the number of asset holdings increases, the level of non-systematic risk is almost eliminated (that is, diversified away). Studies of different asset classes support this. For example, for common stock, several studies suggest that a portfolio size of about 20 randomly selected companies will eliminate non-systematic risk leaving only systematic risk.[4]

Security Market Line

The CML represents an equilibrium condition in which the expected return on a portfolio of assets is a linear function of the expected return of the market portfolio. Individual assets do not fall on the CML. Instead,

[4]The first such study to show this is Wagner and Lau [1971].

Sharpe [1964] demonstrated that the following relationship holds for individual assets:

$$E(R_i) = R_f + \beta_i[E(R_M) - R_f], \tag{4}$$

where β_i is a measure of the sensitivity of asset i's return to the market's return and is the ratio of the covariance of the asset i's return with the market return to the standard deviation of asset i's return.

Equation (4) is called the *security market line* (SML). In equilibrium, the expected return of individual assets will lie on the SML and not on the CML. This is true because of the high degree of non-systematic risk for individual assets, which can be diversified out of portfolios with multiple risky assets. In equilibrium, only efficient portfolios will lie on both the CML and the SML.

According to the SML, given the assumptions of the CAPM, the expected return on an individual asset is a positive linear function of its systematic risk as measured by beta. The higher the beta, the higher the expected return. The beta of an asset is estimated using regression analysis using historical data with the return on asset i as the dependent variable and the market return as the independent variable. Going through the process of estimating β_i here is unnecessary. Estimates for this parameter are available from various financial web sites. Table 1 shows beta estimates for several stocks obtained from *Yahoo!Finance*.

An investor pursuing an active strategy will search for underpriced securities, to purchase or retain, and overpriced securities, to sell or avoid (if held

TABLE 1: Beta Estimates from *Yahoo!Finance* (on July 24, 2018)

Company (Ticker Symbol)	**Beta**
Procter & Gamble (PG)	0.39
Verizon Communications Inc. (VZ)	0.67
Kraft Heinz Company (HKC)	0.78
Facebook, Inc. (FB)	0.89
Anheuser-Busch (BUD)	0.96
International Business Machines (IBM)	1.02
3M Company (MMM)	1.07
Apple Inc. (AAPL)	1.14
Southwest Airlines Co. (LUV)	1.15
Microsoft Corporation (MSFT)	1.24
Alphabet Inc. (GOOG)	1.30
ConocoPhillips (COP)	1.32

in the current portfolio or sold short if permitted). If an investor believes that the CAPM is the correct asset pricing model, then the SML can be used to identify mispriced securities. A security is perceived to be underpriced (i.e., undervalued) if the "expected" return projected by the investor is greater than the "required" return indicated by the SML. A security is perceived to be overpriced (i.e., overvalued), if the "expected" return projected by the investor is less than the "required" return indicated by the SML.

Major Findings of Tests of the CAPM

Now that's the theory. The question is whether the theory is supported by empirical evidence. There have been hundreds of academic papers written on the subject. (Almost all studies use common stock to test the theory.) These papers cover not only the empirical evidence but also the difficulties of testing the theory.[5]

Let's start with the empirical evidence. There are four major findings and these have important implications for formulating investment strategies. They are:

Major finding 1: *The market portfolio outperforms cash.* Over long periods of time (usually 20–30 years), the return on the market portfolio is greater than the risk-free rate.

Major finding 2: *There is a positive relationship between beta and return.* Studies using common stock have consistently found that the larger the beta, the higher the return. That is, high-beta stocks have offered higher returns than low-beta stocks. This finding indicates that the market is compensating investors for taking on systematic risk.

Major finding 3: *Low beta assets offer a better return per unit of risk than predicted by the CAPM.* Although a positive relationship has been reported in all studies, the slope of the estimated relationship between return and beta has been found to be flatter than what the CAPM would predict. As a result, low-beta stocks offer higher returns than

[5]An important paper challenging the validity of these empirical tests of the CAPM is by Roll [1977]. He demonstrates that the CAPM is not testable until the exact composition of the "true" market portfolio is known, and the only valid test of the CAPM is to observe whether the ex ante true market portfolio is mean-variance efficient. As a result of his findings, Roll states that he does not believe there ever will be an unambiguous test of the CAPM.

the CAPM predicts and high-beta stocks offer lower returns than the CAPM predicts.

Major finding 4: *There are other risk factors that the market compensates investors for accepting beyond beta.* The CAPM asserts that the only risk factor that the market rewards investors for accepting is systematic risk and that systematic risk is market risk. Beta is a measure of systematic risk. However, studies have consistently reported that there are other systematic risk factors that the market rewards investors for accepting.

At one time, the CAPM was viewed as the only asset pricing model that academics recommended should be used in constructing portfolios and should be the core of investment strategies. Any study that reported the market was consistently rewarding a risk factor other than market risk was referred to as a "market anomaly". For example, numerous studies reported that the market was compensating investors based on the size of a firm (i.e., market capitalization) and was labeled the "size anomaly". Today, it is recognized that the CAPM does not offer a complete description of all the systematic risks the market compensates investors for accepting. This has led to the search for other systematic or common factors that consistently provide compensation to investors and has led to what is called *factor investing*, which we will describe in Chapter 13. At the end of this chapter, we will describe some of the common factors that have become well established in investment management.

As for the third major finding, we discuss it next because of its implications for investment strategies that we describe in later chapters.

Low-volatility assets versus high-volatility assets

The preponderance of evidence of historical stock returns indicates that low-beta stocks have provided higher returns than predicted by the CAPM, and high-beta stocks have provided lower returns than predicted by the CAPM. This means that low-beta stocks have provided a higher reward per unit of risk than high-beta stocks. This finding is consistent with empirical studies that utilize other measures of risk, the most common measure being some measure of volatility. That is, low-volatility stocks have provided a better reward per unit of risk than high-volatility stocks. When volatility has been used as a measure of risk, this finding has been reported for other asset classes and within asset classes. With respect to asset classes, this means that low-risk asset classes offer a superior return per unit of risk than high-risk asset classes.

This finding is referred to as the *low-volatility anomaly.* It is a key finding that proponents of an asset allocation strategy — the risk parity strategy, described in Chapter 19 — rely upon. There are two reasons that have been offered as an explanation for the low-volatility anomaly.

The first reason is based on the questionable assumption in the CAPM that financial markets are frictionless. If financial markets were indeed frictionless, then there are strategies that would bring the risk-return relationship in line so that no stock or no asset class would offer a superior return per unit of risk. The mechanisms available to market participants to bring the risk/return relationship for all assets and all asset classes in line are short selling and leveraging. There are costs and risks associated with these two mechanisms that make investors reluctant to use them. Consider the impact of the aversion to leveraging on the pricing of high-risk assets and low-risk assets resulting from the demand for these assets. For the pricing of low-risk assets, the reluctance of market participants to leverage low-risk assets reduces their demand. This results in low-risk assets being undervalued and therefore offering a high return relative to risk. One might label low-risk assets in this case as a "neglected asset class". For high-risk assets, market participants in seeking to increase expected return to meet a target return, create increased demand for high-risk assets and therefore causing them to be overvalued. As a result, high-risk assets offer a lower return relative to risk than low-risk assets.

The second reason given to explain the low-volatility anomaly is that some investors prefer lottery-type investments. Since high-risk assets offer a lottery-type payoff, the demand for such assets reduces their return per unit of risk compared to low-risk assets.

CAPM Extensions

There have been several extensions of the CAPM. These extensions include the Consumption CAPM, the Intertemporal CAPM, and the zero-beta CAPM. We describe each one briefly in what follows.

Instead of using a market beta in the CAPM, the *Consumption CAPM* (CCAPM) uses a "consumption beta" in the pricing model. The model was proposed by Lucas [1978] and Breeden [1979]. The consumption beta is based on consumption risk, not market risk. Unlike the CAPM which asserts that the only source of risk is the economy (as measured by the market) but has no underlying theory that provides an explanation for why the market portfolio is risky, the CCAPM is grounded in macroeconomic theory. For example, we know that there is a relationship between overall economic activity and government policy (monetary and fiscal), and the profits generated by firms. Thus, the more appropriate source of risk is not the market, but consumption/savings decisions of households.

The CAPM assumes that the only source of risk that an investor is concerned with is uncertainty about the future price of a security. Investors, however, usually are concerned with other risks that will affect their ability to consume goods and services in the future. Three examples would be the risks associated with future labor income, the future relative prices of consumer goods, and future investment opportunities. Recognizing these other risks that investors face, Merton [1973] extended the CAPM to describe how consumers make their optimal lifetime consumption decisions when they face these "extra-market" sources of risk. His model, referred to as the *Intertemporal CAPM* (ICAPM), assumes more realistic behavior by investors in making investment decisions than the CAPM by seeking to protect their investments in the face of the uncertainty. More specifically, Merton assumes more realistic behavior in making investment decisions by investors than the CAPM because they seek to protect their investments in the face of uncertainty. The term "intertemporal" is used in labeling this model because it recognizes that investors do not make decisions based on investing for one time period but make decisions over multiple time periods and, as a result, formulate a strategy that is revised as market conditions change over time.

The CAPM assumes that there is a risk-free rate. Black [1972] showed how the CAPM can be modified in the absence of a risk-free rate in the financial market. His model is referred to as the *zero-beta CAPM* or the *Black CAPM*. In the absence of a risk-free asset, investors instead use a zero-beta portfolio which is a portfolio of risky assets that has zero covariance with the market portfolio.

Arbitrage Pricing Theory Model

An asset pricing model based purely on arbitrage arguments was derived by Stephen Ross [1976]. This theory, referred to as the *arbitrage pricing theory* (APT), postulates that an asset's expected return is influenced by a variety of risk factors, as opposed to solely market risk as suggested by the CAPM. The APT model states that the return on a security is linearly related to H systematic risk factors. However, the APT model does not specify what these risk factors are, but it is assumed that the relationship between asset returns and the risk factors is linear. Moreover, unsystematic risk can be eliminated so that an investor is only compensated for accepting the systematic risk factors.

The APT model asserts that the return on asset i is given by the following relationship:

$$E(R_i) = R_f + \beta_{i,F1}[E(R_{F1}) - R_f] + \beta_{i,F2}[E(R_{F2}) - R_f] + \cdots + \beta_{i,FH}[E(R_{FH}) - R_f], \quad (5)$$

where $E(Ri)$ is the expected return on asset i, R_f is the risk-free rate, F_h is the hth factor that is common to the returns of all assets ($h = 1, \ldots, H$), $\beta_{i,h}$ is the sensitivity of the ith asset to the hth factor. $[E(R_{F_j}) - R_f]$ is the excess return of the jth systematic risk factor over the risk-free rate, and can be thought of as the price (or risk premium) for the jth systematic risk factor.

The APT model as given by Equation (5) asserts that investors want to be compensated for all the risk factors that systematically affect an asset's return. The compensation is the sum of the products of each risk factor's systematic risk ($\beta_{i,FH}$), and the risk premium assigned to it by the market $[E(R_{Fh}) - R_f]$. As in the case of the CAPM, an investor is not compensated for accepting unsystematic risk.

It turns out that the CAPM is a special case of the APT model obtained without the highly restrictive assumptions made to derive the CAPM. If the only risk factor in the APT model as given by Equation (5) is market risk, the APT model reduces to the CAPM. Now contrast the APT model with the CAPM as given by Equation (3). They look similar. Both say that investors are compensated for accepting all systematic risk and no non-systematic risk. The CAPM states that systematic risk is market risk, while the APT model does not specify the systematic risks.

Supporters of the APT model argue that it has several major advantages over the CAPM. First, it has less restrictive assumptions about investor preferences toward risk and return. As explained earlier, the CAPM theory assumes investors trade off between risk and return solely based on the expected returns and standard deviations of prospective investments. The APT model, in contrast, simply requires that some rather unobtrusive bounds be placed on potential investor utility functions. Second, no assumptions are made about the distribution of asset returns. Finally, since the APT model does not rely on the identification of the true market portfolio, the theory is potentially testable.

Multifactor Models in Practice

The APT model provides theoretical support for an asset pricing model where there is more than one risk factor. Consequently, models of this type are referred to as *multifactor models*. These models provide asset managers with the tools for quantifying the risk profile of a portfolio relative to a benchmark, for constructing a portfolio relative to a benchmark, and controlling risk. Below we provide a brief review of the three types of multifactor risk models: fundamental factor models, macroeconomic factor models, and statistical factor models [Connor, 1995].

Fundamental factor models

There is no shortage of candidates for systematic factors using information about the fundamentals of a company and its industry. Here, we provide a brief description of some well-known systematic factors that have been found to consistently reward investors for accepting the associated risk. In addition to the market factor, there are five other factors, described in what follows: size factor, value factor, profitability factor, investment factor, and momentum factor. The first four factors are referred to as fundamental factors. The size factor and value factor, along with the market factor, make up the well-known Fama–French three factor model introduced by Eugene Fama and Kenneth French [1993]. Carhart [1997] presented a model that added a momentum factor to the three-factor Fama–French model and is referred to as the Fama–French–Carhart model. More recently, Fama and French [2015] added a profitability factor and an investment factor to the three-factor Fama–French factor model, to create what is now referred to as the Fama–French five-factor model.

- *Size factor*: Banz [1981] found that small company stocks (i.e., companies with small market capitalization) outperform large company stocks on a risk-adjusted basis. This empirical observation became known as the "size effect". Small firms are said to be riskier for two reasons. First, stocks of smaller companies tend to be less liquid than the stocks of larger companies. This could be attributable to the fact that small cap firms make up less of the market or that there tends to be less investor demand because the stock of smaller companies are not as well-known as the stock of larger companies (i.e., neglected by market analysts giving rise to the "neglected firm effect"). The second reason offered is that smaller stocks are more sensitive to market movements. If the company has a lower price per share and experiences an increase in demand, the price appreciation will be greater than that for the stock of a larger company. Size was incorporated into the original three-factor Fama–French model.

- *Value factor*: Value investing has been one of the longest-lasting stock selection techniques in investment management. The concept of value investing goes back to the pioneering work of Graham and Dodd [1934]. The idea behind value investing is that investors should buy stocks that are undervalued compared to their fundamental values and therefore the value factor is a fundamental factor.

  To identify stocks that are underpriced, value investors use certain financial measures that compare the stock's price to certain firm-specific variables that provide a good indicator of a stock's future performance. There are a few key financial ratios that value investors will analyze in order to determine whether the stock is underpriced, such as the price-to-earnings ratio and price-to-book ratios. For example, Graham and Dodd provide a few guidelines for selecting stocks of companies that are likely to outperform the market: (1) companies with low price-to-book ratios, (2) companies with low price-to-earnings ratios, and (3) companies that have low debt.

  Companies that exhibit these features are known as *value stocks* because they are underpriced compared to their fundamental values. Conversely, stocks that are priced high compared to their fundamental value are called *growth stocks* because the high price indicates that investors expect the firm to grow in the future. Essentially, value investing is the idea that if two stocks have the same fundamental indicators (i.e., earnings, book value, and leverage), the stock with the lower price is expected to outperform the stock with the higher price.

  Although Graham and Dodd offer general guidelines for stock selection, the financial literature has focused on how these variables that reflect a stock's value affect a stock's expected return. The empirical literature has mainly focused on three ratios that indicate value: earnings-to-price (EP), book-to-market (BM), and debt-to-equity ratios (DER).

  Basu [1977] studied the relationship between EP ratios and expected returns. In this study Basu found a significant and positive relationship between expected returns and EP. This means that as earnings increase relative to its stock price, the stock is expected to have a higher return. Ball [1978], however, explains that EP seems to be a "catch-all" factor because it reflects market risks that are already explained by the market and size factors. Thus, the EP ratio may be too general for a sufficient asset-pricing model that is looking to isolate the effects of the value factor.

Two studies have tested how well BM ratios have impacted a stock's expected returns. BM is the ratio of the firm's book value[6] to the firm's market capitalization. Rosenberg, Reid, and Lanstein [1985] found an inverse relationship between BM and expected returns, which reflects the second guideline provided by Graham and Dodd [1934].

Bhandari [1988] proposed using a firm's debt-to-equity ratio (DER) as a measure of risk. The DER is a variable used to indicate a firm's leverage. While this does not directly relate to the concept of value investing, using DER provides a relative risk measure by measuring debt in terms of a percentage of market value. Bhandari finds that when DER is included with the market risk factor, it proves to be a significant indicator of stock returns. Although it is not surprising that there is a negative relationship between DER and expected returns, it does suggest that a firm's leverage is an additional source of risk even after accounting for the market factor.

- *Profitability factor*: A study by Novy-Marx [2012] found that strategies based on gross profitability performed well in explaining average returns. Novy-Marx measured gross profitability by using the ratio of a firm's gross profits to its assets. (Gross profits are calculated by reducing a company's revenue by its cost of goods sold.) He argues that using gross profits-to-assets compliments the value factor because it identifies the profitable stocks that are also priced at a discount (i.e., value stocks). Thus, it tends to act as a form of quality control when buying stocks that are considered to be cheap. Novy-Marx reported gross profits-to-assets has a significant and positive relationship with average stock returns.
- *Investment factor*: This factor was identified by Fama and French [2015]. They found an inverse relationship between a firm's capital investment and average returns. The idea behind what they refer to as the *investment factor* is that, on average, when a firm increases investment expenditures, the future return generated on investment tends to be less than the present value of the investment expenditure. Essentially, this means that investments tend to produce less value than the cost of the project or

[6]It is calculated as book assets minus liabilities, preferred shares, and intangible assets. For a review of financial accounting concepts, see Chapter 2 in the companion volume.

investment itself. Thus, when the level of investment increases, the stock price tends to decline. Conservative stocks tend to be stocks of companies that have little investment over the past time period, whereas aggressive stocks are considered to be stocks of companies that have increased their investment expenditure in the last period.

- *Momentum factor*: The notion of a stock price momentum impacting its return was originally discovered by Jegadeesh and Titman [1993]. They found that investors could achieve higher returns by buying stocks that have appreciated in the past 6 months and selling stocks that have depreciated in the past 6 months. Because prices tend to persistently go up or down, this factor is referred to as the *momentum factor* and is a non-fundamental factor. The intuition behind the momentum factor is that investors are slow to react to new information causing the price changes to occur over time. For example, if some investors react to positive information right away, the price will receive an initial increase. As more investors react to this information, the price will continue to appreciate until the full price change takes effect.

While we have provided a general description of the well-known factors, we hold off until Chapter 13 to describe how these factors are included in their respective factor model. For example, in the Fama–French model, the size factor is not just tossed in as market capitalization. Rather, the size factor in the model is measured as the difference between the return on portfolios created from small capitalization stocks and the portfolios created from large capitalization stocks. This is because small capitalization stocks are expected to outperform large capitalization stocks. Fama and French denote the size factor by Small Minus Big (SMB). How the model is implemented is described in Chapter 13.

Macroeconomic factor models

In a *macroeconomic factor model*, the factors used are observable macroeconomic variables. These variables can be classified into four groups[7]: (1) general economic condition and business cycle factors (e.g., gross domestic product, employment, industrial production), (2) financial market-related factors (e.g. US yield curve, corporate bond spreads, stock market index, key commodity indexes), (3) monetary policy-related factors

[7]This classification is provided by Tangjitprom (2012).

(e.g., key money market rates, inflation rate), and (4) internationally related factors (i.e., foreign-exchange rate).

The first macroeconomic factor model was pioneered by Chen, Roll, and Ross [1986] who reported that the following macroeconomic variables were statistically significant in explaining stock returns: industrial production, changes in the risk premium, and changes in the shape of the US Treasury yield curve. Other macroeconomic variables that were found to be less strongly related in explaining stock returns were unanticipated inflation and changes in expected inflation.

Models that use financial-market related factors are described in Chapter 15 in the companion book where we describe factor models for managing bond portfolios.

Statistical factor models

In a *statistical factor model*, historical and cross-sectional data on stock returns are tossed into a statistical model. The goal of the statistical model is to best explain the observed stock returns with "factors" that are linear return combinations and uncorrelated with each other. For example, suppose that monthly returns for 5,000 companies for 10 years are computed. The goal of the statistical analysis is to produce "factors" that best explain the variance of the observed stock returns. For example, suppose that there are six "factors" that do this. These "factors" are statistical artifacts and referred to as "latent factors". The objective in a statistical factor model then becomes to determine the economic meaning of each of these statistically derived factors. Because of the problem of interpretation, it is difficult to use the factors from a statistical factor model for valuation, portfolio construction, and risk control. Instead, practitioners prefer the previous two models, which allow an asset manager to pre-specify meaningful observable factors, and thus produce a more intuitive model.

Key Points

- Asset pricing models describe the relationship between risk and expected return.
- The two most well-known pricing models are the capital asset pricing model (CAPM) which is an equilibrium model and the arbitrage pricing theory (APT) model which is based purely on arbitrage arguments.

- In well-functioning capital markets, an investor should be rewarded for accepting the various risks associated with investing in an asset.
- An asset pricing model asserts that the expected return is a function of risk factors.
- An asset pricing model requires the identification of the risk factors that drive asset returns and the determination of the specific relationship between expected return and the risk factors.
- The minimum expected return is the risk-free rate, which is proxied by securities issued by the US government.
- By investing in an asset other than a risk-free asset, investors will demand a premium over the risk-free rate and this risk premium depends on the risk factors associated with investing in the asset.
- Risk factors can be divided into two general categories: systematic risk factors and unsystematic risk factors.
- Systematic risk factors (also referred to as non-diversifiable risk factors) are factors common to all assets and cannot be eliminated through diversification.
- Unsystematic risk factors or diversifiable risk factors can be eliminated via diversification.
- In a well-functioning market, investors should only be compensated for accepting systematic risks.
- The CAPM, the first asset pricing model derived from economic theory, formalizes the relationship that should exist between asset returns and risk if investors behave in a hypothesized manner.
- The CAPM builds on a theory of portfolio selection known as mean-variance analysis.
- The only systematic risk factor according to the CAPM, the risk of the overall movement of the market, is referred to as market risk; in the CAPM, the terms "market risk" and "systematic risk" are used interchangeably.
- Market risk is the risk associated with holding a portfolio consisting of all assets, called the market portfolio.
- According to the CAPM, the risk premium is a product of the quantity of market risk (as measured by beta) and the potential compensation for taking on market risk (as measured by the difference between the expected market return and the risk-free rate).
- Six assumptions are made in the CAPM to make the theory more tractable from a mathematical standpoint.

- The first four assumptions of the CAPM deal with the way investors make decisions: (1) investors construct portfolios using mean-variance analysis, (2) investors are risk averse, (3) investors make investment decisions over some single-period investment horizon, and (4) all investors have the same expectations about future returns and the variance of future returns.
- Two assumptions of the CAPM relate to characteristics of the capital market: (1) there exists in the capital market a risk-free asset and unlimited borrowing and lending at the risk-free rate and (2) the capital market is perfectly competitive and frictionless.
- When investors decide how to construct a portfolio, the inclusion of assets is based on the expected return and variance of asset returns that are candidates for inclusion in the portfolio.
- An efficient portfolio is one that gives the maximum expected return for a given level of risk.
- Since there is an efficient portfolio for every level of risk, there is a set of efficient portfolios, which on a graph is referred to as the efficient frontier.
- Every point on the efficient frontier is the maximum expected portfolio return for a given level of risk.
- In creating an efficient frontier using mean-variance, there is no consideration of a risk-free asset.
- In a capital market with a risk-free rate, the efficient frontier changes, allowing for the construction of portfolios that for a given level of risk provide a higher expected return than on the efficient frontier.
- The capital market line shows all portfolios that an investor can construct by combining the market portfolio with borrowing and lending at the risk-free rate.
- Portfolios that include purchases of risky assets made with funds borrowed at the risk-free rate are referred to as leveraged portfolios.
- The slope of the capital market line is referred to as the equilibrium market price of risk.
- The capital market line says that the expected return on a portfolio is equal to the risk-free rate, plus a risk premium equal to the market price of risk (as measured by the reward per unit of market risk), multiplied by the quantity of risk for the portfolio (as measured by the standard deviation of the portfolio).
- An asset's beta is a measure of the sensitivity of asset i's return to the market's return and is the ratio of the covariance of asset i's return with the market return to the standard deviation of asset i's return.

- While the capital market line represents an equilibrium condition in which the expected return on a portfolio of assets is a linear function of the expected return of the market portfolio, individual assets do not fall on the capital market line.
- In equilibrium, the expected return of individual assets will lie on the security market line and not on the capital market line because of the high degree of non-systematic risk that remains in individual assets that can be diversified out of portfolios.
- According to the security market line, given the assumptions of the CAPM, the expected return on an individual asset is a positive linear function of its systematic risk as measured by beta.
- The four major findings of empirical tests of the CAPM are (1) the market portfolio outperforms cash, (2) there is a positive relationship between beta and return, (3) low beta assets offer a better return per unit of risk than predicted by the CAPM, and (4) there are other risk factors that the market compensates investors for accepting risk that is beyond beta.
- There have been several extensions of the CAPM, including the Consumption CAPM, the Intertemporal CAPM, and the zero-beta CAPM.
- The fact that there are factors that drive returns in addition to the market risk factor has led to the investment strategy known as factor investing.
- The preponderance of evidence of historical stock returns indicates that low-beta stocks have provided higher returns than predicted by the CAPM and high-beta stocks have provided lower returns than predicted by the CAPM.
- The empirically calculated slope of the CAPM indicates that low-beta stocks have provided a higher reward per unit of risk than high-beta stocks.
- When stock price volatility is used as a measure of risk, the finding is consistent with what is reported for the CAPM that uses beta as a risk measure: low-volatility stocks have provided a better reward per unit of risk than high-volatility stocks; this observation is referred to as the low-volatility anomaly.
- Two explanations have been offered to explain the low-volatility anomaly: (1) markets are not frictionless, investors are reluctant to sell short or use leverage and (2) investors have a preference for risky assets that offer lottery-type payoffs.
- The arbitrage pricing theory (APT) postulates that an asset's expected return is influenced by a variety of risk factors, as opposed to solely market risk as suggested by the CAPM.

- The APT model states that the return on a security is linearly related to several systematic risk factors but does not specify these risk factors, only that the relationship between asset returns and the risk factors is linear.
- The APT model asserts that investors want to be compensated for all the risk factors that systematically affect an asset's return with the compensation being the sum of the products of each risk factor's systematic risk and the risk premium assigned to it by the market.
- As in the case of the CAPM, an investor is not compensated for accepting unsystematic risk.
- The APT model provides theoretical support for an asset pricing model where there is more than one risk factor, referred to as a multifactor model.
- Multifactor models provide asset managers with the tools for quantifying the risk profile of a portfolio relative to a benchmark, for constructing a portfolio relative to a benchmark, and controlling risk.
- There are three types of multifactor risk models: fundamental factor models, macroeconomic factor models, and statistical factor models.
- Fundamental factor models derive factors using the fundamentals of a company and its industry.
- In addition to the market factor, there are four fundamental factors that have been found to explain stock returns: size factor, value factor, profitability factor, and investment factor.
- A commonly used non-fundamental factor is the momentum factor.
- The three-factor Fama–French model includes the market factor, size factor, and value factor.
- The five-factor Fama–French model includes the three factors plus the profitability factor and the investment factor.
- The Fama–French–Carhart model includes the three factors in the three-factor Fama–French factor model plus the momentum factor.
- In a macroeconomic factor model, the factors used are observable macroeconomic variables.
- The variables in a macroeconomic factor model include one or more of the following (1) general economic condition and business cycle factors, (2) financial market-related factors, (3) monetary policy-related factors, and (4) internationally related factors.
- In a statistical factor model, historical and cross-sectional data on stock returns are used in a statistical model to determine "factors" that best explain the variance of the observed stock returns.

- In a statistical factor model, the "factors" derived from the analysis (referred to as "latent factors") must be interpreted and this is a major limitation of the use of a statistical factor model for valuation, portfolio construction, and risk control.

References

Ball, R., 1978. "Anomalies in relationships between securities' yields and yield surrogates," *Journal of Financial Economics*, 3: 103–126.

Banz, R. W., 1981. "The relationship between return and market value of common stocks," *Journal of Financial Economics*, 9(1): 3–18.

Basu, S., 1977. "Investment performance of common stocks in relation to their price-earnings ratios: A test of the efficient market hypothesis," *Journal of Finance*, 32(3): 663–682.

Bhandari, L. C., 1988. "Debt/equity ratio and expected common stock returns: Empirical evidence," *Journal of Finance*, 43(2): 507–528.

Black, F., 1972. "Capital market equilibrium with restricted borrowing," *Journal of Business*, 45(3): 444–454.

Breeden, D. T., 1979. "An intertemporal asset pricing model with stochastic consumption and investment opportunities," *Journal of Financial Economics*, 7: 265–296.

Carhart, M. M., 1997. "On persistence in mutual fund performance." *Journal of Finance*, 52(1): 57–82.

Chen, N-F, R. R. Roll, and S. A. Ross, 1986. "Economic forces and the stock market," *Journal of Business*, 59(3): 383–403.

Connor, G. 1995. "The three types of factor models: A comparison of their explanatory power," *Financial Analysts Journal*, 51(3): 42–46.

Fama, E. F., 1970. "Efficient capital markets: A review of empirical work." *Journal of Finance*, 25(2): 383–417.

Fama, E. F. and K. French, 1993. "Common risk factors in the returns on stocks and bonds," *Journal of Financial Economics*, 33(1): 3–56.

Fama, E. and K. French, 2015. "A five-factor asset pricing model," *Journal of Financial Economics*, 116(1): 1–22.

Graham, B. and D. L. Dodd, 1934. *Security Analysis*. New York: McGraw-Hill.

Jegadeesh, N., and S. Titman, 1993. "Returns to buying winners and selling losers: Implications for stock market efficiency," *Journal of Finance*, 48(1): 65–91.

Lintner, J., 1965. "The valuation of risk assets and the selection of risky investments in stock portfolio and capital budgets," *Review of Economics and Statistics*, 47(1): 13–37.

Lucas, R. E., 1978. "Asset prices in an exchange economy," *Econometrica*, 46(6): 1429–1445.

Merton, R. C., 1973. "An intertemporal capital asset pricing model," *Econometrica*, 41(5): 867–887.

Mossin, J., 1966. "Equilibrium in a capital asset market," *Econometrica*, 34: 768–783.

Novy-Marx, R., 2012. "The other side of value: The gross profitability premium," *Journal of Financial Economics*, 108(1): 1–28.

Roll, R., 1977. "A critique of the asset pricing theory's tests," *Journal of Financial Economics*, 4: 129–176.

Rosenberg, B., K. Reid, and R. Lanstein, 1985. "Persuasive evidence of market inefficiency," *Journal of Portfolio Management*, 11(3): 9–16.

Ross, S. A., 1976. "The arbitrage theory of capital asset pricing," *Journal of Economic Theory*, 13: 343–362.

Sharpe, W. F., 1964. "Capital asset prices: A theory of market equilibrium under conditions of risk," *Journal of Finance*, 19(3): 425–442.

Tangjitprom, N., 2012. "Macroeconomic factors of emerging stock market: The evidence from Thailand," *International Journal of Financial Research*, 3(2): 105–114.

Treynor, J. L. , 1961. "Toward a theory of market value of risky assets," Unpublished paper, Arthur D. Little, Cambridge, MA.

Wagner, W. H., and S. Lau, 1971. "The effect of diversification on risks," *Financial Analysts Journal*, 27(3): 48–53.

PART IV
Equity Analysis and Portfolio Management

Chapter 10

Company Equity Analysis*

Learning Objectives

After reading this chapter, you will understand:

- industry analysis and Porter's competitive forces model;
- the difficulties of identifying the industry in which a company operates;
- how the operating performance of a company should be analyzed;
- what is financial ratio analysis;
- how an analyst can use financial ratios to evaluate four aspects of operating performance and financial condition: profitability ratios, asset management ratios, liquidity ratios, and debt management ratios;
- the two types of profitability ratios: return on investment ratios and margin ratios;
- the asset management ratios used to evaluate the benefits produced by specific assets: inventory turnover ratio, accounts receivable turnover ratio, fixed asset turnover ratio, and total asset turnover ratio;
- how liquidity ratios look at the ability of a company to meet its short-term obligations using those assets that are most readily converted into cash and include the current ratio, quick ratio, and the net working capital to sales ratio;
- why debt management ratios indicate how a company is financed and its ability to meet its debt obligations and the two types of financial leverage ratios (component percentages and coverage ratios);
- what common-size analysis is and how it is used in company analysis;
- how the DuPont system is used in explaining company performance;

*Parts of this chapter draw from Frank Fabozzi's writings with Pamela Peterson Drake of James Madison University.

- what cash flow analysis is, its usefulness in company analysis, and the difficulties in measuring a company's cash flow;
- what free cash flow is; and
- other frameworks that are used for assessing the economic merits of a company: Value Chain Analysis, RBV Analysis, and SWOT Analysis.

Company analysis involves the selection, evaluation, and interpretation of economic and financial data and other pertinent information to assist in evaluating the operating performance and financial condition of a company. The information that is available for analysis includes economic, market, and financial information. For publicly traded companies, much of the most important financial data are provided by the company in its annual and quarterly financial statements.

The operating performance of a company is a measure of how well a company has used its resources to produce a return on its investment. The financial condition of a company is a measure of its ability to satisfy its obligations, such as the payment of interest on its debt, in a timely manner. An investor has many tools available in the analysis of financial information. These tools include financial ratio analysis and cash flow analysis.

Cash flows provide a way of transforming net income based on the accrual system of accounting as set forth under the generally accepted accounting principles (GAAP) to a more comparable basis. Additionally, cash flows are essential ingredients in valuation: The value of a company today is the present value of its expected future cash flows — an analytical model that we explain in the next chapter. Therefore, understanding past and current cash flows may help in forecasting future cash flows and, hence, determine the value of the company. Moreover, understanding cash flow allows one to assess a company's ability to maintain current dividends and its current capital expenditure policy without relying on external financing.

In this chapter, we describe and illustrate the basic tools of financial analysis: financial ratio analysis and cash flow analysis. Additional tools for company analysis — Value Chain Analysis, RBV Analysis, and SWOT Analysis — are also described. The discussion in this chapter assumes knowledge of the basics of financial accounting. A review of financial accounting is provided in Chapter 2 in the companion volume to this book.

Industry Analysis

A security analyst does not assess the investment merits of a company in isolation. The analyst must understand the competitive environment in which the company operates and the economic prospects for the industry. Assumptions about the company's growth, the market, and market share must be consistent with the economic projection of the industry. For this reason, the first step in evaluating the investment merits of a company is to analyze the industry in which the company operates. In large portfolio management teams, there is a dedicated individual or group responsible for an industry.

It is critical when analyzing a company, that it is classified in the correct industry. In all industries there are subindustries and the analyst must be sure which subindustry or subindustries the company operates in. For example, consider the pharmaceutical industry. One of the sectors within this industry is manufacturing of end products. In turn, there are three subsectors within the pharmaceutical end products industry: prescription drugs, over-the-counter drugs, and vaccines. Prescription drugs are based on chemical compounds. They are prescribed by physicians or administered by authorized healthcare professionals. Like prescription drugs, over-the-counter drugs are based on chemical compounds. However, unlike prescription drugs, they are freely sold without the need for a prescription. The third subindustry involves vaccines that are based on bacteria and viruses and firms in this subindustry must obtain approval by the US Federal Food and Drug Administration (FDA).

Even within the two drug subindustries, there is a distinction between brand drugs and generic drugs. A brand drug is the one that was developed by the company that obtained the patent for the drug and obtained the initial approval by the FDA. The patent obtained by the original maker of the drug grants the company the exclusive right to sell the drug for a limited time. Generic drugs are those that are copied from the brand drug after the patent expires. A generic drug according to the FDA must have identical active ingredients, dosage form, strength, and same method of administering. Moreover, like brand drugs, generic drugs must be approved by the FDA using identical standards as for brand drugs.

One of the problems in industry analysis is that the products of many companies cut across several industries. For example, consider once again the pharmaceutical end-user industry. There are companies that make brand drugs that have divisions that manufacture generic drugs.

Once the industry is identified, the analyst must perform an economic analysis of the industry. This includes analysis of the historical growth of the industry and projections about the industry's future growth over specified time periods such as the next 5, 10, 15, and 20 years. A description of the regulatory environment should be included and any developments

TABLE 1: Porter's Five Forces

Threat of new entrants: economies of scale; product differentiation; brand identity/loyalty; access to distribution channels; capital requirements; access to latest technology; access to necessary inputs; absolute cost advantages; experience and learning effects; government policies; switching costs; expected retaliation from existing players.

Bargaining power of suppliers: number of suppliers; size of suppliers; supplier concentration; availability of substitutes for the supplier's products; uniqueness of supplier's products or services (differentiation); switching cost for supplier's products; supplier's threat of forward integration; industry threat of backward integration; supplier's contribution to quality or service of the industry products; importance of volume to supplier; total industry cost contributed by suppliers; importance of the industry to supplier's profit.

Bargaining power of buyers: buyer volume (number of customers); size of each buyer's order; buyer concentration; buyer's ability to substitute; buyer's switching costs; buyer's information availability; buyer's threat of backward integration; industry threat of forward integration; price sensitivity.

Threat of substitute products or services: number of substitute products available; buyer's propensity to substitute; relative price performance of substitutes; perceived level of product differentiation; switching costs; substitute producer's profitability and aggressiveness.

Rivalry among existing competitors: number of competitors; diversity of competitors; industry concentration and balance; industry growth; industry life cycle; quality differences; product differentiation; brand identity/loyalty; switching costs; intermittent overcapacity; informational complexity; barriers to exit.

that can adversely impact the outlook for the industry. The analysis should also include the strategies that companies in the industry are employing to facilitate growth. For example, the speed and complexity of product development in the technology industry continues to increase. To deal with this, companies in that industry have found it necessary to develop partnerships to keep pace with consumer and business demands. In the healthcare industry, manufacturers of imaging and monitoring equipment are teaming up with major hospital systems to create networks that assist in diagnosis by allowing medical experts to work with local hospitals and clinics.

Michael Porter [1980] developed a framework for industry analysis. His model can be described as a *competitive forces model*. The five forces that should be investigated are: (1) threat of new entrants, (2) bargaining power of suppliers, (3) bargaining power of buyers, (4) threats of substitute products, and (5) rivalry of existing competitors. Table 1 shows Porter's five forces.

PESTEL Analysis is another commonly used framework to assess and monitor the macro-economic factors that are believed to have a major impact on a company's performance. It is often used together with Porter's Five Forces to identify the internal and external forces that impact the competitive environment in which a company operates. Each letter in the acronym denotes specific factors looked at in the analysis: *p*olitical, *e*conomic, *s*ocial, *t*echnological, *e*nvironmental, and *l*egal. Recently, other factors have been added to the analysis. These factors include demographics, ethical, ecological, and intercultural.

Financial Ratio Analysis

In financial ratio analysis, we select the relevant information — primarily the financial statement data — and evaluate it. We show how to incorporate market data and economic data in the analysis of financial ratios. Finally, we show how to interpret financial ratios, identifying the pitfalls that occur when it's not done properly.

Ratios and Their Classification

A *financial ratio* is a comparison between one bit of financial information and another. Consider the ratio of current assets to current liabilities, which is referred to as the *current ratio*. This ratio, that we discuss in what follows, is a comparison between assets that can be readily turned into cash — current assets — and the obligations that are due in the near future — current liabilities.

Ratios can be classified according to the way they are constructed and the financial characteristic they are describing. There are as many different financial ratios as there are possible combinations of items appearing on the income statement, balance sheet, and statement of cash flows. We can classify ratios according to the financial characteristics that they capture.

When we assess a company's operating performance, a concern is whether the company is applying its assets in an efficient and profitable manner. When an analyst assesses a company's financial condition, a concern is whether the company is able to meet its financial obligations. An analyst can use financial ratios to evaluate four aspects of operating performance and financial condition:

- profitability ratios;
- asset management ratios;

- liquidity ratios;
- debt management ratios.

There are several ratios reflecting each of the four aspects of a company's operating performance and financial condition. The ratios we introduce here are by no means the only ones that can be formed using financial data, though they are some of the more commonly used. After becoming comfortable with the tools of financial analysis, an analyst will be able to create ratios that serve a particular evaluation objective.

In addition to understanding how to compute, interpret, and understand the limitations of the ratio, an analyst must understand that a financial ratio in isolation does not provide sufficient information. The ratio must be compared to some benchmark. The benchmark could be the corresponding ratio in the prior years in order to see how the ratio is changing over time. Another benchmark could be the ratio compared to other companies in the same industry.

Profitability ratios

Profitability ratios are of two types: return on investment ratios and margin ratios.

Return-on-investment ratios: These ratios compare measures of benefits, such as earnings or net income, with measures of investment. For example, if an analyst wants to evaluate how well the company uses its assets in its operations, the analyst could calculate the return on assets — sometimes called the *basic earning power ratio* — as the ratio of *earnings before interest and taxes* (EBIT) (also known as *operating earnings*) to total assets

$$\text{Basic earning power ratio} = \frac{\text{Earnings before interest and taxes}}{\text{Total assets}}.$$

Since the basic earning power ratio does not consider taxes or how the company is financed (i.e., its use of debt), it allows an analyst to compare the effectiveness of management in generating earnings given the assets available to do so.

Another return-on-assets ratio uses net income — operating earnings less interest and taxes — instead of earnings before interest and taxes:

$$\text{Return on assets} = \frac{\text{Net income}}{\text{Total assets}}.$$

This ratio indicates the return, ignoring how the company was financed.

Shareholders are interested in the return the company can generate on their investment. The *return on equity* is the ratio of the net income shareholders receive to their equity:

$$\text{Return on equity} = \frac{\text{Net income}}{\text{Book value of shareholder's equity}}.$$

Return on investment ratios do not provide information on (1) whether the return generated is attributable to profit margins (that is, due to costs and revenues) or to how efficiently management uses its assets and (2) the return shareholders earn on their actual investment in the company, that is, what shareholders earn relative to their actual investment, not the book value of their investment since equity is measured in terms of equity on the balance sheet.

Profit margin ratios: These ratios help an equity analyst gauge how well a company is managing its expenses. Profit margin ratios compare components of income with sales. They give the analyst an idea of which factors make up a company's income and are usually expressed as a portion of each dollar of sales. For example, the profit margin ratios we discuss here differ only in the numerator. It is the numerator that can be used to evaluate performance for different aspects of the business.

For example, suppose the analyst wants to evaluate how well production facilities are managed. The analyst would focus on gross profit (sales less cost of goods sold), a measure of income that is the direct result of production management. Comparing gross profit with sales produces the *gross profit margin*:

$$\text{Gross profit margin} = \frac{\text{Revenue} - \text{Cost of goods sold}}{\text{Revenues}}.$$

Looking at sales and cost of goods sold, we can see that the gross profit margin is affected by:

- Changes in sales volume, which affect cost of goods sold and sales;
- Changes in sales price, which affect revenues;
- Changes in the cost of production, which affect cost of goods sold.

Any change in gross profit margin from one period to the next is caused by one or more of those three factors. Similarly, differences in gross margin ratios among companies are the result of differences in those factors.

To evaluate operating performance, we need to consider operating expenses in addition to the cost of goods sold. To do this, remove operating expenses (e.g., selling and general administrative expenses) from gross profit, leaving operating profit, also referred to as earnings before interest and taxes (EBIT). *The operating profit margin* is therefore

$$\text{Operating profit margin} = \frac{\text{Revenue-Cost of goods sold} - \text{Operating expenses}}{\text{Revenues}},$$

$$\text{Operating profit margin} = \frac{\text{Revenue earnings before interest and taxes}}{\text{Revenues}}.$$

The operating profit margin is affected by the same factors as gross profit margin, plus operating expenses such as:

- Office rent and lease expenses;
- Miscellaneous income (for example, income from investments);
- Advertising expenditures;
- Bad debt expense.

Most of these expenses are related in some way to revenues, though they are not included directly in the cost of goods sold. Therefore, the difference between the gross profit margin and the operating profit margin is due to these indirect items that are included in computing the operating profit margin.

Both the gross profit margin and the operating profit margin reflect a company's operating performance. But they do not consider how these operations have been financed. To evaluate both operating and financing decisions, the analyst must compare net income (that is, earnings after deducting interest and taxes) with revenues. The result is the *net profit margin*:

$$\text{Net profit margin} = \frac{\text{Net income}}{\text{Revenues}}.$$

What these ratios do not indicate about profitability is the sensitivity of gross, operating, and net profit margins to:

- changes in the sales price;
- changes in the volume of sales.

Looking at the profitability ratios for one company for one period gives the analyst very little information that can be used to make judgments regarding future profitability. Nor do these ratios provide the analyst any information about why current profitability is what it is. We need more information to make these kinds of judgments, particularly regarding the future profitability of the company. For that, we turn to asset management ratios, which are measures of how well assets are being used.

Asset management ratios

Asset management ratios can be used to evaluate the benefits produced by specific assets, such as inventory or accounts receivable, or to evaluate the benefits produced by the totality of the company's assets. These ratios include collection period measures for accounts receivable and turnover ratios for other assets.

Inventory Management: There are three measures of the efficiency with which inventory is managed by a company: inventory turnover (period average), inventory turnover (period end), and days inventory.

The *number of days a company* (or simply *days inventory*) ties up funds in inventory is determined by the total amount of money represented in inventory and the average day's cost of goods sold. The current investment in inventory — that is, the money "tied up" in inventory — is the ending balance of inventory on the balance sheet.

The *average day's cost of goods sold* is the cost of goods sold on an average day in the year, which can be estimated by dividing the cost of goods sold by the number of days in the year:

$$\text{Average day's cost of goods sold} = \frac{\text{Cost of goods sold}}{365 \text{ days}}.$$

We compute the *days sales in inventory*, also known as the *number of days of inventory* or simply *days inventory*, by calculating the ratio of the amount of inventory on hand (in dollars) to the average day's cost of goods sold (in dollars per day):

$$\text{Days inventory} = \frac{\text{Amount of inventory on hand}}{\text{Average days cost of goods sold}}.$$

If the ending inventory is representative of the inventory throughout the year, then days inventory indicates the number of days to convert the investment in inventory into sold goods. Why worry about whether the year-end inventory is representative of inventory at any day throughout the year? Well, if inventory at the end of the fiscal year-end is lower than on any other day of the year, we have understated the days inventory. Indeed, in practice most companies try to choose fiscal year-ends that coincide with the slow period of their business. That means the ending balance of inventory would be lower than the typical daily inventory of the year. To get a better picture of the company, we could, for example, look at quarterly financial statements and take averages of quarterly inventory balances.

It should be noted that as an attempt to make the inventory figure more representative, some suggest taking the average of the beginning and ending inventory amounts. This does nothing to remedy the representativeness problem because the beginning inventory is simply the ending inventory from the previous year and, like the ending value from the current year, is measured at the low point of the operating cycle. A preferred method, if data are available, is to calculate the average inventory for the four quarters of the fiscal year.

The *inventory turnover ratio* indicates how quickly a company has used inventory to generate the goods and services that are sold. The inventory turnover is the ratio of the cost of goods sold to inventory:

$$\text{Inventory turnover} = \frac{\text{Cost of goods sold}}{\text{Inventory}}.$$

This ratio indicates how many times per year the company turns over its inventory.

Accounts Receivable Management: In much the same way inventory turnover can be evaluated, an investor can evaluate a company's management of its accounts receivable and its credit policy. The *accounts receivable turnover* ratio is a measure of how effectively a company is using the credit that is extended to customers.

The reason for extending credit is to increase sales. The downside to extending credit is the possibility of default — customers not paying when promised. The benefit obtained from extending credit is referred to as net credit sales — sales on credit less returns and refunds. Then,

$$\text{Accounts receivable turnover} = \frac{\text{Net credit sales}}{\text{Accounts receivable}}.$$

Overall Asset Management: The inventory and accounts receivable turnover ratios reflect the benefits obtained from the use of specific assets (inventory and accounts receivable). For a more general picture of the productivity of the company, an investor can compare the sales during a period with the total assets that generated these revenues.

One way is with the *total asset turnover ratio*, which indicates how many times during the year the value of a company's total assets is generated in revenues:

$$\text{Total assets turnover} = \frac{\text{Revenue}}{\text{Total assets}}.$$

An alternative is to focus only on fixed assets, the long-term, tangible assets of the company. The *fixed asset turnover* is the ratio of revenues to fixed assets:

$$\text{Fixed asset turnover} = \frac{\text{Revenue}}{\text{Fixed assets}}.$$

Here is what these ratios do not indicate about the company's use of its assets:

- the sales not made because credit policies are too stringent;
- how much of credit sales is not collectible;
- the assets that contribute most to the turnover.

Liquidity ratios

Liquidity reflects the ability of a company to meet its short-term obligations using those assets that are most readily converted into cash. Assets that may be converted into cash in a short period of time are referred to as liquid assets; they are listed in financial statements as current assets. Current assets are often referred to as working capital, since they represent the resources needed for the day-to-day operations of the company's long-term capital investments.

Current assets are used to satisfy short-term obligations, or current liabilities. The amount by which current assets exceed current liabilities is referred to as the net working capital.

Operating Cycle: How much liquidity a company needs depends on its operating cycle. The operating cycle is the duration from the time cash is invested in goods and services to the time that investment produces cash. For example, a company that produces and sells goods has an operating cycle comprising four phases:

- purchase raw materials and produce goods, investing in inventory;
- sell goods, generating sales, which may or may not be for cash;

- extend credit, creating accounts receivable;
- collect accounts receivable, generating cash.

The four phases make up the cycle of cash use and generation. The operating cycle would be somewhat different for companies that produce services rather than goods, but the idea is the same — the operating cycle is the length of time it takes to generate cash through the investment of cash.

What does the operating cycle have to do with liquidity? The longer the operating cycle, the more current assets are needed (relative to current liabilities) since it takes longer to convert inventories and receivables into cash. In other words, the longer the operating cycle, the greater the amount of net working capital required.

To measure the length of an operating cycle, we need to know:

- the time it takes to convert the investment in inventory into sales (that is, cash → inventory → sales → accounts receivable);
- the time it takes to collect sales on credit (that is, accounts receivable → cash).

Measures of Liquidity: The analyst can describe a company's ability to meet its current obligations in several ways. The *current ratio* indicates the company's ability to meet or cover its current liabilities using its current assets:

$$\text{Current ratio} = \frac{\text{Current assets}}{\text{Current liabilities}}.$$

A current ratio of 2, for example, would indicate that a company has two times as much as it needs to cover its current obligations during the year. However, the current ratio groups all current asset accounts together, assuming they are all as easily converted to cash. Even though, by definition, current assets can be transformed into cash within a year, not all current assets can be transformed into cash in a short period of time.

An alternative to the current ratio is the *quick ratio*, also called the *acid test ratio*, which uses a slightly different set of current accounts to cover the same current liabilities as in the current ratio. In the quick ratio, the least liquid of the current asset accounts, inventory, is excluded. Hence,

$$\text{Quick ratio} = \frac{\text{Current assets} - \text{Inventory}}{\text{Current liabilities}}.$$

Analysts typically leave out inventories in the quick ratio because inventories are generally perceived as the least liquid of the current assets. By leaving out the least liquid asset, the quick ratio provides a more conservative view of liquidity.

Still another way to measure the company's ability to satisfy short-term obligations is the net working capital-to-sales ratio, which compares net working capital (current assets less current liabilities) with sales:

$$\text{Net working capital to sales ratio} = \frac{\text{Net working capital}}{\text{Sales}}.$$

This ratio tells the analyst the "cushion" available to meet short-term obligations relative to sales. Consider two companies with identical working capital of \$100,000, but one has sales of \$500,000 and the other has sales of \$1,000,000. If they have identical operating cycles, this means that the company with the greater sales has more funds flowing in and out of its current asset investments (inventories and receivables). The company with more funds flowing in and out needs a larger cushion to protect itself in case of a disruption in the cycle, such as a labor strike or unexpected delays in customer payments. The longer the operating cycle is, the more of a cushion (net working capital) a company needs for a given level of sales.

For example, suppose the ratio is 0.20. This tells the analyst that for every dollar of sales, the company has 20 cents of net working capital to support it.

What don't these ratios tell the analysts about liquidity? They don't provide answers to the following questions:

- How liquid are the accounts receivable? How much of the accounts receivable will be collectible?
- What is the nature of the current liabilities? How much of current liabilities consist of items that recur (such as accounts payable and wages payable) each period and how much consist of occasional items (such as income taxes payable)?
- Are there any unrecorded liabilities (such as operating leases) that are not included in current liabilities?

Debt management ratios

A company can finance its assets with equity or with debt. Financing with debt legally obligates the company to pay interest and to repay the principal as promised. Equity financing does not obligate the company to pay anything because dividends are paid at the discretion of the board of directors. There is always some risk, which we refer to as *business risk*, inherent in any business enterprise. But how a company chooses to finance its operations — the particular mix of debt and equity — may add financial risk on top of business risk. *Financial risk* is risk associated with a company's ability to satisfy its debt obligations and is often measured based on the extent to which debt financing is used relative to equity.

Financial leverage ratios are used to assess how much financial risk the company has taken on. There are two types of financial leverage ratios: component percentages and coverage ratios. Component percentage ratios compare a company's debt with either its total capital (debt plus equity) or its equity capital.

Coverage ratios reflect a company's ability to satisfy fixed financing obligations, such as interest, principal repayment, or lease payments.

Component Percentage Ratios: A ratio that indicates the proportion of assets financed with debt is the *total debt-to-assets ratio*, which compares debt (short-term + long-term debt) with total assets:

$$\text{Total debt-to-assets ratio} = \frac{\text{Debt}}{\text{Total assets}}.$$

For example, suppose that this ratio is 45%. Then this indicates that 45% of the company's assets are financed with debt (both short-term and long-term).

Another way to look at the financial risk is in terms of the use of debt relative to the use of equity. The *debt-to-equity ratio* indicates how the company finances its operations with debt relative to the book value of its shareholders' equity:

$$\text{Debt-to-equity ratio} = \frac{\text{Debt}}{\text{Book value of shareholders' equity}}.$$

Both ratios can be stated in terms of total debt, as above, or in terms of long-term debt or even simple interest-bearing debt. And it is not always clear in which form — total, long-term debt, or interest-bearing — the ratio is calculated. Additionally, it is often the case that the current portion of long-term debt is excluded in the calculation of the long-term versions of these debt ratios.

One problem with using a financial ratio based on the book value of equity to analyze financial risk is that there is seldom a strong relationship between the book value and market value of a stock. The distortion in values on the balance sheet is obvious by looking at the book value of equity and comparing it with the market value of equity. The book value of equity consists of:

- the proceeds to the company of all the stock issued since it was first incorporated, less any stock repurchased by the company;
- the accumulated earnings of the company, less any dividends, since it was first incorporated.

Book value generally does not give a true picture of the investment of shareholders in the company because:

- Earnings are recorded according to accounting principles, which may not reflect the true economics of transactions.
- Due to inflation, the earnings and proceeds from stocks issued in the past do not reflect today's values.

Market value, on the other hand, is the value of equity as perceived by investors. It is what investors are willing to pay. So why bother with book value? For two reasons: First, it is easier to obtain the book value over the market value of a company's securities, and second, many financial services report ratios using book value rather than market value.

However, any of the ratios presented in this chapter that use the book value of equity can be restated using the market value of equity. For example, instead of using the book value of equity in the debt-to-equity ratio, the market value of equity to measure the company's financial leverage can be used.

Coverage Ratios: The ratios that compare debt to equity or debt to assets indicate the amount of financial leverage, which enables an investor to assess the financial condition of a company. Another way of looking at the financial condition and the amount of financial leverage used by the company is to see how well it can handle the financial burdens associated with its debt or other fixed commitments.

One measure of a company's ability to handle financial burdens is the interest coverage ratio, also referred to as the *times interest-covered ratio*. This ratio tells us how well the company can cover or meet the interest payments associated with debt. The ratio compares the funds available to pay interest (that is, earnings before interest and taxes) with the interest expense:

$$\text{Interest coverage ratio} = \frac{\text{EBIT}}{\text{Interest expense}}.$$

The greater the interest coverage ratio, the better able the company is to pay its interest expense.

An interest coverage ratio of 5, for example, means that the company's earnings before interest and taxes are five times greater than its interest payments.

The interest coverage ratio provides information about a company's ability to cover the interest related to its debt financing. However, there are other costs that do not arise from debt but that nevertheless must be considered in the same way we consider the cost of debt in a company's financial obligations. For example, lease payments are fixed costs incurred in financing operations. Like interest payments, they represent legal obligations.

What funds are available to pay debt and debt-like expenses? Start with EBIT and add back expenses that were deducted to arrive at EBIT. The ability of a company to satisfy its fixed financial costs — its fixed charges — is referred to as the *fixed charge coverage ratio*. One definition of the fixed charge coverage considers only the lease payments:

$$\text{Fixed charge coverage ratio} = \frac{\text{EBIT} + \text{Lease expense}}{\text{Interest} + \text{Lease expense}}.$$

For example, suppose that the ratio is 2. This tells us that the earnings can cover the company's fixed charges (interest and lease payments) more than two times over.

What fixed charges to consider are not entirely clear-cut. For example, if the company is required to set aside funds to eventually or periodically retire debt — referred to as sinking funds — is the amount set aside a fixed charge? As another example, since preferred dividends represent a fixed financing charge, should they be included as a fixed charge? From the perspective of the common shareholder, the preferred dividends must be covered either to enable the payment of common dividends or to retain earnings for future growth. Because debt principal repayment and preferred stock dividends are paid on an after-tax basis — paid out of dollars remaining after taxes are paid — this fixed charge must be converted to before-tax dollars. The fixed charge coverage ratio can be expanded to accommodate the sinking funds and preferred stock dividends as fixed charges.

Up to now we considered earnings before interest and taxes as funds available to meet fixed financial charges. EBIT includes non-cash items such as depreciation and amortization. If an investor is trying to compare funds available to meet obligations, a better measure of available funds is cash flow from operations as reported in the statement of cash flows. A ratio that considers cash flows from operations as funds available to cover interest payments is referred to as the *cash flow interest coverage ratio* and calculated as follows:

$$\text{Cash flow interest coverage ratio} = \frac{\text{Cash flow from operation} + \text{Interest} + \text{Taxes}}{\text{Interest}}.$$

The amount of cash flow from operations that is in the statement of cash flow is net of interest and taxes. So, we must add back interest and taxes to cash flow from operations to arrive at the cash flow amount before interest and taxes in order to determine the cash flow available to cover interest payments.

Suppose that this ratio is 6.5. This coverage ratio indicates that, in terms of cash flow, the company had 6.5 times more cash than is needed to pay its interest. This is a better picture of interest coverage than the five times reflected by EBIT. The difference is because cash flow considers not just the accounting income, but non-cash items as well.

These ratios do not indicate:

- what other fixed, legal commitments the company has that are not included on the balance sheet (for example, operating leases);
- what the intentions of management are regarding taking on more debt as the existing debt matures.

Common-Size Analysis

An analyst can evaluate a company's operating performance and financial condition through ratios that relate various items of information contained in the financial statements. Another way to analyze a company is to look at its financial data more comprehensively.

Common-size analysis is a method of analysis in which the components of a financial statement are compared with each other. The first step in common-size analysis is to break down a financial statement — either the balance sheet or the income statement — into its parts. The next step is to calculate the proportion that each item represents relative to some benchmark. This form of common-size analysis is sometimes referred to as vertical common-size analysis. Another form of common-size analysis is horizontal common-size analysis, which uses either an income statement or a balance sheet in a fiscal year and compares accounts to the corresponding items in another year. In the common-size analysis of the balance sheet, the benchmark is total assets. For the income statement, the benchmark is sales.

In the income statement, as with the balance sheet, the items may be restated as a proportion of sales; this statement is referred to as the common-size income statement. Looking at gross profit, EBIT, and net income are the profit margins we calculated earlier. The common-size income statement provides information on the profitability of different aspects of the company's business. Again, the picture is not yet complete. For a more complete picture, the analyst must look at trends over time and make comparisons with other companies in the same industry.

Using Financial Ratio Analysis

Financial analysis provides information concerning a company's operating performance and financial condition. This information is useful for an analyst in evaluating the performance of the company as a whole, as well as of divisions, products, and subsidiaries.

But financial ratio analysis cannot tell the whole story and must be interpreted and used with care. Financial ratios are useful but, as noted in the discussion of each ratio, there is information that the ratios do not reveal. For example, in calculating inventory turnover we need to assume that the inventory shown on the balance sheet is representative of inventory throughout the year. Another example is in the calculation of accounts receivable turnover. We assumed that all sales were on credit. If we are on the outside looking in — that is, evaluating a company based on its financial statements only, such as the case of an analyst — and therefore do not have data on credit sales, assumptions must be made that may or may not be correct.

In addition, there are other areas of concern that an analyst should be aware of in using financial ratios:

- limitations in the accounting data used to construct the ratios;
- selection of an appropriate benchmark company or companies for comparison purposes;
- interpretation of the ratios;
- pitfalls in forecasting future operating performance and financial condition based on past trends.

Putting it Altogether: Determinant of Earnings per Share

We've covered a lot of financial ratios in attempting to explain how an analyst assesses the company in terms of its profitability, asset utilization, liquidity, and debt usage. Let's put these ratios together to see how they interact to explain the several key performance measures of a company: earnings per share and return on equity.

The method that is useful to explain performance is the DuPont system. The *DuPont system* is a method of breaking down financial ratios into their components to determine which areas are responsible for a company's performance.

To explain a company's earnings per share, we start with its definition and for convenience we assume no preferred stock:

$$\text{EPS} = \frac{\text{Net income}}{\text{No. of common shares outstanding}}.$$

We will now use a simple mathematical manipulation to break-up a financial ratio into two parts. If we multiple EPS by the amount of equity on the balance sheet, we can rewrite EPS as

$$\text{EPS} = \frac{\text{Net income}}{\text{Equity}} \times \frac{\text{Equity}}{\text{No. of common shares outstanding}}.$$

Here, we have a ratio that we have already seen. The first ratio is the return on equity which we discuss above. The second ratio is one that we have not seen thus far. It is the ratio of the book value of the equity divided by the number of shares of common stock outstanding. This ratio is referred to as the *book value per share of common*; that is,

$$\text{Book value per share of common} = \frac{\text{Equity}}{\text{No. of common shares outstanding}}$$

Thus, EPS can be written as

$$\text{EPS} = \text{Return on equity} \times \text{Book value per share of common}.$$

If management can increase either of the two ratios without reducing the other, there will be an increase in earnings per share. Suppose that management is considering the issuance of additional common stock. The impact on EPS is twofold. Although the book value per share of common will increase, for the EPS to increase the change in the return on equity must be such that this measure cannot decline by more than the increase in book value per share of common. Thus, if management is considering the issuance of additional equity, the opportunities for investments within the company must be such that the return on equity will not decline.

A closer look at return on equity

Let's take a closer look at the return on equity to determine what impacts EPS. We rewrite that ratio as

$$\text{Return on equity} = \frac{\text{Net income}}{\text{Total assets}} \times \frac{\text{Total assets}}{\text{Equity}},$$

The first ratio is the return on assets. As for the second ratio, we know that

$$\text{Total assets} = \text{Equity} + \text{Total liabilities}.$$

or equivalently,

$$\text{Total assets} = \text{Equity} + \text{Debt}.$$

Substituting into the second ratio for the return on equity, we get

$$\begin{aligned}\frac{\text{Total assets}}{\text{Equity}} &= \frac{\text{Equity} + \text{Debt}}{\text{Equity}}\\ &= \frac{\text{Equity}}{\text{Equity}} + \frac{\text{Debt}}{\text{Equity}}\\ &= 1 + \frac{\text{Debt}}{\text{Equity}}.\end{aligned}$$

Now we see why the second ratio for the return on equity is a debt management ratio: the ratio above is the debt-to-equity ratio. Thus, the return on equity can be written as

$$\text{Return on equity} = \text{Return on assets} \times (1 + \text{Debt-to-equity ratio}).$$

This means that to improve EPS by increasing return on equity, management can increase one or both return on assets and the use of greater financial leverage (i.e., more debt). So, a company seeking debt financing (which will increase the debt-to-equity ratio) must be confident that the proceeds received will be used within the firm in such a way as to not reduce return on assets. The reduction in the return on assets will occur if the return earned on the proceeds from the borrowed funds is less than the cost of borrowing the funds. Furthermore, notice that the second measure, (1 + Debt-to-equity ratio), has a magnifying impact.

Analysis of return on assets

For the return on assets, the analysis can be carried further to see the factors that impact that measure. To see how, the return on assets can be rewritten as

$$\text{Return on assets} = \frac{\text{Net income}}{\text{Revenues}} \times \frac{\text{Revenues}}{\text{Total assets}}.$$

The first ratio is a profit margin ratio: net profit margin. The second ratio is an asset efficiency ratio: total asset turnover. Thus, the return on assets can be expressed as

$$\text{Return on assets} = \text{Net profit margin} \times \text{Total asset turnover}.$$

Consequently, to improve the return on assets, which in turn improves the return on equity, and then EPS, a company can improve its profit margin and total asset turnover. An analysis of the asset efficiency ratio for each type of asset can be analyzed to improve total asset turnover.

How does one improve the net profit margin? Let's first concentrate on profit margin based on operations without taking into account interest and taxes, which gives us the net profit margin. Operating income or earnings before interest and taxes (EBIT) reflects earnings from operations ignoring interest and taxes. The ratio of EBIT to total assets is the basic earning power described earlier; that is,

$$\text{Basic earning power} = \frac{\text{EBIT}}{\text{Total assets}}.$$

Multiplying the numerator and denominator by revenues, we get

$$\text{Basic earning power} = \frac{\text{EBIT}}{\text{Revenues}} \times \frac{\text{Revenues}}{\text{Total assets}}.$$

The second ratio is the total asset turnover. The first ratio is a profitability margin ratio, referred to as the operating profit margin, and reflects the profit margin ignoring the capital structure (i.e., the amount paid in interest to borrow funds) and the tax rate that the company must pay to tax authorities.

Consequently, basic earning power can be expressed as

$$\text{Basic earning power} = \text{Operating profit margin} \times \text{Total asset turnover}.$$

Let's take into account taxes. We know that

$$\text{Net income} = \text{Earnings before taxes} - \text{Taxes}.$$

Abbreviating Earnings before taxes as EBT, we can write

$$\begin{aligned}\text{Net income} &= \text{EBT} - (\text{EBT}) \times \text{Effective tax rate} \\ &= \text{EBT} \times (1 - \text{Effective tax rate}) \\ &= \text{EBIT} \times \left[\frac{EBT}{EBIT}\right] \times (1 - \text{Effective tax rate}).\end{aligned}$$

The ratio of EBT/EBIT reflects the *tax burden* of the company based on its capital structure and the interest cost it must pay for debt and therefore equity's share of earnings. The measure (1 – Effective tax rate) is the *tax retention rate* (i.e., the amount that is retained by the company after the payment of taxes).

With some manipulation, the return on assets can be written as

$$\begin{aligned}\text{Return on assets} = &\left[\frac{\text{EBIT}}{\text{Revenues}}\right] \times \left[\frac{\text{Revenues}}{\text{Total assets}}\right] \times \left[\frac{\text{EBT}}{\text{EBIT}}\right] \\ &\times (1 - \text{Effective tax rate}).\end{aligned}$$

The first ratio above is the operating profit margin. The second ratio is the total asset turnover (an asset management ratio). The third ratio is equity's share of earnings after taxes are paid. The last factor is the tax retention rate. Consequently, we can write

$$\begin{aligned}\text{Return on assets} = &\ \text{Operating profit margin} \times \text{Total asset turnover} \\ &\times \text{Equity's share of earnings} \times \text{Tax retention rate}.\end{aligned}$$

Therefore, we can now see the factors that influence the return on assets and in turn EPS.

Cash Flow Analysis

One of the key financial measures that an analyst should understand is the company's cash flow. This is because the cash flow aids the analyst in assessing the ability of the company to satisfy its contractual obligations and maintain current dividends and current capital expenditure policies without relying on external financing (i.e., without relying on the issuance of equity and bonds or the reliance on bank borrowing). Moreover, an analyst must understand why this measure is important for equity analysis. The reason is that the basic valuation principle followed by stock analysts is that the value of a company today is the discounted value of its expected future cash flows. In this section, we discuss cash flow analysis.

Difficulties with Measuring Cash Flow

The primary difficulty with measuring a cash flow is that it is a flow: Cash flows into the company (i.e., cash inflows) and cash flows out of the company (i.e., cash outflows). At any point in time there is a stock of cash on hand, but the stock of cash on hand varies among companies based on the company's size, the cash demands of the business, and a company's management of working capital. What then is cash flow? Is it the total amount of cash flowing into the company during a period? Is it the total amount of cash flowing out of the company during a period? Is it the net of the cash inflows and outflows for a period? Well, there is no specific definition of cash flow — and that's probably why there is so much confusion regarding the measurement of cash flow. Ideally, a measure of the company's operating performance that is comparable among companies is needed — something other than net income.

A simple yet crude method of calculating cash flow requires simply adding non-cash expenses (e.g., depreciation and amortization) to the reported net income amount to arrive at cash flow. That is,

$$\text{Estimated cash flow} = \text{Net income} + \text{Depreciation and amortization.}$$

This amount is not really a cash flow, but simply earnings before depreciation and amortization. Is this a cash flow that stock analysts should use in valuing a company? Though not a cash flow, this estimated cash flow does allow a quick comparison of income across companies that may use different depreciation methods and depreciable lives.

The problem with this measure is that it ignores the many other sources and uses of cash during the period. Consider the sale of goods for credit. This transaction generates sales for the period. Sales and the accompanying cost of goods sold are reflected in the period's net income and the estimated cash flow amount. However, until the account receivable is collected, there is no cash from this transaction. If collection does not occur until the next period, there is a misalignment of the income and cash flow arising from this transaction. Therefore, the simple estimated cash flow ignores some cash flows that, for many companies, are significant.

Another estimate of cash flow that is simple to calculate is earnings before interest, taxes, depreciation, and amortization (EBITDA). However, this measure suffers from the same accrual-accounting bias as the previous measure, which may result in the omission of significant cash flows. Additionally, EBITDA does not consider interest and taxes, which may also be substantial cash outflows for some companies.[1]

These two rough estimates of cash flows are used in practice not only for their simplicity, but because they experienced widespread use prior to the disclosure of more detailed information in the statement of cash flows. Currently, the measures of cash flow are wide-ranging, including simplistic cash flow measures, measures developed from the statement of cash flows, and measures that seek to capture the theoretical concept of free cash flow discussed later.

Cash Flows and the Statement of Cash Flows

In their financial statements, companies must provide a *statement of cash flows*. This statement requires the company to classify cash flows into three categories based on the activity: operating, investing, and financing. Cash flows are summarized by activity and within activity by type (e.g., asset dispositions are reported separately from asset acquisitions).

A company may report the cash flows from operating activities on the statement of cash flows using either the direct method — reporting all cash inflows and outflows — or the indirect method — starting with net income and making adjustments for depreciation, other non-cash expenses, and changes in working capital accounts. Though the direct method is recommended, it is also the most burdensome for a company to prepare. Most companies report cash flows from operations using the indirect method. The indirect method has the advantage of providing the financial statement user with a reconciliation of the company's net income with the change in cash. The indirect method produces a cash flow from operations that is similar to the estimated cash flow measure discussed previously, yet it encompasses the changes in working capital accounts that the simple measure does not.

---

[1]For a more detailed discussion of the EBITDA measure, see Eastman [1997].

The classification of cash flows into the three types of activities provides useful information that can be used by an analyst to see, for example, whether the company is generating sufficient cash flows from operations to sustain its current rate of growth. However, the classification of particular items is not necessarily as useful as it could be. Consider some of the classifications:

- Cash flows related to interest expense are classified in operations, though they are clearly financing cash flows.
- Income taxes are classified as operating cash flows, though taxes are affected by financing (e.g., deduction for interest expense paid on debt) and investment activities (e.g., the reduction of taxes from tax credits on investment activities).
- Interest income and dividends received are classified as operating cash flows, though these flows are a result of investment activities.

Whether these items have a significant effect on the analysis depends on the particular company's situation.

Looking at the relation among the three cash flows in the statement provides a sense of the activities of the company. A young, fast-growing company may have negative cash flows from operations, yet positive cash flows from financing activities (i.e., operations may be financed in large part with external financing). As a company grows, it may rely to a lesser extent on external financing. The typical mature company generates cash from operations and reinvests part or all of it back into the company. Therefore, cash flow related to operations is positive (i.e., a source of cash) and cash flow related to investing activities is negative (i.e., a use of cash). As a company matures, it may seek less financing externally and may even use cash to reduce its reliance on external financing (e.g., repay debts). We can classify companies on the basis of the pattern of their sources of cash flows, as shown in Table 2. Though additional information is required to assess a company's financial performance and condition; examination of the sources of cash flows, especially over time, gives us a general idea of the company's operations.

Though we can classify a company based on the sources and uses of cash flows, more data are needed to put this information in perspective. What is the trend in the sources and uses of cash flows? What market, industry, or company-specific events affect the company's cash flows? How does

TABLE 2: Patterns of Sources of Cash Flows

Cash Flow	Financing Growth Externally and Internally	Financing Growth Internally	Mature	Temporary Finance Downturn	Financial Distress	Downsizing
Operations	+	+	+	−	−	+
Investing	−	−	−	+	−	+
Financing	+	−	+ or −	+	−	−

the company being analyzed compare with other companies in the same industry in terms of the sources and uses of funds?

Free Cash Flow

Cash flows without any adjustment may be misleading because they do not reflect the cash outflows that are necessary for the future existence of a company. An alternative measure, free cash flow, was developed by Jensen [1986] in his theoretical analysis of agency costs and corporate takeovers. In theory, *free cash flow* is the cash flow left over after the company funds all positive net present value projects. Positive net present value projects are those capital investment projects for which the present value of expected future cash flows exceeds the present value of project outlays, all discounted at the cost of capital. (The cost of capital is the estimated cost a company incurs to receive funding from creditors and shareholders. The cost of capital is basically a hurdle: If a project returns more than its cost of capital, it is a profitable project.) In other words, free cash flow is the cash flow of the company, less the estimated capital expenditures necessary to stay in business (i.e., replacing facilities as necessary) and grows at the expected rate (which requires increases in working capital).

The theory of free cash flow was developed by Jensen to explain behaviors of companies that could not be explained by existing economic theories. Jensen observed that companies that generate free cash flow should disgorge that cash rather than invest the funds in less profitable investments. There are many ways in which companies can disgorge this excess cash flow, including the payment of cash dividends, the repurchase of stock, and debt issuance in exchange for stock. The debt-for-stock exchange, for example, increases the company's leverage and future debt obligations, obligating the future use of excess cash flow. If a company does not disgorge this free cash flow, there is the possibility that another company — a company whose cash flows are less than its profitable investment opportunities or a company that is willing to purchase and lever-up the company — will attempt to acquire the free-cash-flow-laden company.

By itself, the fact that a company generates free cash flow is neither good nor bad. What the company does with this free cash flow is what is important. And this is where it is important to measure the free cash flow as the cash flow in excess of profitable investment opportunities.

Consider the simple numerical exercise with the Winner Company and the Loser Company:

	Winner Company	**Loser Company**
Cash flow before capital expenditures	$1,000	$1,000
Capital expenditures, positive net present value projects	(750)	(250)
Capital expenditures, negative net present value projects	0	(500)
Cash flow	$250	$250
Free cash flow	$250	$750

These two companies have identical cash flows and the same total capital expenditures. However, the Winner Company spends only on profitable projects (in terms of positive net present value projects), whereas the Loser Company spends on both profitable projects and wasteful projects. The Winner Company has a lower free cash flow than the Loser Company, indicating that they are using the generated cash flows in a more profitable manner. The lesson is that the existence of a high level of free cash flow is not necessarily good — it may simply suggest that the company is either a very good takeover target or the company has the potential for investing in unprofitable investments.

Positive free cash flow may be good or bad news; likewise, negative free cash flow may be good or bad news:

	Good News	Bad News
Positive free cash flow	The company is generating substantial operating cash flows, beyond those necessary for profitable projects.	The company is generating more cash flows than it needs for profitable projects and may waste these cash flows on unprofitable projects.
Negative free cash flow	The company has more profitable projects than it has operating cash flows and must rely on external financing to fund these projects.	The company is unable to generate sufficient operating cash flows to satisfy its investment needs for future growth.

Therefore, once the free cash flow is calculated, other information (e.g., trends in profitability) must be considered to evaluate the operating performance and financial condition of the company.

Calculating free cash flow

There is some confusion when this theoretical concept is applied to actual companies. The primary difficulty is that the amount of capital expenditures necessary to maintain the business at its current rate of growth is generally not known; companies do not report this item and may not even be able to determine how much of a period's capital expenditures are attributed to maintenance and how much is attributed to expansion.

Some analysts estimate free cash flow by assuming that all capital expenditures are necessary for the maintenance of the current growth of the company. Though there is little justification in using all expenditures, this is a practical solution to an impractical calculation. This assumption allows us to estimate free cash flows using published financial statements.

Another issue in the calculation is defining what truly "free" cash flow is. Generally, we think of "free" cash flow as the amount left over after all necessary financing expenditures are paid. This means that free cash flow is calculated after debt interest has been paid. Some calculate free cash flow before such financing expenditures; others calculate free cash flow after interest, and still others calculate free cash flow after both interest and dividends (assuming that dividends are a commitment, though not a legal commitment).

There is no one correct method of calculating free cash flow and different analysts may arrive at different estimates of free cash flow for a company. The problem is that it is impossible to measure free cash flow as dictated by the theory, so many methods have arisen to calculate this cash flow. A simple method is to start with the cash flow from operations and then deduct capital expenditures.

We can relate free cash flow directly to a company's income. Starting with net income, we can estimate free cash flow using four steps:

Step 1: Determine earnings before interest and taxes (EBIT).
Step 2: Calculate earnings before interest but after taxes.
Step 3: Adjust for non-cash expenses (e.g., depreciation).
Step 4: Adjust for capital expenditures and changes in working capital.

Usefulness of Cash Flows in Financial Analysis

The usefulness of cash flows for financial analysis depends on whether cash flows provide unique information or provide information in a manner that is more accessible or convenient for the analyst. The cash flow information provided in the statement of cash flows, for example, is not necessarily unique because most, if not all, of the information is available through analysis of the balance sheet and income statement. What the statement does provide is a classification scheme that presents information in a manner that is easier to use and, perhaps, more illustrative of the company's financial position.

An analysis of cash flows and the sources of cash flows can reveal the following information:

The sources of financing the company's capital spending: Does the company generate internally (i.e., from operations) a portion or all of the funds needed for its investment activities? If a company cannot generate cash flow from operations, this may indicate future problems. Reliance on external financing (e.g., equity or debt issuance) may indicate a company's inability to sustain itself over time.

The company's dependence on borrowing: Does the company rely heavily on borrowing that may result in difficulty in satisfying future debt service?

The quality of earnings: Large and growing differences between income and cash flows suggest a low quality of earnings.

One use of cash flow information is in financial ratio analysis, primarily with the balance sheet and income statement information. One such ratio is the cash flow-based ratio, the *cash flow interest coverage ratio*, which is a measure of financial risk. There are a number of other cash flow-based ratios that an analyst may find useful in evaluating the operating performance and financial condition of a company.

A useful ratio to help further assess a company's cash flow is the cash flow to capital expenditures ratio, or *capital expenditures coverage ratio*:

$$\text{Cash flow to capital expenditures} = \frac{\text{Cash flow}}{\text{Capital expenditures}}.$$

The cash flow measure in the numerator should be one that has not already removed capital expenditures; for example, including free cash flow in the numerator would be inappropriate.

This ratio provides information about the financial flexibility of the company and is particularly useful for capital-intensive companies and utility companies (see Fridson [1995, p. 173]). The larger the ratio, the greater the financial flexibility. However, one must carefully examine the reasons why this ratio may be changing over time and why it might be out of line with comparable companies in the industry. For example, a declining ratio can be interpreted in two ways. First, the company may eventually have difficulty adding to capacity via capital expenditures without the need to borrow funds. The second interpretation is that the company may have gone through a period of major capital expansion and therefore it will take time for revenues to be generated that will increase the cash flow from operations to bring the ratio to some normal long-run level.

Another useful cash flow ratio is the *cash flow to debt ratio*:

$$\text{Cash flow to debt ratio} = \frac{\text{Cash flow}}{\text{Debt}}.$$

where debt can be represented as total debt, long-term debt, or a debt measure that captures a specific range of maturity (e.g., debt maturing in five years). This ratio gives a measure of a company's ability to meet maturing debt obligations.

Using Cash Flow Information

Cash flow information may help identify companies that are more likely to encounter financial difficulties. Consider the classic example provided by Largay and Stickney [1980] who analyzed the financial statements of W. T. Grant during the 1966–1974 period preceding its bankruptcy in 1975 and ultimate liquidation. They noted that the financial ratios we described in this chapter showed some downward trends but provided no definitive clues to the company's impending bankruptcy. A study of cash flows from operations, however, revealed that company operations were causing an increasing drain on cash, rather than providing cash.[2] This necessitated an increased use of external financing where the required interest payments exacerbated the cash flow drain. Cash flow analysis clearly was a valuable tool in this case since W. T. Grant had been running a negative cash flow from operations for years. Yet none of the earlier financial ratios discussed in this chapter take into account the cash flow from operations. Use of the cash flow to capital expenditures ratio and the cash flow to debt ratio would have highlighted the company's difficulties.

Dugan and Samson [1996] examined the use of operating cash flow as an early warning signal of a company's potential financial problems. The subject of the study was Allied Products Corporation because, for a decade, this company exhibited a significant divergence between cash flow from operations and net income. For parts of the period, net income was positive while cash flow from operations was a large negative value. In contrast to W. T. Grant, which went into bankruptcy, the auditor's report in the 1991 Annual Report of Allied Products Corporation did issue a going-concern warning. Moreover, the stock traded in the range of $2–3 per share. There was then a turnaround of the company by 1995. In its 1995 annual report, net income increased dramatically from prior periods

[2]For the period investigated, a statement of changes of financial position was not required to be reported.

(to \$34 million) and there was a positive cash flow from operations (\$29 million). The stock traded in the \$25 range by the Spring of 1996. As with the W. T. Grant study, Dugan and Samson found that the economic realities of a company are better reflected in its cash flow from operations.

The importance of cash flow analysis in bankruptcy prediction is supported by the study by Ward and Foster [2001], who compared trends in the statement of cash flows components — cash flow from operations, cash flow for investment, and cash flow for financing — between healthy companies and companies that subsequently sought bankruptcy. They observe that healthy companies tend to have relatively stable relations among the cash flows for the three sources, correcting any given year's deviation from their norm within one year. They also observe that unhealthy companies exhibit declining cash flows from operations and financing and declining cash flows for investment one and two years prior to the bankruptcy. Further, unhealthy companies tend to expend more cash flows to financing sources than they bring in during the year prior to bankruptcy. These studies illustrate the importance of examining cash flow information in assessing the financial condition of a company.

Additional Tools for Company Analysis

The field of management offers several other frameworks that are used for assessing the economic merits of a company. These include (1) Value Chain Analysis, (2) RBV Analysis, and (3) SWOT Analysis. We briefly describe each as follows.

Value Chain Analysis

The value chain refers to the activities performed by a company to bring its products and services from conception to distribution to customers/clients. Developed by Michael Porter [1985], *value chain analysis* disaggregates the collection of these activities that a company performs and the interactions of those activities in order to identify the sources of a company's competitive advantage and how the company can improve that competitive advantage by becoming more efficient in one or more of the activities. This, in turn, leads to greater profits by increasing efficiency, by reducing costs, and/or increasing revenues.

To apply Value Chain Analysis, the activities are classified as primary activities and support activities. Primary activities are:

- *Inbound logistics activities* that look at the relationship between the company and its suppliers. These activities include the receiving of inputs, warehousing/storing those inputs, and distributing those inputs.
- *Operations activities* involve activities that transform inputs into the company's products and services.
- *Outbound logistics activities* cover the activities that are needed to store and distribute the products and services.
- *Marketing and sales activities* include the strategies the company employs to promote its products and services to customers and the payment method options that the company uses to allow its customers to pay.
- *Service activities* are the post-sale activities to service the sold products.

Support activities are:

- *Procurement activities* that are related to the acquiring of the inputs and other resources the company needs to produce its products.
- *Human resources activities* involve hiring employees, employee development (including training programs), compensating employees, and firing employees.
- *Technological development activities* include the technologies necessary to transform the inputs into the company's products and services.
- *Infrastructure activities* include the activities performed by the accounting, finance, legal, planning, investor relations, and quality control departments.

RBV Analysis

Resources-based view (RBV) analysis is a framework that views the company's resources as the key to a company's performance and as a way of identifying how to achieve a competitive advantage (see Barney [1991]). The belief is that a company should not look at the competitive environment as suggested at the outset of this chapter (Porter's Five Forces and PESTEL Analysis) when we discussed industry analysis, but rather at the internal characteristics to identify the sources of a company's competitive advantage. Those who support the use of RBV analysis argue that it is more reasonable to modify the use of current resources to exploit externally generated opportunities rather than trying to acquire new resources for each opportunity that may occur.

The four questions that are asked about a resource's ability to create competitive advantages are the (1) question of value, (2) question of rarity, (3) question of imitability, and (4) question of organization (ability to exploit the resource or capability). Since these four questions involve *v*alue, *r*arity, *i*mitability, and *o*rganization, these four questions are referred to as *VRIO attributes*.

SWOT Analysis

SWOT analysis is an acronym that stands for Strengths, Weaknesses, Opportunities, and Threats Analysis of a company. This covers both internal and external factors that impact the competitive position of a company. Strengths (positive attributes) and weaknesses (negative attributes) are internal factors in SWOT analysis. These internal factors can be altered by management over time; that is, management has control over these factors.

Opportunities and threats are the external factors and they can't be changed. Positive opportunities are those external factors that can result in a company prospering. For example, opportunities in the market that the company can capitalize on, or opportunities created by recent economic growth in the industry or other positive changes in the industry. Threats are negative factors from, for example, competition from current or potential competitors, risk factors that cannot be controlled by management, and unfavorable trends in the industry such as increases in input costs or greater regulation.

Key Points

- The analysis of a company begins with an economic and competitive analysis of the industry in which a company operates.
- Identifying the correct industry in which a company operates is not as simple as it may seem.
- Two frameworks for industry analysis are Porter's competitive forces model and PESTEL analysis.

- Porter's competitive forces model requires that the following five forces should be investigated: (1) threat of new entrants, (2) bargaining power of suppliers, (3) bargaining power of buyers, (4) threats of substitute products, and (5) rivalry of existing competitors.
- Financial data from a company's financial statements are used to analyze relationships between different elements of a company's financial statements.
- Financial statement analysis allows an analyst to formulate a picture of the operating performance and financial condition of a company.
- Looking at the calculated financial ratios, in conjunction with industry and economic data, an analyst can make judgments about a company's past and future financial performance and conditions.
- Financial ratios are categorized by the financial characteristic that they seek to measure — profitability, activity, liquidity, and debt ratios.
- Profitability ratios indicate how well a company manages its assets, typically in terms of the proportion of revenues that are left over after expenses.
- Activity ratios identify how efficiently a company manages its assets, that is, how effectively a company uses its assets to generate sales.
- Return-on-investment ratios reveal how much each dollar of an investment has generated in a period.
- Liquidity ratios tell an analyst about a company's ability to satisfy short-term obligations.
- Liquidity ratios are closely related to a company's operating cycle, which indicates how long it takes a company to turn its investment in current assets back into cash.
- Debt ratios indicate (1) to what extent a company uses debt to finance its operations and (2) its ability to satisfy debt and debt-like obligations.
- The DuPont system breaks down return ratios into their profit margin and activity ratios, allowing an analyst to analyze changes in return on investments.
- Common-size analysis expresses financial statement data relative to some benchmark item — usually total assets for the balance sheet and sales for the income statement.
- Representing financial data using common-size analysis allows an analyst to identify trends in investments and profitability.
- Interpretation of financial ratios requires an analyst to put the trends and comparisons in perspective with the company's significant events.

- In addition to company-specific events, issues that can cause the analysis of financial ratios to become more challenging include the use of historical accounting values, changes in accounting principles, and accounts that are difficult to classify.
- Comparison of financial ratios across time and with competitors is useful in gauging performance.
- In comparing ratios over time, an investor should consider changes in accounting and significant company events. In comparing ratios with a benchmark, an analyst must take care in the selection of the companies that constitute the benchmark and the method of calculation.
- The term cash flow has many meanings and the challenge is to determine the cash flow definition and calculation that is appropriate.
- The simplest calculation of cash flow is the sum of net income and non-cash expenses.
- Three frameworks from the field of management that are used for assessing the economic merits of a company are Value Chain Analysis, RBV analysis, and SWOT Analysis.
- Value Chain Analysis disaggregates the collection of activities that a company performs and the interactions of those activities in order to identify the sources of a company's competitive advantage and how the company can improve that competitive advantage by becoming more efficient in one or more of the activities.
- RBV Analysis is a framework that views the company's resources as the key to a company's performance and as a way of identifying how to achieve a competitive advantage.
- SWOT Analysis of a company covers both internal and external factors that impact the competitive position of a company.

References

Barney, J. B., 1991. "Firm resources and sustained competitive advantage," *Journal of Management*, 17: 99–120.

Dugan, M. T., and W. D. Samson, 1996. "Operating cash flow: Early indicators of financial difficulty and recovery," *Journal of Financial Statement Analysis*, 1(4): 41–50.

Eastman, K., 1997. "EBITDA: An overrated tool for cash flow analysis," *Commercial Lending Review*, 12: 64–69.

Fridson, M., 1995. *Financial Statement Analysis: A Practitioner's Guide.* New York: John Wiley & Sons.

Jensen, M. C., 1986. "Agency costs of free cash flow, corporate finance, and takeovers," *American Economic Review*, 76(2): 323–329.

Largay, J. A., and C. P. Stickney, 1980. "Cash flows, ratio analysis and the W. T. Grant Company bankruptcy," *Financial Analysts Journal*, 36: 51–54.

Porter, M. E., 1980. *Competitive Strategy: Techniques for Analyzing Industries and Competitors*. New York: Free Press.

Porter, M. E., 1985. *The Competitive Advantage: Creating and Sustaining Performance*. New York: Free Press.

Ward, T. J. and B. P. Foster, 2001. "The usefulness of aggregated and disaggregated cash flows in signaling financial distress," *Advances in Quantitative Analysis of Finance and Accounting*, 9: 55–80.

Chapter 11

Equity Valuation Models*

Learning Objectives

After reading this chapter, you will understand:

- the two methods for valuing a company's common stock: discounted cash flow model method and valuation by multiples method;
- the assumptions underlying valuation models and the limitations of these models;
- the different types of discounted cash flow models;
- candidates for the measure of cash flow;
- what a dividend discount model is and the economic rationale for this valuation model;
- that dividend discount models include the basic dividend discount model, finite life general dividend discount model, constant growth dividend discount model, constant dividend growth model, and multiphase dividend discount model;
- what a free cash flow discounted cash flow model is;
- how the franchise value valuation model is used;
- what a "price/X ratio," means in the valuation by multiples method;
- what the appropriate cash flow generating performance measure for similar companies should be used in the valuation by multiples method, and;
- what the cyclically adjusted price-to-earnings ratio (CAPE ratio) is.

In this chapter, we discuss popular methods for valuing a firm's equity or the value of a share of common stock. These methods fall into two categories: discounted cash flow model method and valuation by multiples

*Parts of this chapter draw from Frank Fabozzi's writings with Pamela Peterson Drake of James Madison University and Glen Larsen, Jr. of Indiana University.

method. Both methods require strong assumptions and expectations about the future. The product of these models is an estimate of the fair value of a stock. All fair value estimates are subject to model error and estimation error. There is no single valuation model that is perfect.

The individual on an asset management team responsible for valuation is the security analyst, who we refer to simply as the analyst in this chapter. The recommendation that the analyst will make to the senior portfolio manager will be either

- buy the stock if it is not owned;
- purchase additional shares if there is already a position in the stock;
- sell the stock if it is held in the portfolio;
- short the stock if the client's investment guidelines permit short selling.

Discounted Cash Flow Models for Valuation

The discounted cash flow models for estimating the fair value of a stock involve the analyst projecting all future cash flows that will be received from owning the stock and then calculating the present value of each future cash flow. In principle, this is simple in terms of calculations, but the inputs necessary to do the calculations are by far not straightforward to estimate. They include the (1) cash flows, (2) number of future periods over which the cash flows are expected to be received, and (3) the appropriate interest rate for discounting the cash flows.

The cash flows should be an estimate of what the analyst expects to be generated from purchasing the stock. There are several candidates for what the cash flow will be and these lead to the different fair value models discussed in this chapter. These candidates include the following:

- dividends;
- free cash flow;
- earnings;
- sales;
- book-value.

Dividends are the expected cash payments that the company's board of directors declares may be paid to shareholders from the company's earnings. *Free cash flow* is a type of cash flow measure that analysts use as a proxy for the amount of cash available to the company's management after making the necessary expenditures (i.e., capital expenditures) to maintain or expand its business. It is from the free cash flow that cash payments can be made to shareholders. We explained the calculation of free cash flow in the previous chapter.

The earnings measure is the amount based on generally accepted accounting principles (GAAP) that the company has earned for its common stockholders. Earnings are typically reported in terms of a per share amount. GAAP requires that two measures be computed by a company: basic earnings per share and diluted earnings per share. These measures are described in Chapter 2 of the companion book. As in the case of free cash flow, the earnings measure is just an estimate of what might be available for payments that can be made by the company to common stockholders.

The next two cash flow candidates — sales and book-value — are obviously not direct measures of cash flow. A company cannot distribute its sales to shareholders, nor can it distribute its book value. Rather, these measures are proxies for how much a company might be able to generate in cash to pay to common stockholders. These proxy measures are linked to the ability to pay cash. In Chapter 10, where we discuss financial statement analysis, that link is discussed. Consider the case of sales. Sales are related to future real earnings (as opposed to accounting earnings using GAAP). To do that, the analyst must look at the gross margin that can be earned on each dollar of sales. Beginning with projected sales to determine the cash that may be available to pay common stockholders is much more useful than looking at earnings. When analysts think about a company's future sales, they think in terms of sales from their existing operations and sales from potential future business opportunities that differ from its existing business. The profit margin on new business opportunities can be materially different from that of its existing business. Looking at future sales in terms of existing and future business is superior to just thinking in terms of how the growth of existing earnings can affect future payments that the company can distribute to common stockholders.

Based on the above, one way to categorize discounted cash flow models is as follows:

- dividend-based models;
- free cash flow-based models;
- sales-based models;
- earnings-based models;
- book value-based models.

The product of any discounted cash flow model is the stock's fair value. Given the fair value, the assessment of the stock proceeds along the following lines. If the market price is below the fair value derived from the model, the stock is said to be undervalued or cheap. The opposite holds for a stock whose market price is greater than the model-derived price. In this case, the stock is said to be overvalued or expensive. A stock trading at or close to its fair price is said to be fairly valued.

The discounted cash flow model tells us the stock's fair value but does not tell us when the price of the stock should be expected to move to its estimated fair value. That is, the model says that based on the inputs generated by the analyst, the stock may be cheap, expensive, or fair. However, it does not tell us that if it is mispriced, how long it will take before the market recognizes the mispricing and corrects it. As a result, an asset manager may hold on to a stock perceived to be cheap for an extended period of time and may underperform a benchmark designated by a client during that period.

While a stock may be mispriced, an analyst and asset manager must also consider how mispriced it is in order to take the appropriate action (buy a cheap stock and sell or sell short an expensive stock). This will depend on by how far the stock is trading from its fair value and the costs associated with trading that stock (i.e. transaction costs). An analyst and asset manager should also consider that a stock may look as if it is mispriced, but the perceived mispricing may be the result of poor estimates and/or the wrong valuation model coupled with poor estimates.

Dividend-Based Models

Dividend-based models are examples of discounted valuation models and are referred to as *dividend discount models*. The approach involves projecting a company's dividends into the future and discounting the projected dividends at an appropriate discount rate. Most dividend discount models use current dividends, some measure of historical or projected dividend growth for the company, and an estimate of the required rate of return. The required rate of return is the discount rate that is used to compute the discounted (or present value) of the projected future dividends. The greater the risk associated with realizing the projected future earnings, the higher the required rate of return that should be used.

The economic rationale for basing fair value on the dividends is as follows. If an investor buys a company's common stock, the investor has bought shares that represent an ownership interest in that company. Shares of common stock are a perpetual security — that is, there is no maturity. The investor who owns shares of common stock has the right to receive a certain portion of any dividends. However, dividends are not a sure thing since they depend on the company's ability to generate future earnings to support the dividend as well as whether the company's board of directors adopts a policy to pay out earnings in the form of dividends. Typically, we observe some pattern in the dividends that companies pay: Dividends are either constant or grow at a constant rate. But there is no guarantee that dividends will be paid in the future.

It is reasonable to believe that what an investor pays for a share of stock should reflect what the investor expects to receive from it — a return on the investor's investment. What an investor receives are cash dividends in the future. How can we relate that return to what a share of common stock is worth? Well, the value of a share of stock should be equal to the discounted value (present value) of all the future cash flows an investor expects to receive from that share. Therefore, to value the stock, an analyst must project future cash flows, which, in turn, means projecting future dividends. This approach to the valuation of common stock is referred to as the discounted cash flow approach and the models used are what we referred to earlier as dividend discount models.

Popular dividend discount models include the following:

- basic dividend discount model;
- finite life general dividend discount model;
- constant growth dividend discount model;
- constant dividend growth model;
- multiphase dividend discount model.

Basic dividend discount model

The *basic dividend discount model* (DDM) was first suggested by Williams [1938]. In this model, all of the expected future dividends are discounted at an appropriate interest rate. The basic DDM can be expressed mathematically as

$$P = \frac{D_1}{(1+r_1)^1} + \frac{D_2}{(1+r_2)^2} + \frac{D_3}{(1+r_3)^3} + \cdots, \tag{1}$$

where P is the stock's fair value, D is the expected dividend for period t, and r_t is the appropriate discount rate for period t. The assumption is that the dividends are expected to be received forever.

In practice, the assumption that is typically made is that the discount rate is the same for each period and therefore the model becomes

$$P = \frac{D_1}{(1+r)^1} + \frac{D_2}{(1+r)^2} + \frac{D_3}{(1+r)^3} + \cdots. \tag{2}$$

If investors never expected a dividend to be paid, then this model implies that the stock would have no value. To reconcile the fact that stocks not paying a current dividend have a positive market value with this model, one must assume that investors expect that someday, at some time period N, the firm must pay out some cash, even if only a liquidating dividend.

Practitioners rarely use the basic DDM. Instead, one of the DDMs discussed next is typically used.

The finite life general dividend discount model

The basic DDM assuming that the discount rate is the same in each period can be modified by assuming a finite life for the expected dividends rather than assuming dividends to infinity. The cash flow is then the expected dividends for a designated number of periods, say N, and an expected sale price at N. The expected sale price is also called the *terminal price* or *horizon price* and is intended to capture the future value of all subsequent dividend payouts. This model is called the *finite life general dividend discount model*[1] and is expressed mathematically as

$$P = \frac{D_1}{(1+r)^1} + \frac{D_2}{(1+r)^2} + \frac{D_3}{(1+r)^3} + \cdots + \frac{D_N}{(1+r)^N} + \frac{P_N}{(1+r)^N}, \tag{3}$$

where P_N is the expected price (or terminal price) at the horizon period N, N is the number of periods in the horizon, and the other values are the same as in the basic DDM assuming that the discount rate is constant.

Let's illustrate the finite life general DDM based on a constant discount rate assuming each period is a year. Suppose that the following data are determined for stock XYZ by an analyst:

$$N = 5\ D_1 = \$3.24\ D_2 = \$3.50\ D_3 = \$3.78\ D_4 = \$4.08$$
$$D_5 = \$4.41\ P_5 = \$40.00\ r = 5\%,$$

[1]More specifically, because it assumes that all discount rates are the same, it is referred to as a constant discount rate version of the finite life general DDM.

$$P = \frac{\$3.24}{(1.05)^1} + \frac{\$3.50}{(1.05)^2} + \frac{\$3.78}{(1.05)^3} + \frac{\$4.08}{(1.05)^4} + \frac{\$4.41}{(1.05)^5} + \frac{\$40.00}{(1.05)^5}$$
$$= \$3.09 + \$3.17 + \$3.26 + \$3.36 + \$3.45 + \$31.34 = \$47.68.$$

Based on these data, the fair value of this stock is \$47.48.

The terminal price is the most difficult of the three forecasts. According to the theory, the terminal price is the present value of all future dividends after period N. Note that the present value of the expected terminal price becomes very small if N is very large and the discount rate is high.

The forecasting of dividends is somewhat easier. Usually, past history is available, management can be queried, and cash flows can be projected for a given scenario. The discount rate r is the required rate of return. Forecasting r is more complex than forecasting dividends, although not nearly as difficult as forecasting the terminal price (which requires a forecast of future discount rates as well). In practice, for a given company, r is assumed to be constant for all periods and typically generated from the capital asset pricing model (CAPM). As explained in Chapter 9, the CAPM provides the expected return for a company based on its systematic risk (beta).

Constant growth dividend discount model

If future dividends are assumed to grow at a constant rate (g) and a single discount rate (r) is used, then the finite life general dividend discount assuming a constant growth rate becomes

$$P = \frac{D_0(1+g)^1}{(1+r)^1} + \frac{D_0(1+g)^2}{(1+r)^2} + \frac{D_0(1+g)^3}{(1+r)^3} + \cdots + \frac{D_0(1+g)^N}{(1+r)^N} + \frac{P_N}{(1+r)^N}, \tag{4}$$

where D_0 is the current dividend. It can be demonstrated that if N is assumed to approach infinity, the above model reduces to

$$P = \frac{D_0(1+g)}{r-g}. \tag{5}$$

This DDM is called the *constant growth dividend discount model*, a model first formulated by Gordon and Shapiro [1956].

Since the dividend in the first period (D_1) is equal to the current D_0 increased by the assumed dividend growth rate — i.e., $D_1 = D_0(1+g)$ — an equivalent formulation for the constant growth DDM is

$$P = \frac{D_1}{r-g}. \tag{6}$$

Consider a company that currently pays annual dividends of \$3.00 per share (i.e., $D_0 = \$3.00$). The dividend is expected to grow at a rate of 4% per year and therefore D_1 is \$3.00 times (1.04) which is \$3.12. Assuming a discount rate of 9%, the estimated fair value for this stock is

$$P = \frac{\$3.12}{0.09 - 0.04} = \$62.40.$$

Let's apply this model to estimate the price at the end of 2006 of three pharmaceutical companies: Eli Lilly, Schering-Plough, and Wyeth Laboratories.[2] While the example is applied to three companies more than 14 years ago, there is an important point about the limitations of the dividend discount models that comes out of this exercise.

The discount rate for each company was estimated using the CAPM assuming (1) a market risk premium of 5% and (2) a risk-free rate of 4.63%. The market risk premium is based on the historical spread between the return on the market (often proxied by the return on the S&P 500 Index) and the risk-free rate. At the time of this analysis, this spread was approximately 5%. The risk-free rate is often estimated by the yield on US Treasury securities. At the end of 2006, 10-year Treasury securities were yielding approximately 4.63% and we will use this rate in our illustration for the risk-free rate. The beta estimate for each company was: 0.9 for Eli Lilly and 1.0 for both Schering-Plough and Wyeth. The discount rate for each company based on the CAPM is

$$\text{Eli-Lilly: } r = 0.0463 + 0.9(0.05) = 9.125\%;$$

$$\text{Schering-Plough: } r = 0.0463 + 1.0(0.05) = 9.625\%;$$

$$\text{Wyeth: } r = 0.0463 + 1.0(0.05) = 9.625\%.$$

[2]Wyeth Laboratories was purchased by another pharmaceutical company, Pfizer, in 2009.

The dividend growth rate can be estimated using the compounded annual growth rate (CAGR) of historical dividends.[3] CAGR, g, is estimated using the following formula[4]:

$$g = \left(\frac{\text{Last dividend}}{\text{Starting dividend}}\right)^{1/(\text{no. of years})} - 1.$$

Substituting the values for the starting and ending dividend amounts and the number of periods into the formula, we get:

Company	1991 Dividend	2006 Dividend	Estimated Annual Growth Rate (%)
Eli-Lilly	\$0.50	\$1.60	8.063
Schering-Plough	\$0.16	\$0.22	2.146
Wyeth	\$0.60	\$1.01	3.533

The value of D_0, the estimate for g, and the discount rate r for each company are summarized as follows:

Company	Current Dividend (D_0)	Estimated Annual Growth Rate (%)	Required Rate of Return (r) (%)
Eli-Lilly	\$1.60	8.063	9.125
Schering-Plough	\$0.22	2.146	9.625
Wyeth	\$1.01	3.533	9.625

Substituting these values into the model, we obtain

$$\text{Eli Lilly fair value} = \frac{\$1.60(1.08063)}{0.09125 - 0.08063} = \$162.79;$$

[3]See Chapter 7 for an explanation of this measure.

[4]This formula is equivalent to calculating the geometric mean of 1 plus the percentage change over the number of years. Using time value of money mathematics, the 2006 dividend is the future value, the starting dividend is the present value, the number of years is the number of periods; solving for the interest rate produces the growth rate.

$$\text{Schering-Plough fair value} = \frac{\$0.022(1.02146)}{0.09625 - 0.02146} = \$3.00;$$

$$\text{Wyeth fair value} = \frac{\$1.01(1.0533)}{0.09625 - 0.0533} = \$17.16.$$

Comparing the estimated fair value as of the end of December 2006 to the actual market price at the end of December 2006, we see that this model does not do a good job of valuing these stocks:

Company	Estimated Price at the end of 2006	Estimated Price at the end of 2006
Eli-Lilly	$162.79	$49.87
Schering-Plough	$3.00	$23.44
Wyeth	$17.16	$50.52

Note that the constant growth dividend discount model is considerably off the mark for all three companies. The reasons include: (1) the dividend growth pattern for none of the three companies appears to suggest a constant growth rate; and (2) the growth rate of dividends in recent years surrounding the valuation date has been much slower than earlier years (and, in fact, negative for Schering-Plough after 2003), causing growth rates estimated from the long time periods to overstate future growth. And this pattern is not unique to these companies.

Another problem that arises when using the constant growth rate model is that the growth rate of dividends may exceed the discount rate, r. Consider the following three companies and their dividend growth over the 16-year period from 1991 through 2006, with the estimated required rates of return:

Company	1991 Dividend	2006 Dividend	Estimated Growth Rate g (%)	Estimated Required Rate of Return r (%)
Coca Cola	$0.24	$1.24	11.700	7.625
Hershey	$0.24	$1.03	10.198	7.875
Tootsie Roll	$0.04	$0.31	14.627	8.625

For these three companies, the growth rate of dividends over the prior 16 years is greater than the discount rate. If we substitute the D_0 (the 2006 dividends), the g, and the r into the equation for the constant growth dividend discount model, the estimated price at the end of 2006 is negative, which doesn't make sense. Therefore, there are some cases in which it is inappropriate to use the constant growth dividend discount model.

Multiphase dividend discount model

The assumption of constant growth is unrealistic and can even be misleading. Instead, most analysts modify the constant growth DDM by assuming that companies will go through different growth phases. Within a given phase, dividends are assumed to grow at a constant rate.[5] This type of valuation model is called a *multiphase dividend discount model.* There is a two-stage growth model and a three-stage growth model.

Two-Stage Growth Model: The simplest form of a multiphase DDM is the *two-stage growth model.* A simple extension of the constant growth DDM uses two different values for g. Denoting the first growth rate as g_1 and the second growth rate as g_2, and assuming that the first growth rate pertains to the next 4 years and the second growth rate refers to all years following, the constant growth dividend discount model can be modified as

$$\begin{aligned} P = {} & \frac{D_0(1+g_1)^1}{(1+r)^1} + \frac{D_0(1+g_1)^2}{(1+r)^2} + \frac{D_0(1+g_1)^3}{(1+r)^3} + \frac{D_0(1+g_1)^4}{(1+r)^4} \\ & + \frac{D_4(1+g_2)^1}{(1+r)^5} + \frac{D_4(1+g_2)^2}{(1+r)^6} + \cdots, \end{aligned} \tag{7}$$

where $D_4 = D_0(1+g_1)^4$. This simplifies to

$$P = \frac{D_0(1+g_1)^1}{(1+r)^1} + \frac{D_0(1+g_1)^2}{(1+r)^2} + \frac{D_0(1+g_1)^3}{(1+r)^3} + \frac{D_0(1+g_1)^4}{(1+r)^4} + P_4.$$

Because dividends following the fourth year are presumed to grow at a constant rate g_2 forever, the value of a share at the end of the fourth year (that is, P_4) is determined by using Equation (5), substituting $D_0(1+g_1)^4$ for D_0 (because period 4 is the base period for the value at end of the fourth

[5]Molodovsky, May, and Chattine [1965] were some of the pioneers in modifying the dividend discount to accommodate different growth rates.

year) and g_2 for the constant rate g:

$$P = \frac{D_0(1+g_1)^1}{(1+r)^1} + \frac{D_0(1+g_1)^2}{(1+r)^2} + \frac{D_0(1+g_1)^3}{(1+r)^3} + \frac{D_0(1+g_1)^4}{(1+r)^4} + \left\{\frac{1}{(1+r)^4}\left[\frac{D_0(1+g_1)^4(1+g_2)}{r-g_2}\right]\right\}.$$

Suppose a company's dividends are expected to grow at a rate of 4% for the next 4 years and then 8% thereafter. If the current dividend is \$2.00 and the discount rate is 12%,

$$P = \frac{\$2.08}{(1.12)^1} + \frac{\$2.16}{(1.12)^2} + \frac{\$2.25}{(1.12)^3} + \frac{\$2.34}{(1.12)^4} + \left\{\frac{1}{(1.12)^4}\left[\frac{\$2.53}{0.12-0.08}\right]\right\} = \$46.87.$$

If this company's dividends are expected to grow at the rate of 4% forever, the value of a share is \$26.00; if this company's dividends are expected to grow at the rate of 8% forever, the value of a share is \$52.00. But because the growth rate of dividends is expected to increase from 4% to 8% in 4 years, the value of a share is between those two values, or \$46.87.

As can be seen from this example, the basic valuation model can be modified to accommodate different patterns of expected dividend growth.

Three-Stage Growth Model: The most popular multiphase model employed by practitioners appears to be the *three-stage dividend discount model.*[6] This DDM assumes that all companies go through three phases, analogous to the concept of the product life cycle that has been observed. In the growth phase, a company experiences rapid earnings growth as it produces new products and expands market share. In the transition phase, the company's earnings begin to mature and decelerate to the rate of growth of the economy as a whole. At this point, the company is in the maturity phase in which earnings continue to grow at the rate of the general economy.

Different companies are assumed to be at different phases in the three-phase model. An emerging growth company would have a longer growth phase than a more mature company. Some companies are considered to have higher initial growth rates and hence longer growth and transition phases. Other companies may be considered to have lower current growth rates and hence shorter growth and transition phases.

[6]The formula for this model can be found in Sorensen and Williamson [1985].

In a typical asset management team, analysts supply the projected earnings, dividends, growth rate for earnings, and dividend and payout ratios using fundamental security analysis. The basis for the three-stage model is that the current information on growth rates and the like are useful in determining the company's phase and then the valuation model—whether one, two, or three stages—is applied to value the company's stock. Generally, the growth in the mature stage of a company's life cycle is assumed to be equal to the long-run growth rate for the economy.

As a generalization, approximately 25% of the expected return from a company (projected by the DDM) comes from the growth phase, 25% from the transition phase, and 50% from the maturity phase. However, a company with high growth and low dividend payouts shifts the relative contribution toward the maturity phase, while a company with low growth and a high payout shifts the relative contribution toward the growth and transition phases.

Free Cash Flow Based Models

While estimating future cash flows to an individual share of stock can seem daunting, some analysts prefer to estimate the free cash flow to the entire company. Doing this allows analysts to estimate the value of the entire company and then "back out" an estimated value of a share of stock. This is called the *free cash flow model* (FCF model) and it was introduced in Chapter 10. While legitimate accounting rules do enable managers and auditors some range of choices, at the end of the day, good companies wind up looking good and bad companies wind up looking bad.

In short, there is no one number in a company's income statement that truly gives an analyst the necessary information to value a company from a discounted expected future cash flow viewpoint. An analyst still has to select which type of cash flow to look at. But the choice becomes easier once an analyst answers the following question: What is my specific purpose for wanting to know how a company is doing?

There are many different types of users of financial information, and each is best served by concentrating on the most relevant information. Let's look at various kinds of numbers and consider what they say, and what types of investors will find them most useful.

Generally accepted accounting principles (GAAP) is a set of formal rules that produces what most of us have come to accept as the most official, or standard, version of income that a public corporation can report.

Essentially, GAAP is simple: revenues minus costs equal profits. But the world is a complex place. For convenience, we divide activities into time periods. In a simple world, all costs would be incurred in the same period as the revenues with which they are associated. But that is often not the case, so accountants have to find ways to identify which expenses should be matched against which revenues. One example is depreciation, a concept used to allocate multi-period costs of a given expense to all the periods in which the expense is expected to generate revenue (e.g., if a factory can produce revenue for 20 years, charge 5% of the cost to build it against revenue in each year).

Observers correctly note that depreciation rules are artificial, and advocate use of other performance measures that are supposedly more "realistic." But for now, it's important to understand that depreciation rules are motivated by good purpose. They, and other GAAP rules, are designed to paint a picture of the "economic" performance of the business, something that is not necessarily the same as a running tally of physical dollars coming in and going out within a specific period of time.

If an analyst is looking to see how a company is doing in order to form an opinion as to whether it has a track record of "success" (defined however the analyst wishes), GAAP income is very important.

As noted, many analysts do not like GAAP because of the artificial nature of depreciation. Their objection is valid. GAAP is, indeed, imperfect. Companies have latitude to determine how to calculate it. They do not always use an equal allocation for each year. It's difficult, if not impossible, to reliably estimate useful life, especially since assets are usually enhanced (i.e., factories are modernized) as time passes, thereby giving rise to extended life and additional depreciable expenses tacked on. An assumption that at the end of the depreciation period the asset will be worth zero, or some predetermined salvage value, is often untrue in the real world. And besides, there are other kinds of "artificial" revenue–expense matching formulations to cover other situations. But depreciation is usually the biggest objection.

The response is often to add depreciation back to net income to calculate cash flow. This can be a trap for the unwary. The phrase "cash flow" sounds comforting. After all, how much more reliable a gauge of performance can an analyst seek than cash-in minus cash-out? However, is the reported cash flow truly computed by adding depreciation back to net income? If that is what is happening, be very careful. Companies spend money to enhance their assets every year. Because it is understood that the benefits of these expenditures will span many years, they are not put on the income statement in any single year. So, in truth, simple cash flow understates a company's true cash-in minus cash-out situation. The solution lies in the company's free cash flow. To arrive at a company's free cash flow, we start with net income, add back the non-cash depreciation charge, and then subtract the year's capital-spending outlays.[7]

Once an analyst hones in on free cash flow, the analyst is not likely to be misled regarding liquidity. But that does not mean the analyst is learning about general corporate success or failure. Capital spending programs are not "smooth." In some years, expenditures are very large as major programs ramp up. In other years, capital spending shrinks as these programs wind down toward completion. If the company is in a heavy spending year, free cash flow could be negative, even though the company may be having a great year.

Discounted cash flow valuation depends on the construction of pro forma (as if) financial statements in order to estimate a company's future cash flows. This measure shows how a company might perform in the future "as if" it performs as it has in the past, among other assumptions that are made by the analyst. In any event, it is necessary to construct pro forma financial statements in order to estimate future free cash flows that are the basis for total firm valuation.

The free cash flow is used to value the entire firm and is popularly referred to as the *enterprise value*. But the enterprise value is the value that includes the sum of the free cash to equity investors and the free cash flow to creditors. Since the objective is to determine the fair value of the common stock, it is not the enterprise value that should be used in any discount cash flow models based on free cash flow but the free cash flow to equity investors. This free cash flow measure is referred to as the *free cash flow to equity*. In free cash flow to equity discount models, the inputs are the projected free cash flow to equity on a per share basis. This measure is obtained by first calculating the free cash flow of the company (i.e., the enterprise value), reducing it by the free cash to creditors, and then dividing the difference by the number of common shares outstanding. Given the free cash flow to equity projected for each period, it is then discounted by the appropriate discount rate to get the estimated value of the company's common stock.

[7]There are other adjustments, such as those relating to dividends and changes in net working capital; but for now, these simple adjustments will suffice.

The franchise value model

In the late 1980s, Martin Leibowitz and Stanley Kogelman were asked by their then employer, Salomon Brothers, to develop a valuation model to help the firm's analysts to better understand the valuation of the stocks traded on a particular non-US equity market which had realized an exceptional rate of growth. Analysts recognize that not all forms of earnings are significant contributors in valuing a company's stock. Leibowitz and Kogelman [1990] sought to delve more deeply into the future cash flows that determine a firm's P/E ratio. They labeled this valuation approach the *franchise value*. Because of the popularity of the price/earnings ratio (described earlier) as a valuation measure, Leibowitz and Kogelman decided to use that measure as the basis for their franchise value model and build upon the DDM described earlier in this chapter. It improves upon the commonly used DDM, in the sense that it is more flexible and offers greater insight.[8]

The underlying economic idea is that merely extrapolating the realized returns generated in the past based on the company's capital investment is inappropriate. Instead, when valuing a stock with the franchise value model, one must be able to assess the following capital investment returns:

1. sustainable investment returns that the analyst expects can be generated from the company's current business and
2. the capital investment return that can be achieved from what the analyst believes are growth opportunities.

Fundamentally, the franchise value model starts with decomposing a company's value into two components as follows:

$$\begin{aligned}\text{Firm's equity value} &= \text{Firm's current economic value}\\ &\quad + \text{Value of future growth opportunities.}\end{aligned}$$

Leibowitz and Kogelman define the company's tangible value (TV) to be the economic book value associated with its earning stream that can be derived from the current business without the addition of further capital.

[8]Liebowitz and Kogelman went on to publish other franchise value models. These are described in Leibowitz [2004].

TV is calculated as follows[9]:

$$\text{TV} = \frac{\text{ROE}_{eb} \times \text{BVPS}}{r}, \tag{8}$$

where ROE_{eb} is the return on equity for the existing business, BVPS is the book value per share, and r is the required rate of return.

Leibowitz and Kogelman define the company's future value (FV) as the foreseeable future value of its future business. FV is calculated as follows:

$$\text{FV} = \frac{(\text{ROE}_{nb} - r) \times G \times \text{BVPS}}{r}, \tag{9}$$

where ROE_{nb} is the return on equity for the new business and G is the growth rate of book value.

The fair value for the company's equity based on franchise value is the sum of TV and FV and is therefore,

$$\text{Fair value} = \frac{\text{ROE}_{eb} \times \text{BVPS}}{r} + \frac{(\text{ROE}_{nb} - r) \times G \times \text{BVPS}}{r}. \tag{10}$$

Valuation by Multiples Method

In practice, stock valuation of publicly traded companies is strongly tilted toward the use of discounted cash flow models. However, we cannot ignore the fact that many analysts as well as individual investors employ other methods to estimate the price of a company's stock. The primary alternative method is the *valuation by multiples*.

A multiple is just a ratio expressed as follows:

$$\frac{\text{Stock price}}{\text{Cash flow generating performance measure for similar companies}}. \tag{11}$$

These multiples are sometimes referred to as "price/X ratios," where the denominator "X" is the appropriate cash flow generating performance measure for similar companies. For example, the most popular multiple is the *price/earnings ratio* (P/E ratio) where the earnings per share estimate is

[9]The notation used here is different from that used by Leibowitz and Kogelman.

the cash flow generating performance measure used in the denominator. The P/E ratio is called the *earnings multiple.*

The appropriate cash flow generating performance measure for similar companies (i.e., the X in the price/X) ratio can be four of the five measures for the discounted cash flow models we described earlier. The one that is typically not relevant in the case of relative valuation is dividends. Therefore, there are multiples based on free cash flow-based or similar measures, sales-based measures, earnings-based measures, and book value-based measures.

The product of the discount cash flow model is the estimated fair value of the stock. The valuation by multiples is a relative valuation method. This is because the measure used in the denominator is based on similar companies. The "X" selected for calculating the price/X ratio is then applied to the same X of the company being evaluated to assess its relative price. Because valuation by multiples is a relative valuation method, the terms "relative valuation" and "valuation by multiples" are typically used interchangeably.

To explain how the valuation by multiples works, let's use an example. Suppose that an analyst chooses earnings as the scaling measure; that is, the analyst chooses earnings to be the performance measure by which prices of similar companies will be scaled. To scale the observed prices of companies by their earnings, the analyst computes, for each firm, the ratio of its price to its earnings — its P/E ratio or its earnings multiple. The analyst then averages the individual P/E ratios of comparable companies to estimate a "representative" P/E ratio, or a representative earnings multiple. To value a company, the analyst multiplies the projected earnings of the company being valued by the representative earnings multiple, the average P/E.

The key assumption of the valuation by multiples method is that similar (or comparable) companies included in the sample are fairly valued in the market. If this assumption is reasonable, then the "scaled" stock price or value (i.e., the discounted value of expected future cash flows) of similar companies should be much the same. That is, similar companies should have similar price/X ratios. The valuation by multiples is often used in the valuation of private equity (i.e., the equity of private companies whose stock is not traded). The key in applying valuation by multiples is identifying similar firms that can be used for valuing the company of interest.

Valuation by multiples is quick and convenient. However, its simplicity and convenience constitute both the appeal of this valuation method and the problems associated with its use by analysts and individual investors. By simplicity we mean that too many facts about the company are not considered and, as a result, too many questions are unanswered. Multiples should never be an analyst's only valuation method and preferably not even the primary focus because no two companies, or even groups of companies within the same industry, are exactly the same. The term similarly entails just as much uncertainty as the concept of "expected future cash flows" when seeking to apply a discounted cash flow model to value a company. Because the discounted cash flow model forces an analyst to consider the many economic and financial factors impacting the value of a company, it is the preferred valuation method. The use of multiples should be secondary.

Having said this, valuation by multiples can provide a valuable "sanity check." If an analyst has done a thorough valuation, the analyst can compare the predicted multiples to representative multiples of similar firms. If an analyst's predicted multiples are comparable, the analyst can, perhaps, feel more assured of the validity of the analysis performed. On the other hand, if an analyst's predicted multiples are out of line with the representative multiples of the market, then an analyst has some research to do in order to be convinced that the fair value generated from the discounted cash flow model employed is reasonable.

When employing the valuation by multiples, an analyst does not attempt to explain observed prices of companies. Instead, an analyst uses the appropriately scaled average price of similar companies to estimate values without specifying why prices are what they are. That is, the average price of similar companies is scaled by the appropriate "price/X" ratio. Consequently, the analyst is being agnostic about what determines prices. This means that there is no theory to guide the analyst on how best to scale observed market prices. So there is nothing to say that multiple price/X ratios can be used and that each one will generally provide a different estimate of price (value). Hence, the trick in valuing with multiples is selecting truly comparable companies and choosing the appropriate scaling bases — the appropriate "X" measure.

In practice, this means that valuation by multiples requires the use of several scaling factors (i.e., several multiples). Often the best multiples for one industry may not be the preferred multiples in another industry. This implies, for example, that the practice of comparing P/E ratios of companies in different industries is problematic (and in many cases inappropriate altogether). This further implies that when the analyst performs a multiple-based valuation, it is important first to find what the industry considers as the best measure of relative values.

Steps in the Valuation by Multiples Method

The five steps in the valuation by multiples method are:

Step 1: Choose similar (comparable or like-kind) companies;
Step 2: Choose bases for multiples;
Step 3: Determine an appropriate multiple;
Step 4: Project bases for the valued company;
Step 5: Value the company's equity.

Step 1: Choose similar (comparable or like-kind) companies

Since prices of other companies are scaled to value the company being analyzed, the analyst would like to use data of companies that are as similar as possible to the company being valued. The flip side of this argument, however, is that by specifying too stringent a criteria for similarity, the analyst ends up with too few companies to compare. With a small sample of comparable companies, the idiosyncrasies of individual companies affect the average multiples too much so that the average multiple is no longer a representative multiple. In selecting the sample of comparable companies, the analyst has to balance these two conflicting considerations. The idea is to obtain as large a sample as possible so that the idiosyncrasies of a single company do not affect the valuation by much, yet not to choose so large a sample that the "comparable companies" are not comparable to the one being valued.

Financial theory asserts that assets that are of equivalent risk should be priced the same, all else equal. The key idea here is that comparable companies are "assumed" to be of equivalent risk. Thus, the concept of being able to find comparable companies is the foundation for valuation by multiples. If there are no comparable companies, then valuation by multiples is not an option in valuing a company. In the previous chapter where we discussed company analysis, we explained the difficulties of identifying comparable companies.

Step 2: Choose bases for multiples

To convert market prices of comparable companies to a value for the company being analyzed, an analyst has to scale the valued company relative to the comparable companies selected. This is typically done by using several bases of comparison. Some generic measures of relative size often used in valuation by multiples are sales, gross profits, earnings, and book values.

Often, however, industry-specific multiples are more suitable than generic multiples. Examples of industry-specific multiples are price per restaurant for fast-food chains, paid miles flown for airlines, and price per square foot of floor space for retailers.

In general, the higher-up the scaling basis is in the income statement, the less it is subject to the vagaries of accounting principles. Thus, sales is a scaling basis that is much less dependent on accounting methods than earnings per share. Depreciation or treatment of convertible securities critically affect earnings per share calculations but hardly affect sales. On the other hand, the higher-up the scaling basis is in the income statement, the less it reflects differences in operating efficiency across companies — differences that critically affect the values of the comparable companies as well as the value of the firm being analyzed.

Step 3: Determine an appropriate multiple

Once the analyst has a sample of companies considered to be similar companies to the company being valued, an average of the multiples provides a measure of what investors should be willing to pay for comparable companies in order to estimate a fair value for the company whose valuation we seek. For example, after dividing each comparable company's share price by its earnings per share to get individual P/E ratios, the analyst can average the P/E ratios of all comparable companies to estimate the earnings multiple that investors think is fair for companies with these characteristics. The same thing can be done for all the scaling bases chosen, calculating a fair value per dollar of sales, per restaurant, per square foot of retail space, per dollar of book value of equity, and so on.

Note that fair value must be interpreted with care. This is because there is no market for either earnings per share or sales or any other scaling measure. Therefore, the computation of average multiples is merely a scaling exercise and not an exercise in finding how much the market is willing to pay for a dollar of earnings. Investors do not want to buy earnings; they only want cash flows (in the form of either dividends or capital gains). Earnings (or sales) are paid for only to the extent that they generate cash. In computing average ratios for various bases, we implicitly assume that the ability of companies to convert each basis (e.g., sales, book value, and earnings) to cash is the same. Keep in mind that this assumption is more tenable in some cases than in others and for some scaling factors than for others.

Realize that the term "average" is used here to mean the "appropriate" value that is determined by the average company in the comparable group. It may not be the strict average. It may be a mean, median, or mode. The analyst is also free to toss out outliers that do not seem to conform to the majority of companies in the group. Outliers are most likely "outliers" because the market has determined that they are different for any number of reasons.

Step 4: Project bases for the valued company

The average "prices per (Selected base – X measure)" of comparable companies are applied to the projected performance of the company being valued. Therefore, the analyst needs to project the same measures of the relative size used in scaling the prices of the comparable firms for the company being valued. For example:

1. To value a firm, we use earnings as a scaling basis to determine the average earnings multiple (i.e., the average P/E ratio). Thus, the earnings of the company being valued must be projected.
2. To use the average "price per restaurant" to value a fast-food chain, for example, the number of restaurants the chain will have must be projected. Realize the assumption here is that each restaurant in all fast-food chains generates the same cash flow.
3. To use the average "price per dollar of book value" (the market to book or MB ratio), the book value of equity must be projected.

The simplest application of valuation by multiples is by projecting the scaling bases 1-year forward and applying the average multiple of comparable companies to these projections. For example, the comparable company's average P/E ratio to the projected next year's earnings of the company being valued is applied. By applying the average multiple to next year's projections, an analyst overemphasizes the immediate company's prospects and gives no weight to more distant prospects.

To overcome this weakness of the one-step-ahead projections, a more sophisticated approach can be used; that is, apply the average multiples to "representative" projections — projections that better represent the company's long-term prospects. For example, instead of applying the average P/E ratio to next year's earnings, the comparable P/E ratio to the projected average earnings per share over the next 5 years can be projected. In this way, the representative earnings' projections can also capture some of the long-term prospects of the firm, while next year's figures (with their idiosyncrasies) do not dominate valuations.

Step 5: Value the company's equity

In the final step, an analyst combines the average multiples of comparable companies to the projected parameters of the firm to be valued in order to obtain an estimated value. On the face of it, this is merely a simple technical step. Yet often it is not. The values that we obtain from various multiples (i.e., by using several scaling bases) are typically not the same; in fact, frequently they are quite different. This means that this step requires some analysis of its own — explaining why valuation by the average P/E ratio yields a lower value than the valuation by the sales multiple (e.g., the valued firm has higher than normal selling, general, and administrative expenses) or why the market-to-book value ratio yields a relatively low value. The combination of several values into a final estimate of a company's equity value, therefore, requires an economic analysis of both "appropriate" multiples and how multiple-based values should be adjusted to yield values that are economically reasonable.

Cyclically Adjusted Price-to-Earnings Ratio

A popular P/E ratio for assessing whether the overall market is overvalued, undervalued, or fair valued is the *cyclically adjusted price-to-earnings ratio* (CAPE ratio). Developed by Robert Shiller and consequently also referred to as the *Shiller P/E ratio*, the CAPE ratio differs from the standard P/E ratio, in that the earnings per share used are historical earnings per share over a 10-year period adjusted for inflation.[10] That is,

$$\text{CAPE ratio} = \frac{\text{Price}}{\text{10-year average inflation-adjusted earnings per share}}. \tag{12}$$

The purpose of using 10 years of earnings is to smooth out the fluctuations in a company's earnings over the business cycle. The CAPE ratio has been used in looking at valuation in the stock market overall. The denominator in the ratio is calculated for the S&P 500 as follows. First, the annual earnings per share of every company in the S&P 500 is determined for the

[10]The CAPE ratio was introduced in Shiller [2000].

past 10 years. Second, the annual earnings per share are then adjusted for inflation. The Consumer Price Index is used to make the inflation adjustment. Finally, the average of all 500 companies' adjusted earnings per share is computed. Care must be taken to make sure the earnings calculated are properly computed on a historical basis given that GAAP has changed periodically and therefore impacts earnings.

The regular P/E ratio for the S&P 500 uses, in the denominator, the trailing 12-month earnings of each company in the index. To see the difference in the regular P/E ratio for the S&P 500 and the CAPE ratio, on June 23, 2019 the regular P/E was 22 while the CAPE ratio was 30.5. This historical mean for the regular P/E has been 16.1 while for the CAPE ratio it is 17.[11] Tully [2019] points out the two times where the CAPE ratio was at its highest was just before the 1929 stock market crash and during the 1988 to 2001 tech bubble.

Like any ratio, there are criticisms of the use of the CAPE ratio for market valuations. A study by Jeremy Siegel [2018] has found that by using national income and product account (NIPI) after-tax corporate profits rather than the reported earnings of the S&P 500 companies, the forecasting performance of the CAPE model improves. This is because historically changes in GAAP reporting of earnings has resulted in an overpessimistic valuation of the stock market.

Although originally used for valuation for a broad stock market index such as the S&P 500, in conjunction with Barclays, Shiller has developed several equity indices which apply the CAPE ratio as a key driver of valuing stock market sectors.

Franchise Value Price-to-Earnings Ratio

Earlier we provided the franchise valuation model proposed by Leibowitz and Kogelman [1990]. The original intent of their work was to provide a P/E ratio for the valuation of a company's common stock. Their franchise valuation model given by equation (10) is as follows:

$$\text{Fair Value} = \frac{\text{ROE}_{eb} \times \text{BVPS}}{r} + \frac{(\text{ROE}_{nb} - r) \times \text{G} \times \text{BVPS}}{r},$$

[11]Shiller P/E ratio by years is available at https://www.multpl.com/shiller-pe/table/by-year. A CAPE ratio online calculator is available at https://www.caperatio.com/.

where ROE_{eb} is the return on equity for the existing business, ROE_{nb} is the return on equity for the new business, BVPS is the book value per share, G is the growth rate of book value, and r is the required rate of return.

The earnings per share of the company is calculated by multiplying return on equity for the existing business by the book value per share. That is,

$$\text{Earnings per share} = \text{E} = \text{ROE}_{eb} \times \text{BVPS}.$$

We can then substitute E into the franchise valuation model. Denoting the price by P and solving P/E, we get the following P/E ratio based on the franchise model:

$$\text{Franchise P/E ratio} = \frac{\text{P}}{\text{E}} = \frac{1}{r} + \frac{(\text{ROE}_{nb} - r) \times G}{\text{ROE}_{eb} \times}. \tag{13}$$

Key Points

- Discounted cash flow model method and valuation by multiples method are the two major approaches for valuing common stock.
- The output of a valuation model is an estimate of a stock's fair value.
- All fair value estimates are subject to model error and estimation error.
- The recommendation that the analyst will make to the senior portfolio manager will be either buy the stock if it is not owned, purchase additional shares if there is already a position in the stock, sell the stock if it is held in the portfolio, or short the stock if the client's investment guidelines permit short selling.
- The discounted cash flow models for estimating the fair value of a stock involve the analyst projecting all future cash flows that will be received from owning the stock and then calculating the present value of each future cash flow.
- The inputs required for discounted cash flow models include the (1) cash flows, (2) number of future periods over which the cash flows are expected to be received, and (3) the appropriate interest rate for discounting the cash flows.
- The candidates for the cash flow that can be used in a discounted cash flow model are dividends, free cash flow, earnings, sales, and book value.
- If the market price is close to the value derived from a valuation model, the stock is said to be fair valued.

- If the market price is below (above) the fair value derived from a valuation model, the stock is said to be undervalued (overvalued).
- A valuation model suggests the stock's fair value but does not indicate when the price of the stock should be expected to move to its estimated fair value.
- Dividend-discount models are discounted valuation models that use a forecast of a company's future dividends as the cash flow.
- Most dividend discount models use current dividends and some measure of historical or projected dividend growth for the company.
- Dividend discount models include the basic dividend discount model, finite life general dividend discount model, constant growth dividend discount model, constant dividend growth model, and multiphase dividend discount model.
- In the basic dividend discount model, all of the expected future dividends are discounted at an appropriate interest rate.
- The finite life general dividend discount model is a special case of the basic DDM that assumes that the discount rate is the same in each period and that there is a finite life for the expected dividends.
- The constant growth dividend discount model is a special case of the finite life general dividend discount model when future dividends are assumed to grow at a constant rate.
- Because the assumption of constant growth is unrealistic, the constant dividend discount model can be modified to assume the company will go through different growth phases and the resulting model is the multiphase dividend discount model.
- The two most common multiphase dividend discount models are the two-stage growth model and the three-stage growth model.
- An alternative to a dividend discount model is a model based on future free cash flow.
- The free cash flow is used to estimate the enterprise value of a company which includes the sum of the free cash to equity investors and the free cash flow to creditors.
- Since the objective is to determine the fair value of the common stock, only the free cash flow to equity is used.
- The underlying economic idea behind the franchise valuation model is that a company's value is the sum of the sustainable investment returns that is expected to be generated from the company's current business and the capital investment return that can be achieved from what the analyst believes are growth opportunities.

- An alternative to the discounted cash flow models is the valuation by multiples.
- Multiples are sometimes referred to as "price/X ratios," where the denominator is the appropriate cash flow generating performance measure for similar companies.
- There are alternative measures that can be used for the cash flow generating performance measure for similar companies.
- The most popular multiple is the price/earnings ratio where the earnings per share estimate is the cash flow generating performance measure used in the denominator.
- The simplicity of the valuation by multiples makes it an appealing valuation method; however, there are too many facts about the company that are not considered and, as a result, too many questions are left unanswered.
- Multiples should never be an analyst's only valuation method and preferably not even the primary focus because no two companies, or even groups of companies within the same industry, are exactly the same.
- A difficulty in applying the valuation by multiples method is identifying comparable or similar companies.
- A popular P/E ratio for assessing whether the overall market is overvalued, undervalued, or fair valued is the cyclically adjusted price-to-earnings ratio (CAPE ratio) or Shiller ratio.
- The CAPE ratio differs from the standard P/E ratio in that the earnings per share used is historical earnings per share over a 10-year period adjusted for inflation.

References

Gordon, M. and E. Shapiro, 1956. "Capital equipment analysis: The required rate of profit," *Management Science*, 3(1): 102–110.

Leibowitz, M. L., 2004. *Franchise Value: A Modern Approach To Security Valuation*. Hoboken, NJ: John Wiley & Sons.

Leibowitz, M. L. and S. Kogelman, 1990. "Inside the P/E ratio: The franchise factor," *Financial Analysts Journal*, 46(6): 17–35.

Molodovsky, N., C. May, and S. Chattiner, 1965. "Common stock valuation: Principles, tables, and applications," *Financial Analysts Journal*, 21(2): 111–117.

Shiller, R. J., 2000. *Irrational Exuberance*. Princeton, NJ: Princeton University Press.

Siegel, J. J., 2018. "The Shiller CAPE ratio: A new look," *Financial Analysts Journal*, 72(3): 41–50.

Sorensen, E., and D. Williamson, 1985. "Some evidence on the value of dividend discount models," *Financial Analysts Journal*, 41(6): 60–69.

Tully, S., 2019. CAPE fear. *Fortune*, February 13. http://fortune.com/2019/02/15/cape-fear-the-bulls-are-wrong-shillers-measure-is-the-real-deal/.

Williams, J. B., 1938. *The Theory of Investment Value*. Cambridge, MA: Harvard University Press.

Chapter 12

Common Stock Beta Strategies

Learning objectives

After reading this chapter, you will understand:

- the difference between a beta strategy and an alpha strategy;
- the difference between a passive and an active investor;
- what is meant by the pricing efficiency of the stock market and the different forms of pricing efficiency;
- the difference between the efficient market hypothesis and the random walk hypothesis; the evidence on the pricing efficiency of the stock market and the implications for the selection of a common stock strategy (weak, semi-strong, and strong);
- what macro and micro market efficiency are;
- what is meant by indexing and enhanced indexing;
- the issues associated with an indexing strategy;
- methods of constructing a replicating portfolio (capitalization method, stratified sampling, quadratic optimization method);
- the disadvantages of pursing an indexing strategy using a traditional market-capitalization weighted index;
- what a smart beta strategy is and its benefits;
- the two categories of smart beta indexes: alternatively weighted indexes and factor indexes;
- the performance of popular smart beta strategies.

Common stock investment strategies are classified as either beta strategies or alpha strategies. As explained in Chapter 7, the beta of a portfolio or an investment strategy is a measure of the volatility of the portfolio or investment strategy relative to the benchmark. For example, if the benchmark is the Standard & Poor's 500 and the beta of a portfolio is equal to 1, this means that the portfolio will move with the market. So, if the S&P

500 changes in 1 year by 6%, the portfolio is expected to change by approximately 6%. Investors who either manage their own portfolio to match the performance of the benchmark or who engage an asset manager to do so, are referred to as *passive investors* and the strategies that they follow are referred to as *beta strategies*. In contrast, investors who pursue a strategy to outperform a benchmark or who engage an asset manager to do so are referred to as *active investors* and the strategies pursued are referred to as *alpha strategies*. In this chapter, we focus on beta strategies, and in the next chapter, we focus on alpha strategies.

Pricing Efficiency and its Investment Strategy Implications

The decision as to whether a client should use an equity asset manager who pursues a beta strategy or an alpha strategy depends on the client's investment belief about the efficiency of the stock market. More specifically, it is based on the investment belief about the pricing efficiency of the equity market. *Pricing efficiency* refers to a market where prices, at all times, fully reflect all available information that is relevant to the valuation of stocks. That is, relevant information about the stock is quickly integrated into the stock's price. Whether or not the equity market is price efficient is an empirical question and there have been a considerable number of studies that have investigated this issue.

Forms of Pricing Efficiency

Fama [1970] points out that to test whether a market is price efficient, the following two terms must be defined: (1) "fully reflects information" and (2) "relevant information set". Fama defines "fully reflects information" in terms of the expected return from holding a stock. A stock's expected return over some holding period is equal to expected cash distributions plus the expected price change, all divided by the initial price. The price formation process defined by Fama is that the expected return one period from now is a random variable that already takes into account the "relevant information set."

When defining the "relevant information set" stock prices should reflect, Fama classified the pricing efficiency of a market into three forms: weak, semi-strong, and strong. The distinction between these forms lies in the relevant information that is hypothesized to be taken into account in the stock's price. *Weak efficiency* means that the stock's price takes into account the stock's past price and trading history. *Semi-strong efficiency* means that the stock's price fully reflects all public information, which includes but is not limited to historical price and trading patterns. Public information includes the financial statements the company files with the Securities and Exchange Commission and other regulators, if any, and news releases by management. With *strong efficiency* the relevant information set includes all information, regardless of whether it is publicly available.

Empirical Test of Price Efficiency and Implications for Investment Strategies

Since the 1960s, there have been numerous empirical studies of each form of price efficiency. Each form has implications for the types of strategies we discuss in this chapter and the next.

Weak form of price efficiency

Various common stock strategies that involve only historical price movement, trading volume, and other technical indicators have been suggested since the beginning of stock trading in the United States, as well as in commodity markets throughout the world. Many of these strategies involve investigating patterns based on historical trading data (past price data and trading volume) to identify the future movement of individual stocks or the market as a whole. Based on the observed patterns, mechanical trading rules indicating when a stock should be bought, sold, or sold short are developed. Thus, no consideration is given to any factor other than the specified technical indicators. This approach is called *technical analysis*. Because some of these strategies involve the analysis of charts that plot price and volume movements, investors who follow a technical analysis approach are sometimes called *chartists*. The underlying principle of these strategies is to detect changes in the supply of and demand for a stock and capitalize on the expected changes. Edwards and Magee [1948] is widely acknowledged as the bible of technical analysis.

There is considerable debate on the value of technical analysis. Brock, Lakonishok, and LeBaron [1992] investigate some of the trading strategies based on technical analysis discussed in what follows. They conclude that the conclusion reached in the prior three decides that technical analysis had no merit was premature. However, several years later, Sullivan, Timmermann, and White [1999] found that for the best technical analysis strategies reported by Brock, Lakonishok and LeBaron, "there is scant evidence that technical trading rules were of any economic value." Hsu and Kuan [2005] examined the profitability of almost 40,000 technical trading strategies for the period 1989 to 1992 for four stock indexes. They found that the performance of trading strategies depended on the maturity of the indexes (i.e., how long the indexes were outstanding). Basically, they found that technical trading strategies were significantly profitable when applied to the two relatively immature stock indexes they studied but not when applied to the two mature stock indexes studied.

A comprehensive discussion of all of the empirical studies of technical analysis strategies is beyond the scope of this chapter. In what follows we provide a brief description of four technical analysis-based strategies: Dow Theory strategies, simple filter rules strategies, momentum strategies, and market overreaction strategies. But before doing so, let's review such strategies in the context of pricing efficiency. The weak form of pricing efficiency asserts that an asset manager cannot generate abnormal returns by simply analyzing the movements of historical price and volume movements. Thus, if technical analysis strategies can outperform the market, then the market is price-inefficient in the weak form. Another way of viewing this is that if an asset manager or client believes that the stock market is price-efficient in the weak form, then pursuing a strategy based on technical analysis will not consistently outperform the market on a risk-adjusted basis after consideration of transaction costs and management fees.

There are some market observers who believe that the patterns of stock price behavior are so complex that the simple mathematical models that we describe in the following are insufficient for detecting historical price patterns and creating mathematical models for predicting future price movements. As a result, although stock prices may appear to change randomly, there may well be a pattern, but employing simple mathematical tools to identify those patters are insufficient for that purpose. Scientists have developed complex mathematical models for detecting patterns from observations of some phenomena that appear to be random. These models are typically referred to as "nonlinear dynamic models". They are labeled as such because the mathematical equations used for detecting price patterns are nonlinear equations. The particular form of nonlinear dynamic models that has been suggested is *chaos theory*. At this stage, the major insight provided by chaos theory is that stock price movements that may appear to be random may, in fact, have a structure that can be used to generate abnormal returns (see Scheinkman and LeBaron [1989] and Peters [1991]).

Dow Theory strategies

This strategy is based on two assumptions. The first assumption made by Charles Dow, who proposed this strategy, is that "averages in their day-to-day fluctuations discount everything known, everything foreseeable, and every condition which can affect the supply of or the demand for corporate securities." This assumption sounds very much like the efficient market theory, but here is where the second assumption comes into play. The second assumption is that the stock market moves in trends — up and down — over periods of time. According to Charles Dow, it is possible to identify these stock price trends and predict their future movement. If this is so, and an asset manager can realize abnormal returns, then the stock market is not price-efficient in the weak form.

There are three types of trends or market cycles according to the Dow Theory. The primary trend is the long-term movement in the market. These are basically 4-year trends in the market. From the primary trend, a trend line showing where the market is heading can be derived by an asset manager. The secondary trend represents short-run departures of stock prices from the trend line. The short-term fluctuations in stock prices represent the third trend. In the view of Charles Dow, upward movements in the stock market were tempered by fallbacks that lost a portion of the previous gain. A market turn occurs when the upward movement was not greater than the last gain. In assessing whether or not a gain did in fact occur, Charles Dow suggested examining the co-movements in different stock market indexes such as the Dow Jones Industrial Average and the Dow Jones Transportation Average. One of the averages is selected as the primary index, and the other as the confirming index. If the primary index reaches a high above its previous high, the increase is expected to continue if it is confirmed by the other index also reaching a high above its previous high.

Empirically, it is challenging to test the Dow Theory because it is dependent upon identifying turning points. Several studies have attempted to test this theory. The first was by Cootner [1962] who found that it simply did not work. However, Glickstein and Wubbels [1983] found support for the Dow Theory, the authors concluded that "successful market timing is by no means impossible." Brown and van Harlow [1998] revisited the Cowles study by taking into account risk. More specifically, they used the Sharpe ratio and found support for the Dow Theory.

Simple filter rules strategy

The simplest type of technical strategy is to buy and sell on the basis of a predetermined movement in the price of a stock. The rule is basically that if the stock increases by a certain percentage, the stock is purchased and held until the price declines by a certain percentage, at which time the stock is sold. The percentage by which the price must change is called the "filter". Asset managers who want to use this technical strategy must specify their own filter.

A study by Alexander [1961] was the first to investigate the profitability of simple filter rules. Addressing methodological problems of the Alexander study, Fama and Blume [1966] found that price changes do show persistent trends. They found that the trends were too small to exploit after considering transaction costs and other factors that must be considered in assessing the strategy. Two subsequent studies by Sweeney [1988, 1990], however, suggest that a short-term technical trading strategy based on past price movements can produce statistically significant risk-adjusted returns after adjusting for the types of transaction costs faced by floor traders and professional equity managers.

Momentum strategies

Practitioners and researchers alike have identified several ways to successfully predict security returns based on historical returns. Among these findings, perhaps the most popular ones are those of *price momentum strategies* and *price reversal strategies*. The basic idea of a price momentum strategy is to buy stocks that have performed well (referred to as "winners") and to sell the stocks that have performed poorly (referred to as "losers") with the *expectation* that the same trend will continue in the near future. In contrast, in a price reversal strategy stocks that have historically poor performance are purchased (i.e., losers are purchased) with the hope that they will eventually reverse and outperform in the future or short stocks that that have historically good performance (i.e., winners are shorted), hoping that they will underperform in the future. Because a price reversal strategy is one in which the performance in the future is expected to be contrary to the historical performance, it is also referred to as a contrarian strategy.

Basically, the price reversal strategy is the inverse of the price momentum strategy.

Some asset managers are only permitted to buy and not short stocks; these asset managers are referred to as *long-only managers*. As a result, they can only pursue a price momentum strategy in which they buy winners and one in which they sell losers. Asset managers, such as hedge fund managers, that are free to take on both long and short positions can pursue any of the price momentum or reversal strategies. In fact, to create leverage, these asset managers can employ a price momentum strategy such that the value of the portfolio of winners is funded by shorting a portfolio of losers. That is, the net investment to the fund is close to zero. Similarly, in a price reversal strategy, the shorting of the winner portfolio is used to fund the purchase of the loser portfolio.

There is ample evidence supporting price momentum and price reversal strategies. Support for the price momentum strategy in the US stock market was first documented by Jegadeesh and Titman [1993]. Rouwenhorst [1998] found price momentum in other international equity markets. The empirical findings show that stocks that outperformed (underperformed) over a horizon of 6–12 months will continue to perform well (poorly) on a horizon of 3–12 months. Jegadeesh [1990] was the first to identify a short-term (one month) reversal effect and De Bondt and Thaler [1985] identified a long-term reversal effect. Typical backtests of these strategies have historically earned about 1% per month over the following 12 months. However, there is an empirical question regarding the changing nature of markets that suggests price momentum strategies will no longer produce superior returns. This has been documented by Hwang and Rubesam [2015] who, using data from 1927 to 2005, argued that momentum phenomena disappeared during the 2000–2005 period. However, analyzing the S&P 500 index over the 1970–2004 period, Figelman [2007] found new evidence of momentum and reversal phenomena previously not described.

Today, many practitioners rely on momentum strategies — both on shorter as well as longer horizons. Short-term strategies tend to capitalize on intraday buy and sell pressures, whereas more intermediate and long-term strategies can be attributed to overreaction and underreaction of prices relative to their fundamental value as new information becomes available (see Daniel, Hirshleifer, and Subrahmanyam [1998]). Momentum portfolios tend to have high turnover, so transaction and trading costs become an issue. Most studies show that the resulting profits of momentum strategies decrease if transaction costs are taken into account. For example, considering the different costs of buying and short-selling stocks, Korajczyk and Sadka [2004] find that depending on the method of measurement and the particular strategy, profits between 17 and 35 basis points per month (after transaction costs) are achievable.

Momentum is commonly used in factor models that we describe in Chapter 13. Momentum was found to be a systematic factor by Carhart [1997].

While researchers seem to be in somewhat of an agreement on the robustness and pervasiveness of the momentum phenomenon, the debate is still ongoing as to whether the empirical evidence indicates market inefficiency or if it can be explained by rational asset pricing theories.

Market overreaction strategies

To benefit from favorable news or to reduce the adverse effect of unfavorable news, investors must react quickly to new information. Cognitive psychologists tell us that people tend to (1) overreact to extreme events, (2) react more strongly to recent information, and (3) heavily discount older information. The question is, do stock market investors overreact to extreme events? The overreaction hypothesis in finance suggests that when investors react to unanticipated news that will benefit a company's stock, the price rise will be greater than it should be given that information, resulting in a subsequent decline in the price of the stock. In contrast, the overreaction to unanticipated news that is expected to adversely affect the fundamental value of a company will force the price down too much, followed by a subsequent correction that will increase the price.

Suppose that market participants do overreact to unanticipated events. Asset managers can exploit this so as to realize positive abnormal returns if they can (1) identify an extreme event and (2) determine when the effect of the overreaction has been impounded into the market price and is ready to reverse. This theory is what is referred to as the overreaction hypothesis. Asset management teams that have the ability to exploit market overreaction will do the following, depending on whether the news is positive or negative. When unanticipated positive news is identified, the asset manager will buy the stock and sell it before the correction to the overreaction. In the case of unanticipated negative news, asset managers will short the stock and then buy it back to cover the short position before the correction to the overreaction.

As originally formulated by De Bondt and Thaler [1985], the overreaction hypothesis can be described by two propositions. First, the extreme movement of a stock price will be followed by a movement in the stock price in the opposite direction. This is called the *directional effect*. Second, the more extreme the initial price change (i.e., the greater the overreaction), the more extreme the offsetting reaction (i.e., the greater the price correction). This is called the *magnitude effect*. However, as Bernstein [1985] pointed out, the directional effect and the magnitude effect may simply mean that investors overweight short-term sources of information. To rectify this, Brown and van Harlow [1988] added a third proposition which they refer to as the *intensity effect*. According to this effect, the shorter the duration of the initial price change, the more extreme the subsequent response.

There are several empirical studies that support the directional effect and the magnitude effect (see DeBondt and Thaler [1985, 1987] and Brown and van Harlow [1988]). Brown and van Harlow tested for all three effects (directional, magnitude, and intensity) and found that for intermediate- and long-term responses to positive events, there is only mild evidence that market pricing is inefficient; however, evidence on short-term trading responses to negative events is strongly consistent with all three effects. They conclude that "the tendency for the stock market to correct is best regarded as an asymmetric, short-run phenomenon". It is asymmetric because investors appear to overreact to negative, not positive, extreme events.

Semi-Strong Form of Price Efficiency

Empirical analysis on semi-strong price efficiency is mixed. Some studies support the proposition of efficiency when they suggest that investors who select stocks on the basis of fundamental security analysis — which consists of analyzing financial statements, the quality of management, and the economic environment of a company — will not outperform the market. This result is certainly reasonable: so many analysts use the same approach, with the same publicly available data, that the price of the stock remains in line with all the relevant factors that determine value. In contrast, a sizable number of other studies have produced evidence indicating instances and patterns of pricing inefficiency in the stock market over long periods.

Market observers refer to these examples of pricing inefficiencies as pricing anomalies in the market, that is, phenomena that cannot be easily explained and are often persistent.

Semi-strong efficiency remains controversial because of two issues associated with these tests. The first issue is how to measure outperformance relative to some stock market index. Typically, the CAPM is used to estimate the expected return on the market and in using that model, risk is considered so the return is risk adjusted. Thus, these tests depend on a model, the CAPM, that empirical studies have failed to support.[1] The reason is that the risk considered is only one measure of systematic risk — market risk. It ignores all other systematic risk. The abnormal return is the difference between the risk-adjusted return and some stock index return. The decision as to whether the market is efficient is based on whether the abnormal return is statistically significant.

If the market is price-efficient and the CAPM is truly the only way stocks and stock portfolios are priced, then no other factor should impact the return on a stock or a portfolio. When a researcher reported that factors such as market capitalization and volatility are statistically significant, market observers incorrectly thought these results were market anomalies and meant that the market is price efficient. Today, we realize that the market factor as suggested by the CAPM is a major driver of portfolio return but that there are other systematic factors that drive returns, and failure to consider them in empirical testing renders many of the findings questionable.

Strong Form of Price Efficiency

Empirical tests of the strong form of pricing efficiency have primarily focused on the performance of professional money managers. Most studies look at the performance of mutual fund managers. Rather than provide an extensive review of the vast literature on mutual fund performance, we will draw from the work of Berk and van Binsbergen [2016] who provide a comprehensive evaluation of the performance of mutual fund managers. Prior to the work of these two authors, the prevailing view based on empirical studies and anecdotal evidence was that managers of mutual funds that pursue active strategies lacked skill and therefore the management fee paid to active managers was not worth the expense. Yet, the amount of inflows

[1] Moreover, on a theoretical level, Roll [1977] criticized empirical tests of the CAPM arguing that while the CAPM is testable in principle, no correct test of the theory had yet been presented and none are likely in the future. According to Roll there is only one potentially testable hypothesis associated with the CAPM, namely, that the true market portfolio lies on the Markowitz efficient frontier (i.e., it is mean-variance efficient). Furthermore, because the true market portfolio must contain all worldwide assets, the value of most of which cannot be observed (e.g., human capital), the hypothesis is in all probability untestable.

to active management mutual funds has grown significantly and is therefore inconsistent if active management is a futile exercise.

The starting point in investigating performance is establishing a benchmark from which to evaluate the performance of asset managers. Berk [2005] challenges whether the historical alpha metric earned by asset managers, used in previous studies as a measure of managerial skill, is indeed the proper measure for evaluating managerial skill. Berk and van Binsbergen [2016, 131] argue that the appropriate measure of managerial skill is "value added" which they define as "the total number of dollars the manager extracts from markets", providing examples and empirical support. Berk and van Binsbergen provide examples to show the limitations of using traditional alpha measures and why value added is a better measure of managerial skill.

They investigate performance over the period from January 1977 to March 2011. The study looks at mutual funds, not individual managers. The sample included 5,974 mutual funds, a sample that was far larger than previous studies. There are four major findings of their study after adjusting for a fund's benchmark. First, the average value added by mutual fund managers is \$3.2 million per year in 2000 dollars. Second, this value added is attributable to managerial skill rather than luck because superior managerial performance persists for up to 10 years. Third, because investors recognize managerial skill, they compensate mutual fund managers accordingly and therefore the current compensation is a better predictor of future performance than historical performance metrics. Finally, value added is highly predictable because current value added is a reliable predictor of future value. Collectively, these findings explain the growth of capital allocated to mutual fund managers who pursue an active strategy and provide justification for investing in active strategies.

Efficient Market Hypothesis and the Random Walk Hypothesis

The efficient market hypothesis states that the market incorporates new information completely and quickly. In an efficient market, stock prices behave as if they followed a random walk. According to the *random walk hypothesis*, at any time, it cannot be determined whether prices will increase or decrease during the next period.

Expressed mathematically, the next period's price, denoted by P_{t+1}, can be expressed as the current period's price, denoted by P_t, plus a random error term denoted by e_{t+1}:

$$P_{t+1} = \rho P_t + e_{t+1}.$$

The Greek letter rho ρ is a statistical parameter that measures the correlation coefficient between P_{t+1} and P_t. More specifically, it is the serial correlation coefficient (also called the "autocorrelation coefficient"). It quantifies the extent to which the price in one period is related to the next period's price. Consider the case where ρ is equal to zero. In this case, there is no relationship between today's price and the price in the next period. It is in this case that the returns exhibit a random walk relationship and are truly random. If ρ is positive or negative, the returns exhibit a relationship and have positive or negative momentum, respectively. Based on annual returns for large cap and small cap stocks, the serial correlation coefficients over the period 1926 to 2016 are both approximately zero (0.02 and 0.06, respectively) [Ibbotson SBBI, 2017].

Although the random walk hypothesis and the efficient market hypothesis are related, they are not equivalent. This is because for a market to be price-efficient, market prices must exhibit a random walk as prices move toward the efficient level. However, prices could follow a random walk without being efficient. A pricing model, in addition, is necessary to determine the efficiency of a market. Thus, a random walk is a necessary but not sufficient condition for price efficiency. Calculating the degree of randomness in a series is simple but determining the efficiency of a market is difficult and remains a controversial topic.

Overall, if a market is highly price-efficient, it is impossible to outperform the market consistently and, as a result, a passive strategy is ideal. For active strategies to be appropriate, there must be inefficiencies in market prices that can be exploited. Of course, these active strategies would also have to cover transaction costs and management fees to be successful.

Micro vs. Macro Stock Market Efficiency

Paul Samuelson made the following comment about stock market efficiency:

> Modern markets show considerable micro efficiency (for the reason that the minority who spot aberrations from micro efficiency can make money from those occurrences and, in doing so, they tend to wipe out any persistent inefficiencies). In no contradiction to the previous sentence, I had hypothesized considerable macro inefficiency, in the sense of long waves in the time series of aggregate indexes of security prices below

and above various definitions of fundamental values" (cited in Shiller [2001, p. 243]).

According to Samuelson, it is more likely that the efficient market hypothesis is more appropriate for individual stocks than for the aggregate stock market. In other words, Samuelson believes that the stock market is "micro efficient" but not necessarily "macro inefficient." This view is known as "Samuelson's dictum." Studies that have looked for efficiency in the aggregate stock market and in various components of the stock market, such as industries, provide support for Samuelson's dictum (see, for example, Shiller [1981], Jung and Shiller [2005], Campbell and Shiller [1988], and LeRoy and Porter [1981]). Inefficiencies in terms of pricing were measured in these studies on the basis of volatility that should not be excessive in an efficient market. This is referred to as *excess volatility*. The studies found that inefficiencies existed at the aggregate stock market level, providing support for macro inefficiency. However, at the industry, sector, or individual security level, no price inefficiency has been reported, thereby providing support for micro efficiency.

Implications for Selecting Investment Strategies

As mentioned at the outset of this chapter, common stock investment strategies can be classified as beta and alpha strategies. Alpha equity strategies attempt to outperform the market by one or more of the following methods: timing the selection of transactions, such as in the case of technical analysis; identifying undervalued or overvalued stocks using fundamental security analysis; and selecting stocks according to market anomalies. Obviously, the decision to pursue an active strategy rests on the belief that some type of gain can be made from such efforts, even after accounting for transaction costs and management fees, but gains are possible only if pricing inefficiencies exist. The particular strategy chosen depends on what pricing inefficiencies the investor believes are occurring and these are discussed in the next chapter.

Investors who believe that the market is pricing stocks efficiently should accept the implication that attempts to outperform the market cannot be systematically successful, except by luck. This implication does not mean that investors should shun the stock market but instead suggests that they should pursue a beta strategy, which is one that does not attempt to outperform the market. Is there an optimal investment strategy for someone who holds this investment belief in the pricing efficiency of the stock? According to capital market theory described in Chapter 9, the market portfolio offers the highest level of return per unit of risk in a market that is price efficient. A stock portfolio with characteristics similar to those of a portfolio consisting of the entire stock market will capture the market's pricing efficiency.

But how does an asset manager create a portfolio that resembles the market? One approach is to construct a portfolio that holds all stocks based on their market capitalization relative to the capitalization of the stock market. This approach is referred to as *indexing*.

Equity Indexing Strategy[2]

Indexing is a beta strategy where the portfolio is constructed based on the market capitalization of the stocks in a selected stock market index and the market capitalization of all stocks. That is, the percentage of the portfolio allocated to every stock is based on its relative market capitalization. Thus, if the aggregate market capitalization of all stocks included in the market portfolio is \$T and the market capitalization of one of these stocks is \$A, then the fraction of this stock that should be held in the market portfolio is \$A/\$T. While indexing may be a passive form of investing, there are still many issues that the asset manager must address. Here we explain how an indexed portfolio is constructed and maintained.

Selecting the Benchmark

The first step in pursuing an indexing strategy is the selection of the index or benchmark. We described the various stock market indexes in the United States in Chapter 3. There are broad-based indexes and special indexes, or sub-indexes. A pure index fund is a portfolio that is managed so as to perfectly replicate the performance of the market portfolio. The market portfolio in reality is not known with certainty. Nonetheless, the S&P 500 has served as the consensus representative of the market portfolio. The major problem with the use of the S&P 500 as the benchmark is that the stocks are arbitrarily selected by a committee of the Standard & Poor's Corporation. This committee's selection criterion has nothing to do with the growth and earnings potential of a company. Nor is a selection based on

[2]This section is coauthored with Bruce Collins.

whether an issue is undervalued. Thus, asset managers who have a quarrel with indexing do not argue that an active strategy is better than a passive strategy, but rather that the selection of the S&P 500, or any broad-based index, is simply an arbitrary benchmark.

Considerations for Constructing a Replicating Portfolio

Once an asset manager has decided to pursue an indexing strategy and has selected a benchmark, the next step is to construct a portfolio that will track the index. We refer to the portfolio constructed to match an index or benchmark as the *replicating portfolio.* The objective in constructing the replicating portfolio is to minimize the difference in performance between it and the benchmark.

Transaction Costs and Tracking Error Risk

The costs of initiating and maintaining an S&P 500 index fund involve commissions, market impact costs, and rebalancing costs. These costs are explained in the next chapter and in far more detail in Chapter 12 in the companion volume. Asset managers pursuing an indexing strategy usually incur fewer turnovers than alpha strategies described in the next chapter when the benchmark is dominated by large-capitalization issues. Transaction costs may be particularly high for some of the smaller capitalized issues in the benchmark. In formulating an indexing strategy, an asset manager attempts to minimize the costs incurred when trading in some of the smaller-capitalized issues while retaining the replicating portfolio's ability to track the index.

Designing the optimal replicating portfolio may involve holding all the stock issues in the benchmark or a subset of those issues. The number of stock issues in the replicating portfolio affects transaction costs but holding fewer stock issues than contained in the benchmark means that the portfolio is exposed to the risk that the replicating portfolio will underperform the benchmark. This risk is referred to as *tracking error risk.*[3] There is a trade-off between the number of issues in the replicating portfolio and tracking error risk.[4] The trade-off between tracking error risk and number of issues held must also be considered

---

[3]Tracking error is described in Chapter 7.

[4]Chapter 15 in the companion book describes this tradeoff as well as the determinants of tracking error risk.

in terms of transaction costs, which increase with the number of issues traded.

It is next to impossible for a portfolio's returns to exactly match the return on the benchmark. Even if a replicating portfolio is designed to exactly replicate a benchmark by buying all the stock issues, tracking error risk will result.[5] There are several reasons for this.

First, because odd-lot purchases are cumbersome, replicating portfolios usually comprise round lots, and as such the number of shares of each stock in the portfolio is rounded off to the nearest hundred from the exact number of shares indicated by the computer programs that have been developed to build the optimal replicating portfolio. This rounding may affect the ability of smaller replicating portfolios (less than $25 million) to accurately track the index.

Second, and more importantly, the maintenance of a replicating portfolio is a dynamic process. Since most indexes are capitalization-weighted, the relative weights of individual issues are constantly changing. In addition, the stocks that compose the index often change. Thus, the cost of continually adjusting the portfolio, as well as timing differences, hinders an indexer's ability to accurately track a benchmark. The former problem is eliminated by holding all stocks in the benchmark. The portfolio is then self-replicating, which simply means the weights are self-adjusting. If, however, the replicating portfolio contains fewer stocks than the benchmark, the weights are not self-adjusting and may require periodic rebalancing.

Benchmark Construction and the Replicating Portfolio

The method used to construct a replicating portfolio is to formulate a procedure to determine the weight of each issue. There are three basic ways to look at weighting: (1) capitalization or market value, (2) price, and (3) equal dollar weighting. The market value weighting for a single stock in an index is determined by the proportion of its value to the total market value of all stocks in the index. The typical price-weighting scheme assumes equal shares invested in each stock, and the price serves as the weight. Equal dollar weighting requires investing the same dollar amount in each stock.

---

[5]Through the use of relatively inexpensive forms of financing, institutional investors have access to derivative instruments (the subject of Chapter 14) that can achieve close to zero-tracking error risk.

With capitalization weighting, the largest companies naturally have the greatest influence over the index value. Consequently, underweighting or overweighting in a large-capitalization stock can lead to substantial tracking error risk. Also, these stocks tend to be the most liquid. Price weighting endows the highest-priced stock with the greatest influence on the index value. Equal dollar weighting does the opposite. In this case, the lowest-priced stocks have the greatest potential to move the index for a given change in stock price. It is important to understand these properties when constructing a replicating portfolio.

There are two methods of constructing a replicating portfolio: arithmetic and geometric. Typically, stock market indexes use arithmetic averaging. Consequently, we focus only on arithmetic averaging. An arithmetic index is simply the weighted average of all stocks that make up the index where the weights are determined by one of the weighting schemes mentioned; that is,

$$\text{Index} = \text{Constant} \times \sum_{i=1}^{N} (\text{Weight}_i \times \text{Price}_i),$$

where N is the number of stock issues in the index, and the constant represents an arbitrary number used to initialize the value of the index.

Indexes based on arithmetic averages can be easily replicated regardless of the weighting scheme. Over time, however, if there are no changes in the composition of the index, as the price of a stock changes, the weights adjust automatically for consistency with the share amounts. This is true only for an arithmetic index where the share amounts do not change. Consequently, no rebalancing is necessary. However, this is not true for equally weighted indexes because share amounts must change to maintain equal dollar amounts for each stock.

The implication for the management of the replicating portfolio is that holding all the issues in the index reduces the need for rebalancing. But even if the entire index is held, rebalancing may be necessary because changes in the weighting may occur for any of the following reasons:

- Some issues may cease to exist due to merger activity.
- A company may be added to or deleted from the index should it meet or fail to meet capitalization or liquidity requirements for inclusion in an index or listing on an exchange.
- A company may split its stock or issue a stock dividend.

- New stock may be issued.
- Current stock may be repurchased.

Should any of these events occur, the constant term in the index valuation expression may require adjustment to avoid a discontinuous jump in the index value.

Methods of Constructing a Representative Replicating Portfolio

As we discussed, one way to replicate an index is by purchasing all stock issues in the index in proportion to their weightings. Constructing a replicating portfolio with fewer stock issues than the index involves one of three methods.

Capitalization method

Using the capitalization method, the asset manager purchases a number of the largest capitalized names in the index stock issues and equally distributes the residual stock weighting across the index. For example, if the top 200 highest-capitalization stock issues are selected for the replicating portfolio and these issues account for 85% of the total capitalization of the index, the remaining 15% is evenly proportioned among the other stock issues.

Stratified method

The second method for replicating an index is the stratified method. The first step in using this method is to define a factor by which the stocks that make up an index can be categorized. A typical factor is industry sector. Other factors might include risk characteristics such as beta or capitalization levels. The use of two characteristics would add a second dimension to the stratification. In the case of industry sectors, each company in the index is assigned to an industry. This means that the companies in the index have been stratified by industry. The objective of this method is then to reduce residual risk by diversifying across industry sectors in the same proportion as the benchmark. Stock issues within each stratum, or, in this case, industry sector, can then be selected randomly or by some other method such as capitalization ranking, valuation, or optimization.

Quadratic optimization method

The final method uses a quadratic optimization procedure to generate an efficient set of portfolios, and hence is called the quadratic optimization method. This is the same procedure that we described in Chapter 8 to generate the Markowitz (mean-variance) efficient set. The efficient set includes minimum-variance portfolios for different levels of expected returns. The asset manager can select a portfolio among the set that satisfies the client's risk tolerance.

Enhanced Indexing

Some asset managers pursue an indexing strategy that allows for some active management by designing a well-diversified portfolio that takes advantage of superior estimates of expected returns and controlling market risk. Such a strategy is referred to as *enhanced indexing*. Two methods are intended to improve the risk-adjusted portfolio return. The first involves creating a "tilted" portfolio, while the second utilizes the stock index futures market.

The tilted portfolio can be constructed to emphasize a particular industry sector or performance factor — for example, fundamental measures such as earnings momentum, dividend yield, and price/earnings ratio. Or it can be constructed to emphasize economic factors such as interest rates and inflation. The portfolio can be constructed to maintain a strong relationship with a benchmark by minimizing tracking error. An illustration is presented in Chapter 15 in the companion book.

The second method involves the use of stock index futures. The introduction of index-derivative products has provided asset managers with the tools that, when used correctly, may be able to enhance the returns to an index fund. The replacement of stocks with undervalued stock index futures contracts can add value to an indexed portfolio's annualized return without incurring any significant additional risk.

The distinction between active strategies and enhanced indexing is the degree of risk control. In enhanced indexing, the focus is on risk control. The bets that are made by an enhanced indexer do not cause the portfolio's characteristics to depart materially from the benchmark. An active manager's portfolio can deviate materially from the characteristics of the benchmark.

Smart Beta Strategy

Indexing is basically a method for capturing the market risk premium by constructing a portfolio based on market capitalization. This is based on the theory that if the market is price-efficient, then the most efficient way to capture the market risk premium is to construct a portfolio to replicate the performance of the market. However, if markets are not efficient, indexing may not be the best way to capture the market risk premium. Moreover, the drawback of using market-capitalization indexes is that they place greater emphasis on the stock of higher valuation companies and, as a result, produce unintended concentration risk in individual stocks and sectors. By doing so, such indexes neglect the equity of smaller firms that potentially may be the more promising firms that should have a higher allocation.

Alternative methods have been proposed. The most popular strategy for doing so is a *smart beta strategy*. In general, a smart beta strategy is a rule-based construction method where the exposure to each stock is based not on market capitalization but on firm characteristics or systematic factors. The expectation is that the rules established will result in an expected return greater than a market-capitalization based strategy.

There are many terms that are used to describe a smart beta strategy. Morningstar, for example, uses the term *strategic beta*. EDHEC Risk Institute has branded the term *scientific beta*. Several asset management firms refer to it as *alternative beta*. According to Morningstar, there are more than 845 smart (scientific) beta strategies.

Typically, retail investors get exposure to smart beta strategies via exchange-traded funds (ETFs).As of year-end 2017, there was $710 billion invested in smart beta ETFs. A 2019 survey of financial advisors, conducted jointly by ETF.com and Brown Brothers Harriman, found that 83% of survey respondents planned to maintain or increase their exposure to strategic beta in the next year.

Smart Beta Indexes

There are two categories of smart beta indexes: alternatively weighted indexes and factor indexes.[6]

[6]For an excellent discussion of smart beta strategies, see Arnott, Kalesnik, Moghtader, and Scholl [2010].

Alternatively weighted indexes

Typically, *alternatively weighted indexes* are designed to accomplish one or both of the following objectives. First, they can be designed to avoid the concentration of risk associated with market capitalization weighted indexes. Second, they can be designed to reduce the volatility within a traditional index. There are four types of indexes: equally weighted, fundamental, minimum variance, and risk-efficient.

Equally weighted

In an equally weighted index, all stocks that are included in a traditional market-capitalization weighted index are assigned the same weight.[7] There is no regard for any fundamental attribute of the company or any factor characteristics. So, if a traditional market capitalization-weighted index has N stocks, then each stock is assigned a weight of 1/N. The argument for using this weighting scheme is that the risk of concentrating on high price and high valuation stocks that may be overvalued is avoided. The drawback of this type of index is that the risk profile of an equally weighted index is very different from the risk profile of a traditional capitalization-weighted index. Moreover, the transactions for rebalancing may be higher than indexing, thereby reducing the return on a smart beta strategy that uses an equally-weighted allocation.

Fundamental indexes

Arnott, Hsu, and Moore [2005] first proposed fundamental indexation.[8] In the construction of fundamental indexes, the object is to weight stocks based on what the financial economics literature reports influences a company's economic value. This includes measures such as sales, cash flows, book equity, and dividends. These accounting and final measures are described in Chapter 10.

This strategy is just the opposite of an indexing strategy in terms of buying and selling stocks. In an indexing strategy, as the price of a

[7]This strategy, also referred to as the naive strategy, was first tested by DeMiguel, Garlappi, and Uppal [2009]. The reasons why a naive strategy might be expected to outperform a market-capitalization weighted index and a price-weighted index are provided by Plyakha, Uppal, and Vilkov [2012].

[8]This was the first smart beta strategy proposed.

company's stock increases — which means the company's market capitalization increases (decreases) — the asset manager pursuing this strategy would purchase more (less) of that company's stock. This would occur regardless of whether company fundamentals have changed. In the smart beta strategy, increasing or decreasing exposure to a company's stock depends on what happens to the company's fundamentals. When a company's stock increases even though the company's fundamentals have not changed, then there is no reason to increase exposure to the company as would happen in an indexing strategy. Instead, with a smart beta strategy that is based on fundamentals, the exposure to a company is reduced by selling the stock. If, on the other hand, the price of a company's stock declines but there is no deterioration in the company's fundamentals, the exposure to that company is increased. This is in contrast to an indexing strategy where the stock of such a company would be decreased.

Minimum variance

In Chapter 8, we explained how to use an optimization model — more specifically, mean-variance optimization — to construct a portfolio on the efficient frontier that has minimum portfolio volatility. However, if the optimization is done properly, how can the risk-adjusted return be improved since the optimization should provide the highest expected return at the minimum portfolio volatility? It can't if the market is price-efficient and if there is a linear relationship between beta and risk. If there is mispricing and/or there is a nonlinear relationship, a minimum variance index can be created that can potentially generate a higher risk-adjusted return than a market-capitalization index. The minimum variance index that is used in a smart beta strategy is obtained based on an optimization without any reference to the expected return.[9] When the optimization is done without imposing constraints on the allocations to stocks or sectors, high concentration can result. Consequently, in practice there are usually constraints imposed.

[9] This index was first proposed by Haugen and Baker [1991]. They argued that because of market imperfections such as taxes and restrictions on short selling, as well as market expectations, a minimum variance portfolio (index) can outperform a capitalization-weighted index.

Risk efficient

The smart index created for a risk-efficient index assumes that there is a linear relationship between return and some measure of semi-deviation. Using optimization, in this case mean-semi-deviation rather than mean-variance, the maximizing portfolio with the maximum return-risk ratio is sought. The return-risk ratio used is the Sharpe ratio and the resulting portfolio is the risk-efficient index.[10]

Factor indexes

Factor indexes are constructed to replicate the factor risks in a traditional index by using rules that are transparent and such that the constructed index is investable. The factors that numerous studies have found to be drivers of risk and return are value (quality), size, low volatility, dividend yield, and momentum. The three most commonly used factors in smart beta strategies tend to be:

- **Low-Volatility:** Stocks are weighted based on their level of volatility over some specified time period.
- **Momentum:** Stocks are weighted based on their price momentum over a specified time period.
- **Quality:** Criteria used to weight stocks include the strength of balance sheets, consistent earnings performance, and high levels of profit measures such as return on equity.

We describe each of these factors in more detail and how they are measured, as well as other factors, in the next chapter when we describe factor investing.

Performance of Popular Smart Beta Strategies

Is there a best smart beta strategy? A study by Tony Davidow, an alternative beta and asset allocation strategist at the Schwab Center for Financial Research, provides insight as to whether there is a best smart beta

[10]Risk-efficient smart beta indexes were introduced by EDHEC Risk Institute and FTSE Russell. See https://www.ftserussell.com/products/indices/EDHEC-Risk.

strategy.[11] Davidow empirically investigated the annual performance of the five most popular smart beta strategies compared to the annual performance of a market-capitalization weighted index (S&P 500) for the years 2008 through September 2017. The smart beta strategies analyzed were (1) equally weighted, (2) fundamental weighted, (3) low volatility weighted, (4) momentum weighted, and (5) quality weighted. Table 1 shows for each year the year-over-year returns of the best and worst performing smart beta strategies. Also reported is the return for an indexing strategy (the market-capitalization weighted index, the S&P 500).

As can be seen from Table 1, there is no strategy that performed the best in every year. For the 10-year period, the equally weighted strategy was the best performing smart beta strategy in 3 years but the worst performing in 1 year. The low volatility strategy was the best performing in four of the 10 years and the worst performing in only 1 year. Looking at the last column of the exhibit, the S&P 500 return is shown. In parentheses is the ranking of its return out of the six strategies (five smart beta strategies and indexing). The indexing strategy was never the best nor the worst strategy. It is interesting to note that in all but 1 year did the equally weighted index

TABLE 1: Best and Worst Year-over-Year Returns for Five Smart Beta Strategies and for the Market-Weighted Capitalization

Year	Best Performing	Worst Performing	Market Cap, Return (Rank)
2008	Low volatility (−21.4%)	Momentum (−41,1%)	−36.7% (4)
2009	Equal (46.3%)	Momentum (17.1%)	26.5% (4)
2010	Equal (46.3%)	Low volatility (13.4%)	15.1% (4)
2011	Low volatility (14.8%)	Equal weight (−0.1%)	2.1% (5)
2012	Equal (17.6%)	Low volatility (10.3%)	16.0% (4)
2013	Equal (36.1%)	Low volatility (23.6%)	32.4% (4)
2014	Low volatility (17.5%)	Fundamental (12.3%)	13.7% (4)
2015	Momentum (8.7%)	Fundamental (−3.0%)	14.6% (4)
2016	Fundamental (16.3%)	Momentum (4.6%)	12.0% (3)
2017	Momentum (37.4%)	Fundamental (17.3%)	21.8% (3)

Notes: Created by authors from returns reported in The Schwab Asset Class Quilt^{R} (Charles Schwab, "Smart Beta Strategies: Understanding Key Differences", February 16, 2018). The analysis was performed by the Schwab Center for Financial Research with data provided by Morningstar Direct.

[11] "Smart Beta Strategies: Understanding Key Differences", February 16, 2018. Available at https://www.schwab.com/resource-center/insights/content/smart-beta-strategies-understanding-key-differences.

underperform the S&P 500, 2011. In that year, the S&P 500 was the fifth worst performer and the equally weighted index was next.

Smart Beta: Beta or Alpha Strategies?

We have included the smart beta strategy in this chapter that covers beta strategies. The question is whether it is a beta strategy or a form of alpha (active) strategy. The confusion arises because of the different types of smart beta strategies. Morningstar classifies smart beta strategies into return-oriented and risk-oriented strategies. Smart beta strategies that attempt to enhance returns relative to a market-capitalization index are referred to as *return-oriented smart beta* strategies. Fundamental strategies would fall into this category of smart beta strategies and would be considered a true beta strategy. Smart beta strategies that involve changing the level of portfolio risk relative to a market-capitalization weighted index are *risk-oriented smart beta strategies* and are alpha or active strategies.

Key Points

- Common stock investment strategies are classified as either beta strategies or alpha strategies.
- The beta of a portfolio or an investment strategy is a measure of the volatility of the portfolio or investment strategy relative to the benchmark.
- Passive investors either manage their own portfolio to match the performance of the benchmark or engage an asset manager to do so and the strategies that they follow are referred to as beta strategies.
- Active investors pursue a strategy to outperform a benchmark or engage an asset manager to do so and the strategies pursued are referred to as alpha strategies.
- Markets are classified according to their pricing efficiency, referred to as market efficiency.
- A financial market where asset prices rapidly reflect all available information is said to be an efficient market and, in such markets, abnormal returns are precluded.
- There are three levels of market efficiency: weak, semi-strong, and strong forms.
- Weak form of market efficiency means that current asset prices reflect all past prices and price movements.

- Semi-strong form of market efficiency means that current asset prices reflect all publicly available information.
- Strong form of market efficiency means that current asset prices reflect all public and private information.
- Paul Samuelson's dictum asserts that the stock market is "micro efficient" but not necessarily "macro efficient."
- The form of market efficiency has implications for investment management strategies.
- The optimal strategy to pursue when the stock market is perceived to be price efficient is passive indexing because it allows the investor to capture the efficiency of the market.
- Active strategies are characterized by the emphasis on the stock selection process.
- Traditionally speaking, there are two major types of stock selection approaches, those based on fundamental analysis and those based on technical analysis.
- Fundamental analysis tries to assess the viability of a company from a business point of view, looking at financial statements as well as operations.
- The objective of fundamental analysis is to identify companies that will produce a solid future stream of cash flows.
- Technical analysis looks at patterns in prices and returns and assumes that prices and returns follow discernable patterns.
- The underpinning of active portfolio management is the belief that there are market inefficiencies, that is, that there are situations where a stock's price does not fully reflect all available information.
- Indexing is one form of passive equity management.
- The passive approach is supported by the findings that the stock market appears to be sufficiently price-efficient so that it is difficult to consistently outperform the market after adjusting for risk and transaction costs.
- Index fund management involves creating a portfolio to replicate an index.
- The index is selected by the client, the most popular index being the S&P 500.
- In indexing, once an index is selected, the asset manager must decide how to construct the replicating portfolio to minimize tracking error risk.

- In constructing an indexed portfolio, the asset manager must consider the trade-off between the number of stock issues in the index to include in the replicating portfolio and the transaction costs.
- Constructing a replicating portfolio with fewer stock issues than are included in the index involves one of three methods: the capitalization method, stratified method, or quadratic optimization method.
- Some managers utilize active strategies within an index fund management framework in an attempt to enhance returns but still control market risk.
- The two most popular methods are creating a tilted portfolio and utilizing the stock index futures market.
- Indexing is basically a method for capturing the market risk premium by constructing a portfolio based on market capitalization. This is based on the theory that if the market is price-efficient, then the most efficient way to capture the market risk premium is to construct a portfolio to replicate the performance of the market.
- If markets are not efficient, indexing may not be the best way to capture the market risk premium because a drawback of using market-capitalization indexes is that they place greater emphasis on the stock of higher valuation companies and, as a result, produce unintended concentration risk in individual stocks and sectors.
- Using a market-capitalization weighted index neglects the equity of smaller firms that potentially may be the more promising firms that should have a higher allocation.
- The most popular alternative strategy to indexing is a smart beta strategy (also called a strategic beta strategy, scientific beta strategy, and an alternative beta strategy).
- In general, a smart beta strategy is a rule-based construction method where the exposure to each stock is based not on market capitalization but on firm characteristics or systematic factors.
- With a smart beta strategy, the expectation is that the rules established will result in an expected return greater than that of a market-capitalization-based strategy.
- There are two categories of smart beta indexes: alternatively weighted indexes and factor indexes.
- Alternatively weighted indexes are designed to accomplish one or both of the following objectives: (1) avoid the concentration of risk associated with market-capitalization weighted indexes and (2) reduce the volatility within a traditional index.

- There are four types of indexes: equally weighted, fundamental, minimum variance, and risk-efficient.
- Factor indexes are constructed to replicate the factor risks in a traditional index by using rules that are transparent and such that the constructed index is investable.
- The three most commonly used factors in smart beta strategies tend to be (1) low-volatility, (2) momentum, and (3) quality.

References

Alexander, S. S., 1961. "Price movements in speculative markets: Trends or random walks," *Industrial Management Review*, 2: 7–26.

Arnott, R., J. Hsu, and P. Moore, 2005. "Fundamental indexation," *Financial Analysts Journal*, 61(2): 83–99.

Arnott, R., V. Kalesnik, P. Moghtader, and C. Scholl, 2010. "Beyond cap weight: The empirical evidence for a diversified beta," *Journal of Indexes*, 16: 16–29.

Berk, J. B., 2005. "Five myths of active portfolio management," *Journal of Portfolio Management*, 31(3): 27–31.

Berk, J. B. and J. H. van Binsbergen, 2016. "Assessing asset pricing models using revealed preference," *Journal of Financial Economics*, 119(1): 1–28.

Bernstein, P. L., 1985. "Does the market overreact?: Discussion," *Journal of FinanceI*, 40(3): 806–808.

Brock, W., J. Lakonishok, and B. LeBaron, 1992. "Simple technical trading rules and the stochastic properties of stock returns," *Journal of Finance*, 47(5): 1731–1764.

Brown, K. C. and W. van Harlow, 1988. "Market overreaction: Magnitude and intensity," *Journal of Portfolio Management*, 14(2): 6–13.

Brown, S. J., W. A. Goetzmann, and A. Kumar, 1998. "The Dow Theory: William Peter Hamilton's track record reconsidered," *Journal of Finance*, 53(4): 1311–1333.

Carhart, M. M., 1997. "On persistence in mutual fund performance," *Journal of Finance*, 52(1): 57–82.

Cootner, P. H., 1962. "Stock prices: Random vs. systematic risk," *Industrial Management Review*, 3: 24–45.

Campbell, J. Y. and R. J. Shiller, 1988. "Stock prices, earnings, and expected dividends," *Journal of Finance*, 43: 661–676.

Daniel, K. D., D. Hirshleifer, and A. Subrahmanyam, 1998. "Investor psychology and security market under- and overreactions," *Journal of Finance*, 53(4): 1839–1885.

DeBondt, W. and R. Thaler, 1985. "Does the market overreact?" *Journal of Finance*, 40(3): 793–805.

DeBondt, W. and R. Thaler, 1987. "Further evidence on investor overreaction and stock market seasonality," *Journal of Finance*, 42(3): 557–581.

DeMiguel, V., L. Garlappi, and R. Uppal, 2009. "Optimal versus naive diversification: How inefficient is the 1/N portfolio strategy?" *Review of Financial Studies*, 22(5): 1915–1953.

Edwards, R. D. and J. Magee, 1948. *Technical Analysis of Stock Trends*. Boston: John Magee Inc.

Fama, E. F., 1970. "Efficient capital markets: A review of theory and empirical work," *Journal of Finance*, 25(2): 383–417.

Fama, E. F. and M. Blume, 1966. "Filter rules and stock-market trading," *Journal of Business*, 39: 226–241.

Figelman, I. 2007. "Stock return momentum and reversal," *Journal of Portfolio Management*, 34(1): 51–69.

Glickstein, D. and R. Wubbels, 1983. "Dow theory is alive and well!" *Journal of Portfolio Management*, 9(3): 28–32.

Haugen, R. A. and N. L. Baker, 1991. "The efficient market inefficiency of capitalization-weighted stock portfolios," *Journal of Portfolio Management*, 17(3): 35–40.

Hsu, P.-H. and C.-M. Kuan, 2005. "Reexamining the profitability of technical analysis with data snooping checks," *Journal of Financial Econometrics*, 3(4): 606–628.

Hwang, S. and A. Rubesam, 2015. "The disappearance of momentum," *European Journal of Finance*, 21(7): 584–607.

Ibbotson SBBI, 2017. *2017 Classic Yearbook*. Chicago: Morningstar.

Jegadeesh, N., 1990. "Evidence of predictable behavior of security returns," *Journal of Finance*, 45(3): 881–898.

Jegadeesh, N. and S. Titman, 1993. "Returns to buying winners and selling losers: Implications for stock market efficiency," *Journal of Finance*, 48(1): 65–91.

Jung, J. and R. J. Shiller, 2005. "Samuelson's dictum and the stock market," *Economic Inquiry*, 43(2): 221–228.

Korajczyk, R. A. and R. Sadka, 2004. "Are momentum profits robust to trading costs?" *Journal of Finance,* 59(2): 1039–1082.

LeRoy, S. F. and R. D. Porter, 1981. "The present value relation: Tests based on variance bounds," *Econometrica*, 49(3): 555–574.

Peters, E. E., 1991. *Chaos and Order in The Capital Markets: A New View Of Cycles, Prices, and Market Volatility*. New York: John Wiley & Sons.

Plyakha, Y., R. Uppal, and G. Vilkov, 2012. "Why does an equal-weighted portfolio outperform value- and price-weighted portfolios," EDHEC Business School, Working paper.

Roll, R., 1977. "A critique of the asset pricing theory: Part 1. On the past and potential testability of the theory," *Journal of Financial Economics*, 4(2): 129–176.

Rouwenhorst, G. 1998. "International momentum strategies," *Journal of Finance*, 53(1): 267–284.

Scheinkman, J. and B. LeBaron, 1989. "Nonlinear dynamics and stock returns," *Journal of Business*, 62(3): 311–337.

Shiller, R. J., 1981. "Do stock prices move too much to be justified by subsequent changes in dividends?" *American Economic Review*, 71(3): 421–436.

Shiller, R. J., 2001. *Irrational Exuberance*, 2nd edition. New York: Broadway Books.

Sullivan, R., A. Timmermann, and H. White, 1999. "Data-snooping, technical trading rule performance, and the bootstrap," *Journal of Finance*, 24(5): 1647–1691.

Sweeney, R. J., 1988. "Some new filter rule tests: Methods and results," *Journal of Financial and Quantitative Analysis*, 23(3): 285–300.

Sweeney, R. J., 1990. "Evidence on short-term trading strategies," *Journal of Portfolio Management*, 17(1): 20–26.

Chapter 13

Common Stock Alpha Strategies

Learning objectives

After reading this chapter, you will understand:

- what an active or alpha strategy is;
- the top-down approach and bottom-up approach used in formulating an active strategy;
- what traditional fundamental analysis is and fundamental analysis strategies;
- what technical analysis is;
- what equity style investing is;
- what factor investing is and the most well-known factors;
- the difference between a return forecast factor model and a risk forecast factor model;
- what a long-short return forecast factor model is and the three-factor and five-factor Fama–French models;
- what responsible investing (environmental, social, and governance investing) is and the strategies for constructing ESG portfolios;
- the capacity of an equity strategy and how capacity may be measured;
- the different types of transaction costs (implicit and explicit transaction costs);
- what backtesting is and the three methods used for backtesting a proposed investment strategy, and;
- how return attribution models can be used to explain the sources of an asset manager's return.

As explained in Chapter 12, strategies employed by equity portfolio managers are either indexing-type strategies or active strategies. The selection of the type of strategy to pursue depends on a client's view of the pricing efficiency of the stock market. Indexing-type strategies, referred to as beta strategies and the subject of Chapter 12, should be pursued when clients believe that asset managers cannot outperform the stock market after adjusting for risk, transactions costs, and management fees. When a client holds the view that there are equity portfolio managers capable of outperforming the market, then they will seek to retain a manager who pursues an active strategy. Active strategies are called *alpha strategies* and are the subject of this chapter.

Top-Down vs. Bottom-Up Approaches

An equity manager who pursues an active strategy may follow either a top-down or bottom-up approach. With the *top-down approach*, an equity manager begins by assessing the macroeconomic environment and forecasting its near-term outlook. Based on this assessment and forecast, an equity manager decides on how much of the portfolio's funds to allocate among the different sectors of the equity market and how much to allocate to cash equivalents (i.e., short-term money market instruments). The sectors of the equity market are classified as follows: basic materials, communications, consumer staples, financials, technology, utilities, capital goods, consumer cyclicals, energy, healthcare, and transportation.[1] Industry classifications have a finer breakdown and include, for example, aluminum, paper, international oil, beverages, electric utilities, telephone and telegraph, and so on.

In making the allocation decision, a manager who follows a top-down approach relies on an analysis of the equity market to identify those sectors and industries that will benefit the most on a relative basis from the anticipated economic forecast. Once the amount to be allocated to each sector and industry is decided, the manager then looks for the individual stocks to include in the portfolio.

In contrast to the top-down approach, an equity manager who follows a *bottom-up approach* focuses on the analysis of individual stocks and gives little weight to the significance of economic and market cycles. The primary tool of bottom-up portfolio managers is fundamental security analysis. We will discuss this tool in what follows. The product of the analysis is determining a set of potential stocks to purchase that have certain characteristics that the manager views as being attractive. For example, these characteristics can be low

[1]These are the categories used by Standard & Poor's. There is another sector labeled "miscellaneous" that includes stocks that do not fall into any of the other sectors.

price/earnings ratios or small market capitalizations. Three well-known managers who follow or have followed a bottom-up approach are Warren Buffett (Berkshire Hathaway, Inc.), Dean LeBaron (Batterymarch Financial Management), and Peter Lynch (formerly of Fidelity Magellan Fund).

Within the top-down and bottom-up approaches, there are different strategies pursued by active equity managers. These strategies are often referred to as equity styles and will be discussed later in this chapter.

Fundamental vs. Technical Analysis

Within both the top-down and bottom-up approaches, there are two views as to what information is useful in the selection of stocks. These two views are the fundamental analysis view and the technical analysis view.

Traditional fundamental analysis involves the analysis of a company's operations to assess its economic prospects. The analysis begins with the financial statements of the company in order to investigate the earnings, cash flow, profitability, and debt burden. The fundamental analyst will look at the major product lines, the economic outlook for the products (and potential competitors), and the industries in which the company operates. The results of this analysis will be the growth prospects of earnings. Based on the growth prospects of earnings, a fundamental analyst attempts to determine the fair value of the stock using one or more of the equity valuation models discussed in Chapter 11. The estimated fair value is then compared to the market price to determine if the stock is either fairly priced in the market, cheap (a market price below the estimated fair value), or rich (a market price above the estimated fair value). The father of traditional fundamental analysis is Benjamin Graham, who espoused this analysis in his classic book *Security Analysis*.[2] The limitation of fundamental analysis is that it does not quantify the factors associated with a company's stock and how those risk factors affect its valuation. Later in this chapter, we describe models of how different risk factors are quantified.

Technical analysis ignores company information regarding the fundamentals of a firm. Instead, technical analysis focuses on historical prices and/or trading volumes of individual stocks, groups of stocks, and the

[2]There have been several editions of this book. The first edition was printed in 1934 and coauthored with Sidney Cottle. A more readily available edition is Graham, Dodd, and Cottle [1962].

overall market resulting from shifting supply and demand. This type of analysis is not only used for the analysis of common stock, but it is also a tool used in the trading of commodities, bonds, and futures contracts. Technical analysis can be traced back to the seventeenth century, where it was applied in Japan to analyze the trend in the price of rice (see Shaw [1988, p. 313]). The father of modern technical analysis is Charles Dow, a founder of *The Wall Street Journal* and its first editor from July 1889 to December 1902.

Next, we will discuss some of the strategies that are employed by active managers who follow fundamental analysis and technical analysis. We will also look at the evidence regarding the performance of these strategies. It is critical to understand, however, that fundamental analysis and technical analysis can be integrated within a strategy. Specifically, an asset manager can use fundamental analysis to identify stocks that are candidates for purchase or sale, and the manager can employ technical analysis to time the purchase or sale.

Strategies Based on Fundamental Analysis

As explained earlier, fundamental analysis involves an economic analysis of a firm with respect to its earnings growth prospects, ability to meet debt obligations, its competitive environment, and so on. Proponents of semi-strong market efficiency argue that strategies based on fundamental analysis will not produce abnormal returns. The reason is simply that there are many analysts undertaking the same sort of analysis, with the same publicly available data, so the price of the stock always reflects all of the relevant factors that determine value.

Strategies based on fundamental analysis focus on the earnings of a company and the expected change in earnings. In fact, a study by Chugh and Meador [1994] found that two of the most important measures used by analysts are short-term and long-term changes in earnings.

In the rest of this section, we will describe several popular fundamental analysis-related strategies.

Earnings Surprise Strategies

Studies have found that it is not merely the change in earnings that is important to investors. The reason is that analysts have a consensus forecast of a public company's earnings per share that are typically made for the next future quarter, the current fiscal year, and the next fiscal year. For example, Zacks Investment Research follows the earnings per share estimates of sell-side analysts (i.e., analysts from brokerage firms) and uses that information to create a consensus forecast which is the average of the earnings per share estimates.

What might be expected to generate abnormal returns is the extent to which the market's consensus forecast of future earnings differs from actual earnings that are subsequently announced. The divergence between the consensus forecast earnings and the actual earnings announced is called the *earnings per share surprise* (EPS surprise) and is calculated as follows:

$$\frac{(\text{Actual EPS} - \text{Consensus EPS})}{\text{Absolute value of Consensus EPS}} \times 100.$$

When the actual EPS exceeds the market's consensus forecast, this is a *positive earnings surprise*; a *negative earnings surprise* arises when the actual earnings are less than the consensus forecast.

There have been numerous studies of EPS surprises.[3] These studies seem to suggest that identifying stocks that may have positive earnings surprises and purchasing them may generate abnormal returns. Of course, the difficulty is identifying such stocks.

Low Price/Earnings (P/E) Ratio Strategies

The legendary Benjamin Graham proposed a classic investment model in 1949 for the "defensive investor" who he defines as an investor without the time, expertise, or temperament for aggressive investment. The model was updated in each subsequent edition of his book, *The Intelligent Investor*.[4] Some of the basic investment criteria outlined in the 1973 edition are representative of the approach:

1. A company must have paid a dividend in each of the past 20 years.
2. Minimum size of a company is \$100 million in annual sales for an industrial company and \$50 million for a public utility (remember, this is in 1973 dollars).
3. Positive earnings must have been achieved in each of the past 10 years.
4. Current price should not be more than 1.5 times the latest book value.
5. Market price should not exceed 15 times the average earnings for the past 3 years.

[3]The first of these tests was by Joy, Lizenberger, and McEnally [1977].
[4]This model is fully described in Graham [1973, Chapter 14].

Graham considered the price/earnings (P/E) ratio as a measure of the price paid for value received. He viewed high P/Es with skepticism and as representing a large premium for difficult-to-forecast future earnings growth. Hence, lower-P/E, higher-quality companies were viewed favorably as having less potential for earnings disappointments and the resulting downward revision in price.

A study by Oppenheimer and Schlarbaum [1981] reveals that over the period of 1956–1975, significant abnormal returns were obtained by following Graham's strategy, even after allowing for transaction costs. While originally intended for the defensive investor, numerous variations of Graham's low-P/E approach are currently followed by several professional investment advisers.[5]

Market-Neutral Long-Short Strategy

An active strategy that seeks to capitalize on the ability of a manager to solely select stocks is a market-neutral long-short strategy. The basic idea of this strategy is as follows. First, using the models described in Chapter 11, an equity manager analyzes the expected returns of individual stocks from a universe of stocks. Based on this analysis, the manager can classify those stocks as either "high-expected-return stocks" or "low-expected-return stocks." A manager could then follow one of the following three strategies: (1) purchase only high-expected-return stocks, (2) short low-expected-return stocks, or (3) simultaneously purchase high-expected return stocks and short low-expected-return stocks.

The problem with the first two strategies is that movements in the market in general can have an adverse effect. For example, suppose that a manager selects high-expected-return stocks and that the market declines. Because of the positive correlation between the return on all stocks and the market, the drop in the market will produce a negative return even though the manager may have indeed been able to identify high-expected-return stocks. Similarly, if a manager shorts low-expected return stocks and the market rallies, the portfolio will realize a negative return. This is because a rise in the market means that the manager must cover the short position of each stock at a price higher than the price at which a stock was sold.

[5]For a thorough presentation of the low P/E investment strategy, see Dreman [1982].

Let's look at the third alternative strategy of simultaneously purchasing stocks with high expected returns and shorting those stocks with low expected returns. Consider what happens to the long and the short positions when the general market moves. A drop in the market will hurt the long position but benefit the short position. A market rally will hurt the short position but benefit the long position. Consequently, the long and short positions provide a hedge against each other.

Although the long–short positions provide a hedge against general market movements, the degree to which one position moves relative to the other is not controlled by simply going long on the high-expected-return stocks and going short on the low-expected-return stocks. That is, the two positions do not neutralize the risk against general market movements. However, the long and short positions can be created with a market exposure that neutralizes any market movement. Specifically, long and short positions can be constructed to have the same beta, and, as a result, the beta of the long–short position is zero. For this reason, this strategy is called a *market-neutral long–short strategy.* If, indeed, a manager can identify high- and low-expected-return stocks, then neutralizing the portfolio against market movements will produce a positive return regardless of whether the market rises or falls.

Here is how a market-neutral long-short portfolio is created. It begins with a list of stocks that fall into the high-expected-return stock and low expected-return stock group. One or a combination of the models described in Chapter 11 is used. (In fact, we classify this strategy as a fundamental analysis strategy because fundamental analysis is used to identify the stocks that fall into the high- and low-expected return stock categories.) The high-expected-return stocks are referred to as "winners" and are those that are candidates to be included in the long portfolio; the low-expected-return stocks are referred to as "losers" and are those that are candidates to be included in the short portfolio.

Suppose (1) a client allocates \$10 million to a manager to implement a market-neutral long–short strategy[6] and (2) that the manager (with the approval of the client) uses the \$10 million to buy stocks on margin. As explained in Chapter 3, the investor can borrow up to a specified percentage of the market value of the margined stocks, with the percentage determined

[6]This illustration is from Jacobs and Levy [1997].

by the Federal Reserve. Let's assume that the margin requirement is 50%. This means that the manager has $20 million to invest — $10 million in the long position and $10 million in the short position.

When buying securities on margin, the manager must be prepared for a margin call. Thus, a prudent policy with respect to managing the risk of a margin call is not to invest the entire amount. Instead, a liquidity buffer of about 10% of the equity capital is typically maintained. This amount is invested in a high-quality short-term money market instrument. The portion held in this instrument is said to be held in "cash." In our illustration, since the equity capital is $10 million, $1 million is held in cash, leaving $9 million to be invested in the long position; therefore, $9 million is shorted. The portfolio then looks as follows: $1 million cash, $9 million long, and $9 million short.

Market Anomaly Strategies

While there are managers who are skeptical about technical analysis and fundamental analysis, some managers believe that there are pockets of pricing inefficiency in the stock market. That is, there are some investment strategies that have historically produced statistically significant positive abnormal returns. These market anomalies are referred to as the small-firm effect, the low-price/earnings-ratio effect, the neglected-firm effect, and various calendar effects. There is also a strategy that involves following the trading transactions of insiders of a company.

Some of these so-called anomalies are a challenge to the semi-strong form of pricing efficiency because they use the financial data of a company. These would include the small-firm effect and the low-price/earnings-ratio effect. The calendar effects are a challenge to the weak form of pricing efficiency. Following insider activities with regard to buying and selling the stock of their company is a challenge to both the weak and strong forms of pricing efficiency. The challenge to the former is that, as will be explained in what follows, information on insider activity is publicly available and, in fact, has been suggested as a technical indicator in popular television programs such as *Wall Street Week*. Thus, the question is whether "outsiders" can use information about trading activity by insiders to generate abnormal returns. The challenge to the strong form of pricing efficiency is that insiders are viewed as having special information, and, therefore, they may be able to generate abnormal returns using information acquired from their special relationship with the firm.

Small-firm effect

The *small-firm effect* emerges in several studies that have shown that portfolios of small firms (in terms of total market capitalization) have outperformed the stock market (consisting of both large and small firms) (see Reinganum [1981] and Banz [1981]). Because of these findings, several stock market indexes have been produced to serve as a benchmark for managers who want to pursue a small-firm strategy. We will describe this more fully when we discuss equity style management later.

Low-price-earning effect

Earlier, we discussed Benjamin Graham's strategy for defensive investors based on low price/earnings ratios. The low-price/earnings effect is supported by several studies showing that portfolios consisting of stocks with a low price/earnings ratio have outperformed portfolios consisting of stocks with a high price/earnings ratio (see Basu [1977]). However, there have been studies that found that after adjusting for transaction costs necessary to rebalance a portfolio as prices and earnings change over time, the superior performance of portfolios of low-price/earnings-ratio stocks no longer holds (see Levy and Lerman [1985]). An explanation for the presumably superior performance is that stocks trade at low price/earnings ratios because they are temporarily out of favor with market participants. Because fads do change, companies not currently in vogue will rebound at some indeterminate time in the future (see Dreman [1979]).

Neglected-firm effect

Not all firms receive the same degree of attention from security analysts, and one school of thought is that firms that are neglected by security analysts will outperform firms that are the subject of considerable attention. One study has found that an investment strategy based on changes in the level of attention devoted by security analysts to different stocks may lead to positive abnormal returns (see Arbel, Carvell, and Stebel [1983]). This market anomaly is referred to as the neglected-firm effect.

Calendar effects

While some empirical work focuses on selected firms according to some criteria such as market capitalization, price/earnings ratio, or degree of analysts' attention, the *calendar effect* looks at the best time to implement strategies. Examples of anomalies are the January effect, month-of-the-year effect, day-of-the-week effect, and holiday effect. It appears from the empirical evidence that there are times when the implementation of a strategy will, on average, provide a superior performance relative to other calendar time periods. However, since it is not possible to predict when such a strategy will work, this again supports the idea that the market is at least weak-form efficient.

Equity Style Investing[7]

Style investing is the implementation of investment strategies that are designed to earn excess returns from investing in mispriced stocks that result from the empirically observed market anomalies. The two principal anomalies which are used in style investing are value versus growth and market capitalization. These two commonly used styles are depicted in the well-known Morningstar style box shown in Figure 1. There are mutual funds, ETFs, and indexes that correspond to the size and value-growth boxes. While the distinction between market capitalization (size) classes is clear, what is the difference between growth stock managers and value stock managers?

Growth managers seek to perform better than the broad market by buying the stock of companies with high-earnings-growth expectations. The current price of the shares is less important than the company's future fundamentals. That is, the stock will appreciate as the company continues to generate future cash flow increments. In contrast, *value managers* seek to outperform by pursuing a strategy of buying cheap stocks that the stock market has somehow incorrectly priced. It is notable that the growth

Size	Value	Blend	Growth
Large Cap			
Mid Cap			
Small Cap			

FIGURE 1: Morningstar Style Box

[7]Parts of this section on style investing draw from co-authored writing with Eric H. Sorensen, President and Chief Executive Officer of PanAgora Asset Management.

manager terminology emanates from the term "growth company". There is no analog for the value manager—as in "value company".

Clearly there are dramatically differing philosophies among practitioners of these two style camps. Growth managers believe they can identify firms' relative earnings growth rates into the future. They presume that the market is underestimating their perceived value of a stock based on their proprietary forecast of future fundamental corporate potential. As such, they are willing to pay higher prices — price-to-earnings (P/E) or price-to-book-value (P/B) — for what the manager perceives as great companies. Active growth portfolios are generally characterized by consistent and high earnings growth, longer duration[8] (that is, highly sensitive to changes in interest rates), more susceptible to adverse earnings events, have higher market beta, and are in more exciting industries, other things being equal. Basically, the market has underreacted to the positive growth and underestimated this growth.

In contrast, value managers seek to find bargains. They seek stocks that have been sold off for any number of reasons, and on which the market has temporarily given up. Active value managers hold portfolios of stocks with recent unfavorable news, higher dividend yields, lower P/E ratios, and within boring industries with lower general growth prospects, other things being equal. Basically, the market has overreacted to the dull or weak fundamentals and underestimated the potential for improvement or turnaround.

In addition to many generalizations between these two philosophies, the portfolio implementation can also be quite different. Growth managers will often use positive earnings momentum and buy into a rising price scenario. If they are in a hurry, they may be demanders of liquidity as they build positions — driving the price up. In addition, in the event of adverse earnings events, they sometimes unload and are in-part responsible for downward price pressure. In contrast, value managers often buy stocks that are already depressed, and are thus suppliers of liquidity. Often, they might buy early before the stock hits some bottom and sell early as it rises above one's notion of fair value.

Value manager techniques and firm characteristics

In the world of value managers, there are many criteria or firm characteristics to assess in security selection. Some measures of cheapness are at the

[8]We discuss the duration metric in Chapter 16.

top of the list. A so-called *contrarian investor* is often considered a buyer of deep discount securities. These stocks might have extremely low P/E ratios and/or nominally high-dividend yields [Christopherson and Williams, 1997; Schlarbaum, 1997]. Low P/B is also a criterion for certain types of companies. The contrarian investor who pursues a contrarian strategy looks at the book value of a company and focuses on those companies that are selling at a low valuation relative to book value. The companies that fall into this category may be depressed cyclical stocks or companies that have little or no future earnings growth prospects. The expectation is that the stock is on a cyclical rebound or that the company's earnings will turn around. Both of these occurrences are expected to lead to substantial price appreciation.

Many of such oversold stocks in a portfolio may take quarters and even years to realize the hoped-for appreciation. This requires patience and is not typically a good approach for asset managers that seek consistency in outperforming a benchmark on a regular basis.

Other value managers are more moderate in their selection processes. Many focus on relative value, meaning that cheapness is only one, albeit important, consideration. (We discuss relative valuation tools in Chapter 11.) "Relative" sometimes pertains to comparable stocks, like those in the same industry. Therefore, a relative value portfolio may be sector neutral or industry neutral compared to a broad index like the S&P 500. In this instance, the percentages allocated to industries mimic the broad benchmark, but the specific holdings are cheap relative to other stocks in the same industry. This is in sharp contrast to deep value investing that often may result in major industry concentrations (overweights and underweights) relative to the percent of the industry comprising the broad index. Such contrarian portfolios will typically not track the chosen index as consistently as a relative value portfolio.

Another condition the value manager may invoke is growth as a key consideration. Growth is good, but the manager wants to avoid overpaying for a stock. *Growth at a reasonable price* or GARP is a common label for this approach. Here the manager will compare the measure of cheapness selected, say P/E or P/B, with the firm's growth potential, such as dividing the P/E ratio by the projected growth rate. High P/E stocks may be "good value" if the price is supported by expected earnings growth.

Growth manager techniques and factors

Growth managers seek companies with above average growth prospects. In the growth manager style category, there tends to be two major sub-styles

[Christopherson and Williams, 1997]. The first is a growth manager who focuses on high-quality companies with consistent growth. A manager who follows this substyle is referred to as a *consistent growth manager*. These are commonly large-cap growth managers.

The second growth substyle is followed by an *earnings momentum growth manager*. In contrast to a growth manager, an earnings momentum growth manager prefers companies with more volatile, above-average growth. They often seek companies with accelerating growth. These are commonly managers who invest in mid-cap or small-cap stocks.

Factor Investing

In Chapter 9, we discussed the capital asset pricing model (CAPM) and its extensions to explain returns on assets. The CAPM is an equilibrium model. We also discussed a model derived on arbitrage-free arguments, the arbitrage pricing theory (APT). The original CAPM asserts that the only factor that affects asset returns is the general market. In contrast, APT asserts that there are factors other than the market that drive asset returns but the theory fails to identify those factors. These models are conceptual and describe how the world should look based on the underlying model assumptions.

Factor investing in the equity market involves constructing a portfolio based on factors that have consistently been shown to affect the returns on stocks. These factors can be fundamental factors, macroeconomic factors, and/or market factors. BlackRock estimates that the factor industry was roughly \$1.9 trillion as of September 30, 2017 and will grow to \$3.4 trillion by 2022.[9] Morningstar estimates that there are 771 mutual funds and exchange-traded funds that follow a factor investing strategy, with more than \$1 trillion in assets under management.

The quantitative models used in practice in constructing portfolios based on factors fall into two categories. The first is factor models that are used to forecast returns, which we shall refer to as "return forecast factor models". The second is factor models that are used to forecast risk, which we will refer to as "risk forecast factor models". We describe each as follows.

[9] https://www.blackrock.com/us/individual/investment-ideas/what-is-factor-investing.

Return Forecast Factor Models

Empirical tests of the CAPM have found that there are firm characteristics and market information such as a stock's momentum that explain cross-sectional stock returns. That is, for a given time period, a multiple regression is estimated using the return on N publicly traded stocks as the dependent variable, and potential firm characteristics and market information as the independent (explanatory) variables.[10] According to the CAPM, none of these independent variables should be significant. The statistical tests in fact showed that there were some independent variables that were statistically significant across different time period tests.

At one time, the independent variables that were significant were referred to as "anomalies". We described these anomalies earlier. However, they were anomalies only in the sense that the findings were inconsistent with a theoretical model, the CAPM, that was assumed to be the proper model for pricing assets. Today, some of the anomalies, such as the small firm effect discussed earlier, are included in factor models.

A review of the large number of factors identified in empirical tests is beyond the scope of this chapter. Instead, we will briefly discuss the six most popular factors in addition to the market factor according to White and Haghani [2020]: (1) value, (2) size, (3) dividend yield, (4) quality, (5) momentum, and (6) low volatility. The ordering is based on the number of mutual funds and the market capitalization of funds that focus on them. Table 1 describes each factor and the empirical relationship observed between the factor and expected performance.

Fama and French [1993] found value and size (market capitalization) earned a positive risk premium. Carhart [1997] identified a stock's momentum as a factor that explains stock returns. A stock's momentum is the tendency for a stock's price continuing to move in the same direction (i.e., a rising stock price continues to rise, and a declining stock price continues to decline.)

Using the dividend discount model explained in Chapter 11, Fama and French [2015] show that expected profitability and expected investment are also factors that explain stock returns, two factors not shown in Table 1. Empirical evidence about these two factors was provided in subsequent

[10] More specifically, the regression is estimated using the firm characteristics at time t and the firm's return at time $t + 1$.

TABLE 1: Six Most Popular Factors in Addition to Market Factor

Factor	Measurement	Empirical Relationship Observed
Value (V)	Ratio of price per share to book value per share (P/B ratio)	Stocks with a low P/B ratio perform better than stocks with a high P/B ratio
Size (S)	Market capitalization: market price per share times number of shares outstanding	Small capitalization stocks outperform large capitalization stocks
Dividend yield (DY)	Dividend per share divided by price per share	Stocks with a high dividend yield (or a rate of growth of dividends) perform better than stocks with a low dividend (or rate of growth of dividends)
Quality (Q)	Various measures of profitability and investment performance	Stocks with a high profitability and/or conservative investment policy perform better that stocks with a low profitability and/or aggressive investment policy
Momentum (MOM)	Price performance over some specified time period such as six months or a year	Stocks that have outperformed the market over the past specified time period perform better stocks that under perform that market over the past specified period of time
Volatility (VOL)	Various measures of stock price volatility (including beta)	Stocks with low historical volatility (or low beta) perform better than stocks with high historical volatility (or high beta)

Source: Based on information from White and Haghani [2020].

research published in 2013. Novy-Marx [2013] found that a company's current profitability — gross profits-to-assets — is a good predictor of future profitability. Consequently, it is a factor that will explain future returns. The investment factor is based on the study by Aharoni, Grundy, and Zeng [2013] who find that there is an inverse relationship between corporate investments and expected returns.

There are two return forecast factor models that have been proposed by Fama and French. The first includes the market factor, just as in the CAPM, plus value and size as shown in Table 1. This return forecast factor model is called the Fama–French three-factor model. When the profitability and investment factors are added to the three-factor model, the expanded model is referred to as the Fama–French five-factor model. A criticism of these two models is that they do not include the other four factors that have historically been shown to explain cross-sectional returns. Specific to the five-factor model is that the two factors added to the three-factor model do not have the same empirical support as the factors in the three-factor model.[11]

There are two ways in which models incorporating the factors in Table 1 can be used in a return forecast factor model: long-short strategies and long-only strategies. In turn, the strategy can focus only on one factor or more than one factor. The strategies that involve more than one factor use *return forecast multifactor models.*

Long–short strategies

The first way a factor model is used is by looking at the differences in returns from long and short positions in a factor. Long-short strategies can be performed using just one factor to determine the long position and the short position or more than one factor can be used to determine those positions. When more than one factor is used, the model used is referred to as multifactor model.

The following two illustrations are examples of using just one factor in creating the long-short positions. The first illustration uses momentum as a factor and the second uses a fundamental factor. In our first illustration, from a universe of candidate stocks, the stocks are ranked based on price momentum over some specified time period such as 6 months or 1 year. Then the top X% on the list are purchased. These stocks are referred to as "winners". The bottom X% on the list are sold short. These stocks are referred to as "losers". To illustrate how one of the fundamental factors is used in constructing a long–short portfolio, consider a strategy based on the value factor and assume that the metric for value is the book-to-price (B/P) ratios. The higher the B/P ratio is, the higher the value. The top Y% are considered the best value stocks and they are purchased. The lowest Y% are then viewed as growth stocks and are shorted.

For strategies based on return forecast multifactor models, probably the most popular ones are the two developed by Fama and French: the three-factor model and the five-factor model. To explain their model, we'll use

---

[11]The concerns with these models are discussed in Blitz, Hanauer, Vidojevic, and van Vliet [2018].

the following notation used for the three-factor Fama and French model and the meaning of each:

- *Small Minus Big* (SMB) variable is the difference between the return on small-cap stocks minus the return on large-cap stocks. This is done by being long small-cap stocks and short large-cap stocks. The expectation based on the historical performance of small-cap and large-cap stocks is that small-cap stocks will outperform large-cap stocks. This is referred to as the *size premium*. If historical performance is realized in the future, then the long position in small-cap stocks will generate a return that is greater than the return on the large-cap stocks and SMB will be positive for the time period.
- *High Minus Low* (HML) is the difference variable, denoted by HML, is the difference between the return on value stocks ("high") and growth stocks ("low"). This is done by being long value stocks and short growth stocks. The expectation based on the historical performance of value and growth stocks is that value stocks will outperform growth stocks. This is referred to as the *value premium*. If historical performance is realized in the future, then the long position in value stocks will generate a return that is greater than the return on the short positions in growth stocks. A positive value for HML for a given time period means that value stocks outperformed growth stocks.

In the above description of the three variables, we refer to "stocks". That is, there are small-cap stocks, large-cap stocks, value stocks, and growth stocks. The stock groups are measured in terms of portfolios. Fama and French create portfolios as follows:

- *Small-cap portfolio is created from three portfolios*: Small value portfolio, small neutral portfolio, and small growth portfolio. The small-cap portfolio return is the average of the return of these three portfolios.
- *Large-cap portfolio is created from three portfolios*: Large value portfolio, large neutral portfolio, and large growth portfolio. The large-cap portfolio return is the average of the return of these three portfolios.
- *Value portfolio is created from two portfolios*: Small value portfolio and large value portfolio. The value portfolio return is the average of the return of these two portfolios.
- *Growth portfolio is created from two portfolios:* Small growth portfolio and large growth portfolio. The growth portfolio return is the average of the return of these two portfolios.

Long-only return forecast factor models

An alternative approach is to just take long positions based on either one factor or multiple factors. In the case of a single factor, the asset manager decides on which factor is expected to outperform a benchmark and then selects the top ranked stocks based on that factor to hold in the portfolio. For example, if the factor selected is momentum, then only the top X% would be purchased, where X is determined by the asset manager. When there are multifactors involved, then the asset manager will use statistical techniques to determine a model that includes the factors targeted by the asset manager to construct a portfolio.

Risk Forecast Factor Models

There are commercial vendors who have developed models to control the risk exposure of a portfolio to different factors. These are called risk forecast factor models. The commercial vendors of risk models have identified risk factors. These vendors include, for example, the MSCI Barra model, the Northfield XRD model, and Axioma. In Chapter 15 of the companion volume we describe a model developed by Barra. In that model, there are various risk indexes that have been found to be important in determining stock returns. The model begins with *risk indexes* that include volatility, momentum, size, trading activity, growth, earnings yield, value, earnings variability, leverage, currency sensitivity, and dividend yield.

A risk index is the composite of one or more of what are called *risk descriptions*. For example, the growth risk index is made up of (1) payout ratio over 5 years, (2) variability in capital structure, (3) growth rate in assets, (4) earnings growth over the last 5 years, (5) analysts-predicted earnings growth, and (6) recent earnings change. In addition to the risk indexes, the industry in which the company operates is used in the model.

Responsible Investing and Environmental, Social, and Governance Investing

The Principles for Responsible Investment (PRI), established by the United Nations Environment Programme Finance Initiative[12] and the United

[12]https://www.unpri.org/pri/about-the-pri.

Nations Global Compact,[13] defines responsible investing as "a strategy and practice to incorporate environmental, social, and governance (ESG) factors in investment decisions and active ownership". These are the three pillars in measuring sustainability and the impact that a company has on society. There is no shortage of terms to describe responsible investing. Within this broad definition of responsible investing are different themes. For example, *green investing* refers to selecting entities (companies or projects) that commit to conserving natural resources, development of alternative energy sources, and/or development of clean air and water projects.

The growth of mutual funds and ETFs dedicated to responsible investing has increased significantly. More asset management firms are requested by asset owners to formulate strategies that adhere to the principles of responsible investing and these mandates are expected to grow. Greenwich Associates [2018] reported based on global investors in its survey that of those that are not incorporating responsible investing into their investment policy, 75% are considering incorporating it in the future.

Environmental, Social, and Governance Criteria

The ESG criteria are based on how a company is assessed in terms of a wide range of management behavior and are referred to as the three pillars of responsible investing. They include

- *Environmental criteria* consider how a company performs in terms of being a guardian of nature. Examples are a company's policies on the use of energy, its pollution of the environment, its consumption of natural resources, and its impact on the climate.
- *Social criteria* consider how a company manages its relationship with all of its stakeholders (employees, customers, suppliers, and the communities where it operates). Examples covered by the social criteria are the working conditions and the overall well-being of its employees, its dealing with customers, the consistency of it values with that of its suppliers, and the contributions that it makes to the communities such as donations to worthwhile community causes and company personnel volunteering for social events.

[13]This is a strategic initiative by the United Nations to support companies throughout the world based on 10 principles that cover human rights, labor rights, the environment, and corruption.

- *Governance criteria* covers a company's organizational structure and the process by which it makes decisions. This encompasses the accuracy and transparency of its financial accounting system, the opportunity for shareholder voting on key issues and other shareholder rights, and the assembling and effectiveness of its independent board of directors.

ESG Scores

There are several providers of ESG scores for each individual pillar and an aggregate score. Credit rating agencies provide ESG Scores. The two major commercial vendors of ESG scores are Sustainalytics and MSCI.

Comparing ESG scores by these two vendors is difficult because the three pillars do not have standardized factors for the individual ESG criteria nor do they follow a standardized methodology. For example, consider Sustainalytics and MSCI.[14] For Sustainalytics, the focus in deriving each of the ESG scores is the quality and transparency of the disclosures made by the company. For MSCI, the focus is on a company's ESG exposure and the corresponding management policy. The number of factors for each individual pillar differs. Sustainalytics uses a total of 139 factors (52 for Environment, 52 for Social, and 35 for Governance) while MSCI uses 37 factors (13 for Environment, 15 Social, and 9 for Governance) plus 950 sub-factors. Moving from the score on the individual pillar scores to the composite ESG score, Sustainalytics tends to apply an equal weighting of each pillar score to get the composite ESG while MSCI uses a much more complex aggregation scheme.

Strategies for Constructing ESG Portfolios

Constructing an ESG portfolio depends on the targeted objective of the asset owner. Branch, Goldberg, and Hand [2019] suggest quantitative strategies for constructing ESG portfolios given the objective of the asset owner. Each of these strategies involves a different approach to the trade-off that an asset manager must deal with between the targeted ESG attributes and investment performance. Understanding these trade-offs provides asset owners with a guide in selecting the strategy that offers the best match to their ethical view and their investment view.

[14] This information is obtained from Furdak, Gao, Wee, and Wu [2019].

The simplest strategy in constructing ESG portfolios is a *capitalization-weighted exclusion strategy* for a diversified portfolio. This involves screening companies based on one or more ESG attributes and then removing unwanted companies from the list of candidate companies that may be included in the portfolio. The list of candidate companies typically comprises companies included in some market index.

The screening can be based on an asset owner's criteria or based on ESG scores provided by commercial vendors. For example, consider Trillium Asset Management.[15] This asset management firm has developed its own criteria for excluding companies based on its industry, and the following criteria: environment, human rights, animal rights, workplace, product and markets, and governance. Trillium excludes companies involved with or facing ongoing controversies dealing with any of the above criteria.

Once the unwanted companies are removed from the market index (i.e., the candidate list), then the market capitalization of the companies that are permissible investments is determined. The allocation is then made to the permissible companies based on a capitalization-weighted basis. Even though the portfolio is market capitalization weighted, this is not a passive or beta strategy. Rather it is an active strategy since the exclusion of the unwanted companies creates tracking error. When the excluded companies underperform (outperform) the market index, the ESG portfolio that excludes these companies will outperform (underperform) the market index.

An *optimized exclusion strategy* starts by excluding companies just as in the capitalization-weighted exclusion strategy. However, this strategy differs in how the portfolio is constructed from the companies in which the asset manager may invest. Instead of allocating the remaining (permissible) companies based on market capitalization, it is done via an optimization that seeks to minimize tracking error.

The Capacity of an Equity Strategy

Once an equity strategy is implemented by one asset manager, the performance of that strategy may erode for many reasons as it may become more costly to implement the strategy as the amount of assets under management (AUM) devoted to the strategy increases. This impact of applying

[15] https://trilliuminvest.com/trillium-investment-strategies/.

more AUM to a strategy that will eventually result in the erosion of performance is referred to as a *strategy's capacity*. The erosion in performance arises for two reasons. The first is that the trading activity needed to implement the strategy increases. The second is that as AUM increases, the size of the positions that the asset manager must take increases.

Vangelisti [2006] suggests three different definitions of capacity: threshold capacity, wealth-maximizing capacity, and terminal capacity. *Threshold capacity* is the level of AUM beyond which an equity strategy can be relied upon to realize the asset manager's stated return objective. The level of AUM where the amount of wealth is maximized (net of transaction costs) is what Vangelisti defines as *wealth-maximizing capacity*. The level of AUM where transaction costs (which are more than simply commissions and fees) become so high so that no alpha can be delivered (i.e., alpha is equal to zero) is *terminal capacity*.

One concern expressed about factor investing is that these strategies may have reached capacity. Ratcliffe, Miranda, and Ang [2017] investigated the issue of factor strategy capacity in three ways. They define capacity as the "breakeven hypothetical AUM at which the associated turnover transaction costs exactly offset the historically observed style premium". Capacity, in terms of AUM, is based on smart beta strategies — momentum, quality, size, value, and minimum volatility. In addition, they look at multifactor strategies that consist of the momentum, quality, size, and value factors. Their analysis is based on a transaction cost model developed by BlackRock. Their transaction cost approach to analyze the capacity of factor strategies indicates that the capacity is large for factor strategies.

Transaction Costs[16]

Transaction costs are categorized in terms of fixed and variable costs. *Fixed transaction costs* are independent of factors such as trade size and market conditions, whereas *variable transaction costs* depend on some or all these factors. Transaction costs are also categorized in terms of explicit and implicit transaction costs. *Explicit transaction costs* are those costs that are observable and known upfront such as commissions, fees, and taxes. *Implicit transaction costs* are not observable and not known in advance. In general,

[16]A more detailed discussion of transaction costs and how these costs are measured is described in Chapter 14 of the companion volume.

the implicit costs make up the dominant part of the total transaction costs faced by asset managers.

Explicit Transaction Costs

Trading commissions and fees, taxes, and bid-ask spreads are explicit transaction costs. Commissions are paid to brokers to execute trades. Commissions on trades are negotiable. Fees charged by an institution that holds the securities in safekeeping for an investor are referred to as *custodial fees.* When the ownership of a stock is transferred, the investor is charged a *transfer fee.* The difference between the quoted sell and buy order is called the *bid-ask spread.* The bid-ask spread is the immediate transaction cost that the market charges anyone for the privilege of trading.

Implicit Transaction Costs

The two major implicit transaction costs are market impact cost and opportunity cost.

Market impact cost, also referred to as *price impact cost*, is the deviation of the transaction price from the market (mid) price[17] that would have prevailed had the trade not occurred. The price movement is the cost (the market impact cost) of liquidity. The price impact of a trade can be negative if, for example, a trader buys at a price below the no-trade price (i.e., the price that would have prevailed had the trade not taken place).[18]

The cost of not transacting represents an opportunity cost. For example, when a certain trade fails to execute, the asset manager misses an opportunity. Commonly, this cost is defined as the difference in performance between an asset manager's desired investment and the actual investment after transaction costs. *Opportunity costs* are in general driven by price risk or market volatility. As a result, the longer the trading horizon, the greater the exposure to opportunity costs.

Backtesting Investment Strategies

Backtesting is an essential tool in an asset manager's arsenal for evaluating proposed investment strategies. There are various definitions of what

[17]Since the buyer buys at the ask and the seller sells at the bid, this definition of market impact cost ignores the bid/ask spread which is an explicit cost.

[18]There are two kinds of market impact costs, temporary and permanent, and these are described in Chapter 14 in the companion volume.

is meant by a backtest. A reasonable definition is that a *backtest* is a simulation of how a proposed investment strategy would perform subject to certain conditions being true. The major difficulties associated with backtesting are biases in the backtesting process and dealing realistically with implementation issues. These include what is labeled the "Seven Sins of Quantitative Investing" by Deutsche Bank's quantitative team: survivorship bias, look-ahead bias, storytelling, data mining and data snooping, transactions cost, outliers, and shorting (see Luo, Alvarez, Wang, Jussa, Wang, and Rohal [2014]).

The three methodologies for backtesting an investment strategy are the walk-forward method, resampling method, and Monte Carlo method. The *walk-forward method* evaluates the performance of a proposed investment strategy under the assumption that history repeats itself exactly. The two advantages of this method are that it has a clear historical interpretation and its performance can be reconciled with paper trading. There are several disadvantages, however, one of which is that it is based on a single scenario (the historical path) for evaluating potential performance. The second method for backtesting, the *resampling method*, overcomes the single scenario disadvantage of the walk-forward method. The third backtesting method is the *Monte Carlo method* which addresses the disadvantages of the walk-forward method.

In Chapter 17 in the companion book, the advantages and disadvantages of each method are described. The focus of Chapter 17 is on the walk-forward method and the pitfalls associated with each implementation method. In Chapter 5 of the companion book, the Monte Carlo method is described and then applied in Chapter 18 to backtesting.

Evaluating Investment Performance

In Chapter 9, we described measures of investment performance for an active asset manager: Sharpe ratio, Treynor ratio, Sortino ratio, and information ratio. These reward-risk ratios, also referred to as risk-adjusted returns, for measuring investment performance do not answer two important questions: (1) how did the asset manager perform after adjusting for the risk associated with the active strategy employed? And (2) how did the asset manager achieve the reported return?

The answers to these two questions are critical in assessing how well or how poorly the asset manager performed relative to some benchmark. In answering the first question, we must draw upon the various measures of risk that we described in Chapter 7. We can then judge whether the performance was acceptable in the face of the risk accepted. The answer to the second question tells us whether the asset manager, in fact, achieved a return by following the anticipated strategy. While a client would expect that any superior return accomplished is a result of a stated strategy, that may not always be the case. For example, suppose an asset manager solicits funds from a client by claiming he or she can achieve superior common stock performance by selecting underpriced stocks. Suppose also that this asset manager does generate a superior return relative to the client-imposed benchmark, say the S&P 500 Index. The client should not be satisfied with this performance until the return realized by the asset manager is segregated into the various components that generated the return. A client may find that the superior performance was the result of the asset manager's ability to allocate funds among the different sectors while the stocks selected based on what the asset manager thought were underpriced stocks performed poorly. In such an instance, the asset manager may have outperformed the S&P 500 (even after adjusting for risk), but not by following the strategy that the asset manager told the client would generate superior performance.

Return Attribution Analysis

Return attribution analysis (also referred to as *risk decomposition analysis*) is a quantitative framework that can be used to identify the sources of a portfolio's return and therefore how the asset manager performed based on his or her decisions. That is, return attribution analysis partitions the portfolio's return so as (1) to determine whether a superior return was realized and (2) to analyze the actual return of a portfolio to uncover the reasons why a return was realized (i.e., sources of return).

In broad terms, return attribution analysis seeks to explain the sources of return resulting from investment decisions made by an asset manager. The two earliest methodologies, and the ones most commonly used today, were developed by Brinson and Fachler [1985] and Brinson, Hood, and Beebower [1986]. Both are simply referred to as the *Brinson model*. The analysis begins with computing the difference between the actual return on the portfolio and the return realized by the benchmark (which is typically a client-imposed index). The difference is referred to as the *excess return* (or *excess performance*) and is a measure of the value added by the asset manager above the benchmark. It is also referred to as the *active management effect*.

In the Brinson model, the excess return is the result of two investment decisions made by the asset manager: (1) allocation among the sectors of the equity market (i.e., financials, utilities, technology, healthcare, etc.), and (2) selection of individual stocks. These two investment decisions are referred to as the *allocation decision* and *selection decision*, respectively. Reducing the active management effect by the effect of the allocation decision and the selection decision gives the component of the analysis referred to as the *interaction.*

With respect to the allocation decision, every broad market index is divided into sectors and the percentage of each sector in the benchmark (based on market capitalization) can be determined. A deviation of the sector's weight in the portfolio from that of the benchmark represents a bet on the sector. If the percentage in the portfolio exceeds that percentage in the benchmark, then the asset manager is overweighting the sector. If, instead, the percentage in the portfolio is less than the benchmark, the asset manager is underweighting the sector. In an indexed portfolio, the weight assigned to each sector in the portfolio will match the weight in the benchmark. In an actively managed portfolio, there is typically the overweighting or underweighting of sectors.

As for the selection decision, the analysts on the portfolio management team will select the specific companies in the benchmark to include in the portfolio and, in consultation with the senior portfolio manager, the percentage of the portfolio that should be allocated to each company. As with the allocation decision among sectors, there is typically an overweighting or underweighting of companies as well. Not including a company's stock in the portfolio means that the asset manager is underweighting that company. If there are less companies in the portfolio than there are in the benchmark, there will be overweighting of some companies.

Illustration of Brinson-Hood-Beebower model

To illustrate the Brinson model, we will use the data in Table 2. The benchmark in this case is the S&P 500 index. The first column shows the 11 sectors of the S&P 500 index. The portfolio composition (i.e., the portfolio weights) which reflects the allocation decision of the asset manager and the fourth column provides the actual return (net of fees) for each sector in the portfolio over a 1-year period. The third column shows the benchmark weight for each of the 11 sectors of the S&P 500 index. (These are the approximate weights for each sector at year-end 2018.) The benchmark

TABLE 2: Hypothetical Portfolio vs. S&P 500

Sector	**Portfolio Sector Weight (%)**	**Benchmark Sector Weight (%)**	**Portfolio Sector Return (%)**	**Benchmark Sector Return (%)**
Inf tech	25	20	12	13
Health care	15	16	5	5
Financials	12	14	5	4
Consumer discrete	10	10	9	8
Comm services	11	10	7	6
Industrials	7	9	11	11
Consumer staples	7	7	9	8
Energy	4	5	7	7
Utilities	3	3	2	2
Real estate	3	3	9	9
Materials	3	3	8	8
Total	100	100		

return for each sector over the same 1-year period is shown in the last column. The sector returns and therefore the portfolio return in our illustration is net of transaction costs and management fees. There are no such costs with the benchmark return.

Calculation of the portfolio return and the benchmark return is shown in Table 3. In the second column, the portfolio return is calculated using the data in Table 2 as follows:

For a given sector: Portfolio sector weight × Portfolio sector return.

Then these values are summed over the 11 sectors. For our hypothetical portfolio, the actual portfolio return is 8.27% as shown in Table 3.

To compute the benchmark return, the following is first calculated:

For a given sector: Benchmark sector weight × Benchmark sector return.

Then these values are summed over the 11 sectors. For the S&P 500, the actual benchmark return is 7.83% as shown in Table 3.

Given the actual portfolio return and the actual benchmark return over the 1-year period, the value added by the asset manager can be computed. The difference, which is the excess return, is 0.44% or 44 basis points. Therefore, the asset manager has added value. But how did the asset manager do so? Was the 44 basis points excess return due to the portfolio manager's allocation decision, stock selection decision, or both? This is where return attribution comes in.

TABLE 3: Calculation of the Portfolio Return and Benchmark Return

Sector	**Portfolio Sector Return (%)**	**Benchmark Sector Return (%)**
Inf tech	3.000	2.600
Health care	0.750	0.800
Financials	0.600	0.560
Consumer discrete	0.900	0.800
Comm services	0.770	0.600
Industrials	0.770	0.990
Consumer staples	0.630	0.560
Energy	0.280	0.350
Utilities	0.060	0.060
Real estate	0.270	0.270
Materials	0.240	0.240
Portfolio return	8.270	
Benchmark return	7.830	
Excess return	0.440	

Consider first the allocation decision. The formula for calculation of the allocation return for each sector is

For each sector: Portfolio sector weight × Benchmark sector return.

Then the values for the 11 sectors are summed. The calculations are shown in the second column of Table 4. The sum of the second column is the allocation return, 8.12%. The return obtained from the allocation decision is called the *allocation effect*. This is computed as follows:

Allocation effect = Allocation return − Benchmark return.

Since in our illustration the allocation decision resulted in an allocation return of 8.12% and the benchmark return was 7.83%, the allocation effect is 0.29% or 29 basis points. So, of the 44 basis points of excess return, 29 basis points were due to the allocation decision among the sectors.

Now let's look at the stock selection decision. The formula for calculation of the stock selection return for each sector is

For each sector: Benchmark sector weight × Portfolio sector return.

Then the values for 11 sectors are summed. The calculations are shown in the third column of Table 4. The sum of the third column is the stock selection return, 8.04%. The return obtained from the stock selection decision

TABLE 4: Calculation of Allocation Effect, Stock Selection Effect, and Interaction Effect

Sector	Allocation Return (%)	Stock Selection Return (%)
Inf tech	3.250	2.400
Health care	0.750	0.800
Financials	0.480	0.700
Consumer discrete	0.800	0.900
Comm services	0.660	0.700
Industrials	0.770	0.990
Consumer staples	0.560	0.630
Energy	0.280	0.350
Utilities	0.060	0.060
Real estate	0.270	0.270
Materials	0.240	0.240
Allocation Decision		
Allocation return	8.120	
Benchmark return	7.830	
Allocation effect	0.290	
Stock Selection Decision		
Stock selection return	8.040	
Benchmark return	7.830	
Stock selection effect	0.210	
Interaction	0.360	

is called the *stock selection effect* and is computed as follows:

$$\text{Stock selection effect} = \text{Stock selection return} - \text{Benchmark return}.$$

The benchmark return is 7.83% and the stock selection return is 8.04%. Therefore, the stock selection effect is 0.21% or 21 basis points. That is, the asset manager (or the equity analysts on the investment team) added value by selecting individual stocks.

Combining the allocation effect and the stock selection effect in our illustration, we get 50 basis points. However, the excess return is only 44 basis points. The difference between the 44 basis points and the 50 basis points is referred to as the *interaction effect*. That is, recalling that the excess return is also called the active management effect, then

$$\begin{aligned}&\text{Interaction effect}\\&\quad = \text{Active management effect} - \text{Allocation effect} - \text{Stock selection effect}\end{aligned}$$

In our illustration, the interaction effect is −6 basis points (44 bps − 29 bps − 21 bps).

One possible reason for the interaction effect (which is a misnomer and is also referred to as the residual or other in some methodologies) is that the analysis is based on the beginning portfolio composition and does not allow for the changing composition due to trades during the evaluation period.

Other Return Attribution Models

Although the Brinson model is the most used methodology for equity return attribution and other analyses, many more sophisticated models have been developed by commercial vendors and academics. Some of these models provide statistical information to assess whether performance is due to luck rather than skills. There are models that have been proposed for evaluating performance in terms of the contribution by allocation based on factors rather than simply sector allocation and stock selection. These attribution models are typically conducted by regressing the portfolio's returns on the portfolio returns of each of the given factor portfolios. The coefficient in the model represents the portfolio's allocation to or performance attributed to each of the given factors. The intercept in the regression represents the portfolio manager's skill or alpha. This type of performance attribution analysis provides a better idea as to the sources of a portfolio manager's return across multiple periods.

Key Points

- The underpinning of active portfolio management is the belief that there are market inefficiencies, that is, that there are situations where a stock's price does not fully reflect all available information.
- A top-down approach or bottom-up approach can be used by an equity manager pursuing an active strategy.
- There are two major types of stock selection approaches, those based on fundamental analysis and those based on technical analysis.
- Both fundamental and technical analyses attempt to identify situations where the market somehow makes mistakes in processing information, leading to pricing anomalies.
- Technical analysis looks at patterns in prices and returns and assumes that stock prices and returns follow discernable patterns.
- Fundamental analysis tries to assess the viability of a company from a business point of view, looking at financial statements as well as operations.

- The objective of fundamental analysis is to identify companies that will produce a solid future stream of cash flows.
- Strategies based on fundamental analysis include earnings surprise, low price/earnings ratio, market neutral long-short, and so-called market anomalies.
- Market anomaly strategies are based on the small firm effect, low-price-earning effect, neglected firm effect, and various calendar effects.
- Style investing is the implementation of investment strategies designed to earn excess returns from investing in mispriced stocks that result from the empirically observed market anomalies.
- The two principal anomalies which are used in style investing are value versus growth and market capitalization and are commonly depicted in the well-known Morningstar style box.
- Factor investing in the equity market involves constructing a portfolio based on factors that have consistently been shown to affect the return on stocks.
- Factors can be classified as fundamental factors, macroeconomic factors, and/or market factors.
- The quantitative models used in practice for constructing factor-based portfolios are return forecast factor models and risk forecast factor models.
- In addition to the market factor, the six most popular factors are value, size, dividend yield, quality, momentum, and volatility.
- Return forecast factor models may be long-short strategies and long-only strategies;
- A popular long–short strategy that falls into the return forecast factor model is the Fama–French three-factor model where the factors include the market, size, and value.
- The Fama–French five-factor model includes a profitability factor and an investment factor.
- A criticism of the five-factor model is that the two factors added to the three-factor model do not have the same empirical support as the factors in the three-factor model.
- Factor models commonly used also include momentum, a factor identified by Carhart.
- Risk forecast factor models have been developed by commercial vendors to control the risk exposure of a portfolio to different factors.
- Responsible investing is an investment strategy that incorporates environmental, social, and governance (three pillars) in constructing portfolios.

- There are several providers of ESG scores for each individual pillar and an aggregate score.
- Comparing ESG scores by vendors is difficult because the three pillars do not have standardized factors for the individual ESG criteria, nor do they follow a standardized methodology.
- Two strategies that can be used in constructing ESG portfolios are a capitalization-weighted exclusion strategy and an optimized exclusion strategy.
- A strategy's capacity is reached because once an equity strategy is implemented by one asset manager, the performance may erode for many reasons as it may become more costly to implement the strategy as the amount of AUM devoted to the strategy increases.
- Transaction costs are categorized in terms of fixed and variable costs.
- Fixed transaction costs are independent of factors such as trade size and market conditions, whereas variable transaction costs depend on some or all of these factors.
- Transaction costs are also categorized in terms of explicit and implicit transaction costs.
- Explicit transaction costs are those costs that are observable and known upfront such as commissions, fees, and taxes.
- Implicit transaction costs are not observable and not known in advance and typically make up the dominant part of the total transaction costs faced by asset managers.
- The two major implicit transaction costs are market impact cost and opportunity cost.
- Market impact cost is the deviation of the transaction price from the market (mid) price that would have prevailed had the trade not occurred.
- Opportunity costs, the cost of not transacting, are in general driven by price risk or market volatility.
- A backtest is a simulation of how a proposed investment strategy would perform subject to certain conditions being true.
- The major difficulties associated with backtesting are biases in the backtesting process and dealing realistically with implementation issues when backtesting.
- The three methodologies for backtesting an investment strategy are the walk-forward method, resampling method, and Monte Carlo method.
- In evaluating an asset manager's performance, risk-adjusted return (i.e., Sharpe ratio, Treynor ratio, Sortino ratio, and information ratio) is used.
- Risk- returns do not answer two important questions: (1) how did the asset manager perform after adjusting for the risk associated with the

active strategy employed? And (2) how did the asset manager achieve the reported return?

- Return attribution analysis is a quantitative framework used to identify the sources of a portfolio's return and therefore how the asset manager performed based on his or her decisions.
- Return attribution analysis partitions the portfolio's return so as (1) to determine whether a superior return was realized and (2) to analyze the actual return of a portfolio to uncover the reasons why a return was realized (i.e., sources of return).
- In the Brinson model, the excess return is the result of two investment decisions made by the asset manager: (1) allocation among the sectors of the equity market (i.e., financials, utilities, technology, healthcare, etc.), and (2) selection of individual stocks.

References

Arbel, A., S. A. Carvell, and P. Stebel, 1983. "Giraffes, institutions and neglected firms," *Financial Analysts Journal*, 39(3): 57–63.

Aharoni, G., B. D. Grundy, and Q. Zeng, 2013. "Stock returns and the Miller Modigliani valuation formula: Revisiting the Fama French analysis," *Journal of Financial Economics*, 110(2): 347–357.

Banz, R. W., 1981. "The relationship between return and market value of stocks," *Journal of Financial Economics*, 9(1): 103–126.

Basu, S., 1977. "Investment performance of common stocks in relation to their price-earnings ratios: A test of the efficient market hypothesis," *Journal of Finance*, 32(3): 663–682.

Blitz, D., M. X. Hanauer, M. Vidojevic, and P. van Vliet, 2018. "Five concerns with the five-factor model," *Journal of Portfolio Management*, 44(4): 71–78.

Branch, M., L. R. Goldberg, and P. Hand, 2019. "A guide to ESG portfolio construction," *Journal of Portfolio Management*, 45(5): 61–66.

Brinson, G. P. and N. Fachler, 1985. "Measuring non-US equity portfolio performance," *Journal of Portfolio Management*, 11(3): 73–76.

Brinson, G. P., L. R. Hood, and G. L. Beebower, 1986. "Determinants of portfolio performance," *Financial Analysts Journal*, 42(4): 39–44.

Carhart, M. M., 1997. "On persistence in mutual fund performance," *Journal of Finance*, 52(1): 57–82.

Christopherson, J. A., and C. N. Williams, 1997. "Equity style: What it is and why it matters," in *The Handbook of Equity Style Management*, 2nd edition, edited by D. Coggin, F. J. Fabozzi, and R. D. Arnott (pp. 1–20). Hoboken, NJ: John Wiley & Sons.

Chugh, L. and J. W. Meador, 1994. "The stock valuation process: The analysts' view," *Financial Analysts Journal*, 40(6): 41–48.

Dreman, D. N., 1977. *Psychology and the Stock Market: Investment Strategy Beyond Random Walk*. New York: AMACOM.

Dreman, D., 1982. *The New Contrarian Investment Strategy*. New York: Random House.

Fama, E. F. and K. R. French, 1993. "Common risk factors in the returns on stocks and bonds," *Journal of Financial Economics*, 33(1): 3–56.

Fama, E. F. and K. R. French, 2015. "A five-factor asset pricing model," *Journal of Financial Economics*, 116(1): 1–22.

Furdak, R. E., E. Gao, J. Wee, and E. Wu, 2019. "ESG data: Building a solid foundation." Available at https://www.man.com/maninstitute/esg-data-building-a-solid-foundation.

Graham, B. 1973. *The Intelligent Investor*, 4th revised edition. New York: Harper & Row.

Graham, B., D. L. Dodd, and S. Cottle, 1962. *Security Analysis*, 4th edition. New York: McGraw-Hill.

Greenwich Associates, 2018. "ESG investing: The global phenomenon." Summary, methodology, and report, 2018, https://www.greenwich.com/institutional-investing/esg-investing-global-phenomenon.

Jacobs, B. I., and K. N. Levy, 1997. "The long and short on long-short," *Journal of Investing*, 6(1): 78–88.

Joy, M., R. H. Lizenberger, and R. W. McEnally, 1977. "The adjustment of stock prices to announcements of unanticipated changes in quarterly earnings," *Journal of Accounting Research*, 15(2): 207–255.

Levy, H. and Z. Lerman, 1985. "Testing P/E ratio filters with stochastic dominance," *Journal of Portfolio Management*, 11(3): 1–41.

Luo, Y., M. Alvarez, S. Wang, J. Jussa, A. Wang, and G. Rohal, 2014. "Seven sins of quantitative investing," White paper, Deutsche Bank Markets Research, September 8.

Novy-Marx, R., 2013. "The other side of value: The gross profitability premium," *Journal of Financial Economics*, 108(1): 1–28.

Ratcliffe, R., P. Miranda, and A. Ang, 2017. "Capacity of smart beta strategies from a transaction cost perspective," *Journal of Index Investing*, 8(3): 39–50.

Reinganum, M. R., 1981. "Misspecification of capital asset pricing: Empirical anomalies based on earnings yields and market values," *Journal of Financial Economics*, 9(1): 19–46.

Shaw, A. R., 1988. "Market timing and technical analysis," in *The Financial Analyst's Handbook*, edited by S. N. Levine (pp. 944–988). Homewood, IL: DowJones–Irwin.

Schlarbaum, G. G., 1997. "Value-based equity strategies," in *The Handbook Of Equity Style Management*, 2nd edition edited by D. Coggin, F. J. Fabozzi, and R. D. Arnott (pp. 133–150). New York: John Wiley & Sons.

Vangelisti, M., 2006. "The capacity of an equity strategy," *Journal of Portfolio Management*, 32(2): 44–50.

White, J. and V. Haghani, 2020. "Smart beta: The good, the bad, and the muddy," *Journal of Portfolio Management*, 46(1): 11–21.

Chapter 14

Using Equity Derivatives in Portfolio Management

Learning Objectives

After reading this chapter, you will understand:

- the various types of equity derivatives;
- the types of stock index futures products;
- how stock index futures are used to control the risk of a stock portfolio, to hedge against adverse stock price movements, and to construct an indexed portfolio;
- what an equity swap is and its potential use by asset managers;
- the two types of listed equity options: stock options and stock index options;
- how options are used in risk management strategies, management strategies, and return enhancement strategies;
- derivatives available to manage exposure to market volatility of broad-based stock market indexes;
- how market volatility is measured using either historical (realized) volatility or implied volatility from option prices;
- what are stock market volatility indexes;
- what are variance swaps.

In Chapter 6, we reviewed the four types of derivatives — futures/forwards, swaps, options, and caps/floors — and the fundamental features of derivative instruments. We did not focus on any specific underlying or on how they are utilized by asset managers. When the underlying for a derivative is a common stock or some common stock index, the derivative is referred to as an *equity derivative*. In this chapter, we describe the different types of equity derivatives (stock index futures, equity swaps, and listed options on stocks and stock indexes) and derivatives that can be used to obtain exposure to market volatility. We then illustrate how they are used in managing a common stock portfolio.

Stock Index Futures

As we described in Chapter 6, there are futures and forward contracts. In managing common stock portfolios the use of forward contracts is rare.[1] Instead, the popular derivative is stock index futures. These derivatives allow asset managers to obtain exposure (long or short) to the entire market or a sector in one transaction rather than transacting in individual stocks. Thus, they are efficient instruments for transacting at a lower cost than transacting in individual stocks.

Stock Index Futures Products

The underlying for a stock index futures contract can be a broad-based stock market index or a narrow-based stock market index. Examples of US broad-based stock market indexes that are the underlying for a futures contract are the S&P 500 and NASDAQ 100. A narrow-based stock index futures contract is one based on a subsector or components of a broad-based stock market index containing groups of stocks or a specialized sector.

The dollar value of a stock index futures contract is the product of the futures price and a "multiple" that is specified for the futures contract. That is,

$$\text{Dollar value of a stock index futures contract} = \text{Futures price} \times \text{Multiple}.$$

For example, suppose that the futures price for the S&P 500 futures contract is 2800. There are two stock index futures contracts in which the S&P 500 is the underlying. The two contracts are identical except for the multiple. One has a multiple of $250 and the other a multiple of $50. The one with the $250 multiple is referred to as the full contract while the one with the $50 multiple is referred to as the mini contract. The dollar

[1] Also, there are single-stock futures on selected stocks, but these are not used by asset managers in the applications described in what follows. With single stock futures, the underlying is the stock of an individual company. The contracts are for 100 shares of the underlying stock, and at the settlement date, physical delivery of the stock is required.

value of these two contracts is then:

$$\text{Dollar value of full contract: } 2800 \times \$250 = \$700,000,$$

$$\text{Dollar value of mini contract: } 2800 \times \$50 = \$140,000.$$

Stock index futures contracts are *cash settlement contracts*. This means that at the settlement date, cash will be exchanged to settle the contract. For example, if an asset manager buys an S&P 500 futures full contract at 2800 and the futures settlement price is 2850, settlement would be as follows. The investor has agreed to buy the S&P 500 for 2800 times $250, or $700,000. The S&P 500 value at the settlement date is 2850 times $250, or $712,500. The seller of this futures contract must pay the investor $12,500 ($712,500 – $700,000). Had the futures price at the settlement date been 2780 instead of 2850, the dollar value of the S&P 500 futures contract would be $695,000. In this case, the investor must pay the seller of the contract $5,000 ($700,000 – $695,000). (Of course, in practice, the parties would be realizing any gains or losses at the end of each trading day as their positions are marked to market.)

Portfolio Applications with Stock Index Futures

In this section, we will discuss the various ways in which stock index futures can be used by asset managers.

Controlling the risk of a stock portfolio

An asset manager who wishes to alter exposure to the market can do so by revising the portfolio's beta. This can be done by rebalancing the portfolio with stocks that will produce the target beta, but there are transaction costs associated with rebalancing a portfolio. Because of the leverage inherent in futures contracts, asset managers can use stock index futures to achieve a target beta at a considerably lower cost. Buying stock index futures will increase a portfolio's beta, and selling will reduce it.

Hedging against adverse stock price movements

The major economic function of futures markets is to transfer price risk from hedgers to speculators. *Hedging* is the employment of futures contracts as a substitute for a transaction to be made in the cash market. If the cash and futures markets move together, any loss realized by the hedger on one position (whether cash or futures) will be offset by a profit on the other position. When the profit and loss are roughly equal, the hedge is called a *perfect hedge*. (A perfect hedge should generate the risk-free interest rate.)

Short hedge and long hedge

A *short hedge* is used to protect against a decline in the future cash price of the underlying. To execute a short hedge, the hedger sells a futures contract. Consequently, a short hedge is also referred to as a *sell hedge*. By establishing a short hedge, the hedger has fixed the future cash price and transferred the price risk of ownership to the buyer of the contract.

As an example of an asset manager who would use a short hedge, consider a pension fund manager who knows that the beneficiaries of the fund must be paid a total of $30 million four months from now. This will necessitate liquidating a portion of the fund's common stock portfolio. If the value of the shares that the manager intends to liquidate, in order to satisfy the payments to be made, declines in value four months from now, a larger portion of the portfolio will have to be liquidated. The easiest way to handle this situation is for the asset manager to sell the needed amount of stocks and invest the proceeds in a Treasury bill that matures in four months. However, suppose that for some reason the asset manager is constrained from making the sale today. The manager can use a short hedge to lock in the value of the stocks that will be liquidated.

A *long hedge* is undertaken to protect against an increase in the price of stocks that are expected to be purchased in the future. In a long hedge, the hedger buys a futures contract, so this hedge is also referred to as a *buy hedge*. As an example, consider once again a pension fund manager. This time, suppose that the asset manager expects a substantial contribution from the plan sponsor four months from now, and that the contributions will be invested in common stock of various companies. The pension fund manager expects the market price of the stocks in which the contributions will be invested to be higher in four months and, therefore, takes the risk that a higher price for the stocks will have to be paid. The asset manager can use a long hedge to effectively lock in a future price for these stocks now.

Return on a hedged position

Hedging is a special case of controlling a stock portfolio's exposure to adverse price changes. In a hedge, the objective is to alter a current or anticipated stock portfolio position so that its beta is zero. A portfolio with a beta of zero should generate a risk-free interest rate. Thus, in a perfect hedge, the return will be equal to the risk-free interest rate. More specifically, it will be the risk-free interest rate corresponding to a maturity equal to the number of days until settlement of the futures contract.

Therefore, a portfolio that is identical to the S&P 500 (i.e., an S&P 500 index fund) is fully hedged by selling an S&P 500 futures contract with 60 days to settlement that is priced at its theoretical futures price. The return on this hedged position will be the 60-day risk-free return. Notice what has been done. If a portfolio manager wanted to temporarily eliminate all exposure to the S&P 500, the manager could sell all the stocks and, with the funds received, invest in a Treasury bill. By using a stock index futures contract, the manager can eliminate exposure to the S&P 500 by hedging, and the hedged position should earn the same return as that on a Treasury bill reduced by transaction costs. The manager thereby saves on the transaction costs associated with selling a stock portfolio. Moreover, when the asset manager wants to get back into the stock market, rather than having to incur the transaction costs associated with buying stocks, the manager simply removes the hedge by buying an identical number of stock index futures contracts.

Cross hedging

In practice, hedging is not a simple exercise. When hedging with stock index futures, a perfect hedge can be obtained only if the return on the portfolio being hedged with the futures contract produces the risk-free rate.

The effectiveness of a hedged stock portfolio is determined by:

1. The relationship between the cash portfolio and the index underlying the futures contract.
2. The relationship between the cash price and futures price when a hedge is placed and when it is lifted (liquidated).

The difference between the cash price and the futures price is called the *basis*. It is only at the settlement that the basis is known with certainty. At the settlement date, the basis is zero. If a hedge is lifted at the settlement date, the basis is therefore known. However, if the hedge is lifted at any other time, the basis is not known in advance. The uncertainty about the basis at the time a hedge is to be lifted is called *basis risk*. Consequently, hedging involves the substitution of basis risk for price risk.

A stock index futures contract has a stock index as its underlying. Since the portfolio that an asset manager seeks to hedge typically has different characteristics from the underlying stock index, there will be a difference in the return pattern of the portfolio being hedged and the futures contract. This practice — hedging with a futures contract that is different from the underlying being hedged — is called *cross-hedging*. In the commodity futures markets, this occurs, for example, when a farmer who grows okra hedges that crop by using corn futures contracts because there are no futures contracts in which okra is the underlying. In the stock market, an asset manager who wishes to hedge a stock portfolio must choose the stock index (or combination of stock indexes) that best (but imperfectly) tracks the portfolio.

Consequently, cross hedging adds another dimension to basis risk, because the portfolio does not track the return on the stock index perfectly. Mispricing of a stock index futures contract is a major portion of basis risk and is largely random.

The foregoing points about hedging will be made clearer in the illustrations later in this section.

Hedge ratio

To implement a hedging strategy, it is necessary to determine not only which stock index futures contract to use, but also how many of the contracts to take a position in (i.e., how many to sell in a short hedge and buy in a long hedge). The number of contracts depends on the relative return volatility of the portfolio to be hedged and the return volatility of the futures contract. The *hedge ratio* is the ratio of the volatility of the portfolio to be hedged and the return volatility of the futures contract.

It is tempting to use the portfolio's beta as a hedge ratio because it is an indicator of the sensitivity of a portfolio's return to the stock index return. It appears, then, to be an ideal way to adjust for the sensitivity of the return of the portfolio to be hedged. However, applying beta relative to a stock index as a sensitivity adjustment to a stock index futures contract assumes that the index and the futures contract have the same volatility. If futures were always to sell at their theoretical price, this would be a reasonable assumption. However, mispricing is an extra element of volatility in a stock index futures contract. Since the futures contract is more volatile than the underlying index, using a portfolio beta as a sensitivity adjustment would result in a portfolio being overhedged.

The most accurate sensitivity adjustment would be the beta of a portfolio relative to the futures contract. It can be shown that the beta of a portfolio relative to a futures contract is equivalent to the product of the portfolio relative to the underlying index and the beta of the index relative to the futures contract (see Peters [1987]). The beta in each case is estimated using regression analysis in which the data are historical returns for the portfolio to be hedged, the stock index, and the stock index futures contract.

The first regression to be estimated is

$$r_P = \alpha_P + \beta_{PI}\, r_I + e_P,$$

where r_P is the return on the portfolio to be hedged, r_I is the return on the stock index, β_{PI} is the beta of the portfolio relative to the stock index, α_P is the intercept of the relationship, and e_P is the error term. The second regression is

$$r_I = \alpha_I + \beta_{IF}\, r_F + e_I,$$

where r_F is the return on the stock index futures contract, β_{IF} is the beta of the stock index relative to the stock index futures contract, α_I is the intercept of the relationship, and e_I is the error term.

Given β_{PI} and β_{IF}, the minimum risk hedge ratio can then be expressed as

$$\text{Hedge ratio} = \beta_{PI} \times \beta_{IF}.$$

The coefficient of determination of the regression (i.e., R-squared) will indicate how good the estimated relationship is, and thereby allow the asset manager to assess the likelihood of success of the proposed hedge.

The number of contracts needed can be calculated using the following three steps after B_{PI} and B_{IF} are estimated:

Step 1: Determine the equivalent market index units of the market by dividing the market value of the portfolio to be hedged by the current index price of the futures contract:

$$\text{Equivalent market index units} = \frac{\text{Market value of the portfolio to be hedged}}{\text{Current index value of the futures contract}}.$$

Step 2: Multiply the equivalent market index units by the hedge ratio to obtain the beta-adjusted equivalent market index units:

$$\text{Beta-adjusted equivalent market index units} = \text{Hedge ratio} \times \text{Equivalent market index units}.$$

or

$$\text{Beta-adjusted equivalent market index units} \\ = \beta_{PI} \times \beta_{IF} \times \text{Equivalent market index units.}$$

Step 3: Divide the beta-adjusted equivalent units by the multiple specified by the stock index futures contract:

$$\text{Number of contracts} \\ = \frac{\text{Beta-adjusted equivalent market index units}}{\text{Multiple of the contract}}.$$

We will use two examples to illustrate the implementation of a hedge and the risks associated with hedging.

Short hedging illustration

Consider an asset manager who on January 30, 2009 is managing a $100 million portfolio that is constructed to mimic the S&P 500. The asset manager wants to hedge against a possible market decline. More specifically, the asset manager wants to hedge the portfolio until February 27, 2009. To hedge against an adverse market move during the period January 30, 2009, to February 27, 2009, the portfolio manager decides to enter into a short hedge by selling the S&P 500 futures contracts that settled in March 2009. On January 30, 2009, the March 2009 futures contract was selling for 822.5.

Since the portfolio to be hedged is identical to the S&P 500, the beta of the portfolio relative to the index (β_{PI}) is, of course, 1. The beta relative to the futures contract (β_{IF}) was estimated to be 0.745. Therefore, the number of contracts needed to hedge the $100 million portfolio is computed as follows:

Step 1:

$$\text{Equivalent market index units} = \frac{\$100{,}000{,}000}{822.5} = \$121{,}581.$$

Step 2:

$$\text{Beta-adjusted equivalent market index units} \\ = 1 \times 0.745 \times \$121{,}581 = \$90{,}578.$$

Step 3: The multiple for the S&P 500 contract is 250. Therefore,

$$\text{Number of contracts to be sold} = \frac{\$90578}{250} = 362.$$

This means that the futures position was equal to \$74,500,000 (362 × \$250 × 822.5). On February 27, 2009, the hedge was removed. The portfolio that mirrored the S&P 500 had lost \$10,993,122. At the time the hedge was lifted, the March 2009 S&P 500 contract was selling at 734.2. Since the contract was sold on January 30, 2009 for 822.5 and bought back on February 27, 2009 for 734.2, there was a gain of 88.3 index units per contract. For the 362 contracts, the gain was \$7,997,994 (88.3 × \$250 × 362).

This results in a smaller loss of \$2,995,129 (\$7,997,994 gain on the futures position and \$10,993,122 loss on the portfolio). The total transaction costs for the futures position would have been less than \$8,000. Remember, had the asset manager not hedged the position, the loss would have been \$10,993,122.

Let's analyze this hedge to see not only why it was successful but also why it was not a perfect hedge. As explained earlier, in hedging, basis risk is substituted for price risk. Consider the basis risk in this hedge. At the time the hedge was placed, the cash index was at 825.88, and the futures contract was selling at 822.5. The basis was equal to 3.38 index units (the cash index of 825.88 minus the futures price of 822.5). At the same time, it was calculated that, based on the cost of carry, the theoretical basis was 1.45 index units. That is, the theoretical futures price at the time the hedge was placed should have been 824.42. Thus, according to the pricing model the futures contract was mispriced by 1.92 index units.

When the hedge was removed at the close of February 27, 2009, the cash index stood at 735.09 and the futures contract at 734.2. Thus, the basis changed from 3.38 index units at the time the hedge was initiated to 0.89 index units (735.09 – 734.2) when the hedge was lifted. The basis had changed by 2.49 index units (3.38 – 0.89) alone, or \$622.5 per contract (2.49 times the multiple of \$250). This means that the basis alone cost \$225,538 for the 362 contracts (\$622.5 × 362). The index dropped 90.79 index units, for a gain of \$22,698 per contract, or \$8,223,532. Thus, the futures position cost \$225,538 due to the change in the basis risk, and \$8,223,532 due to the change in the index. Combined, this comes out to be the \$7,997,994 gain in the futures position.

Short cross-hedging illustration

We examined basis risk in the first illustration. Because we were hedging a portfolio that was constructed to replicate the S&P 500 index using the S&P 500 futures contract, there was no cross-hedging risk. However, most portfolios are not matched to the S&P 500. Consequently, cross-hedging risk results because the estimated beta for the price behavior of the portfolio may not behave as predicted by β_{PI}.

To illustrate this situation, suppose that an asset manager owned all the stocks in the Dow Jones Industrial Average (DJIA) on January 30, 2009. The market value of the portfolio held was \$100 million. Also assume that the asset manager wanted to hedge the position against a decline in stock prices from January 30, 2009, to February 27, 2009, using the March 2009 S&P 500 futures contract. Since the S&P 500 futures September contract is used here to hedge a portfolio of DJIA to February 27, 2009, this is a cross hedge.

Information about the S&P 500 cash index and futures contract when the hedge was placed on January 30, 2009, and when it was removed on February 27, 2009, was given in the previous illustration. The beta of the index relative to the futures contract (β_{IF}) was 0.745. The DJIA in a regression analysis was found to have a beta relative to the S&P 500 of 1.05 (with an R-squared of 93%). We follow the three steps enumerated above to obtain the number of contracts to sell:

Step 1:

$$\text{Equivalent market index units} = \frac{\$100{,}000{,}000}{822\ 5} = \$121{,}581.$$

Step 2:

$$\text{Beta-adjusted equivalent market index units}$$
$$= 1.05 \times 0.745 \times \$121{,}581 = \$95{,}106.$$

Step 3: The multiple for the S&P 500 contract is 250. Therefore,

$$\text{Number of contracts to be sold} = \frac{\$95{,}106}{250} = 380.$$

During the period of the hedge, the DJIA actually lost \$11,720,000. This meant a loss of 11.72% on the portfolio consisting of the component stocks of the DJIA. Since 380 S&P 500 futures contracts were sold and the gain per contract was 88.3 points, the gain from the futures position was \$8,388,500 (\$88.3 × 380 × 250). This means that the hedged position resulted in a loss of \$3,331,500, or equivalently, a return of −3.31%.

We already analyzed why this was not a perfect hedge. In the previous illustration, we explained how changes in the basis affected the outcome. Let's look at how the relationship between the DJIA and the S&P 500 Index affected the outcome. As stated in the previous illustration, the S&P 500 over this same period declined in value by 10.99%. With the beta of the portfolio relative to the S&P 500 Index (1.05), the expected decline in the value of the portfolio based on the movement in the S&P 500 was 11.54% (1.05 × 10.99%). Had this actually occurred, the DJIA portfolio would have lost only $10,990,000 rather than $11,720,000, and the net loss from the hedge would have been $2,601,500, or −2.6%. Thus, there is a difference of a $730,000 loss due to the DJIA performing differently than predicted by beta.

Constructing an indexed portfolio

As we explained in Chapter 12, some institutional equity funds are indexed to some broad-based stock market index. There are management fees and transaction costs associated with creating a portfolio to replicate a stock index that has been targeted to be matched. The higher these costs are, the greater the divergence between the performance of the indexed portfolio and the target index. Moreover, because an asset manager creating an indexed portfolio will not purchase all the stocks that make up a broad-based stock index, the indexed portfolio is exposed to tracking error risk. Instead of using the cash market to construct an indexed portfolio, the manager can use stock index futures.

Let's illustrate how and under what circumstances stock index futures can be used to create an indexed portfolio. If stock index futures are priced according to their theoretical price, a portfolio consisting of a long position in stock index futures and Treasury bills will produce the same portfolio return as that of the underlying cash index. To see this, suppose that an index fund manager wishes to index a $90 million portfolio using the S&P 500 as the target index. Also assume the following:

- The S&P 500 at the time was 1200.
- The S&P 500 futures index with 6 months to settlement is currently selling for 1212.
- The expected dividend yield for the S&P 500 for the next 6 months is 2%.
- Six-month Treasury bills are currently yielding 3%.

The equation for the theoretical futures price, described in Chapter 6, is as follows:

$$\text{Cash market price} + \text{Cash market price}$$
$$\times(\text{Financing cost} - \text{Dividend yield}).$$

Because the financing cost is 3% and the dividend yield is 2%, the theoretical futures price is

$$1200 + 1200 \times (0.03 - 0.02) = 1212$$

and, therefore, the futures price in the market is equal to the theoretical futures price.

Consider two strategies that the index fund manager may choose to pursue:

Strategy 1: Purchase $90 million of stocks in such a way as to replicate the performance of the S&P 500.

Strategy 2: Buy 300 S&P 500 futures contracts with settlement 6 months from now at 1212, and invest $90 million in a 6-month Treasury bill.[2]

How will the two strategies perform under various scenarios for the S&P 500 value when the contract settles 6 months from now? Let's investigate three scenarios:

Scenario 1: The S&P 500 increases to 1320 (an increase of 10%).
Scenario 2: The S&P 500 remains at 1200.
Scenario 3: The S&P 500 declines to 1080 (a decrease of 10%).

At settlement, the futures price converges to the value of the index. Table 1 shows the value of the portfolio for both strategies for each of the three scenarios. As can be seen, for a given scenario, the performance of the two strategies is identical. This result should not be surprising because a futures contract can be replicated by buying the instrument underlying the futures contract with borrowed funds. In the case of indexing, we are replicating the underlying instrument by buying the futures contract and investing in Treasury bills. Therefore, if stock index futures contracts are

[2]There are two points to note here. First, this illustration ignores margin requirements. The Treasury bills can be used for initial margin. Second, 600 contracts are selected in this strategy because with the current (assumed) market index at 1200 and a multiple of 250, the cash value of 300 contracts is $90 million.

TABLE 1: Comparison of Portfolio Value from Purchasing Stocks to Replicate an Index and a Futures/Treasury Bill Strategy when the Futures Contract is Fairly Priced

Assumptions:
1. Amount to be invested = $90 million
2. Current value of S&P 500 = 1200
3. Current value of S&P futures contract = 1212
4. Expected dividend yield = 2%
5. Yield on Treasury bills = 3%
6. Number of S&P 500 contracts to be purchased = 300

Strategy 1. Direct Purchase of Stocks

	Index Value at Settlement		
	1320	**1200**	**1080**
Change in index value	10%	0%	−10%
Market value of portfolio that mirrors the index	$99,000,000	$90,000,000	$81,000,000
Dividends (0.02 × $90,000,000)	$1,800,000	$1,800,000	$1,800,000
Value of portfolio	$100,800,000	$91,800,000	$82,800,000
Dollar return	$1,080,000	$180,000	$720,000

Strategy 2. Futures/T-Bill Portfolio

	Index Value at Settlement[a]		
	1320	**1200**	**1080**
Gain/loss for 600 contracts (300 × 250 × gain/per contract)	$8,100,000	−$900,000	−$9,990,000
Value of Treasury bills ($90,000,000 × 1.03)	$92,700,000	$92,700,000	$92,700,000
Value of portfolio	$100,800,000	$91,800,000	$82,800,000
Dollar return	$1,080,000	$180,000	$720,000

Note: [a]Because of convergence of cash and futures price, the S&P 500 cash index and stock index futures price will be the same.

properly priced, index fund managers can use stock index futures to create an index fund.

Several points should be noted. First, in strategy 1, the ability of the portfolio to replicate the S&P 500 depends on how well the portfolio is constructed to track the index. On the other hand, assuming that the expected dividends are realized and that the futures contract is fairly priced, the futures/Treasury bill portfolio (strategy 2) will mirror the performance of the S&P 500 exactly. Thus, tracking error is reduced.

Second, the cost of transacting is less for strategy 2. For example, if the cost of one S&P 500 futures is $15, then the transaction costs for strategy 2 would be only \$4,500 for a \$90 million fund. This would be considerably less than the transaction costs associated with the acquisition and maintenance of a broadly diversified stock portfolio designed to replicate the S&P 500. In addition, for a large fund that wishes to index, the market impact cost is lessened by using stock index futures rather than using the cash market to create an index.

The third point is that custodial costs are obviously less for an index fund created using stock index futures. The fourth point is that the performance of the synthetically created index fund will depend on variation margin.

In synthetically creating an index fund, we assumed that the futures contract was fairly priced. Suppose, instead, that the stock index futures price is less than the theoretical futures price (i.e., the futures contracts are cheap). If that situation occurs, the index fund manager can enhance the indexed portfolio's return by buying the futures and buying Treasury bills. That is, the return on the futures and Treasury bill portfolio will be greater than that on the underlying index when the position is held to the settlement date.

To see this, suppose that in our previous illustration, the current futures price is 1204 instead of 1212, so that the futures contract is cheap (undervalued). The futures position for the three scenarios in Table 1 would be \$150,000 greater (2 index units × \$250 × 300 contracts). Therefore, the value of the portfolio and the dollar return for all three scenarios will be greater by \$150,000 by buying the futures contract and Treasury bills rather than buying the stocks directly.

Alternatively, if the futures contract is expensive based on its theoretical price, an index fund manager who owns stock index futures and Treasury bills will swap that portfolio for the stocks in the index. An index fund manager who swaps between the futures and Treasury bills portfolio and a stock portfolio based on the value of the futures contract relative to the cash market index is attempting to enhance the portfolio's return. This strategy, referred to as a *stock replacement strategy*, is one of several strategies used in an attempt to enhance the return of an indexed portfolio.

Transaction costs can be reduced measurably by using a return enhancement strategy. Whenever the difference between the actual basis and the theoretical basis exceeds the market impact of a transaction, the aggressive manager should consider replacing stocks with futures or vice versa.

Once the strategy has been put into effect, several subsequent scenarios may unfold. For example, consider an index manager who has a portfolio of stock index futures and Treasury bills. First, should the futures contract become sufficiently rich relative to stocks, the futures position is sold and the stocks repurchased, with program trading used to execute the buy orders. Second, should the futures contract remain at fair value, the position is held until expiration. When the futures settle at the cash index value, stocks are repurchased at the market at close. Should an index manager own a portfolio of stocks and the futures contract becomes cheap relative to stocks, then the manager will sell the stocks and buy the stock index futures contracts.

Equity Swaps

In Chapter 6, we reviewed swaps. An equity swap requires that the counterparties make periodic exchanges of a schedule of cash flows over a specified time period where at least one of the two payments is linked to the performance of some stock market index. In a plain vanilla equity swap, one of the counterparties agrees to pay the other the total return to an equity index in exchange for receiving either the total return of another asset or a fixed or floating interest rate. All payments are based on a notional amount and payments are made over a fixed time period.

Equity swap structures are very flexible with maturities ranging from a few months to 10 years. The returns of virtually any asset can be swapped for another without incurring the costs associated with a transaction in the cash market. Payment schedules can be denominated in any currency irrespective of the equity asset, and the payments can be exchanged monthly, quarterly, annually, or at maturity. The equity asset can be any equity index or portfolio of stocks, and denominated in any currency, hedged or unhedged.

Equity swaps have a wide variety of applications including asset allocation, accessing international markets, enhancing equity returns, hedging equity exposure, and synthetically shorting stocks.

An example of an equity swap is a 1-year agreement where the counterparty agrees to pay the investor the total return to the S&P 500 Index in exchange for dollar-denominated LIBOR on a quarterly basis. The investor would pay LIBOR plus a spread multiplied by 91/360 multiplied by the notional amount. This type of equity swap is the economic equivalent of financing a long position in the S&P 500 Index at a spread to LIBOR. The advantages of using the swap are no transaction costs, no sales or dividend withholding tax, and no tracking error or basis risk versus the index.

The basic mechanics of equity swaps are the same regardless of the structure. However, the rules governing the exchange of payments may differ. For example, a US investor wanting to diversify internationally can enter into a swap and, depending on the investment objective, exchange payments on a currency-hedged basis. If the investment objective is to reduce US equity exposure and increase Japanese equity exposure, for example, a swap could be structured to exchange the total returns for the S&P 500 Index for the total returns for the Nikkei 225 Index. If, however, the investment objective is to gain access to the Japanese equity market, a swap can be structured to exchange LIBOR plus a spread for the total returns to the Nikkei 225 Index. This is an example of diversifying internationally and the cash flows can be denominated in either yen or dollars. The advantages of entering into an equity swap to obtain international diversification are that the investor exposure is devoid of tracking error, and the investor incurs no sales tax, custodial fees, withholding fees, or market impact associated with entering and exiting a market. This swap is the economic equivalent of being long the Nikkei 225 financed at a spread to LIBOR at a fixed exchange rate.

There are numerous applications of equity swaps, but all assume the basic structure outlined above. Investors can virtually swap any financial asset for the total returns to an equity index, a portfolio of stocks, or a single stock. There are dealers prepared to create structures that allow an investor to exchange the returns of any two assets. The schedule of cash flows exchanged is a function of the assets. For example, an investor wanting to outperform an equity benchmark may be able to accomplish this by purchasing a particular bond and swapping the cash flows for the S&P 500 total return minus a spread.

Equity swaps are a useful means of implementing a multi-asset or asset allocation strategy. One example is an asset swap of the S&P 500 total returns for the total returns to the German DAX index. The investor can reduce US equity exposure and increase German equity exposure through an equity swap, thereby avoiding the costs associated with cash market transactions.

Equity Options

Options provide asset managers with another derivative tool to manage risk and achieve the desired investment objective. As with futures contracts, options can modify the risk characteristics of a portfolio to enhance expected return and reduce transaction costs associated with managing a portfolio. As explained in Chapter 6, there are listed and dealer options. Here we focus on listed equity options.

Listed Equity Options

Listed options include stock options and index options.

Stock options

Stock options refer to listed options on individual stocks. The underlying is 100 shares of the designated stock. All listed stock options in the United States may be exercised any time before the expiration date; that is, they are American-style options. Option contracts for a given stock are based on expiration dates that fit in a cycle, typically 9 months for a stock; for stock options the cycles are two near-term months plus two additional months from the January, February, or March quarterly cycles. Common cycles include January-April-July-October (JAJO) expiring options, February-May-August-November (FMAN) expiring options, and March-June-September-December (MJSD) expiring options.

Index options

Index options are options where the underlying is a stock index rather than an individual stock. An index call option gives the option buyer the right to buy the underlying stock index, while a put index option gives the option buyer the right to sell the underlying stock index. Unlike stock options where a stock can be delivered if the option is exercised by the option holder, it would be extremely complicated to settle an index option by delivering all the stocks that constitute the index. Instead, as with stock index futures, index options are cash settlement contracts. This means that if the option is exercised by the option holder, the option writer pays cash to the option buyer. There is no delivery of any stocks.

The most popular stock index options in terms of trading volume are the S&P 500 Index Option (ticker symbol SPX), the S&P 100 Index Option (ticker symbol OEX), the Nasdaq 100 Index Option (NDX), the Dow Jones Industrial Average Index (ticker symbol DJX), and the Russell 2000 Index Option (RUT). Index options can have a European exercise style and are cash settled.

All stock index options have a multiple. For the four popular stock index options, the multiple is \$100. For the "mini" versions of these contracts, the underlying is one-tenth of the multiple used for the index. Since the multiple for the stock indexes described above is \$100, the mini version's multiple is \$10.

The dollar value of the stock index underlying an index option is equal to the current cash index value multiplied by \$100 or \$10 depending on whether it is the full contract or the mini contract. That is,

$$\text{Dollar value of the underlying index} = \text{Cash index value} \times \text{Multiple.}$$

For example, suppose the cash index value for the S&P 500 is 2800. Since the contract's multiple is \$100, the dollar value of the SPX is \$280,000 (= 2800 × \$100).

For a stock option, the price at which the buyer of the option can buy or sell the stock is the strike price. For an index option, the strike index is the index value at which the buyer of the option can buy or sell the underlying stock index. The strike index is converted into a dollar value by multiplying the strike index by the multiple for the contract. For example, if the strike index for the SPX is 2790, then the dollar value is \$279,000 (= 2790 × \$100). If an investor purchases a call option on the SPX with a strike index of 2700, and exercises the option when the index value is 2800, the investor has the right to purchase the index for \$279,000 when the market value of the index is \$280,000. The buyer of the call option would then receive \$1,000 from the option writer.

Portfolio Applications with Listed Options

In Chapter 6, we explained that the difference between options and futures contracts is that the former have nonlinear payouts that will fundamentally alter the risk profile of an existing portfolio. As a result, investors can use the listed options market to address a range of investment problems. In this section, we consider the use of calls, puts, and combinations in the context of the investment process, which could involve (1) risk management, (2) cost management, or (3) return enhancement.

Risk management strategies

Risk management in the context of equity portfolio management focuses on price risk. Consequently, the strategies discussed in this section in some way address the risk of a price decline or a loss due to an adverse price movement. Options can be used to create asymmetric risk exposures across all or part of the core equity portfolio. This allows an asset manager to hedge downside risk at a fixed cost with a specific limit to losses should the market turn down.

The basic risk management objective is to create the optimal risk exposure and to achieve the target rate of return. Options can help accomplish this by reducing risk exposure. The various risk management strategies will also affect the expected rate of return on the position unless some form of inefficiency is involved. This may involve the current mix of risk and return or be the result of the use of options. In the following, we discuss two risk management strategies: protective put and collar.[3]

Protective put strategies

Protective put strategies are valuable to asset managers who currently hold a long position in the underlying security or investors who desire upside exposure and downside protection by using put options. The motivation is either to hedge some or all of the total risk. Index put options hedge mostly market risk, while equity put options hedge the total risk associated with a specific stock. This allows portfolio managers to use protective put strategies for separating tactical and strategic strategies. Consider, for example, an asset manager who is concerned about exogenous or nonfinancial events increasing the level of risk in the marketplace. Furthermore, assume the portfolio manager is satisfied with the core portfolio holdings and the strategic mix. Put options could be employed as a tactical risk reduction strategy designed to preserve capital and still maintain strategic targets for portfolio returns.

For this reason, a portfolio manager concerned about downside risk is a candidate for a protective put strategy. Nonetheless, protective put strategies may not be suitable for all portfolio managers. The value of protective put strategies, however, is that they provide the investor with the ability to invest in volatile stocks with a degree of desired insurance and unlimited profit potential over the life of the strategy.

The protective put involves the purchase of a put option combined with a long stock position. This is the equivalent of a position in a call option on the stock combined with the purchase of risk-free bond. In fact, the combined

---

[3]Other risk management strategies are discussed in Collins and Fabozzi [1999, Chapter 3].

position yields the call option payout pattern described in Chapter 6. The put option is comparable to an insurance policy written against the long stock position.

The option price is the cost of the insurance premium, and the amount the option is out-of-the-money is the deductible. Just as in the case of insurance, the deductible is inversely related to the insurance premium. The deductible is reduced as the strike price increases, which makes the put option more in-the-money or less out-of-the-money. The higher strike price causes the put price to increase and makes the insurance policy more expensive.

The profitability of the strategy from inception to termination can be expressed as follows:

$$\text{Profit} = N_s(S_T - S_t) + N_p[\max(0, K - S_T) - \text{Put}],$$

where N_s is the number of shares of the stock, N_p is the number of put options, S_T is the price of the stock at the termination date (time T), S_t is the price of the stock at time t, K is the strike price, and Put is the put price.

The profitability of the protective put strategy is the sum of the profit from the long stock position and the put option. If held to expiration, the minimum payout is the strike price (K) and the maximum is the stock price (S_T). If the stock price is below the strike price of the put option, the investor exercises the option and sells the stock to the option writer for K. If we assume that the number of shares $N_s = +N_p$, the number of options, then the loss would amount to

$$\text{Profit} = S_T - S_t + K - S_T - \text{Put} = K - S_t - \text{Put}.$$

Note that the price of the stock at the termination date does not enter into the profit equation.

For example, if the original stock price was \$100 (S_t), the strike price \$95 (K), the closing stock price \$80 (S_T), and the put premium (Put) \$4, then the profit would equal the following:

$$\text{Profit} = \$95 - \$100 - \$4 = -\$9.$$

The asset manager would have realized a loss of \$9 without the hedge.

If, on the other hand, the stock closed up \$20, then the profit would appear as follows:

$$\text{Profit} = S_T - S_t - \text{Put} = \$120 - \$100 - \$4 = \$16.$$

The cost of the insurance is 4% in percentage terms and is manifest as a loss of upside potential. If we add transaction costs, the shortfall is increased slightly. The maximum loss, however, is the sum of the put premium and the difference between the strike price and the original stock price, which is the amount of the deductible. The problem arises when the asset manager is measured against a benchmark and the cost of what amounted to an unused insurance policy causes the portfolio to underperform the benchmark.

Equity managers can use stock selection, market timing, and the prudent use of options to reduce the cost of insurance. The break-even stock price is given by the sum of the original stock price and the put price. In this example, break-even is $104, which is the stock price necessary to recover the put premium. The put premium is never really recovered because of the performance lag. This lag falls in significance as the return increases.

A graphical depiction of the protective put strategy is provided in Figure 1. The figure shows the individual long stock and long put positions and the combined impact, which is essentially a long call option. The maximum loss is the put premium plus the out-of-the-money amount, which is the insurance premium plus the deductible.

Collar strategies

An alternative to a protective put is a collar. A *collar strategy* consists of a long stock, a long put, and a short call. By varying the strike prices, a range of trade-offs among downside protection, costs, and upside potential

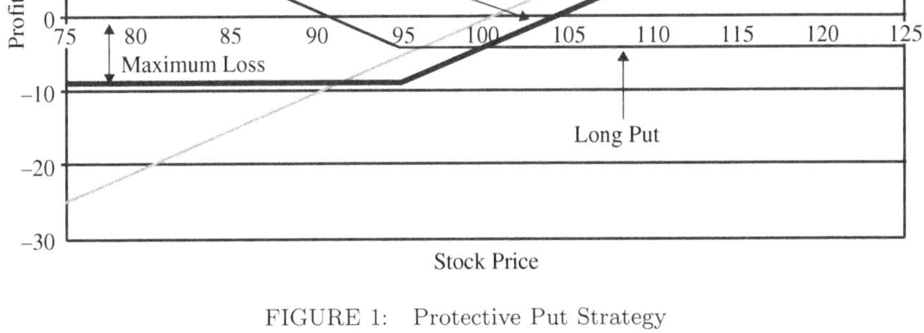

FIGURE 1: Protective Put Strategy

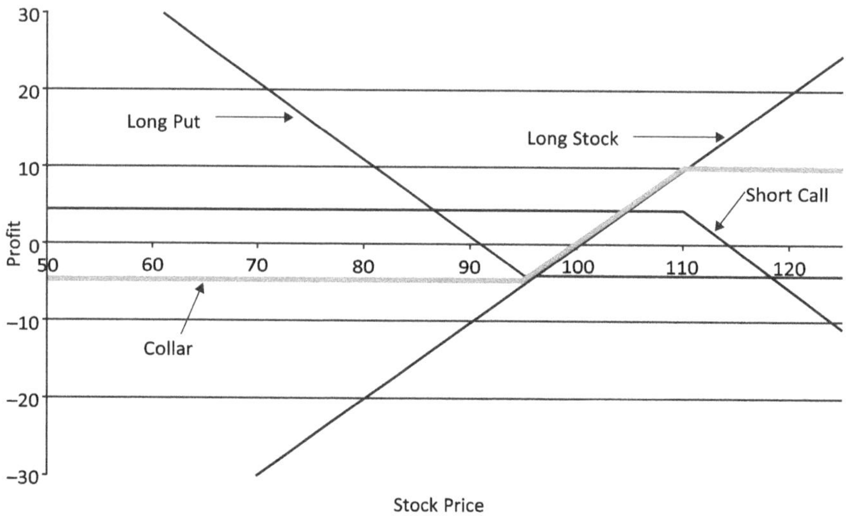

FIGURE 2: Collar Strategy

is possible. When the long put is completely financed by the short call position, the strategy is referred to as a *zero-cost collar*.

Collars are designed for investors who currently hold a long equity position and want to achieve a level of risk reduction. The put exercise price establishes a floor and the call exercise price establishes a ceiling. The resulting payout pattern is shown in Figure 2. The figure includes the components of the strategy and the combined position. This is an example of a near zero-cost collar. In order to pay for the put option, a call option was written with a strike price of \$110. Selling this call option pays for the put premium, but caps the upside to 10.23%. The floor completes the collar and limits downside losses to the out-of-the money amount of the put option. In order to provide full insurance, an at-the-money put option would cost slightly above 6%, which would be paid for by limiting upside potential returns to 5%. Asset managers can determine the appropriate trade-offs and protection consistent with their objectives.

The profit equation for a collar is simply the sum of a long stock position, a long put, and a short call. That is,

$$\text{Profit} = N_s(S_T - S_t) + N_p[\max(0, K_p - S_T) - \text{Put}] - N_c[\max(0, S_T - K_c + \text{Call}],$$

where K_p and K_c are the strike price of the put and call, respectively, and Call is the price of the call option.

Management strategies

Options can be used to manage the cost of maintaining an equity portfolio in a number of ways. Among these strategies is the use of short put and short call positions to serve as a substitute for a limit order in the cash market. *Cash-secured put strategies* can be used to purchase stocks at the target price, while *covered calls* or *overwrites* can be used to sell stocks at the target price. The target price is the one consistent with the portfolio manager's valuation or technical models and the price intended to produce the desired rate of return.

Return enhancement strategies

Options can be used for return enhancement. Here we describe the most popular return enhancement strategy: covered call strategy. Other return enhancement strategies include covered combination strategy and volatility valuation strategy.[4]

Covered call strategy

There are many variations of what is popularly referred to as a *covered call strategy*. If the portfolio manager owns the stock and writes a call on that stock, the strategy has been referred to as an *overwrite strategy*. If the strategy is implemented all at once (i.e., buy the stock and sell the call option), it is referred to as a *buy-write strategy*. The essence of the covered call is to trade price appreciation for income. The strategy is appropriate for slightly bullish investors who don't expect much out of the stock and want to produce additional income. These are investors who are willing either to limit upside appreciation for limited downside protection or to manage the costs of selling the underlying stock. The primary motive is to generate additional income from owning the stock.

Although the call premium provides some limited downside protection, this is not an insurance strategy because it has significant downside risk. Consequently, investors should proceed with caution when considering a covered call strategy.

A covered call is less risky than buying the stock because the call premium lowers the break-even recovery price. The strategy behaves like a long stock position when the stock price is below the strike price. On the other

[4]These strategies are described in Collins and Fabozzi [1999].

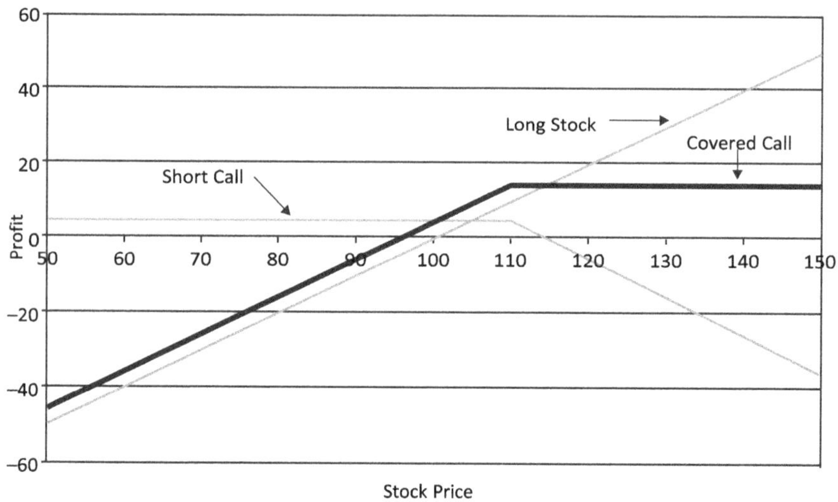

FIGURE 3: Covered Call Strategy

hand, the strategy is insensitive to stock prices above the strike price and is therefore capped on the upside. The maximum profit is given by the call premium and the out-the-money amount of the call option.

The payout pattern diagram is presented in Figure 3, which includes the long stock, short call, and covered call positions.

Market Volatility Derivatives

Asset managers are concerned with the volatility of their common stock portfolio. There are derivatives that asset managers use to buy or sell market volatility to either control a portfolio's volatility or express a view on what future market volatility will be. These include volatility index derivatives, stock index options, and variance swaps. Let's first look at how volatility is measured.

Measuring Stock Market Index Volatility

There are various ways to measure the market's expectation of future volatility for a given broad-based stock market index. One way is by calculating the actual changes and using that measure to calculate the standard deviation. A measure of volatility that uses the changes in the observed values of a stock market index is called *historical volatility* or *realized volatility*.

An alternative way is by using stock index options to obtain that information. In Chapter 6, we identified the factors that impact the value of an option. One of the factors is expected volatility. Basically, with an option pricing model, the six factors that are explained in Chapter 6 that affect the value of an option are entered as inputs and the theoretical option price is computed. Alternatively, one can input into an option pricing model the observed price of the option (i.e., the market price) and the five other factors. The model will then allow for the backing out of the volatility that is consistent with the option pricing model, the observed price of the option, and the five factors. This measure of volatility is referred to as *implied volatility*.

Stock Market Volatility Index Futures and Options

A straightforward way to alter exposure of a portfolio to market volatility is using derivatives where the underlying is some stock market volatility index.

Stock market volatility indexes

The first stock market volatility index that has been commercialized is the CBOE Market Volatility Index (VIX). This index, dubbed the "investor fear index", is based on the S&P 500 index options with 30 days to expiration. The VIX can then be viewed as a measure of the forward-looking volatility of the S&P 500 over the next 30 days. The measure of volatility used is the implied volatility for the S&P 500 index.

The methodology developed for the construction of the VIX has been used by the CBOE to create a market volatility index for the Dow Jones Industrial Average (VXD), the Nasdaq 100 (VXN), and the Russell 2000 (RVX). For all of these, the volatility indexes are based on implied volatility for the market index option.

Volatility index mechanics

There are futures and options on all volatility index measures. These are all cash settlement derivatives because of the inability to deliver the underlying which is the volatility index. We'll use in our discussion futures and options on the VIX.

Consider first the futures product. The buyer of the contract agrees to purchase the index value at the settlement date and the seller agrees to sell the index value at the settlement date. The future price or value is what the two parties agree to transact at. At the settlement date, the difference between the futures index value at that date and the futures price at the time the contract is entered indicates the profit or loss for a party. If the difference is positive, the buyer of the contract realizes a profit and if it is negative the seller realizes a profit. The amount of the profit (which is the amount the party realizing a loss must pay to the other party) is then multiplied by some value (the multiplier). For the VIX, it is \$1,000 and for the mini contract the multiplier is \$100.

Stock Index Options

We described stock index options and strategies in the previous section. In discussing the six factors that impact an option's price in Chapter 6, it was explained that one of the factors is expected volatility of the underlying. Regardless of whether the option is a put or a call, an increase in volatility increases the option's price. Thus, the buyer of an option is buying volatility because if expected volatility increases, the value of the option increases. In contrast, a decrease in volatility decreases the option's price and therefore covered call or secured put option writers are selling volatility. Thus, buying or writing options on a stock index option or a broad-based market index allows an asset manager to alter exposure to market volatility.

The concern with using stock index options for increasing or decreasing exposure to market volatility is that the movements of the underlying stock index will be impacted by the strike index (i.e., strike price) selected. There are ways to control for this, but a discussion of them is beyond the scope of this chapter.

Variance Swaps

A *variance swap* is a forward contract on the annualized variance of the realized returns for a stock market index. The realized returns are calculated as logarithmic returns. The annualized variance is calculated as follows:

First calculate logarithmic returns for the observations of the stock index in the relevant period as follows:

$$r_i = Ln(L_i/L_{i-1}),$$

where L_i is the level of the index on the trade date (i.e., when the investor enters into the contract) and L_{i-1} is the level of the index at the expiration date.

Over the contract's relevant period, calculate the square of the log of the returns and then divide by the relevant number of days to obtain the variance over the relevant time period

$$\text{Realized variance} = \frac{\left[\sum_{i=1}^{N} (r_i)^2\right]}{n}.$$

The relevant number of days for calculating W is the actual number of trading days on which no market disruption event occurs from, but not including, the date of the trade, up to and including the swap's expiration date.

The realized variance is then annualized by multiplying by 252. The number 252 is the factor used to annualize the realized variance based on the fact that this is the standard number of trading days in the year. That is,

$$\text{Annualized realized variance} = V_R = (252) \times \text{Realized variance}.$$

Let V_0 be the specified volatility at which the parties agree to buy and sell volatility at the trade date. Then the payoff for the swap buyer and seller is as follows:

- If $V_R - V_0 > 0$:

  Payoff to swap buyer: \$10,000($V_R - V_0$)profit,
  Payoff to swap seller: – \$10,000(V_R – V_0)loss.

- If $V_0 - V_R > 0$:

  Payoff to swap buyer: – \$10,000($V_0 - V_R$)loss,
  Payoff to swap seller: \$10,000($V_0 - V_R$)profit.

- If $V_0 = V_R$, then the payoff for both parties is zero.

Why is there 10,000 in the payoff formulas above? The 10,000 provides the multiplier for the contract just as there is a multiplier for stock index futures contracts. In the case of a variance swap, the multiplier is 100 and since the realized variance is a squared measure, the multiplier is squared (i.e., $100^2 = 10{,}000$).

Key Points

- When the underlying for a derivative is a common stock or some common stock index, the derivative is referred to as an equity derivative.
- The underlying for a stock index futures contract can be a broad-based stock market index or a narrow-based stock market index.
- The dollar value of a stock index futures contract is the product of the futures price and a "multiple" that is specified for the futures contract.
- Stock index futures contracts are cash settlement contracts.
- Portfolio applications with stock index futures include controlling the risk of a stock portfolio, hedging against adverse stock price movements, and constructing an indexed portfolio.
- Hedging is the employment of futures contracts as a substitute for a transaction to be made in the cash market.
- A short hedge is used to protect against a decline in the future cash price of the underlying; to execute a short hedge, the hedger sells a futures contract.
- A long hedge is undertaken to protect against rising prices of future intended purchases; in a long hedge, the hedger buys a futures contract.
- Hedging is a special case of controlling a stock portfolio's exposure to adverse price changes.
- In a hedge using stock index futures, the objective is to alter a current or anticipated stock portfolio position so that its beta is zero.
- Because a portfolio with a beta of zero should generate a risk-free interest rate, in a perfect hedge, the return will be equal to the risk-free interest rate corresponding to a maturity equal to the number of days until settlement of the futures contract.
- The effectiveness of a hedged stock portfolio is determined by the relationship between (1) the cash portfolio and the index underlying the futures contract and (2) the cash price and futures price when a hedge is placed and when it is lifted (liquidated).
- The basis is the difference between the cash price and the futures price and it is only at the settlement date that the basis is known with certainty.
- The uncertainty about the basis at the time a hedge is to be lifted is called basis risk and therefore hedging involves the substitution of basis risk for price risk associated with the underlying.
- Cross hedging occurs when an asset manager seeks to hedge a stock portfolio that has characteristics different from the underlying of the stock index futures that is used for hedging.

- The hedge ratio is the ratio of the volatility of the portfolio to be hedged and the return volatility of the futures contract and is used to determine the number of contracts that should be used for the hedge.
- An equity swap requires that the counterparties make periodic exchanges of a schedule of cash flows over a specified time period where at least one of the two payments is linked to the performance of some stock market index.
- In a plain vanilla equity swap, one of the counterparties agrees to pay the other the total return to an equity index in exchange for receiving either the total return of another asset or a fixed or floating interest rate.
- Equity swaps have a wide variety of applications including asset allocation, accessing international markets, enhancing equity returns, hedging equity exposure, and synthetically shorting stocks.
- Listed options include stock options (options on individual stocks) and index options.
- Index options are options where the underlying is a stock index rather than an individual stock.
- An index call option gives the option buyer the right to buy the underlying stock index, while a put index option gives the option buyer the right to sell the underlying stock index.
- Options can be used for risk management, cost management, and return enhancement.
- Risk management in the context of equity portfolio management focuses on price risk.
- Options can be used to create asymmetric risk exposures across all or part of the core equity portfolio, allowing an asset manager to hedge downside risk at a fixed cost with a specific limit to losses should the market turn down.
- The basic risk management objective is to create the optimal risk exposure and to achieve the target rate of return; options can help accomplish this by reducing risk exposure.
- Protective put strategies and collar strategies are two risk management strategies.
- Protective put strategies can be used by asset managers who currently hold a long position in the underlying stock or by asset managers who desire upside exposure and downside protection by using put options.
- The protective put involves the purchase of a put option combined with a long stock position; the option price of the put is the cost of the insurance

premium and the amount by which the option is out-of-the-money is called the deductible.

- A collar strategy is an alternative to a protective put strategy that consists of a long stock position, a long put, and a short call.
- In a collar strategy, by varying the strike prices, a range of trade-offs among downside protection, costs, and upside potential is possible.
- Options can be used to manage the cost of maintaining an equity portfolio using a short put and short call positions to serve as a substitute for a limit order in the cash market.
- Cash-secured put strategies can be used to purchase stocks at the target price based on some valuation model, while covered calls or overwrites can be used to sell stocks at the target price.
- Options can be used for return enhancement, the most popular strategy being the covered call strategy.
- There are derivatives that asset managers use to buy or sell volatility to either control a portfolio's volatility or express a view on what future market volatility will be.
- Market volatility derivatives include volatility index derivatives, stock index options, and variance swaps.
- Market volatility derivatives can be based on realized (historical) returns or implied volatility obtained from options based on a stock market index.
- The CBOE Market Volatility Index (VIX), dubbed the "investor fear index", is based on the S&P 500 index options with 30 days to expiration.
- There are futures and options on all volatility index measures.
- A variance swap is a forward contract on the annualized variance of the realized returns for a stock market index.

References

Collins, B. and F. J. Fabozzi, 1999. *Derivatives and Equity Portfolio Management.* Hoboken, NJ: John Wiley & Sons.

Peters, E. E., 1987. "Hedged equity portfolios: Components of risk and return," *Advances in Futures and Options Research* 1, part B: 75–92.

PART V
Bond Analytics and Portfolio Management

Chapter 15

Bond Pricing and Yield Measures

Learning Objectives

After reading this chapter, you will understand:

- how the price of a bond is calculated;
- the inverse relationship between the price of a bond and the required yield;
- how the price of a callable or prepayable bond differs from that of an option-free bond;
- what is meant by a bond characterized by positive convexity and negative convexity;
- the relationship between a bond's coupon rate, required yield, and price;
- the reasons why the price of a bond changes;
- the four bond yield measures commonly quoted: (1) current yield, (2) yield to maturity, (3) yield to call, and (4) yield to put;
- the limitations of yield measures and what is meant by reinvestment risk;
- the different methods for calculating a portfolio's yield and the limitation of these measures;
- calculation of the total return and its applications to horizon analysis;
- what the term structure of interest rates is;
- what are forward rates and spot rates;
- how spot rates and forward rates are used to calculate a debt instrument's arbitrage-free value.

In Chapter 4, we described the fundamental characteristics of debt instruments and the wide range of such investment vehicles available in the market. In this chapter and the one to follow, we discuss the analytics used to evaluate bonds and assess their potential performance. Although we focus on bonds, the bond analytics described here apply equally to other debt instruments. There are special considerations in the case of residential mortgage-backed securities.

We begin by explaining how to determine the price of a bond as well as the relationship between price and yield. Then we discuss various yield measures and their meaning for evaluating the potential performance over some investment horizon. In particular, we explain the various conventions for measuring the yield of a bond, and then demonstrate why conventional yield measures fail to identify the potential return from investing in a bond over some investment horizon. A better measure for assessing the potential return from investing in a bond is the total return. We show how to calculate the potential total return from investing in a bond over some investment horizon. In the last section of this chapter, we discuss the term structure of interest rates and how the rates determined from the term structure are used to value a bond. In the next chapter, we explain bond analytics used in quantifying interest rate risk and credit risk.

Bond Pricing

In this section, we explain how the price of a bond is determined. The approach discussed here is the conventional method that is used. At the end of this chapter when we discuss the term structure of interest rates and the concept of spot or zero-coupon rates, we will see the proper method for computing the theoretical price of a bond. We begin this section with a review of how bond prices are quoted.

Price Quotes

A bond may have any maturity value or par value. Consequently, when quoting bond prices, traders quote the price as a percentage of par value. A bond selling at par is quoted as 100, meaning 100% of its par value. A bond selling at a discount will be selling for less than 100; a bond selling at a premium will be selling for more than 100.

The procedure for converting a price quote to a dollar price is as follows:

$$(\text{Price per \$100 of par value}/100) \times \text{par value}.$$

For example, if a bond is quoted at $96\frac{1}{2}$ and has a par value of \$100,000, then the dollar price is

$$(96.5/100) \times \$100{,}000 = \$96{,}500.$$

If a bond is quoted at $103\frac{19}{32}$ and has a par value of \$1 million, then the dollar price is

$$(103.59375/100) \times \$1{,}000{,}000 = \$1{,}035{,}937.50.$$

As explained in Chapter 4, when an investor purchases a bond between coupon payments, the investor must compensate the seller for the accrued interest.

Pricing of Option-Free Bonds

The price of any financial instrument is equal to the present value of the expected cash flows from the financial instrument. Therefore, determining the price requires:

1. An estimate of the expected cash flows.
2. An estimate of the appropriate required yield.

The expected cash flows for some financial instruments are simple to compute; for others, the task is more difficult. The required yield reflects the yield for financial instruments with comparable risk.

The first step in determining the price of a bond is to estimate its cash flow. We'll consider the simple case where the issuer does not have the option to retire the bond prior to its stated maturity date and there are no options granted to the bondholder to alter the cash flows of the bond. A bond that has no embedded options is referred to as an *option-free bond.*

For an option-free bond, the cash flow is:

1. Periodic coupon interest payments to the maturity date.
2. The par value at maturity.

Our illustrations of bond pricing use three assumptions to simplify the analysis:

1. The coupon payments are made every 6 months. (For most US bond issues, coupon interest is in fact paid semi-annually.)
2. The next coupon payment for the bond is received exactly 6 months from now.
3. The coupon interest is fixed for the term of the bond.

While our focus in this chapter is on option-free bonds, there are more complex models for valuing bonds with embedded options such as the model developed by Kalotay, Williams, and Fabozzi [1993].

Consequently, the cash flows for an option-free bond consist of an annuity of a fixed coupon interest payment paid semi-annually and the par, or maturity, value. For example, a 20-year bond with a 10% coupon rate and a par value (or maturity value) of \$100 has the following cash flows from coupon interest:

$$\text{Annual coupon interest} = \$100 \times 0.10 = \$10,$$
$$\text{Semi-annual coupon interest} = \$10/2 = \$5.$$

Therefore, there are 40 semi-annual cash flows of \$5, and there is a \$100 cash flow in 40 6-month periods from now. Notice the treatment of the par value. It is not treated as if it is received 20 years from now. Instead, it is treated on a basis consistent with the coupon payments, which are semi-annual.

The required yield is determined by investigating the yields offered on comparable bonds in the market. In this case, comparable investments would be option-free bonds of the same credit quality and the same maturity. The required yield typically is expressed as an annual interest rate. When the cash flows occur semi-annually, the market convention is to use one-half the annual interest rate as the periodic interest rate with which to discount the cash flows.

Given the cash flows of a bond and the required yield, we have all the information needed to price a bond. Because the price of a bond is the present value of the cash flows, it is determined by adding these two present values:

1. The present value of the semi-annual coupon payments.
2. The present value of the par, or maturity, value at the maturity date.

In general, the price of a bond can be computed using the following formula:

$$P = \frac{C}{(1+r)^1} + \frac{C}{(1+r)^2} + \cdots + \frac{C}{(1+r)^n} + \frac{M}{(1+r)^n}$$

or

$$P = \sum_{t=1}^{n} \frac{C}{(1+r)^t} + \frac{M}{(1+r)^n}, \tag{1}$$

where P is the price (in \$), n is the number of periods (number of years $\times$ 2), C is the semi-annual coupon payment (in \$), r is the periodic interest rate (required annual yield/2), M is the maturity value, and t is the time period when the payment is to be received.

Because the semi-annual coupon payments are equivalent to an ordinary annuity, the present value of the coupon payments can be determined from the following formula:

$$\text{Present value of coupon payments} = C\left[\frac{1-\frac{1}{(1+r)^n}}{r}\right]. \tag{2}$$

When an investor purchases a bond whose next coupon payment is due in less than 6 months, Equations (1) and (2) can be modified to take this into account.

To illustrate how to compute the price of a bond, consider a 20-year 10% coupon bond with a par value of $100. Let's suppose that the required yield on this bond is 11%. The cash flows for this bond are as follows: (1) 40 semi-annual coupon payments of $5 and (2) $100 to be received for 40 6-month periods from now. The semi-annual or periodic interest rate (or periodic required yield) is 5.5% (11% divided by 2). In terms of our notation: $C = \$5$ $n = 40$ $r = 0.055$.

The present value of the 40 semi-annual coupon payments of $5, discounted at 5.5%, is $80.231, calculated as follows:

$$\text{Present value of coupon payments} = \$5\left[\frac{1-\frac{1}{(1.055)^{40}}}{0.055}\right] = \$80.231.$$

The present value of the par, or maturity, value of $100 received 40 6-month periods from now, discounted at 5.5%, is $11.746, as follows:

$$\frac{\$100}{(1.055)^{40}} = \$11.746.$$

The price of the bond is then equal to the sum of the two present values:

$$\begin{array}{lr} \text{Present value of coupon payments} & = \$80.231 \\ +\text{Present value of par (maturity value)} & = \underline{\$11.746} \\ \text{Price} & = \$91.977. \end{array}$$

Therefore, the bond would be quoted at 91.977.

Suppose that instead of an 11% required yield, the required yield is 6.8%. The price of the bond would then be $134.704, demonstrated as follows: The present value of the coupon payments, using a periodic interest rate of 3.4%

(6.8%/2) is \$108.451. The present value of the par value of \$100 received in 40 6-month periods from now discounted at 3.4% is \$26.253. The price of the bond is then \$134.704, which is the sum of \$108.451 and \$26.253.

If the required yield is equal to the coupon rate of 10%, it can be demonstrated that the price of the bond would be its par value, \$100.

Zero-coupon bonds do not make any periodic coupon payments. Instead, the investor realizes interest as the difference between the maturity value and the purchase price. The price of a zero-coupon bond is calculated by substituting zero for C in Equation (1):

$$P = \frac{M}{(1+r)^n}. \tag{3}$$

Equation (3) states that the price of a zero-coupon bond is simply the present value of the maturity value. In the present value computation, however, the number of periods used for discounting is not the number of years to maturity of the bond, but rather, double the number of years. The discount rate is one-half the required annual yield.

Price-yield relationship of an option-free bond

A fundamental property of a bond is that its price changes in the opposite direction from the change in the required yield. The reason is that the price of the bond is the present value of the cash flows. As the required yield increases, the present value of the cash flows decreases; hence, the price decreases.

The opposite is true when the required yield decreases: The present value of the cash flows increases, and, therefore, the price of the bond increases. This can be seen by examining the price for the 20-year, 10% bond when the required yield is 11%, 10%, and 6.8%. Table 1 shows the price of the 20-year, 10% coupon bond for various required yields.

If we graph the price-required yield relationship for any option-free bond, we will find that it has the bowed shape shown in Figure 1. This shape is referred to as convex. The convexity of the price-yield relationship has important implications for the investment properties of a bond, as we explain later in this chapter.

TABLE 1: Price-Yield Relationship for a 20-Year, 10% Coupon Bond

Yield	Price	Yield	Price
0.045	$1,720.32	0.110	$919.77
0.050	1,627.57	0.115	883.50
0.055	1,541.76	0.120	849.54
0.060	1,462.30	0.125	817.70
0.065	1,388.65	0.130	787.82
0.070	1,320.33	0.135	759.75
0.075	1,256.89	0.140	733.37
0.080	1,197.93	0.145	708.53
0.085	1,143.08	0.150	685.14
0.090	1,092.01	0.155	663.08
0.095	1,044.41	0.160	642.26
0.100	1,000.00	0.165	622.59
0.105	958.53		

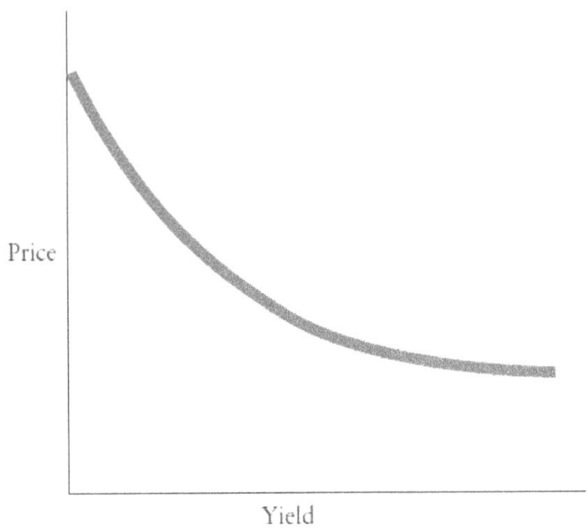

FIGURE 1: Shape of the Price-Yield Relationship for an Option-Free Bond

Relationship between coupon rate, required yield, and price

As yields in the marketplace change, the price of a bond will change. When the coupon rate is equal to the required yield, the price of the bond will be equal to its par value as we stated earlier.

When yields in the marketplace rise above the coupon rate at a given point in time, the price of the bond adjusts so that a new investor can realize some additional interest. This is accomplished by the price falling below its par value. The capital appreciation realized by holding the bond to maturity represents a form of interest to the new investor to compensate for a coupon rate that is less than the required yield. When a bond sells below its par value, it is said to be selling at a discount. In our earlier calculation of a bond's price, we saw that when the required yield is greater than the coupon rate, the price of the bond is lower than the par value.

When the required yield in the market is below the coupon rate, the bond must sell above its par value. This is because a new investor who would have the opportunity to purchase the bond at par value would be getting a coupon rate in excess of what the market requires. As a result, a new investor would bid up the price of the bond because its yield is so attractive. The price would eventually be bid up to a level where the bond offers the required yield in the market. A bond whose price is above its par value is said to be selling at a premium.

The relationship between coupon rate, required yield, and price can be summarized as follows:

$$\text{Coupon rate} < \text{Required yield: Price} < \text{Par (discount bond)},$$

$$\text{Coupon rate} = \text{Required yield: Price} = \text{Par},$$

$$\text{Coupon rate} > \text{Required yield: Price} > \text{Par (premium bond)}.$$

Relationship between bond price and time if interest rates are unchanged

If the required yield does not change between the time the bond is purchased and the maturity date, what will happen to the price of the bond? For a bond selling at par value, the coupon rate is equal to the required yield. As the bond moves closer to maturity, the bond will continue to sell at par value. The price of a bond will not remain constant for a bond selling at a discount or a premium. A discount bond's price increases as it approaches maturity, assuming the required yield does not change. For a premium bond, the price decreases as it approaches maturity. For both bonds, the price will equal par value at the maturity date.

Reasons for the change in the price of a bond

The price of a bond will change for one or more of the following three reasons:

1. There is a change in the required yield owing to changes in the credit quality of the issuer. That is, the required yield changes because the market now compares the bond yield with yields from a different set of bonds with the same credit risk.
2. There is a change in the price of the bond selling at a premium or a discount without any change in the required yield, simply because the bond is moving toward maturity.
3. There is a change in the required yield owing to a change in the yield on comparable bonds. That is, market interest rates change.

Pricing of Callable and Prepayable Bonds

The price-yield relationship for callable bonds and prepayable securities such as residential mortgage-backed securities (RMBS) is shown in Figure 2. As market rates (yields) decline, investors become concerned that they will decline further so that the issuer will benefit from exercising the call option (i.e., calling the bond). (For RMBS, the concern is that homeowners will pay off their mortgage by refinancing at the lower interest rate.) The precise yield level where investors begin to view the issue likely to be

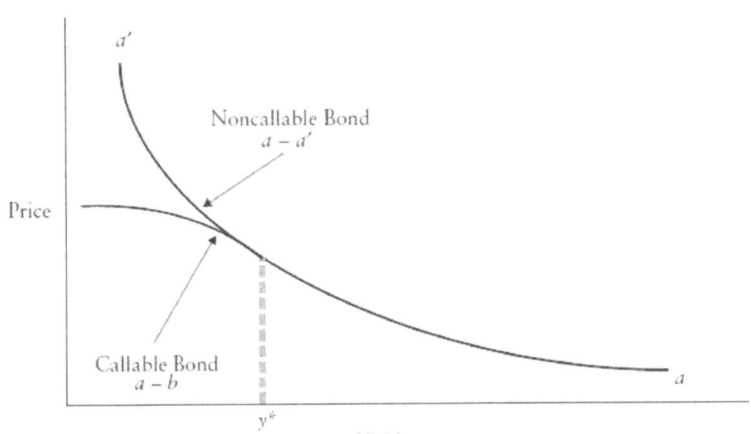

FIGURE 2: Price–Yield Relationship for a Noncallable Bond and a Callable Bond

called may not be known, but we do know that there is some interest rate. In Figure 2, at yield levels below y^*, the price-yield relationship for the callable bond departs from the price-yield relationship for the noncallable bond. For example, suppose that yield in the market is such that an option-free bond would be selling for \$105. However, for a callable bond that can be called at par (\$100), investors would not pay \$105 because of the call option granted to the issuer. If they did, and the bond is called by the issuer, investors would receive \$100 (the call price) for a bond they purchased for \$105. Notice that for a range of yields below y^* in Figure 2, there is price compression (i.e., there is limited price appreciation as yields decline). As explained later in this chapter, the portion of the callable bond price-yield relationship below y^* is said to be *negatively convex*.

Bond Yield and Return Analytics

Related to the price of a bond is its yield. The price of a bond is calculated from the cash flows and the required yield. The yield of a bond is calculated from the cash flows and the market price plus accrued interest. In this section, we discuss various yield measures and their meaning for evaluating the relative attractiveness of a bond.

Yield Measures

There are four bond yield measures commonly quoted by dealers and used by portfolio managers: (1) current yield, (2) yield to maturity, (3) yield to call, and (4) yield to put. In the illustrations that follow, we assume that the next coupon payment is 6 months from now and therefore there is no accrued interest.

Current yield

Current yield relates the annual coupon interest to the market price. The formula for the current yield is

$$\text{Current yield} = \frac{\text{Annual dollar coupon interest}}{\text{Price}}.$$

For example, the current yield for a 15-year, 7% coupon bond with a par value of \$100 selling for \$76.940 is 9.10%, as shown:

$$\text{Current yield} = \frac{\$7.00}{\$76.940} = .091 = 9.1\%.$$

The current yield calculation takes into account only the coupon interest and no other source of return that will affect an investor's yield. No consideration is given to the capital gain that the investor will realize when a bond is purchased at a discount and held to maturity; nor is there any recognition of the capital loss that the investor will realize if a bond purchased at a premium is held to maturity. The time value of money is also ignored.

Yield to maturity

The *yield to maturity* is the interest rate that will make the present value of a bond's cash flows (if held to maturity) equal to the price (plus accrued interest, if any). Mathematically, the yield to maturity, y, for a bond that pays interest semi-annually and that has no accrued interest is found by solving the following equation:

$$P = \sum_{t=1}^{n} \frac{C}{(1+y)^t} + \frac{M}{(1+y)^n}. \tag{4}$$

Since the cash flows are every 6 months, the yield to maturity y found by solving Equation (4) is a semi-annual yield to maturity. This yield can be annualized by either (1) doubling the semi-annual yield or (2) compounding the yield. The market convention is to annualize the semi-annual yield by simply doubling its value. The yield to maturity computed on the basis of this market convention is called the bond-equivalent yield. It is also referred to as a yield on a *bond-equivalent basis.*

The computation of the yield to maturity involves an iterative procedure. Basically, the yield to maturity is nothing more than an internal rate of return calculation. In practice, there are online calculators and software that perform the calculations and report the bond-equivalent yield

To illustrate the computation, consider the bond that we used to compute the current yield. The cash flow for this bond is (1) 30 coupon payments of \$3.50 every 6 months and (2) \$100 to be paid 30 6-month periods from now. To get y in Equation (4), different interest rates must be tried until the present value of the cash flows is equal to the price of \$76.942. When a 5% semi-annual interest rate is used, the present value of the cash flows is \$76.942. Therefore, y is 5%, and is the semi-annual yield to maturity. However, as explained above, the convention in the market is to double the semi-annual yield to obtain an annualized yield. Thus, the yield on a bond-equivalent basis for our hypothetical bond is 10%.

The yield-to-maturity calculation takes into account not only the current coupon income but also any capital gain or loss the investor will realize by holding the bond to maturity. In addition, the yield to maturity considers the timing of the cash flows.

The relationship among the coupon rate, current yield, yield to maturity, and bond price is as follows:

Bond selling at	Relationship
Par	Coupon rate = Current yield = Yield to maturity
Discount	Coupon rate < Current yield < Yield to maturity
Premium	Coupon rate > Current yield > Yield to maturity

Yield to call and yield to put

As explained in Chapter 4, the issuer may be entitled to call a bond prior to the stated maturity date. The price at which the bond may be called is referred to as the *call price*. For some issues, the call price is the same regardless of when the issue is called. For other callable issues, the call price depends on when the issue is called. That is, there is a call schedule that specifies a call price for each call date.

For callable bond issues, the practice has been to calculate a *yield to call* as well as a yield to maturity. The yield to call assumes that the issuer will call the bond at some assumed call date, and the call price is then the call price specified in the call schedule. Typically, investors calculate a *yield to first call* and a *yield to par call*. The yield to first call assumes that the issue will be called on the first call date. The yield to first par call assumes that the issue will be called the first time on the call schedule when the issuer is entitled to call the bond at par value.

The procedure for calculating the yield to any assumed call date is the same as for any yield calculation: Determine the interest rate that will make the present value of the expected cash flows equal to the price plus accrued interest. In the case of yield to first call, the expected cash flows are the coupon payments to the first call date and the call price. For the yield to first par call, the expected cash flows are the coupon payments to the first date at which the issuer may call the bond at par.

Thus, all that must be adjusted in Equation (4) are the two inputs. The first is the maturity value. This should be the call price based on the assumed call date. The second is the number of periods. Rather than the number of periods to maturity, it should be the number of periods to the assumed call date. Once again, online software is available to compute any yield to call.

Investors typically compute both the yield to call and the yield to maturity for a callable bond selling at a premium. They then select the lower of the two as the yield measure. The lowest yield based on every possible call date and the yield to maturity is referred to as the *yield to worst.*

In the same way that the yield to any call date can be computed, a *yield to put* can be calculated for various put dates.

Understanding Bond Yield Measures

What does any bond yield measure mean? Does it mean if one buys a 10-year bond with a yield to maturity of 5%, the investor will realize a 5% annual return? It does not and here we explain why.

An investor who purchases a bond can expect to receive a dollar return from one or more of the following three sources:

1. The periodic coupon interest payments made by the issuer.
2. Income from the reinvestment of the periodic interest payments (the interest-on-interest component).
3. Any capital gain (or capital loss — negative dollar return) when the bond matures, is called, or is sold.

Any measure of a bond's potential yield should take into consideration each of these three potential sources of return. The current yield considers only the coupon interest payments. No consideration is given to any capital gain (or loss) or to interest-on-interest. The yield to maturity takes into account coupon interest and any capital gain (or loss). It also considers the interest-on-interest component; implicit in the yield-to-maturity computation, however, is the assumption that the coupon payments can be reinvested at the computed yield to maturity. The yield to maturity, therefore, is a "promised" yield; that is, it will be realized only if (1) the bond is held to maturity and (2) the coupon interest payments are reinvested at the yield to maturity. If either (1) or (2) fail to occur, the actual yield realized by an investor can be greater than or less than the yield to maturity when the bond is purchased.

Any yield to call or yield to put also takes into account all three potential sources of return. In this case, the assumption is that the coupon payments can be reinvested at the computed yield to call or the yield to put. Therefore, these two yield measures suffer from the same drawback inherent in the implicit assumption of the reinvestment rate for the coupon interest payments. Also, it assumes that the bond will be held until the assumed date, at which time the bond will be called in the case of a callable bond or will be put in the case of a putable bond.

Interest-on-interest dollar return

The interest-on-interest component can represent a substantial portion of a bond's potential return. Letting i denote the semi-annual reinvestment rate we can find the interest-on-interest plus the total coupon payments from the following formula[1]:

$$\text{Coupon interest} + \text{Interest-on-interest} = C[(1+i)^n - 1]/i, \qquad (5)$$

The total dollar amount of coupon interest is found by multiplying the semi-annual coupon interest by the number of periods:

$$\text{Total coupon interest} = nC.$$

The interest-on-interest component is then the difference between the coupon interest plus interest-on-interest and the total dollar coupon interest, as expressed

$$\text{Interest-on-interest} = C[(1+i)^n - 1]/i - nC. \qquad (6)$$

The yield-to-maturity measure assumes that the reinvestment rate is the yield to maturity. For example, let's consider the 15-year, 7% bond with a $100 par value that we have used to illustrate how to compute the current yield and yield to maturity. The yield to maturity for this bond is 10%. Assuming an annual reinvestment rate of 10%, or a semi-annual reinvestment rate of 5%, the interest-on-interest plus total coupon payments using Equation (5) is

$$\begin{aligned} &\text{Coupon interest} + \text{Interest-on-interest} \\ &\quad = \$3.50[(1.05)^{30} - 1]/0.05 = \$232.536. \end{aligned}$$

Using Equation (6), we calculate the interest-on-interest component as

$$\begin{aligned} \text{Coupon interest} &= 30(\$3.50) = \$105.000, \\ \text{Interest-on-interest} &= \$232.536 - \$105.000 = \$127.536. \end{aligned}$$

[1]This is the formula for the future value of an ordinary annuity.

Yield to maturity and reinvestment risk

Let's look at the potential total dollar return from holding this bond to maturity. As mentioned earlier, the total dollar return comes from three sources. In our example:

1. Total coupon interest of \$105.000 (coupon interest of \$3.50 every 6 months for 15 years).
2. Interest-on-interest of \$127.536 earned from reinvesting the semi-annual coupon interest payments at 5% every 6 months.
3. A capital gain of \$23.060 (\$100 par value minus \$76.940 purchase price).

The potential total dollar return if the coupons can be reinvested at the yield to maturity of 10% is then \$255.596.

Notice that if an investor places the money that would have been used to purchase this bond, \$76.940, in a savings account earning 5% semi-annually for 15 years, the future value of the savings account would be

$$\$76.940(1.05)^{30} = \$332.530.$$

For the initial investment of \$76.940, the total dollar return is \$255.596.

So an investor who invests \$76.940 for 15 years at 10% per year (5% semi-annually) expects to receive at the end of 15 years the initial investment of \$76.940 plus \$55.596. This is precisely what we found by breaking down the dollar return on the bond, assuming a reinvestment rate equal to the yield to maturity of 10%. Thus, it can be seen that for the bond to yield 10%, the investor must generate \$127.536 by reinvesting the coupon payments. This means that to generate a yield to maturity of 10%, approximately half (\$127.536/\$255.596) of this bond's total dollar return must come from the reinvestment of the coupon payments.

The investor will realize the yield to maturity at the time of purchase only if the bond is held to maturity and the coupon payments can be reinvested at the yield to maturity. The risk that the investor faces is that future reinvestment rates will be less than the yield to maturity at the time the bond is purchased. This risk is called *reinvestment risk*.

Two characteristics of a bond determine the importance of the interest-on-interest component and, therefore, the degree of reinvestment risk: maturity and coupon. For a given yield to maturity and a given coupon rate, the longer the maturity, the more dependent the bond's total dollar return on the interest-on-interest component in order to realize the yield to maturity at the time of purchase. In other words, the longer the maturity, the greater the reinvestment risk. The implication is that the yield-to-maturity measure for long-term coupon bonds tells little about the potential yield that an investor may realize if the bond is held to maturity. For long-term bonds, the interest-on-interest component may be as high as 80% of the bond's potential total dollar return.

Turning to the coupon rate, for a given maturity and a given yield to maturity, the higher the coupon rate, the more dependent the bond's total dollar return on the reinvestment of the coupon payments in order to produce the yield to maturity anticipated at the time of purchase. This means that when maturity and yield to maturity are held constant, premium bonds are more dependent on the interest-on-interest component than that of bonds selling at par. Discount bonds are less dependent on the interest-on-interest component than are bonds selling at par. For zero-coupon bonds, none of the bond's total dollar return is dependent on the interest-on-interest component. So a zero-coupon bond has no reinvestment risk if held to maturity. Thus, the yield earned on a zero-coupon bond held to maturity is equal to the promised yield to maturity.

Portfolio Yield Measures

Two conventions have been adopted by practitioners to calculate a portfolio yield: (1) weighted-average portfolio yield and (2) internal rate of return.

Weighted average portfolio yield

Probably the most common — and most flawed — method for calculating a portfolio yield is the weighted-average portfolio yield. It is found by calculating the weighted average of the yield of all the bonds in the portfolio. The yield is weighted by the proportion of the portfolio that a security makes up. In general, if we let

w_i = the market value of bond i relative to the total market value of the portfolio,

y_i = the yield on bond i,

K = the number of bonds in the portfolio,

then the weighted-average portfolio yield is

$$w_1y_1 + w_2y_2 + \cdots + w_Ky_K.$$

For example, consider the three-bond portfolio in Table 2. In this illustration, the total market value of the portfolio is \$57,259,000, K is equal

TABLE 2: Three-Bond Portfolio

Bond	Coupon Rate (%)	Maturity (years)	Par Value ($)	Market Value ($)	Yield to Maturity (%)
B1	7.0	5	10,000,000	9,209,000	9.0
B2	10.5	7	20,000,000	20,000,000	10.5
B3	6.0	3	30,000,000	28,050,000	8.5
Total			60,000,000	57,259,000	

to 3, and

$$w_1 = \$9{,}209{,}000/\$57{,}259{,}000 = 0.161 \quad y_1 = 0.090,$$

$$w_2 = \$20{,}000{,}000/\$57{,}259{,}000 = 0.349 \quad y_2 = 0.105,$$

$$w_3 = \$28{,}050{,}000/\$57{,}259{,}000 = 0.490 \quad y_3 = 0.085.$$

The weighted average portfolio yield is then

$$0.161(0.090) + 0.349(0.105) + 0.490(0.085) = 0.0928 = 9.28\%.$$

While it is the most commonly used measure of portfolio yield, the weighted-average yield measure provides little insight into the potential return of a portfolio. To see this, consider a portfolio consisting of only two bonds: a 6-month bond offering a yield to maturity of 11%, and a 30-year bond offering a yield to maturity of 8%. Suppose that 99% of the portfolio is invested in the 6-month bond, and 1% in the 30-year bond. The weighted average yield for this portfolio would be 10.97%. But what does this yield mean? How can it be used within any asset/liability framework? The portfolio is basically a 6-month portfolio even though it has a 30-year bond. Would a portfolio manager of a depository institution feel confident offering a 2-year certificate of deposit with a yield of 9%? This would suggest a spread of 197 basis points above the yield on the portfolio based on the weighted-average portfolio yield. This would be an imprudent policy because the yield on this portfolio over the next 2 years will depend on interest rates 6 months from now.

Portfolio internal rate of return

Another measure used to calculate a portfolio yield is the *portfolio internal rate of return.* It is computed by first determining the cash flows for all the bonds in the portfolio, and then finding the interest rate that will make the present value of the cash flows equal to the market value of the portfolio.

TABLE 3: Cash Flow of Three-Bond Portfolio

Period Cash Flow Received	Bond B1	Bond B2	Bond B3	Portfolio
1	$350,000	$1,050,000	$900,000	$2,300,000
2	350,000	1,050,000	900,000	2,300,000
3	350,000	1,050,000	900,000	2,300,000
4	350,000	1,050,000	900,000	2,300,000
5	350,000	1,050,000	900,000	2,300,000
6	350,000	1,050,000	30,900,000	32,300,000
7	350,000	1,050,000	—	1,400,000
8	350,000	1,050,000	—	1,400,000
9	350,000	1,050,000	—	1,400,000
10	10,350,000	1,050,000	—	11,400,000
11	—	1,050,000	—	1,050,000
12	—	1,050,000	—	1,050,000
13	—	1,050,000	—	1,050,000
14	—	21,050,000	—	21,050,000

To illustrate how to calculate a portfolio's internal rate of return, we will use the three-bond portfolio in Table 2. To simplify the illustration, it is assumed that the coupon payment date is the same for each bond. The cash flow for each bond and the portfolio's cash flows are shown in Table 3. The portfolio internal rate of return is the interest rate that will make the present value of the portfolio's cash flows (the last column in Table 3) equal to the portfolio's market value of $57,259,000. The interest rate is 4.77%. Doubling this rate to 9.54% gives the portfolio internal rate of return on a bond-equivalent basis.

The portfolio internal rate of return, while superior to the weighted-average portfolio yield, suffers from the same problems as yield measures discussed earlier: It assumes that the cash flows can be reinvested at the calculated yield. In the case of a portfolio internal rate of return, it assumes that the cash flows can be reinvested at the calculated internal rate of return. Moreover, it assumes that the portfolio is held until the maturity of the longest-maturity bond in the portfolio. For example, if, in our illustration, one of the bonds had a maturity of 30 years, it is assumed that the portfolio is held for 30 years and that all interim cash flows (coupon interest and maturing principal) are reinvested at a rate equal to 9.54%.

Total Return as a Yield Measure

At the time of purchase, an investor is promised a yield, as measured by the yield to maturity, if both of the following conditions are satisfied: (1) the bond is held to maturity, and (2) all coupon interest payments are reinvested at the yield to maturity.

We focused on the second assumption, and we showed that the interest-on-interest component for a bond may constitute a substantial portion of the bond's total dollar return. Therefore, reinvesting the coupon interest payments at a rate of interest less than the yield to maturity will produce a lower yield than the stated yield to maturity.

Rather than assume that the coupon interest payments are reinvested at the yield to maturity, an investor can make an explicit assumption about the reinvestment rate based on expectations. The *total return* is a measure of yield that incorporates an explicit assumption about the reinvestment rate.

Let's take a careful look at the first assumption — that a bond will be held to maturity. Suppose, for example, that an investor who has a 5-year investment horizon is considering the four bonds shown in Table 4. Assuming that all four bonds are of the same credit quality, which one is the most attractive for this investor? An investor who selects bond C because it offers the highest yield to maturity is failing to recognize that the investment horizon calls for selling the bond after 5 years at a price that depends on the yield required in the market for 10-year, 11% coupon bonds at the time. Hence, there could be a capital gain or capital loss that will make the return higher or lower than the yield to maturity promised now. Moreover, the higher coupon on bond C relative to the other three bonds means that more of this bond's return will be dependent on the reinvestment of coupon interest payments.

Bond A offers the second highest yield to maturity, but matures before the investment horizon is reached. On the surface, it seems to be particularly attractive because it eliminates the problem of realizing a possible capital loss when the bond must be sold prior to the maturity date. Moreover, the reinvestment risk seems to be less than for the other three bonds because the coupon rate is the smallest. However, the investor would not

TABLE 4: Four Alternative Bond Investments

Bond	Coupon	Maturity	Yield to Maturity
A	5%	3 years	9.0%
B	6	20	8.6
C	11	15	9.2
D	8	5	8.0

be eliminating the reinvestment risk because, after 3 years, the proceeds received at maturity must be reinvested for 2 more years. The yield that the investor will realize depends on interest rates after 3 years on 2-year bonds when the proceeds must be rolled over.

The yield to maturity does not seem to be helping us to identify the best bond. So how do we find out which is the best bond? The answer depends on the investor's expectations. Specifically, it depends on the interest rate at which the coupon interest payments can be reinvested until the end of the investor's planned investment horizon. Also, for bonds with a maturity longer than the investment horizon, it depends on the investor's expectations about required yields in the market at the end of the planned investment horizon. Consequently, any of these bonds can be the best alternative, depending on some reinvestment rate and some future required yield at the end of the planned investment horizon. The total return measure takes these expectations into account and will determine the best investment for the investor depending on the portfolio manager's expectations.

Computing the total return for a bond

The idea underlying total return is simple. The objective is first to compute the total future dollars that will result from investing in a bond assuming a particular reinvestment rate. The total return is then computed as the interest rate that will make the initial investment in the bond grow to the computed total future dollars.

The procedure for computing the total return for a bond held over some investment horizon can be summarized as follows:

Step 1: Compute the total coupon payments plus the interest-on-interest based on the assumed reinvestment rate using Equation (4). The reinvestment rate in this case is one-half the annual interest rate that the investor assumes can be earned on the reinvestment of coupon interest payments.
Step 2: Determine the projected sale price at the end of the planned investment horizon. The projected sale price will depend on the projected required yield at the end of the planned investment horizon. The projected sale price will be equal to the present value of the remaining cash flows of the bond discounted at the projected required yield.
Step 3: Sum the values computed in steps 1 and 2. The sum is the total future dollars that will be received from the investment given the

assumed reinvestment rate and the projected required yield at the end of the investment horizon.
Step 4: Obtain the semi-annual total return using the formula:

$$\left(\frac{\text{Total future dollars}}{\text{Purchase price of bond}}\right)^{1/h} - 1, \tag{7}$$

where h is the number of 6-month periods in the investment horizon.
Step 5: The semi-annual total return found in step 4 must be annualized. There are two alternatives. The first is simply to double the semi-annual total return found in step 4. The resulting interest rate is the total return on a bond-equivalent yield basis. The second is to calculate the annual return by compounding the semi-annual total return. This is done as follows:

$$(1 + \text{semi-annual total return})^2 - 1. \tag{8}$$

A total return calculated using the above equation is called a *total return on an effective rate basis.*

Determination of how to annualize the semi-annual total return depends on the situation at hand. The first approach is just a market convention. If an investor is comparing the total return with the return on other bonds or on a bond index in which yields are calculated on a bond-equivalent basis, then this approach is appropriate. However, if the objective is to satisfy liabilities that the institution is obligated to pay, and if those liabilities are based on semi-annual compounding, then the second approach is appropriate.

To illustrate the computation of the total return, suppose that an investor with a 3-year investment horizon is considering purchasing a 20-year, 8% coupon bond with a \$100 par value for \$82.840. The yield to maturity for this bond is 10%. The investor expects to be able to reinvest the coupon interest payments at an annual interest rate of 6% and, at the end of the planned investment horizon, the then-17-year bond will be selling in the market to offer a yield to maturity of 7%. The total return for this bond is found as follows.

Step 1: Compute the total coupon payments plus the interest-on-interest, assuming an annual reinvestment rate of 6%, or 3% every 6 months. The coupon payments are \$4 every 6 months for 3 years, or six periods (the planned investment horizon). Apply Equation (6) for the calculation of total coupon interest plus interest-on-interest, which is \$25.874.

Step 2: Determining the projected sale price at the end of 3 years, assuming that the required yield to maturity for 17-year bonds is 7%, is accomplished by calculating the present value of 34 coupon payments of \$40 plus the present value of the par value of \$100, discounted at 3.5%. The projected sale price is \$109.851.

Step 3: Adding the amounts in steps 1 and 2 gives total future dollars of \$135.725.

Step 4: To obtain the semi-annual total return using Equation (7), compute the following:

$$\left(\frac{\$135.725}{\$82.840}\right)^{1/h} - 1 = 0.0858 = 8.58\%.$$

Step 5: Doubling 8.58% gives a total return on a bond-equivalent basis of 17.16%. Using Equation (8), we get the total return on an effective rate basis:

$$(1.0858)^2 - 1 = 17.90\%.$$

Applications of total return (horizon analysis)

The total return measure allows a portfolio manager to project the performance of a bond on the basis of the planned investment horizon and expectations concerning reinvestment rates and future market yields. This permits the portfolio manager to evaluate which of several potential bonds considered for acquisition will perform the best over the planned investment horizon. As we have emphasized, this cannot be done using the yield to maturity.

Using total return to assess performance over some investment horizon is called horizon analysis. When a total return is calculated over an investment horizon, it is referred to as a *horizon return*. Here we use the terms horizon return and total return interchangeably.

An often cited objection to the total return measure is that it requires the portfolio manager to formulate assumptions about reinvestment rates and future yields, as well as to think in terms of an investment horizon. Unfortunately, some portfolio managers find comfort in measures such as the yield to maturity, yield to call, and yield to put simply because they do not require incorporating any particular expectations. The horizon analysis framework, however, enables the portfolio manager to analyze the performance of a bond under different interest rate scenarios for reinvestment rates and future market yields. This procedure is referred to as *scenario analysis*. Only by investigating multiple scenarios can the portfolio manager see how sensitive the bond's performance will be to each scenario.

To illustrate scenario analysis, consider a portfolio manager who is deciding on whether to purchase a 20-year, 9% option-free bond selling at \$109.896 per \$100 of par value. The yield to maturity for this bond is 8%. Assume also that the portfolio manager's investment horizon is 3 years, and that the portfolio manager believes the reinvestment rate can vary from 3% to 6.5%, and the projected yield at the end of the investment horizon can vary from 5% to 12%. Table 5 shows different projected yields at the end of the 3-year investment horizon, and Panel B gives the corresponding price for the bond at the end of the investment horizon. (This is step 2 in the total return calculation discussed earlier.) For example, consider the 10% projected yield at the end of the investment horizon. The price of a 17-year option-free bond with a coupon rate of 9% would be \$91.9035. Panel C of Table 5 shows the total future dollars at the end of 3 years under various scenarios for the reinvestment rate and the projected yield at the end of the investment horizon. (This is step 3 in the total return calculation discussed above.) For example, with a reinvestment rate of 4% and a projected yield at the end of the investment horizon of 10%, the total future dollars would be \$120.290. Panel D of Table 5 shows the total return on an effective rate basis for each scenario.

Table 5 is useful for a portfolio manager in assessing the potential outcomes of a bond (or a portfolio) over the investment horizon. For example, a portfolio manager knows that the maximum and minimum total return for the scenarios shown in the table will be 16.72% and –1.05%, respectively, and also knows the scenarios under which each will be realized.

Analysis of the Term Structure of Interest Rates

The price of a debt instrument fluctuates over its life as yields in the market change. As explained in Chapter 4 and illustrated in the next chapter, the price volatility of a bond is dependent on its maturity. More specifically, holding all other factors constant, the longer a debt instrument's maturity, the greater the price volatility resulting from a change in market interest rates. The spread between any two maturity sectors of the market is called a *maturity spread*. Although the maturity spread can be calculated for any sector of the market, it is most commonly calculated for the Treasury sector.

TABLE 5: Scenario Analysis

Bond A: 9% coupon, 20-year option-free bond
Price: $109.896

Yield to maturity: 8% Investment horizon: Three years

A. Projected Yield at End of Investment Horizon

5.00%	6.00%	7.00%	8.00%	9.00%	10.00%	11.00%	12.00%

B. Projected Sale Price at End of Investment Horizon

145.448	131.698	119.701	109.206	100.000	91.9035	84.763	78.4478

C. Total Future Dollars

Reinv. Rate	5.00%	6.00%	7.00%	8.00%	9.00%	10.00%	11.00%	12.00%
3.0%	173.481	159.731	147.734	137.239	128.033	119.937	112.796	106.481
3.5%	173.657	159.907	147.910	137.415	128.209	120.113	112.972	106.657
4.0%	173.834	160.084	148.087	137.592	128.387	120.290	113.150	106.834
4.5%	174.013	160.263	148.266	137.771	128.565	120.469	113.328	107.013
5.0%	174.192	160.443	148.445	137.950	128.745	120.648	113.508	107.193
5.5%	174.373	160.623	148.626	138.131	128.926	120.829	113.689	107.374
6.0%	174.555	160.806	148.809	138.313	129.108	121.011	113.871	107.556
6.5%	174.739	160.989	148.992	138.497	129.291	121.195	114.054	107.739

D. Total Return (Effective Rate)

Reinv. Rate	5.00%	6.00%	7.00%	8.00%	9.00%	10.00%	11.00%	12.00%
3.0%	16.44	13.28	10.37	7.69	5.22	2.96	0.87	21.05
3.5%	16.48	13.32	10.41	7.73	5.27	3.01	0.92	20.99
4.0%	16.52	13.36	10.45	7.78	5.32	3.06	0.98	20.94
4.5%	16.56	13.40	10.50	7.83	5.37	3.11	1.03	20.88
5.0%	16.60	13.44	10.54	7.87	5.42	3.16	1.08	20.83
5.5%	16.64	13.49	10.59	7.92	5.47	3.21	1.14	20.77
6.0%	16.68	13.53	10.63	7.97	5.52	3.26	1.19	20.72
6.5%	16.72	13.57	10.68	8.02	5.57	3.32	1.25	20.66

Notes: 1. Price of a 9%, 17-year option-free bond selling to yield the assumed projected yield at the end of the investment horizon.
2. Projected sale price at the end of the investment horizon plus coupon interest plus interest-on-interest at the assumed reinvestment rate.
3. Semi-annual total return calculated as follows:

$$\left(\frac{\text{Total future dollars}}{\text{Purchase price of bond}}\right)^{1/6} - 1$$

$$\text{Total return (effective rate)} = (1 + \text{Semi-annual total return})^2 - 1.$$

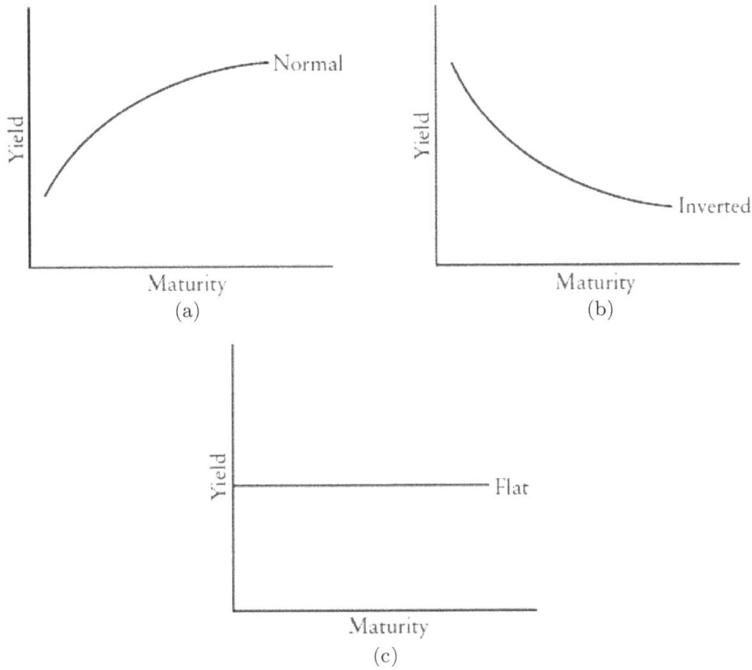

FIGURE 3: Three Observed Shapes for the Yield Curve

The relationship between the yields on comparable securities with different maturities is called the *term structure of interest rates*. The graphic that depicts the relationship between the yields offered on Treasury securities with different maturities is known as the *yield curve* and therefore the maturity spread is also referred to as the *yield curve spread*. Figure 3 shows the shape of three hypothetical Treasury yield curves that have been observed from time to time in the United States.

Forward Rates and Spot Rates

The focus on the Treasury yield curve is due to its role as a benchmark for setting yields in many other sectors of the debt market. However, a Treasury yield curve based on observed yields on the Treasury market is an unsatisfactory measure of the relation between required yield and maturity. The key reason is that securities with the same maturity may actually provide different yields. Hence, it is necessary to develop more accurate and reliable estimates of the Treasury yield curve. Specifically, the key is to estimate the theoretical interest rate that the US Treasury would have to pay assuming that the security issued is a zero-coupon security. Due to its complexity, we will not explain how this is done. However, at this point all that is necessary to know is that there are procedures for estimating the theoretical interest rate or yield that the US Treasury would have to pay for bonds with different maturities. These interest rates are called *Treasury spot rates*.

Valuable information for market participants can be obtained from the Treasury spot rates. These rates are called *forward rates*. First, we will see how these rates are obtained and then we will discuss theories about what determines forward rates. Finally, we will see how asset managers can use forward rates in making investment decisions.

Forward rates

To see how a forward rate can be computed, consider the following two Treasury spot rates. Suppose that the spot rate for a zero-coupon Treasury security maturing in 1 year is 4% and a zero-coupon Treasury security maturing in 2 years is 5%. Let's look at this situation from the perspective of an asset manager who wants to invest funds for 2 years. The asset manager's choices are as follows:

Alternative 1: Asset manager buys a 2-year zero-coupon Treasury security.
Alternative 2: Asset manager buys a 1-year zero-coupon Treasury security and when it matures in 1 year buys another 1-year Treasury security.

With Alternative 1, the investor will earn the 2-year spot rate and that rate is known with certainty. In contrast, with Alternative 2, the asset manager will earn the 1-year spot rate, but the 1-year spot 1 year from now is unknown. Therefore, for Alternative 2, the rate that will be earned over 2 years is not known with certainty.

Suppose that this asset manager expected that 1 year from now the 1-year spot rate will be higher than it is today. The investor might then feel Alternative 2 would be the better investment. However, this is not necessarily true. To understand why it is necessary to know what a forward rate is, let's continue with our illustration.

The asset manager will be indifferent to the two alternatives if they produce the same total dollars over the 2-year investment horizon. Given the

2-year spot rate, there is some spot rate on a 1-year zero-coupon Treasury security 1 year from now that will make the investor indifferent between the two alternatives. We will denote that rate by f.

The value of f can be readily determined given the 2-year spot rate and the 1-year spot rate. If an asset manager placed \$100 in the 2-year zero-coupon Treasury security (Alternative 1) earning 5%, the total dollars that will be generated at the end of 2 years is (i.e., the future value based on compounding):

$$\text{Total dollars at the end of 2 years for Alternative 1} = \$100(1.05)^2$$
$$= \$110.25.$$

The proceeds from investing in the 1-year Treasury security at 4% will generate the following total dollars at the end of 1 year:

$$\text{Total dollars at the end of 1 year for Alternative 2} = \$100(1.04) = \$104.$$

If 1 year from now this amount is reinvested in a zero-coupon Treasury security maturing in 1 year, which we denoted by f, then the total dollars at the end of 2 years would be

$$\text{Total dollars at the end of 2 years for Alternative 2} = \$104(1 + f).$$

The asset manager will be indifferent between the two alternatives if the total dollars are the same. Setting the two equations for the total dollars at end of 2 years for the two alternatives equal, we get

$$\$110.25 = \$104(1 + f).$$

Solving the preceding equation for f, we get 6%.

The forward rate of 6% can be used by an asset manager in two ways. The first is in pricing a debt instrument. We'll explain how this is done later. The second is when an asset manager has a view of future interest rates and wants to select debt instruments based on this view. Let's explain how. If the 1-year spot rate 1 year from now is less than 6%, then the total dollars at the end of 2 years would be higher by investing in the 2-year zero-coupon Treasury security (Alternative 1). If the 1-year spot rate 1 year from now is greater than 6%, then the total dollars at the end of 2 years would be higher by investing in a 1-year zero-coupon Treasury security and reinvesting the proceeds 1 year from now at the 1-year spot rate at that time (Alternative 2). Of course, if the 1-year spot rate 1 year from now is 6%, the two alternatives give the same total dollars at the end of 2 years.

For example, suppose that the asset manager expects that 1 year from now, the 1-year spot rate will be 5.5%. That is, the investor expects that the 1-year spot rate 1 year from now will be higher than its current level. Should the asset manager select Alternative 2 because the 1-year spot rate 1 year from now is expected to be higher? The answer is no. As we explained in the previous paragraph, if the spot rate is less than 6%, then Alternative 1 is the better alternative. Since this asset manager expects a rate of 5.5%, then Alternative 1 should be selected despite the fact that the asset manager expects the 1-year spot rate to be higher than it is today.

This may be a somewhat surprising result for some asset managers. But the reason for this is that the market prices its expectations of future interest rates into the rates offered on investments with different maturities. This is why knowledge of the forward rates is critical. Some market participants believe that the forward rate is the market's consensus of future interest rates. A natural question about forward rates is then how well they do at predicting future interest rates. Studies have demonstrated that forward rates do not do a good job in predicting future interest rates. Then, why the big deal about asset managers understanding forward rates? The reason, as we demonstrated in our illustration of how to select between two alternative investments with different maturities, is that the forward rates indicate how an asset manager's view on future rates must differ from the market consensus in order to make the correct decision.

In our illustration, the 1-year forward rate may not be realized. That is irrelevant. The fact is that the 1-year forward rate indicated to the asset manager that if expectations about the 1-year rate 1 month from now is less than 6%, the asset manager would be better off with Alternative 1.

For this reason, asset managers should not refer to forward rates as being market consensus rates. Instead, forward rates should be interpreted as *hedgeable rates*. For example, by investing in the 2-year Treasury security, the asset manager was able to hedge the 1-year rate 1 year from now.

Shapes of the Yield Curve

At any given point in time, if we plot the term structure — the yield to maturity, or the spot rate, at successive maturities — we would observe one of the three shapes shown in Figure 3. Panel A of the figure shows a yield curve where the yield increases with maturity. This type of yield curve is referred to as an *upward-sloping yield curve* or a *positively sloped yield curve*.

A distinction is made for upward sloping yield curves based on the steepness of the yield curve. The steepness of the yield curve is typically measured in terms of the maturity spread between the long-term and short-term yields. While there are many maturity candidates to proxy for long-term and short-term yields, many market participants use the maturity spread between the 6-month and 30-year yield. In practice, a Treasury with a positively sloped yield curve whose maturity spread as measured by the 6-month and 30-year yields is referred to as a *normal yield curve* when the spread is 300 basis points or less. When the maturity spread is more than 300 basis points, the yield curve is said to be a *steep yield curve.*

Panel B of Figure 3 shows a *downward-sloping or inverted yield curve*, where yields in general decline as maturity increases. Panel C of Figure 3 depicts a *flat yield curve.* While the figure suggests that for a flat yield curve the yields are identical for each maturity, that is not what is observed. Rather, the yields for all maturities are similar. A variant of the flat yield is one in which the yield on short-term and long-term Treasuries are similar, but the yield on intermediate-term Treasuries are much lower than the 6-month and 30-year yields. Such a yield curve is referred to as a *humped yield curve.*

Determinants of the Shape of the Term Structure

There are two major economic theories that have evolved to account for the observed shapes of the yield curve: the *expectations theory* and the *market segmentation theory.*

Expectations theories

There are several forms of the expectations theory: pure expectations theory and biased expectations theory. Both theories share a hypothesis about the behavior of short-term forward rates and assume that the forward rates in current long-term bonds are closely related to the market's expectations about future short-term rates. The two theories differ, however, on whether or not other factors also affect forward rates, and how. The pure expectations theory postulates that no systematic factors other than expected future short-term rates affect forward rates; the biased expectations theory asserts that there are other factors.[2]

[2]This theory was proposed by Lutz [1940].

Pure expectations theory

According to the pure expectations theory, the forward rates exclusively represent expected future rates. Thus, the entire term structure at a given time reflects the market's current expectations of the family of future short-term rates. Under this view, a rising term structure, as in panel A of Figure 3, must indicate that the market expects short-term rates to rise throughout the relevant future. Similarly, a flat term structure reflects an expectation that future short-term rates will be mostly constant, while a falling term structure must reflect an expectation that future short-term rates will decline steadily.

A major shortcoming of the pure expectations theory is that it ignores the risks inherent in investing in debt instruments. If forward rates were perfect predictors of future interest rates, then the future prices of bonds would be known with certainty. The return over any investment period would be certain and independent of the maturity of the debt instrument initially acquired and of the time at which the investor needs to liquidate the debt instrument. However, with uncertainty about future interest rates and hence about future prices, these debt instruments become risky investments in the sense that the return over some investment horizon is unknown.

Similarly, from a borrower's perspective, the cost of borrowing for any required period of financing would be certain and independent of the maturity of the debt instrument if the rate at which the borrower must refinance debt in the future is known. But with uncertainty about future interest rates, the cost of borrowing is uncertain if the borrower must refinance at some time over the periods in which the funds are initially needed.

Biased expectations theory

Biased expectations theories take into account the shortcomings of the pure expectations theory. The two theories are the liquidity theory and the preferred habitat theory.

According to the *liquidity theory*, forward rates will not be an unbiased estimate of the market's expectations of future interest rates because they embody a premium to compensate for risk; this risk premium is referred to as a *liquidity premium*.[3] Thus, an upward-sloping yield curve may reflect expectations that future interest rates either (1) will rise or (2) will be

[3]This theory was proposed by Hicks [1946, pp. 141–145].

flat or even fall, but with a liquidity premium increasing fast enough with maturity so as to produce an upward-sloping yield curve.

The *preferred habitat theory* also adopts the view that the term structure reflects the expectation of the future path of interest rates as well as a risk premium.[4] However, the preferred habitat theory rejects the assertion that the risk premium must rise uniformly with maturity. Proponents of the habitat theory say that the latter conclusion could be accepted if all investors intend to liquidate their investment at the first possible date, while all borrowers are eager to borrow long. However, this is an assumption that can be rejected for a number of reasons. The argument is that different financial institutions have different investment horizons and have a preference for the maturities in which they invest. The preference is based on the maturity of their liabilities. To induce a financial institution out of that maturity sector, a premium must be paid. Thus, forward rates include a liquidity premium and compensation for investors to move out of their preferred maturity sector. Consequently, forward rates do not reflect the market's consensus of future interest rates.

Market segmentation theory

The *market segmentation theory* also recognizes that investors have preferred habitats dictated by saving and investment flows. This theory also proposes that the major reason for the shape of the yield curve lies in asset and liability management constraints (either regulatory or self-imposed) and creditors (borrowers) restricting their lending (financing) to specific maturity sectors. However, the market segmentation theory differs from the preferred habitat theory because the market segmentation theory assumes that neither investors nor borrowers are willing to shift from one maturity sector to another to take advantage of opportunities arising from differences between expectations and forward rates. Thus, for the segmentation theory the shape of the yield curve is determined by the supply of and demand for securities within each maturity sector.

Relationship between Spot and Forward Rates

Earlier we have seen how forward rates are derived from spot rates. The reverse is also true: spot rates can be derived from forward rates. To show

[4]This theory was proposed by Modigliani and Sutch [1966].

the relationship between spot rates and forward rates, we will use the hypothetical Treasury spot rates shown in Table 6. The information in the first column is the period for the Treasury security. Each period is 6 months so that in the second column the number of years is shown. The third column is the annual yield based on the yield curve and the fourth column has the spot rate on an annual basis.

To show the relationship, notation is needed for the spot rates and forward rates. We will let z_m denote the spot rate for period m. Thus, Table 6 shows that the 6-month spot rate for the first period, denoted by z_1, is 3% while the 6-month spot rate in period 6, denoted by z_6, is 4.7520%. For the forward rates, we will let f_m be the 6-month forward rate m periods from now.

In general, the relationship between an m-period spot rate and the 6-month forward rates is as follows:

$$z_m = [(1 + f_1)(1 + f_2) \dots (1 + f_m)]^{1/m} - 1. \tag{9}$$

The relationship between the 6-month forward rate and spot rates is

$$f_m = \frac{(1 + z_m)^m}{(1 + z_{m-1})^{m-1}} - 1. \tag{10}$$

Let's use the spot rates in Table 6 and Equation (10) to compute the 6-month forward rate for the fifth year:

$$f_4 = \frac{(1 + z_5)^5}{(1 + z_4)^4} - 1 = \frac{(1.044376)^{5\ 4}}{1.039164} - 1 = 0.0654 = 6.54\%.$$

This value and the other forward rates are shown in the last column of Table 6.

To see how the forward rates can be used to calculate the spot rate, we use Equation (9) to compute the 5-year spot rate:

$$\begin{aligned} z_5 &= [(1 + f_1)(1 + f_2)(1 + f_3)(1 + f_4) + (1 + f_5)]^{1/5} - 1 \\ &= [(1.030)(1.036)(1.039)(1.052)(1.065)]^{1/5} - 1 = 0.0443 = 4.443\%. \end{aligned}$$

This value is what is shown in Table 6.

Using Spot and Forward Rates to Value a Debt Instrument

At the outset of this chapter, we explained the valuation of an option-free debt instrument. Using that we would value a Treasury security of a given maturity by discounting every coupon and the maturity value by the yield

TABLE 6: Hypothetical Treasury Yield Curve Spot Rate Curve, Spot Rates, and One-Period Forward Rates

Period	Years	Annual Yield to Maturity (BEY) (%)[a]	Spot Rate (BEY) (%)[a]	One Period Forward Rate
1	0.50	3.0	3.0000	3.000
2	1.00	3.3	3.3000	3.600
3	1.50	3.5	3.5053	3.920
4	2.00	3.9	3.9164	5.150
5	2.50	4.4	4.4376	6.540
6	3.00	4.7	4.7520	6.330
7	3.50	4.9	4.9622	6.230
8	4.00	5.0	5.0650	5.790
9	4.50	5.1	5.1701	6.010
10	5.00	5.2	5.2772	6.240
11	5.50	5.3	5.3864	6.480
12	6.00	5.4	5.4976	6.720
13	6.50	5.5	5.6108	6.970
14	7.00	5.6	5.6643	6.360
15	7.50	5.6	5.7193	6.490
16	8.00	5.7	5.7755	6.620
17	8.50	5.7	5.8331	6.760
18	9.00	5.8	5.9584	8.100
19	9.50	5.9	6.0863	8.400
20	10.00	6.0	6.2169	8.720

Notes: [a]The yield to maturity and the spot rate are annual rates. They are reported as bond-equivalent yields. To obtain the semi-annual yield or rate, one half the annual yield or annual rate is used.

offered on a Treasury security with the same maturity. So, for example, consider an 8% coupon Treasury security maturing in 10 years. Table 6 shows the yield in the third column obtained from the yield curve that we used to derive spot rates and forward rates. As can be seen, the yield on a 10-year Treasury is 6%. Using the methodology explained and illustrated earlier in this chapter, every cash flow would be discounted at a 6% rate. To calculate the Treasury security's value, the following equation must be calculated:

$$\frac{\$4.00}{1.03} + \frac{\$4.00}{1.03^2} + \frac{\$4.00}{1.03^3} + \cdots + \frac{\$4.00}{1.03^{19}} + \frac{\$104.00}{(1.03)^{20}}.$$

The cash flow for the 8% coupon is \$4 every 6 months, so the numerator above is \$4 and the maturity value is \$104. The required yield is 6% which is 3% semi-annually and that is used in the denominator. The value of this 8%, 20-year Treasury turns out to be \$114.8775. The Treasury security is trading at a premium because the coupon rate is greater than the required yield.

Now let's look at what the value of this Treasury would be if discounted using the spot rates. The numerator is the same as in the above calculation, but the discount rate varies for each period. Specifically, the following equation should be computed:

$$\frac{\$4.00}{1.0150} + \frac{\$4.00}{1.0165^2} + \frac{\$4.00}{1.0175^3} + \cdots + \frac{\$4.00}{1.0304^{19}} + \frac{\$104.00}{(1.0311)^{20}}.$$

The discount rates here are one-half the spot rates shown in Table 6. The calculation produces a value for this Treasury of \$115.2621. This value is greater than the value when computed by just the required yield of 3%. We can see why there is a greater value when forward rates are used. In the earlier years, the cash flows are discounted at a lower discount rate. In the latter years, there is a higher discount rate used; the impact of the higher discount rate is mitigated by the time value of money. That is, the impact of the higher discount rate is not as significant in future periods.

Thus, it should be clear that discounting at spot rates (or forward rates) would give a different value than discounting by one rate. At which price would this security trade, \$114.8775 or \$115.2621? Is the value using spot or forward rates just a pure theory? The answer is that the price will have to be around the theoretical value using spot rates. The reason is that there is a well-known mechanism in place to force the price towards its theoretical value. This process is known as the stripping and reconstitution process. In the Treasury market, the government facilitates this process.

Stripping is the process that in our example would drive the price of the Treasury security we have just valued to \$115.2621. This is how if the price in the market is \$114.8775, a market participant, say a dealer, would buy the security and then sell each of the cash flows as zero-coupon Treasury securities as described in Chapter 4. The price at which each cash flow can be sold is the present value discounted at the spot rate for that maturity. The aggregate of the value of the cash flows that can be sold will be close to \$115.2621. The action of dealers of buying the Treasury at prices below \$115.2621 will result in an arbitrage profit. For this reason, the theoretical value based on spot (or forward) rates is referred to as the *arbitrage-free value*.

Suppose instead that the market price is greater than the theoretical value of \$115.2621, say \$116.00. In this case, dealers would use the mechanism of *reconstitution* to move the price to \$115.2621. What dealers would do is buy cash flows that match the cash flow of the mispriced Treasury security and sell the package of cash flows for a price of \$116. This activity of selling the package of cash flows would move the price down to the theoretical value of \$115.2621.

Key Points

- The price of any financial instrument is equal to the present value of its expected cash flows.
- Determining the price of any financial instrument requires estimating the expected cash flows and estimating the appropriate required yield.
- For an option-free bond, the cash flow consists of two components: (1) periodic coupon interest payments to the maturity date and (2) the par value at maturity.
- A fundamental property of a bond is that its price changes in the opposite direction from the change in the required yield.
- The reason for the inverse relationship between a bond's price and the required yield is that the price of the bond is the present value of the cash flows: as the required yield increases (decreases), the present value of the cash flows decreases (increases).
- The price-yield relationship for any option-free bond is convex.
- A bond whose price is above (below) its par value is said to be selling at a premium (discount).
- For a bond selling at par value, the coupon rate is equal to the required yield.
- The price-yield relationship for callable and prepayable bonds at high interest rates exhibits positive convexity, but at low interest rates exhibits negative convexity.
- There are four bond yield measures commonly quoted for bonds: (1) current yield, (2) yield to maturity, (3) yield to call, and (4) yield to put.
- Current yield relates the annual coupon interest to the market price.
- The yield to maturity is the interest rate that will make the present value of a bond's remaining cash flows (if held to maturity) equal to the price (plus accrued interest, if any).
- The yield to maturity is a "promised" yield; that is, it will be realized only if (1) the bond is held to maturity and (2) the coupon interest payments are reinvested at the yield to maturity. If either (1) or (2) fail to occur, the actual yield realized by an investor can be greater than or less than the yield to maturity when the bond is purchased.

- The yield to call assumes that the issuer will call the bond at some assumed call date, and the call price is then the call price specified in the call schedule.
- For callable bonds, typically, a yield to first call and a yield to par call are calculated.
- The procedure for calculating the yield to any assumed call date is the same as for any yield calculation: Determine the interest rate that will make the present value of the expected cash flows equal to the price plus accrued interest.
- The interest-on-interest component can represent a substantial portion of a bond's potential return.
- An investor faces reinvestment risk when using the yield to call because future reinvestment rates may be less than the yield to maturity at the time the bond is purchased.
- Two characteristics of a bond determine the importance of the interest-on-interest component and, therefore, the degree of reinvestment risk: maturity and coupon rate.
- For a given yield to maturity and a given coupon rate, the longer the maturity, the more dependent the bond's total dollar return on the interest-on-interest component in order to realize the yield to maturity at the time of purchase.
- For long-term bonds, the interest-on-interest component may be the major component of a bond's potential total dollar return.
- For a given maturity and a given yield to maturity, the higher the coupon rate, the more dependent the bond's total dollar return will be on the reinvestment of the coupon payments to produce the yield to maturity anticipated at the time of purchase.
- For zero-coupon bonds, none of the bond's total dollar return is dependent on the interest-on-interest component and therefore there is no reinvestment risk if held to maturity.
- There are two conventions to calculate a portfolio yield: (1) weighted-average portfolio yield and (2) internal rate of return.
- The weighted average portfolio yield is calculated using the weighted average of the yield of all the bonds in the portfolio.
- While the weighted-average portfolio yield is the most commonly used measure of portfolio yield, this yield measure provides little insight into the potential return of a portfolio.
- The portfolio yield is the portfolio internal rate of return which is calculated by first determining the cash flows for all the bonds in the portfolio,

and then finding the interest rate that will make the present value of the cash flows equal to the market value of the portfolio.

- While superior to the weighted-average portfolio yield, the portfolio internal rate of return suffers from the same problems as yield measures in general: it assumes that the cash flows can be reinvested at the calculated yield.
- Rather than assume that the coupon interest payments are reinvested at the yield to maturity, an investor can make an explicit assumption about the reinvestment rate based on expectations.
- To calculate the potential total return from holding a bond, the objective is first to compute the total future dollars that will result from investing in a bond assuming a particular reinvestment rate and then computing the interest rate that will make the initial investment in the bond grow to the computed total future dollars.
- The total return measure allows a portfolio manager to project the performance of a bond based on the planned investment horizon and expectations concerning reinvestment rates and future market yields.
- In the analysis of the term structure of interest rates, the focus is on the Treasury yield curve because of its role as a benchmark for setting yields in many other sectors of the debt market.
- Treasury yield curve based on observed yields on the Treasury market is an unsatisfactory measure of the relation between required yield and maturity.
- The term structure of interest rates is the relationship between the yields on comparable securities but different maturities.
- The graph that depicts the relationship between the yields offered on Treasury securities with different maturities is known as the yield curve.
- There are procedures for estimating the theoretical interest rate or yield that the US Treasury would have to pay by issuing zero-coupon bonds with different maturities; these interest rates are called Treasury spot rates.
- Valuable information for market participants can be obtained from Treasury spot rates; this information includes forward rates.
- Asset managers should not refer to forward rates as being market consensus rates, but instead they should be interpreted as hedgeable rates.
- The yield curve can have different shapes: upward-sloping yield curve (positively sloped yield curve), downward-sloping yield curve (inverted yield curve), flat yield curve, and humped yield curve.

- There are two major economic theories that have evolved to account for the observed shapes of the yield curve: the expectations theory and the market segmentation theory.
- There are several forms of the expectations theory: pure expectations theory and biased expectations theory.
- The two expectation theories share a hypothesis about the behavior of short-term forward rates and also assume that the forward rates in current long-term bonds are closely related to the market's expectations about future short-term rates.
- The two expectations theories of the shape of the yield curve differ based on whether other factors also affect forward rates, and how.
- The pure expectations theory postulates that no systematic factors other than expected future short-term rates affect forward rates.
- The biased expectations theory asserts that there are other factors.
- Biased expectations theories consider the shortcomings of the pure expectations theory.
- The two biased expectations theories are the liquidity theory and the preferred habitat theory.
- The market segmentation theory also recognizes that investors have preferred habitats dictated by saving and investment flows.
- From the Treasury yield curve, spot and forward rates can be calculated.
- Spot or forward rates should be used to discount the cash flows of a debt instrument.
- The value of a Treasury security discounted using the spot or forward rates is called the arbitrage-free value.
- The market price of Treasury security should trade near its arbitrage-free value because of the stripping and reconstitution processes available in the Treasury market.

References

Hicks, J. R., 1946. *Value and Capital,* 2nd edition. London: Oxford University Press.

Kalotay, A. J., G. O. Williams, and F. J. Fabozzi, 1993. "A model for the valuation of bonds and embedded options," *Financial Analysts Journal*, 49: 35–46.

Lutz, F. 1940. "The structure of interest rates," *Quarterly Journal of Economics,* 55(1): 36–63.

Modigliani, F. and R. Sutch, 1966. "Innovation in interest rate policy," *American Economic Review*, 56: 178–197.

Chapter 16

Interest Rate Risk and Credit Risk Measures

Learning Objectives

After reading this chapter, you will understand:

- the bond characteristics and interest rate environment that impact a bond's interest rate risk;
- measures of interest rate risk: price value of a basis point and duration;
- how duration combined with convexity quantify the interest rate risk of a bond and a bond portfolio;
- the various measures of duration for a parallel shift in interest rates: dollar duration, modified duration, Macaulay duration, and effective duration;
- how to compute portfolio duration and contribution to portfolio duration;
- how key rate duration measures exposure to yield curve changes;
- the different credit analytics measures;
- what default risk is, and credit ratings assigned to debt instruments by credit rating agencies;
- the US bankruptcy process and creditor rights;
- what a default loss rate is and how to measure recovery rates;
- factors considered in rating corporate bonds: character, capacity, collateral, and covenants;
- what is downgrade risk and the meaning of rating migration tables;
- what are credit spread risk and spread duration.

The previous chapter was the first of two chapters on bond analytics. In the previous chapter, the pricing of debt instruments and the various yield measures were explained. In this chapter, we describe bond analytics that address interest rate risk analytics and credit risk analytics.

Interest Rate Risk Analytics

As explained in the previous chapter, a fundamental property of a bond is that its price will change in the opposite direction from the change in the required yield for the bond. This property follows from the fact that the price of a bond is equal to the present value of its expected cash flows. Although all bonds change in price when the required yield changes, they do not change by the same percentage. For example, when the required yield increases by 100 basis points for two bonds, the price of one might fall by 15%, while that of the other might fall by only 1%. To effectively implement bond portfolio strategies, it is necessary to understand why bonds react differently to yield changes. In addition, it is necessary to quantify how a bond's price might react to yield changes. Ideally, a portfolio manager would like a measure that indicates the relationship between changes in required yields and changes in a bond's price. That is, a portfolio manager will want to know how a bond's price is expected to change if yields change by, say, 100 basis points.

In Chapter 4, we stated the characteristics of a bond's price that affect its price volatility. Here we present two measures that are used to quantify a bond's price volatility. One of these measures is duration. Duration, however, provides only an approximation of how the price will change. Duration can be supplemented with another measure that we will discuss, convexity. Together, duration and convexity do an effective job of estimating how a bond's price will change when yields change.

Price Volatility Properties of Option-Free Bonds

Table 1 shows the percentage change in a bond's price for six hypothetical bonds with a $100 par value and trading to a yield of 9% for various changes in the required yield. For example, consider the 9%, 25-year bond. If the bond is selling to yield 9%, its price would be 100. If the required yield declines to 8%, the price of that bond would be 110.741. Thus, a decline in yield from 9% to 8% would increase the price by 10.74% [(110.741 − 100)/100] which agrees with the value shown in Table 1.

An examination of the table reveals several properties concerning the price volatility of an option-free bond.

- **Property 1:** For very small changes in the required yield, the percentage price change for a given bond is roughly the same whether the required yield increases or decreases.

TABLE 1: Instantaneous Percentage Price Change for Six Hypothetical Bonds

Six Hypothetical Bonds, Priced Initially to Yield 9%		
9% coupon,	5 years to maturity,	Price = 100.0000
9% coupon,	25 years to maturity,	Price = 100.0000
9% coupon,	25 years to maturity,	Price = 100.0000
6% coupon,	5 years to maturity,	Price = 88.1309
6% coupon,	25 years to maturity,	Price = 70.3570
0% coupon,	5 years to maturity,	Price = 64.3928
0% coupon,	25 years to maturity,	Price = 11.0710

Required Yield Changes to	**Basis Points Points**	**9%/5**	**9%/25**	**6%/5**	**6%/25**	**0%/5**	**0%/25**
7.00	−200	8.32	23.46	8.75	25.46	10.09	61.73
8.00	−100	4.06	10.74	4.26	11.60	4.91	27.10
8.50	−50	2.00	5.15	2.11	5.55	2.42	12.72
8.90	−10	0.40	1.00	0.42	1.07	0.48	2.42
8.99	−1	0.04	0.10	0.04	0.11	0.05	0.24
9.01	1	−0.04	−0.10	−0.04	−0.11	−0.05	−0.24
9.10	10	−0.39	−0.98	−0.41	−1.05	−0.48	−2.36
9.50	50	−1.95	−4.75	−2.05	−5.09	−2.36	−11.26
10.00	100	−3.86	−9.13	−4.06	−9.76	−4.66	−21.23
11.00	200	−7.54	−16.93	−7.91	−18.03	−9.08	−37.89

- **Property 2:** For large changes in the required yield, the percentage price change is not the same for an increase in the required yield as it is for a decrease in the required yield.
- **Property 3:** For a large change in basis points, the percentage price increase is greater than the percentage price decrease. The implication of this property is that if an investor owns a bond, the price appreciation that will be realized if the required yield decrease is greater than the capital loss that will be realized if the required yield rises by the same number of basis points.

An explanation for these three properties of bond price volatility lies in the convex shape of the price-yield relationship. We will investigate this in more detail later in the chapter.

Factors That Affect a Bond's Price Volatility

In Chapter 4, we stated that there are two features of an option-free bond that determine its price volatility: coupon and term to maturity. In addition, the yield level at which a bond trades affects its price volatility. We can see how the coupon rate and maturity impact price volatility by looking at Table 1.

Consider the three 25-year bonds. For a given change in yield, the zero-coupon bond has the largest price volatility, and the largest coupon bond (the 9% coupon bond) has the smallest price volatility. This is also true for the three 5-year bonds. In general, for a given term to maturity and initial yield, the lower the coupon rate, the greater the price volatility of a bond.

Now consider the two 9% coupon bonds. For a given change in yield, the 25-year bond has the largest price volatility, and the shortest-maturity bond (the 5-year bond) has the smallest price volatility. This is also true for the two 6% coupon bonds and the two zero-coupon bonds. In general, for a given coupon rate and initial yield, the longer the maturity, the greater the price volatility of a bond.

A bond's price volatility is also affected by the level of interest rates in the economy. Specifically, the higher the level of yields, the lower the price volatility. To illustrate this, let's compare the 9%, 25-year bond trading at two yield levels: 7% and 13%. If the yield increases from 7% to 8%, the bond's price declines by 10.3%; but if the yield increases from 13% to 14%, the bond's price declines by 6.75%.

Measures of Interest Rate Risk

Bond price volatility when interest rates change indicates the interest rate risk of a bond. There are two measures of interest rate risk: (1) price value of a basis point and (2) duration and convexity. However, both measures suffer from the problem that they measure only an exposure to a parallel shift in interest rates. That is, it is assumed that the interest rate for all the bonds held will change by the same number of basis points. There are measures that are used to assess the exposure to changes in the yield curve that we discuss later in this chapter.

Price value of a basis point as measure of interest rate risk

The *price value of a basis point* (PVBP), also referred to as the *dollar value of an 01* (DV01), measures the change in the price of the bond if the required yield changes by 1 basis point. Note that this measure of price volatility indicates dollar price volatility as opposed to percentage price volatility (price change as a percentage of the initial price). Typically, the price value of a basis point is expressed as the absolute value of the change in price. Owing to Property 1 of the price-yield relationship, price volatility is the same for an increase or a decrease of 1 basis point in required yield.

To illustrate the calculation, let's calculate the PVBP for a 25-year, 6% coupon bond selling to yield 9%. The price for this bond is \$70.3570. If the yield is increased by 1 basis point to 9.01%, the price would decline to \$70.2824. The difference between the two prices is \$0.0746 and is therefore the PVBP.

Duration and convexity as measures of interest rate risk

The most commonly used approach to measure interest rate risk exposure of a portfolio or a trading position is by approximating the impact of a change in interest rates on a bond or a bond portfolio using duration. Duration is a first approximation. To improve upon this approximation, a second measure is estimated and is referred to as convexity. Here we explain how duration is estimated for bonds and portfolios. There are different types of duration measures for individual bonds and portfolios. We also explain the limitations of duration. We then discuss how the duration measure can be improved by using a measure called convexity.

Duration

The most obvious way to measure the price sensitivity as a percentage of the security's current price to changes in interest rates is to change rates (i.e., "shock" rates) by a small number of basis points and calculate how a security's value will change as a percentage of the current price. The name popularly used to refer to the approximate percentage price change is *duration.*

The following formula can be used to estimate the duration of a security:

$$\text{Duration} = \frac{V_- - V_+}{2V_0\Delta y}, \tag{1}$$

where Δy is the change (or shock) in interest rates (in decimal form), V_0 is the current price of the bond, V_- is the estimated price of the bond if interest rates are decreased by the change in interest rates, and V_+ is the estimated price of the bond if interest rates are increased by the change in interest rates.

Throughout this chapter, we will use "change in interest rate" and "change in yield" interchangeably.

It is important to understand that the two values in the numerator of Equation (1) are the estimated values obtained from a valuation model. Consequently, the duration measure is only as good as the valuation model employed to obtain the estimated values in Equation (1). The more difficult it is to estimate the value of a bond, the less confidence a portfolio manager may have in the estimated duration. We will see that the duration of a portfolio is nothing more than a market-weighted average of the duration of the bonds comprising the portfolio. Hence, a portfolio's duration is sensitive to the estimated duration of the individual bonds.

To illustrate the duration calculation, consider the following option-free bond: a 6% coupon 5-year bond trading at par value to yield 6%. The current price is \$100. Suppose the yield is changed by 50 basis points. Thus, $\Delta y = 0.005$ and $V_0 = \$100$. This is a simple bond to value if the interest rate or yield is changed. If the yield is decreased to 5.5%, the price of this bond would be \$102.1600. If the yield is increased to 6.5%, the value of this bond would be \$97.8944. That is, $V_- = \$102.1600$ and $V_+ = \$97.8944$. Substituting into Equation (1), we obtain

$$\text{Duration} = \frac{\$102.1600 - \$97.8944}{2(\$100)(0.005)} = 4.27.$$

There are various ways that practitioners have interpreted what the duration of a bond is. We believe the most useful way to think about a bond's duration is as the approximate percentage change in the bond's price for a 100 basis point change in interest rates. Thus a bond with a duration of say 5 will change by approximately 5% for a 100-basis-point change in interest rates (i.e., if the yield required for this bond changes by approximately 100 basis points). For a 50-basis-point change in interest rates, the bond's price will change by approximately 2.5%; for a 25-basis-point change in interest rates, 1.25%, and so on.

In estimating the sensitivity of the price of a bond to changes in interest rates, we looked at the percentage price change. However, for two bonds with the same duration but trading at different prices, the dollar price change will not be the same. To see this, suppose that we have two bonds, B_1 and B_2, that both have a duration of 5. Suppose further that the current price of B_1 and B_2 are \$100 and \$90, respectively. A 100-basis-point change for both bonds will change the price by approximately 5%. This means a price change of \$5 (5% times \$100) for B_1 and a price change of \$4.5 (5% times \$90) for B_2.

Here is how duration can be used to approximate the price change and how good the approximation is. The approximate percentage price change of a bond using duration is found as follows:

$$\text{Approximate percentage price change} = -\text{Duration} \times (\Delta y) \times 100, \quad (2)$$

where Δy is the change (or shock) in interest rates (in decimal form). The reason for the negative sign on the right-hand side of Equation (2) is because of the inverse relationship between price change and yield change.

For example, consider the 6%, 25-year bond trading at 70.3570 to yield 9% whose duration can be shown to be 10.6. The approximate percentage price change for a 10-basis-point increase in yield (i.e., $\Delta y = +0.001$) is

$$\begin{aligned}\text{Approximate percentage price change} &= -10.6 \times (+0.001) \times 100 \\ &= -1.06\%.\end{aligned}$$

How good is this approximation? The actual percentage price change is −1.05% (as shown in Table 1 when yield increases to 9.10%). Duration in this case does an excellent job in estimating the percentage price change.

We would come to the same conclusion if we used duration to estimate the percentage price change if the yield declined by 10 basis points (i.e., $\Delta y = -0.001$). In this case, the approximate percentage price change would be +1.06% (i.e., the direction of the price change is reversed, but the magnitude of the change is the same). Table 1 shows that the actual percentage price change is +1.07%.

Let's look at how well duration does in estimating the percentage price change if the yield increases by 200 basis points instead of 10 basis points. In this case, Δy is equal to +0.02. Substituting into Equation (2), we have

$$\begin{aligned}\text{Approximate percentage price change} &= -10.6 \times (+0.02) \times 100 \\ &= -21.2\%.\end{aligned}$$

How good is this estimate? From Table 1 we see that the actual percentage price change when the yield increases by 200 basis points to 11% is −18.03%. Thus, the estimate here is not as good as when we use duration to approximate the percentage price change for a change in yield of only 10 basis points. How about if we use duration to approximate the percentage price change when the yield decreases by 200 basis points? The approximate percentage price change in this scenario is +21.2%, but the actual percentage price change as shown in Table 1 is +25.46%.

Note also in the two scenarios where we changed the yield by 200 basis points that the approximate percentage price change overestimated how much the bond's price would actually decline if the yield increased by 200 basis points and underestimates how much the bond's price would actually increase if the yield decreased by 200 basis points. This will always be the case.

Later we will see how the approximated price change can be improved by using what is called a convexity adjustment.

Dollar duration

The dollar price change of a bond can be measured by multiplying duration by the full dollar price and the number of basis points (in decimal form) and is called the *dollar duration*. That is,

$$\text{Dollar duration} = \text{Duration} \times \text{Dollar price} \times \text{Change in rates in decimal.}$$

The dollar duration for a 100-basis-point change in rates is

$$\text{Dollar duration} = \text{Duration} \times \text{Dollar price} \times 0.01.$$

So, for bonds B_1 and B_2, the dollar duration for a 100-basis-point change in rates is as follows:

$$\text{For bond } B_{1:} \text{ Dollar duration} = 5 \times \$100 \times 0.01 = \$5.0.$$

$$\text{For bond } B_{2:} \text{ Dollar duration} = 5 \times \$90 \times 0.01 = \$4.5.$$

Knowing the dollar duration allows a portfolio manager to neutralize the risk of a bond position. For example, consider a position in bond B_2. If a trader wants to eliminate the interest rate risk exposure of this bond (i.e., hedge the exposure), the trader will look for a position in another financial instrument(s) (for example, an interest rate derivative described in Chapter 18) whose value will change in the opposite direction to bond B_2's price by an amount equal to \$4.5. So, if the trader has a long position in B_2, the position will decline in value by \$4.5 for a 100-basis-point increase in interest rates. To hedge this risk exposure, the trader can take a position in another financial instrument whose value increases by \$4.5 if interest rates increase by 100 basis points.

The dollar duration can also be computed without having to know a bond's duration. This is done by simply looking at the average price change for a bond when interest rates are increased and decreased by the same number of basis points. This can be done easily for interest rate derivatives. For example, the dollar duration for an interest rate futures contract and an interest rate swap can be computed by changing interest rates and determining how the price of the derivative changes on average. This is important because when trying to control the interest rate risk of a position, a portfolio manager or risk manager will employ interest rate derivatives.

Modified duration, Macaulay duration, and effective duration

A popular form of duration that is used by practitioners is modified duration. *Modified duration* is the approximate percentage change in a bond's price for a 100-basis-point change in interest rates, assuming that the bond's cash flows do not change when interest rates change. What this means is that in calculating the values used in the numerator of the duration formula, the cash flows used to calculate the current price are assumed to be unaffected when interest rates change. Therefore, the change in the bond's value when interest rates change by a small number of basis points is due solely to discounting at the new yield level.

Modified duration is related to another measure sometimes referred to in the bond market: *Macaulay duration*. The formula for this measure, first used by Macaulay (1938), is rarely used in practice so it will not be produced here. For a bond that pays coupon interest semiannually, modified duration is related to Macaulay duration as follows:

$$\text{Modified duration} = \text{Macaulay duration}/(1 + \text{yield}/2),$$

where yield is the bond's yield to maturity in decimal form. Practically speaking, there is very little difference in the computed values for modified duration and Macaulay duration.

The assumption that the cash flows will not change when interest rates change makes sense for option-free bonds because the payments by the issuer are not altered when interest rates change. This is not the case for callable bonds, putable bonds, and securitized products such as residential mortgage-backed securities. For these securities, a change in interest rates may alter the expected cash flows.

For bonds with embedded options, there are valuation models that consider how changes in interest rates will affect cash flows. When the values used in the numerator of Equation (1) are obtained from a valuation model that considers both the discounting at different interest rates and how the cash flows can change, the resulting duration is referred to as *effective duration* or option-adjusted duration.

Portfolio duration and contribution to portfolio duration

Portfolio duration can be obtained by calculating the weighted average of the duration of the bonds in the portfolio. The weight is the proportion of the portfolio that a security comprises. Mathematically, portfolio duration can be calculated as follows:

$$\text{Portfolio duration} = w_1 D_1 + w_2 D_2 + \ldots + w_N D_N, \quad (3)$$

where w_i is the market value of bond i/market value of the portfolio, D_i is the duration of bond I, and N is the number of bonds in the portfolio.

To illustrate this calculation, consider the \$240,220,000, 10-bond portfolio shown in Table 2. The table shows the market value of each bond, the percentage that each bond is of the portfolio, and the duration of each bond. The fifth column gives the product of the weight and the duration. The last row in that column shows the portfolio duration of 5.21.

A portfolio duration of 5.21 means that for a 100-basis-point change in the yield for all 10 bonds, the market value of the portfolio will change by approximately 5.21%. But keep in mind that the yield on all 10 bonds must change by 100 basis points for the duration measure to be most useful. The assumption that all interest rates must change by the same number of basis points is a critical assumption, and its importance cannot be overemphasized. Market practitioners refer to this as the "parallel yield curve shift assumption".

TABLE 2: Calculation of Portfolio Duration and Contribution to Portfolio Duration

Bond	Market Value (\$)	Percent of Portfolio	Duration	Contribution to Portfolio Duration[a] (\$)	Dollar Duration (\$)
1	10,000,000	4.1629	4.70	0.20	470,000
2	18,500,000	7.7013	3.60	0.28	666,000
3	14,550,000	6.0569	6.25	0.38	909,375
4	26,080,000	10.8567	5.42	0.59	1,413,536
5	24,780,000	10.3155	2.15	0.22	532,770
6	35,100,000	14.6116	3.25	0.47	1,140,750
7	15,360,000	6.3941	6.88	0.44	1,056,768
8	26,420,000	10.9983	6.50	0.71	1,717,300
9	40,000,000	16.6514	4.75	0.79	1,900,000
10	29,430,000	12.2513	9.23	1.13	2,716,389
Port.	240,220,000	100.0000		5.21	12,522,888

[a]Contribution to portfolio duration = Duration × Percent of portfolio.

Portfolio duration can also be computed by using dollar duration. This is done by computing the dollar duration for each bond in the portfolio. The sixth column of Table 2 gives the dollar duration for each bond in the portfolio. The portfolio duration as shown in the last row of the sixth column of the table is $12,522,888. This means that for a 100-basis-point change in interest rates, the change in the portfolio's value will be approximately $12,522,888. Since the market value of the portfolio is $240,220,000, this means that the percentage change in the value of the portfolio for a 100-basis-point change in interest rates is 5.21% ($12,522,888/$240,220,000). Since duration is the approximate percentage change in value for a 100-basis-point change in interest rates, we can see that the portfolio duration is 5.21%, the same duration obtained from using Equation (3).

To appreciate why it is helpful to know the portfolio dollar duration, suppose that the portfolio manager wants to change the current duration of 5.21 for the 10-bond portfolio to a duration of 4. What this means is that the portfolio manager wants a dollar duration of 4% of $240,220,000 or $9,608,800. But the current portfolio duration is $12,522,888. To get the portfolio to 4, the portfolio manager must get rid of $2,914,088 ($12,522,888 − $9,608,800). To do this, the portfolio manager, if authorized to use interest rate derivatives, will take a position in one or more derivatives whose dollar duration is −$2,914,088.

Portfolio managers commonly assess their exposure to an issue in terms of the percentage of that issue in the portfolio. A better measure of exposure of an individual issue to changes in interest rates is in terms of its *contribution to portfolio duration*. This is found by multiplying the percentage that the individual issue is of the portfolio by the duration of the individual issue. That is,

$$\text{Contribution to portfolio duration} = \frac{\text{Market value of issue}}{\text{Market value of portfolio}} \times \text{Duration of issue.}$$

Note that the contribution to portfolio duration is simply the individual components in the portfolio duration formula given by Equation (3). In Table 2, the contribution to portfolio duration of each bond is shown in the fifth column.

While we show how to compute the contribution to portfolio duration for each bond in a portfolio, the same formula can be used to determine the contribution to portfolio duration for each bond sector represented in a portfolio.

Convexity, convexity measure, and convexity adjustment

As demonstrated earlier, the duration approximation indicates that regardless of whether interest rates increase or decrease, the approximate percentage price change is the same. However, this does not agree with Property 3 of a bond's price volatility. Specifically, while for small changes in yield the percentage price change will be the same for an increase or decrease in yield, for large changes in yield this is not true. This suggests that duration is only a good approximation of the percentage price change for a small change in yield.

The reason for this is that duration is in fact a first approximation for a small change in yield. The approximation can be improved by using a second approximation. This approximation is referred to as "convexity". The use of this term in the industry is unfortunate since the term convexity is also used to describe the shape or curvature of the price-yield relationship given by Figure 1 in the previous chapter. The convexity measure of a security can be used to approximate the change in price that is not explained by duration.

The convexity measure of a bond can be approximated using the following formula:

$$\text{Convexity measure} = \frac{V_+ + V_- - 2V_0}{2V_0(\Delta y)^2}, \tag{4}$$

where the notation is the same as used earlier for duration as given by Equation (1).

For our hypothetical 6%, 25-year bond selling to yield 9%, we know from Table 1 that for a 10-basis-point change in yield ($\Delta y = 0.001$): $V_0 = 70.3570$, $V_- = 71.1105$, and $V_+ = 69.6164$. Substituting these values into the convexity measure given by Equation (4), we obtain

$$\text{Convexity measure} = \frac{69.6164 + 71.1105 - 2(70.3570)}{2(703570)(0001)^2} = 91.67.$$

We will see how to use this convexity measure shortly. Before doing so, there are three points that should be noted. First, there is no simple interpretation of the convexity measure as there is for duration. Second, it is more common for market participants to refer to the value computed in Equation (4) as the "convexity of a bond" rather than the "convexity measure of a bond". Finally, the convexity measure reported by dealers and vendors will differ for an option-free bond. The reason is that the value obtained from Equation (4) will be scaled for the reason explained later.

The procedure for calculating the convexity measure for a portfolio is the same as for calculating a portfolio's duration. That is, the convexity measure for each bond in the portfolio is computed. Then the weighted average of the convexity measure for the bonds in the portfolio is computed to get the portfolio's convexity measure.

Given the convexity measure, the approximate percentage price change adjustment due to the bond's convexity (i.e., the percentage price change not explained by duration) is

$$\begin{aligned}&\text{Convexity adjustment to percentage price change}\\&\quad= \text{Convexity measure} \times (\Delta y)^2 \times 100.\end{aligned}$$

For example, for the 6%, 25-year bond selling to yield 9%, the convexity adjustment to the percentage price change based on duration if the yield increases from 9% to 11% is $91.67 \times (0.02)^2 \times 100 = 3.67\%$. If the yield decreases from 9% to 7%, the convexity adjustment to the approximate percentage price change based on duration would also be 3.67%.

The approximate percentage price change based on duration and the convexity adjustment is found by adding the two estimates. So, for example, if yields change from 9% to 11%, the estimated percentage price change would be

$$\begin{aligned}\text{Estimated change approximated by duration} &= -21.20\%\\ \text{Convexity adjustment} &= \underline{+\ 3.66\%}\\ \text{Total estimated percentage price change} &= -17.54\%.\end{aligned}$$

The actual percentage price change from Table 1 is −18.03%. Hence, the approximation has improved.

For a decrease of 200 basis points, from 9% to 7%, the approximate percentage price change would be as follows:

$$\begin{aligned}\text{Estimated change approximated by duration} &= +21.20\%\\ \text{Convexity adjustment} &= \underline{+\ 3.66\%}\\ \text{Total estimated percentage price change} &= +24.86\%.\end{aligned}$$

The actual percentage price change as can be seen from Table 1 is +25.46%. Once again, we see that duration combined with the convexity adjustment does a good job of estimating the sensitivity of a bond's price change to large changes in yield.

Note that when the convexity measure is positive, we have the situation described earlier that the gain is greater than the loss for a given large change in rates. As explained in the previous chapter, when a bond (or a bond portfolio) exhibits this behavior, it is said to exhibit positive convexity. We can see this in the example above. However, if the convexity measure is negative, we have the situation where the loss will be greater than the gain. When the loss is greater than the gain, a bond is said to exhibit negative convexity.

Positive convexity can be seen in Figures 1 and 2 in Chapter 15. Figure 1 shows the price-yield relationship for an option-free bond. Such a bond exhibits positive convexity for all yields. Figure 2 shows the price-yield relationship for a callable bond or a prepayable security. This type of bond exhibits positive convexity for a range of yields above the yield indicated by y_*. However, for yields below y_*, a callable bond or prepayable security exhibits negative convexity.

Standard convexity and effective convexity

The prices used in Equation (4) to calculate the convexity measure can be obtained by either assuming that when the yield changes, the expected cash flows do not change or they do change. In the former case, the resulting convexity is referred to as *standard convexity.* (Actually, in the industry, convexity is not qualified by the adjective "standard".) *Effective convexity,* in contrast, assumes that the cash flows do change when yields change. This is the same distinction made for duration.

As with duration, for bonds with embedded options, there can be quite a difference between the calculated standard convexity and effective convexity. In fact, for all option-free bonds, either convexity measure will have a positive value. For bonds with embedded options, the calculated effective convexity can be negative when the calculated modified convexity is positive.

Measuring Exposure to Yield Curve Changes: Key Rate Duration

As explained earlier, duration assumes that when interest rates change, all yields on the yield curve change by the same number of basis points. This is a problem when using duration for a portfolio that will typically have bonds with different maturities. Consequently, it is necessary to be able to measure the exposure of a bond or bond portfolio to shifts in the yield curve. There have been several approaches to measuring yield curve risk.

One way is to simply look at the cash flows of the portfolio. The most commonly used measure is *key rate duration* introduced by Ho [1992].[1]

The basic principle of key rate duration is to change the yield for a particular maturity of the yield curve and determine the sensitivity of either an individual bond or a portfolio to that change, holding all other yields constant. The sensitivity of the change in the bond's value or portfolio's value to a change in a specific maturity yield is called *rate duration*. There is a rate duration for every point on the yield curve. Consequently, there is no one rate duration. Rather, there is a set of durations representing each maturity on the yield curve. The total change in the value of a bond or a portfolio if all rates change by the same number of basis points is simply the duration of a bond or portfolio.

Ho's approach focuses on 11 key maturities of the Treasury yield curve. These rate durations are called key rate durations. The specific maturities on the spot rate curve for which a key rate duration are measured are 3 months, 1 year, 2 years, 3 years, 5 years, 7 years, 10 years, 15 years, 20 years, 25 years, and 30 years. Changes in rates between any two key rates are calculated using a linear approximation.

A key rate duration for a particular portfolio maturity should be interpreted as follows: Holding the yield for all other maturities constant, the key rate duration is the approximate percentage change in the value of a portfolio (or bond) for a 100-basis-point change in the yield for the individual maturity whose rate has been changed. Thus, a key rate duration is quantified by changing the yield of the maturity of interest and determining how the value or price changes. In fact, Equation (1) is used. The prices denoted by V_- and V_+ in the equation are the prices in the case of a bond and the portfolio values in the case of a bond portfolio found by holding all other interest rates constant and changing the yield for the maturity whose key rate duration is sought.

Credit Analytics

Credit risk encompasses two forms of risk: default risk and credit spread risk. *Default risk* is the risk that the issuer will fail to satisfy the terms of the

[1]Other measures of yield curve risk are suggested in Klaffky, Ma, and Nozari [1992] and Dattatreya and Fabozzi [1995].

obligation with respect to the timely payment of interest and repayment of the amount borrowed. To gauge default risk, investors rely on credit ratings assigned by credit rating agencies. *Credit spread risk* is the loss or underperformance of an issue or issues due to an increase in the credit spread.

Default risk

We begin our discussion of default risk with a brief description of the US bankruptcy process, creditor rights, and corporate bond default and recovery rates. We then explain the factors used by credit rating agencies in assigning a credit rating and that bond analysts use in gauging the default risk of corporate bonds.

Bankruptcy and creditor rights in the United States

The holder of a corporate debt instrument has priority over the equity owners in the case of bankruptcy of a corporation. There are creditors who have priority over other creditors. Here, we will provide an overview of the bankruptcy process and then look at what actually happens to creditors in bankruptcies. There is a federal law governing bankruptcies in the United States and this law is amended periodically. One purpose of the bankruptcy law is to set forth the rules for a corporation to be either liquidated or reorganized.

The *liquidation* of a corporation means that all the assets will be distributed to the holders of claims of the corporation and no corporate entity will survive. In a *reorganization*, a new corporate entity will result. Some holders of the claim of the bankrupt corporation will receive cash in exchange for their claims, others may receive new securities in the corporation that results from the reorganization, and others may receive a combination of both cash and new securities in the resulting corporation.

The US bankruptcy law comprises 15 chapters, each covering a particular type of bankruptcy. Of particular interest here are two of the chapters, Chapters 7 and 11. Chapter 7 deals with the liquidation of a company; Chapter 11 deals with the reorganization of a company.

When a company is liquidated, creditors receive distributions based on the *absolute priority rule* to the extent assets are available. The absolute priority rule is the principle that senior creditors are paid in full before junior creditors are paid anything. For secured creditors and unsecured creditors, the absolute priority rule guarantees their seniority to equity holders. In liquidations, the absolute priority rule generally holds. In contrast, there is a good body of literature that argues that strict absolute priority has not been upheld by the courts nor the Securities and Exchange Commission (SEC). Studies of actual reorganizations in Chapter 11 bankruptcies have found that the violation of absolute priority is the rule rather than the exception.

Consequently, while investors in the debt of a corporation may feel that they have priority over the equity owners and priority over other classes of debtors, the actual outcome of a bankruptcy may be far different from what the terms of the debt agreement state.

Default loss rate and recovery rate

There is a good deal of research published on default rates by credit rating agencies and academics. From an investment perspective, default rates by themselves are not of paramount significance: It is perfectly possible for a portfolio of corporate bonds to suffer defaults and to outperform Treasuries at the same time, provided the yield spread of the portfolio is sufficiently high to offset the losses from defaults. Furthermore, because holders of defaulted bonds typically recover a percentage of the face amount of their investment, the default loss rate can be substantially lower than the default rate. The default loss rate is defined as follows:

$$\text{Default loss rate} = \text{Default rate} \times (100\% - \text{Recovery rate}).$$

For instance, a default rate of 5% and a recovery rate of 30% mean a default loss rate of only 3.5% (70% of 5%).

Therefore, focusing exclusively on default rates merely highlights the worst possible outcome that a diversified portfolio of corporate bonds would suffer, assuming all defaulted bonds would be totally worthless.

There have been several studies of default rates, particularly for high-yield corporate bonds, and the reported findings at times appear to be significantly different. The differences in the reported default rates are due to the different approaches used by researchers to measure default rates. The differences in reported default rates are not as great as they might first appear once methodologies employed in these studies are standardized.

Several studies have found that the recovery rate is closely related to the bond's seniority. However, seniority is not the only factor that affects recovery values. In general, recovery values will vary with the types of assets and competitive conditions of the firm, as well as the economic environment at the time of bankruptcy. In addition, recovery rates will also vary across industries.

Factors considered in rating corporate bond issues

In conducting its examination of corporate bond issues, the credit rating agencies, as well as bond analysts, consider the "four Cs of credit": character, capacity, collateral, and covenants. The meaning of each is as follows:

- *Character* of management is the foundation of sound credit. This includes the ethical reputation as well as the business qualifications and operating record of the board of directors, management, and executives responsible for the use of the borrowed funds and repayment of those funds.
- *Capacity* is the ability of an issuer to repay its obligations.
- *Collateral* is looked at not only in the traditional sense of assets pledged to secure the debt, but also to the quality and value of those unpledged assets controlled by the issuer. In both senses, the collateral is capable of supplying additional aid, comfort, and support to the debt and the debtholder. Assets form the basis for the generation of cash flow, which services the debt in good times as well as bad.
- *Covenants* set forth restrictions on how management operates the company and conducts its financial affairs. Covenants can restrict management's discretion. A default or violation of any covenant may provide a meaningful early warning alarm, enabling investors to take positive and corrective action before the situation deteriorates further. Covenants have value as they play an important part in minimizing risk to creditors. They help prevent the unconscionable transfer of wealth from debt holders to equity holders.

Character analysis involves the analysis of the quality of management. Moody's, for example, assesses management quality by looking at the business strategies and policies formulated by management. The following factors are considered: (1) strategic direction, (2) financial philosophy, (3) conservatism, (4) track record, (5) succession planning, and (6) control systems.

In assessing the ability of an issuer to pay, an analysis of the financial statements is undertaken. In addition to management quality, Moody's, for example, looks at (1) industry trends, (2) the regulatory environment, (3) basic operating and competitive position, (4) financial position and sources of liquidity, (5) company structure (including structural subordination and priority of claim), (6) parent company support agreements, and (7) special event risk.

In considering industry trends, the credit rating agencies look at the vulnerability of the company to economic cycles, the barriers to entry, and the exposure of the company to technological changes. The credit rating agencies look at the capacity of a firm to obtain additional financing and backup credit facilities. There are various forms of backup facilities.

A corporate debt obligation can be secured or unsecured. In our discussion of creditor rights in a bankruptcy discussed earlier, we explained that in the case of a liquidation, proceeds from a bankruptcy are distributed to creditors based on the absolute priority rule. However, in the case of a reorganization, the absolute priority rule rarely holds. That is, unsecured creditors may receive distributions for the entire amount of their claim and common stockholders may receive something, while secured creditors may receive only a portion of their claim. The reason is that a reorganization requires approval of all the parties. Consequently, secured creditors are willing to negotiate with both unsecured creditors and stockholders in order to obtain approval of the plan of reorganization.

Covenants deal with limitations and restrictions on the borrower's activities. *Affirmative covenants* call on the debtor to make promises to do certain things. *Negative covenants* are those that require the borrower not to take certain actions.

Downgrade risk

Investors gauge the default risk of an issue by looking at the credit ratings assigned to issues by the credit rating agencies. Once a credit rating is assigned to a debt obligation, a credit rating agency monitors the credit quality of the issuer and can reassign a different credit rating. An improvement in the credit quality of an issue or issuer is rewarded with a better credit rating, referred to as a *credit upgrade*; a deterioration in the credit rating of an issue or issuer is penalized by the assignment of an inferior credit rating, referred to as a *credit downgrade*. The actual or anticipated downgrading of an issue or issuer increases the credit spread and results in a decline in the price of the issue or the issuer's bonds. This risk is referred to as *downgrade risk* and is closely related to credit spread risk. A credit rating agency may announce in advance that it is reviewing a particular credit rating and may go further and state that the review is a precursor to a possible downgrade or upgrade. This announcement is referred to as "putting the issue under credit watch".

Occasionally, the ability of an issuer to make interest and principal payments changes seriously and unexpectedly because of an unforeseen event. This can include any number of idiosyncratic events that are specific to the corporation or to an industry, including a natural or industrial accident, a pandemic, a regulatory change, a takeover or corporate restructuring, or even corporate fraud. This risk is referred to generically as *event risk* and will result in a downgrading of the issuer by the credit rating agencies. Because the price of the entity's securities will typically change dramatically or jump in price, this risk is sometimes referred to as *jump risk.*

Rating migration (transition) table

The credit rating agencies periodically publish, in the form of a table, information about how issues that they have rated have changed over time. This table is called a *rating migration table* or *rating transition table.* The table is useful for asset managers to assess potential downgrades (and therefore downgrade risk) and potential upgrades. A rating migration table is available for different lengths of time. Table 3 shows a hypothetical rating migration table for a 1-year period. The first column shows the ratings at the start of the year, and the other columns show the ratings at the end of the year.

Let's interpret one of the numbers. Look at the cell where the rating at the beginning of the year is AA and the rating at the end of the year is AA. This cell represents the percentage of issues rated AA at the beginning of the year that did not receive a change their rating over the year. That is,

TABLE 3: Hypothetical 1-Year Rating Migration Table

Rating at End of Year	**AAA**	**AA**	**A**	**BBB**	**BB**	**B**	**CCC**	**D**	**Total**
AAA	93.20	6.00	0.60	0.12	0.08	0.00	0.00	0.00	100
AA	1.60	92.75	5.07	0.36	0.11	0.07	0.03	0.01	100
A	0.18	2.65	91.91	4.80	0.37	0.02	0.02	0.05	100
BBB	0.04	0.30	5.20	87.70	5.70	0.70	0.16	0.20	100
BB	0.03	0.11	0.61	6.80	81.65	7.10	2.60	1.10	100
B	0.01	0.09	0.55	0.88	7.90	75.67	8.70	6.20	100
CCC	0.00	0.01	0.31	0.84	2.30	8.10	62.54	25.90	100

there were no downgrades or upgrades. As can be seen, 92.75% of the issues rated AA at the start of the year were rated AA at the end of the year. Now look at the cell where the rating at the beginning of the year is AA and at the end of the year is A. This shows the percentage of issues rated AA at the beginning of the year that were downgraded to A by the end of the year. In our hypothetical 1-year rating migration table, this percentage is 5.07%. One can view this figure as a probability. It is the probability that an issue rated AA will be downgraded to A by the end of the year.

A rating migration table also shows the potential for upgrades. Again, using Table 3, look at the row that shows issues rated AA at the beginning of the year. Looking at the cell shown in the column AAA rating at the end of the year, there is the value 1.60%. This figure represents the percentage of issues rated AA at the beginning of the year that were upgraded to AAA by the end of the year.

In general, the following hold for actual rating migration tables. First, the probability of a downgrade is much higher than an upgrade for investment-grade bonds. Second, the longer the migration period, the lower the probability that an issuer will retain its original rating. That is, a 1-year rating migration table will have a lower probability of a downgrade or upgrade for a particular rating than a 5-year rating migration table for that same rating.

Credit spread risk

The credit spread is the premium over the U.S. Treasury yield required by the market for taking on a certain credit exposure. The benchmark is often the on-the-run US Treasury issue for the given maturity. The higher the credit rating, the smaller the credit spread to the benchmark rate, all other factors being constant. *Credit spread risk* is the risk of financial loss resulting from changes in the level of credit spreads used in the marking-to-market of a debt instrument. Changes in market credit spreads affect the value of the portfolio and can lead to losses for traders or underperformance relative to a benchmark for portfolio managers.

Spread duration

Duration is a measure of the change in the value of a bond when rates change. The interest rate that is assumed to shift is the Treasury rate. However, for non-Treasury securities, the yield is equal to the Treasury yield plus a spread to the Treasury yield curve. The price of a bond exposed to credit risk can change even though Treasury yields are unchanged because the spread required by the market changes. A measure of how a non-Treasury issue's price would change if the spread sought by the market changes is called *spread duration*. The contribution to the spread duration of a portfolio can also be computed using the spread duration of an issue in Equation (3). For example, a spread duration of 2.2 for a security means that if the Treasury rate is unchanged but spreads change by 100 basis points, the security's price will change by approximately 2.2%.

Spread duration is calculated using the same formula as calculated for duration using Equation (1). A portfolio spread duration can be calculated and a contribution to spread duration can be computed in the same way as portfolio duration and contribution to portfolio duration that were explained earlier in this chapter.

Key Points

- For very small changes in the required yield, the percentage price change for a given bond is roughly the same, regardless of whether the required yield increases or decreases.
- For large changes in the required yield, the percentage price change is not the same for an increase in the required yield as it is for a decrease in the required yield.
- For a large change in basis points, the percentage price increase for an option-free bond is greater than the percentage price decrease.
- Two characteristics of a bond impact its interest rate risk: coupon rate and maturity.
- A bond's price volatility is affected by the level of interest rates in the economy: the higher the level of yields, the lower a bond's price volatility.
- There are two measures of interest rate risk assuming interest rates shift in a parallel fashion across maturities: (1) price value of a basis point and (2) duration and convexity.
- The price value of a basis point measures the change in the price of the bond if the required yield changes by 1 basis point.
- Duration is the most commonly used measure of the interest rate risk exposure of a portfolio or a trading position.
- Duration is only a first approximation of the percentage change of a bond's value or bond portfolio's value when interest rates change.

- Dollar duration is the dollar price change of a bond measured by multiplying duration by the full dollar price and the change in yield.
- Modified duration is the approximate percentage change in a bond's price for a 100-basis-point change in interest rates, assuming that the bond's cash flows do not change when interest rates change.
- Modified duration is related to Macaulay duration and practically speaking, there is very little difference in the computed values for modified duration and Macaulay duration.
- For bonds with embedded options where the cash flow can change when interest rates change, the duration measure that should be used is effective duration.
- Portfolio duration is computed by calculating the weighted average of the duration of the bonds in the portfolio.
- To assess the interest rate risk exposure of a bond in a portfolio, the contribution to portfolio duration measure is used.
- The convexity measure combined with duration can improve the approximation of how a bond or portfolio reacts to changes in interest rates.
- To measure the exposure of a bond or bond portfolio to a change in the yield curve, rate duration can be used.
- Key rate duration measures the exposure of a bond or a portfolio to a change in key interest rates on the yield curve.
- Credit risk encompasses two forms of risk: default risk and credit spread risk.
- Default risk is the risk that the issuer will fail to satisfy the terms of the obligation with respect to the timely payment of interest and repayment of the amount borrowed.
- To gauge default risk, investors rely on analysis performed by credit ratings assigned by credit rating agencies.
- There is a federal law governing bankruptcies in the United States which covers liquidations and reorganizations of corporations.
- The liquidation of a corporation means that all the assets will be distributed to the holders of claims of the corporation and no corporate entity will survive.
- In a reorganization, a new corporate entity will result with some holders of the claim of the bankrupt corporation receiving cash in exchange for their claims, others may receive new securities in the corporation that results from the reorganization, and others may receive a combination of both cash and new securities in the resulting corporation.

- When a company is liquidated, creditors receive distributions based on the absolute priority rule to the extent that assets are available.
- The absolute priority rule is the principle that senior creditors are paid in full before junior creditors are paid anything.
- For secured creditors and unsecured creditors, the absolute priority rule guarantees their seniority to equity holders.
- In liquidations, the absolute priority rule generally holds while strict absolute priority has not been upheld by the courts in the case of a reorganization.
- Holders of defaulted bonds typically recover a percentage of the face value of their investment; the default loss rate can be substantially lower than the default rate.
- The default loss rate is defined as the product of the default rate and one minus the recovery rate.
- In conducting its examination of corporate bond issues, credit rating agencies, as well as bond analysts, consider the "four Cs of credit": character, capacity, collateral, and covenants.
- Character analysis involves the analysis of the quality of management.
- Covenants deal with limitations and restrictions on the borrowers activities: affirmative covenants call on the debtor to make promises to do certain things while negative covenants are those that require the borrower not to take certain actions.
- Once a credit rating is assigned to a debt obligation, a credit rating agency monitors the credit quality of the issuer and can reassign a different credit rating.
- A credit downgrade occurs when a credit rating agency reduces the credit rating of a bond issue.
- Downgrade risk is the risk that a bond issue will be downgraded.
- A rating migration table is published by credit rating agencies periodically and shows, over some time period, the percentage of issues that are upgraded, downgraded, and unchanged.
- A rating migration table is useful for asset managers to assess potential downgrades and therefore downgrade risk.
- The credit spread is the premium over the U.S. Treasury rates required by the market for taking on a certain assumed credit exposure.
- Credit spread risk is the loss or underperformance of an issue or issues due to an increase in the credit spread.

- Spread duration is a measure of how a non-Treasury issue's price would change if the spread sought by the market changes and is a proxy for credit spread risk.

References

Dattatreya, R. E. and F. J. Fabozzi, 1995. "The risk point method for measuring and controlling yield curve risk," *Financial Analysts Journal*, 51(4): 45–54.

Ho, T. 1992. "Key rate durations measures of interest rate risks," *Journal of Fixed Income*, 2(2): 29–44.

Klaffky, T. E., Y. Y. Ma, and Ardavan Nozari, 1992. "Managing yield curve exposure: Introducing reshaping durations," *Journal of Fixed Income*, 2(3): 1–15.

Macaulay, F., 1938. *Some Theoretical Problems Suggested by the Movement of Interest Rates, Bond Yields, and Stock Prices since 1856*. New York: National Bureau of Research.

Chapter 17

Bond Portfolio Strategies

Learning Objectives

After reading this chapter, you will understand:

- the spectrum of bond portfolio management strategies;
- the risk factors associated with managing a portfolio against an index;
- the difficulties of bond indexing;
- the different forms of enhanced indexing;
- how multifactor risk models can be used to manage a bond portfolio;
- what value-added strategies are in managing a bond portfolio;
- the different types of value-added strategies: interest rate expectations strategies, yield curve strategies, inter- and intra-sector allocation strategies;
- what barbell, ladder, and bullet portfolios are; and
- the different types of liability-driven strategies.

In this chapter, bond portfolio strategies are discussed, drawing on the portfolio analytics described in Chapters 15 and 16. We begin with the spectrum of strategies.

The Spectrum of Bond Portfolio Strategies

A good way to understand the spectrum of bond portfolio strategies and the key elements of each strategy is in terms of the benchmark established by the client. This is depicted in Figure 1. The figure, developed by Volpert [1997] of the Vanguard Group, shows the risk and return of a bond strategy versus a benchmark. He classifies the strategies as follows:

- Pure bond index matching;
- Enhanced indexing/matching primary risk factors approach;
- Enhanced indexing/minor risk factor mismatches;

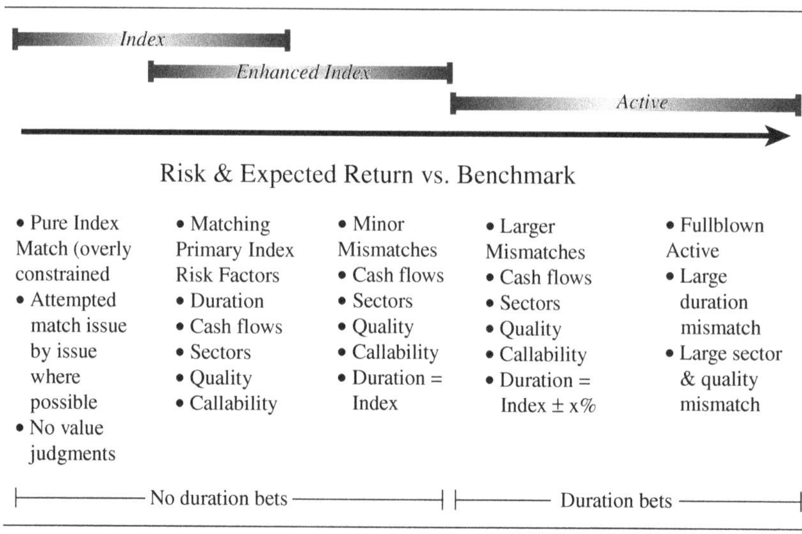

FIGURE 1: Bond Management Risk Spectrum
Source: Exhibit 1 in Volpert [1997, p. 192].

- Active management/larger risk factor mismatches;
- Active/full-blown active management.

The difference between indexing and active management is the extent to which the portfolio can deviate from the primary risk factors that impact the performance of an index.

The primary risk factors associated with an index are as follows:

- The duration of the index.
- The present value distribution of the cash flows;
- Percent in sector and quality;
- Duration contribution of sector;
- Duration contribution of credit quality;
- Sector/coupon/maturity cell weights;
- Issuer exposure control.

The first primary risk factor deals with the sensitivity of the value of the index to a parallel shift in interest rates. The first three strategies listed earlier do not allow for any deviation of the bond's portfolio duration from the duration of the index. The last two strategies allow the duration of the portfolio to deviate from the index. That is, these two bond portfolio strategies allow for duration bets. The second factor is important for controlling the yield curve risk associated with an index.

Pure Bond Indexing Strategy

In terms of risk and return, a *pure bond indexing strategy* involves the least risk in terms of underperforming the index. Several factors explain the popularity of *bond indexing*. First, the empirical evidence suggests that, historically, the overall performance of active bond managers has been poor. The second factor is the lower advisory management fees for an indexed portfolio compared to active management advisory fees. Advisory fees charged by active managers typically range from 15 to 50 basis points. The range for indexed portfolios, in contrast, is 1 to 20 basis points (with the upper range representing the fees for enhanced indexing discussed later). Some pension plan sponsors have decided to do away with advisory fees and to manage some or all of their funds in-house following an indexing strategy. Lower non-advisory fees, such as custodial fees, is the third explanation for the popularity of bond indexing.

Critics of indexing point out that while an indexing strategy matches the performance of some index, the performance of that index does not necessarily represent optimal performance. Moreover, matching an index does not mean that the manager will satisfy a client's return requirement objective. For example, if the objective of a life insurance company or a pension fund is to have sufficient funds to satisfy a predetermined liability, indexing only reduces the likelihood that performance will not be materially worse than the index. The return on the index is not necessarily related to the liability.

The pure bond indexing strategy involves creating a portfolio so as to replicate the issues comprising the index. This means that the indexed portfolio is a mirror image of the index. However, a manager pursuing this strategy will encounter several logistical problems in constructing an indexed portfolio. First of all, the prices for each issue used by the organization that publishes the index may not be execution prices available to the manager. In fact, they may be materially different from the prices offered by some dealers. In addition, the prices used by organizations reporting the value of indexes are based on bid prices. The ask prices of dealers, however, are the ones that the manager would have to transact at when constructing or rebalancing the indexed portfolio. Thus, there will be a bias between the performance of the index and the indexed portfolio that is equal to the bid–ask spread.

Furthermore, there are logistical problems unique to certain sectors in the bond market. Consider first the corporate bond market. There are typically about 5,000 issues in the corporate bond sector of a broad-based bond market index. Because of the illiquidity of many of the issues, not only may the prices used by the organization that publishes the index be unreliable but also many of the issues may not even be available. Next, consider the mortgage sector. There are over 800,000 agency pass-through issues. The organizations that publish indexes aggregate all these issues into a few hundred generic issues. The manager is then faced with the difficult task of finding agency pass-through securities with the same risk–return profile of these hypothetical generic issues.

Finally, recall from Chapter 15 that the total return depends on the reinvestment rate available on interim cash flows received prior to month end. If the organization publishing the index regularly overestimates the reinvestment rate, then the indexed portfolio could underperform the index.

Enhanced Indexing/Matching Primary Risk Factors Approach

An *enhanced indexing strategy* can be pursued so as to construct a portfolio to match the primary risk factors without acquiring each issue in the index. This is a common strategy used by funds because of the difficulties of acquiring all of the issues comprising the index. Generally speaking, the fewer the number of issues used to replicate the index, the smaller the tracking error due to transaction costs, but the greater the tracking error risk because of the difficulties of matching the primary risk factors perfectly. In contrast, the more issues purchased to replicate the index, the greater the tracking error due to transaction costs, but the smaller the tracking error risk due to the mismatch of the primary factors between the indexed portfolio and the index.

There are two methodologies used to construct a portfolio to replicate an index: the stratified sampling and the optimization approach. Both approaches assume that the performance of an individual bond depends on a number of systematic factors that affect the performance of all bonds and on a factor unique to the individual issue. This last risk is diversifiable risk. The objective of the two approaches is to construct an indexed portfolio that eliminates this diversifiable risk.

Stratified sampling approach

With the stratified sampling approach (also referred to as the cellular approach) to indexing, the index is divided into cells representing the primary risk factors. The objective is then to select from all of the issues in the index, one or more issues in each cell that can be used to represent that entire cell. The total dollar amount of the issues purchased from each cell will be based on the percentage of the index's total market value that the cell represents. For example, if X% of the market value of all the issues in the index is made up of corporate bonds, then X% of the market value of the indexed portfolio should be composed of corporate bond issues.

The number of cells that the indexer uses will depend on the dollar amount of the portfolio to be indexed. In indexing a portfolio of less than $50 million, for example, using a large number of cells would require purchasing odd lots of issues. This increases the cost of buying the issues to represent a cell, and thus would increase the tracking error risk. Reducing the number of cells to overcome this problem will also result in an increase in tracking error risk. This is because the major risk factors of the indexed portfolio may differ materially from those of the index.

Optimization approach

In the optimization approach, the manager seeks to design an indexed portfolio that will match the cell breakdown as just described and also satisfy other constraints, but also optimize some objective. An objective might be to maximize convexity or to maximize expected total returns or to minimize tracking error. Constraints, other than matching the cell breakdown, might include not purchasing more than a specified amount of one issuer or group of issuers within the same sector.

The computational technique used to derive the optimal solution to the indexing problem in this approach is mathematical programming.[1] When the objective function that the manager seeks to optimize is a linear function, linear programming (a specific form of mathematical programming) is used. If the objective function is quadratic, then the particular mathematical programming technique used is quadratic programming. When the object is to minimize tracking error in constructing the indexed portfolio, because tracking error is a quadratic function (the difference between the

[1] See Chapter 6 in the companion book.

benchmark return and the indexed portfolio's return, squared), quadratic programming is used to find the optimal indexed portfolio.

Although on the surface the stratified sampling approach is easier to use than the optimization approach, it is extremely difficult to implement the stratified sampling approach when large, diversified portfolios are taken as the benchmark. In this case, many cells are required, and the problem becomes complex. Also, because the handpicking of issues to match each cell is subjective, large tracking errors may result. Mathematical programming reduces the complexity of the problem when well-defined constraints are employed, allowing the manager to analyze large quantities of data optimally.

Enhanced Indexing/Minor Risk Factor Mismatches

Another enhanced strategy is one where the portfolio is constructed so as to have minor deviations from the risk factors that affect the performance of the index. For example, there might be a slight overweighting of issues or sectors where the manager believes there is relative value. However, it is important to point out that the duration of the constructed portfolio is matched to the duration of the index.

Active Management/Larger Risk Factor Mismatches

Active bond strategies are those that attempt to outperform the market by intentionally constructing a portfolio that will have a greater index mismatch than in the case of enhanced indexing. The decision to pursue an active strategy or to engage a client to request a portfolio manager to pursue an active strategy must be based on the belief that there is some type of gain from such costly efforts; for there to be a gain, pricing inefficiencies must exist. The particular strategy chosen depends on why the portfolio manager believes this is the case.

Volpert [1997] classifies two types of active strategies. In the more conservative of the two active strategies, the portfolio manager makes fewer mismatches relative to the index in terms of risk factors. This includes minor mismatches of duration. Typically, there will be a limitation as to the degree of duration mismatch. For example, the portfolio manager may be constrained to be within ± 1 of the duration of the index. So, if the duration of the index is 4, the portfolio manager may have a duration between 3 and 5. To take advantage of an anticipated reshaping of the yield curve, there can be significant differences in the cash flow distribution between the index and the portfolio constructed by the manager. As another example, if the portfolio manager believes that within the corporate sector issues rated A will outperform issues rated AA, the portfolio manager may overweight the A issues and underweight AA issues.

Active/Full-Blown Active Management

In the full-blown active management case, the portfolio manager is permitted to make a significant duration bet without any constraint. The portfolio manager can have a duration of zero (i.e., be all in cash) or can leverage the portfolio to achieve a high multiple of the duration of the index. The portfolio manager can decide not to invest in one or more of the major sectors of the broad-based bond market indexes. The portfolio manager can make a significant allocation to sectors not included in the index. For example, there can be a substantial allocation to non-agency mortgage-backed securities. We discuss various strategies used in active portfolio management in the next section.

Managing a Bond Portfolio Using Factor Models

Factor-based investing is used in equity portfolio management and to a lesser extent in bond portfolio management. Factor models allow an asset manager to construct optimal portfolios based on specified metrics and constraints, control factor exposure, and rebalance a portfolio to minimize transaction costs.[2] In the companion book, Chapter 16 provides an illustration of using factor models in bond portfolio management.

Factor models identify the common or systematic risk factors in a bond portfolio. The risks not captured by the systematic risk factors are called the idiosyncratic risk factors or security-specific risks. The systematic risk factors are then classified as risks that influence all bonds and those risks that affect particular sectors within an asset class. For example, yield curve risk affects the entire asset class of bonds. Prepayment risk, in contrast, affects only securitized products.

[2]For a more detailed description of the use of multifactor models in bond portfolio management, see Lazanas, Baldaque da Silva, Găbudean, and Staal. [2011].

In equity factor models, there are several approaches to estimate the sensitivity of a security to the risk factors. In bond factor models, the sensitivity to risk factors is typically estimated using cross-sectional returns on bond issues. The projected risk of a portfolio is measured relative to that of a benchmark selected by the client. It begins by looking at the exposure of an issue in the portfolio and the exposure of the same issue in the benchmark. The difference in the exposures is then used as a weight to calculate the exposure of an issue to each risk factor. For a given risk factor, the aggregate exposure to the factor is then calculated. This gives the risk exposure of the portfolio to that risk factor. This is done for each risk factor. Also considered in determining the risk exposure of the portfolio to each risk factor is the volatility of that factor and the correlation between risk factors.

Given the total risk of the portfolio and the systematic risks, the portfolio's idiosyncratic risk can be computed. Because there may be more than 5,000 issues in an index that is used as the benchmark while far fewer issues are included in the portfolio, idiosyncratic risk can be high. The idiosyncratic risk can be due to high exposure to a specific company or to a particular sector.

The risk exposure of portfolios based on factor models is measured in terms of tracking error. An indexed portfolio, for example, would have a tracking error that is close to zero. Factor models can be used to create portfolios with the desired risk exposure to each risk factor.

Value-Added Strategies

Active bond portfolio strategies and enhanced indexing/minor risk factor mismatch strategies seek to generate additional return after adjusting for risk. This additional return is popularly referred to as alpha. We shall refer to these strategies as value-added strategies. These strategies can be classified as strategic strategies and tactical strategies.

Strategic strategies, sometimes referred to as *top-down value-added strategies*, involve the following:

1. Interest rate expectations strategies;
2. Yield curve strategies;
3. Inter- and intra-sector allocation strategies.

Tactical strategies, sometimes referred to as *relative value strategies*, are short-term trading strategies. They include:

1. Strategies based on rich/cheap analysis;
2. Yield curve trading strategies;
3. Return enhancing strategies employing futures and options.

Below we discuss these strategies. In addition, there are strategies involving futures and options for potentially adding incremental return.

To help understand strategic strategies, we will use a proposed bond portfolio that a portfolio manager is considering constructing. The proposed portfolio is shown in Table 1. Note that the portfolio is not shown in terms of market value but instead it is in terms of dollar duration, an analytical measure that we described in Chapter 16. The benchmark is a broad-based bond market index.

Interest Rate Expectations Strategies

Portfolio managers who believe that they can accurately forecast the future level of interest rates will alter the portfolio's duration based on their forecast. Because duration is a measure of interest rate sensitivity, this involves increasing a portfolio's duration if interest rates are expected to fall and reducing duration if interest rates are expected to rise. For those portfolio managers whose benchmark is a bond market index, this means increasing the portfolio duration relative to the duration of the benchmark index if interest rates are expected to fall and reducing it if interest rates are expected to rise. The degree to which the duration of the managed portfolio is permitted to diverge from that of the benchmark index may be limited by the client. Interest rate expectations strategies are commonly referred to as *duration strategies*.

A portfolio's duration may be altered in the cash market by swapping (or exchanging) bonds in the portfolio for other bonds that will achieve the target portfolio duration. Alternatively, a more efficient means for altering the duration of a bond portfolio is to use interest rate futures contracts or interest rate swaps. As we explain in Chapter 18, buying futures increases a portfolio's duration, while selling futures decreases it.

The key to this active strategy is, of course, the ability to forecast the direction of future interest rates. The academic literature does not support the view that interest rates can be forecasted so that risk-adjusted excess

TABLE 1: Proposed Bond Portfolio (Values shown on a Duration-Weighted Basis)

Benchmark: Broad-Based Investment-Grade Bond Market Index
Portfolio duration: 4.91 Index duration: 4.81
Portfolio spread duration: 3.80 Index spread duration: 3.66

Approx. Maturity/ Duration	Percent of Market Value by Duration Range												% Over-(+)/ Under Weight(-)	Contribution to						% Over-(+)/ Under Weight(-)
	0–2		2–4		4–7		7–9		9+		Total			Effective Duration			Spread Duration			
	Index	Rec.	Index	Rec.	Index	Rec.	Index	Rec.	Index	Rec.	Index	Rec.		Index	Rec.	Diff.	Index	Rec.	Diff.	
Treasury	5.96	5.05	4.40	0.00	5.67	8.34	2.67	2.38	3.25	1.52	21.95	17.29	–21	1.11	0.95	−0.16	0.00	0.00	0.00	—
Agency	3.55	0.00	3.08	5.37	2.17	4.64	0.60	0.84	0.50	0.00	9.89	10.85	10	0.35	0.43	0.09	0.35	0.40	0.05	16
Mtg.Pass-throughs	2.95	0.05	16.72	14.16	19.29	29.70	0.00	0.00	0.0	0.00	38.95	43.91	13	1.62	1.99	0.37	1.58	2.04	0.46	29
CMBS	0.47	0.00	1.18	0.00	3.35	5.02	0.02	0.00	0.00	0.00	5.02	5.02	0	0.24	0.32	0.09	0.23	0.31	0.08	36
ABS	0.24	0.38	0.31	0.27	0.16	0.09	0.06	0.03	0.01	0.00	0.78	0.78	0	0.03	0.02	−0.28	1.48	1.03	−0.45	–30
Credit	2.00	5.78	6.23	6.85	7.16	5.29	2.90	1.15	5.11	3.11	23.41	22.17	–5	1.47	1.19	−0.28	1.48	1.03	−0.45	–30
Total	15.16	11.26	31.92	26.64	37.80	53.07	6.25	4.41	8.87	4.63	100.00	100.00		4.81	4.91	0.10	3.66	3.80	0.15	4
%Over -(+)/Under weight(-)	–26		–17		40		–29		–48											

returns can be consistently realized. It is doubtful whether betting on future interest rates will provide a consistently superior return.

For the proposed portfolio in Table 1, the portfolio duration is 4.91 and the index duration is 4.81. That is, the portfolio duration is 1.02% of the index, so basically the recommended portfolio is pretty much market neutral.

Yield Curve Strategies

The yield curve for US Treasury securities shows the relationship between maturity and yield. The shape of the yield curve changes over time. A shift in the yield curve refers to the relative change in the yield for each Treasury maturity. A parallel shift in the yield curve refers to a shift in which the change in the yield for all maturities is the same. A non-parallel shift in the yield curve means that the yield for every maturity does not change by the same number of basis points.

Top-down yield curve strategies involve positioning a portfolio to capitalize on expected changes in the shape of the Treasury yield curve. There are three yield curve strategies: (1) bullet strategies, (2) barbell strategies, and (3) ladder strategies. In a *bullet strategy*, the portfolio is constructed so that the maturity of the bonds included in the portfolio is highly concentrated at one point on the yield curve. In a *barbell strategy*, the maturity of the bonds included in the portfolio is concentrated at two extreme maturities. Actually, in practice when managers refer to a barbell strategy, it is relative to a bullet strategy. For example, a bullet strategy might be to create a portfolio with maturities concentrated around 10 years while a corresponding barbell strategy might be a portfolio with 5-year and 20-year maturities. In a *ladder strategy* the portfolio is constructed to have approximately equal amounts of each maturity. So, for example, a portfolio might have equal amounts of bonds with one year to maturity, two years to maturity, and so on.

Each of these strategies will result in different performance when the yield curve shifts. The actual performance will depend on both the type of shift and the magnitude of the shift. Thus, no general statements can be made about the optimal yield curve strategy.

When this strategy is applied by a portfolio manager whose benchmark is a broad-based bond market index, there is a mismatching of maturities relative to the index in one or more of the bond sectors. This can be seen in Table 1, the proposed portfolio is underweighted on the sectors with less than four years to maturity as well as the sectors with greater than seven years to maturity. That is, the short and long ends of the yield curve are underweighted relative to the index. The four- to seven-year maturity sector is overweighted. The proposed portfolio is constructed to be more like a bullet portfolio than the index.

Inter- and Intra-sector Allocation Strategies

A manager can allocate funds among the major bond sectors that is different from that of the allocation in the index. This is referred to as an *inter-sector allocation strategy.* For example, Table 2 shows the portfolio allocation on a duration-weighted basis by sector for the proposed portfolio versus the index. As can be seen, there is an underweighting of the Treasury sector and the credit sector and an overweighting of the agency and mortgage sectors. The portfolio is neutral relative to the index with respect to the CMBS and ABS sectors.

Several duration measures that we discussed in Chapter 16 and showed in Table 2 provide us with information about the level of exposure to spread risk. First is the difference in the spread duration between the index (3.66) and the proposed portfolio (3.80). The spread duration for the proposed portfolio is 104% of that of the index. The second is the difference in the contribution to spread duration for each sector in the index and the corresponding sector in the proposed portfolio.

In an intra-sector allocation strategy, the portfolio manager's allocation of funds within a sector differs from that of the index. Suppose that the intra-sector allocation for the credit sector (corporate sector) is as shown in Table 2. Once again, the values in the table are in terms of contribution to spread duration. They are shown for each credit quality and by sector (financial, utility, industrials, and non-corporates).

Next, we discuss factors that managers consider in making inter- and intra-sector allocations.

Considerations in inter- and intra-sector allocations

In making inter- and intra-sector allocations, a portfolio manager is anticipating how spreads will change. Spreads reflect differences in credit risk, call risk (or prepayment risk), and liquidity risk. When the spread for a particular sector or subsector is expected to decline or "narrow," a portfolio manager may decide to overweight that particular sector or subsector. It will

TABLE 2: Corporate Sector Allocation for the Proposed Bond Portfolio in Terms of Contribution to Spread Duration

	Aaa-Aa			A			Baa			Total			%Over(+)/
	Index	**Rec.**	**Diff.**	**Index**	**Rec.**	**Diff.**	**Index**	**Rec.**	**Diff.**	**Index**	**Rec.**	**Diff.**	**Underweight(-)**
Spread Duration													
0–3	0.11	0.06	−0.05	0.03	0.07	0.04	0.02	0.03	0.00	0.17	0.16	−0.01	−6
3–5	0.09	0.07	−0.02	0.07	0.20	0.13	0.07	0.06	−0.01	0.23	0.32	0.10	43
5–7	0.07	0.00	−0.07	0.10	0.15	0.05	0.10	0.03	−0.07	0.27	0.18	−0.09	−33
7–10	0.10	0.18	0.08	0.08	0.06	−0.02	0.08	0.00	−0.08	0.26	0.24	−0.02	−6
10+	0.11	0.02	−0.10	0.24	0.22	−0.01	0.20	0.09	−0.11	0.55	0.33	−0.22	−40
Total	0.48	0.32	−0.16	0.52	0.70	0.18	0.47	0.20	−0.27	1.47	1.23	−0.24	−16
%Over-(+)/ Underweight(-)			-33			35			-57			-16	
Sector													
Financial	0.22	0.05	−0.17	0.19	0.16	−0.03	0.05	0.00	−0.05	0.46	0.21	−0.25	−55
Utility	0.22	0.05	−0.17	0.19	0.16	−0.03	0.05	0.00	−0.05	0.046	0.21	−0.25	−55
Industrials	0.06	0.09	0.03	0.25	0.41	0.15	0.29	0.12	−0.17	0.61	0.62	0.01	2
Non-Corp.	0.12	0.18	0.06	0.03	0.01	−0.01	0.03	0.08	0.05	0.18	0.28	0.10	52
Total	0.41	0.32	−0.08	0.52	0.71	0.18	0.47	0.20	−0.27	1.40	1.23	−0.17	−12
%Over-(+)/ Underweight(-)			-21			35			-57			-12	

be underweighted if the portfolio manager expects the spread to increase or "widen".

Credit spreads change because of expected changes in economic prospects. Credit spreads between Treasury and non-Treasury issues widen in a declining or contracting economy and narrow during economic expansion. The economic rationale is that in a declining or contracting economy, corporations experience a decline in revenue and cash flow, making it difficult for corporate issuers to service their contractual debt obligations. To induce investors to hold non-Treasury securities, the yield spread relative to Treasury securities must widen. The converse is that during economic expansion and brisk economic activity, revenue and cash flow pick up, increasing the likelihood that corporate issuers will have the capacity to service their contractual debt obligations. Yield spreads between Treasury and federal agency securities will vary depending on investor expectations about the prospects that an implicit government guarantee will be honored.

A portfolio manager, therefore, can use economic forecasts of the economy in developing forecasts of credit spreads. Also, some portfolio managers base forecasts on historical credit spreads. The underlying principle is that there is a "normal" credit spread relationship that exists. If the current credit spread in the market differs materially from that "normal" credit spread, then the portfolio manager should position the portfolio so as to benefit from a return to the "normal" credit spread. The assumption is that the "normal" credit spread has some type of average or mean value and that mean reversion will occur. If, in fact, there has been a structural shift in the marketplace, this may not occur as the "normal" spread may change.

A portfolio manager will also look at technical factors to assess relative value. For example, a manager may analyze the prospective supply and demand for new issues on spreads in individual sectors or issuers to determine whether they should be overweighted or underweighted. This commonly used tactical strategy is referred to as *primary market analysis*.

Now let's look at spreads due to call or prepayment risk. Expectations about how these spreads will change will affect the inter-sector allocation decision between Treasury securities and spread products that have call risk. Corporate and agency bonds have callable and non-callable issues, all mortgages are prepayable, and asset-backed securities have products that are prepayable, but borrowers may be unlikely to exercise the prepayment option. Consequently, with sectors having different degrees of call or prepayment risk, expectations about how spreads will change also affect intra-allocation decisions. They affect (1) the allocation between callable and non-callable bonds within the corporate bond sector and (2) within the agency, corporate, mortgage, and ABS sectors the allocation among premium (i.e., high coupon), par, and discount (i.e., low coupon) bonds.

Spreads due to call risk will change as a result of expected changes in (1) the direction of the change in interest rates and (2) interest rate volatility. An expected drop in the level of interest rates will widen the yield spread between callable bonds and non-callable bonds as the prospects that the issuer will exercise the call option increase. The reverse is true: The spread narrows if interest rates are expected to rise. An increase in interest rate volatility increases the value of the embedded call option and thereby increases the spread between (1) callable bonds and non-callable bonds and (2) premium and discount bonds. Trades where the portfolio manager anticipates better performance due to the embedded option of individual issues or sectors are referred to as *structure trades.*

Individual security selection strategies

Once the allocation to a sector or subsector has been made, the portfolio manager must decide on the specific issues to select. This is because a manager will typically not invest in all issues within a sector or subsector. Instead, depending on the dollar size of the portfolio, the manager will select a representative number of issues.

It is at this stage that a portfolio manager makes an intra-sector allocation decision to the specific issues. The portfolio manager may believe that there are securities that are mispriced within a subsector and therefore will outperform, over the investment horizon, other issues within the same sector. There are several active strategies that portfolio managers pursue to identify mispriced securities. The most common strategy identifies an issue as undervalued because either (1) its yield is higher than that of comparably rated issues; or (2) its yield is expected to decline (and price therefore rises) because credit analysis indicates that its rating will be upgraded.

Once a portfolio is constructed, a portfolio manager may undertake a swap that involves exchanging one bond for another bond that is similar in terms of coupon, maturity, and credit quality, but offers a higher yield. This is called a *substitution swap* and depends on a capital market imperfection. Such situations sometimes exist in the bond market owing to temporary market imbalances and the fragmented nature of the non-Treasury bond market. The risk the portfolio manager faces in making a substitution swap is that the bond purchased may not be truly identical to the bond for which it is exchanged. Moreover, typically bonds will have similar but not identical maturities and coupons. This could lead to differences in the convexity of the two bonds.

What is critical in assessing any potential swaps is to compare positions that have the same dollar duration. To understand why, consider two bonds, X and Y. Suppose that the price of bond X is 80 and has a duration of 5 while bond Y has a price of 90 and has a duration of 4. Since duration is the approximate percentage change per 100-basis-point change in yield, a 100-basis-point change in yield for bond X would change its price by about 5%. Based on a price of 80, its price will change by about \$4 per \$80 of market value. Thus, its dollar duration for a 100-basis-point change in yield is \$4 per \$80 of market value. Similarly, for bond Y, its dollar duration for a 100-basis-point change in yield per \$90 of market value can be determined. In this case, it is \$3.6. So, if bonds X and Y are being considered as alternative investments or in some swap transaction other than one based on anticipating interest rate movements, the amount of each bond involved should be such that they will both have the same dollar duration.

To illustrate this, suppose that a portfolio manager owns \$10 million par value of bond X which has a market value of \$8 million. The dollar duration of bond X per 100-basis-point change in yield for the \$8 million market value is \$400,000. Suppose further that this manager is considering exchanging bond X in its portfolio for bond Y. If the portfolio manager wants to have the same interest rate exposure (i.e., dollar duration) for bond Y that the portfolio currently has for bond X, a market value amount of bond Y with the same dollar duration must be purchased. If the portfolio manager purchased \$10 million of par value of bond Y and therefore \$9 million of market value of bond Y, the dollar price change per 100-basis-point change in yield would be only \$360,000. If, instead, the portfolio manager purchased \$10 million of market value of bond Y, the dollar duration per 100-basis-point change in yield would be \$400,000. Since bond Y is trading at 90, \$11.11 million of par value of bond Y must be purchased to keep the dollar duration of the position for bond Y the same as for bond X.

Failure to adjust a swap so as to hold the dollar duration the same means that the return will be affected by not only the expected change in the spread but also a change in the yield level. Thus, a portfolio manager would be making a conscious spread bet and possibly an unintentional bet on changes in the level of interest rates.

Liability-Driven Strategies

Thus far, the bond portfolio strategies discussed in this chapter have focused on managing funds relative to a benchmark. In a *liability-driven strategy*, the goal is to manage funds to satisfy contractual liabilities. Insurance companies have historically used liability-driven strategies for certain products that they sold. The two strategies are immunization and cash flow matching. Sponsors of defined benefit pension plans have used these strategies. We conclude this chapter with a discussion of the various types of liability-driven strategies.

Immunization Strategy for a Single-Period Liability

Immunization is a hybrid strategy having elements of both active and passive strategies. *Classical immunization* can be defined as the process by which a bond portfolio is created in order to have an assured return for a specific time horizon, irrespective of interest rate changes. In a concise form, the following are the important characteristics of this strategy: (1) a specified time horizon; (2) an assured rate of return during the holding period to a fixed horizon date; and (3) insulation from the effects of potential adverse interest rate changes on the portfolio value at the horizon date.

The fundamental mechanism underlying immunization is a portfolio structure that balances the change in the value of the portfolio at the end of the investment horizon with the return from the reinvestment of portfolio cash flows (coupon payments and maturing securities). That is, immunization requires offsetting interest rate risk and reinvestment risk. To accomplish this balancing act requires controlling duration. By setting the duration of the portfolio equal to the desired portfolio time horizon, the offsetting of positive and negative incremental return sources can, under certain circumstances, be assured. This is a necessary condition for effectively immunizing portfolios. Figure 2 summarizes the general principles of classical immunization.

How often should the portfolio be rebalanced to adjust its duration? On the one hand, the more frequent rebalancing increases transaction costs, thereby reducing the likelihood of achieving the target return. On the other hand, less frequent rebalancing will result in the portfolio's duration wandering from the target duration, which will also reduce the likelihood of achieving the target return. Consequently, a portfolio manager faces a trade-off: Some transaction costs must be accepted to prevent the portfolio

Goal: Lock in a minimum target rate of return and target investment value regardless of how interest rates change over the investment horizon.

Risk when interest rates change: (1) reinvestment risk and (2) interest rate or price risk

Principle:

Scenario 1: Interest rates increase

Implications:
1. Reinvestment income increases.
2. Value of bonds in the portfolio with a maturity greater than the investment horizon declines in value.

Goal: Gain in reinvestment income = Loss in portfolio value

Scenario 2: Interest rates decline

Implications:
1. Reinvestment income decreases.
2. Value of bonds in the portfolio with a maturity greater than the investment horizon increases in value.

Goal: Loss in reinvestment income = Gain in portfolio value

Assumption: Parallel shift in the yield curve (i.e., all yields rise and fall uniformly)

FIGURE 2: General Principles of Classical Immunization

duration from wandering too far from its target, but some maladjustment in the portfolio duration must be lived with, or transaction costs will become prohibitively high.

In the actual process leading to the construction of an immunized portfolio, the selection of the universe is extremely important. The lower the credit quality of the securities considered, the higher the potential risk and return. Immunization theory assumes there will be no defaults and that securities will be responsive only to overall changes in interest rates. The lower the credit rating of the bonds permitted in the portfolio, the greater the likelihood that these assumptions will not be met. Furthermore, securities with embedded options such as call features and mortgage-backed prepayments complicate and may even prevent the accurate measure of cash flows and, therefore, duration, which frustrates the basic requirements of immunization. Finally, liquidity is a consideration for immunized portfolios because, as just noted, the portfolio must be rebalanced over time.

Perhaps the most critical assumption of the classical immunization strategy concerns the assumption regarding the type of interest rate change. A property of a classically immunized portfolio is that the target value of the investment is the lower limit of the value of the portfolio at the horizon date if there is a parallel shift in the yield curve. This would appear to be an unrealistic assumption. According to the theory, if there is a change in interest rates that does not correspond to this shape-preserving shift (i.e., interest rates do not change equally across maturities), matching the duration to the investment horizon no longer assures immunization.

A natural extension of classical immunization theory is a technique for modifying the assumption of parallel shifts in the yield curve. One approach is a strategy that can handle any arbitrary interest rate change so that it is not necessary to specify an alternative duration measure. The approach developed by Fong and Vasicek [1984] introduced a measure of *immunization risk* against any arbitrary interest rate change. The immunization risk measure can then be minimized subject to the constraint that the duration of the portfolio is equal to the investment horizon, resulting in a portfolio with minimum exposure to any interest rate movements.

One way of minimizing immunization risk is shown in Figure 3. The spikes in the two panels of the figure represent actual portfolio cash flows. The taller spikes depict the actual cash flows generated by matured securities, while the smaller spikes represent coupon payments. Both portfolio A and portfolio B are composed of two bonds with a duration equal to the investment horizon. Portfolio A is, in effect, a barbell portfolio — a portfolio comprising short and long maturities and interim coupon payments. For portfolio B, the two bonds mature very close to the investment horizon and the coupon payments are nominal over the investment horizon. As explained earlier in this chapter, a portfolio with this characteristic is called a bullet portfolio.

It is not difficult to see why the barbell portfolio should be riskier than the bullet portfolio. Assume that both portfolios have durations equal to the horizon length, so that both portfolios are immune to parallel rate changes. This immunity is attained as a consequence of balancing the effect of changes in reinvestment rates on payments received during the investment horizon against the effect of changes in the market value of the portion of the portfolio still outstanding at the end of the investment horizon. When

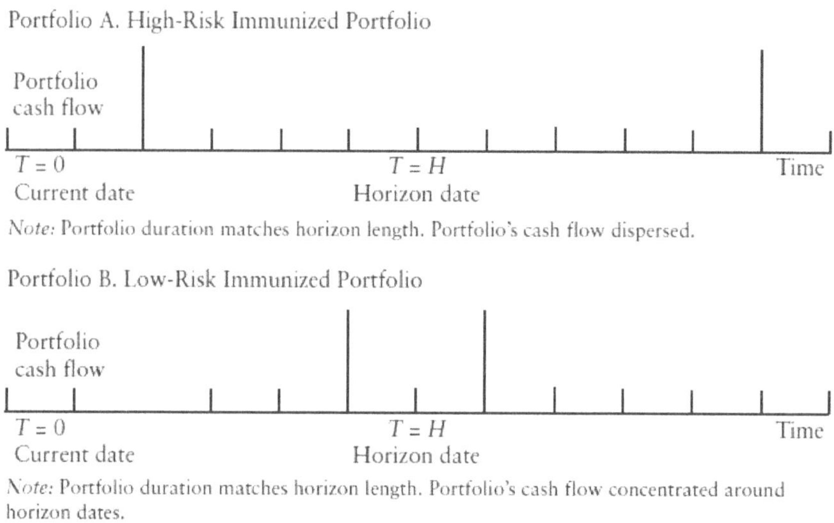

FIGURE 3: Immunization Risk Measure

interest rates change in an arbitrary non-parallel manner, however, the effect on the two portfolios is very different. Suppose, for instance, that short-term rates decline while long-term rates go up. Both portfolios would realize a decline in the portfolio value at the end of the investment horizon below that of the target investment value, since they experience a capital loss in addition to lower reinvestment rates. The decline, however, would be substantially higher for the barbell portfolio for two reasons. First, the lower reinvestment rates are experienced on the barbell portfolio for longer time intervals than on the bullet portfolio, so that the opportunity loss is much greater. Second, the portion of the barbell portfolio still outstanding at the end of the investment horizon is much longer than that of the bullet portfolio, which means that the same interest rate increase would result in a much greater capital loss. Thus, the bullet portfolio has less exposure to the change in the interest rate structure than that of the barbell portfolio.

It should be clear from the foregoing discussion that immunization risk is reinvestment risk. The portfolio that has the least reinvestment risk will have the least immunization risk. When there is a high dispersion of cash flows around the horizon date, as in the barbell portfolio, the portfolio is exposed to higher reinvestment risk. However, when the cash flows are concentrated around the horizon date, as in the bullet portfolio, the portfolio is subject to minimum reinvestment risk.

Contingent immunization strategy

There are variants of the classical immunization strategy. A *contingent immunization strategy* involves the identification of both the available immunization target rate and a lower safety net level return with which the client would be minimally satisfied. The portfolio manager can continue to pursue an active strategy until an adverse investment experience drives the then available potential return — combined active return (from actual past experience) and immunized return (from expected future experience) — down to the safety net level; at such time, the portfolio manager would be obligated to completely immunize the portfolio and lock in the safety net level return.

As long as this safety net is not violated, the portfolio manager can continue to actively manage the portfolio. Once the immunization mode is activated because the safety net is violated, the portfolio manager can no longer return to the active mode unless, of course, the contingent immunization plan is abandoned.

The key considerations in implementing a contingent immunization strategy are (1) establishing accurate immunized initial and ongoing target returns based on market rates; (2) identifying a suitable and immunizable safety net; and (3) implementing an effective monitoring procedure to ensure that the safety net is not violated.

Cash Flow Matching Strategy

The immunization strategy described previously is used to immunize a portfolio created to satisfy a single liability in the future against adverse interest rate movements. However, it is more common in situations to have multiple future liabilities. One example is the liability structure of pension funds. Another example is a life insurance annuity contract. When there are multiple future liabilities, it is possible to extend the principles of immunization to such situations. However, it is more common in practice to use a *cash flow matching strategy*. This strategy is used to construct a portfolio designed to fund a schedule of liabilities from the portfolio return and asset value, with the portfolio's value diminishing to zero after payment of the last liability.

A cash flow matching strategy can be described intuitively as follows. A bond is selected with a maturity that matches the last liability.

An amount of principal equal to the amount of the last liability is then invested in this bond. The remaining elements of the liability stream are then reduced by the coupon payments on this bond, and another bond is chosen for the next-to-last liability, adjusted for any coupon payments of the first bond selected. Going backward in time, this sequence is continued until all liabilities have been matched by payments on the securities selected for the portfolio. Figure 4 provides a simple illustration of this process for a five-year liability stream. Optimization techniques can be employed to construct a least-cost cash flow matching portfolio from an acceptable universe of bonds. This is explained further in Chapter 6 of the companion book.

Liability-Driven Strategies for Defined Benefit Pension Plans

Although some sponsors of defined benefit pension plans have used the cash flow matching strategy, since the dramatic decline in interest rates, this strategy is used less frequently. Moreover, the problem with employing a traditional cash flow matching strategy is that the liabilities are uncertain due to factors such as changes in the contractual benefits provided by the plan sponsor, the decision by plan beneficiaries to retire early, and the impact of inflation on benefits.

A measure of the performance of a pension fund is the *funding ratio* which is equal to

$$\text{Funding ratio} = \frac{\text{Market value of the plan assets}}{\text{Value of the plan liabilities}}.$$

The value of the liabilities is the discounted cash flow of the liabilities (i.e., present value of the liabilities) using a suitable discount rate.

Despite the importance of the funding ratio, historically, plan sponsors have focused on the plan's assets, using market benchmarks as a measure of performance without considering the relationship between the plan's liability profile and that of the market benchmark.

Historically, a commonly used allocation was a traditional 60/40 stock/bond mix. Today other asset classes such as alternative assets are included. There are two views as to the appropriate investment strategy that plan sponsors should utilize in the allocation of plan funds to different asset classes: bond-only view and multiple asset class view. Proponents of the bond-only view favor the cash flow matching strategy discussed earlier. Proponents of the multiple asset class view argue that the liability

Assume: Five-year liability stream and cash flow from bonds are annual.

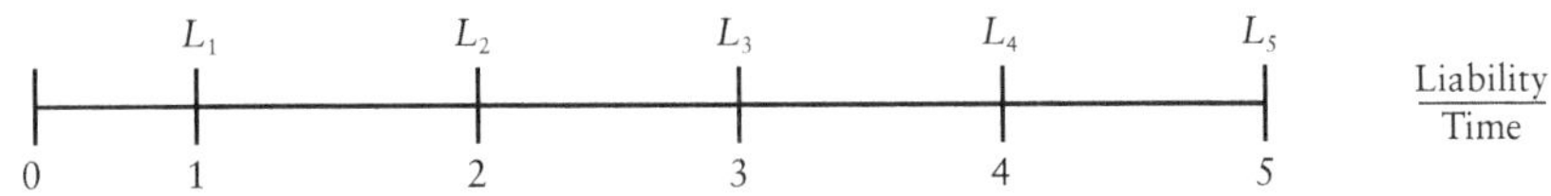

Step 1:
Cash flow from Bond A selected to satisfy L_5
Coupons = A_C; Principal = A_p and $A_C + A_p = L_5$
Unfunded liabilities remaining:

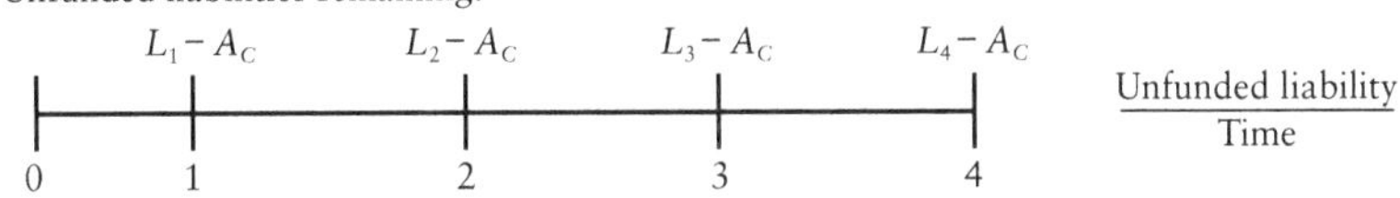

Step 2:
Cash flow from Bond B selected to satisfy L_4
Unfunded liability = $L_4 - A_C$
Coupons = B_C; Principal = B_p and $B_C + B_p = L_4 - A_C$
Unfunded liabilities remaining:

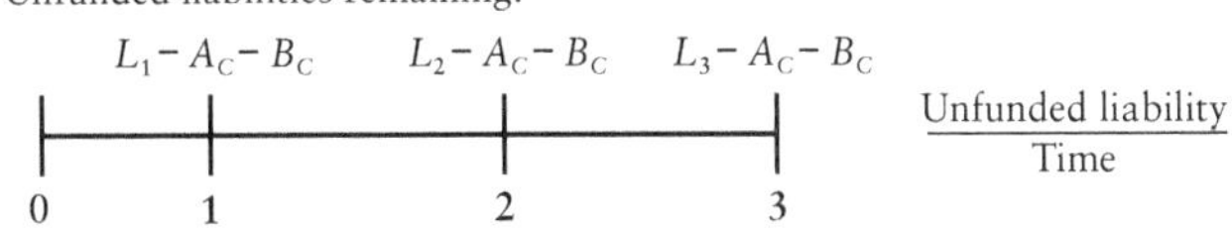

Step 3:
Cash flow from Bond C selected to satisfy L_3
Unfunded liability = $L_3 - A_C - B_C$
Coupons = C_C; Principal = C_p and $C_C + C_p = L_3 - A_C - B_C$
Unfunded liabilities remaining:

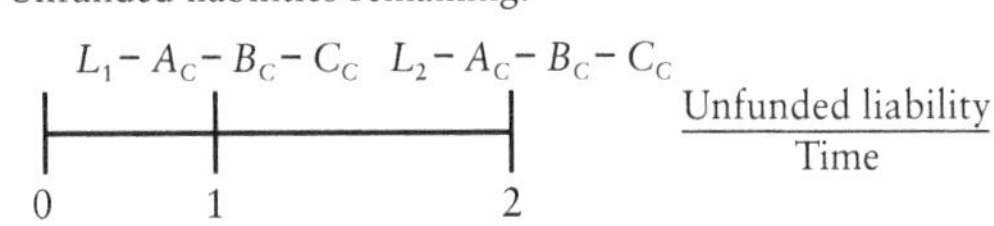

Step 4:
Cash flow from Bond D selected to satisfy L_2
Unfunded liability = $L_2 - A_C - B_C - C_C$
Coupons = D_C; Principal = D_p and $D_C + D_p = L_2 - A_C - B_C - C_C$
Unfunded liabilities remaining:

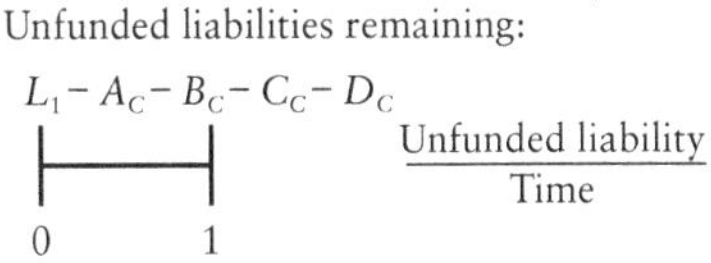

Step 4:
Select Bond E with a cash flow of $L_1 - A_C - B_C - C_C - D_C$

FIGURE 4: Illustration of Cash Flow Matching Process

characteristics of pension funds require an exposure to all asset classes. Both views, however, agree that the benchmark should be the liabilities, not general market benchmarks for asset classes that are too often used.

Basically, those who espouse the multiple asset class view believe that the plan sponsor should use the classical mean-variance optimization framework but that the liability benchmark must be incorporated into the analysis. In mean-variance optimization, as described in Chapter 8, a portfolio manager determines the efficient frontier. The efficient frontier is the set of efficient portfolios where an efficient portfolio is the portfolio with the highest expected return for a given level of risk. To determine which efficient portfolio to select, the Sharpe ratio is used. As explained in Chapter 7, the Sharpe ratio is the excess return of the portfolio divided by the standard deviation of the excess return. The excess return is the difference between the expected return of the portfolio minus the risk-free rate, with the risk-free rate being a Treasury rate. Proponents of the multiple asset class view argue that rather than measuring the excess return in terms of a benchmark such as the risk-free rate, the benchmark should be an index that reflects the liability structure of the pension plan.

Ross, Bernstein, Ferguson, and Dalio [2008] propose the following liability-driven strategy for a pension plan which involves two steps. In the first step, the plan sponsor, in consultation with its advisor, creates a cash flow matched strategy in order to hedge the adverse consequences associated with the exposure to the liabilities attributable to a change in interest rates. In the second step, the plan sponsor in consultation with its advisor works with asset managers to create portfolios that generate a return that exceeds the return on the immunizing portfolio. Such portfolios are referred to as "excess return portfolios". The total return for the pension plan is then

$$\begin{aligned}\text{Total plan return} &= \text{Return on liability-immunizing portfolio}\\ &\quad + \text{Return on excess return portfolios}\\ &\quad - \text{Return on liabilities.}\end{aligned}$$

The return on liabilities is the change in the present value of the liabilities. If the immunizing portfolio is properly created, its return should be close to the return on the liabilities. (Recall it is not a simple task to completely immunize.) Hence, the volatility of the liabilities is neutralized to a great extent. What remains is then the return on the excess return portfolio.

Key Points

- The spectrum of bond portfolio strategies and the key elements of each strategy can be understood in terms of the risk and return of a strategy versus a benchmark established by the client.
- Strategies can be classified as follows: (1) pure bond index matching; (2) enhanced indexing/matching primary risk factors approach; (3) enhanced indexing/minor risk factor mismatches; (4) active management/larger risk factor mismatches; and (5) active/full-blown active management.
- The difference between indexing and active management is the extent to which the portfolio can deviate from the primary risk factors associated with the index.
- The primary risk factors associated with an index are: (1) the duration of the index; (2) the present value distribution of the cash flows; (3) percent in sector and quality; (4) duration contribution of sector; (5) duration contribution of credit quality; (6) sector, coupon, or maturity cell weights; and (7) issuer exposure control.
- A pure bond index matching strategy involves the least risk of underperforming the index and involves creating a portfolio so as to replicate the issues comprising the index.
- A portfolio manager pursuing a pure index matching strategy will encounter several logistical problems in constructing an indexed portfolio that will cause tracking error.
- An enhanced indexing strategy can be pursued so as to construct a portfolio to match the primary risk factors without acquiring each issue in the index.
- There are three methodologies used to construct a portfolio to replicate an index: the stratified sampling or cellular approach, the optimization approach, and the variance minimization approach.
- Enhanced indexing/minor risk factor mismatches is an enhanced strategy where the portfolio is constructed so as to have minor deviations from the risk factors that affect the performance of the index, but the duration of the constructed portfolio is matched to the duration of the index.
- Active bond strategies are those that attempt to outperform the market by intentionally constructing a portfolio that will have a greater index mismatch than in the case of enhanced indexing.
- One active bond strategy the portfolio manager can pursue involves larger mismatches relative to the index in terms of risk factors, including minor mismatches of duration.

- In the full blown active management case, the portfolio manager is permitted to make a significant duration bet without any constraints and can make a significant allocation to sectors not included in the index.
- A factor model can be used in bond portfolio management for the purpose of constructing a portfolio, controlling for risk in terms of the exposure to the factors, and rebalancing a portfolio.
- A factor model allows an asset manager to identify the exposure to systematic risk factors and idiosyncratic risk.
- Value-added strategies are those that seek to enhance return relative to an index and can be strategic or tactical.
- Strategic strategies include interest rate expectations strategies, yield curve strategies, and inter- and intra-sector allocation strategies.
- Tactical strategies are short-term trading strategies that include strategies based on rich/cheap analysis, yield curve trading strategies, and return enhancing strategies employing futures and options.
- Interest rate expectations strategies involve adjusting the duration of the portfolio relative to the index based on expected movements in interest rates.
- Top-down yield curve strategies involve positioning a portfolio to capitalize on expected changes in the shape of the Treasury yield curve following either a bullet strategy, barbell strategy, or ladder strategy.
- An inter-sector allocation strategy involves a portfolio manager's allocation of funds among the major bond sectors.
- In making inter- and intra-sector allocations, a portfolio manager is anticipating how spreads will change due to differences in credit risk, call risk (or prepayment risk), and liquidity risk.
- In undertaking a potential swap to enhance returns via intra-sector allocation, it is critical that the trade be constructed so as to maintain the same dollar duration as the initial position, so as to avoid an unintentional interest rate bet.
- In a liability-driven strategy, the goal is to manage funds to satisfy contractual liabilities.
- Immunization is a hybrid strategy having elements of both active and passive strategies.
- Classical immunization is the process by which a bond portfolio is created in order to have an assured return for a specific time horizon irrespective of interest rate changes.
- The fundamental mechanism underlying immunization is the creation of a portfolio structure that offsets interest rate risk and reinvestment risk.

- To protect an immunized portfolio against a parallel shift in interest rates, the portfolio's duration must be such that it is equal to that of the desired portfolio time horizon.
- A critical assumption of the classical immunization strategy is that the interest rates change in a parallel fashion; an extension of classical immunization theory is a strategy that can handle any arbitrary interest rate change.
- One approach for dealing with any arbitrary interest rate change is to use an immunization risk measure and minimize that measure.
- A contingent immunization strategy involves the identification of both the available immunization target rate and a lower safety net level return with which the client would be minimally satisfied.
- A cash flow matching strategy is used to construct a portfolio designed to fund a schedule of projected future liabilities using the portfolio's return and asset value, with the portfolio's value diminishing to zero after payment of the last liability.
- The liability structure of defined benefit pension plans is uncertain.
- There are two liability-driven strategies advocated for defined benefit pension plans.
- One approach argues that only bonds should be acquired, and a dedicated portfolio strategy should be used; the other approach is a liability-driven strategy that uses all asset classes but uses the liabilities as a benchmark in determining the best asset allocation.

References

Fong, H. G. and O. A. Vasicek, 1984. "A risk minimizing strategy for portfolio immunization," *Journal of Finance*, 30: 1541–1546.

Lazanas, A., A. Baldaque da Silva, R. Găbudean, and A. D. Staal, 2011. "Multifactor fixed income risk models and their applications," in *The Theory and Practice in Investment Management: Second Edition*, edited by F. J. Fabozzi and H. M. Markowitz, Chapter 21 (pp. 585–622). Hoboken, NJ: John Wiley & Sons, 2011.

Ross, P., D. Bernstein, N. Ferguson, and R. Dalio, 2008. "Creating an optimal portfolio to fund pension liabilities," in *Handbook of Finance*, vol. 2, edited by F. J. Fabozzi (pp. 463–484). Hoboken, NJ: John Wiley & Sons.

Volpert, K. E., 1997. "Managing indexed and enhanced indexed bond portfolios," in *Managing Fixed Income Portfolios,* edited by F. J. Fabozzi (pp. 191–211). Hoboken, NJ: John Wiley & Sons.

Chapter 18

Using Derivatives in Bond Portfolio Management

Learning Objectives

After reading this chapter, you will understand:

- the different types of interest rate futures contracts;
- the two types of interest rate futures contracts available to asset managers: Treasury-based futures and Eurodollar futures;
- how interest rate futures are used to control interest rate risk;
- what a long (buy) hedge and a short (sell) hedge are;
- what the hedge ratio is and how it is calculated;
- the complications in hedging with Treasury-based futures;
- what an exchange-traded futures option is and the mechanics of this derivative;
- how to use Treasury futures options in a protective put buying strategy and covered call writing strategy;
- what an interest rate swap is and its interest rate sensitivity;
- how to hedge with an interest rate swap;
- what a credit default swap is and the two types of credit default swaps;
- how to take a position in a credit default swap to buy or sell credit insurance.

For many portfolio strategies, derivative instruments provide a more efficient vehicle for obtaining the objective sought by the asset manager. We explained how this is done for equity strategies in Chapter 14. In this chapter, we explain how interest rate derivatives — futures, options, swaps — and credit derivatives can be used in bond portfolio management.

Interest Rate Futures Contracts

As with stock index futures described in Chapter 14, interest rate futures provide asset managers with opportunities to implement investment strategies and control risk. In this section, we describe the major interest rate futures contracts and show how one type of contract can be used in asset management.

Types of Interest Rates Futures

There are two types of interest rate futures contracts used by asset managers: Treasury-based futures contracts and Eurodollar futures contracts. Each type is described as follows.

Treasury-based futures

There are three Treasury-based futures contracts: Treasury bond futures, Treasury note futures, and ultra Treasury bond futures. The underlying instrument for the Treasury bond futures contract is $100,000 par value of a hypothetical 20-year, 6% coupon bond. This hypothetical bond's coupon rate is called the *notional coupon.* There are three Treasury note futures contracts: 10-year, 5-year, and 2-year. All three contracts are modeled after the Treasury bond futures contract. The underlying instrument for the 10-year Treasury note contract is $100,000 par value of a hypothetical 10-year, 6% Treasury note. For the Treasury bond futures, acceptable deliverable bond issues have a maturity of at least 15 years but no more than 25 years. The deliverable specification for the ultra Treasury bond futures contract calls for the acceptable deliverable bonds to have at least 25 years to maturity. All of the other specifications for the contract are the same as for the Treasury bond futures contract, so we use this Treasury futures contract in our discussion here.

Treasury futures contracts have March, June, September, and December settlement months. The futures price is quoted in terms of par being 100. Since the bond and notes futures contract are similar, for the remainder of our discussion we focus on the bond futures contract.

We have been referring to the underlying instrument as a hypothetical Treasury bond. While some interest rate futures contracts can only be settled in cash, others can be physically settled. Thus, the seller (the short) of a Treasury bond futures contract, who chooses to make delivery rather than liquidate his/her position by buying back the contract prior to the settlement date, must deliver some Treasury bond. This begs the question "which Treasury bond?" The exchange where these contracts are traded, the Chicago Mercantile Exchange Group (CME), allows the seller to deliver one of several Treasury bonds that the CME specifies are acceptable for delivery. A trader who is short a particular bond is always concerned with the risk of being unable to obtain sufficient securities to cover a position.

The bond issues that meet the delivery requirements for a particular contract are referred to as *deliverable issues*. The CME makes its determination of the Treasury issues that are acceptable for delivery from all outstanding Treasury issues that have at least 15 years to maturity from the first day of the delivery month. For settlement purposes, the CME specifies that a given issue's term to maturity is calculated in complete 3-month increments (that is, complete quarters). For example, if the actual maturity of an issue is 15 years and 5 months, it would be rounded down to a maturity of 15 years and 1 quarter (3 months). Moreover, all bonds delivered by the seller must be of the same issue.

Keep in mind that, while the underlying Treasury bond for this contract is a hypothetical issue and therefore cannot itself be delivered into the futures contract, the bond futures contract is not a cash settlement contract. The only way to close out a Treasury bond futures contract is to either initiate an offsetting futures position or to deliver one of the deliverable issues.

The delivery is as follows. On the settlement date, the seller of the futures contract (the short) is required to deliver to the buyer (the long) $100,000 par value of a 6%, 20-year Treasury bond. As noted, no such bond exists, so the seller must choose one of the deliverable issues to deliver to the long. Suppose the seller selects a 5% coupon, 20-year Treasury bond to settle the futures contract. Since the coupon of this bond is less than the notional coupon of 6%, this would be unacceptable to the buyer who contracted to receive a 6% coupon, 20-year bond with a par value of $100,000. Alternatively, suppose the seller is compelled to deliver a 7% coupon, 20-year bond. Since the coupon of this bond is greater than the notional coupon of 6%, the seller would find this unacceptable. How does the exchange adjust for the fact that deliverable issues have coupons and maturities that differ from the notional coupon of 6%?

To make delivery equitable to both parties, the CME publishes conversion factors for adjusting the price of each deliverable issue for a given contract. Given the conversion factor for a deliverable issue and the futures price, the adjusted price is found by multiplying the conversion factor by the futures price. The adjusted price is called the *converted price*. That is,

$$\text{Converted price} = \text{Contract size} \times \text{Futures settlement price} \\ \times \text{Conversion factor}.$$

For example, suppose the settlement price of a Treasury bond futures contract is 110 and the deliverable issue selected by the short has a conversion factor of 1.25. Given the contract size is \$100,000, the converted price for the deliverable issue is

$$\$100{,}000 \times 1.10 \times 1.25 = \$137{,}500.$$

The price that the buyer must pay the seller for the deliverable issue is called the *invoice price*. The invoice price is the converted price plus the deliverable issue's accrued interest. That is, the invoice price is

$$\text{Invoice price} = \text{Contract size} \times \text{Futures settlement price} \\ \times \text{Conversion factor} + \text{Accrued interest}.$$

In selecting the issue to be delivered, the short will select from all the deliverable issues the one that will give the largest rate of return from a *cash-and-carry strategy*. In the case of Treasury bond futures, a cash-and-carry strategy is one in which a cash bond that is acceptable for delivery is purchased with borrowed funds and simultaneously the Treasury bond futures contract is sold. The bond purchased can be delivered to satisfy the short futures position. Thus, by buying the Treasury issue that is acceptable for delivery and selling the futures, an investor has effectively sold the bond at the delivery price (that is, the converted price).

A rate of return can be calculated for this strategy. This rate of return is referred to as the *implied repo rate*. Once the implied repo rate is calculated for each deliverable issue, the issue selected for delivery will be the one that has the highest implied repo rate (i.e., the issue that gives the maximum return in a cash-and-carry strategy). The issue with the highest return is referred to as the cheapest-to-deliver issue (CTD issue). This issue plays a key role in the pricing of a Treasury futures contract and in developing hedging strategies.[1]

[1]While a particular Treasury bond may be the CTD issue today, changes in interest rates, for example, may cause some other issue to be the CTD issue at a future date. A sensitivity analysis can be performed to determine how a change in yield affects the CTD issue. In particular, sensitivity analysis identifies which deliverable issue is cheapest to deliver following various shocks to the yield curve.

In addition to the choice of which acceptable Treasury issue to deliver — sometimes referred to as the *quality option* or *swap option* — the short has at least two more options granted under CME delivery guidelines. The short is permitted to decide when in the delivery month the delivery will actually take place. This is called the *timing option.* The other option is the right of the short to give notice of intent to deliver up to 8 pm Chicago time after the closing of the exchange (3.15 pm Chicago time) on the date when the futures settlement price has been fixed. This option is referred to as the *wildcard option.* The quality option, the timing option, and the wildcard option — in sum referred to as the *delivery options* — mean that the long position can never be sure which Treasury bond issue will be delivered or when it will be delivered.

Eurodollar futures

The Eurodollar futures contract is used to take a position in the short end of the yield curve. Asset managers have found it to be an effective vehicle for a wide range of hedging situations.

A Eurodollar futures contract represents a commitment to pay/receive a quarterly interest payment determined by the level of 3-month LIBOR. The contract is based on a notional principal of $1 million. Various quarterly settlement dates for Eurodollar futures contracts are available extending out 10 years. The Eurodollar futures contract is a cash settlement contract.

This contract is traded on an index-price basis. The index-price basis on which the contract is quoted is equal to 100 minus the annualized futures LIBOR. For example, a Eurodollar futures price of 97.50 means a 3-month LIBOR of 2.5%. Since the minimum price fluctuation (tick) for this contract is 0.01 (or 0.0001 in terms of LIBOR), the price value of a basis point for this contract is $25, found as follows. The simple interest on $1 million for 90 days is equal to $1,000,000 × (LIBOR ×90/360). If LIBOR changes by one basis point (0.0001), then $\$1,000,000 \times (0.0001 \times 90/360) = \$25$.

Bond Portfolio Management Applications with Treasury Bond Futures

There are various ways an asset manager can use interest rate futures contracts in addition to speculating on the movement of interest rates. Prior to the introduction of Treasury bond and note futures contracts, Treasury securities were used. Before describing the use of Treasury futures, let's first address why these contracts are used rather than using Treasury securities.

There are four reasons why it is preferable to use Treasury futures rather than Treasury securities. First, Treasury futures are more liquid than Treasury securities and therefore executing in the Treasury futures market results in lower transactions costs. Second, often when taking a position in Treasury securities it may be expensive if the instrument used to control interest rate risk is a Treasury security that is on "special," or if an off-the-run Treasury needs to be utilized. Under such circumstances, the cost of establishing a position in a Treasury security may be expensive because of low reverse-repo rates or wide bid–ask spreads. Third, margin requirements for establishing futures positions are less than margin requirements for buying Treasury securities on margin. Finally, if the position that is required involves a short position in the market, it is far easier to short Treasury futures than Treasury securities.

Controlling the interest rate risk of a portfolio

Asset managers can use interest rate futures to alter the interest rate sensitivity, or duration, of a portfolio. Those with strong expectations about the direction of the future course of interest rates will adjust the duration of their portfolios so as to capitalize on their expectations. Specifically, an asset manager who expects rates to increase will shorten duration; an asset manager who expects interest rates to decrease will lengthen duration. While asset managers can use cash market instruments to alter the durations of their portfolios, using futures contracts provides a quicker and less expensive means for doing so (on either a temporary or permanent basis).

A formula to approximate the number of futures contracts necessary to adjust the portfolio duration to some target duration is

$$\frac{\text{Target portfolio dollar duration} - \text{Current portfolio dollar duration}}{\text{Dollar duration of the futures contract}}.$$

Dollar duration was described in Chapter 16. The dollar duration of the futures contract is the dollar price sensitivity of the futures contract to a change in interest rates.

Note that if the asset manager wishes to increase the portfolio's current duration, the numerator of the formula will be positive. This means that futures contracts will be purchased. That is, buying futures increases the duration of the portfolio. The opposite is true if the objective is to shorten the portfolio's current duration: The numerator of the formula will be negative, and this means that futures must be sold. Hence, selling futures contracts reduces the portfolio's duration.

Hedging

Hedging is a special case of risk control where the target duration sought is zero. If cash and futures prices move together, any loss realized by the hedger from one position (whether cash or futures) will be offset by a profit on the other position. When the net profit or loss from the positions is such that the return earned from the position over the hedging period is the risk-free rate, the hedge is referred to as a perfect hedge as explained in Chapter 14.

In practice, hedging is not that simple as demonstrated in Chapter 14 for stock index futures. In bond portfolio management, typically the bond to be hedged is not identical to the bond underlying the futures contract and therefore there is cross-hedging. This may result in substantial basis risk.

Conceptually, cross-hedging is somewhat more complicated than hedging deliverable securities because it involves two relationships. In the case of Treasury bond futures contracts, the first relationship is between the CTD issue and the futures contract. The second is the relationship between the security to be hedged and the CTD issue.

The key to minimizing risk in a cross hedge is to choose the right hedge ratio. The hedge ratio depends on volatility weighting, or weighting by relative changes in value. The purpose of a hedge is to use gains or losses from a futures position to offset any difference between the target sale price and the actual sale price of the security.

Accordingly, the hedge ratio is chosen with the intention of matching the volatility (that is, the dollar change) of the Treasury bond futures contract to the volatility of the bond to be hedged. Consequently, the hedge ratio for a bond is given by

$$\text{Hedge ratio} = \frac{\text{Volatility of bond to be hedged}}{\text{Volatility of Treasury bond futures contract}}. \tag{1}$$

For hedging purposes, we are concerned with volatility in absolute dollar terms. To calculate the dollar volatility of a bond, one must know the precise time that volatility is to be calculated (because volatility generally declines as a bond moves toward its maturity date), as well as the price or yield at which to calculate the volatility (because higher yields generally reduce dollar volatility for a given yield change). The relevant point in the life of the bond for calculating volatility is the point at which the hedge will be lifted. Volatility at any other point is essentially irrelevant because the goal is to lock in a price or rate only on that particular day. Similarly, the relevant yield at which to calculate volatility initially is the target yield. Consequently, the "volatility of bond to be hedged" referred to in Equation (1) for the hedge ratio is the price value of a basis point for the bond on the date the hedge is expected to be delivered.

Illustration: We will use an illustration to show how to calculate the hedge ratio and then verify that it will do an effective job in hedging a bond position. We will assume that on December 24, 2007, a bond portfolio manager wants to hedge a position in a Procter & Gamble (P&G) 5.55% of 3/5/2037 bond that the manager anticipates selling on March 31, 2008.[2] The par value of the P&G bond is $10 million. The portfolio manager decides that she will use the March 2008 Treasury bond futures to hedge the bond position which she can settle on March 31, 2008. Because the portfolio manager is trying to protect against a decline in the value of the P&G bonds between December 24, 2007 and the anticipated sale date, she will short (sell) a number of March 2008 Treasury bond futures contracts. Because the bond to be hedged is a corporate bond and the hedging instrument is a Treasury bond futures contract, this is an example of a cross hedge.

On December 24, 2007, the P&G bond was selling at 97.127 and offering a yield of 5.754%. Since the par value of the P&G bond held in the portfolio is $10 million, the market value of the bond is $9,712,700 (97.127 × $10,000,000). The price of the March 2008 Treasury bond futures contract on December 24, 2007 was 114.375. The portfolio manager determines that the Treasury 6.25% of 8/15/2023 issue was the CTD issue for the March 2008 Treasury bond futures contract. The price of this Treasury issue is 117.719 (a yield of 4.643%) and the conversion factor for this Treasury issue is 1.0246. The yield spread between the P&G bond and the CTD issue was 111.1 basis points (5.754% − 4.643%). To simplify the analysis, the portfolio manager assumes that this 111.1 yield spread will remain the same over the period the bond is hedged.

What target price is the portfolio manager seeking to lock in for the P&G bonds? One might think it is the current market price of the P&G

[2]We thank Peter Ru for providing this illustration.

bonds, 97.127. However, that is not correct. The target price is determined by the March 2008 Treasury bond futures contract that is being shorted. Some calculations are required to determine the target price. We begin by determining the target price for the CTD issue. Given the conversion factor for the CTD issue (1.0246) and the futures price for the March 2007 contract (114.375), the target price for the CTD issue is found by multiplying these two values. That is, the target price for the CTD issue is 117.1886.

But there is a target yield for the CTD issue that corresponds to the price of 117.1886. For the Treasury 6.25s of 8/15/2023 issue, the yield if the price is 117.1886 on March 31, 2008 (the settlement date) is 4.670%. Thus, the target yield for the CTD issue is 4.670%.

Given the target yield for the CTD issue of 4.670%, the portfolio manager can calculate the target yield for the P&G bond. Here the portfolio manager makes use of the assumption that yield spread between the P&G bond and the CTD issue remains at 111.1 basis points. For the target yield for the CTD issue of 4.670%, the portfolio manager adds the 111.1 basis point spread, giving a target yield for the P&G bond of 5.781%. The final step to estimate the target price for the P&G bond as of March 31, 2008 is to determine the price for the P&G bond on the settlement date given a target yield of 5.781%. This is a straightforward calculation given the coupon and maturity date of the P&G bond. The target price is 96.788. For a $10 million par value holding of the P&G bond, the target market value that the portfolio manager seeks is about $9,678,000.

To calculate the hedge ratio, the portfolio manager needs to know the volatility of the March 2008 Treasury bond futures contract. Fortunately, knowing the volatility of the bond to be hedged relative to the CTD issue and the volatility of the cheapest-to-deliver bond relative to the futures contract, we can modify the hedge ratio given by Equation (1) as follows:

$$\text{Hedge ratio} = \frac{\text{Volatility of bond to be hedged}}{\text{Volatility of CTD issue}} \times \frac{\text{Volatility of CTD bond}}{\text{Volatility of Treasury bond futures contract}}. \tag{2}$$

The second ratio above can be shown to equal the conversion factor for the CTD issue. Assuming a fixed yield spread between the bond to be hedged and the CTD issue, Equation (2) can be rewritten as

$$\text{Hedge ratio} = \frac{\text{PVBP of bond to be hedged}}{\text{PVBP of CTD issue}} \times \text{Conversion factor for CTD issue}, \tag{3}$$

where PVBP is equal to the price value of a basis point. As explained in Chapter 16, the PVBP is computed by changing the yield of a bond by one basis point and determining the change in the bond's price. It is a measure of price volatility to interest rate changes and related to duration.

The portfolio manager can calculate the PVBP of the P&G bond and the CTD issue from the target yield and the target price for the bonds at the settlement date. For the CTD issue it is 0.1207 and for the P&G bond it is 0.1363. Substituting these two values plus the conversion factor for the CTD issue (1.0246) into Equation (3), we get

$$\text{Hedge ratio} = \frac{0.1363}{0.1207} \times 1.0246 = 1.157.$$

Given the hedge ratio, the number of contracts that must be short is determined as follows:

$$\text{Number of contracts} = \text{Hedge ratio} \times \frac{\text{Par value to be hedged}}{\text{Par value of the futures contract}}.$$

Because the amount to be hedged is $10 million and each Treasury bond futures contract is for $100,000 par value, this means that the number of futures contracts that must be sold is

$$\begin{aligned}\text{Number of contracts} &= \text{Hedge ratio} \times \frac{\$10{,}000{,}000}{\$100{,}000} \\ &= 1.157 \times 100 = 116 \text{ contracts (rounded).}\end{aligned}$$

Table 1 shows that if the simplifying assumptions that were made in this illustration to calculate the hedge ratio are satisfied, a futures hedge wherein 116 futures contracts are shorted very nearly locks in the target market value of $9,678,000 for $10 million par value of the P&G bond. There are refinements that can be made to the hedging procedure to improve this hedge. However, these are unimportant for a basic understanding of hedging with Treasury bond futures contracts.

Use of Interest Rate Options in Bond Portfolio Management

Interest rate options can be written on a bond or an interest rate futures contract. The former options are called *options on physicals* and the latter are called *futures options*. The most liquid exchange-traded option on bonds is an option on Treasury bonds traded on the CME. Options on interest rate

TABLE 1: Hedge of the $10 million Par Value of Procter & Gamble 5.55% 3/5/2037 with March 2008 Treasury Bond Futures Contract with Settlement on March 31, 2008

Actual Sale Price of P&G Bond	Yield at Sale (%)	Yield of Treasury[a] (%)	Price of Treasury	Futures Price[b]	Gain (loss) on 116 contracts	Effective Sale Price[c]
8,000,000	7.204	6.093	101.544	99.106	1,771,194	9,771,194
8,200,000	7.010	5.899	103.508	101.023	1,548,862	9,748,862
8,400,000	6.824	5.713	105.438	102.907	1,330,323	9,730,323
8,600,000	6.645	5.534	107.341	104.764	1,114,875	9,714,875
8,800,000	6.472	5.361	109.224	106.601	901,748	9,701,748
9,000,000	6.306	5.195	111.071	108.404	692,606	9,692,606
9,200,000	6.144	5.033	112.914	110.203	484,008	9,684,008
9,400,000	5.989	4.878	114.714	111.960	280,164	9,680,164
9,600,000	5.838	4.727	116.504	113.707	77,476	9,677,476
9,800,000	5.691	4.580	118.282	115.442	(123,809)	9,676,191
10,000,000	5.550	4.439	120.021	117.139	(320,633)	9,679,367
10,200,000	5.412	4.301	121.755	118.831	(516,925)	9,683,075
10,400,000	5.278	4.167	123.469	120.505	(711,032)	9,688,968
10,600,000	5.149	4.038	125.149	122.144	(901,256)	9,698,744
10,800,000	5.022	3.911	126.832	123.787	(1,091,785)	9,708,215
11,000,000	4.899	3.788	128.490	125.405	(1,279,473)	9,720,527
11,200,000	4.780	3.669	130.120	126.996	(1,464,047)	9,735,953
11,400,000	4.663	3.552	131.749	128.586	(1,648,452)	9,751,548
11,600,000	4.550	3.439	133.347	130.145	(1,829,358)	9,770,642

Notes:
[a]By assumption, the yield on the CTD issue (6.25% of 8/15/2003) is 111.1 basis points lower than the yield on the P&G bond.
[b]By convergence, the futures price equals the price of the CTD issue divided by 1.0246 (the conversion factor).
[c]Transaction costs and the financing of margin flows are ignored.

futures have been far more popular than options on physicals.[3] However, portfolio managers have made increasingly greater use of over-the-counter (OTC) options. Typically, they are purchased by institutional investors who want to hedge the risk associated with a specific security or index. Besides options on fixed income securities, there are OTC options on the shape of the yield curve, or the yield spread between two securities. A discussion of these OTC options is beyond the scope of this chapter.

[3]Futures options are believed to be "cleaner" instruments because of the reduced likelihood of delivery squeezes.

Exchange-Traded Futures Options

A futures option gives the buyer the right to buy from or sell to the writer a designated futures contract at the strike price. If the futures option is a call option, the buyer has the right to purchase one designated futures contract at the strike price. That is, the buyer has the right to acquire a long futures position in the designated futures contract. If the buyer exercises the call option, the writer acquires a corresponding short position in the futures contract.

A put option on a futures contract grants the buyer the right to sell one designated futures contract to the writer at the strike price. That is, the option buyer has the right to acquire a short position in the designated futures contract. If the put option is exercised, the writer acquires a corresponding long position in the designated futures contract.

These positions are summarized as follows:

Type	Buyer Has the Right to:	If Exercised, the Seller Has:	If Exercised, the Seller Pays the Buyer:
Call	Purchase one futures contract at the strike price	A short futures position	Current futures price — Strike price
Put	Sell one futures contract at the strike price	A long futures position	Strike price — Current futures price

The CME's Treasury-based futures contracts have delivery months of March, June, September, and December. There are futures options on all the Treasury-based futures contracts.

Mechanics of trading futures options

Because the parties to the futures option will realize a position in a futures contract when the option is exercised, the question is, what will the futures price be? That is, at what price will the long be required to pay for the instrument underlying the futures contract, and at what price will the short be required to sell the instrument underlying the futures contract?

Upon exercise, the futures price for the futures contract will be set equal to the strike price. The position of the two parties is then immediately marked to market in terms of the then-current futures price. Thus, the futures position of the two parties will be at the prevailing futures price. At the same time, the option buyer will receive from the option seller the economic benefit from exercising the option. In the case of a call futures option, the option writer must pay to the buyer of the option the difference between the current futures price and the strike price. In the case of a put futures option, the option writer must pay the option buyer the difference between the strike price and the current futures price. The last column of the table above summarizes the positions of the two parties to a futures option.

For example, suppose an investor buys a call option on some futures contract in which the strike price is 85. Assume also that the futures price is 95 and that the buyer exercises the call option. Upon exercise, the call buyer is given a long position in the futures contract at 85, and the call writer is assigned the corresponding short position in the futures contract at 85. The futures positions of the buyer and the writer are immediately marked to market by the exchange. Because the prevailing futures price is 95 and the strike price is 85, the long futures position (the position of the call buyer) realizes a gain of 10, while the short futures position (the position of the call writer) realizes a loss of 10. The call writer pays the exchange 10, and the call buyer receives 10 from the exchange. The call buyer, who now has a long futures position at 95, can either liquidate the futures position at 95 or maintain a long futures position. If the former course of action is taken, the call buyer sells a futures contract at the prevailing futures price of 95.

There is no gain or loss from liquidating the position. Overall, the call buyer realizes a gain of 10. The call buyer who elects to hold the long futures position will face the same risk and reward of holding such a position, but still realizes a gain of 10 from the exercise of the call option.

Suppose, instead, that the futures option is a put rather than a call, and the current futures price is 60 rather than 95. If the buyer of this put option exercises, the buyer would have a short position in the futures contract at 85; the option writer would have a long position in the futures contract at 85. The exchange then marks the position to market at the then-current futures price of 60, resulting in a gain to the put buyer of 25, and a loss to the put writer of the same amount. The put buyer, who now has a short futures position at 60, can either liquidate the short futures position by buying a futures contract at the prevailing futures price of 60 or maintain the short futures position. In either case, the put buyer realizes a gain of 25 from exercising the put option.

Applications to Bond Portfolio Management

In our explanation of how to use options in equity portfolio management, we explained how they can be used in risk management and return enhancement. We will not repeat an explanation of the applications here. Instead, we will illustrate how futures options can be used for hedging and return enhancement. More specifically, we will illustrate a protective put buying strategy (a risk management application) and a covered call writing strategy (a return enhancement application). As will be seen, the applications are complicated by the fact that the option is not an option on a physical but rather a futures option.

Protective put buying strategy with futures options

Buying puts on Treasury futures options is one of the easiest ways to purchase protection against rising rates. As explained in Chapter 14, this strategy is called a protective put buying strategy. To illustrate this strategy, we use the P&G bond that we used earlier in this chapter to demonstrate how to use Treasury bond futures for hedging. We also compare hedging using Treasury bond futures with hedging using Treasury futures options.

In our illustration, we assumed that the portfolio manager owns $10 million par value of the P&G 5.55%, 3/5/2037 bond and used Treasury bond futures to lock in a sale price for those bonds on a future delivery date. The P&G bond was selling at a yield of 5.74%. The specific contract used for hedging was the Treasury bond futures contract with settlement in March 2008. The CTD issue for the Treasury bond futures contract was the Treasury 6.25%, 8/15/2023 bond selling to yield 4.643%.

Now we want to show how the portfolio manager could have used Treasury bond futures options instead of Treasury bond futures to protect against rising rates. In this illustration, we will assume that the portfolio manager uses a put option on the March 2008 Treasury bond futures contract. The put options for this contract expire on February 22, 2008.

For simplicity, we assumed that the yield spread between the CTD issue and the P&G bonds remains at 111.1 basis points.

To hedge using puts on Treasury bond futures, the portfolio manager must determine the minimum price for the P&G bond. In the illustration, it is assumed that the minimum price is 96.219 per bond or $9,621,900 for $10 million of par value. Thus, 96.219 becomes the target price for the P&G bond. However, the problem is that the portfolio manager is not purchasing a put option on the P&G bond but a put option on a Treasury bond futures contract. Therefore, the hedging process requires that the portfolio manager determine the strike price for a put option on a Treasury bond futures contract that is equivalent to a strike price of 96.219 for the P&G bond.

The process involves several steps. These steps are shown in Figure 1. Because the minimum price is 96.219 (Box 1 in Figure 1) for the P&G bond, this means that the portfolio manager is seeking to establish a maximum yield of 5.821%. We know this because given the price, coupon, and maturity of the bond, the yield can easily be computed. This gets us to Box 2 in Figure 1. Now we have to make use of the assumption that the yield spread between the P&G bond and the CTD issue is 111.1 basis points. By subtracting this yield spread from the maximum yield of 5.821%, we get the maximum yield for the CTD issue of 4.710%. This gets us to Box 3 in Figure 1.

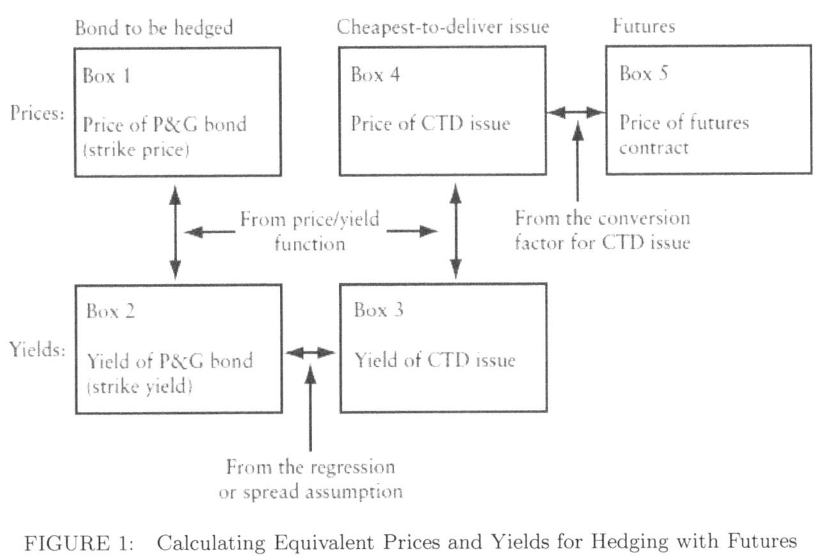

FIGURE 1: Calculating Equivalent Prices and Yields for Hedging with Futures

Now we move on to Box 4 in Figure 1. Given the yield of 4.710% for the CTD issue, the minimum price can be determined. Because the CTD issue is the Treasury 6.25%, 8/15/2023, a 4.710% yield means that the target price for that issue is 116.8044. The corresponding futures price is found by dividing the price of the CTD issue by the conversion factor. This gets us to Box 5 in Figure 1. The conversion factor for the CTD issue is 1.0246. Therefore, the futures price is about 114.373 (116.8044 divided by 1.0246). Now the portfolio manager must look to the options market to determine what strike prices are available because there are a limited number of strike prices available on the exchange. In this illustration, we will assume that the strike price available to the portfolio manager is a strike price of 114 for a put option on a Treasury bond futures contract. This means that a put option on a Treasury bond futures contract with a strike price of 114 is roughly equivalent to a put option on the P&G bond with a strike price of 96.219.

The steps identified in Figure 1 and described above are always necessary to identify the appropriate strike price on a put futures option. The process involves simply (1) the relationship between price and yield; (2) the assumed relationship between the yield spread between the bonds to be hedged and the CTD issue; and (3) the conversion factor for the CTD issue. As with hedging with Treasury bond futures illustrated earlier in this chapter, the success of the hedging strategy will depend on (1) whether the CTD issue changes as market yield changes and (2) the yield spread between the bonds to be hedged and the CTD issue.

The hedge ratio is determined using Equation (3) because we will assume a constant yield spread between the bond to be hedged and CTD issue. To compute the hedge ratio, the portfolio manager must calculate the price value of a basis point at the option expiration date (assumed to be February 22, 2008) and at the yields corresponding to the futures' strike price of 114 (4.710% yield for the CTD issue and 5.821% for the P&G bond). The price value of a basis point per $100 par value for the P&G bond and the CTD issue were 0.1353 and 0.1208, respectively. This results in a hedge ratio of 1.148 for the protective put hedge, or 1.15 with rounding. Because the par value of the futures option is $100,000 and the par value to be protected is $10,000, then 115 put options on the Treasury bond futures contract should be purchased. At the time of the hedge, December 24, 2007, the price quote for this put option was 1.972. This means the dollar cost of each option is

\$197.2. Since 115 contracts would have to be purchased, the total cost of the put options (ignoring commissions) would have been about \$22,678.

To create a table for the protective put hedge, we can use some of the numbers from Table 1. The first column in Table 3 repeats the numbers in the first column of Table 1; the second column in Table 3 reproduces the futures price from the fifth column of Table 1. The rest of the columns in Table 3 are computed. The value of the put options shown in the third column of the table is easy to calculate because the value of each option at expiration is the strike price of the futures option (114) minus the futures price (or zero if that difference is negative). The difference is then multiplied by \$1,000. Let's see why by looking at the first row that corresponds to a future price of 99.139. Since the strike price for the put option is 114, the value of the put option is 14.861 (114.000 – 99.139) per \$100 of par value. Because the par value for the Treasury bond futures contract is \$100,000, the 14.861 must be multiplied by \$1,000. Thus, the value of the contract is 14.861 times \$1,000 or \$14,861. For the 115 contracts purchased for this strategy, the total value is \$1,709,015. The value of the 115 put options shown in the third column of \$1,709,040 differs by \$25 due to rounding in earlier calculation.

The next-to-the-last column of Table 2 shows the cost of the 115 put options. The effective sale price for the P&G bond can then be computed. It is equal to the sum of the actual market price for the P&G bond and the value of the 115 put options at expiration, reduced by the cost of the 115 put options. The effective sale price is shown in the last column of the table. This effective sale price is never less than \$9,601,824. Recall that we established a minimum price of \$9,621,900. This minimum effective sale price is something that can be calculated prior to the implementation of the hedge. Note that as prices decline, the effective sale price actually exceeds the projected effective minimum sale price by a small amount. This is due to rounding and the fact that the hedge ratio is left unaltered, although the relative price values of a basis point that go into the hedge ratio calculation change as yields change. As prices increase, however, the effective sale price of the P&G bond increases as well; unlike the futures hedge shown in Table 3, the protective put buying strategy protects the portfolio manager if rates rise but allows the portfolio manager to profit if rates fall.

Table 3 compares the hedging strategy involving shorting Treasury bond futures with that of the protective put buying strategy.

TABLE 2: Hedge of the $10 Million Par Value of Procter & Gamble 5.55%, 3/5/2037 Using a Protective Put Option Strategy

Actual Sale Price of P&G Bonds	Futures Price[a]	Value of 115 Put Options[b]	Cost of 115 Put Options	Effective Sale Price[c]
8,000,000	99.139	1,709,040	22,678	9,686,362
8,200,000	101.054	1,488,827	22,678	9,666,149
8,400,000	102.946	1,271,207	22,678	9,648,529
8,600,000	104.812	1,056,651	22,678	9,633,973
8,800,000	106.647	845,619	22,678	9,622,941
9,000,000	108.469	636,036	22,678	9,613,358
9,200,000	110.265	429,516	22,678	9,606,838
9,400,000	112.042	225,118	22,678	9,602,440
9,600,000	113.787	24,502	22,678	9,601,824
9,800,000	115.519	0	22,678	9,777,322
10,000,000	117.237	0	22,678	9,977,322
10,200,000	118.938	0	22,678	10,177,322
10,400,000	120.608	0	22,678	10,377,322
10,600,000	122.269	0	22,678	10,577,322
10,800,000	123.908	0	22,678	10,777,322
11,000,000	125.522	0	22,678	10,977,322
11,200,000	127.135	0	22,678	11,177,322
11,400,000	128.721	0	22,678	11,377,322
11,600,000	130.303	0	22,678	11,577,322

Notes:
[a]These numbers are approximate because futures trade in even 32nds.
[b]From $115 \times 1,000 \times \mathrm{Max}[(114 - \text{futures price}), 0]$.
[c]Does not include transaction costs or the financing of the options position.

Covered call writing strategy with futures options

To see how covered call writing with futures options works, we assume that the portfolio manager owns the P&G bond used in our previous illustration. With futures selling around 114.375, a futures call option with a strike price of 120 might be appropriate. The price for the March call options with a strike of 120 expiring on 2/22/2008 was 0.512. As before, it is assumed that the P&G bond will remain at a 111.1 basis point spread off the CTD issue. The number of options contracts sold will be the same as in the protective put buying strategy, 115.

Table 4 shows the results of the covered call writing strategy given these assumptions. To calculate the effective sale price of the bonds in the covered call writing strategy, the premium received from the sale of the call options is added to the actual sale price of the bonds, and the liability associated with the short call position is subtracted from the actual sale

TABLE 3: Comparison of Hedging with Treasury Bond Futures and Protective Put Buying Strategy

Actual Sale Price of P&G Bonds	Effective Sale Price with Futures Hedge	Effective Sale Price with Protective Puts
8,000,000	9,767,401	9,686,362
8,200,000	9,745,273	9,666,149
8,400,000	9,725,761	9,648,529
8,600,000	9,709,339	9,633,973
8,800,000	9,696,472	9,622,941
9,000,000	9,685,066	9,613,358
9,200,000	9,676,751	9,606,838
9,400,000	9,670,575	9,602,440
9,600,000	9,668,215	9,601,824
9,800,000	9,667,281	9,777,322
10,000,000	9,668,034	9,977,322
10,200,000	9,670,700	10,177,322
10,400,000	9,676,990	10,377,322
10,600,000	9,684,253	10,577,322
10,800,000	9,694,165	10,777,322
11,000,000	9,706,975	10,977,322
11,200,000	9,719,797	11,177,322
11,400,000	9,735,913	11,377,322
11,600,000	9,752,347	11,577,322

price. The liability associated with each call is the futures price minus the strike price of 120 (or zero if this difference is negative), all multiplied by \$1,000. The middle column in the table is just this value multiplied by 115, the number of options sold.

Just as the minimum effective sale price can be calculated beforehand for the protective put buying strategy, the maximum effective sale price can be calculated beforehand for the covered call writing strategy. The maximum effective sale price will be the price of the P&G bond corresponding to the strike price of the call option sold, plus the premium received. In this case, the strike price on the futures call option was 120. A futures price of 120 corresponds to a price of 122.9520 (from 120 times the conversion factor of 1.0246), and a corresponding yield of 4.126% for the CTD issue.

The equivalent yield for the P&G bond is 111.1 basis points higher, or 5.3271%, for a corresponding price of 103.273. Adding on the premium received, 0.512, the maximum effective sale price will be about 103.785 or \$10,378,500. While not shown here, it can be demonstrated that if the P&G bond does trade at 111.1 basis points over the CTD issue as assumed, the

TABLE 4: Hedge of the $10 million Par Value Procter & Gamble 5.55%, 3/5/2037 Using Calls on Futures

Actual Sal Price of P&G Bonds	Futures Price[a]	Liability of 115 Call Options[b]	Premium for 115 Call Options	Effective Sale Price[c]
8,000,000	99.139	0	5,888	8,005,888
8,200,000	101.054	0	5,888	8,205,888
8,400,000	102.946	0	5,888	8,405,888
8,600,000	104.812	0	5,888	8,605,888
8,800,000	106.647	0	5,888	8,805,888
9,000,000	108.469	0	5,888	9,005,888
9,200,000	110.265	0	5,888	9,205,888
9,400,000	112.042	0	5,888	9,405,888
9,600,000	113.787	0	5,888	9,605,888
9,800,000	115.519	0	5,888	9,805,888
10,000,000	117.237	0	5,888	10,005,888
10,200,000	118.938	0	5,888	10,205,888
10,400,000	120.608	69,902	5,888	10,335,986
10,600,000	122.269	260,978	5,888	10,344,910
10,800,000	123.908	449,427	5,888	10,356,461
11,000,000	125.522	635,003	5,888	10,370,885
11,200,000	127.135	820,568	5,888	10,385,320
11,400,000	128.721	1,002,866	5,888	10,403,022
11,600,000	130.303	1,184,850	5,888	10,421,038

Notes:
[a]These numbers are approximate because futures trade in even 32nds.
[b]From 115 × $1,000 × Max[(futures price −120), 0].
[c]Does not include transaction costs or the financing of the options position.

maximum effective sale price for the P&G bond is, in fact, slightly more than that amount. The discrepancies shown in the table are due to rounding and the fact that the position is not adjusted even though the relative price values of a basis point change as yields change.

Using Interest Rate Swaps in Bond Portfolio Management[4]

In Chapter 14, we explained equity swaps. The use of such swaps is far less common than interest rate swaps. In this section, we explain how bond portfolio managers can control interest rate risk using interest rate swaps. Although different types of interest rate swaps exist, including

[4]This section is coauthored with Shrikant Ramamurthy.

vanilla swaps, basis swaps, indexed-amortizing swaps, and callable swaps, to name a few, here our focus is on generic interest rate swaps as hedge instruments.

We begin with a brief description of the characteristics of interest rate swaps and how a swap can be viewed as a financed bond position. This alternate view is particularly useful for understanding how interest rate swaps can be used to control interest rate risk. We then focus on the interest rate sensitivity of swaps and go on to develop hedge ratios and hedge strategies using swaps. As we shall illustrate, hedging with swaps is very similar to hedging with Treasury securities and interest rate futures contracts. An example of constructing a hedge for corporate bonds is provided.

Characterizing Interest Rate Swaps

In its most basic form, an interest rate swap is an agreement between two parties to exchange cash flows periodically. In a plain vanilla swap, one party pays a fixed rate of interest based on a notional amount in return for the receipt of a floating rate of interest based on the same notional amount from the counterparty. These cash flows are exchanged periodically for the life of the swap (also known as the tenor of the swap). Typically, no principal is exchanged at the beginning or end of a swap.

The fixed rate on a swap is ordinarily set at a rate such that the net present value of the swap's cash flow is zero at the start of the swap contract. This type of swap is also known as a *par swap* and the fixed rate is called the *swap rate*. The difference between the swap rate and the yield on an equivalent-maturity Treasury is called the *swap spread*.

The floating rate on a swap has historically been benchmarked off of a money market rate, typically the London Interbank Offered Rate (LIBOR).[5] In a plain vanilla swap, the floating rate is 3-month LIBOR, which resets and pays quarterly in arrears[6] on an actual/360 daycount

[5]LIBOR is the average interbank interest rate at which leading banks in London are willing to lend to one another. There are seven maturities: overnight (1 day), 1 week, 1 month, 2 months, 3 months, 6 months, and 12 months. Because it was determined that the select banks that reported LIBOR misstated the rate in order to enhance profits, in the U.S. and U.K. the use of LIBOR will end by December 2021.

[6]Quarterly payment in arrears means the interest payment made by the issuer on the first day of each quarter pays the interest for the quarter that just ended.

basis. The fixed rate is paid semiannually,[7] which is similar to the convention in the corporate bond market.[8]

Conceptually, from the perspective of the fixed-rate receiver (floating-rate payer), a position in an interest rate swap can be viewed as a long fixed-rate bond position that is totally financed at short-term interest rates, such as term repurchase (repo) rates or LIBOR. In a fully financed long bond position, fixed-rate interest payments are received, and floating-rate financing costs are paid periodically, with the final principal payment from the bond used to repay the initial financing of the bond purchase. On a net basis, a fully financed bond position has zero cost, like a swap, and the periodic cash flows replicate the cash flows on a swap. In fact, a swap from the perspective of the fixed-rate receiver is a fully leveraged bond position where the financing rate is equivalent to the floating-rate on a swap. Hence, this alternate view of an interest rate swap from the perspective of the fixed-rate receiver is appealing because it implies that a swap can be used as an alternative hedging vehicle to Treasury securities and futures contracts to manage interest rate risk.

The position of a floating-rate payer (fixed-rate receiver) is equivalent to shorting a fixed-rate bond and investing the proceeds in a floating-rate bond. Once again, this is appealing because it suggests that swaps can be used as an alternative instrument to manage interest rate risk.

Interest Rate Sensitivity of a Swap

Although the value of a swap is a function of both long- and short-bond positions, it is still very sensitive to changes in interest rates. Figure 2 shows the price profile of a currently par priced swap to changes in interest rates. The tenor of the swap is 2 years, the swap rate (i.e., the fixed rate) is 6.225% and is paid semiannually, and the reference rate is 3-month LIBOR and is paid quarterly. The notional amount is $100. For comparison purposes, the values of the fixed-rate and floating-rate bonds that make up the equivalent portfolio are shown as well.

---

[7] There are conventions in the bond market for the assumed number of days in the month and number of days in the year for computing interest on a debt instrument. These are called daycount conventions. The daycount convention used in the swap market is 30/360 which means 30 days in a month and 360 days in a year.

[8] Paid in arrears means that the floating rate for a particular quarter is set at the beginning of the quarter and the associated cash flow is exchanged at the end of the quarter.

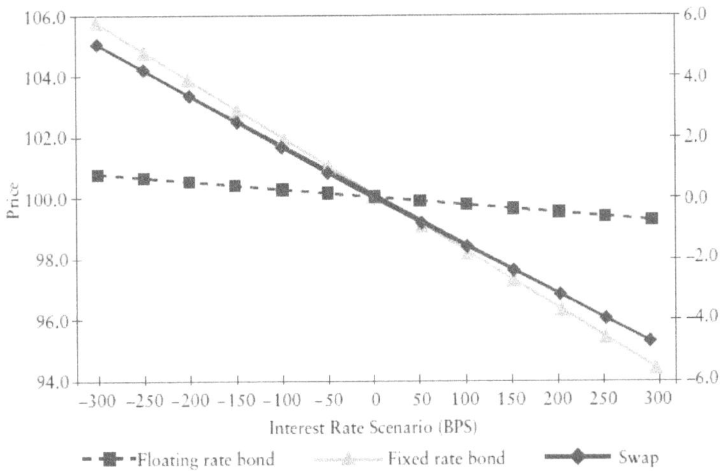

FIGURE 2: Price Sensitivity of a 2-Year Interest Rate Swap

Note: The pricing on the floating rate bond assumes that the coupon of the first period has already been set.

The swap currently has no value and both the fixed- and floating-rate bonds are priced at par. As rates decline, the value of the swap increases because the fixed rate cash-flow receipts become more valuable in the lower-rate environment. The value of the swap does not increase as much as that of the fixed-rate bond because the increase in the value of the swap in declining rate scenarios is constrained by the increase in the value of the floating-rate bond. However, given that the increase in the floating-rate bond is minimal, the change in the value of the swap is similar to the change in the value of the fixed-rate bond. In environments where rates rise, the value to the swap falls like that of the fixed-rate bond; however, the decline in value is slightly reduced by the short floating-rate position.

Like a fixed-rate bond, an interest rate swap displays positive convexity, which, as explained in Chapter 16, means that the increase in the value of a swap for a decline in rates is larger than the loss associated with a similar increase in rates. The similar price profile between a fixed-rate bond and a swap is important to note because it is this similarity that makes swaps an efficient and alternate hedge instrument for bonds.

PVBP of a Swap

As explained in Chapter 16, the price value of a basis point (PVBP) of a swap measures the dollar sensitivity of a swap to changes in interest rates.

The PVBP of a swap is the change in the value of a swap for a 1-basis-point change in rates. As it was for using Treasury futures and options for hedging, the PVBP is the key measure in developing a hedge ratio when using interest rate swaps.

The PVBP of a swap can be computed as follows:

$$\text{PVBP(Swap)} = \text{PVBP(Fixed rate bond)} - \text{PVBP(Floating rate bond)}. \tag{4}$$

The PVBP using Equation (4) is usually computed on a notional amount of \$1 million. Implicitly, the PVBP computation assumes that rate movements are parallel, with the entire yield curve shifting in equal fashion. Typically, PVBP is computed using increments of 10 to 25 basis points. Since PVBP is computed using scenarios where rates rise and fall, the PVBP computation is an average sensitivity measure and will not measure exactly the sensitivity in either scenario.

It can be shown that the PVBP of the swap is \$160.71 — slightly less than the PVBP of a 2-year fixed-rate bond at \$185.36. The PVBP of a swap is slightly less than that of a fixed-rate bond to account for the short position in the floating-rate bond, which has a PVBP of \$24.65.

Equation (4) provides the PVBP for the swap. In general, the PVBP of a swap is approximately equal to the PVBP of a fixed-rate bond with maturity spanning from the next reset date to the maturity date of the swap. The PVBP of a 5-year swap is similar to the PVBP of a 4.75-year fixed-rate bond; the PVBP of a 2.25-year swap is similar to the PVBP of a 2-year fixed-rate bond.

Although the PVBP of a swap is similar to that of a slightly shorter fixed-rate bond, the PVBP of a swap will change differently over time from the PVBP on a fixed-rate bond. This is important to note in the context of hedging. The PVBP of a swap just prior to a reset date will be identical to the PVBP of a fixed-rate bond because, at this time, the PVBP of the floating-rate bond is zero. However, just after the reset date, the floating-rate bond will have a PVBP that is similar to the PVBP of a fixed-rate bond to the next reset date.

As a result, just after the reset date, the PVBP on a swap will immediately decline by the PVBP of the floating-rate bond. Between reset periods, the PVBP of the swap will not change much as both the PVBP of the fixed-rate bond and the floating-rate bond will decline in similar fashion. This is very different from the PVBP of a fixed-rate bond that declines steadily over time.

Hedging with Interest Rate Swaps

Hedging bonds with interest rates swaps is similar to hedging bonds with Treasury-based futures contracts as we illustrated earlier in this chapter. To hedge a long position in a bond, an asset manager needs to establish a pay-fixed swap position since changes in the value of a swap are inversely related to changes in the value of the bond being hedged. Recall that in a pay-fixed swap position, which is analogous to a short-bond position, the asset manager pays a fixed rate to receive a floating rate. In designing a hedge using interest rate swaps, the maturity of the interest rate swap should match the maturity of the instrument that is used as the pricing reference for the security being hedged. This is analogous to hedging in the Treasury market.

For example, if a 2-year corporate bond is priced relative to the 2-year Treasury security, the corporate bond's price changes as yield spreads change and as the yield on the 2-year Treasury changes. The appropriate swap hedge for this corporate bond is a 2-year swap since it is also priced relative to the 2-year Treasury. A 2-year swap's value changes as swap spreads change and as the 2-year Treasury's yield changes. As a result of using a 2-year swap to hedge the corporate bond, the interest rate risk of the 2-year corporate bond that is attributable to movements in 2-year Treasury yields can be mitigated. To the extent that the 2-year corporate bond's yield spread is correlated to 2-year swap spreads, credit spread risk also may be mitigated.

Hedge ratio

The hedge ratio for hedging a bond using interest rate swaps is a function of the PVBPs of the swap and the security to be hedged, and is expressed as

$$\text{Hedge ratio} = \frac{\text{PVBP of security to be hedged}}{\text{PVBP of swap}}. \tag{5}$$

Recall that the PVBP of an interest rate swap is similar to that of a fixed-rate bond with a maturity from the swap's next reset date to the swap's maturity date. Thus, the hedge ratio using interest rate swaps, generally, will be slightly higher than the hedge ratio using Treasury securities.

Corporate bond swap hedge illustration

Table 5 describes a hedge for a long position in TCI Corporation 9.25% of April 15, 2002, as of June 16, 1997. Since the TCI notes are priced off

TABLE 5: Hedging a Corporate Bond Using Interest Rate Swaps

Objective: Hedge $1 million par amount TCI Corp 9.25% of April 15, 2002, using five-year interest rate swaps.

Issue	Coupon/ Swap Rate (%)	Maturity	Price[a]	Yield (%)	Spread (bps)	PVBP per $1 million Par Amount ($)
TCI Corp	9.25	04/15/02	107.915	7.27	+100	420.27
5-Year Swap	6.53	06/19/02	0.000	—	+26	396.20

$$\text{Hedge Ratio} = \frac{420.27}{396.20} = 1.061$$

Change in Portfolio Value[a]

	Unhedged Portfolio	Hedged Portfolio
Rates increase by 50 basis points	1,058,390 − 1,079,150 = −20,760	(1,058,390 − 1,079,150) −1,061(−19,550) = 17.45
Rates decrease by 50 basis points	1,100,420 − 1,079,150 = 21,270	(1,100,420 − 1,079,150) −1.061(20,080) = −34.88

Note: [a]Prices as of June 16, 1997.

5-year Treasury rates, the appropriate hedge instrument using swaps is a 5-year interest rate swap, which is similarly affected by movements in 5-year yields. The hedge ratio using swaps is 1.061, implying that approximately $1.061 million notional amount of 5-year swaps need to be sold in order to hedge $1 million TCI corporate notes. If 5-year Treasury securities are used as a substitute, the hedge ratio will be slightly smaller because the 5-year Treasury has a higher PVBP.

If the TCI position is not hedged, the portfolio can gain or lose approximately $21,000 if rates move 50 basis points. In contrast, the hedged portfolio provides substantial protection against interest rate movements. If rates move 50 basis points, the hedged portfolio moves minimally in value. This analysis assumes that yield spreads are unchanged and does not account for any bid-offer spread in the markets. If spread changes on the corporate bond position are accompanied by similar spread changes on the 5-year swap, the swap hedge will also eliminate credit spread risk. If corporate spreads are negatively correlated with swap spreads, then a swap-based hedge will increase the exposure to credit spread risk. Generally, though, swap spreads move in the same direction as corporate spreads and provide protection against general movements in corporate spreads. Of course, given the generic nature of swap spreads, they will never provide protection against the idiosyncratic risk of any particular corporate credit.

One point to note when using swaps as a hedge instrument is that the PVBP of a swap declines on a reset date. This implies that on swap reset dates, the existing swap position may need to be adjusted by shorting additional swaps with the same remaining term-to-maturity to match the PVBP of the security being hedged.

Using Credit Default Swaps to Manage Credit Risk

Thus far, our focus has been on using derivatives to control interest rate risk. Another major risk exposure of a bond portfolio is credit risk. There are derivatives that are available to provide credit protection or to obtain credit exposure. The general name for these types of derivatives is *credit derivatives.* The type of credit derivative that is most commonly used is a *credit default swap* (CDS). Here, our focus will be only on this type of credit derivative. It is important to emphasize that a CDS is an OTC instrument. Therefore, while this derivative can be used to control credit risk, there is counterparty risk in a CDS trade that must be considered.

There are two types of CDS: single-name CDS and credit default swap index. We will describe the features of these two credit default swaps and how they can be used to manage credit risk.

Single-Name Credit Default Swaps

A CDS is employed to shift credit exposure to a credit protection seller. A CDS that involves only one entity for which credit protection is being transferred is called a *single-name credit default swap.* The entity that is the underlying for the contract is either referred to as the reference entity or reference obligation. The *reference entity* is the issuer of the bond and hence is also referred to as the *reference issuer.* For example, the reference issuer could be Procter & Gamble. Rather than a reference entity, the underlying for a single-name CDS could be a specific bond issue. In such cases, the underlying is referred to as the *reference obligation.* For example, Procter & Gamble has many bond issues outstanding. Any one of those issues could be the reference obligation for a single-name CDS. Typically, the underlying for a single-name CDS involving a corporate entity is a reference entity.

The mechanics of a single-name CDS are as follows. There are two parties to the contract: the buyer of the CDS and the seller of the CDS. The buyer of the CDS is the party that is seeking credit protection for the reference entity. The seller of the CDS is the party that is providing protection to the CDS buyer for the reference entity. The credit protection being sought is against the occurrence of a *credit event*. That is, if a credit event occurs with respect to the reference entity, the protection seller (i.e., seller of the CDS) must compensate the protection buyer (i.e., buyer of the CDS). To understand the mechanics of the contract, we need to understand: (1) what a credit event is and (2) what the potential cash flows are for the two parties to the contract.

Credit event

One might think that a credit event is the default or bankruptcy of the reference entity. However, that is not true. Default and bankruptcy are only two types of credit events. What constitutes a credit event is defined in the legal documentation for a CDS trade. That documentation, which is the standard contract for a CDS trade developed by the International Swap and Derivatives Association (ISDA), defines eight credit events that attempt to capture every type of situation that could cause the credit quality of the reference entity to deteriorate, or cause the value of the bonds of the reference entity to decline in value. These eight events include (1) bankruptcy, (2) failure to pay, (3) repudiation/moratorium, (4) downgrade, (5) restructuring, (6) credit event upon merger, (7) cross acceleration, and (8) cross default.[9] In the documentation for a specific CDS trade, there are checkboxes whereby the counterparties to the trade specify the credit events that are applicable.

Equivalent economic positions in cash bond market

Now let's look at the cash flows for a single-name CDS trade with the goal of understanding how a position taken in a CDS equates to a position in the cash bond market. The protection buyer pays a premium periodically (typically every quarter) to the credit protection seller in return for the right

[9]The definition for each credit event is set forth in more detail in the 1999 *ISDACredit Derivatives Definitions* as modified in 2001 by the *Restructuring Supplement to the 1999 ISDA Credit Derivatives Definitions* and then in 2003 by the 2003 *ISDA Credit Derivative Definitions*.

to receive a payment conditional upon the occurrence of a credit event by the reference entity. The premium is called the *swap payment*. If no credit event occurs over the life of the contract, then the credit protection buyer makes the payments up to the contract's maturity date. At that time, the contract terminates. If a credit event occurs, the credit protection buyer is responsible for the accrued premium up to the date of the credit event and the credit protection seller must perform depending on the settlement procedure set forth in the legal documentation. The contract terminates after the credit event occurs.

The most obvious way for an asset manager to use a single-name CDS is to acquire credit protection for the holding of a credit name in its portfolio. The question is why doesn't the asset manager just sell the bonds? There are two reasons. First, the market for corporate bonds is not very liquid. The asset manager may find it beneficial to acquire protection rather than sell the bond when there is poor liquidity. Second, there may be a tax reason for doing so. For example, the asset manager may have to hold a corporate bond for say 2 months in order to benefit from a favorable capital gains treatment. A single-name CDS can be used to provide protection against credit risk during that 2-month period.

If an asset manager wants to purchase the obligation of a corporate entity (i.e., gain long exposure), then the most obvious way to do so is to purchase the bond in the cash market. However, as just noted, because of the illiquidity of the corporate bond market, there may be better execution by transacting in the CDS market. More specifically, the selling of credit protection on a corporate entity provides long credit exposure to that entity. To understand why, consider what happens when an asset manager sells credit protection on a reference entity. The asset manager receives the swap premium and if there is no credit event, the swap premium is received over the life of the CDS contract. However, this is equivalent to buying the bond of the corporate entity. Instead of receiving coupon interest payments, the asset manager receives the swap premium payments. If there is a credit event, then the asset manager, under the terms of the CDS, must make a payment to the credit protection buyer. However, this is equivalent to a loss that would be realized if the bond was purchased. Hence, selling credit protection via a single-name CDS is economically equivalent to a long position in the reference entity.

Suppose that an asset manager wants to short a corporate bond because it is believed that the corporation is going to experience a credit event that will cause a decline in the value of the bond. In the absence of a CDS, the asset manager would have to short the bonds in the cash market. However, it is extremely difficult to short corporate bonds. With a liquid single-name CDS, it is easy to effectively short the bond of a corporate entity. Remember that shorting a bond involves making payments to another party and then if the investor is correct and the bond's price declines, selling the bond at a higher price (i.e., realizes a gain). That is precisely what occurs when a single-name CDS is purchased: the investor makes payments (the swap premium payments) and realizes a gain if a credit event occurs. Hence, buying credit protection via a single-name CDS is equivalent to shorting.

Finally, for an asset manager seeking a leveraged position in a corporate bond, this can be achieved by selling credit protection. As just noted, selling credit protection is equivalent to a long position in the reference entity. Moreover, as with other derivatives, a CDS allows this to be done on a leveraged basis.

Credit Default Swap Index

Unlike a single-name CDS, the underlying for a *credit default swap index* (CDX) is a standardized basket of reference entities. There are standardized CDX compiled and managed by Dow Jones. For the corporate bond indexes, there are separate indexes for investment-grade corporate entities, the most actively traded being the North America Investment Grade Index (denoted by DJ.CDX.NA.IG). As the index name suggests, the reference entities in this index are those with an investment-grade rating. The index includes 125 corporate names in North America with each corporate name having an equal weighting in the index (0.8%). The index is updated semi-annually by Dow Jones.

The mechanics of a CDX are different from that of a single-name CDS. For both types of CDS, there is a swap premium that is paid periodically. If a credit event occurs, the swap premium payment ceases in the case of a single-name CDS and the contract is terminated. In contrast, for a CDX, the swap payment continues to be made by the credit protection buyer. However, the amount of the quarterly swap premium payment is reduced. This is because the notional amount is reduced as a result of a credit event for a reference entity.

For example, suppose that a portfolio manager is the protection buyer for a DJ.CDX.NA.IG and the notional amount is $100 million. The formula given earlier for the quarterly swap premium payment is used to compute the payment for a CDX. At the outset of the CDX trade (before a credit event), the premium would be based on a notional amount of $100 million. If a credit event occurs for one of the reference entities, the notional amount for computing future swap premium payments is reduced by $80,000 (0.8% times $100 million)[10] to $99,920,000.

What we said earlier about how an asset manager can use a single-name CDS applies equally to CDX. However, rather than managing exposure to a single entity, a CDX allows a portfolio manager to reduce exposure to a diversified portfolio of investment-grade corporate names. Thus, an asset manager seeking credit protection for the investment-grade corporate sector of a portfolio can obtain that protection by buying a CDX. This is the same as reducing credit exposure to that sector. A corporate bond portfolio manager seeking to increase exposure to the investment-grade corporate sector can do so by selling a CDX.

Key Points

- There two types of interest rate futures contracts used by asset managers: Treasury-based futures contracts and Eurodollar futures contracts.
- There are three Treasury-based futures contracts: Treasury bond futures, Treasury note futures, and ultra Treasury bond futures.
- The underlying for the Treasury-based futures is a hypothetical Treasury that grants the seller (the short) of the contract the option to deliver several Treasury issues, referred to as the quality option or the swap option.
- The Treasury issue that is best to deliver against a specific Treasury futures contract is called the cheapest-to-deliver issue and is the issue with the largest implied repo rate.
- In addition to the choice of which acceptable Treasury issue to deliver, the short is permitted to decide when in the delivery month the delivery actually takes place (called the timing option) and to give notice of intent to deliver up to 8 pm Chicago time after the closing of the exchange (called the wildcard option).
- The quality option, the timing option, and the wildcard option — in sum, referred to as the delivery options — mean that the long position

[10]Since there are 125 companies in the index, removing one means that 1/125 or 0.8% of the notional amount will be reduced.

can never be sure of which Treasury bond issue will be delivered or when it will be delivered.

- The Eurodollar futures contract is used to take a position in the short end of the yield curve.
- Asset managers have found the Eurodollar futures contract to be an effective vehicle for a wide range of hedging situations.
- A Eurodollar futures contract represents a commitment to pay/receive a quarterly interest payment determined by the level of 3-month LIBOR and is quoted on an index-price basis.
- Asset managers can use interest rate futures to alter the interest rate sensitivity, or duration, of a portfolio.
- Buying Treasury-based futures increases the portfolio's duration; selling Treasury-based futures contracts reduces the portfolio's duration.
- Hedging is a special case of risk control where the asset manager's target duration is zero.
- Cross-hedging with Treasury-based futures is more complicated than hedging deliverable securities because it involves two relationships: (1) between the CTD issue and the futures contract and (2) the security to be hedged and the CTD issue.
- The key to minimizing risk in a cross hedge is to choose the right hedge ratio.
- The hedge ratio depends on volatility weighting, or weighting by relative changes in value.
- Interest rate options can be written on a fixed income security (options on physicals) or an interest rate futures contract (futures options).
- A futures option gives the buyer the right to buy from or sell to the writer a designated futures contract at the strike price.
- For a futures option that is a call option, the buyer has the right to purchase one designated futures contract at the strike price (i.e., the buyer has the right to acquire a long futures position in the designated futures contract); if the buyer exercises the call option, the writer acquires a corresponding short position in the futures contract.
- A put option on a futures contract grants the buyer the right to sell one designated futures contract to the writer at the strike price (i.e., the option buyer has the right to acquire a short position in the designated futures contract); if the put option is exercised, the writer acquires a corresponding long position in the designated futures contract.

- Futures options are used in a protective put buying strategy (a risk management application) and a covered call writing strategy (a return enhancement application).
- In its most basic form, an interest rate swap is an agreement between two parties to exchange cash flows periodically.
- In a plain vanilla swap, one party pays a fixed rate of interest based on a notional amount in return for the receipt of a floating rate of interest based on the same notional amount from the counterparty.
- Credit default swaps are the most popular type of credit derivative for providing credit protection or to obtain credit exposure.
- The two types of CDS are single-name CDS and credit default swap index.
- Selling credit protection via a single-name CDS is economically equivalent to a long position in the reference entity; buying credit protection via a single-name CDS is equivalent to shorting the reference entity.
- An asset manager seeking credit protection for the investment-grade corporate sector can use a credit default swap index.

PART VI

Multi-asset Portfolio Strategies

Chapter 19

Multi-asset Portfolio Strategies

Learning Objectives

After reading this chapter, you will understand:

- what a balanced fund strategy is;
- criticisms of a balanced fund investment vehicle;
- what a multi-asset fund is and why multi-asset strategies are popular today;
- the different types of multi-asset strategies;
- the different types of asset allocation strategies: strategic, tactical, and dynamic;
- the risk-parity allocation and factor-based allocation;
- the difference between passive asset allocation strategies and active asset allocation strategies;
- the difference between conventional strategic allocation, risk-parity allocation, and factor-based allocation;
- the characteristics of multi-asset strategies;
- the investment objectives of multi-asset funds.

At one time, a popular strategy for achieving diversification was a *balanced fund strategy* with the objective of income and capital appreciation. This strategy, offered to investors in the form of a mutual fund, invests in US equities and US bonds. The key in a balanced fund strategy — also referred to as *a hybrid fund strategy* and an *allocation fund strategy* — is the allocation among these two asset classes. In this strategy, the fund manager has a target allocation, the "stock/bond mix". Morningstar classifies balanced funds into five categories according to a fund's percentage of equities: (1) 15% to 30%, (2) 30% to 50%, (3) 50% to 70%, (4) 70% to 85%, and (5) 85%+.

There are criticisms of a balanced fund as an investment vehicle. Lustig [2017] summarizes the three main criticisms of balanced funds:

1. "While the word "balanced" appears in the name of some funds, often their exposure to equity markets explains over 90% of their risk and returns — hardly balanced.
2. Some funds' rigid asset allocation lacks dynamism, as it is driven mainly by long-term, strategic allocation without the ability to shift nimbly across markets (often referred to as "tactical positioning" or "market timing").
3. The universe of asset classes included in some funds is limited to traditional equities and bonds, without sufficient exposure to alternative investments and sophisticated investment methods."

For these reasons, there has been reduced interest in balanced funds. Today, a well-structured diversified portfolio involves going beyond stocks and bonds. Such funds that include multiple asset classes beyond just that of bonds and equities are called *multi-asset funds*. The strategies that the managers of these portfolios pursue are called *multi-asset strategies*. These strategies differ from a balanced fund strategy in two ways. First, in order to provide better diversification, multi-asset strategies cover far more asset classes such as global equities, global debt instruments, commodities, currencies, and real estate. Second, multi-asset strategies are much more sophisticated in structuring the portfolio, using systematic strategies such as tactical asset allocation and risk-controlled strategies to hedge against tail risk (i.e., the risk of major market declines).

Multi-asset funds are now an important feature of the investment landscape. They provide diversification benefits, offer the opportunity to enhance risk-adjusted returns, and enable the fund manager to customize the strategy to satisfy a wide range of investment objectives.

According to Cao [2015], there were few multi-asset strategies prior to the 2008–2009 Global Financial Crisis. One obvious reason is the recognition of the importance of expanding beyond equities and bonds to provide better diversification. Cao offers two other reasons for the rise in the development of multi-asset strategies. The need of the asset management industry to create products that were different from those traditionally offered to clients was one of the reasons. Second, following the Global Financial Crisis, tactical asset allocation strategies became popular and, as explained later in this chapter, this offers the fund manager far greater flexibility in selecting an asset allocation.

In this chapter, we describe the broad categories of multi-asset strategies and how they differ from the strategies used by traditional balanced funds. Because all managers of multi-asset portfolios use various asset allocation strategies, we begin by describing these strategies.

Asset Allocation Strategies

In Chapter 1, we briefly described two studies that have demonstrated the importance of the asset allocation decision when asset managers invested primarily in only two asset classes, equities and bonds. An objective in multi-asset funds is to use asset allocation strategies to specifically drive returns. Here, we will describe the different asset allocation strategies. They include the following:

- Strategic asset allocation.
- Tactical asset allocation.
- Dynamic asset allocation.

We briefly described these asset allocation strategies in Chapter 1.

Strategic Asset Allocation

A *strategic asset allocation* is a long-term asset allocation decision that uses a top-down approach to determine a long-term "normal" asset mix that offers the greatest prospects for strong long-term rewards to accomplish investment objectives. Typically, a strategic asset allocation strategy, also referred to as a *policy asset allocation*, allows for a narrow range for the deviation from the specified allocation for each asset class. However, once the portfolio is outside of that range, the fund manager must rebalance the portfolio's allocation to bring the asset allocation into compliance.

In addition to considering the client's risk tolerance, the allocation is based on capital market forecasts of three key inputs: average long-term returns for each asset class, average return volatility of each asset class, and the average return correlation for each pair of asset classes. The key issue with strategic asset allocation is forecasting these inputs. This is no simple task. As mentioned in Chapter 8, these inputs which are used in mean-variance analysis can result in substantially different strategic asset allocations when different input values are assumed. Mean-variance analysis assumes that the average value for the inputs is unchanged over time, ignoring the fact that average values are not realized during periods of market stress as was observed during the Global Financial Crisis. Moreover, the resulting allocation is often highly concentrated in a sub-set of asset classes.

With strategic allocation, there are various strategies that can be employed to determine the asset allocation. The conventional approach is based on capital market inputs on historical returns, variances, and correlations for each asset class. Even within the mean-variance framework, as explained in Chapter 8, there is not one allocation but an allocation for each level of risk (variance or standard deviation). The portfolios that provide the maximum return for a given level of risk are called efficient portfolios. The most common efficient portfolio is the one with the global minimum variance. However, there are limitations to this approach as we have just noted and explained in more detail in Chapter 8. Commonly used approaches to overcome the problems associated with conventional strategic asset allocation are risk-parity allocation and factor-based allocation. With the introduction of multi-asset strategies, there has been a migration from the conventional asset allocation to risk-based allocation or factor-based allocation.

Risk-parity allocation

In conventional strategic asset allocation, the inputs are expected returns, variances, and correlations using mean-variance analysis to determine the allocation. A strategic asset allocation using *risk-parity allocation* is based solely on equalizing the risk contribution of each asset class and ignoring expected returns and correlations. This approach, also referred to as *equally-weighted risk allocation*,[1] uses leverage such that the portfolio is equally risk weighted for each asset class. This is done by taking the least volatile asset class (i.e., government bonds) and leveraging the exposure to it. The contribution to portfolio risk from the leveraged position in government bonds is like the volatility exposure of the unleveraged position in other asset classes included in the portfolio. The combined leveraged government bond position and unleveraged exposure in an asset class can result in a portfolio that exhibits lower volatility than an unleveraged portfolio.

[1]Empirical evidence supporting an equally-weighted risk allocation was found by Maillard, Roncalli, and Teïletche [2010].

The risk contribution of an asset class is computed as follows. First, the market value of asset class i is divided by the total value of the portfolio. This is the weight of asset class i. Second, the *marginal risk contribution* is calculated by changing, by a small amount, how much is allocated to asset class i and determining how the total portfolio risk changes. Finally, the product of the weight of asset class i and the marginal risk contribution gives the risk contribution of asset class i. Allocating based on risk contribution is referred to as *risk budgeting*. When the risk budget is based on an equal allocation of risk across asset classes, it is referred to as *risk parity*.

Factor-based allocation

Strategic asset allocation assumes that the attributes of asset classes should be used as the foundation to construct multi-asset portfolios. Since the turn of the century, however, studies have suggested that a better building block for constructing portfolios is to do so using factors, not asset classes.[2] A *factor-based allocation strategy*, it is argued, is the best method for capturing risk premiums that a fund manager has identified.[3] The idea is to target the allocation based on common risk factors and then identify the asset classes that provide the optimal exposure to those risk factors. Implementing this strategy involves not only identifying the factors but also obtaining good forecasts of expected factor returns, factor variances, and correlations of factor returns. This is the same criticism leveled against the traditional strategic asset allocation approach.

Tactical Asset Allocation

A client seeking to pursue a strategic asset allocation strategy may not permit the fund manager to deviate from the fixed asset mix specified (or violate the boundaries for a specific asset class). That is, once the allocations are made to each asset class, no changes are permitted. Consequently, a strategic asset allocation strategy that offers the fund manager no flexibility to modify the initial asset allocation is a *passive asset allocation*

[2]See, for example, Bender, Sun, and Thomas [2019], Clarke, de Silva, and Murdock [2005], and Page and Taborsky [2011].

[3]Bergeron, Kritzman, and Sivitsky [2018] propose a model for integrating traditional asset allocation and factor-based investing. Bass, Gladstone, and Ang [2017] propose a strategic factor allocation framework. Greenberg, Babu, and Ang [2016] propose a methodology that maps factor exposures to different asset classes.

strategy. However, investors may allow a fund manager to deviate from the fixed allocation to an asset class in order to enhance the expected return through short-term gains to a given asset class. This asset allocation strategy is referred to as *tactical asset allocation*. Perceived short-term gains can be realized based on a variety of strategies that we described in earlier chapters.

Tactical asset allocation is not a single, clearly defined strategy. There are many variations and nuances that are involved in building a tactical allocation strategy. Given that the goal of the strategy is to seek short-term return enhancement opportunities, it is referred to as an *active asset allocation strategy*. The risk to this asset allocation strategy is that there could be considerable short-term losses that result in the strategic asset allocation strategy failing to meet the investment objectives.

Dynamic Asset Allocation Strategy

A criticism of the strategic asset allocation strategy is that it considers only capital market conditions at the outset of the investment period and thereby fails to adapt to changes in capital market conditions. In contrast to a strategic asset allocation strategy, in a *dynamic asset allocation strategy*, the asset mix (i.e., the allocation among the asset classes) is mechanistically shifted in response to changing capital market conditions. Also, unlike a strategic asset allocation strategy, no fixed allocation is established for each asset class. The fund manager is free to alter the asset mix based on expectations about each asset classes' performance. The fund manager shifts funds out of the asset classes that are expected to perform poorly and into those expected to perform the best. The performance of the portfolio is, of course, determined by the fund manager's skill in assessing the future performance of each asset class. Moreover, transaction costs are higher than that of a strategic asset allocation strategy because of the rebalancing of the portfolio to capitalize on the expected performance of asset classes.

Like the tactical asset allocation strategy, the dynamic asset allocation strategy is an active asset allocation strategy. The difference between these two active asset allocation strategies is that tactical asset allocation strategy requires that the fund manager return to the fixed allocation as specified by the strategic asset allocation strategy; the fund manager using a dynamic asset allocation strategy does not have a fixed allocation to an asset class that must be adhered to.

Characteristics of Multi-asset Strategies

Multi-asset strategies have the following characteristics[4]:

- The fund manager's mandate (i.e., set of instructions for managing the fund) is broad.
- The broad mandate gives the fund manager the flexibility to invest in a broad range of asset classes that have a wide spectrum of risk–return profiles.
- Because of the broad mandate, the fund manager can construct the portfolio with investment vehicles ranging from low-risk government bonds to high-risk investment vehicles such as emerging market equities, or low-grade fixed-income securities or high-dividend paying stocks.
- The fund manager seeks to provide diversification by holding asset classes with low correlations with each other and with assets that have a high degree of liquidity.
- The broad mandate combined with high liquidity allows the fund manager to take advantage of perceived opportunities by adjusting the asset allocation.
- There may be some benchmark based on a combination of asset class benchmarks or, as commonly is the case, there may be no benchmark but instead an absolute return that is expected to be earned over the business cycle.

General Classification of Multi-asset Strategies

There are various ways to classify the wide range of multi-asset strategies. We describe two classification systems here.

Mercer Classification of Multi-asset Strategies

As of 2014, the consulting firm Mercer tracks more than 400 strategies and provides four broad categories of multi-asset strategies:

- core strategies;
- risk parity strategies;

[4]https://www.aegonassetmanagement.com/netherlands/news-and-insights/Multi-asset-an-all-weather-investment-solution/.

- diversified inflation strategies;
- idiosyncratic strategies.[5]

We already covered risk-parity strategies, so we will just discuss the other three multi-asset strategies as follows.

Core strategies

Core strategies include strategies where most of the fund's growth depends on market returns. Either a target long-term strategic asset allocation for the equity/bond mix is established or an implicit mix is pursued. A dynamic asset allocation strategy is followed to allow the fund manager to alter the allocation to asset classes. This is typically implemented using derivatives and exchange-traded funds so that the rebalancing can be executed in a cost-effective manner.

The fund manager seeks to enhance returns through allocations to other asset classes. According to the strategies tracked by Mercer, this includes exposure to exotic credits such as high-yield bonds and emerging market debt, mortgage-backed securities, and alternative investment vehicles.

Typically, an asset management firm will use its in-house capabilities to manage its equity and investment-grade bond exposure, but retains one or more sub-advisors to manage the exposure to more exotic investment products. Thus, the strategy is managed by multiple asset managers.

Diversified inflation strategies

The focus of a *diversified inflation strategy* is to use asset classes that can generate growth but have high sensitivity to inflation. The types of assets included are liquid real assets and inflation sensitive bonds combined in such a way as to achieve a balance between fund growth and a defensive position. Liquid real assets are exchange-traded products such as commodity futures, natural resource equities, and real estate investment trusts (REITS). Inflation-sensitive bonds include primarily US Treasury Inflation Protection Securities (TIPS) and in some cases corporate inflation-linked bonds.

[5]The general framework for the discussion that follows draws from Mercer, "Multi-Asset Strategies: The Choices Available — A Guide," October 2014.

Idiosyncratic strategies

An *idiosyncratic strategy* is a multi-asset strategy that does not rely on traditional market return but instead focuses on returns generated from tactical asset allocation and/or specific trades. Of the four categories, this is the broadest category of multi-asset strategies. According to Mercer (p. 13), the following are the types of trades that can be included:

- "Baskets of equities to focus on specific sectors, markets, or types of stock (e.g. emerging market consumer-oriented stocks).
- Relative value trades between the equity markets in different countries (e.g. France vs. Germany).
- Relative value trades between the government bond markets in different countries.
- Playing a theme across multiple asset classes (focus on periphery Europe via equity, currency, and/or interest rates).
- Trades hedged indirectly (e.g., Japan equity alongside a gold position).
- Tactical use of alternative risk premia (e.g. implied vs. realized volatility trades)."

BlackRock Classification of Multi-asset Strategies

Most major asset management firms have their own way of classifying multi-asset strategies. According to BlackRock Financial Management, the largest asset management firm in the world, the three major categories of multi-asset funds are:

> "**Global macro allocation:** These multi-asset funds offer investors broad diversification across a wide spectrum of asset classes. They trade assets in a flexible approach to adapt to shifting macro-economic conditions.
> **Risk tolerance:** These funds tailor their allocation toward a desired level of risk, whether it's conservative, moderate, or aggressive.
> **Target date:** Typically geared toward retirement investing, these multi-asset funds gradually adjust their allocation to match a specific investment horizon."[6]

[6] https://www.blackrock.com/us/individual/education/multi-asset-strategies.

Examples of Multi-asset Investment Strategy Objectives

To see the different objectives that can be pursued in their mutual fund offerings by asset management firms, Table 1 provides some examples of mutual funds that are multi-asset funds and their stated investment objectives. Panel A shows three multi-asset funds managed by Lazard Asset Management, and Panel B, three managed by PIMCO. The funds identified in Table 1 are just examples and are not recommendations by the authors.[7]

TABLE 1: Multi-Asset Funds Stated Investment Objective and Strategy/ Overview

Panel A: Managed by Lazard Asset Management

Fund name: Global Dynamic Multi-Asset
Stated investment objective and strategy/fund overview: "a stable pattern of returns utilizing a process designed to control for market volatility and reduce the probability of extreme outcomes. The Multi-Asset team allocates the strategy's assets among various global equity and fixed-income baskets of securities managed by Lazard's security selectors. As market conditions and volatility expectations change, the team dynamically shifts the strategy's allocation."
Source: https://www.lazardassetmanagement.com/us/en_us/investments/strategy/global-dynamic-multi-asset-strategy/S205/.

Fund name: Opportunistic Strategies
Stated investment objective and strategy/fund overview: "specialize in investments in global capital markets that offer unique investment characteristics, outsized opportunity for excess return, and correlation or risk benefits. These investments can be in equity, debt, commodity, real assets, currency, or market hedging instruments. Typically, these investments are not clearly defined by asset allocation limitations and are unconstrained by region, size, or style. The strategy is available in global and global (UK) implementations."
Source: https://www.lazardassetmanagement.com/us/en_us/investments/strategy/capital-allocator-series---opportunistic-strategies/S51/.
Fund name: Lazard Real Assets and Pricing Opportunities
Stated investment objective and strategy/fund overview: "strategy aims to provide a multi-faceted approach to different inflationary forces while seeking to generate current income and capital appreciation. The strategy invests in liquid real assets, including real estate investment trusts (REITs), listed infrastructure companies, commodity futures, companies affected by commodity prices and broader inflation trends, and global inflation-linked bonds."
Source: https://www.lazardassetmanagement.com/us/en_us/investments/strategy/real-assets-and-pricing-opportunities-strategy/S193/.

---

[7]BlackRock mutual funds are not included here because one of the authors is a trustee for that asset management firm's multi-asset strategy funds.

TABLE 1: (*Continued*)

Panel B: Managed by PIMCO

Fund name: Inflation Response Multi-Asset Fund
Stated investment objective and strategy/fund overview: "By investing in a blend of inflation-related strategies, the strategy seeks to help preserve and grow purchasing power, enhance portfolio diversification, and guard against market shocks across varying inflation environments."
Source: https://www.pimco.com/en-us/investments/mutual-funds/inflation-response-multi-asset-fund/inst.

Fund name: Multi-Strategy Alternative Fund
Stated investment objective and strategy/fund overview: "invests across the full suite of PIMCO's liquid alternative strategies as it targets attractive risk-adjusted returns through various market environments, while potentially limiting portfolio downside during large corrections in equity or bond markets."
Source: https://www.pimco.com/en-us/investments/mutual-funds/multi-strategy-alternative-fund/inst.

Fund name: Global Core Asset Allocation Fund
Stated investment objective and strategy/fund overview: "designed to serve as a flexible, comprehensive asset allocation solution. It seeks to benefit from global opportunities while also limiting downside risks created by today's evolving and sometimes turbulent marketplace."
Source: https://www.pimco.com/en-us/investments/mutual-funds/global-core-asset-allocation-fund/inst.

Key Points

- Balanced funds, also called hybrid funds, invest in US stocks and US bonds and are offered to investors in the mutual fund format.
- The investment objective of balanced funds is income and capital appreciation.
- A balanced fund has a target allocation for the stock/bond mix.
- There are criticisms of the balanced funds which have reduced investor interest in this type of investment vehicle.
- Today, a well-structured diversified portfolio involves investing in more than just US stocks and US bonds and are called multi-asset funds.
- Strategies used by managers of multi-asset funds differ from a balanced fund strategy in two ways: (1) they provide better diversification and (2) they are much more sophisticated in constructing portfolios by using systematic strategies such as tactical asset allocation and risk-controlled strategies to hedge against the risk of major market declines.
- Multi-asset funds were motivated by the need of the asset management industry to create products that were different from those traditionally

offered to clients, and after the Global Financial Crisis, tactical asset strategies became popular, offering asset managers greater flexibility in selecting an asset allocation mix.

- Asset allocation strategies include strategic asset allocation, tactical asset allocation, and dynamic asset allocation.
- A strategic asset allocation is a long-term asset allocation decision that uses a top-down approach to determine a long-term "normal" asset mix that offers the greatest prospects for strong long-term rewards to accomplish investment objectives.
- Typically, a strategic asset allocation strategy allows for a narrow range for the deviation from the specified allocation for each asset class.
- In strategic asset allocation strategies, the allocation is based on capital market forecasts of the average long-term returns for each asset class, average return volatility of each asset class, and the average return correlation for each pair of asset classes.
- Because of the problems associated with conventional strategic asset allocation, there has been a migration to risk-based allocation or factor-based allocation.
- A strategic asset allocation using risk-parity allocation is based solely on equalizing the risk contribution of each asset class and ignoring expected returns and correlations, and is accomplished by leveraging the least volatile asset class (i.e., government bonds).
- When a risk-based asset allocation is employed, the combined leveraged government bond position and unleveraged exposure in an asset class can result in a portfolio that exhibits lower volatility than an unleveraged portfolio.
- A factor-based allocation strategy, it is argued, is the best allocation approach to capture risk premiums that a fund manager has identified.
- The idea of a factor-based allocation strategy is to base the allocation on the exposure of the portfolio to common risk factors and then identify the asset classes that provide the optimal exposure to those risk factors.
- Implementing a factor-based allocation strategy requires not only the identification of the factors but also obtaining good forecasts of expected factor returns, factor variances, and correlations of factor returns.
- In a tactical asset allocation strategy, the fund manager may deviate from the fixed allocation mandated by a strategic asset allocation strategy in

order to enhance the expected return through short-term gains from a given asset class.

- A strategic asset allocation strategy that offers the fund manager no flexibility to modify the initial asset allocation is a passive asset allocation strategy, whereas a tactical asset allocation strategy is an active asset allocation strategy.
- Unlike a conventional strategic asset allocation strategy that considers only capital market conditions at the outset of the investment period and ignores changes in capital market conditions, in a dynamic asset allocation strategy the asset mix is mechanistically shifted in response to changing capital market conditions and the fund manager does not have to comply with a fixed allocation to each asset class.
- Dynamic asset allocation and tactical asset allocation are active asset allocation strategies.
- The difference between a dynamic and tactical asset allocation strategy is that in managing the latter, a fund manager must return to the fixed allocation as specified by the strategic asset allocation strategy, while in the former the fund manager does not have a fixed allocation to an asset class that must be adhered to.
- Because of the broad mandate for multi-asset funds, the fund manager has the flexibility to invest in asset classes with a wide range of risk–return profiles.
- In a multi-asset fund, there may be some benchmark used to evaluate the performance of the fund manager based on a combination of asset class benchmarks or, as commonly is the case, there may be no benchmark but instead an absolute return that is expected to be earned over the business cycle.
- One consulting firm provides four broad categories of multi-asset strategies: core strategies, risk parity strategies, diversified inflation strategies, and idiosyncratic strategies.
- With a core strategy, most of the fund's growth depends on market returns.
- The focus of a diversified inflation strategy is to use asset classes that can generate growth but have high sensitivity to inflation.
- An idiosyncratic strategy does not rely on traditional market returns but instead focuses on returns generated from tactical asset allocation and/or specific trades.

- A major asset management firm classifies multi-asset strategies as global macro allocation strategies, risk tolerance strategies, and target date strategies.

References

Bass, R., S. Gladstone, and A. Ang, 2017. "Total portfolio factor, not just asset, allocation." *Journal of Portfolio Management*, 43(5): 38–53.

Bender, J., J. L. Sun, and R. Thomas, 2019. "Asset allocation vs. factor allocation — Can we build a unified method?" *Journal of Portfolio Management*, 45(2): 9–22.

Bergeron, A., M. Kritzman, and G. Sivitsky, 2018. "Asset allocation and factor investing: An integrated approach," *Journal of Portfolio Management*, 44(4): 32–38.

Cao, L., 2015. "Multi-asset strategies: A primer," CFA Institute Bogs. Available at https://blogs.cfainstitute.org/investor/2015/03/03/multi-asset-strategies-a-primer/.

Clarke, R. G., H. de Silva, and R. Murdock, 2005. "A factor approach to asset allocation," *Journal of Portfolio Management*, 32(1): 10–21.

Greenberg, D., A. Babu, and A. Ang, 2016. "Factors to assets: Mapping factor exposures to asset allocations," *Journal of Portfolio Management*, 42(5): 18–27.

Lustig, Y., 2017. "Asset allocation: The battle of the multi-asset strategies: Balanced vs. absolute return," T. Rowe Price. Available at https://www4.troweprice.com/gis/content/dam/tpd/Articles/PDFs/231903_GAF_vs_Absolute_Return.pdf.

Maillard, S., T. Roncalli, and J. Teïletche, 2010. "The properties of equally weighted risk contribution portfolios," *Journal of Portfolio Management*, 36(4): 60–70.

Page, S., and M. A. Taborsky, 2011. "The myth of diversification: Risk factors versus asset classes: Invited editorial comment," *Journal of Portfolio Management*, 37(4): 1–2.

Author Index

M

N

O

P

R

S

Subject Index

B

D

E

G

J

N

O

Q

R

T

U

V

W

Y

Z

www.ingramcontent.com/pod-product-compliance
Lightning Source LLC
LaVergne TN
LVHW010539300926
849162LV00002B/176
* 9 7 8 9 8 1 1 2 2 0 0 2 9 *